MW00963804

FIELDING TRAVEL GUIDES

FIELDING'S EASTERN CARIBBEAN

Other Fielding Titles

Fielding's Alaska Cruises/Inside Passage
Fielding's Amazon
Fielding's Australia
Fielding's Bahamas
Fielding's Belgium
Fielding's Bermuda
Fielding's Borneo
Fielding's Brazil
Fielding's Britain
Fielding's Budget Europe
Fielding's Caribbean
Fielding's Caribbean Cruises
Fielding's Caribbean East
Fielding's Caribbean West
Fielding's Europe
Fielding's European Cruises
Fielding's Far East
Fielding's France
Fielding's Freewheelin' USA
Fielding's Guide to the World's Most Dangerous Places
Fielding's Guide to Kenya's Best Hotels, Lodges & Homestays
Fielding's Hawaii
Fielding's Holland
Fielding's Italy
Fielding's Las Vegas Agenda
Fielding's London Agenda
Fielding's Los Angeles Agenda
Fielding's Malaysia and Singapore
Fielding's Mexico
Fielding's New York Agenda
Fielding's New Zealand
Fielding's Paris Agenda
Fielding's Portugal
Fielding's Rome Agenda
Fielding's San Diego Agenda
Fielding's Scandinavia
Fielding's Southeast Asia
Fielding's Southern Vietnam on Two Wheels
Fielding's Spain
Fielding's Thailand Including Cambodia, Laos, Myanmar
Fielding's Vacation Places Rated
Fielding's Vietnam
Fielding's Worldwide Cruises
The Indiana Jones Survival Guide

FIELDING'S EASTERN CARIBBEAN

Fielding's guide to the best Eastern Caribbean escapes

By
Joyce Wiswell

Fielding Worldwide, Inc.

308 South Catalina Avenue

Redondo Beach, California 90277 U.S.A.

FIELDING WORLDWIDE INC.

PUBLISHER AND CEO	**Robert Young Pelton**
GENERAL MANAGER	**John Guillebeaux**
MARKETING DIRECTOR	**Paul T. Snapp**
ELECTRONIC PUBLISHING DIRECTOR	**Larry E. Hart**
PUBLIC RELATIONS DIRECTOR	**Beverly Riess**
ACCOUNT SERVICES MANAGER	**Christy Harp**
PROJECT MANAGER	**Chris Snyder**
DATABASE PUBLISHING MANAGER	**Jacki VanderVoort**

CONTRIBUTING WRITER
David Swanson

EDITORS

Linda Charlton   **Kathy Knoles**

PRODUCTION

Ron Franco	**Martin Mancha**
Gini Sardo-Martin	**Ramses Reynoso**
Craig South	**Janice Whitby**

COVER DESIGNED BY	**Digital Artists, Inc.**
COVER PHOTOGRAPHERS — Front Cover	**Mark Lewis & Donald Nausbaum/Tony Stone Images**
Back Cover	**Julie Houck/Westlight**
INSIDE PHOTOS	**Carol Lee, Benford Associates, Grenada Tourist Office, Karen Weiner, Escalera Associates, Robinson, Yesavich & Pepperdine, Inc., Saba Tourist Office, Trombone Associates, Corel Professional Photos**

Inquiries should be addressed to: Fielding Worldwide, Inc., 308 South Catalina Ave., Redondo Beach, California 90277 U.S.A., ☎ *(310) 372-4474*, Facsimile *(310) 376-8064*, 8:30 a.m.–5:30 p.m. Pacific Standard Time.

ISBN 1-56952-071-2

Printed in the United States of America

Letter from the Publisher

The Caribbean can be a daunting place when it comes to choosing the perfect island getaway. Our focus is making sure you get the best experience for your time and money. To assist you we have created handy comparison tables for accommodations and restaurants complete with highest rated and budget listings so you can get the most for your money. You'll also find the introductions tighter and with a definite accent on the romantic and adventurous. Loyal readers will be pleasantly surprised to find the entire book rewritten and with every listing checked for accuracy just before presstime.

Author Joyce Wiswell, faced with covering and reviewing hundreds of "tropical getaways on white sandy beaches," brings a youthful enthusiasm along with a true love of the Caribbean to this book. She has tackled the daunting task of giving the reader a balanced overview of the region as well as highlighting the unique personality of each island. In these 750-plus pages you will find the famous, the hidden and the overlooked all rated and reviewed in our new easy-to-use format. Supporting her efforts have been the staff and researchers at Fielding Worldwide who have done an impressive job of gathering, checking, sorting and compiling more than 1500 attractions, hotels and restaurants. Special thanks to our staff for making it all come together. If it helps you find that one perfect place for your once-a-year getaway, then we have done our job.

Today, the concept of independent travel has never been bigger. Our policy of *brutal honesty* and a highly personal point of view has never changed; it just seems the travel world has caught up with us.

Enjoy your Caribbean adventure.

RYP

Robert Young Pelton
Publisher and CEO
Fielding Worldwide, Inc.

Trouble in Paradise

Luis and Marilyn—sounds like an odd couple starring in a cheesy sitcom. If only they were that dismissable. In September 1995, the innocuous-sounding pair of hurricanes reduced several idyllic island paradises into twisted heaps of rubble, stripped trees of virtually every leaf and left islanders scrambling to rebuild in time for the all-important winter tourist season.

As this book was going to press, the Eastern Caribbean was under the spell of the worst hurricane season since the 1930s. The two major September storms cut a swath of destruction that decimated the infrastructure of several islands and left few others completely untouched. Hurricane Luis rolled over Antigua, Barbuda, St. Barthélémy, St. Martin/Sint Maarten, Guadeloupe and Anguilla, while just a week later, Hurricane Marilyn roared through the U.S. Virgin Islands and the Puerto Rican island of Culebra.

Luis virtually totaled Antigua and St. Martin/Sint Maarten, while Marilyn's fury was unleashed mainly on St. Thomas. As residents of both islands are completely dependent on tourism for their livelihood, they are currently pouring every possible resource into repairing, replenishing, renovating and repainting for visitors.

In Antigua, damage was considerable. Most private and commercial buildings were heavily ravaged. Several popular resorts, including Galley Bay, Runaway Beach Club and the Tradewinds Hotel, were completely destroyed and not expected to reopen until at least the summer of 1996. Other properties, such as the Half Moon Bay Club, Sunset Cove and Pineapple Beach Club, suffered considerable damage but expected to reopen by the end of 1995.

St. Martin/Sint Maarten, the small island shared by the French and Dutch, also suffered greatly. Luis tossed boats onto the island's shores, sunk some 200 others into the depths of Simpson Bay and created 40-foot waves that generally wreaked havoc. Waves crashed onto the third-floor restaurant of the Great Bay Beach Hotel, where 200 guests sat out the storm. At least 2000 people were left homeless by the storm on the Dutch side alone. Hotels greatly damaged include Great Bay Beach Hotel, which hopes to reopen by Fall 1996, and Divi Little Bay, which is closed until further notice. Dutch tourism officials initially tried the ultimate in spin control by banning news crews from recording the horrible scenes of destruction and looting in the days following the hurricane.

On the French side, Grand Case was particularly hard hit, with several beachfront restaurants washed away. In hotel news, La Belle Creole is closed until further notice, while Club Orient, the island's nudist resort was completely wiped out. Rebuilding is uncertain at this point. Also heavily damaged, but anticipating December reopenings, are Captain Oliver's Hotel, Golden Tulip and Orient Bay Hotel.

Cupecoy and Maho beaches suffered erosion, while the strands at Dawn and Philipsburg actually grew. Damage to the island's scrubby interior was extensive, but nature has an amazing way of rejuvenating what it tears down.

In Anguilla, winds of more than 200 miles per hour ripped the roofs off many private homes, while most hotels suffered mainly from flooding, broken glass and devastated landscaping. Casablanca and Frangipani were badly hit, but both are expected to be ready for guests in December. Some beaches suffered from erosion while others have gotten larger. The hurricane caused no deaths or serious injury on the island—and the one baby born during the storm will NOT be named Luis, according to the Tourist Board.

On St. Barthélémy, the hurricane wiped out the beach at Flamands, while St. Jean Beach also suffered serious erosion. Badly damaged were the Taiwana and Baie des Flamands, while the Emeraude Plage lost some beachfront bungalows. The tony villas at Castelets were severely ravaged and reopening is uncertain, while Taiwana was also badly hit.

Dominica experienced minimal damage, as did Guadeloupe (although a French tourist was washed out to sea while photographing the storm's fury). On Martinique, man-made beaches at the Bakoua and Meridien hotels were completely lost but are being replaced. As can be expected, all three islands suffered damage to vegetation and some beach erosion, Hotels on Saba, St. Eustatius, St. Kitts, Nevis and Montserrat were generally spared the brunt of Luis' fury.

While we've contacted each property in this book to learn of its future plans, readers are advised to check with the tourist board or individual hotels before planning a visit. Hurricanes are nothing new to the Caribbean and these islands will persevere, but many scheduled reopening dates are probably optimistic at best.

On the other hand, don't let Luis or Marilyn automatically cross an effected island off your list. The silver lining in those literal dark clouds, at least to tourists, is that most accommodations will be like new, and probably a bargain to boot as hoteliers try to convince vacationers to come back. And while it's not your duty to combine altruism with your Caribbean holiday, keep in mind that these islands have been severely financially strained by the storms, so tourists are assured of an especially warm welcome.

DEDICATION

To all those rebuilding their slices of paradise.

Mohala ka oua, ua wehe kaiao
The blossoms are opening, for dawn is breaking
—Hawaiian Proverb

ACKNOWLEDGEMENTS

So many people assisted in this project it is impossible to list them all, but you know who you are and how much I appreciate your help. In particular, special thanks to Richard Kahn and Stephen Bennett of Kahn Travel Communications who assisted in planning my itinerary, Gloria Gumbs who went above and beyond the call of duty in assisting with my travel to the U.S. Virgin Islands and Fielding's John Guillebeaux. Cheers to all the hoteliers, tourist board personnel, restaurateurs, bartenders, waitstaff, locals and tourists who befriended a wandering traveler and made her feel at home.

ABOUT THE AUTHOR

Joyce Wiswell

Joyce Wiswell has been writing about travel for more than 15 years. Various writing assignments have taken her to nearly every state in the union, as well as China, Hong Kong, the Philippines, Thailand, Europe, and, of course, throughout the Caribbean. Her work has appeared in numerous magazines and newspapers. Wiswell is also the author of *Fielding's Las Vegas Agenda*, *Fielding's Western Caribbean* and *Fielding's Caribbean*.

A native of New Jersey, she is a magna cum laude graduate of Connecticut's Quinnipiac College. After paying her dues as a magazine writer and editor in New York City for eight years, she fled for life in California, where she lives happily in Santa Barbara. When not traveling, she putters in the garden and pampers her cats, and worries unduly about both when on the road.

Fielding Rating Icons

The Fielding Rating Icons are highly personal and awarded to help the besieged traveler choose from among the dizzying array of activities, attractions, hotels, restaurants and sights. The awarding of an icon denotes unusual or exceptional qualities in the relevant category.

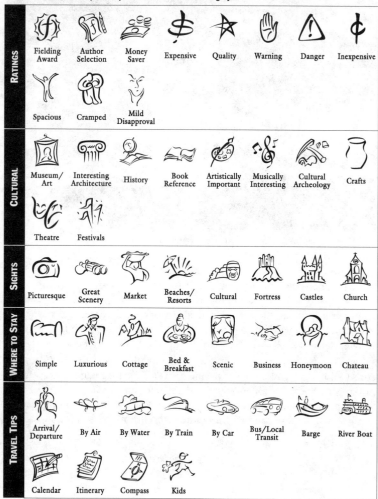

RATINGS

Fielding Award · Author Selection · Money Saver · Expensive · Quality · Warning · Danger · Inexpensive

Spacious · Cramped · Mild Disapproval

CULTURAL

Museum/ Art · Interesting Architecture · History · Book Reference · Artistically Important · Musically Interesting · Cultural Archeology · Crafts

Theatre · Festivals

SIGHTS

Picturesque · Great Scenery · Market · Beaches/ Resorts · Cultural · Fortress · Castles · Church

WHERE TO STAY

Simple · Luxurious · Cottage · Bed & Breakfast · Scenic · Business · Honeymoon · Chateau

TRAVEL TIPS

Arrival/ Departure · By Air · By Water · By Train · By Car · Bus/Local Transit · Barge · River Boat

Calendar · Itinerary · Compass · Kids

ACTIVITIES

Downhill Skiing	X–country Skiing	Water Sports	Sailing
Scuba Diving	Snorkeling/ Diving	Deep-sea Fishing	Freshwater Fishing
Swimming	Hiking	Walking	Relaxing
Golf	Tennis	Horseback Riding	General Sports
Cycling	Workout		

SPECIAL INTEREST

Nightlife	Singles	Romantic	Nude Beaches
Lecture	Spectacular Cuisine	Wine Tasting	Shopping
Cafe Stops	Gardening	Pro Sports	Mystery

What's in the Stars

Fielding's Five Star Rating System for the Caribbean

★ ★ ★ ★ ★ Exceptionally outstanding hotels, resorts, restaurants and attractions.

★ ★ ★ ★   Excellent in most respects.

★ ★ ★   Very good quality and superior value.

★ ★   Meritorious and worth considering.

★   Modest or better than average.

Restaurants are star rated and classified by dollar signs as:

$	Inexpensive	$1–$9
$$	Moderate	$9–$15
$$$	Expensive	$15 and up

A NOTE TO OUR READERS:

If you have had an extraordinary, mediocre or horrific experience we want to hear about it. If something has changed since we have gone to press, please let us know. Those business owners who flood us with shameless self-promotion under the guise of readers' letters will be noted and reviewed more rigorously next time. If you would like to send information for review in next year's edition send it to:

Fielding's Caribbean
308 South Catalina Avenue
Redondo Beach, CA 90277
FAX: (310) 376-8064

TABLE OF CONTENTS

LIST OF MAPS

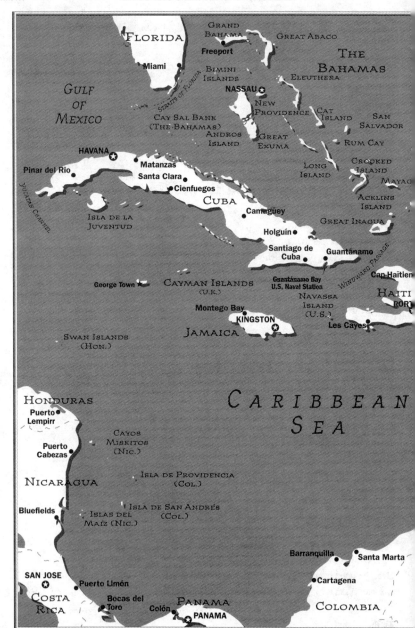

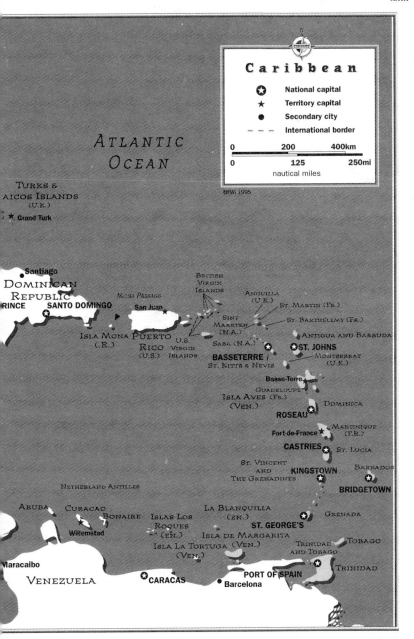

EASTERN
CARIBBEAN INTRO

What is it about the idea of a tropical island that sets our pulses racing and hearts swooning? It's the lure of palm tree-dotted beaches, no doubt, and a sea so incredibly clear you can inspect your pedicure in five feet of water. It's balmy evenings when trade winds caress your hair, soothe your spirit and make everyone look and feel sensuous. It's the sheer romance of escaping the bills and the boss, not worrying about windchill factors, and having only to decide if it's time to turn over and tan your back or if you're up to a night dive.

While a rose may still be a rose no matter what it's called, lumping the Caribbean islands together under one category is, categorically, unfair. Each island has its own history, its own culture, its own unique personality. Seen one, seen them all is not the reality of the Eastern Caribbean.

Caribbean Planner

By Air

Many airlines fly to the Caribbean, though for island-hoppers, American and American Eagle are probably the best bet, as they service many destinations and give good deals on multi-island tickets. (On one swing, I hopped to eight islands, and the fare was only about $1250, including round-trip from California.) On the other hand, many flights connect through San Juan, Puerto Rico, which means it can take many hours to get where a crow can fly in minutes. TACA is also good for short hops between islands.

Other airlines with service from the U.S. to the Caribbean are Aeromexico, Air Jamaica, ALM, Avensa, Avianca, BWIA, Cayman Airways, Continental,

Delta, Dominicana, Lacsa, LanChile, Mexicana, Northwest, TWA, United, USAir and Viasa.

How much you'll pay depends on how demanding you are. If you're counting pennies, obviously you'll fly coach. If you're willing to spend more, upgrade to business or first class, but be aware you'll pay dearly for the wider seat and better food, in most cases, several hundred dollars more. When island hopping, you'll be on small craft with no separate classes of service.

To save money, buy your ticket as far in advance as possible, and be on the lookout for special promotions. It's cheaper all the way around to travel to the Caribbean in the summertime—everything from air to hotels are generally discounted. Also consider a package deal that includes air, transfers, hotel accommodations and sometimes meals and a rental car. Charter flights are also worth investigating, but have the distinct disadvantage of extremely limited schedules and a disturbing propensity to cancel flights. Unlike a commercial carrier, if your charter flight is canceled, you're usually left on your own to scramble for an alternate.

The Affordable Caribbean, *(8403 Colesville Road, Silver Spring, MD 20910;* ☎ *(301) 588-2300)* is a monthly newsletter that reports on last-minute deals and other Caribbean bargains. If you travel to the Caribbean frequently and have a flexible schedule, it's well worth the $49 annual subscription cost.

By Sea

There's nothing like a cruise for relaxing and really getting away from it all. These floating hotels pamper guests and provide lots of onboard activities for those who get bored just laying on deck soaking up the rays. Cruise ships stop at virtually every island, and several, such as Princess, have their own private islands where passengers spend the day enjoying watersports and a beach barbecue.

Life at sea is so pleasant it can be hard to drag yourself off the ship at the ports of call. Obviously you're not going to soak up much island flavor in five or six hours, but there's still plenty to do and see—besides the requisite shopping—at each island. (See the chart on Island Excursions) for ideas. Take note that if you sign up for one of the official cruise line excursions, you'll pay much more than if you venture off alone. The disadvantage is that if you don't get back on time, you're in trouble—ships sail exactly when they say they will, and don't take a head count first. Always bring your passport ashore just in case you literally miss the boat.

A cruise can be as short as three days and as long as several weeks; seven-day trips are most popular in the Caribbean. What you pay varies widely upon what type of cabin you snag. The most expensive are the suites with balconies—a true treat if you can afford it—while the cheapest fares go to those who have a tiny inside cabin (no window) on a lower deck. Generally, the higher up you are, the higher the price. Watch the papers for deals on last-minute cruises—cruise lines will slash fares a few weeks out rather than sail empty.

Once you cruise with a line, it will try hard to get you back. The major lines reward frequent cruisers with deep discounts and two-for-one fares. While it's fun to try out different cruise lines, these promotions go a long way to assure brand loyalty. Also note the loyalty of your travel agent (cruises are virtually always booked through an agent rather than directly through the line). A good travel agent will send flowers and/or a bottle of wine to your cabin. If you've used the same agent a few times and have not received these perks, it's time to try an agency that will let you know your business is appreciated.

For general information on cruising, contact the **Cruise Lines Association** *(500 Fifth Avenue, New York, NY 10110;* ☎ *(212) 921-0066)*. Also see Fielding's *Worldwide Cruises* for honest reviews of each ship and line.

By Land

Some islands are so tiny you'll easily get around on foot. Others use the golf cart as the preferred mode of transportation. Several have excellent bus systems and good taxi fleets—it varies widely by island. For details, see the "Getting Around" section in the directory in the back of each island chapter.

The biggest decision will be whether or not to rent a car. Chain and locally owned rental companies are available on virtually every island, and summer rates are often cheaper than during the prime winter season.

If you're staying at an all-inclusive resort and plan to rarely leave the property, there's no need to rent a car. If, however, you plan to explore and try different restaurants each evening, you're often better off renting a car than paying lots of taxi fares. You'll also be more independent.

Road conditions vary from island to island. Some have modern paved roads, but too often, the roadways are narrow, rutted and filled with hairpin turns. Driving is often on the left side of the road, which can be dangerous if you're not used to it. On the plus side, most islands have few major roads so getting lost is rarely a problem. Consider renting a convertible so you can soak up every possible ray of sunshine, or a four-wheel drive to easily navigate the often torturous roads on some islands.

A few tips on car rentals: Always reserve as far in advance as possible, as the cars do get snatched up during prime tourist seasons. Check to see if they'll deliver the car to your hotel—many do at no extra charge, and it's a nice perk. Before leaving home, check your car insurance policy to see if rental cars are covered. They often are, and this allows you to refuse the rental company's outrageously priced insurance, which saves big bucks. If you're not covered, seriously consider buying the rental insurance, as island drivers can be wackier than even those in Boston, and, as stated, the roads are often awful.

Taxi service also varies. Some islands have metered cabs, but many more use standardized fares. In those cases, always ask what the trip will cost before you get in. If you're hiring a cabby for a day's sightseeing, you'll usually be able to negotiate a fare. On some islands, such as St. Martin, fares increase dramatically at night. In others, they disappear by midnight. If you're relying on taxis, be sure you'll be able to catch a cab if you plan to stay out late. Always treat your cab driver with courtesy and respect. You should anyway, but it can especially pay off when you hit it off and the cabby—virtually always a native—turns you on to interesting facts and places you'd never otherwise find. If you're a business traveler on an expense account, tote along a small notebook for receipts, as most cabbies don't carry them.

Lodging

Some of the world's best resorts are found in the Caribbean. So, alas, are some sleazy and roach-ridden dumps. Most fall in between.

Once you decide on an island—no easy choice in itself—your next task is to pick accommodations. The choices are immense—luxury resorts that cater to every whim, all-inclusive properties when everything from soup to nuts is included in the price, glamorous villas with your own butler and pool, budget motels with limited amenities, atmospheric inns with rich history and often colorful owners, cheap guest houses where you'll get little more than a clean (or not so) room, and apartments and condominiums where you can save money by preparing your own meals.

Many hotels offer the same rates for single and double occupancy, with a surcharge for a third or fourth person in the room. Children under 17 or 12 (it varies by company) often stay and even eat for free. Larger resorts offer supervised children's activities during the high season, and it's often complimentary. They can also arrange for a nighttime baby-sitter for a nominal charge.

Always ascertain if you are paying for the Full American Plan (FAP, three meals), Modified American Plan (MAP, two meals), Breakfast Plan (BP, full breakfast), Continental Plan (CP, continental breakfast) or European Plan (EP, no meals). The latter is the most common. Many resorts offer optional meal plans that for, say, $40 to $60 a day, include three meals. Unless you really have no plans to venture off-site, eschew these since it can be terribly dull to eat all your meals at the same spot, no matter how good the food. Also, unless you're a very hardy eater, you can probably save money by dining a la carte. As you spend a few days on your vacation, you'll inevitably hear about some great restaurant you must try, so it's better not to be locked in with a meal plan.

Also be sure exactly what is included in the rates. Watersports are sometimes complimentary, but often are not, and that snorkel equipment and float can really add up. Other nonmotorized watersports are free, but you'll pay to rent a jet ski or take a sunset cruise. Even the coffeemaker in your room can't be taken for granted. It's usually free to make a cup of joe, but sometimes (and ironically, at the most expensive resorts) you'll get a charge tacked onto the room. When it comes to the minibar, assume that you're paying (dearly) for anything you use. Some hotels and resorts, however, will tuck a bottle of champagne or wine in your refrigerator as a welcome gift. If in doubt, call the front desk. (I once assumed a delicious box of bon-bons was graciously supplied to each guest, until I saw the $20 charge on my final tab when checking out.)

No matter what class of lodging you choose, you can generally assume you'll pay a premium for an oceanfront room. Slightly less are rooms with a view of the sea, though not necessarily on it. Cheapest are the "garden view" rooms—but beware—that "garden" may actually be a parking lot. In cases where rooms are on multiple levels, request a unit on the upper floor(s) for increased privacy and better views.

Never assume a hotel has air conditioning—it's not nearly as common in the Caribbean as throughout the U.S. You can usually count on having a ceiling fan—and trade winds often do a good job in keeping things cool—but if you're set on air, be sure to ask. Some places charge a $10 or $20 daily fee for the use of air conditioners. Also keep in mind that central air is very rare; most hotels use individual units that can be quite noisy, enough to drown out the soothing sounds of the surf. Television and telephones are also not often available—if it's important to you, ask first.

All-Inclusive

One fast-growing Caribbean trend is the all-inclusive property, which means that for one price, you get lodging, all meals, drinks, activities and entertainment. They also frequently include gratuities and surcharges.

Sounds great, but there are definite disadvantages to such a resort. Generally, as with Club Meds, the rooms are quite basic and nothing to get excited about. There are usually just a few restaurants (and sometimes only one), so meals can become routine. Some can overdo the camaraderie angle to the point where you're made to feel almost guilty if you don't join in corny group activities.

The biggest drawback is that when everything is made so easy and accessible, it can be hard to tear yourself off the grounds. This is fine if you're just looking to escape the world for a while, but if you're interested in really getting to know an island and its people, it won't happen at an all-inclusive. Often they have fences and guards to keep the locals out—good for security but hardly conducive to a cultural exchange. Many times all-inclusives are so generic they could be located anywhere—the same feel on Anguilla as in St. Thomas—two very distinct destinations.

Resorts like Sandals and Couples (whose logo, oddly enough, is a copulating pair of lions) accept only same-sex couples. Honeymooners and other lovers staring dreamily into each other's eyes and making out in the pool is the norm. At the other extreme, the properties that cater to singles are tropical meat markets where scoring with the opposite sex is a top priority. Club Med, which started the whole all-inclusive phenomenon nearly 30 years ago, used to be known as the premiere singles spot, but lately is courting families with lots of special activities for kids.

Several all-inclusive resorts are quite luxurious and cater to the well-heeled crowd. Others are relatively tiny (Anguilla's Pineapple Beach Club comes to mind) and you'll really get a chance to know the staff and your fellow guests. Most fall in between, with a hundred or so rooms, several restaurants and decent nightlife. Nearly all have well-manicured grounds and a wealth of watersports, arts and crafts activities, talent shows, sports competitions and theme nights. Most also offer diving and sightseeing excursions that cost extra, and a few don't include alcohol in the price. Be sure to ask exactly what you're getting before making your reservations.

The biggest thing to keep in mind is that if you're not interested in socializing, don't stay in an all-inclusive! If, on the other hand, you only have a set amount of money to spend and don't want to worry about carrying cash, an all-inclusive can be perfect for a relaxed, hassle-free holiday.

Lots of properties throughout the Caribbean offer all-inclusive packages in addition to European and American plans. In these cases, you're probably better off booking your room under the European Plan (no meals), then seeing how you feel once you check the resort out in person. It's the rare hotel that won't let you switch to an all-inclusive plan, but rarer still are the ones that will let you get out of it once you make the commitment.

Packing the Suitcase

First and foremost, try to pack lightly enough so you can carry your luggage on the plane, as opposed to checking it in. That way you'll whisk through customs (where applicable) well ahead of your fellow travelers waiting forlornly at the luggage carousel. Everything goes slower in the Caribbean—and luggage retrieval is certainly no exception. Most airlines will only let you carry on two bags (and sometimes one on a very crowded flight) that measures no more than 62 inches (width plus length plus height). In all cases, carry-ons must fit under your seat or in the overhead compartment. This is impossible on the tiny planes that hop from island to island, but if you hand your bag to them on the runway rather than check it, you'll still get it back more quickly.

As humidity is quite high throughout the Caribbean, bring natural fabrics; lightweight cotton is the best. Casual clothes are fine just about anywhere both day and night (when it's not, it's noted in the hotel or restaurant description). An exception are historic churches, which generally have a no-shorts rule. Respect this custom; it's especially easy for women, who can wear a light sundress.

The nights are generally warm and sultry, but some clubs and restaurants will invariably overdo the air conditioning, so tuck in a jacket or sweater. If you're going to be trekking through the jungle or rainforest, obviously you want sturdy shoes and raingear. The nicer hotels equip their rooms with umbrellas; you may want to tuck in a small portable one just in case. Don't forget to bring a beach bag to hold your suntan lotion, hat or visor and a few dollars for lunch (your carry-on bag can serve this purpose).

Bring sandals or flip-flops for the beach (the sand gets hot!) and good sneakers for touring around. Lots of villages have cobblestone streets, and the old forts usually have dubious pathways, so you'll appreciate sturdy shoes. Unless you're into tottering around on high heels, you can leave them at home; flat dressy sandals will do even at the finer resorts.

Consider buying a sarong once you arrive. These large, colorful pieces of rectangular cloth can be tied in a variety of ways, from halter dress to shirt, fold up into practically nothing, are easy to handwash and make great souvenirs to boot. You'll find them in all the shops and marketplaces.

You'll also find lots of hats, mainly straw, and it's a good idea to pick one up. The sun is very strong throughout the region, and just because you are dutifully sightseeing rather than lazing on the street doesn't mean you won't get burnt.

The sunbathers on many islands go topless; whether or not you do too is a personal choice. However, it's considered rude to go to a nude beach and keep your clothes on. In any event, wearing swimsuits anywhere but the pool or beach is generally a no-no, and men, please spare us the sight of your hairy (or otherwise) chest in public places.

Other essentials include mosquito repellent, a portable water bottle, strong sunscreen and film. You'll generally save a lot of money by buying these items stateside rather than on the island. Smokers, on the other hand, can usually score cigarettes much cheaper on the islands, often even compared to the duty-free shops. (Remember you can legally bring only one carton back into the U.S.)

Finer hotels outfit their bathrooms with hairdryers, shampoo, conditioner and body lotion, but these products are usually cheap, so if you're particular, bring your own. It's well worth checking out the "introductory" or travel sizes of personal care items at the drug store or supermarket, or buying small plastic containers to fill. There's no need to lug your whole bottle of Prell, just bring what you'll need for your length of stay.

Women should pack a few tampons or sanitary pads...just in case. Also bring a small sewing kit, extra eyeglasses, condoms if you're planning to get extra friendly with new acquaintances and motion-travel wristbands or medication if you're prone to seasickness and will be boating. There's nothing like the fit of your own snorkel mask, so bring that along, too. Men who use electric shavers may need an electric converter (see the "Directory" under each island for electrical currents). Prescription medications and eyeglasses should always be carried on your person when traveling, not checked with your luggage.

What not to bring: travel iron (virtually all hotels supply one on request, and besides, this is the Caribbean and wrinkles are acceptable), expensive jewelry (Why add to the myth that Americans are all rich, and the possibility of getting ripped off?), cowboy boots (too hot) and beach towels (unless you're staying in the cheapest of guest houses). Rather than dragging your whole address book along, which you'd hate to lose anyway, copy the addresses of friends to whom you plan to send postcards and tuck it into your wallet.

Fanny packs are excellent for carrying your money and camera, and a lot cooler than backpacks. Always lock your passport, extra money, plane ticket and other valuables in the in-room safe or check them at the front desk.

Remember, unless you're extremely fashion conscious, it's inevitable you'll wear the same comfortable clothes again and again, so pack lightly. And be sure to leave room in your suitcase for souvenirs!

Money Managing

Unless you plan to bring huge sums of money with you or are staying a very long time, it's much more convenient to NOT bring traveler's checks. There are two reasons for this advice: many establishments tack on at least a five percent surcharge when cashing them; and worse, many places don't take them at all. On the other hand, you always run a risk when carrying cash, so it basically comes down to a personal decision. If you do opt for traveler's checks, be sure to carry the numbered receipts separately from your money—you'll need them for a refund in the event of loss or theft. Members of the Automobile Club of America (AAA) can get free traveler's checks, as can American Express cardholders.

A credit card is essential, even if you don't plan to use it. Most hotels won't give you a room without a credit card imprint, even if you're paying in cash. The same is true for car rental companies. This may be annoying, but perfectly understandable as hotels get ripped off constantly and with a credit card, they at least have a chance of recouping their losses. Also, you never know what emergencies may arise, so always carry a credit card. Visa and MasterCard are the most widely accepted and American Express is often honored, but the still relatively new Discover card has yet to make much of an inroad in the Caribbean.

Except for Puerto Rico and the U.S. Virgin Islands, each island has its own currency, but U.S. dollars are accepted virtually everywhere. In most cases, you won't even need to change money. If you do want to convert to local dollars, you're best off doing so at a bank, where the rate of exchange is invariably better than at hotels. In all instances, avoid the black market. In poorer nations, you're setting yourself up for scams or outright robbery.

Unless you're a whiz at division and multiplication, it's a good idea to carry a small calculator when shopping to figure out how prices translate into U.S. dollars. The calculator can also be used to communicate and negotiate when you're dealing with someone who doesn't speak English.

Automatic Teller Machines (ATMs) are becoming more common throughout most islands, but not so that you can really rely on them, except in San Juan and the U.S Virgin Islands. If you're island hopping and need cash, seek out the ATM at the San Juan airport. It's also a good idea to tuck a few blank checks into your wallet—if you really get into trouble cash-wise, some major hotels will cash one for you (after a lot of begging). If you're really stuck, you can always get a cash advance on your credit card at a casino, but be warned that the service charges are exorbitant (about $17 for each $100).

When traveling about the island, always carry small bills. They are much more convenient for paying taxi and restaurant fares. Plus, it's rude to dicker over a price at the marketplace, get the seller down from $18 to $9, then present a $20 bill. Keep a supply of singles for tipping doormen and other personnel at your hotel, as necessary.

Above all, use your in-room safe (they are becoming increasingly standard) or check your valuables with the front desk. Nothing will ruin a vacation faster than getting ripped off—it's worth the few minutes of hassle to play it safe.

Documents

Each island requires some sort of identification to enter; details are given in the directory at the back of each chapter. Generally, you're best off with a passport, though some nations accept a photo I.D. such as a driver's license. (Often, expired passports are also acceptable.) Visas are generally not required for citizens of the U.S., Canada and the European Economic Community, but again, rules vary by island.

You'll often need to show proof that you're just a visitor and are not planning to make the island your new home, (a return plane ticket.) Sometimes you're even required to prove you have enough funds for your length of stay.

When you purchase your plane ticket, the agent will inform you of any special documents needed. If he or she fails to volunteer this information, ask. Cruise ship passengers need to bring a passport along, but usually don't need to show it at ports of call. Still, it's a good idea to take it along with you when debarking the ship, just in case.

Customs and Duties

As if coming home from a glorious Caribbean holiday isn't depressing enough, you have to go through customs, unless Puerto Rico was your vacation spot. (In that case, you don't pass through customs and can bring back as much stuff as you want.) You'll fill out a simple form stating how much you spent on goods you're bringing back—if it's over $400, you'll have to list each item. When shopping in duty-free stores, be sure to save the receipts to show proof of purchase.

Rules vary by region, but here's the general scoop on duty-free shopping:

You can bring $1200 worth of stuff back from the U.S. Virgin Islands; $600 for Antigua, Barbuda, Barbados, British Virgin Islands, Dominica, Grenada, Montserrat, Saba, St. Eustatius, St. Kitts, Nevis, St. Lucia, St. Maarten (the Dutch side), St. Vincent, the Grenadines, Trinidad and Tobago; $400 for Anguilla, Guadeloupe, Martinique, St. Martin (the French side) and St. Barthélémy.

If you stay on an island less than 48 hours or have been outside the U.S. within 30 days of your current trip, you can only bring back $25 worth of duty-free goods (except, again, for Puerto Rico).

If you've gone over the limit, you'll be taxed at a flat rate of 10 percent (5 percent for the U.S. Virgin Islands) on the first $1000 of merchandise. Except for gifts under $50 sent directly to the recipient, all items shipped home are considered dutiable.

Some people try to beat customs by wearing their new Rolex or emerald earrings and acting as if they've always owned them. This is not especially recommended—you may need to show proof you did indeed leave the U.S. with these expensive items. Conversely, if you're traveling with a Rolex or huge rock on your finger, it's a good idea to bring the receipt along to prove you already owned it.

A NOTE ON DRUGS: Don't even think of trying to get illegal drugs into an island or back to the U.S. It's just not worth the risk, and while few people busted in the Caribbean have *Midnight Express*-style horror stories to tell, remember you are in a foreign country and you're under its rules. Carry prescription drugs in their original containers to avoid hassles.

For more information on duty-free allowances, contact the **U.S. Customs Service** *(P.O. Box 7404, Washington, DC 20044; for taped information, call* ☎ *(202) 927-2095).*

Insurance and Refunds

You can insure everything from your valuables being stolen to your rental car crashing to bad weather ruining your trip—it's up to you and how much of a gambler you are. A must: car rental collision insurance, unless your car owner's policy covers rental cars (many do, and it's well worth checking before you leave home, as this is a big savings).

Always check the small print when booking a hotel and airline ticket. These days most airlines charge anywhere from $30 to $50 (and more) if you change your flight times; if you decide to scrap the whole trip, airline tickets are often nonrefundable. Most hotels require at least 48 hours' notice (and as much as two full weeks in the high season) to refund your deposit. When cruising, consider the optional insurance policy that lets you cancel at the last minute, for any reason, and still get a refund.

When to Go

Common holidays such as Christmas and Easter are celebrated throughout the Caribbean. In addition, virtually every island has a large carnival, usually in February before Lent. These giant parties consist of parades, imaginative costumes, food festivals, sports competitions and general fun. Trinidad and Martinique's are among the most elaborate. The following guide summarizes the holidays and festivals unique to each island.

Anguilla

Carnival takes place in late July and runs through mid-August. Special street lighting, buntings, troupes and colorful costumes abound during parades, boat races, family reunions, beach barbecues and the nightly Carnival Village where locals compete for the titles of Prince and Princess and bands duke it out in calypso competitions. Other public holidays include Good Friday, Easter Monday, Anguilla Day (May 30), Whit Monday (June), Queen's Birthday (June 19), August Monday (first Monday in August), August Thursday (first Thursday in August), Constitution Day (August 11), Separation Day (December 19) and Boxing Day (December 26).

Antigua

Carnival is late July to early August, a time when locals celebrate their nation's heritage with dancing, parades and calypso bands. The last week of April is Sailing Week, one of the premiere sailing events of the world. Other holidays are Easter Monday, Labor Day (May 1), Whit Monday (June), Caricom Day (July 3), Independence Day (November 1) and Boxing Day (December 26).

Barbados

Crop Over, which celebrates the completion of the sugarcane harvest, takes place for three weeks in July, with special events such as a large parade, craft exhibitions, the Bajan Cultural Village, folk concerts, calypso competitions and the Grand Kadooment, the grand finale with street dancing and fireworks. There's also the Jazz Festival (January), Gospelfest (May), Holetown Festival (February) and the Oistins Fish Festival (Easter weekend). Also observed are Good Friday, Easter Monday, Whit Monday, Errol Barrow Day (January 21), May Day (May 1), United Nations Day (first Monday in October), Independence Day (November 30) and Boxing Day (December 26).

Barbuda

Carnival is late July to early August, a time when locals celebrate their nation's heritage with dancing, parades and calypso bands. The last week of April is Sailing Week, one of the premiere sailing events of the world. Other holidays are Easter Monday, Labor Day (May 1), Whit Monday (early June), Caricom Day (July 3), Independence Day (November 1), and Boxing Day (December 26).

British Virgin Islands

The Spring Regatta takes place in mid-April. The three-day race is the second leg of the Caribbean Ocean racing Triangles. The first week of August is given over to the Summer Festival, with parades, street dancing, bands and more. BVI also celebrates Commonwealth Day (March), Easter Monday, Whit Monday, Sovereign's Birthday (June), Territory Day (July 1), St. Ursula's Day (October 21) and Boxing Day (December 26).

Dominica

Carnival occurs the Monday and Tuesday before Ash Wednesday, with the usual costumes, parades and merriment. Other holidays are Good Friday, Easter Monday, May Day (May 1), Whit Monday, August Monday (first Monday in August), Independence day (November 3), Community Service Day (November 4) and Boxing Day (December 26).

Grenada

Carnival takes place each August and includes five days of steelband competitions, the crowning of the king and queen, street dancing and jump ups, costumed bands and a parade. The Carriacou Regatta, also held each August, is three days of boat races between Grenada and Carriacou and Big Drum Dance performances. The Rainbow City Festival, also in August, takes place in Grenville with cultural events and street dancing. Other holidays: Independence Day (February 7), National Day (March 13), Labor Day (first Monday in May), Emancipation Day (first Monday in August), Thanksgiving (October 25) and Boxing Day (December 26).

Guadeloupe

Carnival starts in early January and runs through Lent, with a giant party on Ash Wednesday. The Mardi Gras-style celebration is among the Caribbean's wildest. The Cook's Festival (Fete des Cuisinieres) takes place each August and includes a five-hour banquet (tourists welcome), singing, dancing and women parading in Creole costumes with baskets filled with island specialties and trimmed with miniature kitchen utensils. Other holidays include Easter Monday, Labor Day (May 1), VE Day (May 8), Slavery Abolition Day (May 22), Ascension Thursday (late May), Pentecost Monday (June), Bastille Day (July 14), Assumption Day (August), All Saints Day (November 1) and Armistice Day (November 11).

Martinique

Carnival is among the best in the West Indies. It starts each January and includes six weeks of pageants, parades, special events and all-night parties called zouks. The festival is especially lively as Ash Wednesday nears, and, unlike most other islands, continues on this day. On Shrive Tuesday (also known as Mardi Gras), revelers costumed as "red devils" parade around La Savane in Fort-de-France. Other holidays include Easter Monday, Labor Day (May 1), Slavery Abolition Day (May 22), Ascension Thursday (late May), Pentecost Monday (June), Bastille Day (July 14), Assumption Day (August), All Saints Day (November 1) and Armistice Day (November 11).

Montserrat

St. Patrick's Day (March) is a week-long party with a masquerade, jump ups, street theater, music and Irish marching bands and music. In August, the annual Pilgrimage is a 10-day event with cultural and sporting activities. Other holidays: Good Friday, Easter Monday, Labor Day (May 1), Whit Monday (early June), Queen's Birthday (June 10), August Monday (first Monday in August) and Boxing Day (December 26).

Nevis

Carnival, which happens in late December-early January, is a week-long festival with queen shows, calypso competitions, float and costume parades and street dancing. It takes place on both Nevis and sister island St. Kitts. Culturama happens each August, a week-long event that celebrates local culture with string band competitions, beauty pageants, art shows, a cultural parade, a food fair and daily street jamming. Public holidays are Carnival Last Lap (January 3), Good Friday, Easter Monday, Labor Day (first Monday in May), Whit Monday, Queen's Birthday (second Saturday in June), August Monday (first Monday in August), Culturama Last Lap Day (August 8), Independence Day (September 19) and Boxing Day (December 26).

Saba

The Queen's Birthday (April 30) is saluted with fireworks, parades and sports competitions. The Saba Summer Festival is a 10-day event each July with steel band competitions, dancing, games and general partying. Each December sees Saba Days, a festival with maypole dancing and other games.

St. Barthélémy

Carnival occurs in late February with a week of celebrations, including a pageant for Prince and Princess and a Mardi Gras costumed parade. The Festival of St. Barthélémy takes place each August to honor the island's patron saint. Boats are blessed and there's a regatta, public ball and fireworks. Fete-du-Vent takes place in the late summer with fishing contests, lotteries, dances and fireworks in the village of Lorient. Other public holidays: Easter Monday, Labor Day (May 1), Armistice Day (May 8), Ascension Thursday, Pentecost Monday, Slavery Abolition Day (June 27), Bastille Day (July 14), Assumption Day (August), All Saints Day (November 1), All Souls Day (November 2) and Armistice Day (November 11).

St. Croix

Christmas is celebrated over 12 days, from December 25 through January 6. Besides the big day itself and New Year's Eve, there's the Feast of the Three Kings, a colorful parade through Christiansted on January 6. There's also two carnival days on the last Friday (for children) and Saturday (for adults) in April. Besides the holidays celebrated in the U.S. the island observes Three King's Day (January 6), Transfer Day (March 31), Organic Act Day (June 20), Emancipation Day (July 3), Hurricane Supplication Day (July 25), Hurricane Thanksgiving Day (October 17), Liberty Day (November 1) and Christmas Second Day (December 26).

St. Eustatius

Statia/America Day, November 16, features parades and pageants to celebrate the day the island first saluted the American flag after the Revolutionary War. St. Eustatius was the first foreign government to recognize the fledgling U.S., earning it the nickname "America's Childhood Friend."

St. John

Carnival is celebrated on the last Friday (for children) and Saturday (for adults) in April. The Atlantic Blue Marlin Tourament, held each August, draws anglers from around the globe. Besides the holidays celebrated in the U.S., the island observes Three King's Day (January 6), Transfer Day (March 31), Organic Act Day (June 20), Emancipation Day (July 3), Hurricane Supplication Day (July 25), Hurricane Thanksgiving Day (October 17), Liberty Day (November 1) and Christmas Second Day (December 26).

St. Kitts

Carnival, which happens in late December-early January, is a week-long festival with queen shows, calypso competitions, float and costume parades and street dancing. Public holidays are Carnival Last Lap (January 3), Good Friday, Easter Monday, Labor Day (first Monday in May), Whit Monday,

Queen's Birthday (second Saturday in June), August Monday (first Monday in August), Culturama Last Lap Day (August 8), Independence Day (September 19) and Boxing Day (December 26).

St. Lucia

Carnival is a two-day affair in February with parades, music, costumes and partying. National Day in December is celebrated with cultural and special events. Public holidays are New Year's (January 1 and 2), Independence Day (February 22), Good Friday, Easter Monday, Emancipation Day (August 7), Thanksgiving (October 2) and National Day (December 13).

St. Martin/Sint Maarten

On the French side, Halloween is a wild affair in Grande Case, where everyone dresses up and goes wild. Carnival occurs in February right up through Ash Wednesday with parades, election of the Queen, and Shrove Thursday, a Mardi Gras-style festival with street dancing in Marigot and Grande Case. On the Dutch side, carnival is celebrated in late April and early May with beauty contests, food competitions, calypso concerts, parades, bright costumes and jump ups. Other holidays include Queen's Birthday (April 30), Labor Day (May 1), Ascension Thursday, Pentecost Monday, Bastille Day (July 14, French side), Assumption Day (August) and Concordia Day, when both sides celebrate their peaceful coexistence (November 11).

St. Thomas

Carnival, held just after Easter, is an island-wide event with steel bands, jump ups, parades and Mocko Jumbies—people dressed as spirits and perched precariously on very high stilts. Charlotte Amalie sees most of the fun. Besides the holidays celebrated in the U.S., the island observes Three King's Day (January 6), Transfer Day (March 31), Organic Act Day (June 20), Emancipation Day (July 3), Hurricane Supplication Day (July 25), Hurricane Thanksgiving Day (October 17), Liberty Day (November 1) and Christmas Second Day (December 26).

St. Vincent

The large Carnival takes place each July with steel and calypso bands in fevered competition, the crowning of the king and queen, jump ups and lots of fun. Other holidays include St. Vincent and Grenadines Day (January 22), Good Friday, Easter Monday, Labor Day (May 2), Whit Monday, August Monday, Independence Day (October 27) and Boxing Day (December 26).

Trinidad & Tobago

Carnival, which is centered on Trinidad but also spills over to Tobago, is among the Caribbean's greatest celebrations. Held each year on the Monday and Tuesday right before Ash Wednesday (February or early March), it's a huge party with amazing handmade costumes, parades, calypso competitions and a Kiddie Carnival (held the previous Saturday). Other holidays are Good Friday, Easter Monday, Whit Monday (June 7), Corpus Christi (June 18), Labor Day (June 19), Emancipation Day (August 1), Independence Day (August 31), Republic Day (September 24) and Boxing Day (December 26).

Secret Tips for Caribbean Survival

Duty-Free Does Not Necessarily Mean Cheaper

The term "duty-free" (a shopper's best friend) means that retailers are not required to pay import taxes on certain items, so they can pass these savings directly along to the consumer. Often that translates to prices 30 to 40 percent cheaper than in the U.S. Even islands not officially duty-free still often have duty-free shops at the airport or around the island, such as St. Lucia's Pointe Seraphine. Furthermore, on your way to an island, you can shop duty-free in major U.S. airports by showing your boarding pass.

While most duty-free items are truly a bargain, it isn't always necessarily so. Cigarettes, for example, often cost close to $17 per carton at airport duty-free shops, and you can often do better on the island itself (and even in some U.S. supermarkets). If you're planning to buy expensive French perfume or a good piece of jewelry, do some comparison shopping before leaving the U.S. to see how prices stack up. Remember, if the product is defective, you'll have a much easier time getting satisfaction from your local store than a little shop in the Caribbean.

Good duty-free bargains can generally be found on French perfumes, Dutch porcelain, Swiss crystal, fine bone china and woolens from England, linens and gemstones, especially emeralds. Prices are especially good on European-owned territories such as St. Martin. St. Barts, Martinique and Guadeloupe for French items and Anguilla, Antigua, Montserrat, Nevis, St. Kitts, Grenada, St. Lucia, St. Vincent and the British Virgin Islands for goods from England.

Those Damn Surcharges

Most folks are genuinely amazed when checking out of a hotel and seeing their final hotel tab. Where did all these charges come from? What's this government tax? What on earth is a "service charge?"

While it's always a good idea to go over your bill with a fine-tooth comb, most of these charges, alas, are legitimate.

All hotels (even all-inclusive) charge a government tax of anywhere from 5-10 percent of your nightly room rate. The service charge, which averages 10-

15 percent, is supposedly for maids and other staff—whether they actually ever see it or not is another matter. Still, don't feel obligated to tip extra if the service charge is included. Many hotels automatically tack on a service charge whenever you charge a meal or drink to your room, and room service checks virtually always include a service charge. In these cases, it's not necessary to tip the bartender or waiter. If you're not sure, ask. Energy surcharges are sometimes added to the bill to help defray the costs of electricity when prices are quite high. Note that all these charges are rarely, if ever, mentioned in the brochure or when you inquire about rates.

The biggest killers are the telephone surcharges. Ironically, it seems the more expensive the hotel, the higher the telephone rates. Many charge around $1 per local phone call, even if you're calling an 800 number to use your credit card. If you dial direct to the U.S., be prepared for exorbitant fees—double or triple the amount of your call. If you must call the States direct, have your party immediately call you back—you'll save a lot of money that way. Also consider buying a phone card, which are springing up all over the islands, wherein you pay a flat fee (say, $10) for a prescribed amount of time. When you can use your stateside carrier's credit card (such as ATT, Sprint and MCI) you'll invariably save, but note that their 800 access numbers are often not reachable from the Caribbean, even with operator assistance.

Beware of the minibar—that tempting bottle of Red Stripe probably costs double or triple the usual price. If you don't trust your will power regarding raiding the fridge and gobbling down all those $5 candy bars (which cost 50 cents in the store) leave the minibar key at the front desk.

If you're a drinker, you'll really drop dead when you get your cruise ship bill. (Most lines give you a preliminary statement a few days before the end of the trip to help ease the final shock.) The cruise fare usually doesn't include drinks—alcohol and otherwise—and while the prices are reasonable, they really add up. You'll also pay port taxes (about $75 per person), any shopping you did aboard, those tempting pictures snapped by the ship's photographers, casino chips charged to your cabin (an especially dangerous habit to fall into) and any ship-run shore excursions.

The biggest expense, and one you must plan for, are the tips given out at the end of the cruise. Most cruise lines hand out printed guidelines and even give formal talks on the art of tipping, but the general rule of thumb is that waiters and cabin stewards get $3 per day per person and busboys (they're rarely female) and wine stewards get $1.50 per day per person. You may be tempted to skip the tips, after all, you're leaving and will never see these people again—but keep in mind that the service staff's salary is virtually nil, with tips making up the vast majority of their income. So bring aboard enough cash for tips, then forget about it until the last night, when tips are usually distributed in envelopes provided by the cruise line. You may also want to tip the bartender and maitre'd if he took special care of you, but that's completely optional. It's never necessary to tip those higher up the chain such as the cruise director and shore excursions manager.

Ten Ways to Save Money

1) Choose a cheap island.

Just as a vacation in the Midwest is usually a lot cheaper than one in New York or California, prices vary widely from island to island. Among the cheapest in the East are Saba and St. Eustatius. (Conversely, among the most expensive are Anguilla, the British Virgin Islands and, unless you're camping, St. John.) Remember, just because it costs less, it doesn't mean you're settling for second best. See the descriptions of each island to see if you're a good fit.

2) Consider a self-catering holiday.

Securing lodging with a kitchenette or full kitchen can save you big bucks over eating in restaurants. Food establishments at resorts can be particularly expensive—you may pay as much as $10 just for a bagel and cup of coffee. Be sure to ask before making your reservation exactly what the kitchen contains. Some come equipped with microwaves, dishwashers and high-quality dishes and cookware, while others consist of little more than a hot plate and refrigerator.

3) Go with another couple.

If you're a couple chummy with another twosome, consider taking your holiday together and staying in a two-bedroom condo or villa. You'll save big on lodging and also a rental car—but be sure you like these people enough to spend your hard-earned vacation with them.

4) Swap houses.

This requires a lot of lead time (generally a year) but can be well worth it if you find a Caribbean homeowner who wants to swap houses or apartments for a week or two. Two organizations (**Intervac**, ☎ *(800) 756-4663* and **Vacation Exchange** Club, ☎ *(800) 638-3841*) publish a directory of interested homeowners. It costs from $46 to $60 to be listed. These services will also supply you with guidelines—obviously, you want to check out the person carefully to avoid getting ripped off, and want to get as many details as possible about their home.

5) Travel in the off season.

You'll save big on airfare, lodgings and even rental cars if you travel to the Caribbean during the summertime. Yes, it can be very hot, but then again you have that splendid sea in which to spend the day. Off-season travel also has the distinct advantage of sharing the beaches, museums and attractions with fewer people. But note that many shops and restaurants reduce their hours in the summer, so your choices may be more limited. Among the all-inclusive properties that offer deep summer discounts are St. Kitts' **Jack Tar Village Royal** (20 percent), Anguilla's **Pineapple Beach Club** (19 percent) and St. Lucia's **Le Sport** (20 percent). Hotels offering great deals include Anguilla's **Cinnamon Reef** (40 percent), Barbados' **Royal Pavil-ion** (48 percent) and Nevis' **Hermitage** (43 percent).

6) Book a package deal.

Virtually every resort offers packages that include meals, rental cars, sightseeing and so on. Divers especially should look to properties that cater to them—Bonaire's Harbour Village and Captain Don's come to mind—while golfers can be kept happy with packages on St. Thomas, St. Croix and Dutch St. Maarten that include greens fees.

7) Don't be too quick to sign up for the meal plan.

Major hotels and resorts often offer, and heavily promote, meal plans that keep their guests on site, which keeps stockholders happy. But they are not necessarily such a great deal. At the fine new Tropical Club Hotel in Guadeloupe, for example, you'll pay $224 per person for a week's worth of dinners. That works out to an average of $32 per person per meal—not outrageous (and it should be pointed out that the restaurant is excellent), but not exactly a bargain, either. Just as importantly, buying a meal plan locks you into eating in the same restaurant or two night after night—hardly the way to get to know the island. If you're unsure about the meal plan, wait until you arrive and can scope out the scene before committing.

8) Try a guest house.

Sure you'll sacrifice room service, free postcards and usually a swimming pool, but you'll gain a wealth of island flavor and lots of inside tips, assuming the owner is friendly and chatty (most are). Tobago has some especially charming inns (**Rich-mond Guest House** is the tops), and several in St. Thomas **(Heritage Manor** for one) offer great savings over full-service hotels and resorts. You'll especially save if you're willing to share a bath. If you're unsure about the property, ask to see a room before checking in—no reputable operation will refuse.

9) Be flexible.

If you're lucky enough to have a schedule that allows for last-minute trips, you can score big in the savings department. Scan the travel sections of your local newspaper for promotions and ask your travel agent to be on the lookout for good deals. This can especially pay off with cruises—lines hate to sail empty, so will often offer deep discounts a few weeks out.

10) Stock your refrigerator.

Even most of the cheapest hotels outfit their rooms with a refrigerator; if not, invest in a Styrofoam cooler. Keep it stocked with beer, wine, juice and soft drinks and you'll save a lot of money over using the minibar or room service. If the hotel has jammed your minibar to the gills (most do), buy identical drinks at the liquor or grocery store and simply restock it yourself. Carry your cooler to the pool or beach so you don't have to buy drinks from the roving waitstaff. Buying a sackful of gro-ceries such as donuts, cereal, fruit, bread and cheese can save big bucks on breakfast and lunch.

Health Precautions

There are very few health risks throughout the Eastern Caribbean. In most cases, the water is safe to drink (even if it doesn't taste so great); always inquire at your hotel if you're not sure. They'll give you an honest answer—the last thing these people want is a bunch of sick guests on their hands.

The biggest health threat in the Caribbean—as, alas, the world over these days—is from AIDS and other sexually transmitted diseases. Use condoms! It's best to bring them from home because they are not always as readily available on smaller islands as we've grown accustomed to seeing them in the U.S. Latex condoms offer much more protection than those made of lambskin.

It's always a good idea to carry along a small bottle of stomach medicine such as Mylanta, diarrhea aids such as Pepto Bismol or Imodium and pain relievers like aspirin or Tylenol. Don't assume you'll be able to find such items on the island. (No problem in St. Thomas, but lots of luck on Saba.) If you require injections, bring your own sterile syringes and consider buying disposable ones from a U.S. pharmacy before you leave.

Fortunately, malaria is generally no longer a threat (except possibly in the Dominican Republic and Haiti), which is good news, since you can count on providing lots of free meals for mosquitoes and no-see-ums.

Watch out for the sun, it's going to be a lot stronger than you think, especially on overcast days when you may forget to apply sunscreen. Though getting a killer tan is high on many tourists' list of things to do, start slowly with a strong sunscreen, then once you work up a good base tan, gradually switch to a lower number. (Of course dermatologists recommend no tan at all, but let's deal with reality.)

The high humidity will probably make you perspire more than usual. Drink lots of fluids to avoid dehydration (water is best) to replace the sweat you're oozing through your pores.

Guests at all-inclusive properties invariably go wild the first night with all those free drinks, then pay dearly for it the next day. Keep that in mind as you order your fourth pina colada.

Buying prepared food from street vendors is generally safe, but do check out the operation. Is the meat kept refrigerated? Are the utensils clean? When buying bottled water, especially on the street, check that the tamperproof band is intact. Some unscrupulous vendors will refill bottles with tap water.

Illegal Drugs

If you're a recreational drug user, you'll generally have no problem scoring high-quality marijuana (called ganga on many islands) at prices much cheaper than the U.S. We're not endorsing this, but if you are intent on buying drugs, use common sense and stay away from dim alleyways, deserted parking lots and the like. You can often ask your trusty bellboy or bartender where it's okay to score. Bring your own pipe or rolling papers because they can be hard to find on some islands. It's incredibly stupid to buy anything stronger than pot because heaven only knows what they are lacing cocaine, crystal meth and other potent drugs with. As stated earlier, don't even think of trying to bring drugs into another country or back into the U.S.—it's just not worth the risk.

Weather—or Not

Californians cope with earthquakes and mudslides, East Coasters deal with blizzards and ice storms and Midwesterners have bitter cold and flash floods. In the Caribbean the enemy is the hurricane.

Hurricane season is an annual event that generally runs from June to September. Most turn out to be little more than pesky rainstorms or dramatic electrical displays, but some are deadly and should be taken dead serious. Thirty years ago, Hurricane Hattie was strong enough to literally rip a Belizean island in two, and Hugo devastated St. Croix, St. Eustatius, and other islands in 1989. In September, 1995, Luis and Marilyn wreaked havoc on several islands. (See "Trouble in Paradise," p. vi.) Heed warnings of locals in regard to threatening weather.

Mother Nature's other biggest drawback is the high humidity that lingers on the islands all year long and is especially uncomfortable in the summer. It won't kill you (though it sometimes feels like it will) but take care to avoid overexertion and drink lots of water to keep hydrated.

Island Etiquette

While some of your best vacation photos will be candid shots of locals, keep in mind that many folks—older ones especially—often don't appreciate being part of your tourist experience. Always ask before snapping someone's photo and take a refusal with grace. (Although I do find it annoying that the old woman who makes johnny cakes at St. Croix's Whim Plantation refuses photos—rudely at that—since she is part of the attraction and you pay a hefty admission price to get in.) Kids, on the other hand, usually love to get the attention and will often ask YOU to take their picture. Indulge them, even if you're down to your last shot (better to fake taking the picture than hurt their feelings), and besides, you'll probably get some really cute shots.

Carry small bills when dealing with street vendors and in marketplaces where you'll be negotiating prices.

In museums and restaurants, keep your negative feelings to yourself (or at least whisper them to your companion) about the lousy artwork or crappy food. You may find you just hate conch, but remember that it's a staple in many island diets, so try not to be judgmental. On the other hand, if the food is truly inedible, you have every right to send it back.

No one should have to endure lousy service, but extra patience will be required in the Caribbean. Everything is on a slower pace, and that, alas, includes waitresses and cooks.

Respect local rules and customs regarding the formality of dress. In most cases shorts and T-shirts are just fine, but most churches ban them, even if you're just ducking in for a quick peek. Bathing suits are nearly always improper anywhere but on the beach or at the pool. If you want to go topless, make sure it's considered acceptable on the island.

Make a genuine effort to speak the language on islands such as Guadeloupe, where English speakers are rare. No matter how terrible your syntax or pronunciation, such efforts are greatly appreciated, and people will be much more apt to help you out than if you just walk up expecting them to speak your language.

Above all, do your fellow countrymen a big favor, and don't act like the Ugly American. It's no wonder everyone thinks we're all rich the way some U.S. travelers flash around large bills and expensive jewelry. (And actually, if we can afford a Caribbean vacation—even on the cheap—we are pretty rich compared to most locals.) Be sensitive to the fact that on most of these islands, life is much simpler and less materialistic. Remember, too, that you are a guest in this foreign land. Sure, you're paying for it, but that doesn't mean you've bought the right to impose your values on people of different cultures.

Here's a huge generalization, but it does apply: Islanders are usually quite reserved and will often avoid eye contact, especially on the street. However, it's amazing how far a smile and a "good day" will go. Try it, and you'll be pleasantly surprised—and left all atingle in good feelings.

ISLAND SNAPSHOTS

They may be grouped closely together and lumped into the "Caribbean" label, but each island has its own history, culture, topography and lifestyle. Here's a quick look at what you can expect; for more details, see the chapter devoted to each island.

Anguilla

If you're longing for picture-perfect beaches with sand as soft and white as baby powder, this is the spot. Anguilla, a British colony just a short ferry ride from St. Martin, boasts some of the Caribbean's best stretches of sand. The island is small, features just a handful of stoplights and probably has more resident goats than people. It also boasts some astoundingly luxurious resorts, a slew of more moderately priced accommodations and some great restaurants. Nightlife consists of grooving to the reggae beat at a number of clubs where you're apt to see more locals than tourists. Shopping is limited, though, and there are no real attractions such as historic forts or museums.

Antigua

This former British colony, located to the south of Guadeloupe, has more than 350 beaches—so there are at least 350 reasons people flock here. As throughout most of the Caribbean, all are open to the public, but you'll have no problem finding a deserted stretch for a romantic tête-à-tête, one where folks shun swimsuits, and others abuzz with activity. Lodging ranges from the ultra-decadent to budget motels; there are also some glorious inns that practically ooze charm. Dining and nightlife are sophisticated and a handful of museums and historic sites add diversity to this pretty, but somewhat reserved, island.

Barbados

This jewel, located southeast of St. Lucia, is among the Caribbean's most sophisticated spots. Though it has been independent from Great Britain for more than 30 years, it still retains much from its former motherland, including high tea served each afternoon at the fancier resorts, a tradition of dressing for dinner and a fierce love of cricket. There are lovely beaches as well as sloping hills, picturesque valleys, lush rainforests, a wildlife preserve, miles of undulating sugarcane fields and even limestone caves. Add to that botanical gardens, vintage churches and plantations and diverse lodging, and it's no wonder Barbados remains a top destination.

Barbuda

A small and sparsely populated island, Barbuda caters mostly to the very rich who can afford the high tariffs (for which they are treated like royalty) at its two pricy resorts. There's also one lone hotel with more reasonable—though not cheap—rates for wannabes. Besides the Frigate Bird Sanctuary, there's little to see and do on this little sister to Antigua save soak up the luxury of its resorts.

British Virgin Islands

Life is laid-back and unassuming on BVI, a complex of more than 40 islands, rocks and cays. Located northeast of St. John, the most important islands are Tortola, Virgin Gorda, Anegada and Jost van Dyke. Tortola, which measures just 12 by three miles, has the vast majority of residents and facilities for tourists. Eight-square-mile Virgin Gorda has some wonderful resorts and the famed Baths, where snorkelers float among giant boulders and clear pools. A handful of tiny other islands are given over to upscale resorts. If price is no object, you can even rent the entire Necker Island, a remarkable mansion with two guesthouses set on a 74-acre estate. Islanders are friendly and welcoming, and good food and spirits abound on BVI. Another plus is that it's easy to hop between islands and over to the U.S. Virgin Islands via ferry.

Dominica

Located between Guadeloupe and Martinique, Dominica (pronounced dom-in-EE-ka) is not for everyone—to the delight of the adventure travelers who do come here. While most of the Caribbean continues to develop and rely on tourism, this rocky isle, which has few beaches, has changed little since it was created by volcanic eruptions eons ago. The attraction here is nature pure and pristine, with virgin rainforests, verdant mountains, the second-largest lake in the world, Boiling Lake (with temperatures of 180–197°F!), spectacular waterfalls, and some 400 inches of rain a year. Vacationers wear themselves out scaling mountains, diving among the coral reefs, trekking through the jungle and swimming in rivers. The people on this former British colony are friendly and peaceful.

Grenada

There's a real spiciness to Grenada—literally. The tiny island, set between St. Vincent and Trinidad, is a major producer of cinnamon, nutmeg, cocoa, mace and other pungent spices. Their aroma lingers in the air, just another charming feature of this thoroughly enjoyable island. The former British colony (which was notoriously invaded by U.S. troops in 1983) is simply beautiful, with great beaches, lush forests and lovely hillsides. Sunning, diving and exploring the national park make up most tourists' itineraries. Most of the action takes place on Grenada proper, and there's also a sprinkling of resorts on Carriacou (pronounced carry-a-COO), which lies 40 miles offshore. The people are friendly and just love Americans—they consider Ronald Reagan their savior for squashing that 1983 attempted coup.

Guadeloupe

If you don't parles francais, you may feel a bit lost on this butterfly-shaped French "departement," the most northerly of the West Indies' Windward Islands. Outside of the major hotels, most residents don't speak English—though the standard reply to "parlez-vous anglais?" is always "a little," when in fact the truthful answer is "non!" Still, you'll get around okay armed with a phrase book and a sense of humor. Guadeloupe attracts mainly eco-travelers who hike its national park, climb its volcano, cycle its hills and valleys and dive in its clear waters. If you're looking for beaches, stay on Grande-Terre; if it's the mountains and rainforest you seek, head for Basse-Terre. (Both sides are easily accessible, wherever you stay.)

The two nearby islands of Marie-Galante and Les Saintes, reached via plane or ferry, are not to be missed. Marie-Galante is a lovely spot of rolling hills, pristine beaches and old plantations, while picturesque Les Saintes appeals to romantic types who revel in its quaint village and warm, hospitable people.

Martinique

It's tres French on this stunning island, the largest of the Windwards at 425 square miles. Most of the tourists come from the mother country of France, and little English is spoken outside the hotels. The island is quite mountainous—there's even an active volcano—and there's also a huge rainforest, acres of sugarcane, black sandy coves and white and gray sand beaches. Flowers grow everywhere and trees are rich with papayas, cherries, lemons, limes and mangoes. Man-made attractions include an impressive array of museums and good duty-free shopping. This is the most French of that country's islands so you'll invariably run into some of that infamous French snobbery—but nearly everyone responds to courtesy and a smile.

Montserrat

Mother Nature has often taken out her bad moods on this tiny island southeast of Antigua. The worst was overwhelming devastation brought by Hurricane Hugo in 1989, though you'd hardly know it today as proud locals have fixed everything up and most of the vegetation has grown back. The British colony's 39.5 square miles include three mountain ranges, an extinct volcano and beaches of dark brown or gray—many inaccessible by road. Life here is peaceful and relaxing; most tourists busy themselves with hiking, trekking and diving. Locals are friendly and superstitious on this relatively undiscovered island. Nightlife and shopping are extremely limited.

Nevis

St. Kitts' sister island is intent on keeping its natural beauty (white and black sand beaches, mineral spas, lagoons, lush foliage and a towering volcano) intact with some of the world's strictest ecological laws. Many accommodations are found in historic inns and restored plantations, though Four Seasons opened one of its typically smashing resorts here a few years ago. It and St. Kitts, which is separated by a two-mile channel, are former British colonies. Nevis' few thousand residents are gentle and superstitious. Life is slow and laid-back here.

Saba

There are virtually no beaches on this volcanic island, which boasts exactly one road and more goats and chickens than people. Pronounced SAY-bah, the island lies between St. Martin and St. Eustatius. The entire island is an extinct volcano—there's no flat land except at the tiny airport, just one beach that's hard to reach and, save a few atmospheric inns, little in the way of accommodations. Obviously, you won't find much in the way of shopping (besides lovely handmade lace) or nightlife either. It's the excellent diving that keeps tourists coming back for more. A marine park circles the island with a depth of 200 feet and the underwater sites are grand. Healthy types scamper (or at least limp) up the 1065 steps to the top of Mount Scenery.

St. Barthélémy

St. Barts (or Barths, depending on who you talk to) is straight out of the pages of "Lifestyles of the Rich and Famous." The French "departement" is a free port with good deals on fine perfumes and fashions direct from the motherland. The island, located south of St. Martin and north of St. Kitts, totals just 9.5 square miles and is a dependency of Guadeloupe, some 125 miles away. Everything is squeaky clean and meticulously manicured on the charming isle, comprised mostly of rocky terrain and postcard-perfect beaches. Besides fine resorts and restaurants, there's little in the way of man-made diversions. Much is owned by expatriates, all of whom, unfortunately, did not leave their superior attitudes back in France.

St. Croix

The largest of the U.S. Virgin Islands is an interesting mix of its two siblings. St. Croix, which was particularly hard-hit by 1989's Hurricane Hugo but has recovered admirably, has the fine resorts, good nightlife and excellent duty-free shopping found on busier St. Thomas, but a much more serene feel and unspoiled nature akin to St. John. There's a wealth of fine beaches, a large rainforest, good golf courses, restored plantations, verdant countryside and two charming villages that recall their Dutch heritage. The residents may be U.S. citizens, but retain their own relaxed lifestyle.

Sint Eustatius

Most often called Statia (pronounced STAY-sha), this Dutch island southeast of Saba totals just 12 square miles. This is one of the Caribbean's least developed and touristic islands as its beaches are only fair and there are not many man-made attractions save a fort and museum. You won't find good shopping or fancy resorts here, but if you're into hiking and diving (there are lots of submerged shipwrecks) you'll be content. Many tourists come for the day from St. Martin. People are welcoming and there is virtually no crime, but that may change as the island goes after increased tourism. The time to come is now.

St. John

Life on St. John, the smallest of the U.S. Virgin Islands, is about as good as it gets. The vast majority of the island is given over to a national park perfect for trekking and snorkeling the underwater trail at Truck Bay. St. John has two smashing (and expensive) resorts, a handful of more reasonable accommodations and two excellent campgrounds. Despite its small size (19 square miles) and underdevelopment, there is excellent dining and duty-free shopping. If you're looking for great nightlife, though, you'll be happier on St. Thomas. Many of the residents hail from the mainland U.S. and are hopelessly in love with their new home.

St. Kitts

Beautiful St. Kitts is just starting to come on as a tourist destination, as is its little sister, Nevis, which lies just two miles offshore. The island, now independent of Great Britain, is divided by three volcanic mountains split by deep ravines. The southeast peninsula has excellent white sand beaches while at other areas the sand is black, the product of long-ago eruptions. The island is also home to a rainforest, undulating sugarcane fields and an impressive fortress. There's much nightlife in the hotels; one sports the island's lone casino. Life is pretty laid-back here, with most tourists happily scaling mountains, inspecting one of the Caribbean's best fortresses or exploring the forest on horseback. The people retain much of their British roots, including a fanaticism for cricket.

St. Lucia

Lying between Martinique and St. Vincent, St. Lucia is a large island—238 square miles—and remarkably lush, dominated by rainforests and twin mountain peaks. There are also natural sulfur springs, countless fields of banana trees and fine beaches, mostly of black sand. Diving, snorkeling and hiking are all excellent. All-inclusive properties are the rage on this independent state within the British Commonwealth of Nations, much to the dismay of local restaurateurs and other businesspeople who find it hard to compete. The people are friendly and helpful and just love to dance—you'll have no problem finding places to party.

Sint Maarten/St. Martin

You get two distinct cultures in one when visiting this 37-square-mile island, the smallest piece of land in the world shared by two nations. St. Martin has a decidedly French flavor with its excellent gourmet restaurants, fine duty-free shopping and afternoon siestas wherein virtually all stores and businesses close down. It's also less developed than the teeming Dutch side, but still too busy for those seeking the ultimate escape. St. Maarten, as the Dutch side is known, has a golf course, a slew of hotels, lots of nightlife and a dozen casinos, but is so overdeveloped only dedicated party animals will be really happy. English is generally spoken everywhere, and just a marker on the side of the road lets you know you've switched countries.

St. Thomas

St. Thomas, the busiest and most developed of the U.S. Virgin Islands, is one of the Caribbean's most cosmopolitan destinations. It's quite hilly and stunning views abound at every turn. The beaches are good—Magen's Bay is among the Caribbean's most gorgeous—but many are quite narrow. Shoppers go crazy in the capital city of Charlotte Amalie (pronounced ah-MAHL-ya) with its dense proliferation of duty-free stores and upscale boutiques. The island has excellent lodging and a ton of attractions to keep sun avoiders happy. It's a beautiful island, but a bit too frenetic for some, and traffic can be a real problem. Like the other two U.S. Virgin Islands (Sts. Croix and John), the people are U.S. citizens who pay taxes and must honor federal laws, but are not allowed to vote for the president.

St. Vincent and The Grenadines

This string of islands between Grenada and St. Lucia (with Barbados to the east) are relatively undeveloped, with much of the land dominated by lush mountains, family farms and fields of banana, coconut and breadfruit trees. St. Vincent is by far the largest (133 square miles) and most populated (about 99,000). Most beaches are of black sand, though you'll find a few white ones as well. Diving is one of the island's chief attractions with shallow reefs surrounding nearly every one of the Grenadines. St. Vincent's dominant feature is Soufriere Volcano, which has been active for centuries and last erupted in 1979 (the same year, incidentally, that the islands became independent from Great Britain); hiking to the top is popular, though strenuous. The Grenadines, which together total 17 square miles, offer a peaceful holiday with a smattering of hotels and restaurants.

Tobago

Lying off the Venezuela coast close to its sister island of Trinidad, Tobago is relatively undiscovered, which suits those in the know just fine. Thanks to great foresight by the British residents in 1765, more than 27,000 acres of rainforest are protected from development. The island, which measures 27 miles long by seven miles wide, is lovely with fine beaches, little fishing villages, steep, verdant hillsides and small hotels. Diving is good but a bit rugged. Life is much more peaceful here than on Trinidad—it can be hard to remember the two islands, former British colonies, are actually one independent nation.

Trinidad

If you're looking for good beaches, head elsewhere, as there are few on this busy island. If, however, you want to shop till you drop, party all night, be pampered in fine hotels and rub elbows with international business travelers, this is the spot for you. Best known to tourists for its amazing Carnival and its array of steel band music, Trinidad is as different from Tobago as guppies are to barracuda. More than a million souls live on Trinidad, most quite prosperous and literate. The island was the wealthiest of the Caribbean after oil was discovered offshore in the 1970s; the subsequent drop of prices has led the government to give tourism a big push.

EASTERN CARIBBEAN ADVENTURE

By David Swanson

On Foot

No example sums up the joy and frustration of hiking in the Eastern Caribbean better than my first visit to **Antigua**. A government official had eagerly informed me prior to my trip that the Ministry of Agriculture had identified three new trails into the heart of the island's limited wilderness area. An appointment was set with a guide who would take me to one or more of the hikes.

My first couple of days on Antigua were disappointing because I found the island crassly overdeveloped, and escape seemingly unattainable. The idea of heading for the hills became more and more appealing. My guide, Dennis, arrived exactly as scheduled and we went on a pleasant morning tour of the island by car. Then he took me over to Fig Tree Drive, the greenest, prettiest part of the island, for the hiking portion of the tour. Near the pass leading over Fig Tree Hill, he veered off onto a dirt road which led to an empty reservoir tucked neatly into the hillside. Dennis explained this was a popular picnic area for Antiguans, and we then walked to a trail which marched around and up the slopes of Leafy Mountain.

After a mile of hiking, it became apparent we were lost. Not lost in the sense that we couldn't make our way back, but lost in that it was apparent that the trail was nothing more than a goat path which would divide and merge with another goat path every 50 feet or so. There was no real trail to the summit; it was simply a matter of fumbling our way to the top like wayward goats through Antigua's lightly forested hillsides.

We eventually found the summit, which relinquished stunning views of the island's capital to the north, the plains to the east, and of sugary coves of sand juxtaposed against baby blue Caribbean waters. I sat down to breathe in the humidity, silently applauding my success at escaping the drunken sailors and mammoth cruise ships which had previously defined this trip to Antigua. Dennis disappeared into the woods and returned a few minutes later, his shirt wrapped around a dozen or more huge lemons, picked from a nearby tree and hoisted over his shoulder.

The point is not that we got lost; we had a great time exploring. You will too, if you delve into this lovely area. The reality is that, as much as the government wanted to oblige my interest, it really had little to show me.

This isn't always the case in the Caribbean: **Guadeloupe**, **Martinique** and **St. John** furnish literally dozens of trail options; most of these hikes are regularly maintained, with trailhead signs providing distances and directions. At the other extreme is **St. Kitts**, which has a verdant rainforest and a splendid volcanic summit, but essentially no maintained or marked trails, leaving visitors largely at the beck and call of the very good, but not inexpensive local guide service. The norm is somewhere in between, with island governments slowly integrating nature's bounty into their infrastructure, largely because of the financial dividend ecotourism offers.

The geographical appearance of Eastern Caribbean islands falls into two general categories: those which were formed by continuing volcanic evolution, producing steep flanks which climb to the summit of both dormant and active volcanoes, and those which were created by an uplift of coral limestone, creating a gentler, usually drier, landscape of rolling hills, scalloped by coves of white sand. The twin-island nation of **Trinidad** and **Tobago** are the exception; they were once linked to South America (Trinidad's mountains are an extension of the Andes). As a rule, the volcanic islands have the greatest quantity and diversity of hiking options with ambitious treks through rain forests and over mountains, while the limestone islands offer quieter walks visiting beaches, forts and bird sanctuaries.

A number of the region's volcanoes are still very much alive. The most famous eruption during modern times was that of Martinique's **Mt. Pelee** in 1902, which exploded in a torrent of hot ash and gas, and suffocated the thriving city of Saint-Pierre and its entire population of 30,000. More recently, **La Soufriere** on St. Vincent erupted in 1979 sending clouds of ash and steam ten miles into the air, while the like-named Soufriere on Guadeloupe thundered to life in 1976 and encouraged the evacuation of the island's capitol, Basse-Terre. However, don't let these facts alarm you too much. Although one or two wake up for a period every decade or so—most recently, Montserrat's **Tar River Soufriere** in July, 1995—the activity typically remains more benign than that of Mt. Pelee almost a century ago. The region's volcanic summits generally appear to be sleeping peacefully and invite exploration on foot. Details of these hikes, among the most challenging in the Caribbean, are given in each chapter. (You'll see the term *soufriere* a lot in this book; it's a French word for volcanic crater that has found its way into common usage within the Eastern Caribbean).

Most of the hikes we've listed can be made on your own. On occasion, however, there will be recommendations regarding the use of local guides, obtained either through a guide service or, sometimes, by inquiring in the vicinity of the trailhead. The availability of independent guides in the Eastern Caribbean is more a by-product of ecotourism in the region, rather than locals looking for free handouts. On the more impoverished islands, there is less government money to spend on trail upkeep and markers, making guides a prerequisite for first-time visitors. In some areas island tourism offices will strongly encourage using a guide for trails of only moderate difficulty; the hidden agenda is indirect support of the local economy. There are at least three main reasons for using a guide:

1. The guide will help lead you through genuinely difficult or dangerously exposed areas.

2. A good guide will add to your trek by explaining the natural environment you are exploring and the historical significance of ruins you may encounter, as well as providing an inside glimpse into the local character of the island.

3. Hiring a guide contributes to the local economy by directly supporting an individual, some of whom spend a good deal of their "spare" time maintaining trails.

There are at least three reasons *against* hiring guides:

1. Many of the trails where guides are recommended by tourist offices are not that difficult for hikers of reasonable ability.

2. If you're looking for escape and solitude, the well-meaning conversation a guide might engage in may detract from your desired interaction with the natural environment.

3. Guides are usually expensive; it's not uncommon to spend over a hundred dollars for a guide on a major trail.

While the quality of guides available on various islands differs greatly, and trail conditions are constantly evolving, we urge you to use your own judgment, keeping in mind that a good guide will do much more than point you to your destination, and can greatly add to the experience of the hike. If you plan to hike several major trails on an island, hire a guide for at least the first day so that you gain a sense of the difficulties you will be encountering, as well as an appreciation for the plant life and history of the area. You may decide that you'll want to use that guide's services for the remainder of your visit.

There are a few precautions which hikers should take into account before embarking on any trail. First, carry plenty of fresh water. Rivers, as clean and refreshing as they may appear, are not generally safe to drink from. The parasite bilharziasis is frequently found in slow-moving streams and lakes, and the illness it causes can even result in death (islands to be particularly wary of the parasite are Guadeloupe, Martinique and St. Lucia). Let the heat and humidity of the tropics be a constant reminder to drink bottled water regularly while exercising. If you feel dehydrated at the end of a day, slightly increase the salt in your diet, which will help you retain fluids when exercising.

If you're walking through areas where shade is minimal (the coraline islands in particular), the sun will be intense. Even in moderate doses of an hour or two, it can cause severe sunburns which will crimp your style for an entire vacation and, in extreme cases, can cause sunstroke (and we won't even start on the skin cancer topic). For the former, use sun block at all times, taking into account that much of the lotion will drip off during sweat-inducing activities. For the latter, minimize your time in the sun, particularly at the start of a trip, wear sunglasses and a wide-brimmed hat and, again, always drink plenty of fluids. If you plan to do more than a day or two of hiking, consider bringing along a Gatorade-style drink (available in powdered form) which will help replace lost electrolytes. For severe cases of dehydration, consult a doctor.

Watch out for the ghastly manchineel tree, amply offered throughout the Eastern Caribbean. Its fruit, which looks something like a green crab apple, is very poisonous. But problems with the tree don't end there: if you stand under a manchineel during rainfall, the runoff from the leaves can cause blisters. Like the fruit, the tree's sap is also quite potent and was once used by Carib Indians to dip their arrowheads in before heading out for a missionary slaughter. In more heavily traveled areas, particularly around beaches, locals will frequently post warning signs on the trees (some manchineels are marked with red paint). However, in more remote areas, you're on your own. Have an islander point out the tree shortly after arrival so you can avoid it on your explorations. Also note that the sap from the oleander is also poisonous.

Snakes are not generally a problem in the Caribbean, but one variety, the fer-de-lance, deserves attention; its powerful bite can be deadly or, at least, extremely painful. The snake is most predominant on Martinique, typically in the dry coastal areas, and has also been seen on St. Lucia and Trinidad. The fer-de-lance really doesn't want to have anything to do with people and bites are infrequent, but it's prudent to be aware of its presence. They are most likely to attack when cornered or surprised, so the best way to keep the fer-de-lance away is to tap a stick in front of your feet as you hike. Heavy shoes and long pants are a good idea if you plan to be exploring the bush. Another problematic encounter is that with a scorpion, recognized by the stinger arching over its back. Although generally not fatal, scorpions boast a painful defense strategy and are best avoided. Like the fer-de-lance, they are usually found in hot, dry areas. Finally, two mere nuisances are mosquitoes and sand-flies, found principally in areas of stagnant water and on beaches, respectively. They are best combated with insect repellent.

Wear appropriate clothing for your treks, temperatures drop as one climbs into cloud-wrapped mountains. Combined with perspiration, brisk wind, and humidity or rain, these conditions can be ideal for hypothermia. For any hike ascending elevations above 3000 feet, we recommend packing a pair of long pants and a light windbreaker jacket. Although heavy hiking boots aren't really necessary in the Caribbean, a sturdy pair of walking shoes, broken in before your trip (to avoid blisters), is generally sufficient. Before investing in a pair of new shoes, remember that you may be hiking on muddy paths or through streams which are sure to alter the appearance of the most colorful designs! As appealing as it might be at some points, walking barefoot is not a good idea; hookworms can penetrate skin.

By Pedal

It makes sense that, following the explosion of mountain biking in the United States, it would catch on sooner or later in the Caribbean. And why not? What could be more inviting than riding through charming island villages, past rolling fields of sugarcane and down to silky white beaches? Those interested in more demanding explorations will find an ample quantity of steep hills and challenging forest trails on most islands. Though the sport is still in its nascent stages, there are biking organizations on most of the larger islands, as well as an increasing quantity of rental shops carrying a variety of the better brands known at home.

With over 1200 paved miles to ride, **Guadeloupe** is the regional capital of road riding and features the Tour de la Guadeloupe every August, a sort of miniature Tour de France-gone-tropical. Although cars race by on the main roads at breakneck speeds, islanders embrace cyclists enthusiastically. Other islands which encourage road biking include Martinique, Trinidad and Barbados although each of these islands feature their share of heavy vehicular traffic. The quality of paved roads varies greatly within the region and it's best to check with a local rider or biking outfit before importing a road bike for touring an island.

Mountain biking is spreading throughout the region, from **St. Vincent** and tiny **Montserrat** where old goat paths and plantation trails lace the hillsides, to the **British Virgin Islands**, where every direction appears to be up or down, except for the ferry which leads to another island and more trails. When off-roading through drier sections—and this includes the lower elevations of virtually all the islands—you'll want to have a patch-kit handy for stickers and thorns.

It is possible to ship your bike into the Caribbean on the same plane you are arriving on, although the disadvantages may far outweigh the relative ease of renting from a local shop. If your bike uses exotic parts, you may want to bring the unique items and a toolkit with you. Don't ship anything fragile (like a top-of-the-line road bike) that you wouldn't want banged around. I watched as one island baggage handler tossed a boxed bicycle onto the airport's baggage conveyer-belt hard enough to have the handlebars puncture the cardboard. Moments later, as the bike turned a corner, it flopped off the belt and onto the floor where it sat unattended while its owner stood trapped in a long customs line.

The rental agencies we've listed on each island differ greatly in what they provide, and rental prices vary even more wildly, from a very reasonable $7 to a breathtaking $32 per day. And don't expect that the price relates to what you get; it's all supply and demand. Most of the businesses we've listed are set up specifically to cater to tourists, while a few are stores which focus primarily on sales to locals, renting to visitors as a way of supplementing business. The number of bikes the shops carry also varies significantly, from two (at the lone bike supplier on St. Eustatius, a local dive shop) to several dozen. However, if the current trend continues, the number of bikes available to rent in the Eastern Caribbean could easily double in the next couple of years.

In a few cases, the rental stores have well-staffed repair shops and can handle virtually any problem you may encounter with your own bike on the island. On other islands, the shops may be strictly a rental agency and limited to servicing only what they rent in their repair facilities. Many of the better shops are happy to substitute your peddles and clips if you are bringing your own shoes, but call in advance if you want to count on it.

When renting a bike, check to make sure the seat and handlebars are adjusted for your height. Verify that tires are adequately filled and learn how to use the air pump for the bike you are renting (it may be foreign to what you are used to). If you don't know how to patch a tire, have someone in the shop spend a few minutes showing you how; if you're planning a long ride, carry a spare tube, if possible.

In addition to carrying plenty of bottled water, "hydrate" your body by guzzling a quart or two of water before you hit the road. You may find it helpful to bring along energy bars or powdered drinks which help maintain your stamina and replace cherished electrolytes. Heed prior warnings concerning the sun, which can be relentless on some treeless roads (see "On Foot"). Helmets are an essential component of safe riding; although most or all of the shops provide them, bring one from home if you can.

Bike and Cruise Tours

☎ *(503) 667-4053.*

If you are willing to dedicate your entire Caribbean vacation to cycling, Oregon-based Linda Thompson offers biking tours in conjunction with Norwegian Cruise Line sailings out of Puerto Rico. Bikes are provided in Puerto Rico, loaded onto the ship, and a leader and preset riding itinerary—averaging 20-25 miles each day—greets cyclists on each island. Group size varies but usually averages a couple dozen riders and prices start at about $1850 (from the east coast) including airfare, seven-day cruise, bike rental and port taxes.

Underwater

When divers dream of the Caribbean, typically they fantasize about Bonaire, the Caymans, Belize, Cozumel. While we won't discourage you from visiting any of these locations—each covered in Fielding's *Guide to the Western Caribbean*—there's plenty to keep most any diver, beginner to advanced, happily occupied in the Eastern Caribbean. Wall dives and pinnacles, wrecks and reefs are found throughout the region and, though the diving can be dramatic and dynamic, the experience tends to be more relaxed, less-crowded.

With so many unheralded destinations to choose from where does one go? Wall enthusiasts should head for **St. Croix**, **Saba**, **Dominica** or **St. Lucia**, where steep drop-offs provide canyons, pinnacles and more. If investigating wrecks is your pleasure, you need look no further than the **Virgin Islands**, **Anguilla** or **Barbados**, destinations which have proven a magnet for both planned and unexpected disasters, creating artificial reefs for the pleasure of divers. And if reefs call to you, the plateau-shaped underwater landscapes of **Antigua**, the **Virgin Islands**, and the **Grenadines** will hit the right notes. Shore diving is not widely available in the Eastern Caribbean, but you'll find opportunities on **St. Croix** and **St. Lucia**. Finally, if heading well off the beaten track is your objective, try **St. Eustatius** or **Montserrat**, islands with ample sights and few visitors, or better yet, head for **Barbuda's** desolate shores, where diving on pristine reefs is possible only from the decks of a live-aboard situation.

Learning to dive is a less complicated, and more available exercise, than many people imagine. One can try diving by signing up for a resort course. These half-day introductions into the world of diving are available through most major dive shops, generally for around $75. While there is some classroom-style information, the course culminates, usually in a pool or shallow reef, with actual diving in full regalia. In the French West Indies, a similar overture, referred to as a "Baptism" is available, although their introduction actually takes you down onto the reefs for a short spin, in the hands of an able instructor.

If you are certain that diving is something you're willing to fall in love with, then you'll want to obtain certification—your "C" card—which allows you to dive on your own, without needing an instructor to tag along (although all diving should be done with a buddy). You can take the entire course at home spread out over several weeks or months (usually starting in a pool, graduating to a lake or ocean dive), or you can do it all in the Caribbean, concentrated into five or six days. An increasingly popular option is a combination of the two, allowing you to review the classroom material at home (usually via video), and save the actual water training for your vacation. Another route is to obtain your certification one dive at a time, spread over several vacations and different destinations; NAUI calls this their "Passport Diver" program and it allows you to pick up the course wherever you left off, spread out over a period of months or even years.

Diving is a serious and potentially dangerous sport. There are universal risks, which won't be addressed here, and there are those which are fairly unique to the Caribbean. The shark activity common in the Bahamas is actually rare in the nearby Eastern Caribbean. Nurse sharks are spotted throughout the region, but they are typically shy and unproblematic, content to nap under ledges. On rare occasions, hammerheads will be seen where deeper waters approach dive sites, but they tend to stay at a distance.

The huge, graceful whale shark is rarely observed in the Eastern Caribbean, but the timid creature is affably tolerant of human interaction. Barracudas and moray eels also tend to be shy and won't usually bite unless provoked or cornered.

There are several, more innocuous creatures which do create problems. One is fire coral, which is found throughout the region. Although the nasty sting you'll feel after touching it will eventually go away, it can be inflamed by scratching the area of your skin which came into contact (quickly fanning your hands around the affected area while underwater helps to dispel the coral darts which cause the pain). Avoid the beautiful fireworm which also defends itself with bunches of tiny daggers. The black sea urchin has dozens of sharp needles protruding from its body like a pincushion. These spines can grow up to a foot long and will back up their sting with a dose of venom. More serious is the scorpionfish, which frequently appears to be just another rock, until it's stepped on, at which point it releases a potentially fatal toxin; medical attention should be sought immediately.

As a rule, dive sites are clustered on the western coasts of most islands, away from the brisk currents of the Atlantic. The primary exception is around the Virgin Islands, where the numerous tiny islands provide shelter for reefs and divers.

The four destinations of the French West Indies adhere to different dive standards than those commonly practiced at PADI or NAUI style outfits. You should familiarize yourself with their methods and styles before boarding a boat; a good grasp of conversational French is necessary for some of the shops on Guadeloupe and Martinique (St. Barthelemy and St. Martin dive shops are more fluent in English). One key difference is that while Americans consider 130 feet the depth limit for safe recreational diving, the French allow advanced divers to descend to about 195 feet. You will be expected to produce a medical certificate before diving with a French operation. Instead of a standard resort course, the French offer *le baptism*, a hand-held submersion into the dive experience.

The dive sites we have listed are by no means comprehensive, and even aren't necessarily "the best" a given island has to offer. We have tried to create a representative sample of the kinds of dives available, avoiding, what one operator referred to obliquely as "proprietary" sites which aren't known to others. Where we've graded sites as being suitable for beginners, note that few of these locations are appropriate as a first dive. A beginner or novice site is usually for divers who have completed their certification or, at least, are in the company of a trained instructor.

The pricing information we have provided for the various dive operators is meant primarily for comparison purposes; every dive shop has an assortment of packages and hotel tie-ins available which reduce the per-dive cost. Although we have noted whether individual shops are PADI or NAUI affiliated and to what level they offer instruction, these facts should not be an overriding factor in comparing dive shops.

CRUISE PORTS

Charlotte Amalie in St. Thomas is one of the most popular cruise ship ports.

Cruising can be so addicting that it's sometimes hard to even get off the ship at a port of call. If you do choose to do so, you have several options for exploring that day's island. The cruise company will try hard to get you to take one of their organized shore excursions, which often include lunch. The advantage is that you'll be shown around safely and you'll always be back on time to catch the ship. The drawback, however, is that their prices can be quite high, often as much as 100 percent above what you'd pay on your own. If you're adventurous, it's better to explore on your own, but keep a sharp eye on the time, as cruise ships set sail promptly as scheduled with or without straggling passengers.

Anguilla

Cruise ships do not stop at the port on this island.

Antigua

Island Tour

A visit to the island's Interpretation Center focuses on local history, followed by visits to historic sites, notably Nelson's Dockyard National Park and English Harbour, where Horatio Nelson once plied the waters. Day trips are also available to Barbuda, 25 miles away and inaccessible by cruise ship.

Jolly Roger Cruise

On this veritable floating pirate theme park, you can hang out at the open bar, learn the latest Caribbean dances, watch a staged "pirate wedding," snorkel, or walk the plank.

Catamaran Cruise

Sail the northwest coast of the island, stopping to snorkel, swim or relax on the beach.

Snorkeling

Various snorkeling adventures are available on the island, notably to Prickly Pear Island, often accompanied by lunch.

Golf

The Cedar Valley Golf Course, a 6142-yard, par-70 facility, welcomes you to its native grass fairways and greens.

Barbados

Island Tours

Historic sites and breathtaking vistas are on the agendas of several island tours that emphasize historical sites such as Gun Hill Signal Station, Villa Nova, Sam Lord's Castle, St. John's Church and local plantations. Tours focusing on natural wonders take you to the Flower Forest and/or Andromeda Gardens.

Jolly Roger Tour

Pretend you're a pirate and sail the west coast, anchoring in Holetown Bay to walk the plank, snorkel or land on the beach. Free rum and a staged pirate wedding add to the merriment.

Carlisle Beach Excursion

You'll find everything you need (towels, chairs, showers, lockers) for a day at the beach at the Carlisle Beach Center. A barbecue lunch is included, along with live island music and access to a bar and gift shop.

Pub-Hopping

It's bar-hopping in the English tradition, but with a Caribbean flavor. A guide will accompany you to all the local hot spots such as the Bamboo Beach Bar, Rumors and the Coach House. A complimentary drink is available at each stop. (All pub-hoppers must be 18 or older.)

Photography Tour

Serious photographers will enjoy the many photo opportunities on this excursion, which takes in Bathsheba Beach and Skeete's Bay.

Harrison's Cave

Not for claustrophobics, this tram ride takes you on an underground ride past dramatic waterfalls, tranquil pools and stalactites and stalagmites.

Atlantis Submarine

The air-conditioned Atlantis II takes you down more than 100 feet for a look at a shipwreck, coral reefs, sponge gardens and other marine life.

Snorkeling

Explore the waters (and a shipwreck) at Carlisle Bay or sail on a catamaran to Bridgetown Deep Water Harbour for some serious snorkeling.

SCUBA

Certified divers are invited to explore parts of the island's western coast, including a coral reef, on this one-tank dive. Equipment and experienced guides provided.

Golf

The Sandy Lane Resort is home to this 18-hole, par-72 course. The cost for a ship excursion includes transportation and greens fees; carts and lunch are extra.

Barbuda

Cruise ships do not stop at the port on this island.

British Virgin Islands

Virgin Gorda

It's a 40-minute boat ride to Virgin Gorda from the Tortola port of Road Town. Once you get there, visit Baths, where you can explore marine caves with equipment provided.

Tortola Island Tour

Visit Tortola's Botanical Gardens, Cane Garden Bay and the island's most panoramic vistas aboard an open-air safari bus.

Mount Sage

One of the island's most famous viewpoints, Mount Sage is the highest mountain in the Virgin Islands. Walk the fairly strenuous trail to the top, enjoying the rainforest flora and fauna on the way up.

Glass-Bottom Boat

Watch marine life from a dry perch in a 21-foot glass-bottom boat.

Snorkeling

Peter Island is one of the most beautiful of Tortola's islands—perfect for snorkeling.

Dominica

Nature Tour

The island's Botanical Gardens, Trois Pitons National Park and the Emerald Pool are the destinations on this nature-lover's tour. Some tours proceed to Trafalgar Falls.

Grenada

Island Tour

Driving tour includes a visit to the capital of St. George, Westerhall Point, a sugar factory, and Flamboyant Beach, where drinks, swimming, and sun are complimentary.

Grand Etang National Park

Everything is uphill on this tour, which takes in Annandale Falls and continues to 1910 feet to Grand Etang National Park. Explore the rainforest, view Grand Etang Lake (set in an extinct volcano) and visit Fort Frederick—built by the French in 1779—on the way down. Naturalists also may enjoy a visit to Bay Gardens, located in St. Paul.

Party Raft

Raft along the coast of Grenada, sip rum punch and stop at a deserted beach for swimming or snorkeling.

Helicopter Tour

See the island from above on a helicopter tour. The pilot narrates; you take the pictures.

St. Pauls/Westerhall

Sugar and spice and everything nice on this tour, which checks on the growing and processing of sugar, cocoa and nutmeg (among other species), then stops briefly at the white-sand Grand Anse Beach.

Catamaran Tour

Aboard the double-deck catamaran Rhum Runner your guide will brief you on the history of the island while you drink rum punch. View a coral reef through the glass bottom, then relax or swim at Morne Rouge Beach.

Guadeloupe

Island Tour

Enjoy the gorgeous island scenery, walk up to Crawfish Falls, and tantalize your taste buds with a visit to the Severin Distillery, where you can imbibe on the spot or buy at factory prices for later consumption.

Carbet Falls

This half-day excursion takes in banana plantations, tropical forest, Carbet Falls (the walk to the falls takes approximately one hour), La Soufriere volcano, and lunch at a typical Creole restaurant.

Domaine de Valombreuse

Flower enthusiasts won't want to miss an excursion to this stunning floral park where there are varieties of flowers from all over the world. Birders also may find this a hot spot.

Martinique

Island Tour

An overview of the island and rainforest, plus a stop at St. Pierre, destroyed by the eruption of Mount Pelee in 1902, and various other historical sites. Some island tours include a visit to the Butterfly Farm, set in a beautiful botanic park.

Calypso Tour

This double-deck party boat cruises across the Bay of Fort-de-France, stops at a beach for swimming, and allows you to look down on a coral reef through its glass-bottom viewers.

Walking Tour

If you're tired of water-related transportation and are in good physical condition, use your feet to explore the capital's historic and architectural sites. An English-speaking guide accompanies you.

Balata Gardens

Caribbean flora is highlighted at Balata Gardens, where footpaths wind through one of the best collections of native plants and flowers in the islands. Also visit Balata Church, modeled after the Sacred Heart Basilica in Paris, and the Creole House. Other nature-oriented stops worth a look include Les Ombrages and the Parc des Floralies.

St. Pierre/Plantation de Leyritz

Visit St. Pierre and stop at the historic Plantation de Leyritz, a restored sugar plantation converted into an inn and restaurant. Enjoy a complimentary beverage and lunch in the restaurant, do some exploring, or swim in the pool. On the trip back, stop for a look at a local rum factory.

Snorkeling

Equipment and instruction are provided as you explore one of the island's coral reefs.

Golf

The Country Club de la Martinique welcomes you to its par-71 course, designed by Robert Trent Jones. The scenery is as exciting as the game is challenging, and a constant 15–20-mph wind keeps things interesting.

Montserrat

Galaways Plantation

This estate, touted as the only Irish plantation in the New World, is now mostly ruins, but it provides an interesting look at life on the island in the 17th and 18th centuries.

Great Alps Waterfalls

It's a bit of a hike, but there is much tropical flora and fauna to be enjoyed along the way. You may be able to find a guide at Shooter's Hill Village, where the trail begins.

Nevis

Island Tour

There's not all that much to see on Nevis, but you may wish to take in the area around Charlestown and historical sites such as the Montpelier Plantation and the Nelson Museum.

Saba

Cruise ships do not stop at the port on this island.

St. Barthélémy (St. Barts)

Island Tour

Tour downtown Gustavia by minibus, then take in the local historical sites and scenic views, with a short shopping stop in La Savone.

SCUBA

Many dive sites in the area lend themselves to both scuba diving and snorkeling. Some favorites are Pain de Sucre and Les Petits Saints.

St. Croix

Island Tour

A driver/guide takes you around the island in an air-conditioned van, stopping to tour the Whim Great House and to enjoy the lush rainforest on St. Croix's north shore.

Botanical Gardens

See St. George Village and Botanical Gardens in Christiansted and other scenic and historical highlights—including the 1493 Columbus landing site at Salt River—on this guided tour.

Catamaran Tour

A 52-foot catamaran takes passengers to Buck Island for snorkeling, and to Coakley Beach for a barbecue lunch prepared by the crew.

Buck Island Snorkeling

Buck Island Reef, part of the Buck Island National Monument, is the destination on this excursion, led by experienced guides and appropriate for snorkelers of all levels. Highly recommended!

Butler Bay Hike

Nature lovers shouldn't miss this hike through 225-acre Butler Bay preserve, which begins at the Ghut Bird Sanctuary and includes the ruins of the Estate Mount Washington Plantation, and panoramic views of Frederiksted Harbor, Sandy Point Beach and the rainforest. Wear comfortable footwear and bring bottled water for this moderately strenuous hike.

Sail and Snorkel

Gear and instruction are provided in this one-hour dive just off the island's coast.

Party Cruise

Complimentary rum and fruit punch add to the party atmosphere on the double-decked, glass-bottomed Reef Queen, but you also can look down on shipwrecks, coral reefs, and marine life. A stop at Sandy Point Beach for swimming or sunning is included.

Golf

Robert Trent Jones' par-72, 18-hole Carambola course is one of the Caribbean's finest, and was featured on "Shell's Wonderful World of Golf," when Chi Chi Rodriguez burned up the links with a 69.

Sint Eustatius

The Quill

The climb up the side of this volcanic cone yields plenty of birds and other fauna—including an occasional iguana. Degree of difficulty varies, depending on which trail you take.

St. John

Island Tour

A narrated driving/walking tour of the island that departs from the ship's pier. Highlights include island history and panoramic overlooks.

Beach Tour

Tour Virgin Island National Park and other sights of interest, then snorkel or swim at Trunk Bay, which boasts its own underwater snorkel trail.

Island Cruise

Explore the island by sea on this guided tour that takes you around the island and focuses on both history and current events. After the tour, anchor near the beach for swimming and snorkeling.

St. Kitts

Brimstone Hill Tour

Christopher Columbus' 1493 landing site at Old Road Town is just one of the intriguing stops on this tour, which also visits the Romney Estate, an old West Indian plantation home where the Caribelle Batik Industry is now located. The main attraction is Brimstone Hill, site of a 17th-century fortress that houses a museum and offers panoramic views of the coastline.

Rainforest Excursion

After a stop at a Caribelle workshop to watch batiks being created, venture into a rainforest valley for a naturalist-led hike and look at the tropical flora and fauna.

Horseback Riding

What better way to experience the beach than astride a gentle, well-trained horse! After the one-hour ride, enjoy a complimentary cocktail.

Catamaran Adventure

Sail along the southern coast of the island, then disembark for snorkeling—gear and instruction provided.

Golf

The 18-hole Royal St. Kitts Golf Course welcomes you to its 6918-yard championship links.

St. Lucia

Sea Safari

Travel by boat to the Soufriere, where you can peer over the edge into the volcano's hissing abyss (it's dormant, not to worry). Enjoy the gorgeous Diamond Mineral Baths and surrounding botanical garden, then stop at Anse Cochon Beach for a swim.

Helicopter Tour

Enjoy the view over Castries Harbor, the Pitons (volcanic mountains), Jalousie Plantation, and the tropical rainforest.

Plantation Tour

Island history is highlighted on a tour of the restored, 600-acre Invergoil Sugar Mill. See the settlement villages, the stone mill, and hear stories of plantation life. Great photo ops along the way. Variations of this tour include exploration of the local rainforest accompanied by a naturalist.

Rodney Bay/Pigeon Island

Visit Rodney Bay and Pigeon Island, site of Fort Rodney. Tour the fort, then head to Reduit Beach for recreation and relaxation.

Sint Maarten/St. Martin

Island Tour

A bus ride from the capital city of Philipsburg takes you to both the French and Dutch sides of the island, and includes historical sites, shopping and refreshments.

Beach Rendezvous

Get away from it all at Orient Bay, sometimes called the French Riviera of the Caribbean. A barbecue lunch with all the trimmings will be served while you relax in lounge chairs.

Le Privelege

This exclusive resort, located on the French side of the island, overlooks Anse Marcel Bay. Enjoy use of all the resort's sports facilities and have lunch by the pool.

Sun and Sea Cruise

Board the 60-foot Maison Maru for a coastal cruise that includes both the French and Dutch sides of the island. The rum punch is on the house.

See and Sea

See the sights on the French part of St. Maarten, then board a semi-submarine for a 45-minute narrated tour of coral reefs and Crole Rock. Watch a diver feed the moray eels, then—if you still have the stomach for it—stop for a complimentary drink, do some shopping and enjoy plenty of photo ops on the way back.

Golden Eagle Sailing

The 76-foot catamaran Golden Eagle sweeps you across the shimmering waters to Tintamar, an island where you can swim, snorkel or relax on the beach. A continental champagne breakfast or afternoon snack is included, and there's an open bar for your enjoyment on the return trip.

Champagne Brunch Tour

Board the Lady Mary and sip champagne as you sail through Simpson Bay Lagoon. Enjoy authentic Creole dishes, listen to the steel band or watch local artisans on the yacht, who carve and make weavings before your eyes.

Explorer Cruise

See the sights on the Dutch side of the island, then board the Explorer for a cruise through a French lagoon and into the Port la Royale Marine. Visit the Explorer's private island for swimming, jet skiing or parasailing.

America's Cup Sailing

Wannabe America's Cup sailors can get a taste of the action in an actual race aboard 70-foot America's Cup yachts. Go along for the ride or assist the crew if you have the stamina for it.

Pinel Island

Visit the secluded isle de Pinel, where you can swim, snorkel, play volleyball, or sunbathe—au naturel if you wish.

Deep Sea Fishing

Marlin, sailfish, tuna and shark are a few of the possibilities when you fish onboard one of the island's fishing boats.

Shipwreck Cove

With the help of a professional staff, snorkel your way through a sunken ship, explore the coral or feed the fish.

SCUBA

Certified divers only on this shallow water, one-tank dive in the company of a divemaster, who will give you a guided tour. Equipment provided or bring your own.

Golf

The par-70 Mullet Bay Golf Club is more challenging that its 6200 yards would imply. Try out your over-water shots—and watch those tricky greens!

St. Thomas

Island Tour

A driver will take you on a narrated tour to St. Peter's Greathouse, where you can explore the former getaway estate of the "rich and famous." Then enjoy the spectacular view from the island's highest point, Mountain Top, where shopping also is available.

Charlotte Amalie

It takes a couple of hours to walk this historic district, but the beautifully restored homes are worth seeing, and the area is a window into the island's past. See Fort Christian, the oldest building in the Virgin Islands, along with other historic landmarks, and visit the Emancipation Garden, Market Square and the fishing village of Frenchtown.

St. John Island

Take a ferry from the eastern tip of St. Thomas to the St. John Island. Then enjoy the sights on a scenic drive to Trunk Bay, where you can swim or snorkel (there's an underwater trail for snorkeling enthusiasts). Not to be missed.

The Arboretum at Magens' Beach

Although the arboretum is touted as one of St. Thomas' "best-kept secrets," it's no secret to the cruise lines, which regularly list it on their excursion agendas. Highlights include the 100-foot Puerto Rico palms and other magnificent trees planted in the restored arboretum and the opportunity to swim in the crystal clear waters of Magens' Beach.

Skyline Drive

Yo, ho ho! This tour takes you past old hideouts of the notorious Bluebeard the pirate and others of his ilk, then sweeps you up the mountain to the Saint Peter House for dozens of photo ops and a stroll around the estate.

Coral World

A good way for landlubbing tourists to see the marvels of the coral reef without getting wet. A visit to this underwater observatory includes a 90-minute tour. Some excursions also include a ride on a semi-submarine and/or snorkeling at Coki Point.

Windsong Sailing Tour

Get off the boat and into a yacht for this approximately three-hour sailing tour of the island. Lots of scenery and plenty of opportunities for swimming or soaking up the sun.

Sunset Sail

It doesn't get more romantic than this: a sunset, gorgeous scenery and complimentary wine and munchies.

Charter Sail

Have your own private party aboard a 65-foot schooner or 36-foot sloop available for half-day charter. Captain and crew are included, but you plan the trip, with stops for snorkeling if you wish.

Kon Tiki

The Kon Tiki is about as touristy as you can get, offering sightseeing above and below water (it has glass-bottomed tanks for your viewing pleasure), music for dancing and a never-ending supply of rum punch.

Atlantis Submarine

Moderately expensive as shore excursions go, this one offers a narrated underwater excursion aboard the 65-foot submarine Atlantis.

Seaplane Vistaliner

It's up, up and away on the Seaplane Vistaliner, an excursion that will put a bit of a bite in your vacation budget, but allows you to view the island chain from a completely different perspective. The 40-minute flight originates from St. Thomas Harbor. Great views, so bring your camera.

Helicopter Tour

A 25-minute flight takes you over Thatch and Grass cays and past other local landmarks. Some tours combine a helicopter flight with a 90-foot submarine dive into the waters off Charlotte Amalie.

Snorkeling

Everything is provided for you on this underwater adventure, including snorkeling gear, instructions and food to feed the fish. Weather permitting, the destination is St. John, where you can "snuba" as well as snorkel. Other snorkeling adventures are available to Turtle Cove on Buck Island.

SCUBA

If you are a certified SCUBA diver, board a custom dive boat for a one-tank dive to one of several island locations. Most lines also offer SCUBA adventures for noncertified divers that involve instruction and a dive to a coral reef.

Golf

Mahogany Run is one of the most famous golf courses in the Caribbean, and also one of the most challenging. The par-70 course is surrounded by gorgeous vistas, which takes your mind off the difficulty you're having staying on the fairways.

St. Vincent/Grenadines

Falls of Baleine

Approximately 20 miles from Kingstown, the falls are accessible by boat. Great scenery, and opportunities for swimming, snorkeling and exploring.

Sights around Kingstown include Fort Charlotte, the St. Vincent Museum and the St. Vincent Library.

Mayreau/Palm Island

Sail past the Tabago Cays to Palm Island, where you can swim or explore to your heart's content. Lunch is served aboard the sailboat.

Mayreau/Glass-bottom Boat

View coral reefs from above on this guided tour of local waters.

Catamaran Sailing

Sail past Petit St. Vincent and Palm Island on the Jetset, one of the fastest catamarans in the Caribbean.

Snorkeling

Dive at one of the island's most colorful reefs. Equipment and instruction are included.

SCUBA

One-tank dives are available for both certified and noncertified divers.

Tobago

Island History and Culture

Survey this island's historical and cultural sites, including Fort King George, Fort James, and plantations of coconut palms. Final stop is the famous Flambeaux Club, where you'll be immersed in the island's cultural side in the form of Tobagonian music and dance.

Beach Excursion

Spend the day at Mount Irvine Beach, one of the island's most exclusive private beaches. A barbecue lunch is included.

Glass-bottom Boat Tour

View Buccoo Reef and Coral Gardens from above, with a guide pointing out the undersea flora and fauna. Then anchor at Nylon Pool, where you can swim or relax.

Catamaran Cruise

Take a cruise along the coast in the 50-foot catamaran Loafer, which makes stops at Nylon Pool and Bon Accord Point. Opportunities for swimming—and an open bar—are available along the way.

Golf

The 18-hole, par-72 championship Mount Irvine course is gorgeous, and your golf excursion includes transportation, greens fees and a shared golf cart.

Trinidad

Island Tour

Begin your island tour at Port of Spain, with stops at the National Museum and Art Gallery and at various historic churches and homes.

Asa Wright Nature Centre

It's an hour's drive from Port of Spain, but both the flora and fauna are worth the trip—especially for birders and other nature lovers. Serious birders may want to visit the Caroni Bird Sanctuary, 10 miles south of Port of Spain.

ANGUILLA

The children of Anguilla are polite, proud and friendly.

Long, flat and skinny, Anguilla looks like an anchovy—indeed the name in Italian means "eel," a nickname reportedly bestowed on the island by Christopher Columbus when he cruised past in 1493. Today imbued with a British gentility, the island is a model of peace, quiet and pristine beauty; poets fall over themselves trying to describe the three blues of sea, sky and horizon. With no casinos, cinema, duty-free shopping, museums or golf courses, there's not much to do in Anguilla but surrender to nature; celebs like Robert De Niro and Princess Stephanie of Monaco find it quite easy. A dry climate has always rendered Anguilla the least populous of the British Crown Colonies in the Eastern Caribbean, but the swell of tourists in the past decade (17,000 in 1982 to 94,000 in 1994), has turned the economy from its former sea orientation to tourism. And yet, even though everyone wants to buy land here, no one seems able to, since the tight control of property and its very inaccessibility has saved Anguilla from the kind of overdevelopment that's nearly drowned nearby St. Martin. The result is an island where the beaches are still clean, the brew is still local, and the local scratch bands haven't succumbed to pretension. In short, an island to love.

Sometimes called the South Beach of the Caribbean, Anguilla boasts a remarkable clarity of light that throws a sparkling glow over everything. Even at peak season, it's easy to find secluded strands perfect for walking, snoozing, snuggling or snorkeling. There are offshore reefs and water sports galore, with fish pots and lobster traps and handcrafted racing boats boasting designer driftwood and exotic walls made of conch shells. Underwater is a Fujichrome spectacular of corals and fish. The landscape buzzes with wildlife—diving pelicans, mischievous frigate birds and noisy tropical birds. Everywhere you'll see hummingbirds feasting on flowering hibiscus and your breakfast table might even be visited by bananaquits, a little yellow bird with an unabashed appetite. There's even one local residence where snowy egrets stroll through the backyard.

Bird's Eye View

This 16-by- 3.5 mile island is scrubby, flat and often dusty. It rises from the Anguilla Bank 180 feet below sea level to only 213 feet above at its highest point. A frequent location for some of the most luxurious fashion shoots in the world, Anguilla boasts more than 33 brilliantly white beaches and no real city; instead the island is dotted with small villages. Refreshing wind rustles through the golden meadows full of towering savannah grass and migrating birds alight on serene ponds and around the picturesque bay. With the advent of spring, Anguilla bursts into flame with flamboyant trees shading gingerbread houses and hanging over seaside cliffs.

Anguilla's main road starts at West End, a village in the southwest and runs to The Quarter, a small settlement in the center of the island. The same road connects to island harbor. Turnoffs will take you to isolated beaches and fishing villages. The Department of Tourism is located in the Valley, at the center of the island. Nearby is Wallblake Airport. The port of entry is at Sandy Ground at Road Bay, on the north coast. There are just six traffic lights on the island—but unfortunately, numerous speed bumps.

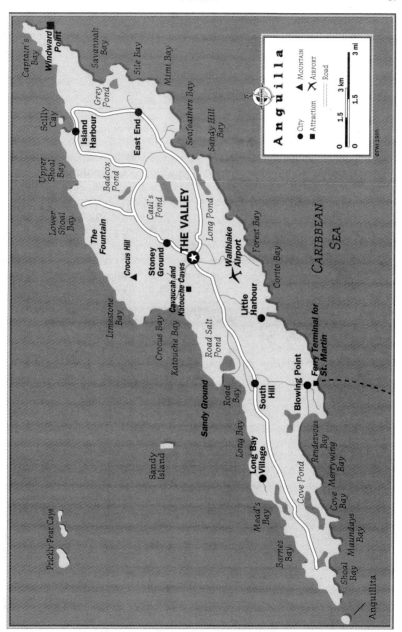

People

The natives of Anguilla are polite, proud and friendly. Nearly everywhere else in the Caribbean, natives seem sleepy; here they are wide awake and look you straight in the eye. Industrious and hardworking, many toil at several jobs, taking pride in their work and helping each other out during hurricanes and drought. (Many native-borns actually work abroad and send money home). Since Anguilla never had a big plantocracy, the shadow of slavery doesn't hover; hence, there are few racial tensions and little class pretension. Anguilla is the sort of place where both the British governor and the hotel clerk ride their bikes to work. Anguillian goats, who never seem to know when to get out of the way of oncoming traffic, seem to hold the real power here. Most natives are boat racing fanatics; in fact, Anguilla is the only British isle in the Caribbean where cricket is *not* the number one sport.

Fielding Tip:

It's considered rude to meet anyone without the prerequisite greeting: a gentle good morning or good afternoon, or more informally "okay" or "awrigh" (meaning, "hello-how- are-you-everything okay-allright?"

History

Long before the Europeans arrived in the Caribbean, Arawak Indians inhabited Anguilla's hot and dusty scrubland. Over the past 10 years, some 40,000 Amerindian artifacts have been uncovered by the Anguilla Archaeological and Historical Society from some 50 sites, indicating Anguilla may have been an important ceremonial site, even a pilgrimage, for this native American tribe. By the time the English settled in the 1650s, the Arawaks had vanished—probably decimated by European conquistadors and marauding pirates. When the dry climate foiled all British attempts at farming, their former slaves divided up the land, cultivated pigeon peas and corn, and then finally turned to the sea, building and trading sloops and schooners and fishing in rich waters. In the late '60s, the British forced Anguilla into an uncomfortable triisland alliance when the Associated State of St. Kitts-Nevis-Anguilla was signed into law. The single act stimulated a determined, if not exactly violent, rebellion, which found Anguillians marching a coffin around the island, burning the Government House, and sending its 12 policemen packing. World headlines roared with news of "The Eel that Squeeled" (sic) as the Brits sent in paratroopers, only to be met on the shore by cheering Anguillians singing the British national anthem and waving Union Jacks. Finally the Brits succumbed and gave Anguilla what it really wanted—a benevolent overlord who took the pains to build a badly needed phone system, a new pier and roads. Today Anguilla is a happy British dependent with its own elected governing body.

Beaches

Windsurfing and sailing are readily available at many Anguilla hotels.

Anguilla boasts some of the best beaches in the entire Caribbean, with sand as soft and white as talcum powder. **Rendezvous Bay**, one of the island's most spectacular strands, is two miles of pure sand dunes facing the rolling hills of

St. Martin. Good for long, lonely walks, the beach is studded with pretty sea-shells and monstrous-shaped driftwood as well as coconuts that have dropped from the palm trees that shade the strand. **Shoal Bay**, on the western tip, boasts an expansive sweep and silvery glow. The sea is full of iridescent fish who beg for snorkelers. **Savannah Beach**, rife with palms, is where you go when you are looking for unadulterated privacy. **Captain's Bay**, tucked on the island's northeast edge, offers good treks past a field of wild frangipani; from here you get an excellent view of crashing waves among the coral reefs. A climb across the karst takes you to **Windward Point** on the easternmost tip. **Limestone** is good for a snooze or quiet reading time. **Crocus or Little Bay**, home to the boat races, is best for snorkeling; here you'll find lobster, turtles and huge shoals of fishes, armies of sergeant majors, butterflyfish, iridescent blue doctorfish, grunts, squirrelfish, and *wrasses*. **Cove Bay's** white strands are terribly secluded except for fishing boats. Maunday's Bay Home is home to **Cap Juluca**, the luxurious resort, and sports some of the largest seagrape trees on the island. **Sandy Ground,** on Road Bay, is a must-see village of picturesque proportions, located between the big salt pond and the island's commercial and yacht harbor on Road Bay.

Underwater

Swimming through the carcasses of downed ships provides a delightful scuba conundrum: the wrecks are dead, yet teeming with life as the sea consumes their skeletal remains. Anguilla is a decidedly low-key dive destination, happily content to sink abandoned ships off its northern coast for the delight of visitors and fish alike. Seven of these artificial reefs have been put down over the past decade—four in 1990 alone during the island's offshore clean-up campaign—allowing Anguilla to proclaim itself the "wreck dive capital of the Caribbean." The most exciting wreck activity is somewhat less deliberate: a pair of Spanish galleons were recently discovered off **Junk's Hole Bay** for which excavation is just starting for bronze religious medallions (the site is unlikely to be open to the public until 1997). Because the remaining wrecks are more recent, they are a number of years away from true encrustation but, combined with an assortment of attractive nearby reefs, Anguilla is a pleasurable dive destination. The island's waters have not suffered from overuse, and the government recently created a Marine Parks system and instituted a mooring permit policy to minimize damage to reefs. An added attraction in

March is the humpback whales which navigate the straight between Windward Point and Scrub Island. Snorkeling is excellent at a number of north coast locations and on the nearby reefs; check out Frenchman's Reef and the east side of Shoal Bay, both accessible from shore.

Prickly Pear Reef

The idyllic Prickly Pear Cays, located four miles off the northern coast of Anguilla, are home to a lush reef (30-70 feet) that features canyons, ledges, caverns and a forest of elkhorn coral inhabited by colorful parrotfish. Nurse sharks are usually seen resting on the sandy floor, and barracudas cruise nearby.

Sandy Island and Sandy Deep

Sea fans and soft coral highlight the island portion of this dive site, while Sandy Deep is a mini wall that drops from 15 to 60 feet and is decorated with hard coral and an abundance of fish, lobster and occasional stingrays. Surface conditions permitting, this is an ideal novice site.

Frenchman's Reef

A delightful introductory dive, Frenchman's lies below a limestone coastal cliff which is tumbling slowly into the ocean, creating a field of boulders festooned with soft corals and vivid reef fish (to 40 feet). The surface is unusually calm here and the site draws a sprinkling of many smaller reef fish.

Paintcan Reef

Named for the bright swaths of colored sponges sloshed across a patch reef formation, Paintcan is known for its large pelagics, sparkling schools of silversides, copper sweepers and occasional Hawksbill turtles. Situated about three miles north of Road Bay, the reef sprawls over several acres and makes a terrific advanced dive location (55-80 feet).

The Steps

Located off Scrub Island on the east end of Anguilla are several newer dives, including this popular one, descending to 70 feet. The coral structure features grottoes, tunnels and pathways; at its deeper end, the sea life includes trigger fish, green eels, hawk fish, hawksbill and green turtles and the occasional barracuda.

Wreck of the *Oosterdiep*

Anguilla's best wreck dive, the 130-foot *Oosterdiep* was sunk in 1990 as part of the Old Road Bay cleanup project, which removed some of the abandoned ships sitting off the shores of Sandy Ground. Lying upright at 75-80 feet, the *Oosterdiep* seduces a wide variety of fish into its hold, including French angels, schooling yellowtail and flying gurnards (penetration recommended for advanced divers only). A few hundred feet from the wreck is a reef that can be included as part of the same dive; the sands between the wreck and reef are inhabited by shy garden eels and rays, and sprinkled with conch.

Dive Shops

Tamariain Watersports, Ltd.

Sandy Ground; ☎ (809) 497-2020.

The island's oldest dive shop (since 1985), a PADI Five Star facility working with all levels of divers. Resort courses, $80. Two-tank dive, $70.

Anguillan Divers

Island Harbor; ☎ *(809) 497-4750.*

Smaller PADI facility, with courses to Divemaster; open since 1991. Dives the adventurous reefs off Windward Point and the eastern channel. Two-tank dive, $70. Resort course, $75.

On Foot

Being slender in shape, and only modestly endowed with gentle limestone hills, coraline Anguilla would hardly seem to boast a wealth of hiking options. Scrubby **Crocus Hill** represents the island's high-point, a mere hiccup in the Eastern Caribbean at just 213 feet above sea level, which helps keep the island's focus firmly glued on its stunning beaches. However, a topo map from the Land and Survey Department will display some of the tracks that cross Anguilla's interior, while several offshore islands can be reached by charter boats and provide additional exploration possibilities. Although there are no companies that specialize in touring the island on foot, the Anguilla Archeological and Historical Society conduct walks (typically on Friday afternoons) and can be reached through your hotel's receptionist. Keep in mind that the island's beaches and brushy interior are scrubby and dry; bring ample water and sunscreen for any excursions.

Caul's Pond

A brackish inland swamp providing excellent bird-watching, Caul's Pond is best located using the main road out of The Valley and watching for one of several dirt roads that lead right (southeast) toward the sight (roadsigns on Anguilla are few and it may be necessary to ask for directions in the vicinity of Stoney Ground). After reaching the northern end, park and locate the ill-defined road that circles Caul's, although the path soon becomes overgrown and more difficult to follow as you round the southern edge of the water. Caul's is visited by many of the island's 80-odd permanent and visiting birds, including the white-cheeked pintail, black-necked stilts and other waders. Additional birding opportunities can be found at nearby Long Salt Pond and Grey Pond behind Savannah Bay.

Captain's Bay and Windward Point

Leading east out of Island Harbour, a sheltered fishing village, is a dirt road frequented by more goats than cars, which nonetheless makes for a romantic evening stroll. About a mile down the road is dramatic Captain's Bay, a short, steep beach with rough surf; its seclusion has made it the island's unofficial nude beach. Continuing further, you'll arrive at remote Windward Point, the northeastern tip of Anguilla, where waves crash splendidly onto the rocks overlooking nearby Scrub Island. Around the corner is Windward Point Bay, the island's most isolated stretch of sand, although swimmers should be wary of large breakers and a toothy undertow. Two Spanish wrecks have been recently located off the rugged coast here.

Cavanah and Katouche Caves

Anguilla's most famous cavern, Fountain Cave, is closed while the National Trust develops a plan for reopening it to visitors while protecting its contents. However, Cavanah and Katouche, two smaller caves nearby are open to amateur spelunkers. From the Government House just west of the Valley, look for a track behind (east of) the residence. After a short walk through a lightly forested area (watch for wild orchids), you will locate the entrances. Cavanah was once a phosphate mine, while Katouche, identified by the large tree at its mouth, is home to an extended family of bats. A flashlight is necessary for exploration beyond the entrances.

Rendezvous Bay to Maunday's Bay

A series of coves lining the southern coast can be followed for a casual beach walk featuring views across the channel to St. Martin. From the eastern edge of shell-laden Rendezvous Bay, follow the one-and-a-half mile sweep of sand west to narrow Merrywing Bay, a small beach protected by a shoal. Beyond Merrywing is pearl-white and unadorned Cove Bay, where palm trees lurk seductively just past the dunes. A short distance farther is Maunday's Bay, possibly Anguilla's most beautiful beach, and home to Cap Juluca, the extravagant Moorish-style resort. Although the next beach west, Shoal Bay, is also stunning, this popular cove is well-developed by Anguilla standards and a frequent objective of St. Martin day-trippers. Bring light footwear for the rocky points between bays.

By Pedal

Anguilla is relatively flat and the main roads can easily be explored in a relaxing day or two. For a pleasant tour of the island's more remote parts, head north out of The Valley to Island Harbor on rolling hills, then south to **Sandy Hill Bay**, an excellent rest point for a swim in the quiet cove before heading back to The Valley. It's also possible to ride from Island Harbor out to **Windward Point** on mountain bikes on the foot trail mentioned above, but watch out for stickers and carry a patch kit if you plan to do much exploring off the main roads.

Bike Rental Shops

Multiscenic Tours

    George Hill; ☎ *(809) 497-5810.*

    Rents 15- and 18-speed Diamond Backs, Raleighs and Giants at $10 per day, including locks (provided strictly for visitor peace-of-mind, we're told). Delivery and pickup is available for an additional $10.

Boothes

    South Hill; ☎ *(809) 497-2075.*

    Rents Outbacks for $8 per day.

What Else to See

Anguilla's gorgeous natural beach scene overshadows any other man-made sights, so spend most of your extra time either slung out in local bars or discovering new beaches. In the afternoon, catch the local fishermen spilling their sacks of spiny lobster on the sand for prospective buyers. For the most spectacular view, cross the crest of the little hill on the final stretch of the Shoal Bay road and look toward the horizon, particularly at sunset.

The Fountain, near Shoal Bay, is the island's only natural spring, today considered a site of ceremonial pilgrimage after archaeologists discovered numerous 2000-year-old petroglyphs of an Arawak god. The large-dome-shaped cavern stands on a ridge 70 feet above sea level. A steel ladder was added many years ago for easier access to the cave, whose entrance is quite small, allowing in very little natural light.

Island Harbour is a disarmingly charming fishing village peopled with descendants of the marauding Irish mixed with African slaves. That means green eyes and chocolate skin—a devastating combination, and with a lively spirit to match. Don't miss catching the strains of local bands at Smitty's bar.

Scilly Cat, only two minutes by boat from the island's harbor, is a wonder of coral, sand and exotic vegetation. You can spend the whole day there plying a variety of water sports and chowing down on native-style barbecue. Don't miss **Gorgeous Scilly Cay** restaurant, an island tradition, where you can hear the best local bands.

Johnno, the famous beach bar at Sandy Ground, is the place to be on Sunday, when the entire island turns out for a rock-out party. It's usually a local's scene, but visitors are welcome to join in the maddening calypso and reggae beat. Also try **Smithy's** and **Island Harbour** for good dancing and friendly folks.

Fielding Tip:

Learn the language of land directions in Anguilla, inspired by the winds. East is "up." West is "down." And both north and south are "over."

City Celebrations

Festival

Various locations, The Valley.

To celebrate Emancipation Day, or "August Monday" when the slaves were freed, Anguillans throw a week-long party each year that begins the first week of August. Festivities include boat races—the island's national sport—cultural events and general acts of merriment.

Historical Sites

Wallblake House   ★★★

Crossroads, The Valley, ☎ *(809) 497-2405.*

This plantation house, circa 1787, can be toured only by appointment, but even if you just get to see the outside, it's worth a look. Great tales of intrigue, murder, a French invasion and dysfunctional family history surround the place, which is now owned by the Catholic Church. While you're here, check out the newer church next door with its open-air side walls. The best time to come is Saturday mornings in the winter, when local artisans display their works on the grounds.

Tours

Sandy Island   ★★★★

Off the northwest coast, near Sandy Ground, Sandy Ground, ☎ *(809) 497-5643.*

This tiny island, which measures just 650 by 160 feet, is surrounded by a living reef with depths to 10 feet. Besides the obvious snorkeling and diving possibilities, you can enjoy all kinds of watersports, including deep-sea fishing, parasailing and glass-bottom boat rides. There's also a bar and restaurant. To get there, go to Sandy Ground at the top of the hour from 10 a.m. to 3 p.m., or call them and they'll pick you up at your hotel's beach. Fun, but keep in mind that Anguilla has such gorgeous beaches it's not really necessary to travel to one. The ferry ride costs $8; bring extra money to rent watersports equipment.

Sports

The sea is king when it comes to sports in Anguilla. Sailboat-racing is a mania, sometimes merely the excuse for riotous beachside parties and barbecues. (Look for them on New Year's Day, Anguilla Day and Easter, as well as spontaneously.) There are also excellent scuba, sailing and snorkeling possibilities. Most hotels have some kind of activities program; the best will always be connected with the largest resorts. Some of the top hotels have numerous courts. Free playing time is available at the Scouts Headquarters (For more information, call the **Anguilla Drugstore ☎** *2738.*

El Rancho Del Blues

Next to Anguilla Gases on the Blowing Point main road, Road Bay, ☎ *(809) 497-6164.*
Hop on a horse and take a beach or trail ride through gorgeous scenery. Beach rides depart daily at 9 a.m. and 2 p.m., while trail rides leave at 11 a.m. and 4 p.m. One-hour rides cost $25; two hours go for $45. One-hour private beach rides and full-moon beach rides are also available for $45. English and Western saddles are available, as are riding lessons.

Tamariain Watersports

Road Bay, The Valley, ☎ *(809) 497-5125.*
The island's only full-service PADI (Professional Association of Diving Instructors) dive facility offers dives to a variety of underwater sites, as well as a course that takes beginners on one open-water dive ($80). They also offer Sunfish sailboats for rent and host water-skiing excursions. Dive prices are $40 for a one-tank dive, $70 for two, and $50 for a night dive.

Where to Stay

Fielding's Highest Rated Hotels in Anguilla

★★★★★	Malliouhana Beach Hotel	$240
★★★★	Cap Juluca	$275
★★★★	Cinnamon Reef Beach Club	$155–$330
★★★★	La Sirena	$100–$280
★★★	Arawak Beach Resort	$100–$300
★★★	Carimar Beach Club	$130–$630
★★★	Cove Castles Villa Resort	$350–$990
★★★	Fountain Beach	$100–$365
★★★	Frangipani Beach Club	$195
★★★	Paradise Cove	$310–$425

Fielding's Most Romantic Hotels in Anguilla

★★★	Fountain Beach	$100–$365
★★★★★	Malliouhana Beach Hotel	$240–$1240
★★★	Pineapple Beach Club	$260–$460

Fielding's Budget Hotels in Anguilla

★★★	Lloyd's Guest House	$70–$94
★★	Inter-Island Hotel	$35–$135
★★	Ferryboat Inn	$70–$225
★★	Rendezvous Bay Hotel	$90–$240
★★★★	La Sirena	$100–$280

In Anguilla you can sleep stinking rich (like the luscious five-bedroom villa at the Cap Juluca) or "rough" it in a bed and breakfast for under $100. The latest trend is to stay in newly built cottages and villas designed to reflect the island's all-seasonal lifestyle, particularly good for return visitors who already know the island. For bed and breakfast digs (usually located along or near the main road of the island) contact the tourist offices in Anguilla and New York. Best bargains are found in the summer when you can rack up to 60 percent discounts. If you have no car, choose lodgings near and in Sandy Ground, Shoal Bay and Island Harbour, since restaurants and shops will be within walking distance. Most hotels, except for the cheapest, usually have air conditioning, phones, TVs and private baths. Crime has been considered so nonexistent that some hotels actually boast they have no locks on the doors. If you haven't evolved to such transcendental levels of trust, inquire before you book yourself in.

Hotels and Resorts

Paradise Cove, Anguilla's newest luxury property, located in the cove on the western end of the island, is sporting a new restaurant for breakfast and light meals, and an expanded children's playground, making the 14 fully furnished suites fully adaptable for families. La Sirena Hotel, overlooking Meads Bay, has added a fifth villa—three-bedrooms that can comfortably accommodate six adults or a large family. New athletic and entertainment facilities have been added to Cap Jaluca, and a 32-foot speedboat is available for excursions. A putting green on the southern shore of Maundays Bay Lagoon was installed as was an English-regulation croquet court.

Arawak Beach Resort $100–$300   ★ ★ ★

P.O. Box 98, The Valley, Island Harbour, ☎ *(800) 553-4939, (809) 497-4888, FAX (809) 497-4898.*
Single: $100–$300. Double: $300.
Located on the site of an ancient Arawak Indian village, this newer resort consists of two-story villas furnished with Amerindian replicas. Lots of interesting touches here: A small museum exhibits artifacts found on the site; the courtyard is planted with traditional island crops like cotton and papaya; and the watersports include canoe rentals. No smoking throughout, and though you can bring your own, no liquor is served.

Cap Juluca $275–$2085   ★ ★ ★ ★

Maunday's Bay, ☎ *(800) 323-0139, (809) 497-6666, FAX (809) 497-6617.*
Single: $275–$2085. Double: $275–$2085.

It doesn't get much better than here at Cap Juluca, the epitome of resort living at its swankest. Guestrooms, housed in whitewashed villas, are exquisitely decorated and boast giant walk-in closets, walnut louvered doors and windows and huge patios. They come in four categories, and some even include solariums, roof terraces and private pools. Breakfast is served by two maids; when you return from dinner, you'll find they left flickering candles when they turned down the beds. The imaginatively landscaped grounds include scenic lagoons, two restaurants, three tennis courts with a resident pro, a fitness center, media room and the gorgeous beach. There's entertainment four nights a week. If you're dying to watch TV or a video, they'll install one for $20 per day, which seems a bit expensive considering the high rates. Still, the well-heeled guests here aren't worried about being nickled and dimed. This resort is more laid back and casual than its chief competitor, Malliou-hana. No kids under six.

Casablanca Resort $205–$600 ★★★

Rendezvous Bay West, ☎ *(800) 231-1945, (809) 497-6999, FAX (809) 497-6899.*
Single: $205–$475. Double: $255–$600.
This Moorish-influenced, pink and green resort is a rather incongruous sight on this laid-back island, but if you like pizazz, Casablanca delivers. The $20-million, 200-acre resort boasts three miles of beach, two lit tennis courts, a 1200-square-foot pool, games room, library, three restaurants, gymnasium and such special touches as hand-carved and handpainted mosaics created by Moroccan artisans. Beach wing rooms have the best views, but the garden rooms are bigger and have more luxurious baths. All are simply gorgeous with Moroccan rugs, lovely fabrics, stenciled accents on the walls and small marble baths. The rates include watersports (they have only non-motorized toys), breakfast, free tennis lessons from the pro who visits each week and such pampering touches as fresh fruit four times each day on the beach. All-inclusive packages are also available. By far Anguilla's glitziest resort, and quite nice at that. No kids under 16.

Cinnamon Reef Beach Club $155–$330 ★★★★

Little Harbour, ☎ *(800) 223-1108, (809) 497-2727, FAX (809) 497-3727.*
Single: $155–$330. Double: $155–$330.
Pleasantly informal is the atmosphere at this intimate 40-acre resort. Accommodations are in whitewashed villas set on the beach or perched on a bluff; each has living and dining rooms, a raised bedroom, patio complete with hammock, and tiled sunken showers (no baths). For recreation, there's a huge pool (40 by 60 feet), three tennis courts and all kinds of complimentary watersports. Located on Anguilla's southern coast, this excellent resort's only downfall is its relatively small beach, though its calm waters make for great windsurfing. Rooms include a Continental Breakfast.

Coccoloba $225–$425 ★★★

Barnes Bay, ☎ *(800) 982-7729, (809) 497-6871, FAX (809) 497-6332.*
Single: $225–$425. Double: $225–$425.
A true tropical hideaway, chic Coccoloba is nestled on a rocky headland between two picture-perfect beaches. Most guest rooms are in cottages on a bluff above the beach, though seven units are housed in a beachside villa. All have sea views, but some are better than others. Each room is done in traditional West Indian decor, with bright Caribbean colors, marble baths and individual, though not secluded, patios. All watersports are free, and extras like complimentary soft drinks on the beach and high tea daily keep you pampered.

Frangipani Beach Club $195–$1200 ★★★

Meads Bay, ☎ *(800) 892-4564, (809) 497-6442, FAX (809) 497-6440.*
Single: $195–$555. Double: $250–$1200.
This newer enclave of Spanish-style pink stucco and red-tile roof villas offers one- to three-bedroom suites on gorgeous Meads Bay Beach. All units have air conditioning, full kitchens, natural rattan furnishings and a patio or balcony; some boast

Jacuzzis as well. The restaurant is open only for breakfast and lunch. Watersports cost extra.

Malliouhana Beach Hotel $240–$1240   ★★★★★

Meads Bay, ☎ *(800) 835-0796, (809) 497-6111, FAX (809) 497-6011.*
Single: $240–$810. Double: $240–$1240.

Every little detail is in place at this impeccable resort, set atop a hill overlooking two beaches. Just perusing the lovely Indian and Haitian artwork in the lobby is a treat in itself. Guestrooms are spacious and nicely decorated with high-quality rattan furniture, Haitian art, marble baths with oversized tubs and patios or balconies. There are four tennis courts, three pools, complimentary watersports (you'll pay extra for windsurfing and waterskiing lessons) and an open-air exercise pavilion with lovely ocean views to keep you motivated. Mellow live music is offered each night during the winter (and three times a week in the summer), and parents can leave the little ones in free supervised programs. You'll pay $25 extra per day for a TV and VCR. But gorgeous as this spot is—and it is lovely—the staff can be a bit cool, and the overall atmosphere a bit snooty and reserved.

Mariners, The $115–$535   ★★★

Sandy Ground, ☎ *(800) 848-7938, (809) 497-2671, FAX (809) 497-2901.*
Single: $115–$190. Double: $115–$535.

A true West Indian-style resort, complete with gingerbread cottages and handcrafted lattice. Accommodations have pitched ceilings, Haitian wicker furniture painted in pastels, and modest bathrooms. The nicer cottages boast living rooms and well-equipped kitchenettes. Be warned that not all units have air conditioning. This all-inclusive resort is situated at the far end of Anguilla's busiest beach, near a deep-water port. True couch potatoes can rent a TV and VCR for an added fee. Service is friendly but sometimes lacking.

Pineapple Beach Club $260–$460   ★★★

Rendezvous Bay, ☎ *(800) 345-0356, (809) 497-6061, FAX (809) 497-6344.*
Single: $260–$360. Double: $350–$460.

A solid choice for those watching their pocketbooks, this cozy, all-inclusive resort is set on Anguilla's southernmost tip. Connected one-story bungalows set around a central courtyard open to a beautiful beach and have a distinctive West Indian style, with wide verandas, trellises and whimsical gingerbread trim. Rooms are spacious and nicely though sparsely done in mahogany furnishings, handcrafted linens ceiling fans and air conditioning. Formerly the Anguilla Great House, this pleasant spot offers complimentary watersports, great dining and lots of resident bunnies and turtles. There are many more luxurious resorts on the island, but this spot has its own very lovely charm and a wonderfully friendly staff. Highly recommended!

Rendezvous Bay Hotel $90–$240   ★★

Rendezvous Bay, ☎ *(800) 274-4893, (809) 497-6549, FAX (809) 497-6026.*
Single: $90–$240. Double: $90–$240.

Set among 60 acres of coconut trees, this is the island's first resort, and though it draws a lot of repeat customers, it does show its age. Not a bad choice for the price, though, with the lovely beach making up for a lack of amenities—-no pool, for example. The original rooms are simple and lack air conditioning, while the newer villas have spacious one-bedroom suites and air; some also have kitchenettes. There are two lighted tennis courts, a game and TV room and, best of all, an elaborate electric train setup in the lounge. Decent value, and pleasantly informal.

Apartments and Condominiums

Independent-minded folks with time on their hands will enjoy the villa life in Anguilla, though there are drawbacks. Some staples might need to be bought in neighboring St. Martin/Sint Maarten. In general, prices will be much higher than at home. Check yearly for new listings since new properties are always being built. **Anguilla Connections** (☎ *(809) 497-4403)* specializes in villa rentals.

Carimar Beach Club   **$130–$630**   ★★★

Meads Bay, ☎ (800) 235-8667, (809) 497-6881, FAX (809) 497-6071.
Single: $130–$630. Double: $250–$630.
These comfortable one- and two-bedroom apartments (and one three-bedroom) are owned as condominiums and rented out when the owners aren't using them. The villas are Mediterranean style and nicely done with wicker and rattan furniture, TVs, full kitchens, large living rooms, dining areas and balconies or patios. Most offer only partial views of the magnificent beach. The tropical grounds include two tennis courts but no pool. There's no restaurant or bar on site, but the complex is within walking distance of Malliouhana and Coccoloba.

Cove Castles Villa Resort   **$350–$990**   ★★★

Shoal Bay West, ☎ (800) 348-4716, (809) 497-6801, FAX (809) 497-6051.
Single: $350–$590. Double: $350–$990.
This ultramodern apartment resort may take some getting used to at first, with its futuristic white structures a somewhat jarring site. Accommodations are in eight 2 bedroom beach houses and four 3 bedroom villas. All have two baths, cable TV, a well-stocked and very modern kitchen, living and dining rooms, skylights, nice furnishings and a covered beachfront veranda. There's a restaurant and bar on the premises, and unlike other apartment complexes, limited room service. The beach is fantastic.

Easy Corner Villas   **$90–$295**   ★★★

Road Bay, ☎ (800) 223-9815, (809) 497-6433, FAX (809) 497-6410.
Single: $90–$295. Double: $90–$295.
Families are prevalent at this complex of one- to three-bedroom apartments with combination living and dining areas, full kitchens and a patio; only three are air-conditioned. A restaurant and coffee shop are located on-site, and daily maid service is available for an extra fee. Located on a bluff overlooking Road Bay, this simple spot represents good value for the price.

La Sirena   **$100–$280**   ★★★★

Meads Bay, ☎ (800) 331-9815, (809) 497-6827, FAX (809) 497-6827.
Single: $100–$160. Double: $1200.
Accommodations at this pleasant property are in two- and three-bedroom apartments in Mediterranean-style white stucco buildings. Units are nicely done with rattan furnishings, ceiling fans and Caribbean pastels. There are two pools on-site, plus

a formal restaurant and a casual poolside cafe. The beach is a two-minute walk. Not the most exciting place around, but good value for the rates.

Paradise Cove $310–$425   ★★★

P.O. Box 135, ☎ *(800) 728-0784, (809) 497-3559, FAX (809) 497-2149.*
Single: $310–$425. Double: $425.

An intimate and romantic hideaway nestled among palm trees and lush tropical gardens just a five-minute walk from beautiful Cove Beach. Centrally air-conditioned one- and two-bedroom units are quite spacious elegantly furnished and include fully equipped kitchens, telephones, private laundry facilities, huge bathrooms, cable TV, high beamed ceilings and two large balconies. This is one of Anguilla's few locally owned properties, and it's a real winner, despite its slightly off the beach locale. The grounds include a barbecue area, a large but plain pool, two Jacuzzis, a restaurant that serves breakfast and lunch and a playground for the kids. Request an end unit for more privacy. Watersports await at nearby beaches. Very, very fine—it's especially neat that you can hire a private cook in the evenings for just $5 an hour (plus ingredients). Indulge! A seven-night package costs $1315–$2400 for a one-bedroom suite, $1840–$3205 for two bedrooms, and includes a rental car for the week.

Sea Grape Beach Club Villas $180–$450   ★★

Meads Bay, ☎ *(800) 223-9815, (809) 497-6433, FAX (809) 497-6410.*
Single: $180–$450. Double: $280–$450.

These modern two-bedroom condominiums are very nicely appointed; each has three bathrooms, ultra-large closets and private decks with sweeping ocean views. They're especially suited for those who like to spread out —- each unit encompasses some 2000 square feet. The grounds include a restaurant, bar, watersports (for a fee) and two tennis courts.

Shoal Bay Villas $147–$385   ★★★

P.O. Box 81, North Coast, North Coast, ☎ *(800) 722-7045, (809) 497-2051, FAX (809) 497-3631.*
Single: $147–$385. Double: $147–$385.

Contemporary villa-style condominiums located on the beach west of Island Harbour. The one- and two-bedroom units have kitchenettes and painted rattan furniture, but no air conditioning. The palm-studded beach is a tropical dream, and there's a restaurant and bar on-site with occasional live music. No children in the winter.

Inns

The lifestyle is breezier and more casual at Anguilla's handful of inns; management is often more attentive. Travelers young in spirit and weak on wallet should also check out the small properties in "Budget Bunks."

Ferryboat Inn $70–$225   ★★

Blowing Point, ☎ *(809) 497-6613, FAX (809) 497-6713.*
Single: $70–$125. Double: $85–$225.

This family-owned and operated inn, near the ferry dock and beach, is a solid choice for those on a budget. Accommodations are comfortable and simple, consisting of one- and two-bedroom suites that are not air conditioned and a two-bedroom beach house that is; all have full kitchens. There's a bar and restaurant on-site, and the views at night of neighboring St. Martin are enchanting.

Fountain Beach   **$100–$365**   ★★★

Shoal Bay, ☎ (800) 523-7505, (809) 497-3491, FAX (809) 497-3493.
Single: $100–$280. Double: $285–$365.
Set on a scrumptious beach along the rural north coast, this secluded resort appeals to those who like privacy. Accommodations are in oversized studios and one- and two-bedroom suites with Caribbean antique artwork, colorful rattan and wicker furniture, large marble baths and full kitchens. The grounds include two tennis courts and a pool. Decent digs for the rates.

Inter-Island Hotel   **$35–$135**   ★★

Lower South Hill, ☎ (809) 497-6259, FAX (809) 497-5381.
Single: $35–$40. Double: $55–$135.
This small villa-style guest house, located near Sandy Ground, is a quarter mile from the beach, but at these rates, who's complaining? Rooms are simple but very clean and comfortable with ceiling fans (no air conditioning) and tiny bathrooms; one- and two-bedroom suites are also available. Not much in the way of amenities, but an excellent choice for those who really can't afford Anguilla to begin with.

Low Cost Lodging

You'll find best bargains on lodging anytime during low season (mid-April to December). During high season, the cheapest small hotel will bed two (no meals) for about $50, but you're risking seediness. In this very low-cost range, you'll find either cotlike beds and shared bathrooms in guest houses, or basic furnishings in no-atmosphere edifices. Don't even think about being near a beach.

Lloyd's Guest House   **$70–$94**   ★★★

Crocus Hill, ☎ (809) 497-2351, FAX (809) 497-3028.
Single: $70. Double: $94.
The only drawback to Lloyd's, which has been operational since 1959, is that the beach is a mile and a quarter away. You can walk it in five minutes or so, but it's down a steep hill, so leave some energy for the return trip. Besides that, all is fine at this family-run guest house, where the rooms are small but sweet and very clean and accented with pretty fabrics, private baths and fans (no air conditioning). The rates include breakfast.

Where to Eat

Fielding's Highest Rated Restaurants in Anguilla

★★★★★	Pimms	$20–$35
★★★★	Dunes, The	$5–$10
★★★★	Hibernia	$17–$30
★★★★	Malliouhana Hotel Restaurant	$11–$40
★★★★	Palm Court	$12–$26
★★★★	Scilly Cay	
★★★	Barrel's Stay	$8–$30
★★★	Koal Keel	$8–$30
★★★	Lucy's Harbour View	$8–$30
★★★	Mango's	$20–$35

Fielding's Special Restaurants in Anguilla

★★★★★	Pimms	$20–$35
★★★	Barrel's Stay	$8–$30
★★★	Ferryboat Inn	$7–$26
★★★	Koal Keel	$8–$30
★★★	Mango's	$20–$35

Fielding's Budget Restaurants in Anguilla

★★★★	Dunes, The	$5–$10
★★★	Old House	$5–$20
★★★	Ferryboat Inn	$7–$26
★★★	Roy's	$4–$30
★★★	Paradise Cafe	$8–$27

When Anguilla was discovered in the mid-'80s by the cream of Carib connoisseurs, the taste for lobster exploded. Fishermen now go farther and farther from shore to catch the island's prized marine treasure. It's usually readily available except during the brief hibernating and spawning season, which coincides with the slow tourist season of early summer. Most restaurants keep an ample supply of crayfish and lobster in live pots offshore. At the **Palm Court Restaurant** at the Cinnamon Reef Resort, two lobster dishes are true competitors: simply grilled in a delicate essence of cilantro and a unique lobster salad with plantains and baby artichokes in a peanut dressing. No matter where you're lodged, alternate your meals between tony French elegance found at the island's most expensive resorts, such as Cap Jaluca, and budget creole cooked by talented locals at primitive-looking shacks. Local chefs do wonders also with red snapper, whelk and conch. For meat-eaters, a favorite is Island Mutton Stew with native vegetables. West Indian dishes are prepared superbly here, especially pumpkin soup. Don't miss the island's traditional brew—Perry's Soda Pop.

Arlo's Place $ ★★★

☎ *(809) 497-6810.*
Italian cuisine.
This trattoria draws a local crowd hungry for authentic Italian cuisine like homemade lasagna and fettuccini in a lobster tomato sauce, as well as tasty pizzas. Set right on the beach with great sunset views.

Barrel's Stay $$$ ★★★

Road Bay, ☎ *(809) 497-2831.*
French cuisine.
Lunch: 11 a.m.–3 p.m., entrees $8–$30.
Dinner: 6:30–9:30 p.m., entrees $8–$30.
The name becomes obvious when you see this spot fashioned from old rum barrels and disassembled barrel stays. Tasty seafood and meat entrees dressed in creative sauces are served outside on a terrace. Some say the food is overpriced, but the French wines are reasonable.

Dunes, The $ ★★★★

Near Pineapple Beach Club, ☎ *(809) 497-6699.*
Casual cuisine.
Lunch: entrees $5–$10.
First of all, you'll need a four-wheel drive, or at least a sturdy rental car, to get to this unique spot on the beach. As they say, "follow the funky signs from the Pineapple Beach Club turnoff," and don't give up as you bump and grind down a dirt path that barely deserves to be called a road. It's worth it once you get here. The Dunes is owned and run by Bankie Banx, a talented reggae musician who is recently getting a lot of deserved recognition. Lunch is a casual affair—just the basics—but the setting on a windswept beach is fantastic. The best time to come, however, is the open-mike Friday and Sunday nights, when Bankie and friends let the music rip.

Ferryboat Inn   **$$$**   ★★★

Cul de Sac Rd., ☎ (809) 497-6613.
Latin American cuisine.
Lunch: Noon–2:30 p.m., entrees $7–$26.
Dinner: 7–10 p.m., entrees $7–$26.

Set on the beach near the Blowing Point Ferry Pier, this tres romantic spot special-izes in French/Caribbean dishes. Wonderful soups like French onion and black bean; lobster thermidor is the house favorite. The Ferryboat is especially inviting at night, with the flickering lights of St. Martin weaving an enchanting spell.

Hibernia   **$$$**   ★★★★

Island Harbour, ☎ (809) 497-4290.
Seafood cuisine.
Lunch: Noon–2 p.m., entrees $17–$30.
Dinner: 7–9 p.m., entrees $20–$30.

There are just 10 tables at this lovely spot, set in a West Indian-style cottage with a wide porch, on the island's northeast corner. Specialties include grilled and smoked seafood, creatively enhanced with fresh local ingredients. They whip up their own breads and ice cream daily. Closed September and October.

Koal Keel   **$$$**   ★★★

The Valley, ☎ (809) 497-2930.
EuroCaribe cuisine.
Lunch: Noon–2:30 p.m., entrees $8–$28.
Dinner: 7–10:30 p.m., entrees $20–$30.

This lovely spot is situated in a beautifully restored plantation great house from the 18th century, with service as gracious as the surroundings. Especially fanciful is the bed, all dressed up in white lace, sitting smack in the middle of the courtyard. The cuisine is based on foods abundant in Anguilla: fresh fish, coconut, corn, pigeon peas, potatoes, mangos, sugars, limes and native herbs and seasonings. Fresh breads and roast meats are prepared in a large rock oven, and the lobster crepes are to die for. The new wine cellar, located 17 feet below sea level, has a capacity for 25,000 bottles, so you're sure to find something tasty. The restaurant hosts daily wine tast-ings and tours of the grounds; after dinner, you can sample more than 30 different rums in a complimentary tasting. A neat spot to try "EuroCaribe" cuisine.

Lucy's Harbour View   **$$$**   ★★★

South Hill, ☎ (809) 497-6253.
Latin American cuisine.
Lunch: 11:30 a.m.–3:30 p.m., entrees $8–$16.
Dinner: 7–10 p.m., entrees $15–$30.

Like the name implies, diners enjoy wonderful views from this casual cafe set high on a steep hill overlooking Sandy Ground. The menu focuses on fresh vegetables and lobster and fish dishes. Whole red snapper and pumpkin soup are house special-ties.

Malliouhana Hotel Restaurant   **$$$**   ★★★★

Meads Bay, ☎ (809) 497-6111.
French cuisine.
Lunch: 12:30–3:30 p.m., entrees $11–$30.

Dinner: 7–10:30 p.m., entrees $30–$40.

Set in an open-air pavilion on a rocky promontory overlooking the sea, the feel here is wonderfully elegant, with gracious service, fine china and crystal and gourmet goodies. Famed French chef Michel Rostang created the menu and occasionally whips up the dishes himself. It'd be easy to make an entire meal of the imaginative hors d'oeuvres, but save room for the catch of the day. The wine cellar stocks some 25,000 bottles, most priced in the $25.00–$35.00 range.

Mango's $$$ ★★★

Barnes Bay, ☎ (809) 497-6491.
American cuisine.
Dinner: 6:30–9 p.m., entrees $20–$35.

Make reservations far in advance to get into this hot spot, which has two seatings for dinner, at 6:30 and 8:30. They use the freshest ingredients, grill-cook meat and fish, offer up some tasty vegetarian selections, make their own bread, desserts and ice cream daily—and best of all, do it all with an absolute minimum of calories. You'd never know by the taste that you're actually eating healthy food!

Old House $$$ ★★★

George Hill, ☎ (809) 497-2228.
West Indian cuisine.
Lunch: 11 a.m.–5 p.m., entrees $5–$12.
Dinner: 6–11 p.m., entrees $16–$20.

Yes, this eatery really is situated in an old house, set on a hill near the airport. The decor is simple but the food's just fine. West Indian specialties include conch, local lamb, curry goat and Anguillan pot fish; the fruit pancakes keep the locals coming. It's nice to sit on the porch and watch the planes come and go. Also open for good, cheap breakfasts from 7–11:30 a.m.

Palm Court $$$ ★★★★

Cinnamon Reef Resort, ☎ (809) 497-2727.
Latin American cuisine.
Lunch: Noon–2:30 p.m., entrees $12–$18.
Dinner: 7–9:30 p.m., entrees $20–$26.

Haitian furniture, colorful murals and huge picture windows overlooking the sea make this place special. The nouvelle Caribbean food is good too, with items like grouper encased in toasted pumpkin seeds or banana rum sauce. Lunch is more casual, with good salads, soups and sandwiches. Save room for the mango puffs in caramel sauce.

Paradise Cafe $$$ ★★★

Shoal Bay West, ☎ (809) 497-6010.
Indian cuisine.
Lunch: Noon–2:30 p.m., entrees $8–$14.
Dinner: 7–9:30 p.m., entrees $10–$27.

Ocean breezes set many windchimes tinkling, a nice backdrop to tasty dishes with unique French and Asian influences. Try the West Indian bouillabaisse, individual pizzas or the catch of the day. Reservations are suggested; for better or worse, the rich and famous have discovered this spot. Closed in September.

Pimms　　　　　　　　　　　$$$　　　　　　　★ ★ ★ ★ ★

Cap Juluca Hotel, Maunday's Bay, ☎ *(809) 497-6666.*
French cuisine.
Dinner: 7–10 p.m., entrees $20–$35.
One of the finest restaurants in all the Caribbean, located in the wonderful resort of Cap Juluca. Candlelit tables overlook the gorgeous beach, and the Continental-style cuisine, spiced with West Indian accents, is fabulous. Try the local lobster or grouper. Dress up for this spot, and don't even think about getting in without reservations.

Riviera Bar & Restaurant　　　　$$$　　　　　　　★ ★

Road Bay, ☎ *(809) 497-2833.*
French cuisine.
Lunch: 11 a.m.–3 p.m., entrees $6–$16.
Dinner: 6–9:30 p.m., entrees $20–$35.
This bistro on the beach compliments its French and Creole dishes with distinctive Asian accents—oysters sauteed in sake and soy sauce, for instance. There's occasional live music at this casual site, and the daily happy hour, 6–7, is happening.

Roy's　　　　　　　　　　　$$$　　　　　　　★ ★ ★

Crocus Bay, ☎ *(809) 497-2470.*
English cuisine.
Lunch: Noon–2 p.m., entrees $4–$16.
Dinner: 6–9 p.m., entrees $14–$30.
Two British expatriots set up this little slice of their home land, and they got it right, all the way down to the English beers (thankfully served cold) and dart board. Dine al fresco on the veranda, with nice sea views, on fish and chips and Caribbean favorites like barbecued chicken and lobster Creole.

Scilly Cay　　　　　　　　　$　　　　　　　★ ★ ★ ★

Just off the coast from Island Harbour, ☎ *(809) 497-5123.*
cuisine.
Wonderful (but extremely expensive) fresh lobster, crayfish and marinated chicken are the reasons to hop the free ferry for the short ride over to this picture-perfect island. Live music varies—on Wednesdays, it's romantic ballads, Fridays steel pans and Sundays reggae. After lunch, you can stroll the gardens, snorkel (bring your own equipment) or just laze on one of the complimentary lounge chairs.

Where to Shop

There is little to speak of, in terms of shopping; most of the young female locals head for the trendy shops of St. Martin to dress themselves. Anything of value is to be found in the top-of-the-crop resorts and hotels. One of the most renowned local artists is **Courtney Deonish** (imported from Barbados), whose impressive carvings are sold at the airport.

For local crafts try **Elsie's in Stoney Ground** for embroidery and crochet, and the **Anguilla Craft Shop**, also in Stoney Ground, for straw artisanry, jams, jellies and local shellwork.

The latest craze on Anguilla are tiny wooden house plaques painted by **Lucia Butler**, sometimes known as the Caribbean's Grandma Moses. On layered pieces of wood she paints whimsical pastels and ornate gingerbread details of typical West Indian cottages. Houses of different sizes range from $18–$45 at the **Arts and Crafts Center** or at the artist's home studio (☎ *(809) 497-4259* for an appointment).

Anguilla Directory

ARRIVAL AND DEPARTURE

American Airlines offers direct service from the United States to San Juan, Puerto Rico, where you can change to American Eagle for the one-hour hop to Anguilla. There are two American Eagle flights daily. You can also fly American or Continental to Dutch Sint Maarten's Juliana Airport, where connections to Anguilla can be found on WINAIR or LIAT. For about the same fee ($25 one way), Anguilla's own **Tyden Air** (☎ *(800) 842-0261* or *(809) 497-2719*) makes the five-minute flight offering "Immediate Pickup" service that saves passengers baggage handling, all check-in procedures, and waiting. During high season (mid-December to mid-April), the Sint Maarten/Anguilla fare on Tyden is raised to $45, due to the chaos at Juliana, but the return trip remains $25. You can also take a taxi from Juliana Airport to Marigot on the French side (about $10) and catch one of the Anguilla power boats ($10) departing every 30–40 minutes for the 15-minute ride. If returning by boat with a lot of luggage, ask the French immigration officials in Marigot to call you a cab; the taxi stand is a ten-minute walk away. Note that in the evening there are only two ferry rides.

The **Link Ferry** *(☎ (809) 497-2231)* offers the fastest ferry ride from Anguilla to St. Martin.

Upon leaving the island by air, all travelers are charged a $6 departure tax.

BUSINESS HOURS

Stores open Monday–Saturday 8 a.m.–5 p.m. or 6 p.m. A few open on Sundays. Banks open 8 a.m.–3 p.m. Monday–Thursday and until 5 p.m. Friday.

CLIMATE

Anguilla has one of the driest climates in the region—a bane to farmers, but a boon to tourists. As a result, vegetation is short and sparse, with few palm trees. With the lowest average annual rainfall in the Leeward Islands, Anguilla receives only 30-45 inches annually. Hurricane season is intense.

CURRENT

Most outlets are 110 AC, as in the U.S.

DOCUMENTS

Visitors must show ID with a photo, preferably a passport, and an on-going ticket. Departure tax is $6 at the airport and $2 at the ferry port.

GETTING AROUND

You'll need a car or open-air jeep called a mini-moke to visit more than one beach; hitchhiking is safe and accepted. Taxis are readily available at both Wallblake Airport and Blowing Point dock. You won't find any rental car agencies there; a taxi can deliver you there. Good local agencies are **Triple K** (representing Hertz), ☎ *(809) 497-2934*; **Maurice Connors** ☎ *(809) 497-6410*; and **Roy Rogers Rental,** ☎ *(809) 497-6290*, FAX *809-497-3345*. Note well that driving is on the left and you must obtain a local driver's license from your rental agency. If you're game to cycle, try **Boo's Cycle Rental**.

The island bus service begins from a roadside stop a few steps from the pier at Blowing Point.

LANGUAGE

The official language is English spoken with a West Indian lilt.

MEDICAL EMERGENCIES

For serious problems, head for a hospital in Puerto Rico. The small hospital at Crocus Bay is usually overflowing with natives.

MONEY

Official currency is the Eastern Caribbean dollar (EC), usually marked by "$" sign in stores and restaurants. Before you shell out any dough, however, make sure the price is not referring to American dollars. Traveler's checks, personal checks (sometimes, with picture ID) and American dollars are also readily accepted.

TELEPHONE

From North America to Anguilla, dial *809* (area code) + *497* (country code) + local number (4 digits). Faxes are widely used by hotels and other businesses. To save money when calling home from Anguilla, go to the Cable & Wireless office and buy a phone card. Before leaving home, check with your own telephone service to see how you can most cheaply call home using your own special card.

TIME

Anguilla is on Atlantic standard time, one hour ahead of Eastern standard time in winter (that means 1 p.m. in New York, 2 p.m. in Anguilla). During the summer, it's the same time.

TIPPING AND TAXES

Service charges (10–15 percent) and an 8 percent government tax are usually included in hotel bills; 10 percent on all food and beverage tabs. Some establishments charge a fee for credit cards. Waiters and waitresses appreciate tips, but don't expect any. If a young boy carries your bag at the airport, one dollar per bag will put a smile on his face. More often, your taxi driver will tote them.

TOURIST INFORMATION

Contact the **Anguilla Tourist Office** ☎ *(800) 553-4939*. Before you go, you can get an updated list of rates for accommodations and a map. Better maps are available in local stores.

WHEN TO GO

The Miller Genuine Draft Moonsplash Tour in January is a well-attended music festival. Anguilla Day is celebrated by a huge boat race on May 30. The Queen's Birthday is feted by celebrations in the month of June. The Anguilla National Summer Festival takes place on Aug. 4–12. The Christmas Fair at the Governor's Residence occurs in December. On holidays and during Carnival, the whole island turns out to bet on spectacular boat races. Carnival itself, in the month of August, is celebrated with early morning dancing, beachside barbecues and special pageants.

ANGUILLA HOTELS	RMS	RATES	PHONE	CR. CARDS
Road Bay				
★★★★★ **Malliouhana Beach Hotel**	53	$240–$810	(800) 835-0796	A, MC, V
★★★★ **Cap Juluca**	91	$275–$2085	(800) 323-0139	A, MC, V
★★★★ **Cinnamon Reef Beach Club**	22	$155–$330	(800) 223-1108	A, MC, V
★★★★ **La Sirena**	24	$100–$280	(800) 331-9358	A, MC, V
★★★ **Arawak Beach Resort**	14	$100–$300	(800) 553-4939	A, MC, V
★★★ **Carimar Beach Club**	23	$130–$630	(800) 235-8667	A, MC, V
★★★ **Casablanca Resort**	88	$350–$1100	(800) 231-1945	A, MC, V
★★★ **Coccoloba**	51	$225–$425	(800) 982-7729	A, MC, V
★★★ **Cove Castles Villa Resort**	12	$350–$990	(800) 348-4716	A
★★★ **Easy Corner Villas**	15	$90–$295	(800) 223-9815	A, D, MC, V
★★★ **Fountain Beach**	10	$100–$365	(800) 523-7505	A, D, MC, V
★★★ **Frangipani Beach Club**	21	$195–$1200	(800) 892-4564	A
★★★ **Lloyd's Guest House**	11	$70–$94	(809) 497-2351	
★★★ **Mariners, The**	25	$115–$535	(800) 848-7938	A, D, MC, V
★★★ **Paradise Cove Hotel**	14	$310–$425	(800) 728-0784	A, MC, V

ANGUILLA HOTELS		RMS	RATES	PHONE	CR. CARDS
★★★	Pineapple Beach Club	27	$270–$660	(800) 345-0356	A, D, MC, V
★★★	Shoal Bay Villas	13	$147–$385	(800) 722-7045	A, D, MC, V
★★	Ferryboat Inn	7	$70–$225	(809) 497-6613	A, MC, V
★★	Inter-Island Hotel	14	$35–$135	(809) 497-6259	A, V
★★	Rendezvous Bay Hotel	47	$90–$240	(800) 274-4893	D, MC, V
★★	Sea Grape Beach Club Villas	10	$180–$450	(800) 223-9815	A, MC, V

ANGUILLA RESTAURANTS		PHONE	ENTREE	CR. CARDS
Road Bay				
	American			
★★★ Mango's		(809) 497-6491	$20–$35••	A, MC, V
	English			
★★★ Roy's		(809) 497-2470	$4–$30	MC, V
	French			
★★★★★ Pimms		(809) 497-6666	$20–$35••	A, MC, V
★★★★ Malliouhana Hotel Restaurant		(809) 497-6111	$11–$40	A, MC, V
★★★ Barrel's Stay		(809) 497-2831	$8–$30	A, MC, V
★★ Riviera Bar & Restaurant		(809) 497-2833	$6–$35	A, D, MC, V
	Indian			
★★★ Paradise Cafe		(809) 497-6010	$8–$27	A, MC, V
	Latin American			
★★★★ Palm Court		(809) 497-2727	$12–$26	A, MC, V
★★★ Ferryboat Inn		(809) 497-6613	$7–$26	A, MC, V
★★★ Koak Keel		(809) 497-2930	$6–$40	A, MC, V
★★★ Lucy's Harbour View		(809) 497-6253	$8–$30	A, MC, V
★★★ Old House		(809) 497-2228	$7–$20	A, MC, V
	Seafood			
★★★★ Hibernia		(809) 497-4290	$17–$30	A, MC, V

Note: • Lunch Only

•• Dinner Only

ANTIGUA

Farming on Antigua has shifted from sugarcane to fruits and vegetables.

Antigua starts with an A—a letter that could be easily used to spell either attitude or adventure. Formerly a British Colony, Antigua comes wrapped with a British frostiness that finds its way into the cool, distant smiles of waiters, hotel clerks and even shopkeepers. But, with nary a day of rain, and miles and miles of glorious beaches, the island still boasts enough attributes of paradise to keep American, Canadian, British and German millionaires heading for the super-deluxe resorts on its southern and western shores. Today, the island also attracts a broader base of tourists, and can accommodate all budgets, from the backpacker to the honeymooner, the latter always looking to save money at no sacrifice of romance. Color and music explode in August when Carnival comes to the streets of Antigua, filling the air with calypso competitions, steel bands and fanciful costumes. Since flying is the easiest way to reach the Caribbean—some airlines fly direct—Antigua is the best place to start a Caribbean vacation; from here, you can always charter a sailboat and fan out to neighboring islands. In fact, during the last weeks of April (or beginning of May), when international yachting fans congregate for Antigua's annual Sailing Week—the premier nautical event in the Caribbean—some hearty travelers actually chuck their flight ticket home and hitch a ride on one of the many colorful sailboats bobbing in the harbor.

Bird's Eye View

Sprawling over about 108 square miles, Antigua is the largest, most developed and most visited of the Leeward Islands. Together with Barbuda and Redonda, an uninhabited rocky inlet, it forms the independent nation of Antigua and Barbuda, within the Commonwealth of Nations. To the south lies the French island of Guadeloupe; to the southwest lies the British dependency of Montserrat and to the west, the island of Nevis. The capital is St. John's, with a population of about 36,000. The island of Antigua itself is divided into six parishes. Travelling through the island, you will be able to discern clearly the variety of regions as you pass from the hilly ranges in the southwest to the almost desertlike cacti in the northeast to the enormous bush and woodland in the interior. **Boggy Peak**, its highest elevation, rises to 1330 feet. There are 365 talcum-soft white beaches fringed with palm trees, among the most beautiful in the West Indies.

History

The Siboney Stone people were the first to graze the terrain of Antigua with settlements dating back to 2400 BC. Arawaks lived on the islands between A.D. 35 and 1100. Columbus discovered the island on his second voyage in 1493, naming it Santa Maria de la Antigua. The absence of freshwater springs persuaded French and Spanish colonists to sail on, and by 1632, the English had successfully established colonization. Apart from a

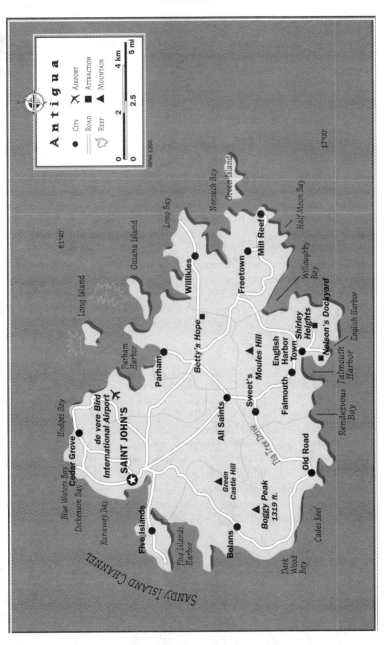

brief French invasion in 1666, the three islands of Antigua, Barbuda and Redonda have all remained British. The first large sugar estates were established in Antigua by Sir Christopher Codrington in 1674, who convinced the natives on Barbuda to raise provisions for the plantations (a village in Barbuda bears his name). As production increased forests were cleared for cultivation and African slaves were imported by the boatloads. (Today many Antiguans trace the lack of rainfall to this early forest devastation.) A vicious cycle of drought led eventually to barren lands, testimony of which can be seen in the ruined towers of sugarcane throughout the island. Abolition arrived in 1834, but the former slaves found they could barely subsist due to a lack of surplus farming and an economy that was based on agriculture and not manufacturing. Poor labor conditions and growing violence led to the organization of unions in 1939. A strong political Labor Party emerged seven years later, catapulting Antiguans into the 20th century. During World War II, Antigua was selected as a military base and American servicemen arrived in droves. Until 1959, Antigua was administered as part of the Leeward Islands, until attaining associated status with full self-internal government in 1967.

Since 1990 scandal and accusations of corruption have rocked the Antiguan government, including misuse of public funds and a series of arson attacks and murders investigated by Scotland Yard. In 1990 the governments of Antigua and Barbuda became embroiled in a scandal where they were accused of being involved in the sale of weapons to the Medellin cartel of drug traffickers in Colombia.

Today Antigua maintains strong links with the U.S., having actively assisted in the U.S. military intervention in Grenada in 1983. Since 1982, both Antigua and Barbuda have intensified their programs of foreign relations and have agreed that the People's Republic of China could open an embassy. In 1990 Antigua opened relations with Russia and in April 1983 with the Ukraine. Today both islands are constitutional monarchies, with executive power invested in the British sovereign and exercised by the Governor-General, who is appointed on the advice of the Antiguan prime minister.

Since the sugarcane industry fell off completely in 1972, tourism has monopolized the economy. In recent years, touristic activities have undergone a tremendous expansion, bringing the number of tourists who visit yearly to nearly half a million (half of which are cruise passengers).

People

As of a 1993 census, 65,000 people live in Antigua, 85 percent of them of African descent, although there is a small minority of English, Portuguese, Lebanese and Syrian. On first glimpse, the natives of Antigua may seem formal and distant, but once you crack the facade of formality, a warm, generous character surfaces. Because Antigua has an excellent harbor and easy access to the outside world, its people are quite used to traveling and are well aware of current events. The relative stability of the democracy has been reflected in the nature of the people, who are considered among the leaders in the Caribbean family. About one-third of all Antiguans live in or around the capital of St. John's, on the northwest coast. The remainder are spread evenly throughout the island, in more than 40 small towns and villages. Most own some kind of property, even if it is just a small shack in the countryside.

To delve more deeply into the Antiguan character, read Jamaica Kinkaid's devastating profile of the island and its people called *A Small Place* (1988).

Beaches

You could spend several lifetimes exploring the 365 beaches in Antigua. Beyond West Bay's Seven Mile Beach, the nearest beach to St. John's is Fort James, not conducive to swimming because of its milky film and rough waters. Nevertheless, on weekends, it gets very crowded. Farther out is Dickenson Bay, with numerous hotels along the strand section off the beach. On the peninsula west of St. John's, past the Ramada Royal Antiguan Hotel, are several picturesque beaches. **Galley Bay**, past Five Islands, is secluded and pristine, especially popular with joggers at sunset. A spectacular beach is **Galleon**, near English Harbour, though you'll need a car or taxi to get there. One of the most beautiful in the Caribbean is **Shoal Beach**, famous for its uninterrupted stretch of silvery powder. The four **Hawksbill** beaches at the end of the peninsula are attractive crescent shapes (one is a nudist beach). **Dark**

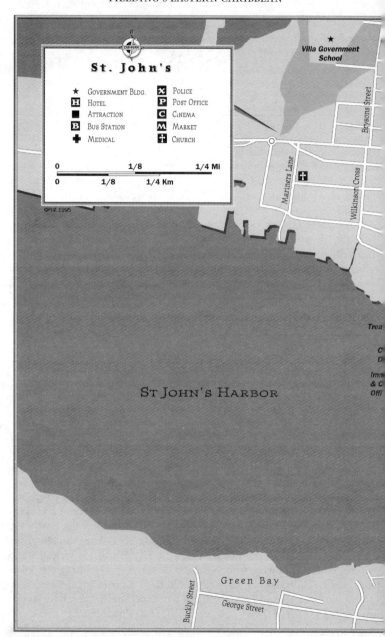

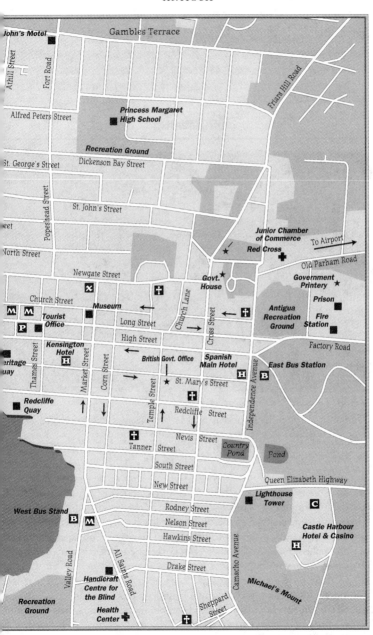

Wood Beach, on the road from St. John's to Old Round around the southwest coast, is quite pleasant, with a bar and overpriced restaurant.

Underwater

Advanced divers head for 122 ft. deep Sunken Rock.

Similar in topography to nearby St. Martin, the coral reef surrounding Antigua and Barbuda—estimated to be upward of 1000 square miles in size—is part of a giant, sloping underwater platform. As such, there are no real wall dives, although the area below Shirley Heights does offer relatively sheer drop-offs exceeding 100 feet; most dive spots tend to be shallow in nature, typically bottoming out at 60 feet or so. The best sites line the south and west coasts, though the area just northeast of the airport is now being explored with some success. Underwater visibility is somewhat limited, averaging 70 to 80 feet due primarily to the healthy plankton growth which thrives over the shallow reefs. Additionally, the government doesn't actively enforce the fishing ban within National Parks, meaning that marine life can be skimpy, even at the island's best sites (like Cades Reef). The island's massive, offshore reef structure provides many underexplored areas; some of the charted sites lie several miles off the coastline, requiring long boat rides but, in the words of *Undercurrent Magazine*, these dives are "well worth it."

Snorkelers can head to the remains of the *Andes*, in shallow water off Hawks-bill Beach in front of the Royal Antiguan Hotel; it's one of the few Caribbean wrecks that's easily accessible from shore (though not particularly interesting for divers).

Cades Reef

Located on the sleepy southern coastline between Urlings and Old Road, Cades is an extensive formation surrounded by calm waters that stretches for five miles. The outer edge of this fringe reef tilts casually downward; smaller barracuda, parrotfish and blue tang are among the regulars. One area, named Monkshead, is an attractive sand channel inhabited by garden eels. When other locations are stirred up, Cades offers the island's best visibility.

Wreck of the *Jettias*

The *Jettias* is a 310-foot steamer that crashed onto the reefs in 1917, leaving its deep end in 28 feet of water. Although the wreck is starting to break up, the atmospheric wheelhouse is still intact; the *Jettias* makes an excellent night dive when visitors are almost guaranteed to meet the 60- to 70-year-old resident turtle.

Pillars of Hercules

Conveniently located at the mouth of English Harbor, the Pillars make an ideal second dive (20-45 feet) in a dramatic setting. The site features big boulders encrusted with coral, reef ledges, crevices and an old anchor, all peppered with a diverse collection of smaller reef fish.

Sunken Rock

Probably the most popular site on the island, Sunken Rock is an advanced dive dropping to more than 120 feet amid choppy seas. Positioned in the Indian Harbor channel, just east of English Harbor, the site's architecture is truly memorable, a series of clefts and overhangs that lead to a sand floor. Majestic gorgonians and brilliant sponges abound, with an assortment of larger barracuda, rays and amberjack tooling through the depths.

Dive Shops

Dockyard Divers

English Harbor; ☎ *(809) 460-1178.*

Dockyard specializes in the south coast surrounding Shirley Heights, with most dives 10-15 minutes from the shop. Resort course available. Groups average 5–10 divers; two-tank dive $63.

Dive Runaway

Runaway Beach Hotel; ☎ *(809) 462-2626.*

Caters to Europeans; PADI training courses up to and including Divemaster. Dives west side of the island. Two-tank dive $60.

Dive Antigua

Rex Halcyon Cove Hotel; ☎ *(809) 462-3483.*

Boasts a logbook containing more than 200 dive sights, many of which are "exclusive, proprietary locations." Integrates marine biology orientation into all dives.

Oldest shop on the island (since 1970), featuring PADI and NAUI courses to Assistant Instructor. Resort courses, $85 (including a reef dive). Two tank dive $60.

On Foot

Having amply exploited its insupportable claim to 365 beaches, and now egged on by the green-backed bellow of the ecotourism monster, Antigua is attempting to mine its hillsides and coasts for trails and exploration possibilities. Instead, the island may be playing "catch-up" with the ecological advances made on other islands for a long time. Most of Antigua's interior, once covered in sugarcane, is dry and unappealing, which limits the hiking opportunities available. But the National Trust claims to be trying to identify trails, primarily in the southern region between Boggy Peak and English Harbor and may have finally produced a hiking brochure by the time you visit.

Boggy Peak

Capped by a mass of radio towers, Boggy Peak is Antigua's highest point, rising to a modest 1319 feet. Although it's possible to drive to the top, the summit represents a worthy goal on foot. Leading away from the main road along the coast, about a half-mile east of the village of Urlings, is a worn track leading toward the obvious mountain above. Follow this road to the gates at the Cable and Wireless buildings; it's possible to wander around the summit area to take in the panoramic view, which includes Guadeloupe, Montserrat, St. Kitts and Nevis.

Monk's Hill

From the village of Liberta, hike to Table Hill Gordon. Here, a steep climb ascends an old jeep trail for about a mile to the ruins of Great George Fort, where the views south encompass English and Falmouth Harbors, Nelson's Dockyard and Shirley Heights. The early 18th-century British fort was designed as a refuge for women and children in case of attack, but was never utilized as such. An alternate return route is available by following the path leading down the east side of Monk's Hill to the village of Cobb's Cross.

Green Castle Hill

This small volcano a few miles south of St. John's boasts a series of megaliths at its summit that have inspired some debate; some view the rock formations as unusual geological phenomena while others call them the remains of an Indian worship sight. Either way, the ascent rewards hikers with a lush view of the coastline and surrounding volcanic hills. The steep trail begins at the brick factory in the village of Jennings and takes a little more than an hour round-trip.

By Pedal

After slowly developing a local following, visitors are now beginning to rely on bikes as a way to explore the country's many and varied beaches and as an alternative to the expensive local taxi service. Fig Tree Drive, a road leading through Antigua's greenest hills, is a beautiful ride of moderate difficulty; the loop leading south from St. John's to Swetes, over Fig Tree Hill, and back north via the vivid western coastline makes an excellent trip that passes one breathtakingly white cove after another (about 25 miles; allow the whole day for ample beach-sampling). The area surrounding Five Islands is also popular for bicycling, but be wary of cars, particularly approaching and within busy St. John's. Mountain biking through the former cane fields should be fun, but carry a patch kit for the ever-present stickers you're guaranteed to encounter (and lucky to miss).

Bike Rental Shops

Cycle Krazy

St. Johns; ☎ *(809) 462-9253.*
$15 per day for Raleighs and Diamond Backs. Owners Dimples and Noreen Gonsalves are active in the local biking community, schedule the island's races and have a son training for the Olympics.

Sun Cycles

Hodges Bay; ☎ *(809) 461-0324.*
18- or 21-speed Raleighs are $18 for the first day, $13 for each subsequent.

What Else to See

Although St. John's, the capital of Antigua, looks a bit tatty these days, there are areas being developed for tourism and worthy of a stroll, particularly **Redcliffe Quay**, a picturesque district full of historical buildings and now duty-free stores, souvenir shops and new restaurants. Cruise ship passengers tend to crowd into **Heritage Quay**, off the harbor, where there is also a casino and a big-screen TV satellite.

If you're looking for a cool interior to escape from the sun, dip into the city's **Anglican Cathedral**, rebuilt several times due to earthquakes. No matter where you stand in St. John's, you can see the twin towers. The present building was rebuilt in 1843.

Fascinating weekly lectures are given at the **Museum of Marine and Living Art**, where you can view exhibits of sea shells, shipwrecks and even pre-Columbian history. A tour of the English Harbour is a must if you have any sort of maritime fetish. The area has been designated as a national park. The best view of the harbor is from **Limey's Bar**. Take the footpath that leads round the bay to **Fort Berkeley** for a great view that you'll share with grazing goats. Nearby, the future King William IV spent his nights at **Clarence House** when he served in the Navy during the 1780s. Overlooking the English Harbour, at Shirley Heights, are the ruins of 18th-century fortifications. It's best to go on Sundays when the steel bands play at the bar on the lookout point called the Battery. Prepare yourself for very loud music.

Best View:

Even Antiguans still flock to the top of the Shirley Heights installations to view the fabulous sunsets. You can see the English and Falmouth harbors in the foreground and the hills and coast of Antigua in the distance. On a clear day you can see as far as Redonda, Montserrat and Guadeloupe.

City Celebrations

Carnival

Various locations, ☎ *(809) 462- 194.*

What began some 20 years ago as a celebration to welcome Queen Elizabeth II has become a full-fledged annual festival with 11 days of art shows, parades and partying. The main event is "Juve," when some 400 locals dance behind steel and brass bands. Held in late July and early August, you can pick up a full program once on the island.

Sailing Week   ★★★★

English Harbour.

The Caribbean's premiere yachting event is now in its 27th year. Some 200 boats from 25 countries pour into English Harbour for five races, and there's lots going on for landlubbers as well—food vendors, beach dancing and above all, lots of partying (and lots of cops to keep things from getting out of hand). For $30 you can dress up and attend Lord Nelson's Ball at the Admiral's Inn, but those in the know say it's a bit too stuffy compared to the unabashed goings-on elsewhere. Held the last week of April.

Historical Sites

Nelson's Dockyard National Park ★★★★★

Nelson's Dockyard, English Harbour, ☎ (809) 460-1005.

Hours open: 8 a.m.–6 p.m.

This pretty spot is the only Georgian-style naval dockyard left in the world. It has a rich history as home base for the British fleet during the Napoleonic Wars and was used by Admirals Nelson and Hood. The area includes colonial naval buildings, nice beaches, ancient archeological sites and lots of nature trails. Short dockyard tours, nature walks of varying length and boat cruises are offered daily. Check out the Admiral's House, a lovely inn and museum of colonial history, then have a drink at their popular bar. Children under 16 admitted to the park for free.

St. John's Cathedral ★★

Newgate Street and Church Lane, St. John's, ☎ (809) 461- 82.

This Anglican cathedral has a sorrowful history. Originally built of wood in 1683, it was replaced by a stone building in 1745, then destroyed by an earthquake in 1843. Replaced in 1847, it was once again heavily damaged by earthquake in 1973. Restoration continues as funds are available. The figures of St. John the Baptist and St. John the Divine were taken from a French ship in the early 19th century, and the iron railing entrance dates back to 1789.

Museums and Exhibits

Dow's Hill Interpretation Center ★★

Near Shirley Heights, English Harbour.

Hours open: 9 a.m.–5 p.m.

The multimedia presentations of the island's six periods of history, from Amerindians to slavery to independence, are unique to the Caribbean. Bring your camera, as the views from the observation platforms are spectacular. $2 for kids under 16.

Museum of Antigua and Barbuda ★★

Church and Market Street, St. John's, ☎ (809) 462-1469.

Hours open: 8 a.m.–4 p.m.

Mainly intended for the island's children but worth a look if you're in the neighborhood, this small museum spotlights Antigua's geological and political past. Some interesting exhibits include a lifesize Arawak house, a wattle and daub house, models of sugar plantations and Arawak and pre-Columbian artifacts. There's also a decent giftshop selling local arts and crafts, books and historic artwork. Donation requested.

Tours

Jolly Roger

Redcliff Quay, English Harbour, ☎ (809) 462-2064.

This is the largest sailing ship in local waters—108 feet long—and a great way to spend the day. A "pirate" crew will have you walking the plank, dancing the limbo, eating, drinking, and in general making merry as you sail the seas.

Sports

The **Antigua Sailing Week** is a major Caribbean event, held at the end of April through the beginning of May.

All you have to do is head for the English Harbour to meet some of the hundreds of yachties who cruise in from all over the world. Most hotels now arrange day-sailing excursions. Numerous dive facilities are located along **Dickenson Bay**, and certification courses are available. The watersports concession located there can also reserve a deep-sea fishing expedition. Windsurfing is generally best accomplished on the eastern shores; regattas are regularly planned, so ask about. Most of the big hotels have tennis courts, and many visitors return for the Antigua Tennis Week in late April or May. Rates for balls and rackets are exorbitant. Golfers will find an 18-hole course at the **Great Valley Course**, near St. John's. Horseback riding can be arranged through your hotel, as there are several stables and resorts with their own horses and equipment. The southeast countryside is rife with trails and a great half-day trek can be made to **Monks Hill**. Also attractive is the ride around **Half Moon Bay** that circles around Mannings and overlooks Soldier Point on the Atlantic.

Golf

Two locations, English Harbour.

Hours open: 8 a.m.–6 p.m.

The island has only two golf courses, so it won't be hard to make your choice. At **Half Moon Bay Hotel** ☎ *(460-4300)* there are nine holes (2410 yards, par 34), with more challenging conditions at **Cedar Valley Golf Club** ☎ *(462-0161)*. Their 18-hole, par-70 course has some lovely views of the north coast. Green fees are $30 and cart rental is an additional $30.

Watersports

Long Bay Hotel, Long Bay, ☎ *(809) 463-2005.*

If it involves getting wet, they have it at the **Long Bay Hotel**, where nonguests can rent equipment for scuba (experienced only), snorkeling, sailing, etc. They also offer snorkel trips (four minimum) to a few small islands, though conditions are great just off the beach, thanks to Long Bay's double reef. Also check out **Shorty's** ☎ *(462-6066)* where they have all kinds of watersports and glass-bottom excursions; and **Halycon Cove Watersports** ☎ *(462-0256)*, where you can water ski. Both are at Dickenson Bay.

Windsurf Shop

Lord Nelson Beach Hotel, Dutchman's Bay, ☎ *(809) 462-3094.*
Here's your chance to try this ever-popular sport; they guarantee you'll be whisking around on your own after $50 and a two-hour lesson. (And in case you mess up, they have radio-assisted rescues.)

Where to Stay

Fielding's Highest Rated Hotels in Antigua

★★★★★	Curtain Bluff	$330–$600
★★★★★	Jumby Bay	$650–$980
★★★★	Copper and Lumber Store	$85–$325
★★★	Club Antigua	$170–$325
★★★	Galley Bay	$210–$520
★★★	Half Moon Bay Club	$245–$325
★★★	Pineapple Beach	$305–$425
★★★	Siboney Beach Club	$135–$275
★★★	St. James Club	$250–$655
★★★	Trade Winds Hotel	$194–$250

Fielding's Most Romantic Hotels in Antigua

★★	Antigua Village	$100–$475
★★★★	Copper and Lumber Store	$85–$325
★★★★★	Curtain Bluff	$330–$600
★★★★★	Jumby Bay	$650–$980

Fielding's Budget Hotels in Antigua

★	Barrymore Hotel	$53–$75
★	Antigua Sugar Mill Inn	$55–$105
★★	Lord Nelson's Beach Hotel	$60–$100
★	Blue Heron Beach Hotel	$63–$140
★★★	Admiral's Inn	$79–$149

Antigua offers an enormous array of resorts, hotels and self-catering accommodations, including those on close-by Barbuda (see "Barbuda"). Construction is a constant reality, but conservation groups are taking the issue in hand to preserve the coastline. Most properties focus around St. John's, along the coast to the west, and to the north in clockwise direction to the airport. There are also options near English Harbour and Falmouth Harbour in the southeast. Some hotels close in September and October to spruce up for winter. If you arrive on the island without a reservation, the tourist office will help you book a room. Most hotels don't have air conditioning, though the combination of ceiling fans and swift breezes keeps things cool.

Hotels and Resorts

Hotel rooms run from the gloriously luxurious ($500 and up at Jumby Bay) to so-called inexpensive hostelry rooms (about $75 at Admiral's Inn), which are pleasantly simple. Jumby Bay, now open year-round, was voted the Caribbean's No. 2 best all-inclusive resort by the *Caribbean Travel and Life* readership. It is a private island resort two miles off Antigua's northeastern coast, and is open year-round. The upscale Half-Moon Bay Club on the southeast coast has gone all-inclusive, and the Long Bay Hotel has been refurbished. Hawksbill Beach Resort, a longtime favorite for its four superb beaches, has added new beachfront cottages. Sandals Antigua was voted No. 3 for all-inclusive resorts in the *Caribbean Travel and Life* reader's poll.

Antigua Sugar Mill Inn $55–$105   ★

Coolidge, English Harbour, ☎ (809) 462-3044, FAX (809) 462-4790.
Single: $55–$95. Double: $65–$105.

Because it is the closest hotel to the airport, this spot does a big business with overnight guests on their way to hither and yon. Rooms are simple but do have air conditioning, and there's a pool, restaurant, bar and historic stone sugar mill with an observation tower on-site. The beach is nearly a mile away, which helps explain the very reasonable prices.

Barrymore Hotel $53–$75   ★

Old Fort Road, English Harbour, ☎ (809) 462-1055, FAX (809) 462-4062.
Single: $53–$61. Double: $68–$75.

Lots of business travelers stay at this low-frills hotel, which consists of very basic rooms with motel-like furnishings; only some have air conditioning. The grounds are quite nice, though, and there's a pool and restaurant on-site. The beach is a mile away.

Blue Heron Beach Hotel $63–$140   ★

Johnson's Point Beach, English Harbour, ☎ (809) 462-8564.
Single: $63–$120. Double: $63–$140.

This very basic and somewhat rundown beach hotel appeals mainly to Europeans on a budget. The best units are right on the beach and have balconies; all are simply furnished with wood and formica. Watersports are free, and there's a nice beach bar. Nothing quaint or especially charming here, but the rates keep 'em coming.

Blue Waters Beach Hotel $125–$290   ★★★

Soldier Bay, English Harbour, ☎ (809) 462-0292, FAX (809) 462-0293.
Single: $125–$255. Double: $145–$290.

Lots of repeat visitors, mainly Europeans, flock to this classic island property. The setting is its greatest asset—-14 acres of meticulously manicured gardens and a small palm-fringed beach that, while pretty, is not great for swimming. Accommodations are set along the beach and have air conditioning, pastel-colored rattan furniture, and a small patio or balcony. Villas offer two or three bedrooms with kitchens, living and dining rooms, and Jacuzzis. Afternoon tea is an especially nice ritual, but the overall service sometimes lags.

Club Antigua $170–$325   ★★★

Jolly Beach, English Harbour, ☎ (800) 777-1250, (809) 462-0068, FAX (809) 462-4900.
Single: $170–$225. Double: $225–$325.

This all-inclusive resort, set on 38 acres with a half-mile beach, hums with action and attracts mainly young people who don't mind the busy beach—-lined with vendors hawking everything from jewelry to joints—-and noisy nightlife. Lots to do here, including four restaurants, five bars, a slot casino, happening disco, all watersports, eight tennis courts and, for the kids (and their parents), a supervised children's club. The cheapest rooms, called minimums, are just so and quite small; the other classes are larger and worth the extra bucks.

Curtain Bluff $330–$600   ★★★★★

Morris Bay, English Harbour, ☎ (809) 462-8400, FAX (809) 462-8452.
Single: $330–$500. Double: $430–$600.

Antigua's most famous resort has earned its reputation for lavish accommodations and excellent service. Extras like fresh flowers daily, bidets and plush robes accent the spotless rooms and suites. The best bets are the bluffside split-level apartments, which offer up great views from two balconies. The all-inclusive rates include all watersports—-even scuba—-drinks, tennis, fitness center and putting green. The only thing missing is a pool. This is one of the Caribbean's prettiest settings, but the atmosphere can be a bit too refined for laid-back types.

Galley Bay $210–$520   ★★★

Five Islands, English Harbour, ☎ (809) 462-0302, FAX (809) 462-4551.
Single: $210–$440. Double: $330–$520.

This all-inclusive resort is set on 40 lovely acres adjacent to a bird sanctuary. Accommodations are on the beach in Polynesian thatched huts and modern cottages; all lack air conditioning but do have coffee makers, robes and hair dryers. The best rooms are built around a salt pond and coconut grove; request these "Ganguin Village" units. The beach is great and the hotel offers most watersports as well as one tennis court, a restaurant, bar and the very popular afternoon tea. This spot is popular with Europeans who aren't looking for much of a nightlife.

Halcyon Cove Beach Resort $110–$475   ★★

Halcyon Cove, Dickenson Bay, ☎ (800) 255-5859, (809) 462-0256, FAX (809) 462-0271.
Single: $110–$210. Double: $110–$475.

Lots of group tours from the U.S. and Europe congregate at this busy spot, made even more crowded by the many cruise passengers who spend the day at its excellent beach. The expansive complex includes several restaurants, four bars and a night-club, a casino, and extensive watersports including scuba, water skiing and glass-bottom boat rides. Rooms are just adequate with standard furnishings and air con-ditioning; only the beachside units have TVs, and many rooms lack views. Not great, but the rates are reasonable.

Half Moon Bay Club $245–$325   ★★★

Half Moon Bay, English Harbour, ☎ *(809) 460-4300, FAX (809) 460-4306.*
Single: $245–$285. Double: $285–$325.
A decent all-inclusive beach resort, located next to the Mills Reef Club on a nice beach. Suites are luxurious if a bit worn, and there's no air conditioning. In addition to the usual watersports there is an excellent windsurfing school, nine holes of golf and five tennis courts.

Hawksbill Beach Hotel $130–$375   ★★★

Five Islands, English Harbour, ☎ *(809) 462-1515, FAX (809) 462-0302.*
Single: $130–$310. Double: $165–$375.
This lively spot is frequented by Europeans and young babyboomer couples. The atmosphere is nicely informal, and restaurant prices are quite reasonable. Accom-modations are in West Indian-style cottages near the beach with nice lawns; all have tropical decor, pleasant furnishings and modern baths. There's also a Colonial-style Great House with three bedrooms and a kitchenette. The 37 acres include an old sugar mill that has been transformed into a boutique, tennis, watersports and four beaches, one where you can shuck your bathing suit.

Jumby Bay $650–$980   ★★★★★

Jumby Bay Island, English Harbour, ☎ *(800) 421-9016, (809) 462-6000, FAX (809) 462-6020.*
Single: $650–$980. Double: $650–$980.
Situated on its own 300-acre private island, this glorious Mediterranean-style all-inclusive resort attracts mature, affluent travelers who like everything just so. The original former home, some 230 years old, is now the main Great House with a lounge, library, games room and restaurant. Accommodations are in circular bun-galows and cottages, all spacious with separate sitting areas and expensive furnish-ings, though no phone, air conditioning or TV. Most guests get around the expansive grounds on bikes, and yachters pull in for dinner. Heavenly!

Long Bay Hotel $155–$370   ★★

Long Bay, English Harbour, ☎ *(809) 463-2005, FAX (809) 463-2439.*
Single: $155–$290. Double: $255–$370.
This intimate resort, run by the Lafaurie family, is set far out on Antigua's northeast coast. Guest rooms, situated in motel-style wings, are large but simple; the cottage units, with gabled ceilings, nice artwork and small but fully equipped kitchens, are nicer. For recreation, there's one tennis court, free watersports (scuba costs extra), a library and games room. This is an authentic Caribbean retreat—-not some cor-

poration's idea of one. Lots of American families are attracted by the warm and friendly service.

Pineapple Beach   **$305–$425**   ★★★

Long Bay, English Harbour, ☎ (800) 345-0271, (809) 463-2006, FAX (407) 994-6344.
Single: $305–$425. Double: $305–$425.

This all-inclusive resort flanks a beautiful beach, but bring your written confirmation notice, as they have a distressing tendency to overbook. A good spot for those who want all-inclusive amenities without sacrificing an arm or leg. Accommodations front the ocean and are of average size with wicker furniture, local artwork, large balconies and Mexican tile floors. This place teems with action, with folks running from tennis to volleyball to croquet to the casino, which has only one-armed bandits.

Royal Antiguan   **$115–$165**   ★★★

Deep Bay, English Harbour, ☎ (800) 228-9898, (809) 462-3733, FAX (809) 462-3733.
Single: $115. Double: $165.

Owned by Ramada, this ugly high-rise is the island's most American-like resort and has yet to meet its full potential. It does a bang-up business, though, by offering modern conveniences like direct-dial phones, TV and air conditioning. Set on 150 acres, there's a lot to keep visitors occupied, including a full casino, enormous pool with swim-up bar, lots of tennis and watersports and a supervised children's program. It's a few minutes' walk to the beach, which is frequented by local artists displaying their wares.

Runaway Beach   **$65–$280**   ★★

Runaway Bay, English Harbour, ☎ (809) 462-1318, FAX (809) 462-4172.
Single: $65–$85. Double: $65–$280.

This small resort puts up its guests in cottages perched on a mile-long, reef-protected beach. The lower units sacrifice views for air conditioning and kitchenettes; the upper units have sleeping lofts and ceiling fans instead. The beach gets crowded when cruise ships are in port. Service can be slow and indifferent, but rates are reasonable.

Sandals Antigua   **$3190–$4375 per week for two**   ★★

Dickenson Bay, ☎ (800) 726-3257, (809) 462-0267, FAX (809) 462-4135.
Rack rate Per Week: $3190–$4375.

Only heterosexual couples are allowed at this all-inclusive resort, set on a small, lively beach lined with palms and local vendors. Most accommodations are in motel-like units that are small but adequate; the 17 rooms in rondovals are better. There's tons going on here, and the staff will cheerfully badger you to participate—this is not the spot for discreet liaisons. Most of the couples are young, and many are honeymooning. One week's minimum stay costs $3190–$4375 per couple.

St. James Club   **$250–$655**   ★★★

Marmora Bay, English Harbour, ☎ (800) 274-0008, (809) 460-5000, FAX (809) 460-3015.

Single: $250–$600. Double: $305–$655.

Set on 40 lush acres, this very nice resort does not necessarily live up to its reputation as a playground for the rich and famous, and chances are slight you'll actually see tennis pro Martina Navratilova. Nevertheless, this is a great spot, with two pretty beaches, an attractive European-style casino, tony boutiques and a lively disco. Rooms are beautifully furnished, and the two-bedroom villas are wonderful. Guests can choose from watersports, horseback riding, working out in the gym, playing tennis or frolicking in three pools. Nice!

Apartments and Condominiums

Self-catering units are available throughout the island, but many complain that staples in St. John's are expensive and not worth the trouble to discover and buy. (Truth is, eating out in Antigua can be just as expensive, or more). If you're still interested, options range from simply furnished studio apartments to glorious homes rented by the owner. Booking is generally through the unit itself. Be wary of booking units from abroad before you actually see what you have rented: Surprises can include thin walls that give no privacy and strangely built rooms with little beach view. One general booker for several different complexes is **La Cure Villas** *(11661 San Vincente Blvd., Los Angeles, CA 90049.)*

Antigua Village $100–$475   ★★

Dickenson Bay, ☎ *(809) 462-2930, FAX (809) 462-0375.*
Single: $100–$475. Double: $100–$475.

This rambling complex of red-roof condominiums is located on a peninsula along a busy beach. Choose from spacious studios or one- and two-bedroom units, all with kitchenettes, bright tropical decor, air conditioning and daily maid service; only a few have TVs. Watersports are free, and there's a restaurant, bar and minimarket on-site. A reliable spot, but nothing too exciting.

Barrymore Beach Club $75–$240   ★★

Runaway Bay, English Harbour, ☎ *(800) 542-2779, (809) 462-4101, FAX (809) 462-4101.*
Single: $75–$105. Double: $120–$240.

This recently renovated beachfront complex consists of hotel rooms and one- and two-bedroom apartments with kitchenettes but no air conditioning. There's also a three-bedroom villa for rent with its own pool. There's a restaurant and bar on-site, but not much else to get excited about.

Galleon Beach Club $130–$365   ★

Freeman's Bay, English Harbour, ☎ *(809) 460-1024, FAX (809) 460-1450.*
Single: $130–$365. Double: $130–$365.

This is a time-share complex of cottages scattered about the beach or a steep hillside. Accommodations are in one-bedroom suites or two-bedroom cottages; all have rattan furnishings, living and dining areas and kitchenettes, but lack air conditioning, TVs and phones. There's a good Italian restaurant on the premises. Maintenance and housekeeping can be sloppy.

Hodges Bay Club Resort $99–$147   ★★★

Hodges Bay, English Harbour, ☎ *(809) 462-2300, FAX (809) 462-1962.*
Single: $99–$115. Double: $124–$147.

Located in an exclusive residential neighborhood, this recently renovated complex has picturesque beachfront villas with one or two bedrooms, air conditioning, full kitchens and nice views off the balconies. The beach is excellent for snorkeling, and day trips are offered to Prickley Pear Island, one mile offshore. There's a bar and restaurant on-site, as well as a pool, two tennis courts and free watersports.

Marina Bay Beach Hotel   **$80–$255**   ★★

Corbinsons Point, Dickenson Bay, ☎ (809) 462-3254, FAX (809) 462-2151.
Single: $80–$125. Double: $130–$255.

A pleasantly basic spot, with spacious and bright studios and one- and two-bedroom villas. All have air conditioning, cable TV, full kitchens and Italian-tiled baths. Located on a public beach with watersports available. There's no restaurant on-site, but several within an easy walk.

Siboney Beach Club   **$135–$275**   ★★★

Dickenson Bay, ☎ (800) 533-0234, (809) 462-0806, FAX (809) 462-3356.
Single: $135–$275. Double: $135–$275.

This three-story apartment building, enhanced by lots of greenery, is near a good but busy beach. The one-bedroom suites are nicely furnished with rattan, kitchenettes and ceiling fans; there's also a maid to tidy things up and limited room service. There's entertainment most nights at the bar, and extensive watersports including excursions via catamaran or glass-bottom boat. The service is very friendly at this well-run spot.

Trade Winds Hotel   **$194–$250**   ★★★

Dickenson Bay, ☎ (809) 462-1223, FAX (809) 462-5007.
Single: $194–$250. Double: $194–$250.

This all-suite hotel is located above Dickenson Bay with great ocean views. The beach is nearly a mile away, but the management will take you to and fro. There's a small pool on-site, as well as a restaurant and piano bar. Accommodations, in Spanish-style villas, are decent. Lots of Europeans like this spot.

Yepton Beach Resort   **$115–$500**   ★★

Deep Bay, English Harbour, ☎ (800) 361-4621, (800) 462-2520, FAX (809) 462-3240.
Single: $115–$500. Double: $115–$500.

This condominium resort consists of Mediterranean-style white stucco buildings with nice views of the beach and lagoon. All units have air conditioning and kitchenettes and include studios with Murphy beds or one- and two-bedroom apartments. All line the excellent beach. There's a restaurant and bar with live music three nights a week, with lots of other eating choices within walking distance. All-inclusive plans are offered on request.

Inns

Most inns on Antigua are expensive, but they provide a charming ambience and down-home hospitality. The most authentically historical is **Admiral's Inn**, set in an 18th century building, overlooking the harbor; here you might find billionaire yachties sipping drinks with grungy sailors in the breezy patio bar. Windsurfers who don't mind the basic furnishings like to congregate at the **Lord Nelson Club**. The **Inn at English Harbour**, near Galleon Beach, tends to best capture the seaside hominess most travelers seek in an inn.

Admiral's Inn $79–$149 ★★★

Villa Olga, English Harbour, ☎ *(809) 460-1027, FAX (809) 774-8010.*
Single: $79–$149. Double: $79–$149.

Housed in a Georgian brick building dating back to 1788, this intimate inn has a nautical theme and is loaded with charm. Rooms are small but very nice with beam ceilings and antiques; some have air conditioning and patios. This spot is a tourist attraction in its own right, so it can get crowded with folks coming through to take a look. Management transports guests to two nearby beaches. A great spot if you don't mind sacrificing resort amenities for a quaint, distinctive atmosphere.

Copper and Lumber Store $85–$325 ★★★★

English Harbour, ☎ *(809) 460-1058, FAX (809) 460-1529.*
Single: $85–$195. Double: $175–$325.

Studios and duplex suites have authentic or reproduction 18th-century furnishings, canopy beds, brass chandeliers and hand-stenciled floors. The charm extends to the bathrooms, which boast mahogany-paneled showers. No air conditioning, but ceiling fans provide a breeze. There's no beach or pool but guests are whisked via ferry to nearby Galleon Beach. A wonderful spot, but also a busy tourist attraction.

Inn at English Harbour $135–$445 ★★

English Harbour, ☎ *(809) 460-1014, FAX (809) 460-1603.*
Single: $135–$295. Double: $185–$445.

Set on ten acres of beach and hillside overlooking colorful Nelson's Dockyard, this small inn has rooms in cottage-style buildings on the beach or atop a hill. All are nicely done with island-style rush rugs, wicker and modern furniture and ceiling fans. There are two restaurants and bars, and free watersports. The clientele is mostly English.

Lord Nelson's Beach Hotel $60–$100 ★★

Dutchman's Bay, English Harbour, ☎ *(809) 462-3094, FAX (809) 462-0751.*
Single: $60–$77. Double: $70–$100.

This family-run inn, small and informal, could use a renovation to bring it fully into the 1990s. Rooms are simple but at least have balconies, and there's a restaurant and bar on-site. Basic watersports are offered, and this spot is loved by windsurfers. Located on a rather isolated spot on the northeast coast, there's virtually nothing within walking distance, so you'll need a rental car.

Low Cost Lodging

Finding a budget room on Antigua is not impossible. A good source is *A Guide to Small Hotels and Guest Homes*, provided by the Tourist Office (ask them for one). Of course, no money pays for no ambience; most low-cost lodgings are in modern, stucco buildings with only basic furnishings. A location beachside will be rare. As such, you'll probably have to throw the extra bucks into renting a car.

Where to Eat

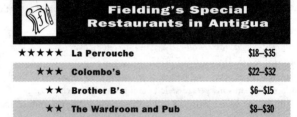

Fielding's Highest Rated Restaurants in Antigua

★★★★★	La Perrouche	$18–$35
★★★	Chez Pascal	$22–$29
★★★	Coconut Grove	$15–$30
★★★	Colombo's	$22–$32
★★★	Le Bistro	$22–$26
★★★	Le Cap Horn	$10–$20
★★★	Redcliffe Tavern	$7–$20
★★★	Warri Pier	$7–$40

Fielding's Special Restaurants in Antigua

★★★★★	La Perrouche	$18–$35
★★★	Colombo's	$22–$32
★★	Brother B's	$6–$15
★★	The Wardroom and Pub	$8–$30

Fielding's Budget Restaurants in Antigua

★★	Brother B's	$6–$15
★★	Hemingway's	$7–$15
★★	G & T Pizza	$7–$19
★★★	Redcliffe Tavern	$7–$20
★★★	Le Cap Horn	$10–$20

Antigua has rarely suffered for the lack of good restaurants, but new additions are always cropping up. Prices for a top-class dinner aren't cheap; expect to fork over at least $95 for two in the most expensive places. Spices, influenced by East Indian and creole cooking, are liberally added and tend to run on the hot side. Look for specialties such as banana and cinnamon pancakes with Antiguan rum syrup, sea urchin flan, and lump crabmeat with avocado and lemongrass.

For steel bands and a barbecue on Sundays, reserve first and then head to **Shirley Heights Lookout**, housed in a restored 18th century fort with a memorable view of Nelson's Dockyard and English Harbour.

Admiral's Inn $$$ ★ ★

Nelson's Dockyard, English Harbour, ☎ (809) 460-1027.
American cuisine. Specialties: Pumpkin soup, red snapper.
Lunch: Noon–2:30 p.m., entrees $10–$25.
Dinner: 7–9:30 p.m., entrees $10–$25.
Like the Copper and Lumber Store Hotel alongside it, the Admiral's Inn is so long on atmosphere and history, the food doesn't have to be good to be worth a visit. But thankfully, that is not the case here, especially for a silky pumpkin soup. Some never get as far as the restaurant, preferring to stay in the dark bar or sit under the old trees outdoors, looking out at the convoys of ships in the harbor. Those so inclined can eat here three times a day, and breakfast, served daily from 7:30 to 10:00 a.m., is a terrific deal. Closed September through mid-October.

Big Banana Holding Co. $$$ ★ ★

Redcliffe Quay, St. John's, ☎ (809) 462-2621.
Italian cuisine. Specialties: Pizza, conch salad.
Lunch: Noon–4 p.m., entrees $6–$30.
Dinner: 4 p.m.–midnight, entrees $6–$30.
A lot of locals and tourists homesick for pizza flock here at all hours. The pies in question are rather pricey and not very exciting, but the location, in the interesting and trendy Redcliffe Quay shopping center, helps. All in all it's considered very proper to sit under the whirring fans and just sip a cool tropical drink (these are bright, frothy and potent). Salads, seafood dishes and fruit plates are also available.

Brother B's $$ ★ ★

Long Street, St. John's,
Indian cuisine. Specialties: Pepperpot soup and fungi, pelleau, bull's foot soup.
Lunch: entrees $6–$15.
Dinner: entrees $6–$15.
A not-to-be missed touch of local color, Brother B's in Soul Alley (near the Museum) is the place to be to experience a taste of real Antiguan culture, hear the live buzz of other diners amiably feasting on local West Indian eats and freshly squeezed juices, and to tap to the beat of a hired band at noon.

Calypso $$$ ★ ★

Redcliffe Street, St. John's, ☎ (809) 462-1965.
International cuisine. Specialties: Pumpkin soup, baked chicken with cornmeal.
Lunch: 10 a.m.–4 p.m., entrees $8–$25.
This open-air, lunch-only spot jumps weekdays, and is an accessible, friendly location to try West Indian specialties. These often include fresh seafood, sauteed or prepared in batter. Homey stews and soups with pumpkin or okra satisfy; the less adventurous can chow down on burgers and sandwiches.

Chez Pascal   **$$$**   ★★★

4 Tanner Street, St. John's, ☎ *(809) 462-3232.*
French cuisine. Specialties: Bisque de langouste, croustade de fruits de mer.
Dinner: 6:30–10 p.m., entrees $22–$29.

Lyon-born Pascal Milliat, previously the chef de cuisine at La Sammana, the swank five-star resort on St. Martin, owns and toils in the kitchen of this, his own chez with the ever-pleasant assistance of his spouse, Florence, who seats patrons. Dishes are classic French with a twist of "Antiguaise" sprinkled hither and yon. Vichyssoise is a popular starter.

Coconut Grove   **$$$**   ★★★

Dickenson Bay, St. John's, ☎ *(809) 462-1538.*
International cuisine. Specialties: Grilled local lobster, chilled gazpacho.
Lunch: 11:30 a.m.–3 p.m., entrees $15–$30.
Dinner: 6:30–10 p.m., entrees $15–$30.

A simple beachfront spot surrounded by tall coconut palms swaying in the breeze, this eatery is a choice spot for privacy, moonlight and a nicely grilled lobster caught fresh that day. Chicken, hearty chops, tangy soups and salads are also on offer.

Colombo's   **$$$**   ★★★

Galleon Beach, English Harbour, ☎ *(809) 463-1452.*
Italian cuisine. Specialties: Veal Scaloppine, carpaccio.
Lunch: 12:30–2:30 p.m., entrees $22–$32.
Dinner: 7–10 p.m., entrees $22–$32.

Only in the Caribbean can one eat spaghetti Bolognese or carpaccio in a fancy, thatched-roof hut and dance to a reggae band on the beach. But everything here is scrupulously good and the service is amiable. There are daily specials and a variety of wines.

G & T Pizza   **$$**   ★★

East Falmouth Harbor, Falmouth Harbour,
Italian cuisine. Specialties: Pizza, salads.
Lunch: Noon–4:30 p.m., entrees $7–$19.
Dinner: 4:30–10:30 p.m., entrees $7–$19.

Blend in with the seafaring crowd at this popular restaurant on the waterfront at the Antigua Yacht Club in Falmouth Harbour that serves tasty pizzas and salads for under $20. Seating is on informal picnic tables framed by palm trees, and day or night, entertainment is provided by sailboats and motorcraft on the oceanfront. G&T stays open until midnight for drinks, and there's a happy hour from 5-6 p.m.

Hemingway's   **$$**   ★★

St. Mary's Street, St. John's, ☎ *(809) 462-2763.*
International cuisine. Specialties: Lobster soup, tropical chicken with fruit salsa.
Lunch: 11:30 a.m.–4:30 p.m., entrees $7–$15.
Dinner: 4:30–10 p.m., entrees $7–$15.

Not very far from the sea in the traditional West Indian town of St. John's is this tropical Victorian house with a restaurant on the second floor. There's a lot of activity and people-watching opportunities on the porch, where frothy tropical drinks can be sipped. Nibble on lobster, salads, burgers and spicy chicken. Vegetarian specialties are also available.

La Perrouche $$$ ★★★★★

Falmouth Harbour, ☎ (809) 460-3040.
International cuisine. Specialties: Whitefish with polenta, lobster with Bordelaise sauce.
Dinner: 6–10 p.m., entrees $18–$35.

This charmer is an ideal splurge restaurant, one of a handful on the island that boasts native French or French-trained chefs. The artist in question at this bloom-bedecked outdoor establishment is David Wallach, who served a stint at L'Esper-ance. Together with partner Mona Frisell, he creates a culinary palette of tropical colors and tastes each evening. Wallach imports a special whitefish chosen for its del-icacy, and local lobster is used as a sauce ingredient. Desserts involve a small orchard of exotic fruits, including sweet "black" pineapple. Well-chosen wine list.

Le Bistro $$$ ★★★

Hodges Bay, St. John's, ☎ (809) 462-3881.
French cuisine. Specialties: Red snapper baked in foil, seafood in puff pastry.
Dinner: 6:30 p.m.–10:30 p.m., entrees $22–$26.

Le Bistro, on the island's north shore, caters to residents with expensive villas in the area, but anyone with a fancy for fine cuisine can repair here for classic French dishes prepared with care. Lobster and red snapper are usually available, and made with cream, white wine and fresh herb sauces. The dining room is attractive and plant-filled.

Le Cap Horn $$$ ★★★

Falmouth Harbour, ☎ (809) 460-3336.
French cuisine. Specialties: Seafood, pizzas, steak.
Lunch: Noon–6:30 p.m., entrees $10–$13.
Dinner: 6:30–11 p.m., entrees $13–$20.

A highly recommended Italian and French restaurant in a verdant outdoor setting en route to Nelson's Dockyard. Snacks, wood-fired pizza or more substantial meat dishes are available for decent prices. Dine early or late on the porch on daily specials for under $20.

Lemon Tree $$$ ★★

Long and Church Streets, St. John's, ☎ (809) 462-1969.
International cuisine. Specialties: Cajun garlic shrimp, burritos.
Lunch: 10 a.m.–4 p.m., entrees $15–$25.
Dinner: 4–11 p.m., entrees $15–$25.

The atmosphere here is very South Seas, with a lot of wicker and wooden blinds, good for a cool-off drink or meal after a visit to the Museum of Antigua and Bar-buda nearby. Graze Caribbean-style from a long menu of finger foods, Tex-Mex items and the usual lobster and chicken dishes, which vary in quality. Unfortunately, with a cruise crowd in attendance, service can be rushed. Good for music in the evening.

Lobster Pot $$$ ★★

Runaway Bay, St. John's, ☎ (809) 462-2856.
Seafood cuisine. Specialties: Chicken in coconut milk and curry, fresh fish.
Lunch: entrees $7–$12.
Dinner: entrees $15–$25.

Even picky diners will find something to their liking at this airy eatery in Runaway Bay that does creative things with chicken and lobster at prices that won't leave you breathless. The substantial menu runs the gamut from hearty breakfasts to leafy salads, sandwiches and fresh local fish and shellfish. Commune with nature at tables on the seaside veranda; come early for these or reserve a seat.

Redcliffe Tavern $$ ★★★
Redcliffe Quay Street, St. John's, ☎ *(809) 461-4557.*
Italian cuisine. Specialties: Barbecued chicken, pasta, fresh local seafood.
Lunch: 8 a.m.–3 p.m., entrees $7–$20.
Dinner: 3–7:30 p.m., entrees $10–$20.

Begin or end a shopping tour at the charming Redcliffe Quay complex in St. John's harbor with lunch or dinner or a snack at the Redcliffe Tavern. It's one of a handful of vintage structures that have been restored for commercial usage. Once an old warehouse, the Tavern sports antique hardware for decor, and the waitstaff serves good burgers or barbecue or pastas and freshly caught lobster. Architecture buffs and Anglophiles should find the surroundings especially appealing.

Shirley Heights Lookout $$$ ★★
Shirley Heights, English Harbour, ☎ *(809) 463-1785.*
Seafood cuisine. Specialties: Pumpkin soup, lobster with lime sauce.
Lunch: 9 a.m.–4 p.m., entrees $15–$26.
Dinner: 4–10 p.m., entrees $15–$26.

Something festive is always happening in this two-story pub-restaurant amidst the ruins of Fort Shirley—especially on Sunday, when there's dancing and live bands that play for free from mid-afternoon on. Barbecued meats at decent prices accompany the tunes, and the views behind the Lookout are superb. The rest of the week, eat in peace upstairs or downstairs for breakfast, lunch or dinner. The second-floor dining room is a very intimate trysting spot.

The Wardroom and Pub $$$ ★★
Nelson's Dockyard, English Harbour, ☎ *(809) 460-1058.*
International cuisine. Specialties: West African groundnut soup, shepherd's pie.
Lunch: 11:30 a.m.–4:30 p.m., entrees $8–$25.
Dinner: 6–11 p.m., entrees $18–$30.

Old Antigua hands will be pleased with the new face given the 18th-century Copper and Lumber Store Hotel in Nelson's Dockyard. Others should come at least once to savor the atmosphere and eat remarkably fine food at remarkably high prices, especially at dinner in the Wardroom on the ground floor. But American-style or English lunches and cool drinks are within most everyone's reach at the hotel's pub.

Warri Pier $$$ ★★★
Dickenson Bay, St. John's, ☎ *(809) 462-0256.*
International cuisine. Specialties: Seafood linguine, marlin.
Lunch: Noon–6 p.m., entrees $7–$35.
Dinner: 6–10 p.m., entrees $7–$40.

Dine on marlin—"warri" is the local name—on a private pier belonging to the Halcyon Cove Beach Resort. This is a lovely setting poised high above the sand like a great wooden bird on the northern edge of Dickinson Bay, about a mile and a half from the airport. Undoubtedly, it's an excellent perch from which to observe the setting sun. Light meals of chunky fruit salads or burgers and seafood soups are substantial at lunch. Dinner gets somewhat fancier with grilled lobster and the like and luscious desserts.

Where to Shop

Redcliffe Quay and **Heritage Quay** now compete for tourist shoppers (though if you want to avoid the cruise crowd, park yourself at Redcliffe).The best shops are clustered on **St. Mary's Street** or **High Street** in St. John's. Duty-free items are omnipresent, and there are also some special Antiguan crafts such as rum, silk-screened fabrics, native straw work, and curios made from shells. Hot new clothing stores have also sprung up or expanded in the last year. Check easy-to-wear cotton and cotton/lycra styles for men, women and children at BAE stores in Redcliffe Quay. Also in Redcliffe Quay is the chic Debra Moises boutique, which carries husband-and-wife-designed sensations in flowing gauze and one-of-a-kind hair accessories (carried by Bergdorf's and Saks in Manhattan). For some strange reason, some shops in Antigua close on Thursday at noon.

Check out the Saturday fruit and vegetable market at the West Bus Station. You can also find a good selection of local handicrafts.

Antigua Directory

ARRIVAL AND DEPARTURE

BWIA has daily flights from Miami and New York. American Airlines also flies from Baltimore, Washington, Miami, Puerto Rico and New Orleans. Air Canada flies from Toronto. Continental Airlines now operates six times a week from Newark, New Jersey (every day but Tuesday, with one stop in St. Maarten).

The V.C. Bird airport, just 4.5 miles from St. John's, receives all air traffic. LIAT and American Airlines operate frequent air service to neighboring islands, such as Anguilla, Barbados, Barbuda, Dominica, Martinique, Grenada, Jamaica, Montserrat, Nevis, Guadeloupe, Trinidad, St. Croix, St. Kitts, St. Lucia, St. Maarten, St. Thomas, St. Vincent, Puerto Rico and Tortola. Carib Aviation also arranges charters (for 5–9 passengers), which often works out much cheaper than a regular airline. They are located at the **V.C. Bird Airport**; ☎ *462-3147*;

after office hours ☎ *461-1650*. Consider a day trip to Montserrat, which is only an 18-minute flight away.

The departure tax is U.S. $12.

BUSINESS HOURS

Shops open Monday–Friday 8:30 a.m.–4 p.m. and Saturday 8 a.m.–noon or 3 p.m. Banks generally open Monday–Thursday 8 a.m.–2 and Friday 8 a.m.–4 p.m.

CLIMATE

The Antiguan climate is probably the best in the Caribbean, with so little rainfall that water shortage sometimes becomes a problem. Any rainfall is usually restricted to brief heavy showers. Constant sea breezes and trade winds keep the air fresh and the temperatures hovering around 81 degrees F, except in the hot season (May-November), when temperatures can rise to 93 degrees F. The mean annual rainfall of 40 inches is slight for the region.

DOCUMENTS

U.S. and Canadian citizens must show proof of citizenship (passport, birth certificate, or voter's registration) plus a photo ID, and an ongoing or return ticket.

ELECTRICITY

The majority of hotels use 110 volts, 60 cycles, same as the U.S. Some shaver outlets are 110-volt. Hotels generally have adapters.

GETTING AROUND

The best guides in Antigua are generally taxi drivers. Or stop by the taxi rank on St. Mary's Street. Buses don't go to the airport, or to very many beaches. Look for one outside Dew's or Bryson's supermarket. Barter for a price beforehand since there are no meters. And make sure you are both talking about the same dollars (Antiguan or American).

Buses tend to leave only when there are enough riders.

Hitchhiking during the day seems fashionable and safe.

Car rental agencies are numerous. Some hotels have their own rental car services. Others found at the airport include **Titi Car Rental** ☎ *(809) 460-1452*; and **Jonas Rent-A-Car** ☎ *(809) 462-3760*. If you plan to drive, be careful since Antiguan roads are notorious for potholes, crumbling shoulders and bad signs. Antiguan drivers are about as courteous as French ones, so drive defensively.

If you want to rent a car, you must purchase a license (about US $12), valid for three months by showing your own valid license to the agency.

Motorcycles and mountain bikes are probably the easiest way to see the island. Try **Ivor's** at English Harbour or **Sun Cycles** in Hodges (for bikes only).

LANGUAGE

English is the official language, though the special Antiguan lilt may make some words indistinguishable.

MEDICAL EMERGENCIES

Holberton Hospital, on the outskirts of St. John's, is a 220-bed hospital. Serious medical emergencies are usually flown off the island to Miami. Ask if your hotel has a doctor on call.

MONEY

The official currency is the Eastern Caribbean dollar (known as Bee Wee or EC). You get the best exchange rates at banks. Most establishments will accept American and Canadian dollars. Credit cards and traveler's checks are accepted at top hotels and many shops and eateries.

TELEPHONE

From the U.S., dial 809.

TIME

Atlantic Standard Time.

TIPPING AND TAXES

Most hotels and restaurants add a 10 percent service charge. When not included, tip 10–15 percent for waiters, $1 per room per day for maids, and 50 cents per bag for bellhops. Tip taxi drivers 10 percent.

TOURIST INFORMATION

The official tourist office is located on Long Street in St. John's. You can also find information centers at the airport, at the ship terminal in St. John's and at Heritage Quay. For more information call ☎ *(809) 462-0480; FAX (809) 462-2483*. In the United States call ☎ *(212) 541-4117*.

WHEN TO GO

Men's Tennis Week, a professional and amateur tournament is held in January. Women's Tennis Week, a professional and amateur tournament, is held in early April. Race Week, a week of boat races between sailors from all over the Caribbean, is held in late April. The Queen's Birthday is celebrated in June. Carnival is held during the week before the first Monday of August. Independence Day is Nov. 1. Independence Week Half Marathon is held in early November. Christmas and Boxing Day is Dec. 2 and 26.

ANTIGUA HOTELS	RMS	RATES	PHONE	CR. CARDS
St. John's				
★★★★★ **Curtain Bluff**	62	$330–$600	(809) 462-8400	A
★★★★★ **Jumby Bay**	50	$650–$980	(800) 421-9016	A, MC, V
★★★★ **Copper and Lumber Store**	38	$85–$325	(809) 460-1058	A, MC, V

ANTIGUA HOTELS	RMS	RATES	PHONE	CR. CARDS
★★★ Admiral's Inn		$79–$149	(809) 460-1027	A, MC, V
★★★ Blue Waters Beach Hotel	67	$125–$290	(809)462-0290	A, MC, V
★★★ Club Antigua	472	$170–$325	(800) 777-1250	A, MC, V
★★★ Galley Bay	30	$210–$520	(809) 462-0302	A, MC, V
★★★ Half Moon Bay Club	100	$245–$325	(809) 460-4300	A, DC, MC, V
★★★ Hawksbill Beach Hotel	88	$130–$375	(809) 462-1515	A, DC, MC, V
★★★ Hodges Bay Club Resort	26	$99–$147	(809) 462-2300	A, MC, V
★★★ Pineapple Beach	130	$305–$425	(800) 345-0271	A, MC, V
★★★ Royal Antiguan	282	$115–$165	(800) 228-9898	A, DC, MC, V
★★★ Siboney Beach Club	12	$135–$275	(800) 533-0234	A, DC, MC, V
★★★ St. James Club	178	$250–$655	(800) 274-0008	A, DC, MC, V
★★★ Trade Winds Hotel	41	$194–$250	(809) 462-1223	A, DC, MC, V
★★ Antigua Village	100	$100–$475	(809) 462-2930	D, MC, V
★★ Barrymore Beach Club	36	$75–$240	(800) 542-2779	A, MC, V
★★ Halcyon Cove Beach Resort	135	$110–$475	(800) 255-5859	A, D, MC, V
★★ Inn at English Harbour	28	$135–$445	(809) 460-1014	A, CB, D, DC, MC, V
★★ Long Bay Hotel	26	$155–$370	(809) 463-2005	A, MC, V
★★ Lord Nelson's Beach Hotel	16	$60–$100	(809) 462-3094	A, MC, V
★★ Marina Bay Beach Hotel	27	$80–$255	(809) 462-3254	A, DC, V
★★ Runaway Beach	33	$65–$280	(809) 462-1318	A, D, DC, MC, V
★★ Sandals Antigua	207		(800) 726-3257	A, MC, V
★★ Yepton Beach Resort	38	$115–$500	(800) 361-4621	A, MC, V
★ Antigua Sugar Mill Inn	24	$55–$105	(809) 462-3044	A, D, DC, MC, V
★ Barrymore Hotel	36	$53–$75	(809) 462-1055	A, D, DC, MC, V
★ Blue Heron Beach Hotel	40	$63–$140	(809) 462-8564	A, D, MC, V
★ Galleon Beach Club	36	$130–$365	(809) 460-1024	A, MC, V

ANTIGUA RESTAURANTS   PHONE   ENTREE CR. CARDS

St. John's

	American			
★★	Admiral's Inn	(809) 460-1027	$10–$25	A, MC, V
	French			
★★★	Chez Pascal	(809) 462-3232	$22–$29●●	A, DC, MC, V
★★★	Le Bistro	(809) 462-3881	$22–$26●●	A, MC, V
★★★	Le Cap Horn	(809) 460-3336	$10–$20	A, MC, V
	Indian			
★★	Brother B's		$6–$15	None
	International			
★★★★★	La Perrouche	(809) 460-3040	$18–$35●●	A, MC, V
★★★	Coconut Grove	(809) 462-1538	$15–$30	A, DC, MC, V
★★★	Warri Pier	(809) 462-0256	$7–$40	A, MC, V
★★	Calypso	(809) 462-1965	$8–$25●	A, DC, MC, V
★★	Hemingway's	(809) 462-2763	$7–$15	None
★★	Lemon Tree	(809) 462-1969	$15–$25	A, DC, MC, V
★★	The Wardroom and Pub	(809) 460-1058	$8–$30	A, MC, V
	Italian			
★★★	Colombo's	(809) 463-1452	$22–$32	A, DC, MC, V
★★★	Redcliffe Tavern	(809) 461-4557	$7–$20	A, MC, V
★★	Big Banana Holding Co.	(809) 462-2621	$6–$30	A, DC, MC, V
★★	G & T Pizza		$7–$19	A, MC, V
	Seafood			
★★	Lobster Pot	(809) 462-2856	$7–$25	DC, MC, V
★★	Shirley Heights Lookout	(809) 463-1785	$15–$26	AE, MC, V

Note: • Lunch Only

●● Dinner Only

Hurricane Updates

The damage from Hurricane Luis, which stormed over Antigua in September, 1995, was considerable. Several popular resorts, Galley Bay, Runaway Beach Club and the Tradewinds Hotel were not scheduled to reopen until Summer, 1996 or later. The hotels listed in the book were open or minimally damaged at presstime. Those listed below sustained major damage.

Barrymore Beach Club

Severely damaged by Hurricane Luis, but apartments were expected to gradually open, a few at a time, by November, 1995.

Blue Heron Beach Hotel

Hurricane damage, no reopening date available.

Blue Waters Beach Hotel

Extensive hurricane damage; anticipating a February, 1996 reopening.

Galley Bay

Significant hurricane damage; reopening date tentatively set for Christmas, 1996.

Hodges Bay Club Resort

The hotel restaurant and some rooms were damaged by Hurricane Luis; full operation date to be determined.

Inn at English Harbor

Extensive water damage from hurricane; reopening date to be determined.

Runaway Beach

Significant hurricane damage; reopening tentatively set for Summer, 1996.

Tradewinds Hotel

Extensive damage. Reopening set for Summer, 1996.

BARBADOS

Large numbers of sailboats are available for charter in Barbados.

Three centuries ago, Barbados was called the "Brightest Jewel in the English Crowne," and today, this tiny coral island still gleams, not just as a "veddy British" trinket, but as a Caribbean treasure in its own right. After a long struggle to balance itself politically after declaring independence from Britain 30 years ago, Barbados is returning to a celebration of its own Bajan culture, interlacing the passion for cricket and afternoon teas with the more boisterous native traditions of rum, calypso and Rastafarianism. In 1993, the Human Development Report of the United Nations placed Barbados first among all developing nations in the world—the third year in a row—and tourists can't help but feel blessed by the efficiency of service, the top-class cuisine and the general enthusiasm of spirit. Long one of the most cosmopolitan and sophisticated islands in the Caribbean, Barbados is looking even spiffier these days as a building boom creates new hotels and restaurants by the dozens. Spearheaded by the Pemberton Resorts' new **Royal Westmoreland Golf and Country Club**, the construction of golf facilities, including an international school and six multimillion-dollar courses, will rank Barbados among the top destinations for golf in the world. Carnival and the annual Crop Over festival are the times when Barbados truly hangs loose, but those interested in getting away from it all can still find a wild and rugged Barbados tucked in the backcountry. A new Concorde charter service will allow travelers to reach Barbados in less the flight time normally required and will reap hundreds of saved dollars in an 8 day/7 night package at one of 15 luxury hotels on the island.

Bird's Eye View

A pear-shaped coral island that stretches 21 miles north and 14 miles east to west, Barbados is the most easterly of the complex of West Indies islands—a series of stepping stones that arch from South Florida to South America. Spanning a total of 166 square miles, Barbados boasts a remarkably varied topography—in an hour you can pass through the lush rain forest of St. Thomas, the rugged rocky coast of St. Joseph, and the gentle sloping capped hills of St. Andrew. The northernmost parish of St. Lucy is where the Caribbean and the Atlantic coast meet. Because Barbados is the first land hit by the westerly trade winds traversing the Atlantic, the air is fresh and invigorating, so much so that in the 19th century the island became known as the "sanitarium of the West Indies" because boatloads of Brits came to air out their vaporous lungs. Perhaps the good air explains the longevity of Barbadians, who on the average live well into their 70s.

History

When the Portuguese explorer Pedro a Campos discovered Barbados in the 17th century, he found the island totally uninhabited. As the sailor took in

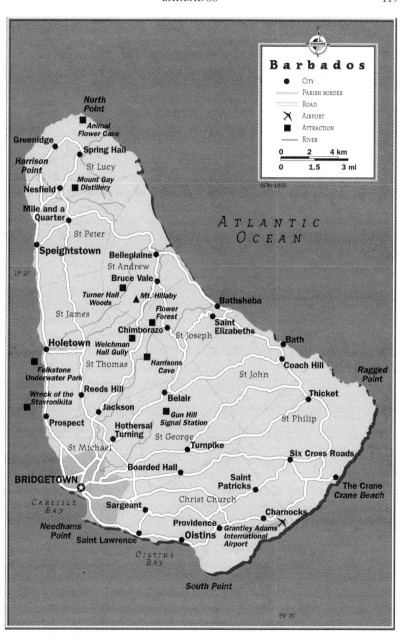

Barbados

- ● City
- ┈┈┈ Parish border
- ┈┈┈ Road
- ✕ Airport
- ■ Attraction
- ┈┈┈ River

0   2   4 km
0   1.5   3 mi

©PWI 1998

North Point

■ Animal Flower Cave

Greenidge

Spring Hall

Harrison Point

St Lucy

Mount Gay Distillery

Nesfield

Mile and a Quarter

St Peter

ATLANTIC OCEAN

13° 15'

Speightstown

Belleplaine

St Andrew

Bruce Vale

Turner Hall Woods

▲ Mt. Hillaby

Bathsheba

Flower Forest

Chimborazo

St Joseph

Saint Elizabeths

Bath

St James

Welchman Hall Gully

Holetown

St Thomas

Harrisons Cave

Coach Hill

St John

Folkstone Underwater Park

Wreck of the Stavronikita

Reeds Hill

Belair

Ragged Point

Thicket

Jackson

Gun Hill Signal Station

St Philip

Prospect

Hothersal Turning

St George

Boarded Hall

St Michael

Turnpike

Six Cross Roads

BRIDGETOWN ✕

Saint Patricks

CARLISLE BAY

Sargeant

Christ Church

Charnocks

The Crane Crane Beach

Needhams Point

Providence

Oistins

Grantley Adams International Airport

Saint Lawrence

OISTINS BAY

South Point

59° 30'

the lush tropical surroundings, he spotted fig trees with clumps of bushy roots hanging from branches that resembled beards. From that came the name Barbados, which in Portuguese means "the bearded ones." Long before the first European contact, Arawak Indians were said to be living on the island, but they were long gone by the time of the first British expedition in 1625. Two years later, 80 British settlers under the leadership of Captain John Powell settled at Jamestown (later renamed Holetown). Soon, conditions proved highly favorable for tobacco, cotton and sugarcane production, and thousands of African and European slaves were shipped over to till the fields. A strong fortress system (26 forts along 21 miles of coast) kept the island from invasion, and Barbados became the only island in the Caribbean to be under uninterrupted British rule for more than three centuries. In 1937, economic problems caused by the fluctuating price of sugar led to demonstrations in Bridgetown, which resulted in the establishment of a British Royal Commonwealth to the West Indies—a gesture that proved instrumental in bringing about social and political reform, including universal adult suffrage in 1951. Fifteen years later, Barbados received its full sovereignty.

Today Barbados is a British Commonwealth nation with a parliamentary system of government headed by an appointed governor-general and an elected prime minister. British influence extends to the courts, laws, language and place names.

People

Barbados is still a place where stately women carry umbrellas with pride, children peer from shutters, and men slam down dominoes on rickety tables. About 80 percent of the native population hail from African origin, another 15 percent are of mixed blood. Although Europeans represent only about 5 percent of the total population, a strong sense of British tradition still pervades, including a profound commitment to education (the island boasts a whopping literacy rate of 99 percent). Schoolchildren descended from slaves were taught to think of Barbados as Little England, and even in the most inland roads, you'll see children dressed in the mandatory school uniforms (pressed shirt and ties for both sexes), all color-coded in true British fashion. So strong is the Brit lifestyle here the afternoon tea is still habitually enjoyed, and passions for cricket and polo run deep. Along esplanades and streets,

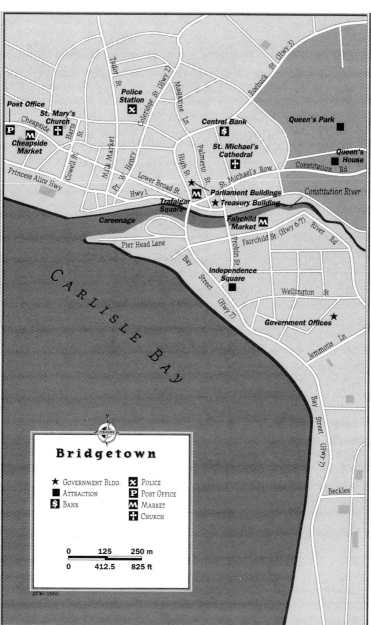

Bridgetown

★ GOVERNMENT BLDG.   ✗ POLICE
■ ATTRACTION   P POST OFFICE
$ BANK   M MARKET
✝ CHURCH

| 0 | 125 | 250 m |
| 0 | 412.5 | 825 ft |

©TW 1996

however, you might see locals playing *warri*, a traditional bead game from West Africa.

Driving around aimlessly is a way of life in Barbados—there's even a word for it: "buttin' 'bout." In fact, the best thing to do in Barbados is to throw away your map because asking and receiving directions can often be the prelude to new friendships or a spontaneous game of road tennis. If you really want to delve into the soul of Barbados, pick up a copy of the highly acclaimed novel *In the Castle of My Skin* by George Lamming.

One sad note: due to high unemployment, U.S. advisories have warned about purse-snatching, sexual crime and armed robbery. Avoid flashing jewelry and keep an eye on wallets and packs carried on the back.

Beaches

All beaches in Barbados are open to the public, even those abutting the high-priced hotels; local law requires that access to the beaches be open, either through the road or through the hotel's entrance. A beautiful drive through sugarcane fields will take you to the rugged, surf-pounding beaches of the east coast (North Point, Cove Bay and Archer's Bay), but most people prefer the calmer western beaches called the **Gold Coast** (Paradise Beach, Paynes Bay and Sandy Lane Bay, Treasure Beach, Gibbs Bay, Heywoods Beach, Rockley and Bentson Beach). The water most everywhere stays a comfortable few degrees below body temperature. The most secluded and charming hotel beach is behind the **Coconut Creek Club**, in St. James. **Mulins Bay**, just south of Speightstown, is a particularly pleasant nonhotel beach with a good restaurant-bar and a free outdoor shower. Parking is in the lot across the road. The most dramatic beach is most likely **Batsheba**, on the rugged northeast side, where foamy waves pound the shores with huge salt sprays. Here you'll see lots of old Barbadian families taking their weekend and holiday escapes.

Underwater

Busy, industrious Barbados has long been preoccupied with maintaining its commercial needs, frequently at the expense of the marine life lying just off its shores. Pollution, dynamite fishing and anchors have each taken their toll on the reefs, so it should be no surprise that the best underwater attractions the island offers are of the unnatural kind: wrecks. There are rolling plains of coral along the west and south coasts, but divers expecting extensive formations or reasonable quantities of marine life inhabiting them will be in for a disappointment. Barbados' coral structures tend to lie flat, rather than producing the caves and caverns found on other islands. But, if you come for the wrecks, there are a number to hold your interest, including the huge *Stavronikita*, a freighter now developing a forest of black coral on its decks. Visitors who come to the island in fall may be able to dive the pristine and beautiful northern coast, which is otherwise fairly inaccessible due to rough water. Sharks are rare, islandwide, and this includes at misnamed Shark Reef. The inner fringe reef averages 40 to 60 feet deep and provides decent breeding ground, particularly along the southern coast, while some of the best diving lies right off **Bridgetown** in **Carlisle Bay**. Barbados has a recompression chamber available at St. Anne's Fort. Snorkelers can visit the *Pamir*, a 150-foot vessel resting in shallow waters (easily visible from the shoreline near Mullins Bay), while Holetown's **Folkestone Park** offers a popular underwater trail.

Brightledge

Named for the sheen the narrow reef casts when viewed from above, Brightledge is a lovely formation near Six Men's Bay. The reef sits at about 60 feet, with drop-offs on either side, and offers turtles, abundant barracudas and schooling jacks, and a barrel sponge large enough to encase divers.

Carlisle Bay

A good beginner dive (20–40 feet) featuring three wrecks, one of them a coral-encrusted tug dating back to 1919. A few anchors and cannons have been added to spruce up the floor, while sea horses, flying gurnards and frog fish are among the more unusual specimens inhabiting the reef. Much of this site can be snorkeled.

Dottins Reef

Probably the island's best reef, Dottins is situated off Sandy Lane Bay; its shallow sections (averaging 40 feet) are ideal for beginners, but advanced divers will be entertained by the drop-offs leading to 130 feet. The lovely reef features brown coral trees and healthy barrel sponges, enhanced by schooling tropicals, parrotfish, blue chromis, amberjacks and turtles.

South Winds Fringe

Located off St. Lawrence on the southern coast, this appealing area features flying gurnards, kettle fish and several tame moray eels that eat from your hands; sea horses are not uncommon. This area provides breeding grounds for many of the island's reef fish and showcases many juvenile species.

Wreck of the *Stavronikita*

A 365-foot Greek freighter the government sunk in 1981, the huge *Stav* lies on a bank 137 feet down, although its rigging towers to within 12 feet of the surface. Most visitors descend to the 100-foot level, but can choose from 17 different dive profiles; the ship is firmly situated and was opened up so divers are never far from an exit, making exploration suitable for less-experienced wreck divers. The limited sea life weaving through the sight includes chubbs and barracuda.

Dive Shops

Coral Isle Divers

Bridgetown; ☎ *(809) 431-9068.*
PADI affiliated with courses through Divemaster, but serves many beginners. Dives inner and outer reefs from a 40-foot catamaran with full amenities; north and east coast dives in fall as weather permits. Two-tank dive, $60.

Dive Boat Safari

Bridgetown; ☎ *(809) 427-4350.*
PADI five-star facility; provides free introductory classes in the Hilton pool; Resort Courses, $45 (including easy wreck dive). Three dives daily and snorkeling trips to Carlisle Bay. Two-tank dive, $50; snorkeling trips, $15.

The Dive Shop

Aquatic Gap; ☎ *(809) 426-9947.*
PADI and NAUI affiliated and the oldest shop on the island (since 1965). Dives Carlisle Bay, where divers can pick up 18th-century antique bottles, as well as bigger wrecks and reefs. Resort course, $50. Two tank dive $55.

Exploresub

St. Lawrence; ☎ *(809) 435-6542.*
Island's only PADI five-star facility, includes an Instructor Development Center. Organizes underwater weddings, providing staff as witnesses. Dives south coast reefs and wrecks. One-tank dive $35; two-tank dives $70.

Hightide Watersports

Sandy Lane Hotel, Holetown; ☎ *(809) 432-1311, ext. 264.*
Works with smaller groups of six to eight, focusing on the northern half of the west coast. PADI facility teaching most specialty courses including underwater photography; uses a 36-foot-long dive boat with full amenities. Two-tank dive, $65. Resort course, $70.

On Foot

Walking is a beloved pastime for many locals. Indeed, the activity may remind visitors of country excursions in England: rolling green hills and breezy coastlines with scheduled, punctual walks. Thigh-challenging hikes are at a minimum; the island is one of the most densely populated countries in the world, its fields extensively cultivated and, owing to the limestone-based topography, the hillsides slope gently toward the muted summit of **Mount Hillaby** (1116 feet). Be sure to connect up with the local National Trust (☎ *(809) 426-2421)* which organizes free Sunday walks. These depart at 6 a.m. and 3:30 p.m. year-round, average three hours and provide visitors a chance to mingle with locals. The excursions are so well attended they break up the group into three speeds, from casual (termed "stop and stare," and guided with an educational p.o.v.) to breakneck. Several dedicated forest reserves (that charge admission) provide Barbados' most scenic natural environments, although solitude is probably best located on the broad east coast

The Railway Track

Barbados had a 37-mile public train system (built in 1883) that ran along the east coast as far as Belleplaine. The line eventually closed in 1937 due to erosion problems (both sea and land) and funding issues. Although some of the coastal sections where tracks were laid has since crumbled into the sea, most of the right-of-way between Bath and Bathsheba still exists and provides an ideal way to experience the dramatic coastline.

By Pedal

Although its 800-plus miles of paved roads are busy with motor traffic, Barbados has a dedicated local cycling club and world class riders. While many islands in the Eastern Caribbean are either limited in their road network or laced with killer hills, the Bajan countryside can be ridden for days with a variety of new challenges. One word of caution: the industrious area in and around Bridgetown and along the west coast is always choked with cars. Try taking Highway 6 out of Bridgetown, taking a right at Six Cross Roads and then left a couple miles later to Crane Bay; returning via Highway 7 (passing the airport) will provide a circuit of about 33 miles. A 55-mile tour of the island's perimeter on the main highway is geared toward seasoned cyclists. The area around Bathsheba provides beautiful coastal hills and quieter riding. Although major intersections are generally well-marked, it's easy to get lost on the maze of roads which navigate the interior; pick up an Ordnance Survey map that details the lattice of paved possibilities. Better yet, ride with Bajans who know their island's many twists and turns like the back of their hand. The Barbados Cycling Union holds rides and competitions nearly every weekend; contact Mario or Larry Williams at M.A. Williams for information.

Bike Rental Shops

Club Mistral

> *Maxwell, near Oistins Bay; (809) 428-7277.*
> Provides Raleigh mountain bikes for $20/day.

M. A. Williams Rentals

> *Hastings; (809) 427-3955.*
> Rents Mongoose Cross Trainers for $10 a day or $50 per week.

Taylor's Cycle Center

> *Bridgetown; (809) 436-2142.*
> Owner Alan Taylor has been cycling on Barbados for more than 50 years. No rentals, but does repairs; specializes in Raleighs.

Barbados' limestone foundation has created several caves of note. **Harrison's Cave** is the most famous, but visitors must experience the cave via a 20-minute electric tramride that winds down into the cave's depths. There are stalactites and stalagmites dripping peacefully, and waterfalls leading to an underground lake. Spelunkers may be happier with nearby **Coles Cave** which, though well-explored, has not been turned into a ride and allows for a more personal experience. Bring a flashlight; ask for directions to Cole's at the Harrison gift shop. Finally, an underground experience of a different nature is provided at the **Animal Flower Cave** at the northern tip of Barbados. The caves are at sea level (and below) and the titular animals are sea anemones, referred to locally as animal flowers, which are found at water level throughout the caverns. Wear well-soled shoes as the rocks inside the cave are slippery.

With big swells landing on the east coast almost year-round, Barbados is one of the few legitimate surfing destinations in the Eastern Caribbean. The best action is found in **Bathsheba** (where the Barbados International Surfing Championship is held early November), although **South Point** and **Needham's Point** (just outside Bridgetown) are also good spots. Waves die down for the summer, with winter providing the best rides.

What Else to See

Barbadian history and culture still lives vibrantly in the art and architecture of the island. Most visitors only visit the capital, **Bridgetown**, for shopping forays, but there are a few sights for which you might consider sacrificing precious time at the beach. **The Careenage**, a haven for the old clipper ships, still exudes an air of intrigue, although these days it has lost some of its former glory. Cars usually whiz by **Trafalgar Square**, but the stained glass windows of the **Public Building** represent the crowned heads of England, and are worth a quick look. The monument, dedicated to Admiral Horatio Nelson, celebrates his contributions to the island. It's rare to find Jewish houses of worship in the Caribbean, but the synagogue on Synagogue Lane is one of the oldest in the Western Hemisphere, erected on the site of an even older synagogue established by Brazilian Jews. From here, you could take a taxi to visit the garrison Savannah, especially if a cricket game or horse race is in full force.

Speightstown, on the west coast, has retained much of its colonial look and flavor. Two-story shops with Georgian-style galleries propped up by two-by-four pillars line the narrow street. Just to roam the sidewalks clogged with food vendors is an education in the vast variety of exotic tropical fruits that are available on the island.

An interesting excursion is to take a tram through **Harrison's Cave**, home of geologic formations of crystallized limestone. Streams, pools and waterfalls—one of them 40 feet—cause slow but steady erosion of the rock.

Anyone interested in antiques should visit a few plantation houses, some of which date back to the 17th century. **Drax Hall** is considered the oldest plantation house on the island, and many of the bedrooms and parlor of **Sunbury Plantation** look as if someone is still living there. **St. Nicholas Abbey** boasts an owner, Lt. Col. Stephen Cave, who will prove a true living legend if you corner him into conversation. To round out the history lesson, visit the **Barbados Museum**, which houses a fine collection of Barbadian furnishings, fine art and artifacts from the early days. The Barbados Heritage Passport, a package program, was recently expanded to 15 of the most outstanding cultural sites on the island (plantations, gardens, museums, mills, etc.). Run by the Barbados National Trust, the package offers entrance to all sites for $35, a 50 percent discount from regular admission prices.

BEST VIEW:

Grenade Hall, a restored 19th century signal station, surrounded by a user-friendly tropical forest, offers the most spectacular panorama of the island.

Historical Sites
Bridgetown

Francia Plantation   ★★★

Highway X, St. George, ☎ (809) 429- 474.
Hours open: 10 a.m.–4 p.m.
This family house, still home to descendants of the original owner, provides an authentic look at old Barbados. Also worth checking out is the Sunbury Plantation Home in St. Philip (423-6270), a 300-year-old home filled with fine antiques.

Gun Hill Signal Station   ★★

Highway 4, St. George, ☎ (809) 429-1358.
Hours open: 9 a.m.–5 p.m.
This 1818 signal station was used by the British Army. Even if you're not into such things, the views from atop the highland are worth the trip.

Old Synagogue   ★★★

Synagogue Lane, Bridgetown, ☎ (809) 426-5792.
Hours open: 9 a.m.–4 p.m.
Built by Jews from Brazil in 1654, the synagogue is the second-oldest in North America. It was partially destroyed by hurricane and rebuilt to its present state in 1833. The grounds include a cemetery, still used today, with graves of early Jewish settlers from as far back as the 1630s.

St. Peter

Morgan Lewis Sugar Windmill   ★

Highway 2, St. Andrew, ☎ (809) 426-2421.
Hours open: 9 a.m.–5 p.m.
This historic spot provides a fine example of the windmills used to process sugarcane in the 17th-19th centuries. Nice views of the "Scotland District."

St. Nicholas Abbey   ★★★

Cherry Tree Hill, St. Peter, ☎ (809) 422-8725.
Hours open: 10 a.m.–3:30 p.m.
This is Barbados' oldest structure, dating back to 1650, though it was actually an abbey only in the mind of a former owner, who dubbed it so in the 1800s. Two hundred acres of sugarcane surround the Jacobean-style great house of wood and stone.

Museums and Exhibits
Bridgetown

Barbados Museum   ★★★★

St. Ann's Garrison, St. Michael, ☎ (809) 427- 201.
Hours open: 9 a.m.–5 p.m.

This unusually fine museum, housed in a former military prison, traces the island's history from prehistoric times to the present. Good exhibits on natural history, West Indian maps and arts and the slave trade. The grounds also include a decent gift shop and an excellent cafe.

Parks and Gardens
Bridgetown

Welchman Hall Gully   ★★★
Highway 2, St. Thomas, ☎ *(809) 438-6671.*
Hours open: 9 a.m.–5 p.m.
A peaceful oasis owned by the Barbados National Trust, with acres of labeled trees and flowers, and possibly even a green monkey. The breadfruit trees are said to be descended from seeds brought by Captain Bligh.

St. Peter

Andromeda Gardens   ★★★
Bathsheba, St. Joseph, ☎ *(809) 433-9261.*
Hours open: 9 a.m.–5 p.m.
This unique spot encompasses eight acres of gardens set into oceanfront cliffs. The emphasis is on unusual plants from around the world, and they have those aplenty, plus hundreds of orchids, hibiscus and palm varieties—plus a babbling brook winding throughout.

Farley Hill   ★★★★
Farley Hill, St. Peter.
Hours open: 8:30 a.m.–6 p.m.
Very rugged grounds and the ruins of a once-grand plantation house mark this picturesque national park.

Flower Forest
Highway 2, St. Joseph, ☎ *(809) 433-8152.*
Hours open: 9 a.m.–5 p.m.
Set on an old sugar plantation in the scenic Scotland District, this park encompasses eight acres of flowering trees and shrubs. Great views of Mt. Hillaby, too.

Tours
Bridgetown

Atlantis Submarines Barbados   ★★★★★
McGregor Street, Bridgetown, ☎ *(809) 436-8929.*
Hours open: 9 a.m.–6 p.m.
The perfect way to see the world below, without getting wet, is aboard an Atlantis submarine, which takes its passengers in air-conditioned comfort some 150 feet beneath the water's surface. The two-hour tour includes the sighting of a shipwreck. Recommended for everyone but the claustrophobic.

Harrison's Cave   ★★★★★
Highway 2, St. Thomas, ☎ *(809) 438-6640.*
Hours open: 9 a.m.–4 p.m.
This is the island's biggest tourist attraction, and rightfully so, as these limestone caverns are unique to the Caribbean. Better yet, it's all tastefully done with discreet

lighting that preserves the feel of the place. Don a hard hat (more for drama than necessity) and ride an electric tram through the immense caverns, which come complete with waterfalls and streams. Reservations are recommended.

Highland Outdoor Tours

Bridgetown, ☎ *(809) 438-8069.*
Experience the real Barbados—far from the glittery resorts and tony restaurants—with this new tour operator that specializes in adventure travel. Options include a 2.5-hour Horseback Trek to the island's east coast for a bareback ride in the surf and a Caribbean lunch on the beach ($100); the Scenic Safari Hike, a five-mile walk through the pristine Scotland district and lunch on the beach ($70); and the Plantation Tour, a two-hour jaunt on a tractor-driven open jitney through some of the Barbados' great plantations ($25). You can also tour the plantations via horseback ($50).

Jolly Roger Cruises

Shallow Draft, Bridgetown, ☎ *(809) 436-2149.*
Lots of options for multihour cruises, including the Bajan Queen, a Mississippi riverboat replica that is the largest cruise ship of its kind and the only one offering sit-down dining. There are also two very fun pirate frigate replicas that offer snorkel trips and general merrymaking. Prices start at $52.50 and include transport from your hotel.

St. Peter

Animal Flower Cave

Highway 1B, North Point, ☎ *(809) 439-8797.*
Hours open: 9 a.m.–4 p.m.
The cavern takes its name from the small sea anemones that prettily open their tentacles, but don't expect to see too many nowadays.

Barbados Wildlife Preserve

Highway 1, St. Peter, ☎ *(809) 422-8826.*
Hours open: 10 a.m.–5 p.m.
This walk-through preserve, essentially a monkey sanctuary run by the Barbados Primate Research Center, features free-roaming land turtles, peacocks, parrots—even a kangaroo. They also have good exhibits on the island's natural history and an interesting walk-in aviary.

Where the Rum Comes From ★★★★

Pick up from your hotel, St. Peter.
The wonderful world of rum is the focus of this tour, held each Wednesday from 12–2:15 p.m. You'll tour Cockspur, manufacturers of Barbadian rum for more than 200 years, then sip the potable and groove to a steel band while supping on a buffet meal.

Sports

Barbados is a perfect island for surf and turf sports. Hiking, as sponsored by the Barbados National Trust and the Duke of Edinburgh's Award Scheme, has nearly become a national pastime on Sunday mornings from January-May when group treks are arranged, according to skill and endurance. (For more information, see "Treks" above.) Horseback riders can enjoy a variety of trails through tropical forests; one spectacular ride is the 3-4 hour tour of the Villa Nova Plantation, which includes a hearty lunch. Tennis courts can be found at most of the major hotels, and there are usually facilities for night-playing.

Conditions for all watersports in Barbados rank among the finest in the Caribbean, especially windsurfing, which takes advantage of the sturdy trade winds between November and May and the shallow offshore reef off Silver Sands. Deep-sea fishermen have raved about the variety of barracuda, sailfish, marlin and wahoo. Resort certification in scuba can be arranged through **Sandy Beach Watersports**; check out its most recent scuba-holiday packages. Snorkeling is also favorable, especially in **Folkstone Underwater Park**, where visibility can range up to 100 feet most of the year.

Pemberton Resort's new **Royal Westmoreland Golf and Country Club**, is presently building a $30 million-dollar, 27-hole course over 500 acres in the hills overlooking the two adjacent Pemberton hotels—Royal Pavilion and Glitter Bay. Sandy Lane also updated its course and opened an international golfing school in 1993. The Barbados government has approved five more courses on the island's south coast.

Bridgetown

Dive Shop, The

Aquatic Gap, St. Michael, ☎ *(809) 426-9947.*
Hours open: 8:30 a.m.–4:30 p.m.
They offer great scuba excursions to colorful reefs and wrecks, with prices starting at $40 per one-tank dive. Beginners can take a resort course for $50, and deep-sea fishers can arrange a charter for $300 per boat per half-day.

Christ Church

Barbados Windsurfing Club

Silver Sands Hotel, Christ Church, ☎ *(809) 428-6001.*
Rent a windboard for $20 an hour, $40 per half day, or partake in a lesson to learn this challenging sport.

Fun Seekers, Inc.

78 Old Chancery Lane, Christ Church, ☎ *(809) 435-9171.*

You can rent motorbikes or bicycles here, or better yet, partake of a cruise aboard the 44-foot *Limbo Lady.* Lunch cruises cost $50 and include snorkeling; sunset sails are $40. They'll pick you up at your hotel if need be.

St. Peter

Caribbean International Riding

Auburn, St. Joseph, ☎ *(809) 433-1453.*

Hours open: 7:30 a.m.–6 p.m.

Trail rides on handsome horses range from a 75-minute jaunt ($28) to a three-hour tour of the historic Villa Nova Plantation, complete with lunch, for $88.

Heywoods Golf Course

St. Peter, ☎ *(809) 422-4900.*

Only guests of the Almond Beach Village can golf at this nine-hole, par-three course. Fees are $35, and if the mood suits you, you can go around twice without paying for the privilege.

Sandy Lane Golf Course

Sandy Lane Hotel, St. James, ☎ *(809) 432-1311.*

This is the island's best, an 18-hole championship course with a famed 7th hole that has an elevated tee and wonderful views. Greens fees are $120 for $18 holes, $90 for nine.

Where to Stay

Fielding's Highest Rated Hotels in Barbados

★★★★★	Glitter Bay	$200–$325
★★★★★	Royal Pavilion	$235–$330
★★★★★	Sandy Lane Hotel	$500–$955
★★★★	Barbados Hilton	$149–$201
★★★★	Cobblers Cove Hotel	$135–$625
★★★★	Coral Reef Club	$74–$250
★★★★	Marriott's Sam Lord's	$110–$225
★★★★	Sandals Barbados	$105–$335
★★★★	Sandpiper Inn	$110–$445
★★★	Almond Beach Club	$259–$395

Fielding's Most Romantic Hotels in Barbados

★★★	Ocean View Hotel	$34–$71
★★★★★	Royal Pavilion	$235–$330
★★★★★	Sandy Lane Hotel	$500–$955

Fielding's Budget Hotels in Barbados

★	Fairholme	$35–$65
★★★	Ocean View Hotel	$34–$71
★	Benston Windsurfing Hotel	$50–$70
★★	Sugar Cane Club	$40–$85
★	Yellow Bird Apartments	$55–$105

Accommodations in Barbados range from the fabulously chic (villas with private pools, sprawling resorts, beachfront mansions built like a fort) to inexpensive rooms in simple hotels with basic amenities. Since brochures don't always do justice (or too much justice!) to properties, do your best to learn everything you can before making a reservation. If you're seeking high fashion, **St. James Beach** is where you'll want to roost; lesser budgets should try the studio apartments in Hastings and Worthing in the south. The best bargains for the best price are small inns run intimately by live-in managers; look for these in "The Inns" section. Unfortunately prices during high season soar skyward due to the high demand, but great bargains can be found in off-season.

For easy booking, take advantage (or ask your travel agent to) of a central reservation service operated by the Barbados Hotel Association; first call toll-free ☎ *(800) 462-2526* or *(800) GO-BAJAN.*

Hotels and Resorts

Barbados' hotels are among the poshest in the Caribbean and resorts such as the Royal Pavilion, and Sandy Lane compete with the world's best while Treasure Beach perhaps boasts the most repeat visitors. Like everything else in Barbados, many hotels have been renovated in recent years to gleaming effect. The **Coral Reef Club** and the **Sandpiper Inn** have gotten facelifts. The Moorish-style **Tamarind Cove** has added suites, shops and a classy seafood restaurant. The first all-inclusive resort, once called Pineapple Beach Club, now the **Almond Beach Club**, features one of the best authentic Bajan restaurants, **Enid's**, as well as upgraded fitness facilities and an "All-inclusive Plus" program.

A new **Concorde** charter service package offers a two-hour flight from JFK Airport on a Concorde and an 8 day/7-night package in one of 15 luxury hotels. Prices range from $2800–$5500. For more information call ETM Travel Group at ☎ *(203) 454-0090*, or toll-free *(800) 992-7700*. This is a fine (and easy!) deal for honeymooners since most of the finer resort hotels also offer on-staff consultation for wedding arrangements.

Bridgetown

Barbados Hilton $149–$201 ★★★★

Needhams Point, St. Michael, ☎ (800) 445-8667, (809) 426-0200, FAX (809) 436-8946.
Single: $149–$184. Double: $161–$201.
A good, safe choice—but don't expect a lot of Caribbean flavor at this hotel. Surrounded by nice beaches and near an oil refinery that sometimes produces pungent odors, this spot has all the modern conveniences you'd expect from a Hilton—plus lots of conventioneers running around in name tags. The pool is excellent but for unknown reasons closes at 6:00 p.m. There's a health club and tennis courts on site, as well as an old British Fort for exploring. Accommodations are fine and the service is professional.

Coconut Creek Club Hotel $240–$350 ★★★

St. James Street, Bridgetown, ☎ (800) 462-2566, (809) 432-0803, FAX (809) 432-0272.
Single: $240–$310. Double: $280–$350.
Set amid beautifully landscaped grounds, this very private resort attracts lots of European celebrities. Accommodations, in Spanish-style cottages, are small but very

clean and chic, with tropical decor, air conditioning, and walk-in closets. They sit on a low bluff overlooking two quite secluded beaches that almost disappear during high tide. Somehow, Coconut Creek manages to be both informal and sophisticated, and the service is outstanding.

Colony Club Hotel $271–$480   ★★★

St. James Street, Bridgetown, ☎ (809) 422-2335, FAX (809) 422-0667.
Single: $271–$371. Double: $300–$480.
A simple but gracious resort lining one of Barbados' best beaches, Colony Club puts guests up in Mediterranean-style bungalows with private patios and the usual amenities. TVs can be rented for those who can't go without. Watersports are complimentary, as is the shuttle that runs guests into town. A nice, quiet spot that appeals mainly to travelers from England.

Crane Beach Hotel $105–$300   ★★

Crane Beach, St. Philip, ☎ (800) 462-2526, (809) 423-6220.
Single: $105–$300. Double: $105–$300.
Set on a remote area overlooking a gorgeous beach, the Crane has the feel of a private estate. Oceanview rooms are stocked with antiques (but no air conditioning); some have kitchenettes. The picturesque Roman-style pool and a statue-punctuated grassy courtyard add a nice touch of class. The grounds include four tennis courts and a few restaurants. Novice swimmers beware: the surf here can be rough.

Ginger Bay Beach Club $80–$205   ★★★

Crane, St. Philip, ☎ (809) 423-5810.
Single: $80–$205. Double: $80–$205.
Situated on a small bluff overlooking one of Barbados' best beaches, Ginger Bay is a lovely property, but its remote location is not for everyone. All accommodations are in spacious one-bedroom suites with kitchens, modern baths and canopied king beds. They open onto private terraces complete with hammocks—a nice touch. The beach is reached via a staircase though a cave. Except for a pool and tennis court, there's not much happening here, but beach lovers are kept happy.

Grand Barbados Beach $125–$605   ★★★

Aquatic Gap, St. Michael, ☎ (800) 462-2526, (809) 426-0890, FAX (809) 426-0890.
Single: $125–$605. Double: $135–$605.
Set on Carlisle Bay, one mile from Bridgetown, this sophisticated hotel does big business with leisure as well as business travelers, who like the full-service amenities lacking at many other island resorts. Guest rooms are small but modern and come equipped with the usual creature comforts, including air and satellite TV. The pool is too small if everyone decides to partake, but the beach is nice and surprisingly quiet given its near-city locale. All watersports are free, including sailing. The long pier adds atmosphere.

Marriott's Sam Lord's $110–$225   ★★★★

St. Philip, ☎ (800) 228-9290, (809) 423-5918, FAX (809) 423-5918.
Single: $110–$225. Double: $110–$225.
Marriott's Sam Lord's Castle takes its name from the 1820 great house built by Samuel Hall Lord, known as the "Regency Rascal" for his penchant for tricking

ships to his jagged shore, then looting the smashed cargo. Today's resort is set among 72 acres with formal gardens and all the resort amenities you'd expect from a fine Marriott property. Accommodations are quite varied; choose a cottage if budget permits. All runs smoothly, but the overabundance of conventioneers can leave individual travelers feeling forgotten and overwhelmed.

Sandals Barbados $105–$335 ★★★★

Black Rock, St. Michael, ☎ *(800) 726-3257, (809) 424-0888, FAX (809) 424-0889.*
Single: $105–$235. Double: $125–$335.

A complete overhaul has left Sandals looking shiny and spiffy. This all-inclusive resort, open only to heterosexual couples, provides all meals, drinks and recreational diversions in one price. The activity is there for the taking—those who would rather leave it may be happier at a less-organized resort. Everything you'd ever want to do is there for the asking, and guests work frantically to earn a tiny pair of sandals to show what good sports they are. Lots of honeymooners.

Christ Church

Benston Windsurfing Hotel $50–$70 ★

Maxwell, Christ Church, ☎ *(809) 428-9095, FAX (809) 428-9095.*
Single: $50–$70. Double: $55–$70.

You know the windsurfing's gotta be good if an entire (albeit small) hotel is dedicated to it. Those staying at this basic property are devoted to the sport, and, as such, are generally young and lively. Accommodations are spacious but bare-bones; everyone's always out zipping along the surf, anyway. They'll teach you how to do it, but most who come here are already pretty darn good.

Caribbee Beach Hotel $60–$105 ★★

Hastings, Christ Church, ☎ *(800) 462-2526, (809) 436-6232, FAX (809) 436-0130.*
Single: $60–$90. Double: $65–$105.

There's no beach at this beach hotel, just the ocean slamming into a seawall. Oh well. . . the rates are low, though they probably should be even lower. Rooms are air-conditioned and furnished in basic motel style. The absence of both a beach and a pool make other budget properties a better choice.

Divi Southwinds Resort $115–$245 ★★

St. Lawrence Gap, Christ Church, ☎ *(800) 367-3484, (809) 428-8076, FAX (809) 428-4674.*
Single: $115–$245. Double: $115–$245.

Set on 20 acres, this resort partially lines the beach, though most of the complex is inland. Accommodations, in white stucco buildings, are mostly suites with full kitchens, living areas, air conditioning and attractive tropical furnishings. For fun, there are two tennis courts, two pools and a private beach. Lots of entertainment attracts a clientele of mostly young families.

Southern Palms $69–$265 ★★★

St. Lawrence Gap, Christ Church, ☎ *(800) 462-2526, (809) 428-7171, FAX (809) 428-7175.*
Single: $69–$265. Double: $94–$265.

Set on six acres surrounding an old plantation-style manor house, Southern Palms attracts a fun-loving set. The resort sprawls with a variety of buildings of different influence, including Italian, Spanish and West Indian styles. Lots of organized activities keep guests busy, from miniature golf tournaments to steel band dances. All the usual watersports are free, and accommodations are pleasant.

St. Peter

Almond Beach Club $259–$395 ★ ★ ★

Vauxhall, St. James, ☎ (809) 432-7840, FAX (809) 423-2115.
Single: $259–$295. Double: $305–$395.
This all-inclusive resort is refreshingly free of pressure to join in activities, but if you're game, there's a slew of stuff going on, from island tours to shopping trips to watersports. Half the accommodations are in one-bedroom suites with island decor. The grounds include three pools, tennis and squash, and lots of dining options. The beach is narrow and not great for swimming, but better ones are close by.

Buccaneer Bay Hotel $90–$330 ★ ★ ★

Paynes Bay, St. James, ☎ (809) 432-7981.
Single: $90–$200. Double: $200–$330.
Set on one of the best beaches on the west coast, this small hotel has large air-conditioned rooms with refrigerators, toasters and tea kettles, plus TV sets on request. The pool has a swim-up bar but other diversions, such as watersports, are lacking, though they can be arranged nearby.

Cobblers Cove Hotel $135–$625 ★ ★ ★ ★

Road View, St. Peter, ☎ (800) 223-6510, (809) 422-2291, FAX (809) 422-1460.
Single: $135–$625. Double: $135–$625.
Built on the site of a former British fort, this lovely and intimate all-suite hotel keeps guests pampered, earning its reputation as one of the island's finest resorts. Suites are nicely decorated and come with kitchenettes. The lush tropical grounds include a tennis court, pool and nice beach. If you're up for splurging, book the Camelot Suite, fit for a king with marble floors, its own small pool and a spiral staircase leading to a private sundeck.

Coral Reef Club $74–$250 ★ ★ ★ ★

St. James Beach, St. James, ☎ (800) 525-4800, (809) 422-2372, FAX (809) 422-1776.
Single: $74–$134. Double: $117–$250.
Small cottages with spacious accommodations are scattered about the nicely landscaped grounds here at Coral Reef, one of Barbados' best bets. Flawlessly run by the O'Hara family—which does indeed give a damn—the grounds are lushly maintained and the beach is terrific, attracting a loyal following. All rooms come equipped with refrigerators, hair dryers, a small library of paperbacks and air conditioning. Most watersports are free, and tennis courts are a short stroll away.

Crystal Cove $100–$335 ★ ★

Fitt's Village, St. James, ☎ (800) 462-2426, (809) 425-1440, FAX (809) 438-4697.
Single: $100–$335. Double: $110–$335.
Set on a sandy beach, this complex includes a mix of standard rooms and deluxe units with living areas, kitchens and separate bedrooms; all have motel-like furnish-

ings, air conditioning and high ceilings. Typical resort recreational diversions are offered, though maintenance and service can be shoddy.

Discovery Bay Hotel			**$120–$375**					★★★

Holetown, St. James, ☎ (800) 462-2526, (809) 432-1301, FAX (809) 432-2553.
Single: $120–$375. Double: $170–$375.

This plantation-style hotel, set on four tropical acres, consists of two-story structures around an attractive courtyard. Accommodations are spacious and modern, though the air conditioning doesn't always keep up. There's also a three-bedroom villa for those who don't mind splurging. The grounds include watersports (most free), two tennis courts, a pool and a windsurfing school. The welcome drink you receive on arrival portends the excellent, friendly service. A good choice in the price range.

Glitter Bay				**$200–$325**				★★★★★

Porter's, St. James, ☎ (800) 283-8666, (809) 422-4111, FAX (809) 422-3940.
Single: $200–$325. Double: $200–$325.

This refined beachfront resort, which sports an impressive Great House as its centerpiece, is top-drawer in every aspect. All accommodations are in suites set among beautifully landscaped grounds, and include air conditioning, marble baths, bidets, kitchenettes, living rooms and great views. The large free-form pool comes complete with waterfall, and the two tennis courts are in top condition. All watersports are complimentary, and guests can partake of the facilities at the Royal Pavilion next door. Luxury all the way!

King's Beach Hotel			**$105–$245**					★★

Road View, St. Peter, ☎ (800) 462-2526, (809) 422-1690.
Single: $105–$245. Double: $105–$245.

This Spanish-style beachfront hotel does a good business with families, with a playground and kid's club wooing the younger set. Guest rooms are air-conditioned and sport TVs and minibars as well as floor-to-ceiling windows affording great views. All the usual watersports, plus a pool and tennis court, round out the action.

Royal Pavilion				**$235–$330**				★★★★★

Porters, St. James, ☎ (800) 283-8666, (809) 422-5555, FAX (809) 422-3940.
Single: $235–$330. Double: $235–$330.

This elegant Mediterranean-style enclave is Barbados' best, with gorgeous grounds and excellent accommodations, all in junior suites with marble floors, lovely furnishings and lots of perks. Virtually all have ocean views. Use of the two lighted tennis courts and watersports is complimentary, as are afternoon tea and occasional evening cocktails. The beach is fine. Guests can use facilities at the neighboring Glitter Bay, which is a bit more informal. Those opting for the Royal Pavilion are indeed treated like royalty. Wonderful!

Sandpiper Inn				**$110–$445**				★★★★

St. James Beach, St. James, ☎ (800) 223-1108, (809) 422-2251, FAX (809) 422-1776.
Single: $110–$141. Double: $285–$445.

There's a real island feel to this charming hotel, set right on the beach among coconut trees. Accommodations are in suites with kitchens, one or two bedrooms, air conditioning and nice local artwork. Two lighted tennis courts, a pool and free watersports (except skiing, which costs extra) round out the picture.

Sandy Lane Hotel $500–$955   ★ ★ ★ ★ ★

St. James, ☎ *(800) 223-6800, (809) 432-1311, FAX (809) 432-2954.*
Single: $500–$955. Double: $500–$955.
Luxury doesn't come cheap here, but it's worth every hard-earned cent to retreat to Sandy Lane, one of the island's best choices. A recent refurbishment has put this place back on top, and all is impeccable. Accommodations are lovely with antique and local-style furnishings and lots of extras. There are all the usual watersports and complimentary golf on 18 holes. Lots of old money and Britains here, and while the service befits the rates, the atmosphere can be a tad snooty. Casual types will be happier (and spend lots less) elsewhere.

Tamarind Cove Hotel $280–$640   ★ ★ ★

St. James, ☎ *(800) 462-2526, (809) 422-1726, FAX (809) 432-6317.*
Single: $280–$490. Double: $320–$640.
Classic Spanish architecture marks this romantic beachfront resort, which is nestled among coconut trees and coral sands. Guest rooms and suites are very nice; the newer suites have Roman tubs and bidets. Three pools, once complete with waterfall, enhance the grounds. All watersports are free, including sailing and skiing. There's lots of nightlife here, including a Barbadian revue and boisterous barbecues.

Treasure Beach Hotel $155–$445   ★ ★ ★

Paynes Bay, St. James, ☎ *(800) 462-2526, (809) 432-1094.*
Single: $155–$445. Double: $155–$445.
This small hotel is set on a nice coral beach, but its small grounds and tiny pool are definite drawbacks. Nevertheless, the hotel has a very loyal following and lots of repeat visitors. Accommodations are in suites (but lack kitchens) and are very nicely done with tropical art and furnishings; toasters and kettles are available on request. Request a unit on an upper floor for more privacy.

Apartments and Condominiums

Noting the uneven supply and demand for Barbados accommodations, local businessmen have turned to building apartments and renovating private homes that suit many different lifestyles. Depending on your budget, you can choose to stay in a private home worthy of an exiled contessa or in a small, inexpensive apartment. A three-bedroom property on the west coast, on the beach but without sultanic amenities, could run $1500–$3000 a week in high season; $950–$2000 off season. Many homes come with built-in household help who often act quite proprietary. If you do your own cooking, stock the larder with provisions form **Eddie's and Jordan's**, supermarkets located in Speightstown. They offer nearly everything you're used to along with interesting local products like a fiery hot yellow sauce, which makes a great gift to take home.

Christ Church

Casuarina Beach Club $80–$165   ★ ★ ★

St. Lawrence Gap, Christ Church, ☎ *(809) 428-3600, FAX (809) 428-1970.*
Single: $80–$165. Double: $80–$165.

Set on seven acres of well-tended tropical palms and shrubs, this family-owned hotel has air-conditioned studios and apartments of one or two bedrooms, all with kitchenettes and spiffy accessories. Resort-style amenities include two tennis courts, squash, an Olympic-size pool, a few bars and a restaurant. Nice beach, too, but the choppy water isn't for everyone. The lovely gardens are reason enough to enjoy this very fine spot; another are the extremely reasonable prices.

Club Rockley Barbados $180–$535   ★ ★

Worthing, Christ Church, ☎ (800) 462-2526, (809) 435-4880, FAX (809) 435-8015. Single: $180–$535. Double: $180–$535.

This condominium resort consists of modest townhouses set along the fairway of a nine-hole golf course, in a predominantly residential neighborhood. Units come with one or two bedrooms, kitchens, air conditioning and uninspired decor. The grounds are extensive, with seven pools, five tennis courts, lawn games and two air-conditioned squash courts. A shuttle runs guests to a private beach club every half hour when the usual water diversions are available, included in the all-inclusive package.

Half Moon Beach Hotel $75–$215   ★ ★

St. Lawrence Gap, Christ Church, ☎ (800) 462-2526, (809) 428-7131, FAX (809) 428-4674. Single: $75–$215. Double: $90–$215.

Set on tropical Dover Beach, this small complex consists of one- and two-bedroom apartments with kitchens and modern furnishings. There's a pool and restaurant on-site, but not much else, though the friendly staff and reasonable rates make Half Moon worth a look if you're on a budget.

Sand Acres Beach Club $75–$125   ★ ★

Maxwell Coast Road, Christ Church, ☎ (800) 462-2526, (809) 428-7141, FAX (809) 428-6089. Single: $75–$125. Double: $75–$125.

Accommodations at this beachfront property are in studios or one-bedroom apartments with kitchens. The grounds include a simple restaurant, standard pool and a beach bar, as well as one tennis court and watersports for an additional fee. The beach is nice, but service can be harried.

Sandy Beach $100–$175   ★ ★ ★

Worthing, Christ Church, ☎ (800) 462-2526, (809) 435-8000. Single: $100–$175. Double: $100–$175.

This informal all-suite hotel offers units with one or two bedrooms; all have kitchens, satellite TV and air conditioning. There's a pool and restaurant on-site, and watersports can be had for an additional fee. The beach is small but pleasant.

Sea Breeze Beach Hotel $45–$245   ★ ★

Maxwell Coast Road, Christ Church, ☎ (800) 822-7223, (809) 428-2825, FAX (809) 428-2872. Single: $45–$245. Double: $50–$245.

Located on two secluded beaches, this apartment complex has air-conditioned studios with kitchenettes and balconies overlooking gardens or the beach. There are also three 2 bedroom units for those who need the space. Two restaurants and a pool complete the scene.

Sea Foam Haciendas   **$70–$93**   ★ ★

Worthing, Christ Church, ☎ *(800) 822-7223, (809) 435-7380, FAX (809) 435-7384. Single: $70–$93. Double: $70–$93.*

Very comfortable two-bedroom apartments with kitchens, living/dining areas, air conditioning and full maid service. Many sport nice ocean views, and watersports are available. No restaurant on site, but several nearby.

Woodville Beach Apartmens   **$47–$129**   ★ ★ ★

Hastings, Christ Church, ☎ *(800) 462-2526, (809) 435-9211, FAX (809) 435-9211. Single: $47–$129. Double: $47–$129.*

Accommodations at this oceanfront complex range from studios to one- and two-bedroom units, each with full but tiny kitchens, though only some have air conditioning. They are rather spartan, but clean and comfortable. The beach is quite rocky and recommended only for strong swimmers; better bathing is found at Rockley Beach, a five-minute walk.

Yellow Bird Apartments   **$55–$105**   ★

St. Lawrence Bay, Christ Church, ☎ *(809) 435-8444, FAX (809) 435-8522. Single: $55–$105. Double: $65–$105.*

Situated across the street from the bay and a small beach, this apartment complex offers air-conditioned studios with full kitchens and ocean-view balconies. There's a poolside bar and restaurant, but little else in the way of extras.

St. Peter

Asta Apartment Hotel   **$50–$235**   ★ ★

Palm Beach, Hastings, ☎ *(800) 462-2526, (809) 427-2541, FAX (809) 426-9566. Single: $50–$235. Double: $50–$235.*

Studios and apartments of one and two bedrooms offer guests the option of cooking in to save money. (There's also a restaurant on-site and several within walking distance when you tire of your own fare.) There's a pool on the grounds but little else, as reflected in the rates. One nice extra: the maid does the dishes.

Beachcomber Apartments   **$80–$300**   ★ ★

Paynes Bay, St. James, ☎ *(809) 432-0489, FAX (809) 432-2824. Single: $80–$195. Double: $155–$300.*

Basic apartments are air-conditioned and come in studios or one- or two-bedroom configurations. Though they call themselves luxury apartments that may be stretching it. No pool or restaurant on-site, but the beach is nice and maid service is available.

Sandridge Beach Hotel   **$60–$195**   ★ ★

Roadview, St. Peter, ☎ *(800) 462-2526, (809) 422-2361, FAX (809) 422-1965. Single: $60–$195. Double: $70–$195.*

This apartment hotel has studios and one-bedroom units with air conditioning, kitchenettes and TV rentals. There's a pool and restaurant, plus complimentary watersports, including free glass-bottom boat rides. A good choice for families.

Settler's Beach Hotel   **$555–$705**   ★★★

Holetown, St. James, ☎ *(800) 462-2526, (809) 422-3052, FAX (809) 422-1937.*
Single: $555–$705. Double: $555–$705.

Accommodations are in bi-level townhouses or cottages, each with large living/dining areas, kitchens, two bedrooms and spacious terraces; all are sunny and colorfully decorated. The lush grounds include a small pool, access to two tennis courts and a restaurant. Kids under 18 stay free, so expect to see lots of families.

Sugar Cane Club   **$40–$85**   ★★

Maynards, St. Peter, ☎ *(809) 422-5026, FAX (809) 422-0522.*
Single: $40–$85. Double: $40–$85.

Located in a remote region on a hilltop overlooking the Caribbean, the small hotel offers studios and apartments with modern touches like air conditioning and color TV. There's a bar and restaurant on-site, as well as a pool, sauna and putting green. Nothing too exciting, but at those rates, it doesn't have to be.

Inns

The best inns in Barbados offer an intimate, relaxing escape from the bustle of top-class resorts and package deals. The most attractive are housed in buildings that date back to the 18th and 19th centuries. Furnishings are more often than not simple, but views, such as those from the **Kingsley Club**, sometimes rate as stupendous. **Sugar Cane Club** is best if you're seeking total peace and quiet.

Bridgetown

Island Inn   **$130–$230**   ★★★

Aquatic Gap, St. Michael, ☎ *(809) 436-6393, FAX (809) 437-8035.*
Single: $130–$170. Double: $180–$230.

This intimate all-inclusive resort, housed in an 1804 former rum store for the British Regiment, has lovely guest rooms for those who like modern luxury (all rooms are air-conditioned, for example) combined with historic charm. Accommodations are situated around a picturesque courtyard with gurgling fountains, and include Persian rugs, limestone brick walls and white rattan furniture. The all-inclusive rates include such extras as picnic baskets and a two-hour cruise. Nice!

Christ Church

Ocean View Hotel   **$34–$71**   ★★★

Hastings, Christ Church, ☎ *(809) 427-7871.*
Single: $34–$44. Double: $55–$71.

Don't be put off by the faded exterior along a busy street; the Ocean View's considerable charms lie within. This is Barbados' oldest hotel, dating back to 1898, and if you don't mind forgoing modern conveniences, a stay here will live on in your memory. Guest rooms are individually decorated with a decidedly funky slant, with lots of genuine antiques mixing with the merely old. Bunches of tropical flowers add to the ambience. This special spot is not for everyone, but well loved by those who appreciate its unique flair.

Seaview Hotel   **$95–$305**   ★★

Hastings Main Road, Christ Church, ☎ *(809) 426-1450, FAX (809) 436-1333.*
Single: $95–$305. Double: $95–$305.

Housed in a historic building from 1776, the Seaview is one of Barbados' oldest hotels. Rooms are air-conditioned and decorated in a faux-Georgian style that meshes nicely with the high ceilings and shuttered windows. The grounds include a small pool, tennis and squash. A bit overpriced for what you get.

St. Peter

Kingsley Club   **$85–$106**   ★★

St. Joseph, ☎ *(809) 433-9422, FAX (809) 433-9226.*
Single: $85–$97. Double: $89–$106.
This remote and peaceful spot appeals to Barbadians and those who savor a true island experience. Rooms in the historic house are simple but clean, and the views are spectacular. It's best not to attempt the very strong surf, although the beach is glorious.

Low-Cost Lodging
Christ Church

Fairholme   **$35–$65**   ★

Maxwell, Christ Church, ☎ *(809) 428-9425.*
Single: $35–$65. Double: $35–$65.
A combination of hotel and apartment complex, the Fairholme consists of a converted plantation house that holds standard guest rooms and 20 Spanish-style studio apartments with air conditioning. There's a restaurant, bar and pool, but little else. Still, it's hard to beat the rates.

Where to Eat

Fielding's Highest Rated Restaurants in Barbados

★★★★	Bagatelle Great House	$30–$35
★★★★	Carambola	$20–$40
★★★★	David's Place	$9–$30
★★★★	Ile de France	$18–$38
★★★★	La Cage aux Folles	$25–$38
★★★★	Pisces	$15–$30
★★★★	Raffles Old Towne	$25–$35
★★★★	The Fathoms	$6–$29
★★★	La Maison	$23–$40
★★★	Reid's	$21–$40

Fielding's Special Restaurants in Barbados

★★★★	Bagatelle Great House	$30–$35
★★★★	David's Place	$9–$30
★★★★	La Cage aux Folles	$25–$38
★★★★	Raffles Old Towne	$25–$35
★★★	Reid's	$21–$40

Fielding's Budget Restaurants in Barbados

★★	Chicken Barn, The	$3–$11
★★	Carib Beach Bar	$6–$16
★★	T.G.I. Boomers	$4–$17
★★	Atlantis Hotel	$12–$17
★★★	Koko's	$12–$22

Barbados' restaurants are world-class, and can hold their own against any international cuisine.

Bajan cooking blends the ethnic influences of the British colonists, the Arawak Indians in residence on the island at the time of their arrival, and the African slaves imported between 1640 and 1807.

Flying fish—boiled, baked, stewed, fried, steamed or stuffed—is the island specialty, available on many menus. One of the hot spots is **La Maison**, tucked inside an old coral-stone Bajan house where the red snapper marinated in herbs and honey is reportedly sublime.

Wine bars and tapas are now the rage in Barbados. Tapas fanatics should head for the **Waterfront Café** in a restored coral-limestone warehouse on Bridgetown's inner harbor, where the young and gorgeous chow down on "fish-melts" (batter-fried flying fish roe) and lime squash while listening to great jazz. Lunch is also good since the view of the bay is spectacular.

Among the most romantic spots are **Carambola**, on the west coast (catch the sunset), and **The Mews** on the Gold Coast, where you can dine on the patio under a starry sky or inside the white stucco house brimming with tropical plants. Even more romantic is **Reid's**, a St. Peter restaurant with open sides that overlook manicured gardens filled with fountains and singing tree frogs called *coquis.*

Do stop by the supermarket and check out the huge variety of island spices. You'll also discover nine different brands of *mauby*, the local sugar-and-tree bark drink. Hot-sauce addicts can choose from at least 12 brands of local brew made from scotch-bonnet peppers, mustard, garlic, scallions and spices; visitors have been known to chug home a gallon or two.

Bridgetown

Bagatelle Great House $$$ ★★★★

Highway 2A, St. Thomas Parish, ☎ *(809) 421-6767.*
French cuisine.
Dinner: 7-9:30 p.m., entrees $30–$35.
Diners too timid to experience the vibrant street scene on the Baxter Road, an open-air market in the heart of Bridgetown where vendors cook fish on hot fires, come to Bagatelle Great House, which duplicates this method with whatever's fresh that day. The restaurant is located within the former residence of the first governor of Barbados, and this is probably one of the island's more elegant dining experiences, with stellar service—though the food is less distinguished than the surroundings. Guests can eat downstairs or on a small terrace one flight above.

Brown Sugar $$$ ★★★

Aquatic Gap, St. Michael Parish, ☎ *(809) 426-7684.*
Latin American cuisine. Specialties: Flying fish, Creole orange chicken.
Lunch: Noon-2:30 p.m., prix fixe $14–$25.
Dinner: 6–9:45 p.m., entrees $10–$25.

One of the better values on the islands, and a lovely one to boot, is this lush, terraced, tropical-style restaurant located a few miles south of Bridgetown. Smart businesspeople and others in the know dine here at lunch on weekdays when a West Indian buffet is available for $14.00. There are various soups, salads and stews to choose from, including pepper pot. Other offerings include flying fish, jerk chicken and pork and luscious desserts. Dinner is more of a Continental affair, with international touches added to local ingredients, like the popular Creole orange chicken.

Carib Beach Bar   **$$**   ★★

Sandy Beach, Worthing,
International cuisine. Specialties: Fish fry, barbecue.
Lunch: 11:30 a.m.–3 p.m., entrees $6–$16.
Dinner: 3–10 p.m., entrees $6–$16.
One of a string of economical beach bars that pop up on several locations around the islands, Carib is right on the sand at Sandy Beach, offering fish sandwiches and fresh seafood in a comfortable upstairs restaurant, and potent rum punches in the lower-level bar. Better yet are the Wednesday night fish fries and Friday barbecue buffet, which both start at 7:30 p.m. and cost around $10 for a substantial amount of food. A happening place that stays open fairly late. The restaurant closes at 7:30 on Sundays.

Chicken Barn, The   **$**   ★★

Highway 7, Worthing,
American cuisine. Specialties: Fried chicken.
Lunch: 10 a.m.–3:30 p.m., entrees $3–$11.
Dinner: 3:30–10:30 p.m., entrees $3–$11.
The Chicken Barn is a convenient quick lunch stop that serves fried chicken and decent burgers for a little over $1. In fact, the Barn is one of a group of inexpensive faster food establishments on Highway 7 not far from Sandy Beach in the town of Worthing, a great place for budget-minded travelers. You can also get salads and fish and chips for under $4.

Josef's   **$$$**   ★★★

Waverly House, St. Lawrence Gap, ☎ (809) 435-6541.
International cuisine. Specialties: Toast skagen, dolphin meuniere.
Lunch: Noon–2:30 p.m., entrees $10–$13.
Dinner: 6:30–9:30 p.m., entrees $25–$40.
Although Austrian chef and restaurateur extraordinaire Josef Schwaiger sold his well-loved namesake restaurant to open two other fashionable spots, the flame has passed splendidly to Swedish chef Nils Ryman. Ryman has kept Josef's more stellar creations on the mostly seafood menu, including the sublime dolphin meuniere, but has added some fine dishes of his own, namely a smorrebrod of shrimp with dill mayonnaise. It might be difficult to snag a dinner reservation, but a weekday lunch is a viable option for a smoked fish or chef's salad. No lunch served on weekends.

Waterfront Cafe   **$$$**   ★★

The Careenage, Bridgetown, ☎ (809) 431-0303.
International cuisine.
Lunch: 10 a.m.–2 p.m., entrees $8–$25.

Dinner: 2–10 p.m., entrees $8–$30.

The Waterfront Cafe is an inexpensive cool-off eatery on the Careenage, a small inlet for light craft. It serves Bajan-inspired quick meals like pepper pot soup, a copious appetizer platter and flying fish interspersed with familiar burgers and English pub food. There's music every evening, usually jazz, and a relaxed bar scene. Seating is either outdoors facing the water or in the dining room.

Christ Church

Da Luciano's   **$$$**

Staten, Christ Church, ☎ (809) 437-7544.
Italian cuisine.
Dinner: 6:30-10:30 p.m., entrees $19–$33.

A lot of care goes into the presentation and preparation of the Italian food served here in a handsome old home, Staten, a historical landmark near a white sand beach popular with locals. Starters include a mixed seafood platter and antipasto, and main courses and pastas are hearty and often infused with plenty of garlic.

David's Place   **$$$**   ★★★★

St. Lawrence Main Road, Christ Church, ☎ (809) 435-6550.
Latin American cuisine. Specialties: Baxter Street fried chicken.
Lunch: 11 a.m.–3 p.m., entrees $9–$13.
Dinner: 6-10 p.m., entrees $14–$30.

Wear loose clothing to eat this delicious Bajan food in a pretty cottage beside St. Lawrence Bay, where every table has an ocean view. A spicy fried chicken named in honor of the Baxter Street food vendors is a specialty, as is pepperpot and pumpkin soup. Huge helpings of rice and peas, cheese bread, potatoes and vegetables come with all the entrees, but you can't stop there. Make room for fantastic desserts like coconut cream pie if you can—you won't regret it.

Ile de France   **$$$**   ★★★★

Hastings, Christ Church, ☎ (809) 435-6869.
French cuisine. Specialties: Foie gras.
Dinner: 6:30-10 p.m., entrees $18–$38.

An innovative French restaurant located on the lush grounds of one of Barbados' traditional hotels, the Windsor Arms, Ile de France brings Gallic intensity to its slower-paced, old-fashioned surroundings. Many classic dishes are represented, including a definitive foie gras and ballotine de canard (one of the owners is from Toulouse), escargots de Bourgogne, and crepes flambeed at tableside. The atmosphere is sublime and unobtrusive, with candlelight, subtle lighting and music.

Pisces   **$$$**   ★★★★

St. Lawrence Gap, Christ Church, ☎ (809) 435-6564.
Seafood cuisine. Specialties: Red snapper caribe.
Dinner: 6-10 p.m., entrees $15–$30.

Flowers, greenery, an oceanfront table and an impeccable reputation for fresh seafood draws visitors to Pisces again and again. Red snapper caribe with tomatoes and shrimp is an ongoing special, although it may be difficult to choose an entree from the long and varied menu that invariably includes the catch of the day served any style, with a butter sauce or with Jamaican jerk seasonings. There's a refreshing gazpacho and a few meat, chicken and vegetarian dishes.

T.G.I. Boomers $$ ★★

St. Lawrence Gap, Christ Church, ☎ *(809) 428-8439.*
International cuisine. Specialties: Flying fish.
Lunch: 11:30 a.m.–6 p.m., entrees $4–$11.
Dinner: 6-10 p.m., entrees $11–$17.

This very welcome (for variety and bargain prices) bar-restaurant near Rockley Beach serves three meals a day, including an all-American breakfast of bacon and eggs, french toast or an omelette (with coffee and juice) for $6.50. At lunch, burgers, deli and fish sandwiches and vegetarian dishes are offered for under $10. Dinner plates of steak or seafood are garnished with vegetables, rice or potatoes and soup or salad. It also serves the needs of party types and barhoppers with daiquiris and other blender drinks at the bar, which stays open until midnight.

Witch Doctor $$$ ★★

St. Lawrence Gap, Christ Church, ☎ *(809) 435-6581.*
Latin American cuisine. Specialties: Pumpkin soup.
Dinner: 6:15-9:45 p.m., entrees $13–$30.

You'll think you're on another island when dining at this wild jungle-themed dining room serving spicy, innovative and traditional island cuisine. If the decor doesn't get to you, the good food will satisfy, including creamy pumpkin soup, seafood cocktail marinated in lime and flying fish.

St. Peter

Atlantis Hotel $$$ ★★

Bathsheba, St. James Parish, ☎ *(809) 433-9445.*
Latin American cuisine. Specialties: Pepper pot stew, flying fish.
Lunch: Noon–3 p.m., prix fixe $12–$17.
Dinner: 7–9 p.m., prix fixe $15–$17.

You might go without a full meal for a week after the enormous Sunday brunch at the Atlantis Hotel, a traditional hostelry with a breathtaking sea vista. Although this dining room operated by owner Enid Maxwell serves set lunches and dinners at very reasonable prices, Sunday is when everyone (including tour groups) blows in. The tables groan with authentic "Bajan" specialties, including pepper pot stew (assorted meats in a rich broth, simmered for days), breadfruit, flying fish and rice and peas. If lines are overwhelming, try the Edgewater Hotel dining room nearby ☎ *(433-9902).*

Carambola $$$ ★★★★

Derricks, St. James Parish, ☎ *(809) 432-0832.*
French cuisine.
Dinner: 6:30–9:30 p.m., entrees $20–$40.

This old favorite is still wowing a select group who ooh and aah over the spicy Thai-French cuisine (a unique combination) served in a cliffside dining room, with the sea lapping 10 feet below. Carambola is located in a converted old home north of Bridgetown in St. James Parish, where chef Paul Owens and owner Robin Walcott have prepared and planned such delights as green or red curry chicken or filet of dolphin with dijon mustard sauce. It's too bad that only dinner is served, because the view is spectacular.

Koko's $$$ ★★★

Prospect House, St. James Parish, ☎ *(809) 424-4557.*
Latin American cuisine. Specialties: Pepper pot soup, seafood.
Dinner: 6:30–10 p.m., entrees $12–$22.

The chef here is a talented saucier, creating a symphony of flavors that accentuate the freshly caught shellfish and game garnishing the colorful plates. The beach setting is pretty, with tables set on the patio of a traditional Bajan house on the west coast of the island. The food is largely island-style, with pepper pot soup often on hand, as well as lightly fried shellfish cakes in a tangy citrus and mayonnaise sauce.

La Cage aux Folles $$$ ★★★★

Summerland Great House, St. James Parish, ☎ *(809) 424-2424.*
International cuisine. Specialties: Sesame prawn pate, orange peel chicken.
Dinner: 7–10:30 p.m., entrees $25–$38.

There aren't any showgirls with feathered plumes anywhere in sight at this eclectic Asian-Caribbean restaurant. The setting, in the Summerland Great House, a restored plantation, is entertainment enough. The food, luckily, plays a stellar role, with Chinese crispy duck, sesame prawn pate and orange peel chicken as predominant examples. There's a balcony for cocktails and a view of lush gardens, and an intimate antique-filled room for private parties within. Owners are experienced restaurateurs with establishments in London.

La Maison $$$ ★★★

Balmore House, St. James Parish, ☎ *(809) 432-1156.*
Seafood cuisine.
Dinner: 6:30–10 p.m., entrees $23–$40.

Comfortably positioned in yet another Great House on the St. James coast (will they ever run out of them?), La Maison has been wowing visitors and residents alike since it opened in the early 1990s with sophisticated, French-inspired seafood. Dining here is likened to a posh beach camp-out, with tables set out on the sand under a tent or indoors in a courtyard exposed to ocean breezes and views. The ever-changing menu may feature salmon with cream sauce, marinated flying fish and rich ice cream or chocolate desserts.

Raffles Old Towne $$$ ★★★★

1st Street, St. James Parish, ☎ *(809) 432-6557.*
International cuisine. Specialties: Curries.
Dinner: 7–10 p.m., entrees $25–$35.

Named after the Raffles Hotel in Singapore and inspired by British colonial exploits abroad, this highly regarded restaurant employs a big-game hunter theme in an intimate room close to the ocean in Holetown. Naturally, there are curries and chutneys, blackened fish and chicken, and a full-course dinner for $40. Raffles rates three "knives and forks" (the highest culinary honor) from the Barbados Tourism Authority.

Reid's $$$ ★★★

Derricks, St. James Parish,
International cuisine. Specialties: Lobster.
Dinner: 7–10 p.m., entrees $21–$40.

Fresh fish, lobster and escargots in white wine and garlic are served to diners at this plantation building south of Holetown. Reservations should be made a few days in advance to enjoy manicured garden views, gurgling fountains and a well-chosen wine list.

The Fathoms $$$ ★★★★

Paynes Bay, St. James Parish, ☎ *(809) 432-2568.*
International cuisine. Specialties: Lobster, octopus.
Lunch: 11 a.m.–3 p.m., entrees $6–$8.
Dinner: 6:30–10 p.m., entrees $15–$29.

Daring seafood dishes are the hallmark of this ocean-view, red-roofed spot on Paynes Bay, near Holetown. You can stick with a grilled lobster, stuffed crab or catch of the day, but octopus and sea eggs (white sea urchins' roe, prepared deviled or breaded) are sometimes on the menu. At night it's romantic with candlelight and crashing waves for sound effects; other times it's Bajan casual. Besides seafood, there are burgers, salads and pork crepes. With less than 25 tables in the dining area, make reservations well in advance.

The Mews $$$ ★★★

Second Street, St. James Parish, ☎ *(809) 432-1122.*
Seafood cuisine. Specialties: Fresh fish.
Dinner: 7–10 p.m., entrees $20–$30.

This is one of two new restaurants opened by award-winning chef Josef Schwaiger, who sold his popular Josef's in St. Lawrence Gap. It's already very successful among his many admirers and assorted fish fanciers (Josef's specialty) who like to dine in a trellised garden on paupiettes of snapper and a sublime lime mousse. Before or apres dinner, walk across the street to **Nico's Champagne and Wine Bar**, ☎ *(809) 432-0832* for some bubbly or chablis by the glass.

Where to Shop

Even the shopping scene in Barbados has been recently spruced up, with the addition of more stores to an already bulging array of specialty boutiques, departments stores and resort-wear shops spread throughout the island. Even the beach peddlers have new kiosks. At the newly renovated cruise terminal (probably the best in the Caribbean), you can stroll through an attractive indoor shopping and entertainment arcade lined with 20 duty-free shops, crafts boutiques and restaurants—all designed to resemble a West Indian town with gingerbread cottages in pastel colors. Cruise passengers (and other foreign tourists) can choose among jewelry, liquor, china, electronics, perfume and leather goods, all duty-free for U.S. citizens (with savings of up to 40 percent off U.S. prices). There are also shops of Barbadian woodcarvings and fine art galleries as well as clothing and souvenir boutiques. Here you can also find a tourist information center, car and bike rentals, automated teller machines, florists, dive shops and a communications center with fax and phones.

Most resort hotels have a bevy of boutiques at their entrance or on premises, but prices are usually marked way up; you pay for the convenience (the Hilton and Sandy Lane do have interesting stock, however). If you're looking for department stores (and impressive ones for an island), head for downtown (especially **Da Costas Mall** with more than 50 stores), but branches can usually be found in resort communities as well as at **Holetown** and **Speightstown**, where you also find specialty boutiques of top quality and resort-wear shops. On the west coast, there is the **Sunset Crest** shopping mall.

Perhaps the most outstanding Bajan art you can take home is **pottery**. Native potters use clay from the area, eschewing cheap souvenir figurines and instead fashioning the traditional shapes used in Bajan kitchens, such as the monkey pot that actually makes water taste better since it can be stored at the proper temperature. The ramshackle town of **Chalky Mount**, high on a cliff overlooking Barbados' northeastern St. Andrew parish, is considered to be the epicenter of Bajan folk art. Here, every home has a potter's wheel and fathers pass down the craft techniques to their sons, a tradition that dates back 300 years. Best pottery can be found at **Chalky Mount Potter** ☎ *(809) 422-9619* and also at **Springer's Pottery** ☎ *(809) 422-9682.*

Other local crafts include black-coral jewelry, attractive wall hangings made from dried grasses and flowers, and straw mats, baskets and bags. Leatherwork is just beginning to find its place among Bajan craft art.

Barbados Directory

ARRIVAL

American Airlines, Air Canada and BWIA are the principal carriers to Barbados, flying from New York, Toronto, Miami and San Juan to Grantley Adams Airport. Good connections can be made with other Caribbean islands, especially via British Airways, which has good deals between Antigua, St. Lucia, Barbados and Trinidad. It's best to buy ongoing tickets ahead of time as Barbados agents add a 20 percent service tax. Reserve months in advance for the Christmas season and during the

Crop Over Festival in August. A departure tax, payable at the airport upon leaving, is U.S. $12.50.

BUSINESS HOURS

Stores open weekdays 8 a.m.–4 p.m., Saturday 8 a.m.–1 p.m. Banks open Monday–Thursday 8 a.m.–3 p.m. and Friday 9 a.m.–5 p.m.

CLIMATE

Constant northeast trade winds keep temperatures between 75-85 degrees F year-round. The wet season, from June to November, is more humid than at any other time; September and October are the rainiest months. Weather can change quickly—in a cross trip on the island from west to east, you can start out with sunny skies and end up in a raging storm. Rainfall varies from 50 inches on the coast to 75 inches in the higher interior.

CRUISES

Cruise ships dock at the Deep Water Harbour's pier. Most folks on a limited time schedule head for Pelican Village to do some shopping. You can easily catch a taxi waiting at the dock. (The walk can get long and hot!) If you want to catch a smaller ship or sailboat to another island, hang around the port here and see who you can meet; ships are arriving all the time on their way to other islands.

DOCUMENTS

U.S.and Canadian citizens need to show proof of citizenship (passport, birth certificate, or voter's registration card, along with a government-issued photo ID, like a driver's license). Also required is an ongoing or return ticket.There is a departure tax of U.S. $12.50.

ELECTRICITY

The current is 100 volts, 50 cycles, as in the U.S., though the speed is somewhat slower. Hotels with 220 volts usually provide adapters.

GETTING AROUND

From the airport it's a good hour's drive to the part of the west coast where many (but not all) of the best hotels and houses to let are located. You can rent a car at the airport, but only local agencies are available. Since the road from the airport is a bit hairy, visitors are better off taking a taxi to the hotel, and then renting a car from there. If you rent a car, you'll need your own license, plus a driver's permit issued at the airport by the police or your rental agency for a $5 fee. Take the insurance ($5 a day) if you're not sure you are already covered. Note that driving is on the left.

The most highly recommended car-rental agency is **National Car Rental**, Bush Hall, Main Road, St. Michael; ☎ *(809) 426-0603*. Cars will be delivered to a location anywhere on the island.

Also try **P&S Car Rentals** ☎ *(809) 424-2052 or 424-2907*, Pleasant View, Cave Hill, St. Michael; **Sunny Isle Motors**, ☎ *(809) 435-7979*.

In general, roads are well paved and locations well marked.

Taxi drivers are no longer naive on Barbados and know their way around know-nothing tourists. Ask your concierge or hotel management how much a particular trip should cost before you get in the taxi; otherwise you could get bilked.

Public buses are reliable and safe, but unbearably crowded at rush hours (8:30–9:30 a.m. and 3:30–6 p.m.). The route that runs down the south and west coast is an inexpensive way to see the island.

GUIDES

Although the more independent traveler prefers to rent his own car and toddle around on his own, hotels can arrange a personal guide for you if you want to see more of the island. Excellent service is offered by **Sally Shearn's VIP Tour Service** ☎ *(809) 429-4617*.

LANGUAGE

English is the official language, spoken with a pronounced island lilt.

MEDICAL EMERGENCIES

Top-class hotels usually have a doctor on call. Queen Elizabeth Hospital, located on Martinsdale Road in Bridgetown, is the preeminent training hospital in the Caribbean.

MONEY

The official currency is the Barbados dollar, worth about 50 cents in American currency. Most stores will accept American dollars and traveler's checks. However, to get your best rate, it's better to exchange your American dollars for Bajan ones at a bank.

TELEPHONE

Area code is 809.

TIPPING AND TAXES

Most hotels and restaurants add a 10 percent service charge. Feel free to tip extra if the service is especially fine.

TOURIST INFORMATION

The tourist office is located in the Harbour Industrial Park near the Deep Water Harbour in Bridgetown. You'll also find information posts at the airport and at the cruise ship pier at the Deep Water Harbour. They are only open weekdays. From the U.S. call ☎ *(213) 380-2198*.

WATER

Water is safe to drink in Barbados, pumped from an underground source in the island's coral reefs.

WHEN TO GO

Crop Over Festival in July and August is an islandwide celebration of Barbadian arts, food, music and dance, which harks back to the 19th century when the last of the year's sugarcane crop was feted. Three weeks of competitions, festivities, feasts and fairs celebrate the culture and history of the island. Kaddoment Day, a national holiday held on

Aug. 1, is the culmination of the Crop Over Festival, with costumes, music, street dancing and fireworks. The Holetown Festival in February, commemorating the first settlement in 1627, is celebrated by a big street party, as is the Oistins Fish Festival at Easter. In November the National Independence Festival of Creative Arts (NIFCA) usually sponsors an annual month-long celebration of Barbadian talent competitions in art, music, song and dance. In July, the Sir Garfield Sobers International School's Cricket Tournament, named after a famous Barbadian cricketer, has become an international event, attracting worldwide participation.

Every Sunday year-round, traditional Sunday hikes are cosponsored by various charities, encouraging participants to walk at their own pace. Walks start at 6 a.m. and 3:30 p.m. Call the **Barbados National Trust** ☎ *(809) 428-5889*. On Sundays in January, **Barbados Horticultural Society's Open Garden Program** presents local gardeners displaying their gardens from 2–6 p.m. For more information, call ☎ *(809) 428-5889*. On Wednesday afternoons, January-April, **Barbados National Trust Open House Program** invites visitors to browse through the private homes of architectural and historical importance to the island.

The period between Christmas and Easter is the most popular time for tourists, though the British summer is busier than it used to be.

BARBADOS HOTELS		RMS	RATES	PHONE	CR. CARDS
Bridgetown					
★★★★	**Barbados Hilton**	184	$149–$201	(800) 445-8667	MC, V
★★★★	**Marriott's Sam Lord's**	234	$110–$225	(800) 228-9290	A, D, DC, MC, V
★★★★	**Sandals Barbados**	178	$105–$335	(800) 726-3257	A, MC, V
★★★	**Coconut Creek Club Hotel**	53	$240–$350	(800) 462-2566	A, MC, V
★★★	**Colony Club Hotel**	76	$271–$480	(809) 422-2335	A, MC, V
★★★	**Ginger Bay Beach Club**	16	$80–$205	(809) 423-5810	A, D, DC, MC, V
★★★	**Grand Barbados Beach**	133	$125–$605	(800) 462-2526	A, DC, MC, V
★★★	**Island Inn**	23	$130–$230	(809) 436-6393	A, D, DC, MC, V
★★	**Crane Beach Hotel**	18	$105–$300	(800) 462-2526	A, DC, MC, V
Christ Church					
★★★	**Casuarina Beach Club**	129	$80–$165	(809) 428-3600	A, D, MC, V
★★★	**Ocean View Hotel**	35	$34–$71	(809) 427-7871	A, MC, V
★★★	**Sandy Beach**	89	$100–$175	(800) 462-2526	A, D, DC, MC, V
★★★	**Southern Palms**	92	$69–$265	(800) 462-2526	A, D, DC, MC, V

BARBADOS HOTELS	RMS	RATES	PHONE	CR. CARDS
★★★ Woodville Beach Apartmens	28	$47–$129	(800) 462-2526	None
★★ Caribbee Beach Hotel	55	$60–$105	(800) 462-2526	A, D, DC, MC, V
★★ Club Rockley Barbados	108	$180–$535	(800) 462-2526	A, D, DC, MC, V
★★ Divi Southwinds Resort	160	$115–$245	(800) 367-3484	A, DC, MC, V
★★ Half Moon Beach Hotel	36	$75–$215	(800) 462-2526	A, MC, V
★★ Sand Acres Beach Club	37	$75–$125	(800) 462-2526	A, MC, V
★★ Sea Breeze Beach Hotel	60	$45–$245	(800) 822-7223	A, D, DC, MC, V
★★ Sea Foam Haciendas	12	$70–$93	(800) 822-7223	D, MC, V
★★ Seaview Hotel	25	$95–$305	(809) 426-1450	A, MC, V
★ Benston Windsurfing Hotel	15	$50–$70	(809) 428-9095	A, D, DC, MC, V
★ Fairholme	31	$35–$65	(809) 428-9425	None
★ Yellow Bird Apartments	21	$55–$105	(809) 435-8444	A, D, MC, V

St. Peter

	RMS	RATES	PHONE	CR. CARDS
★★★★★ Glitter Bay	81	$200–$325	(800) 283-8666	A, D, DC, MC, V
★★★★★ Royal Pavilion	75	$235–$330	(800) 283-8666	A, D, DC, MC, V
★★★★★ Sandy Lane Hotel	121	$500–$955	(800) 223-6800	A, DC, MC, V
★★★★ Cobblers Cove Hotel	39	$135–$625	(800) 223-6510	MC
★★★★ Coral Reef Club	71	$74–$250	(800) 525-4800	A, MC, V
★★★★ Sandpiper Inn	45	$110–$445	(800) 223-1108	A, MC, V
★★★ Almond Beach Club	147	$259–$395	(809) 432-7840	A, DC, MC, V
★★★ Buccaneer Bay Hotel	29	$90–$330	(809) 432-7981	A, MC, V
★★★ Discovery Bay Hotel	85	$120–$375	(800) 462-2526	A, MC, V
★★★ Settler's Beach Hotel	22	$555–$705	(800) 462-2526	A, MC, V
★★★ Tamarind Cove Hotel	116	$280–$640	(800) 462-2526	A, MC, V
★★★ Treasure Beach Hotel	26	$155–$445	(800) 462-2526	A, DC, MC, V
★★ Asta Apartment Hotel	60	$50–$235	(800) 462-2526	A, MC, V
★★ Beachcomber Apartments	9	$80–$300	(809) 432-0489	MC, V
★★ Crystal Cove	88	$100–$335	(800) 462-2426	A, D, DC, MC, V
★★ King's Beach Hotel	57	$105–$245	(800) 462-2526	A, D, MC, V
★★ Kingsley Club	7	$85–$106	(809) 433-9422	A, MC, V
★★ Sandridge Beach Hotel	52	$60–$195	(800) 462-2526	A, MC, V
★★ Sugar Cane Club	23	$40–$85	(809) 422-5026	A, D, DC, MC, V

BARBADOS RESTAURANTS	PHONE	ENTREE	CR. CARDS
Bridgetown			
American			
★★ **Chicken Barn, The**		$3–$11	None
French			
★★★★ **Bagatelle Great House**	(809) 421-6767	$30–$35••	A, MC, V
International			
★★★ **Josef's**	(809) 435-6541	$10–$40	A, MC, V
★★ **Carib Beach Bar**		$6–$16	MC, V
★★ **Waterfront Cafe**	(809) 431-0303	$8–$30	A, MC, V
Latin American			
★★★ **Brown Sugar**	(809) 426-7684	$14–$25	A, DC, MC, V
Christ Church			
French			
★★★★ **Ile de France**	(809) 435-6869	$18–$38••	MC, V
International			
★★ **T.G.I. Boomers**	(809) 428-8439	$4–$17	A, MC, V
Italian			
★★ **Da Luciano's**	(809) 437-7544	$19–$33••	MC, V
Latin American			
★★★★ **David's Place**	(809) 435-6550	$9–$30	A, MC, V
★★ **Witch Doctor**	(809) 435-6581	$13–$30••	A, MC, V
Seafood			
★★★★ **Pisces**	(809) 435-6564	$15–$30••	A, MC, V
St. Peter			
French			
★★★★ **Carambola**	(809) 432-0832	$20–$40••	A, MC, V
International			
★★★★ **La Cage aux Folies**	(809) 424-2424	$25–$38••	MC, V
★★★★ **Raffles Old Towne**	(809) 432-6557	$25–$35••	A, DC, MC, V
★★★★ **The Fathoms**	(809) 432-2568	$6–$29	A, MC, V

BARBADOS RESTAURANTS	PHONE	ENTREE	CR. CARDS
★★★ Reid's		$21–$40••	A, MC, V
Latin American			
★★★ Koko's	(809) 424-4557	$12–$22••	MC, V
★★ Atlantis Hotel	(809) 433-9445	$12–$17	A
Seafood			
★★★ La Maison	(809) 432-1156	$23–$40••	MC, V
★★★ The Mews	(809) 432-1122	$20–$30••	A, MC, V

Note: • Lunch Only

•• Dinner Only

BARBUDA

Barbuda is the perfect place to indulge in the "deserted island" experience.

Barbuda is not a "Wow" island. It's flat and featureless, with about as much excitement as a bird-watcher could take. Who's it for, then? The *totally* rich and reclusive. For years, only one resort, Coco Point, dominated the island, until fashion mogul Mariuccia Mandelli, alias Krizia of Milan, chose tiny Barbuda for her personal Eden. Club K, Krizia's $30 million dream resort, today totally reflects her taste, at the same time capturing the evanescent sense of space and breeze that defines the island. Any entertainment and sports activities are dependent on these two resorts, where you will feel as close to being on a deserted island-cum-butler as you can get. If the first-class attention gets you down or the top-notch cuisine starts to get boring, a boatman can always deposit you, a picnic basket, and a two-radio signal in hand, on the isolated beach at Spanish Point. Leave the cellular phones at home.

Bird's Eye View

Barbuda offers soft white sand, gorgeous sea views and a relaxed lifestyle.

Barbuda lies 30 miles north of Antigua, some 68 square miles of flat, coral terrain. Only about 1500 people live here, the majority in the town of Codrington on the edge of the lagoon. An impressive frigate bird colony is located in the mangroves of the Codrington Lagoon, where hundreds of birds mate between August and December. The River Road runs from Codrington to Palmetto Point, about three miles, past Cocoa Point, and on to Spanish Point, a half-mile finger of land that divides the Caribbean from the Atlantic.

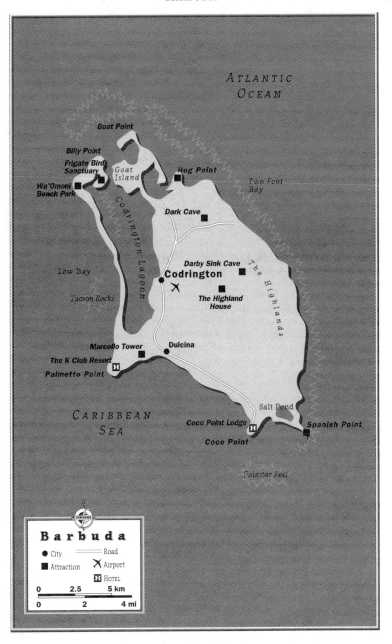

People

The natives of Barbuda are unusually tall, a trait they have inherited from their descendants in the Corramante tribe in Africa. Most people live in Codrington, the only village on the island, located on the edge of the lagoon.

Beaches and Other Natural Wonders

Lush, tropical vegetation is all but nonexistent on Barbuda's coral rock terrain, but beaches are generally glorious. The **Wa'Omoni Beach Park** is the hub of beach activities, perfect for a day trip, where you can barbecue freshly caught lobster on the beach and visit the **Frigate Bird Sanctuary**. Here, you can actually witness the miracle of seeing birds, the *fregata magnificicens* (frigate birds), hatch their eggs deep within the mangrove bushes. Ask your hotel to arrange a tour, which can only be accomplished in a small motorboat. Bird-watchers will also be delighted with numerous sightings of tropical mockingbirds, pelicans and herons, plus about 150 more species throughout the island. Other sights include a fascinating system of caves in the northeast where Indian carvings have been found, and **River Fort**, a martello tower on the south coast.

Underwater

Although several excellent reefs can be found in the waters off Barbuda, this low-key island has no professional dive facility at present. On the down side, visitors are strongly advised to have tanks supplied and filled on Antigua, 27 miles away; visibility is generally limited to 40-50 feet due to the rougher Atlantic weather conditions. There is a 20-mile-long barrier reef fronting the eastern coastline (too dangerous for snorkeling), while coral formations off Coco Point swarm with tropical fish and crustaceans in the absence of local fishing. Snorkelers can charter a boat from fishermen to visit Tuson Rock, about three miles straight west of Codrington and a half-mile off the thin spit of sand which represent the western border of the lagoon; a few other good sites lie just north of here. All told, Barbuda is a challenging, isolated dive frontier for serious adventurers, and is best served by a live-aboard dive boat.

Palaster Reef

A Marine Park one mile off one of the Caribbean's choicest beaches, Palaster Reef houses at least 60 wrecks, including the 1000-ton *Payson Tucker* and several warships (look for cannons and anchors). The reef boasts voluminous quantities of fish and lobster, and divers are virtually assured of eyeing the nurse, lemon and gray-tipped sharks that frequent Barbuda's shallow depths.

On Foot

Barbuda is one of the flattest of all Caribbean islands, peaking at a series of hills, termed the **Highlands**, about 100 or 200 feet in elevation (depending on whose estimate you rely on). As such, well-defined trails are basically non-existent. Dry and unremarkable in appearance, greenery is limited to low-lying scrub with mangroves fringing the numerous saltwater ponds. But for travelers with a true explorer's zeal, this backwater has 62 square miles of marginally charted territory, pale pink beaches that stretch unbroken as far as the eye can see, and **Codrington Lagoon**, a nearly unrivaled location that the magnificent frigatebird calls home. Additional wildlife, though sparse, includes fallow deer, guinea fowl and wild pigs and donkeys.

Five miles north of Codrington, at the end of the Highlands and inland from Two Foot Bay, is **Dark Cave**. Difficult to locate without a guide and impossible to explore without a flashlight, the entrance is near the north side of a scrubby sinkhole. An awkward descent though a narrow slot to a cavern leads to a passage involving a clamber under overhangs; the bottom of the cave is a huge chamber with deep pools containing blind shrimp. Easier to locate is **Darby Sink Cave**, a sinkhole approximately 300 feet in diameter which drops down 70 feet. The cave is two miles east of the ruins of the **Highland House** (the 18th-century estate of the Codrington family). The descent to the bat-guano floor is relatively easy and reveals stalagmites and a miniature tropical rain forest environment—the lushest spot of all on barren Barbuda.

Investigating Barbuda's backcountry—which is to say, seeing anything on foot—is serious business, by Caribbean standards, anyway. Once you leave the town of Codrington or venture far from the south coast beaches, you're on your own. There is no shade on the island, making the sun a significant consideration; bring a hat, ample sunscreen and more water than you ever think you'll need. Give the wild donkeys wide berth; the males are quite protective of their mates. Lastly, although the details it provides on an island unscarred by pavement may be sparse, the maps available at the Codrington post office can be helpful. If you are a day-tripper visiting Barbuda, you are best advised to hook up with the taxi drivers who greet each plane arrival, negotiating for a tour featuring some combination of caves, birdwatching and snorkeling. Oh, and sunning.

Tours

Frigate Bird Sanctuary   ★ ★ ★
North End, Codrington Lagoon.

Reached only via small boat, this pristine spot is one of the world's largest bird sanctuaries and the spot where *fregata Magnificens* (frigate birds) brood their eggs in mangrove bushes. These impressive birds have eight-foot wingspans and soar to 2000 feet. Mating season, September to February, is the best time to come; chicks hatch from December to March and remain in the nest for up to eight months. Also look out for pelicans, warblers, snipes, ibis, herons, kingfishers, tropical mockingbirds and cormorants.

Sports

All sports activities are arranged through the two resorts on the island. Your only problem will be what to choose. You might consider hanging around the dock of the K Club and hitching a ride on one of the many schooners that dock regularly.

Where to Stay

| ★★★★ | Coco Point Lodge | $455 |
| ★★★★ | The K Club | $900 |

Fielding's Most Romantic Hotels in Barbuda

| ★★★★ | Coco Point Lodge | $455 |
| ★★★★ | The K Club | $900 |

Fielding's Budget Hotel in Barbuda

| ★★ | Palmetto Beach Hotel | $181–$352 |

You basically have two choices in Barbuda: extravagantly expensive resorts or a bed in a local home. There is one self-catering unit, but it is extremely basic.

Hotels and Resorts

The two resorts on Barbuda give you the kind of beach experience you will never forget. **Coco Point Lodge** is situated on one of the most fabulous beaches in the Caribbean, and the K Club, created in loving detail by the Italian designer Krizia, is where the haughtiest of the haute couture go to be reborn. If you stay at any of these places, make sure your bank account can withstand the beating.

Coco Point Lodge $455–$1000   ★★★★

Coco Point, ☎ (809) 462-3816.
Single: $455–$905. Double: $555–$1000.
This secluded resort, set on a 164-acre peninsula at the island's southern tip, is for those who really do want to get away from it all, and don't mind the lack of bells and whistles at more commercial properties. Set on one of the Caribbean's most glorious beaches, Coco Point accommodates guests in ranch-style villas that are comfortably though simply furnished. The all-inclusive rates include everything from soup to nuts (and drinks), but there's very little action at night—people come here to relax, not party. They'll even do your laundry every other day. The athletic-minded will find two tennis courts and all watersports. Unwind!

Palmetto Beach Hotel   **$181–$352**   ★ ★

Palmetto's Peninsula, ☎ *(809) 460-0326.*
Single: $181–$352. Double: $181–$352.

Located on the island's southwestern side, this small hotel offers an alternative to Barbuda's two other much pricier resorts. Guest rooms are air-conditioned and have separate living areas; the nine cottages offer more privacy but rely on sea breezes for cooling. A pool, tennis court and watersports round out the activities, and two restaurants keep guests sated.

The K Club   **$900–$2700**   ★ ★ ★ ★

Coco Point, ☎ *(809) 460-0300, FAX (809) 460-0300.*
Single: $900–$2000. Double: $900–$2700.

Most everything is perfect at this stylish enclave of white cottages set on a spectacular beach. Accommodations are spacious and beautifully decorated by owner Krizia, the Italian fashion designer, who oversaw every detail of development, down to the cotton lounging robes in each room. The all-inclusive rates include wonderful meals and all activities, but splendid as everything is, it's still overpriced. Those who can afford the ultimate escape won't be disappointed, though service is not always up to par and management is on a revolving-door basis.

Apartments and Condominiums

There is one lone apartment complex on the island, but furnishings are extremely casual; it's best to have a camper's enthusiasm. If you plan to do your own cooking, bring as many staples from home as possible—prices run high in Barbuda. You can always bargain with fishermen bringing in their daily catch of fresh fish and lobster.

Inns

There's only one "inn" on the island, but the condition of rooms is often iffy. It's also a long hot haul from the middle of town.

Low Cost Lodging

Visitors have been known to bargain for a room in local homes. The best way is to come in person to make the contact. Hot water is not always guaranteed and you will probably have to share the bathroom.

Where to Eat

Restaurants at the two resorts are considered spectacular. If you're staying there, meals are included in the all-inclusive rate. The K Club specializes in Mediterranean cuisine.

Where to Shop

Forget Codrington for anything worth taking home; the boutiques at both resorts carry the traditional Caribbean trinkets and sportswear. Even Antigua's airport won't offer up much, so you might arrange a stop in St. John's before flying home the same day.

Barbuda Directory

ARRIVAL

LIAT ☎ *(809) 462-0701* makes the 15-minute flight from Antigua's V.C. Bird Airport to Barbuda's Codrington Airport in two daily runs (morning and afternoon). There is also a private airport, the Coco Point Airstrip, at Coco Point Lodge, 8 miles from Codrington.

BUSINESS HOURS

Shops open Monday–Friday 8:30 a.m.–4 p.m. and Saturday 8 a.m.–noon or 3 p.m. Banks generally open Monday–Thursday 8 a.m.–2 p.m. and Friday 8 a.m.–4 p.m.

CLIMATE

Average temperatures hover around 75–85 degrees F. year-round.

DOCUMENTS

U.S. and Canadian citizens need to present a valid passport (or original birth certificate and photo ID), plus an ongoing ticket. British citizens need to show a valid passport.

ELECTRICITY

Most of the island uses 220 volts AC/60 cycles. Some hotels in the Hodges Bay area run on 110 volts AC/60 cycles. Check your hotel's conditions before you come.

GETTING AROUND

Taxis are omnipresent outside major hotels and the airport. However, jeeps are the best way to zip about the island; most people prefer small Suzuki four-wheel drives. You'll need an Antiguan driver's license (available for purchase when you rent a vehicle). Negotiate like crazy for a good price.

Both Coco Point Lodge and K Club can arrange a day tour of the island. Profit Burton, a private guide, usually meets visitors at the airport and will design personal tours for you in his minivan.

LANGUAGE

The official language is English.

MEDICAL EMERGENCIES

Don't get sick in Barbuda or you'll have to fly to Puerto Rico or Miami. Make sure you bring your own medicines if you have a chronic condition. Some basic care can be found at the small Springview Hospital, funded by a New York not-for-profit organization.

MONEY

Official currency is the Eastern Caribbean dollar, but most establishments welcome American dollars. Exchange houses are hard to find here; exchange before you come.

TELEPHONE

Area code is *809*. Phone service is limited. Make sure you bring your own calling card from home to save money on long-distance calls.

TIPPING AND TAXES

Most hotels add a 10 percent service charge; tip extra if the service is especially nice.

TOURIST INFORMATION

Antigua and Barbuda Tourist Office Box 363, Long St., Antigua, W.I., ☎ *(809) 462-0480* or *(809) 462-2105*, FAX *(809) 462-2483*. In the United States ☎ *(212) 541-4170*.

WATER

Officially, you can drink tap water, but most visitors feel safer downing the bottled variety.

WHEN TO GO

See the calendar in the "When to Go" section of Antigua.

BARBUDA HOTELS	RMS	RATES	PHONE	CR. CARDS
Codrington				
★★★★ **Coco Point Lodge**	34	$455–$1000	(809) 462-3816	None
★★★★ **The K Club**	27	$900–$2700	(809) 460-0300	A, DC, MC, V
★★ **Palmetto Beach Hotel**	35	$181–$352	(809) 460-0326	A, D, MC, V

Hurricane Update

Although Antigua and Sint Maarten/St. Martin received most of the press, Barbuda was hit hard enough by Hurricane Luis to splinter parts of the island's low-lying lagoon area. All of the island's hotels sustained considerable damage, but the Palmetto Beach Hotel anticipated being closed indefinitely.

BRITISH VIRGIN ISLANDS

Up close views of marine life await novice and experienced divers on the British Virgin Islands.

BVI refer to themselves as Nature's Little Secrets. The country has never sought nor desired mass tourism, preferring to let the discerning traveler discover it. The quiet, unassuming attitude is felt the moment you step off the plane, reflected in the gentle nature of the people and the laid-back way of life. The *dolce far ninete* (nothing-to-do) philosophy reigns in the BVI, and those who require high-rise resort amenities, late-night bars and other externally generated entertainment should not even buy a ticket. Even at The Baths, BVI's most famous beach on its second-largest island, Virgin Gorda, there are no bustling beach cafes, souvenir shops or crowds. What BVI does have are miles and miles of nearly deserted, uninterrupted beaches, tiny coral coves perfect for diving, and even a few islands where the only place to stay is a luxurious private home that can rent for up to $8000 a day. For more reasonable budgets, a full week on the water in the BVI, sailing from island to island, under the direction of a well-trained captain, can run under $450 per person summer and fall. Essentially, the compactness of the BVI, the purity of the waters and the accessibility of facilities offer an unparalleled opportunity to experience as many different dive, snorkeling and trekking sites as possible in the shortest amount of time.

Bird's Eye View

Boats and kayaks are available for rent on BVI.

More than 40 islands, rocks and cays make up the complex called the British Virgin Islands, the most important being Tortola, Virgin Gorda, Beef Island, Anegada and Jost van Dyke. Lying 60 miles east of Puerto Rico and directly northeast of St. John, the islands harbor a population of only about 12,000 people stretched over 16 inhabited islands. From nearly any advantage point, the view is that of seemingly endless tropical islands stretching off into the horizon. The appearances of these islands range from sloping moun-

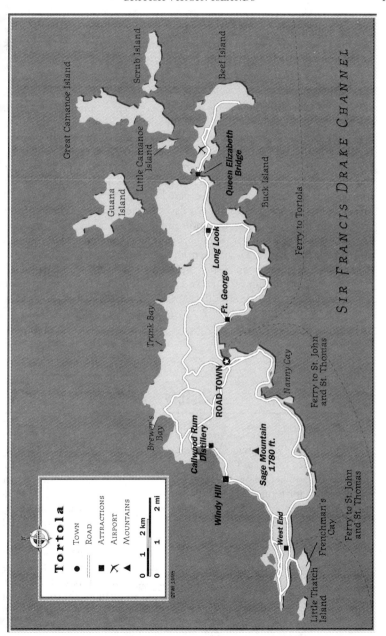

Tortola

● TOWN
  ROAD
■ ATTRACTIONS
✕ AIRPORT
▲ MOUNTAINS

0   1   2 km
0   1   2 mi

tains cloaked with verdant green growth to scrub and cactus-covered hills layered with massive rounded boulders. Long stretches of palm-shaded beaches border much of the island's perimeters. Offshore rough-hewn rock formations poke their heads out of the water, providing perches for seabirds.

Tortola, the capital and largest island, is a good base for exploring the archipelago. The coastline snakes in and out, providing a wealth of anchorages and long, fine beaches. Hills angle up to a rocky spine, running the length of the island. On the moist north side of the island (exposed to the Atlantic), vegetation takes the form of a jungle, with aromatic flowering bushes.The highest point is the 1740-foot Mount Sage, a rain forest that is part of the BVI National Trust. The north side retains the air of old Tortola, with its quaint inns, rustic bars and isolated beaches. The island's West Indian roots can be seen in Road Town, where pastel-colored wood shops line Main Street and local chefs add Caribbean flavor to dishes such as conch fritters and shrimp creole. Here, on the arid southern coast, facing the Sir Francis Drake Channel, one finds the stark beauty of foothills decorated with cactus and scrub bush. Protected yearlong from the brunt of the trade winds, this is perfect sailing territory, considered among the best in the world. Although the ocean is calm for much of the year, certain bays are famous worldwide among surfers for the fine waves during January and February.

History

The Virgin Islands were discovered by Christopher Columbus on his second voyage in 1493. Fascinated by the exquisite natural beauty of the islands, he named them *Las Once Mil Virgines* (the 11,000 Virgins) in honor of St. Ursula and her followers. The truth is, Columbus was the not the first human to set forth on the island. Prior to the European invasion, these islands had been populated by successive waves of Indian tribes migrating north from the Orinoco region of South America. Unfortunately, the arrival of the Europeans spelled the end of the native population; within a generation, there was not a trace of them. The occupation of the island by the Spanish and other Europeans followed a pattern similar to that of other Caribbean islands. For two centuries, control of the island was passed from one country to another while the islands remained mostly uninhabited. Many of those who balked at directly challenging the Spanish chose instead the path of piracy and pirateering, the most famous of whom were Sir John Hawkins,

Henry Morgan, Jost Van Dyke and Edward Teach, better known as Black-beard. These islands provided a secluded and safe anchorage for these brig-ands. Even today the legacy of piracy survives in the names of many islands and in the ever-persistent legends of buried treasure. Control of the Virgin Islands finally equalized with the Danish taking control of the western islands, now known as the U.S. Virgin Islands, while the British controlled the eastern set—so-named the British Virgin Islands. In fact, Tortola (BVI) is separated from St. John (USV) by less than two miles. From the 1700s to the mid-1800s, a plantation economy supported these islands. The remnants of the sugar industry can still be seen in the ruins of sugar mills hidden in the bush. In 1967, the BVI became a self-governing member of the British Commonwealth.

People

The people of the British Virgin Islands have an extraordinarily friendly reputation and will naturally extend you greetings as you stroll down the street. In fact, an islander can become quite hurt if you don't return the greeting. At the same time, Gordians and Tortolans are said to be somewhat retiring and not exactly prone to inviting travelers into their homes. Those who live in the interior mountains definitely tend to by shyer, but their life-style is also comparatively less pressured by touristic demands; these are older people in the mountain communities who still ride donkeys, make their own charcoal and harbor age-old superstitions about *duppies* or spirits. As tourism blossomed due to the efforts of established black families as well as spunky individuals, some of the island's women have become renowned for their cooking skills, in particular Mrs. V. Thomas who was decorated by the Queen of England for her guava jelly and mango chutney. As construction demands rise, traditional island occupations, such as stonemasonry and gardening, have begun returning, and sailors in the old school of sloops are finding another kind of work in more progressive boating. Because of the generous economic assistance received from Great Britain, islanders enjoy a considerable enthusiasm for, and strong identification with, their mother country.

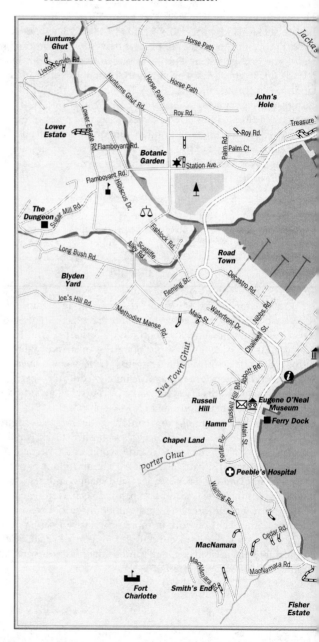

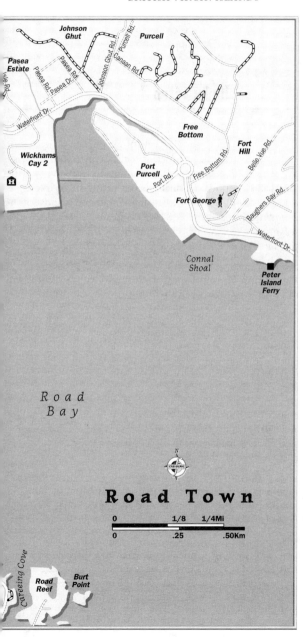

Underwater

The abundance of tiny islands which comprise the British Virgins create a host of varied diving opportunities for all levels of experience. There's not much in the way of wall diving, but wrecks and reefs are plentiful, and visibility can top a crystalline 130 feet. Anegada is off limits to boat dives for the moment due to overfishing (and shore diving is not easy); the snorkeling is fine. BVI's best is found mostly among the small, uninhabited islands southeast of Tortola including the spectacular 310-foot steamer, *The Rhone*, the Caribbean's most famous wreck, which sunk theatrically off the rocks of Salt Island in 1867 with most of its 300 passengers on board. Diving is more expensive here than in most of the Eastern Caribbean, but the British Virgins feature a nice concentration of worthy sites, even after one has taken in the must-see *Rhone*.

Blonde Rock

A pinnacle rising to within 15 feet of the surface, this is an advanced site that requires calm seas for diving. The top of the rock is wrapped in fire coral, but the dive continues down rock ledges to a depth of 60 feet and lead to a series of tunnels, caves and overhangs that contain moray eels, large crabs and lobsters, while fan coral wave gently nearby.

The Indians

Four jagged pinnacles rise dramatically above sea level near Pelican Island. The dive (to 50 feet) circumnavigates the pinnacles and underwater arches using a narrow canyon, and visits one cave brimming with copper sweepers; nurse sharks, spotted eagle and southern rays also ply the waters.

Painted Walls

An excellent and unique beginner's dive off Dead Chest Island (30-50 feet) through four canyons, each vividly "painted" with different encrusting corals and sponges. Turtles and nurse sharks occasionally lurk quietly just outside the canyons.

Wreck of the *Chikuzen*

The BVI's other wreck, the Chikuzen is a Japanese refrigeration ship scuttled six miles north of Beef Island in 1981. Lying on her side 75 feet down, the 246-foot hull has become home to a monstrous jewfish, along with pelagics, octopus and numerous schooling fish. Black tip sharks are occasionally spotted, while big rays ply the sands surrounding the wreck. Only drawback: the Chikuzen is a long ride from the nearest dock.

Wreck of the *RMS Rhone*

The Caribbean's great wreck dive lies in two sections; the bow sits in 80 feet of water and contains the massive cargo hold and other chambers. The stern settled at 30 to 65 feet and showcases the engine, prop shaft and her overwhelming propeller (if seas are calm, beginners can safely explore this part of the ship). The *Rhone* is a new world at night, as pufferfish and squid take the stage and the brilliant orange cup coral that covers the skeletal steel remains blossom, like flowers. This is possibly the single most popular dive site in the Eastern Caribbean and can be attended by dozens of eager explorers at once (local operators refer to it as "The Office," as in, I work at the...); try to visit the *Rhone* early in the morning, or on an off day.

Dive Shops

Baskin in the Sun

Road Town; ☎ *(800) 233-7938 or (809) 494-5854.*

Features courses in Caribbean reef ecology and historical ship wrecks. Two tank dive $80; also has a shop at West End, which accesses dives in the sleepier waters around Jost Van Dyke.

Blue Water Divers

Nanny Cay, Tortola; ☎ *(809) 494-2847.*

PADI facility, handles SSI referrals; courses to Instructor in September. Utilizes a 47-foot catamaran with full diving amenities. Two tank dive including all equipment, $80. Resort course, $80.

Kilbrides Underwater Tours

Bitter End Yacht Club; ☎ *(800) 932-4286, (809) 495-9638.*

The oldest shop on the island, situated in a quiet location at Gorda's North Sound Bay (closest to the *Chikuzen*). PADI and NAUI affiliated, with courses to Divemaster. Two tank dive $80, including equipment. Resort courses, $95.

On Foot

Quiet and uncrowded, well-tended yet off-the-beaten track, the natural environments of the British Virgin Islands are a lot of things their American counterparts aspire to, but only attain on protected St. John, lying a scant mile off Tortola's southern coast. There are actually about 60 islands in the BVIs, but almost all are uninhabited, which allows the option to travel to an island for a day of private exploration and contemplation. There are delightful, mostly short trails on the main islands (outlined below), while the outer destinations boast a wealth of unmarked possibilities.

The Anegada Beach Walk

The one coral-formed mass in the British Virgins, pancake flat Anegada is out of the way for most tourists, even though it's the second largest island in the archipelago. The "summit" is a measly 28 feet above sea level, which makes the long northern coastline Anegada's most appealing walk. How long? How about nearly 20 miles of unblemished, unbroken, undeveloped white sand? On this little visited, barely populated outpost, you're sure to locate a few miles you can call your own for the day. This is actually a relatively serious undertaking; there are no facilities and little shade, so a substantial water supply and sunscreen is required. A road parallels the western part of the coast, so that it's possible to coordinate a pickup at a predetermined location to avoid a round-trip trek.

Cow Hill

Immediately left of the ferry dock on Virgin Gorda is a striking, triangular-shaped hill. The trail to its summit begins at the parking lot for Little Dix Bay Resort. The half-hour ascent winds through cactus and scrubby woodlands to a beautiful view encompassing most of the BVI chain. This exposed trail can be hot and dry; bring water and attempt the hike early or late in the day to avoid direct sun.

Gorda Peak

Several trails wind through the Virgin Gorda forests to the island's 1370-foot summit, but the main path is marked by a sign off North Sound Road, four miles from the ferry dock. Watch for a junction following the stone steps where the hike begins; the main trail to the summit heads right. All land above 1000 feet on Virgin Gorda is a National Park.

Norman Island

Believed to be the setting for Robert Louis Stevenson's *Treasure Island*, this uninhabited location seven miles south of Tortola's Road Town will stir your best pirate fantasies. Although the vague trails are strictly unmarked, one leads up the ridge above the bay east for over a mile, while another ascends sheer Spy Glass Hill for excellent views. A salt pond provides bird-watching, and there are striking sea-level caves at Treasure Point that yield snorkeling opportunities. Norman Island is reached only by private boat or charter.

Sage Mountain National Park

Using land donated by the Rockefellers in the 1960s, the government has been reforesting this prime Tortola parcel which encompasses the major hills west of Road Town, including Sage Mountain (1780 feet, the highest point in the Virgins). Although the park receives a relatively modest 100 inches of rain a year, at first glance it looks like a rainforest, with deep green elephant ear philodendrons, tree ferns and bromeliads growing beneath mahogany and white cedar trees. A gravel path leads from the parking lot to a wooden gate; take the path on the left marked Mahogany Forest Trail, which in turn leads to a spur to the top of the peak. The trek to stimulating views is steep, but short, and can be completed in well under and hour. Two other trails also begin at the gate using on the gravel path to the right (leading away from the peak), and lead into the rainforest with signs identifying the native foliage.

By Pedal

In 1995, Christopher Ghiorse opened Last Stop Mountain Biking and a new island sport was born. Although a friend described it as "one big hill," Tortola is home to his shop. Tranquil **Virgin Gorda** offers the best riding and can easily be reached by ferry; the beautiful ride to the Baths is about as scenic as biking comes in the Caribbean, but time your ride to miss the midday onslaught of day-trippers and reschedule entirely if a cruise ship is docked nearby. Tortola can be circumnavigated in a half-day (40 miles, all paved); a shorter version of this trip leads west out of Road Town to Nanny Cay, West End and around Steel Point. More challenging is the sweaty ride up **Sage Mountain**. Local traffic is swift and requires caution on Tortola, but bikers are welcomed and respected, so far. Smaller Jost Van Dyke and Peter Island also can be toured using the local ferry service. Anegada features miles of flat sandy roads, but no easy access for day visitors with bikes.

Last Stop Mountain Biking

Road Town; ☎ *(809) 494-0564.*
Still building his inventory, Ghiorse rents Gary Fishers for $20 per day and invites visiting bikers to join the biweekly races put on by the BVI Bicycling Club.

Tortola

Twelve miles long by three miles wide, Tortola is home to three-fourths of the residents of the BVI. It's a refreshingly unaffected combination of the young and new, a reflection of a refined and contemporary approach to West Indian culture. Years of British rule have given Tortola a well-educated and worldly population, one largely unaffected by tourism. Nevertheless, most of the hotels are located here, about a dozen around Road Town. There are a couple of places to stay near Wickam's Cay I and II, on the southeast shore, and on the northwest shore at Apple Bay. In general, the crime rate is low and many residents seldom lock their doors, but it's not suggested that tourists follow their habit.

Beaches

The finest beaches and bays are located on the north side of Tortola. At the **West End**, where the majority of hotels are situated, are the Pirate's Pub and the Pusser's Pub; **Smuggler's Cove** to the north is an exquisite crescent-shaped strand. **Long Bay** and **Apple Bay** are notable; the latter is where surfers find their biggest waves (check out Bomba's Surfside shack made out of driftwood). **Cane Garden Bay** has a gently curving beach and is a popular anchorage. Good beaches are also located around **Beef Island**, the site of Tortola's airport, including the extremely dramatic **Josiah's Bay** and **Elizabeth Beach**. Outstanding, powdery beaches can be found on all the islands of the BVI. Snorkelers and divers can take full advantage of the crystal clear waters.

What Else to See

The best sights in the British Virgin Islands have to do with sun, surf and beach; anything else should be left for a rainy or hazy day. The Tourist Office can arrange a visit to **Road Town's Folk Museum** or the **rum factory**. Consider taking a frog-jumper's flight or quick cruise to one of the surrounding islands—you can make it back the same day. Most people come back from

Cooper Island raving about the beauty, and if you get tired of the beach you can always trek through some fascinating trails. **Anegada**, reached best by small plane from Tortola's Beef Island, can also turn into a memorable day excursion, mostly for divers.

Museums and Exhibits

British Virgin Islands Folk Museum ★★★

Main Street, Road Town.
Hours open: 10 a.m.–4 p.m.
Housed in a traditional West Indian building, this museum showcases artifacts from Arawak Indians and the island's plantation and slave eras. There are also some interesting relics salvaged from the wreck of the RMS Rhone, a British mail ship that sank off Salt Island in 1867.

Parks and Gardens

J.R. O'Neal Botanical Gardens ★★★

Station Avenue, Road Town, ☎ *(809) 494-4557.*
Hours open: 8 a.m.–4 p.m.
Indigenous and exotic plants are beautifully showcased at this four-acre garden, which includes an herb garden and hothouses for orchids and ferns.

Mount Sage National Park ★★★★

Ridge Road, West End.
Located on the peak of a volcanic mountain, this 92-acre national park protects the remains of a primeval rain forest—most, alas, was cut down over the years. A graveled path will take you to the top, some 1780 feet up, the highest elevation in the British and U.S. Virgin Islands. A nice day trip.

Tours

Travel Plan Tours ★★★

Waterfront Plaza, Road Town, ☎ *(809) 494-2872.*
Island tours take about 2.5 hours and include all the hot spots. $50 per person.

Sports

Why bother with other sports when the sea treasures are as spectacular as they are on these islands? There are tennis courts at some hotels and horseback riding can be arranged through your hotel. Bare-boating (self-crew yacht chartering) is one of the biggest pastimes here, or you can charter a boat that comes equipped with a crew. Navigation is not difficult and the weather is usually so clear you can't get lost. (Note that bareboaters aren't allowed to travel to Anegada because of the dangerous route through the reef.) If you're not an educated sailor, think about taking a few classes at the **Nick Trotter Sailing School** at the **Bitter End Yacht Club, North Sound ☎ 494-2745**. The best centers for fishing are **Salt Island, Anegada, Jost Van Dyke, West End, Tortola** and **Peter Island**. Bird-watchers should have a blast on **Virgin Gorda** and **Guana Island**, off Tortola.

Boardsailing B.V.I.

Long Look, West End, ☎ *(809) 495-2447.*

Learn the popular sport of windsurfing for $20 for a one-hour lesson. Boards can be rented for $155 a week. On Virgin Gorda, the Nick Trotter Sailing School at the *Bitter End Resort* ☎ *(809-872-2392)* offers courses and rentals.

Boating

Road Town, ☎ *(809) 494-2331.*

At the Moorings Resort, you can rent all manner of sailing yachts, from bareboat (no crew) to the works, with a skipper, cook and crew. Try Virgin Island Sailing, also in Road Town, for charters. Call from the States: ☎ *800-233-7936.*

Deep-Sea Fishing

Various locations, Road Town.

Sport fishers can arrange a charter or join a scheduled excursion. Captain Dale ☎ *(809-495-5225)* arranges trips out of Virgin Gorda.

Scuba Diving

Various locations, Road Town.

Several outfits will teach you the ropes and take you to the best underwater sports. On Tortola: **Baskin in the Sun** ☎ *(809-494-5854)* and **Underwater Safaris** ☎ *(809-494-3235)*. On Virgin Gorda, try **Kilbrides Underwater Tours** at the Bitter End Resort ☎ *(809-495-9638)*; two-tank dives cost $80–$90.

Shadow's Ranch

Todman's Estate, Road Town, ☎ *(809) 494-2262.*

Hop aboard a horse and venture along the beach or up to Mount Sage National Park. Prices start at $25 per hour.

Where to Stay

∬	**Fielding's Highest Rated Hotels in British Virgin Islands**	
★★★★★	Guana Island	$485–$635
★★★★★	Necker Island	$5500
★★★★★	Peter Island Resort	$195
★★★★	Biras Creek Hotel	$340–$840
★★★★	Drake's Anchorage	$223–$600
★★★★	Little Dix Bay Hotel	$225
★★★	Bitter End Yacht Club	$295–$405
★★★	Olde Yard Inn	$85–$180
★★★	Sugar Mill Hotel	$115–$320
★★★	Treasure Isle Hotel	$85–$230

♡	**Fielding's Most Romantic Hotels in British Virgin Islands**	
★★★★★	Guana Island Club	$485–$635
★★★★	Little Dix Bay Hotel	$225–$1000
★★★★★	Peter Island Resort	$195–$3900

	Fielding's Budget Hotels in British Virgin Islands	
★★	Fort Burt Hotel	$60–$95
★★	Moorings-Mariner Inn	$80–$165
★★	Nanny Cay Resort	$50–$195
★★★	Olde Yard Inn	$85–$180
★	Sebastian's on the Beach	$75–$190

Accommodations in the British Virgin Islands are the antithesis of the big-island resort; for the most part, they are intimate and casual and reflect the style of the owner/management, usually husband-and-wife teams. The tiny isles of the BVI are rarely overrun with tourists during the peak season, but those travelers seeking maximum solitude will want a copy of *Intimate Inns & Villas*. The colorful booklet lists more than two dozen small properties on the islands of Virgin Gorda, Tortola Anegada and Jost Van Dyke. Copies are available from the **British Virgin Islands Tourist Board** in NY ☎ *(800) 835-8530*.

Wherever you stay, check your final bills; many a tourist here has been charged for snorkeling gear that they had already returned. Also remember that ordering from the minibar will spell instant death to your wallet: a six-pack of Jamaican beer, a couple of bottles of mineral water, and a couple of colas ran someone we know about $75. Also check your credit charges after you've been home for several months—you might have had your number stolen.

Hotels and Resorts

Most of the hotels in the BVI are located in Tortola, situated around Road Town (one grand exception is the exquisite Little Dix on Virgin Gorda). However, room rates seem to be competitive with big resort hotels, with no real relation to quality. The premier property is **Long Bay**, which acts as the social hub of the island. The only thing marring its beachfront is the heavy presence of coral, which can be dangerous to unsuspecting bathers. Staying on Tortola will save you (hopefully) from some of the disasters that hit other islets, power losses and low water supplies. At all hotels, the lifestyle is casual outdoors. Note that outside of beaches, skimpy attire tends to offend residents.

Long Bay Beach Hotel $55–$295   ★★★

Road Town, ☎ (800) 729-9599, (809) 495-4252, FAX (914) 833-3318.
Single: $55–$265. Double: $110–$295.
Situated on a 52-acre estate that slopes down to a powdery mile-long beach, Long Bay offers a variety of accommodations, ranging from standard guest rooms to villas of two to five bedrooms, some with their own private pool. Some units are located along a hillside (great views), others are right on the beach. All come equipped with air conditioning, ceiling fans, refrigerators, wet bars, hair dryers and phones, while the most expensive units also boast full kitchens, VCRs and huge decks. Active types are kept happy with the complimentary pitch-and-putt golf course, pool, tennis court and new fitness/massage center. The restaurant, housed in an old sugar mill, offers fine gourmet fare and live music most nights. Villa dwellers can arrange to have a chef prepare a private dinner—nice!

Prospect Reef Resort $91–$279   ★★★

Road Town, ☎ (800) 356-8937, (809) 494-3311.
Single: $91–$270. Double: $91–$279.
Set on lush grounds overlooking a channel (but lacking a beach of note), the choices here range from standard guest rooms to studios to villas and townhouses with kitchenettes; only some have air conditioning. Lots going on, including six tennis courts, a par-three golf course and a health club with pampering treatments. Several pools include one that is junior-Olympic sized and another that contains

saltwater. Sailboats can be rented at the small harbor. Those with difficulty walking should note that there are lots of steep stairs and climbs.

Sugar Mill Hotel   **$115–$320**   ★ ★ ★
Road Town, ☎ *(800) 462-8834, (809) 495-4355.*
Single: $115–$320. Double: $125–$320.
The dining room is housed in a 360-year-old sugar mill and rum distillery, hence the name. All is quite nice at this lushly landscaped estate, with accommodations in simple cottages scattered about a hillside. Furnishings are basic but adequate; some have kitchens but none have air conditioning. One air-cooled villa is available for rent complete with a full kitchen, large balcony and spacious stone terrace. There's a small pool for those who don't want to cross the street to get to the compact beach. The property is owned by an American couple who used to write about travel and food, so you know they know what they're doing. Great meals, and wonderful service to match. Just the spot for those who really want to get away from it all but don't want all the trappings of a full resort.

Treasure Isle Hotel   **$85–$230**   ★ ★ ★
Road Town, ☎ *(800) 334-2435, (809) 494-2501, FAX (809) 494-2507.*
Single: $85–$220. Double: $95–$230.
All the air-conditioned rooms at this pretty resort overlook the harbor and marina, and include tropical art and pleasant rattan furniture. Situated on 15 acres of hillside, the grounds include a festive free-form pool, a full dive facility, and water sports for an extra fee. Management is friendly, and guests here are kept happy. Lots of evening entertainment for the partying set.

Village Cay Marina Hotel   **$115–$330**   ★ ★
Road Town, ☎ *(809) 494-2771.*
Single: $115–$330. Double: $115–$330.
This small hotel is located downtown in the Village Cay Marina Complex. Rooms are air conditioned and have cathedral ceilings, Oriental rugs, cable TV with VCRs and hair dryers. There's a restaurant and bar on site, as well as a small pool and watersports. The clientele is largely comprised of yachtsmen, and there's lots to do within walking distance.

Apartments and Condominiums

Yacht owners and vacationers prepared to settle for a long stay take advantage of the lovely private homes rented by owners during high season. Apartments and cottages also offer the opportunity for independent living, especially if you want to do your own cooking. Bring your best staples from home since prices on Tortola run high. Several townhouse units along the southeast shore are excellent for romantic sunset viewing, and in some villas, maid service is included (**Fort Recovery Estates**). Tortola's premier villa rental is **Shannon House**, built into a hill, and boasting a network of romantic trails, large boulders, and luscious gardens; the kicker is the split-level pool with a water slide that plunges into the sea off a cliff. If you're just looking for a place to store your luggage before you head out to the beach, the cottages at **Over the Hill** will serve nicely. For luxury rentals, contact **McLaughlin Anderson Vacation** at ☎ *(800) 537-6246* or *(809) 776-0635.*

Admiralty Estate Resort $110–$275   ★★

Road Town, ☎ *(809) 494-0014.*
Single: $110–$275. Double: $110–$275.

Perched on a hillside, this condominium hotel has one- and two-bedroom units that are attractively furnished and include air conditioning, full kitchens, living and dining areas and balconies with a view. There's a restaurant on site with limited room service available, and nightly entertainment in the pool bar. Four tennis courts and a pool complete the picture.

Fort Recovery Estates $125–$295   ★★

Road Town, ☎ *(800) 367-8455, (809) 495-4467, FAX (809) 495-4036.*
Single: $125–$295. Double: $200–$295.

The fieldstone tower is about all that remains of this 17th-century fort, today a small enclave of attractive villas with full kitchens and air-conditioned bedrooms. Larger parties can rent a four-bedroom, three-bathroom house. The small beach makes for good swimming and watersports, or unwind in a yoga class. Daily maid service keeps things looking fresh. The grounds are nice and bright, with lots of colorful flowers scattered about.

Frenchman's Cay Resort $107–$270   ★★

West End, Road Town, ☎ *(800) 235-4077, (809) 495-4844.*
Single: $107–$185. Double: $113–$270.

Set on its own small cay and connected via bridge to Tortola, this luxury enclave of villas has nice views of the channel and neighboring islands. One- and two-bedroom villas include a full kitchen, ceiling fans (no air conditioning), and island art. The small beach is good for snorkeling, but rocks make wading difficult. There's also a small pool, hammocks meant for snoozing, a tennis court and an open-air restaurant. A nice, quiet spot.

Nanny Cay Resort $50–$195   ★★

Nanny Cay Marina, Road Town, ☎ *(809) 494-2512, FAX (809) 494-0555.*
Single: $50–$80. Double: $85–$195.

Set on a private 25-acre inlet on Sir Francis Drake Channel, Nanny Cay houses guests in studio apartments with kitchenettes, West Indian decor and air conditioning. Lots of yachtsmen come here, lured by the 180-slip marina. Extras include two restaurants and bars, a pool and tennis. Service can be uneven.

Rockview Holiday Homes $100–$755   ★★

Road Town, ☎ *(800) 621-1270, (809) 494-2550.*
Single: $100–$755. Double: $100–$755.

This informal villa complex is set in lush tropical gardens. Accommodations range from one- to five-bedroom villas situated on a hillside or overlooking the beach, all with full kitchens. Some even have their own pool. Maid service is available, and you can hire a chef if you're not up for cooking.

Inns

Since everything in the BVI practically resembles an inn, the following properties are more notable for their management, usually run by owners, who like to get involved in their client's vacations. The best is **Sugar Mill Estate**, which also serves fine meals in surroundings that will make you want to stay longer than planned. If you want to meet yacht owners, they tend to hang out at the bar at the **Cane Garden Beach Hotel**.

| **Fort Burt Hotel** | **$60–$95** | ★★ |

Road Town, ☎ *(809) 494-2587, FAX (809) 494-2002.*
Single: $60–$85. Double: $80–$95.
Set on a hillside and incorporating a 300-year-old Dutch-English fort, this small inn's guest rooms are dark, sparse and greatly in need of renovation. Still, the atmosphere is fun and friendly, with interesting tales of its long past. Great views of the harbor. The site includes a restaurant and small pool.

| **Moorings-Mariner Inn** | **$80–$165** | ★★ |

Road Town, ☎ *(800) 535-7289, (809) 494-2331, FAX (809) 494-2226.*
Single: $80–$150. Double: $90–$165.
It's a yachting crowd here, dahling, but the hospitality is still warm, friendly and blessedly informal. Facing the busy marina and within walking distance of shops and restaurants, this small hotel houses guests in lanai-style rooms with island decor and kitchenettes, but no air conditioning (sea breezes do the job). Landlubbers are kept happy with a pool and tennis court, but may feel out of place among all the seafaring folk. A good dive center rounds out the scene.

| **Sebastian's on the Beach** | **$75–$190** | ★ |

Little Apple Bay, Road Town, ☎ *(800) 336-4870, (809) 495-4212, FAX (809) 495-4466.*
Single: $75–$180. Double: $85–$190.
Set on its own beach, this small hotel is split in two by a road; request a room on the beach side for obvious reasons, but ask that it not be one of the rear units, as they have no view. Just two rooms have air conditioning; the rest make do with ceiling fans. The beach is fine for swimming, a good thing since there's no pool. There's a bar and restaurant, plus a fun weekly barbecue.

Low Cost Lodging

Budget accommodations are now available here, usually in a good location that won't require a car. **Sea View**, a popular local restaurant, merely added rooms (with a view) and studios to its property. Campers who don't need much more than a bed and hangers should head for the **Jolly Roger** Inn or **Harbour View Guest House** (the latter has a simple kitchenette).

Where to Eat

Fielding's Highest Rated Restaurants in British Virgin Islands

★★★★	Biras Creek	$40–$40
★★★★	Brandywine Bay	$20–$28
★★★★	Capriccio di Mare	$8–$15
★★★★	Skyworld	$7–$40
★★★★	The Tradewinds Restaurant	$18–$36
★★★★	The Upstairs	$10–$27
★★★	Olde Yarde Inn	$18–$30
★★★	Sugar Mill	$6–$28
★★★	The Apple	$15–$35
★★★	The Bath and Turtle Pub	$7–$30

Fielding's Special Restaurants in British Virgin Islands

★★★★	Biras Creek	$40–$40
★★★★	Brandywine Bay	$20–$28
★★★★	Skyworld	$7–$40
★★★★	The Tradewinds Restaurant	$18–$36
★★★★	The Upstairs	$10–$27

Fielding's Budget Restaurants in British Virgin Islands

★★	Kilumba	$8–$15
★★★	Green Parrot	$5–$20
★★★	Toys Grand Cafe	$5–$23
★★★	China Garden	$5–$24
★★★★	Classic Eatery	$5–$25

Excellent West Indian cuisine is available throughout Tortola; however, prices here are extravagant and can even give New York prices a run for the money, though the casual settings often belie the reality of the final bill. To save time, you'll probably want to stay around **Road Town**, where the majority of restaurants are located, but an excursion out to Sugar Mill on the northwest coast can end up a spectacular experience; even though the owners are American ex-pats, they've been highly acclaimed for their curried banana soup and cold rum soufflés. One of the best views, overlooking the town, can be had at **Skyworld** on the Ridge Road.

Resort food is not to be sniffed at on BVI, and some of the best dining can be found at both Virgin Gorda's **Bitter End Yacht Club** and **Biras Creek**, where diners will have breathtaking views. The menu at the **Peter Island Resort** changes every day, a combination of West Indian delicacies and continental favorites. For home-cooked meals and a big, generous heart, head for **Mrs. Scatlife's**, east of Sugar Mill at Carrot Bay, whose owner might serenade you with gospel music after dinner. English pub food can be had at **Pussers**, with locations in both Tortola and Virgin Gorda; while you're there, don't miss downing a Painkiller, made from Pusser's Rum, a local product, orange and pineapple juice, and coconut creme. Reservations at most popular restaurants are essential, especially at the smaller ones, which can book up fast.

Bing's Drop Inn $$ ★★

Fat Hog's Bay, East End, ☎ *(809) 495-2627.*
Indian cuisine. Specialties: Conch fritters, fish stew.
Dinner: 6:30 p.m.–midnight, entrees $10–$20.
Do drop in to Bing's—and you'll probably make a local friend or two. Tasty home-style conch fritters and fish stew are specialties and more elaborate lobster, chicken and steak dishes are served as well. Come to dance and kibitz here after a meal elsewhere; it's a very unpressurized environment that stays open for snacks and drinks until midnight.

Brandywine Bay $$$ ★★★★

Sir Francis Drake Highway, West End, ☎ *(809) 495-2301.*
Italian cuisine. Specialties: Homemade mozzarella, beef and lobster carpaccio, tiramisu.
Dinner: 6:30–9 p.m., entrees $20–$28.
For a special occasion, drive out a little east of Road Town to this hillside spot owned by Cele and David Pugliese for Tuscan food that's very widely praised. Whether it's local fish simply grilled with homegrown fresh herbs or an elaborately sauced roast duckling, everything is superb. Dining is on the terrace outside the once-private home that overlooks the Sir Francis Drake Channel. Hostess Cele will personally describe each entree on the menu while David prepares and arranges everything picture-perfectly (he's a former fashion photographer). Closed August-October.

Capriccio di Mare $$ ★★★★

Waterfront Drive, West End, ☎ *(809) 494-5369.*

Italian cuisine. Specialties: Pastries, pasta and pizza, frozen granite.
Lunch: 11:30 a.m.–4 p.m., entrees $8–$15.
Dinner: 4–9 p.m., entrees $8–$15.

This new arrival is a welcome taste treat for seafood-dominated Tortola. A little sister operation to the popular Brandywine Bay, a bastion of *cucina fiorentina*, Capriccio di Mare is an informal Italian cafe—a place to sit and sip espresso or cappuccino and nibble pastries or sandwiches on foccacia bread. Pizzas with a choice of vegetable or meat toppings are also available, as well as pastas.

Chopsticks $$ ★★
Wickham's Cay, ☎ *(809) 494-3616.*
Asian cuisine.
Lunch: entrees $10–$20.
Dinner: entrees $10–$20.

When you have a yen for Japanese (no pun intended), Chinese and other Asian (crossbred with West Indian) foods, and it's after 10 p.m., where you gonna go? Chopsticks, a cool spot with a veranda situated across from the Cable and Wireless office in Wickham Cay (you can also call mamma), has a good reputation for local fish and conch. All dishes are available for take-out. Open from 7:30 a.m. until late; hours vary.

Mrs. Scatliffe's $ ★★★
Carrot Bay, West End, ☎ *(809) 495-4556.*
Indian cuisine. Specialties: Pot roast, chicken or pork, spicy papaya soup.

The former chef of the well-regarded Sugar Mill, a native Tortolian, operates this West-Indian restaurant on the deck of her home, a pastel-colored building with a tin-roof in Carrot Bay. Diners come for the set meal of four courses, which are prepared with fruits and vegetables from her own garden. Popular starters are fresh fruit daiquiris, followed by soup, home-baked bread, chicken in a coconut shell or curried goat, and more of that fresh fruit in her imaginative ice cream desserts. Entertainment follows, usually, a family sing-out.

Pusser's Landing $$$ ★★
Sopers Hole, ☎ *(809) 495-4554.*
International cuisine. Specialties: Beef Wellington, guava chicken, nightly dessert specials.
Lunch: 11 a.m.–3 p.m., entrees $5–$9.
Dinner: 6–10 p.m., entrees $13–$25.

Diners can look out to the lights of St. Thomas from this waterfront restaurant in Tortola's West End, a fancier link in the Pusser's chain, serving black bean soup, West Indian ribs, roasted half-chicken in guava sauce and the signature Pusser's dishes, Beef Wellington with Bearnaise sauce and mud pie for dessert. Special events include dancing under the stars to a live band on Saturdays and all-you-can-eat shrimp dinners on Tuesday nights for $17.95. The potent Pusser's Painkiller may cure what ails you, but don't quaff too many or you'll be back in pain in the morning.

Pusser's Outpost and Pub $$$ ★★
Main Street, ☎ *(809) 494-4199.*
International cuisine. Specialties: Beef Wellington, lobster club sandwich, mud pie.

Lunch: 11 a.m.–3 p.m., entrees $7–$9.
Dinner: 5–10 p.m., entrees $15–$25.

Enjoy varied international cuisine with the yachting set in this second link in the Pusser's (local rum) chain of eateries. The two-story establishment has a downstairs pub where the namesake libation can be quaffed, accompanied by sandwiches and snacks amid a boisterous atmosphere. Escape upstairs later to the Outpost for Beef Wellington prepared with choice cuts of beef tenderloin, mushroom duxelle and homemade pastry, served with Bearnaise sauce. Later, if you have room, down Pusser's famous mud pie, dessert-style or in a rum-Irish cream concoction.

Skyworld $$$ ★★★★

Ridge Road, West End, ☎ (809) 494-3567.
International cuisine.
Lunch: 10 a.m.–5:30 p.m., entrees $7–$13.
Dinner: 6:30–10 p.m., entrees $23–$40.

A perfect remembrance of a Tortola visit is dining or having a drink before sunset and watching a technicolor movie in the sky at this dining room perched some 1000 feet above sea level. You can partake from chef George Petcoff's international menu of veal with capers, beautifully grilled local fish, passion fruit sorbets or less elaborate conch fritters or french fries and onion rings. At lunch enjoy the view from a different perspective with a sandwich on homebaked bread while casting an eagle eye on neighboring islands in the distance. Closed in September.

Spaghetti Junction $$$ ★★

Waterfront Drive, West End, ☎ (809) 494-4880.
Italian cuisine. Specialties: Chilled roasted eggplant and plum tomatoes, veal scaloppine.
Dinner: 6–10 p.m., entrees $10–$25.

You can get spaghetti and other pastas in this cute joint located upstairs in a small blue building, built back a little ways from the sea in Road Town. Formerly a bar that overlooked the water, it is now separated from the ocean by new roads and office buildings—all in the name of progress. Yachties and others like it for its infectious grooves. The caesar salad, served with sun-dried tomatoes, isn't bad, either. Daily chalkboard specials and desserts.

Sugar Mill $$$ ★★★

Apple Bay, West End, ☎ (809) 495-4355.
International cuisine.
Lunch: Noon–2 p.m., entrees $6–$12.
Dinner: 7–8:30 p.m., prix fixe $18–$28.

Bon Appetit columnists Jefferson and Jinx Morgan spent a lot of years cooking and writing about food and wine before they decided to buy a 300-year-old sugar mill in Apple Bay, converting it to a world-class inn and restaurant. The Morgans have wisely kept their menu small, allowing them to concentrate on the details of each dish, which usually includes a cold fruit soup and fresh fish in banana leaves with herbs from the Mill's own garden. Leave room for a scrumptious banana bread pudding with rum sauce when it's available.

The Apple $$$ ★★★

Zion Hill Road, ☎ (809) 495-4437.

Indian cuisine. Specialties: Whelks in garlic butter.
Dinner: 6:30–9 p.m., entrees $15–$35.

An enterprising and talented Tortolian, Liston Molyneux, has opened a restaurant in his home in Little Apple Bay, on Zion Hill, preparing local dishes like uncommonly served whelks (a type of snail), and the more familiar conch. Lunches are varied and include curried chicken rotis (West Indian burritos), or crepes. An interesting Sunday barbecue of West Indian treats is also offered from 7-9 p.m. Closed in September.

The Fish Trap $$$ ★★★

Columbus Centre, ☎ *(809) 494-3626.*
Seafood cuisine. Specialties: Prawns provencale, prime rib, teriyaki chicken.
Lunch: 11:30 a.m.–3 p.m., entrees $8–$14.
Dinner: 6:30–8 p.m., entrees $14–$25.

An informal, open-air terrace restaurant in Wickham's Cay that always has some good-value meals happening, the Fishtrap features barbecues on Saturdays and Sundays, prime rib on Sundays and local fish, shellfish, teriyaki chicken and other hearty, honest food the rest of the week.

The Upstairs $$$ ★★★★

West End, ☎ *(809) 494-2228.*
International cuisine. Specialties: Filet mignon, roast duck.
Lunch: Noon–2 p.m., entrees $10–$16.
Dinner: 6–8:30 p.m., entrees $16–$27.

An intimate dining room with lovely views of the harbor, The Upstairs has received kudos from the likes of *Gourmet* magazine. The star of the Prospect Reef Resort, which is built on a coral reef, the restaurant offers simple but exceptionally well-prepared (and pricey) meals like local lobster served grilled as an entree or gratine as an appetizer. Service is attentive and gracious. Ask for a window table for stargazing.

Virgin Queen $$ ★★★

Fleming Street, ☎ *(809) 494-2310.*
English cuisine. Specialties: Queen's pizza, shepherd's pie, bangers and mash.
Lunch: Noon–2 p.m., entrees $7–$12.
Dinner: 6–9 p.m., entrees $8–$16.

The Queen's pizza has been nominated for best in the islands, but it's also great finger food for sailors and other active types who like to quaff a few, throw darts at a board and shoot the breeze. There's a TV for background noise to go with the other fare offered—mostly English pub and West Indian food like bangers and mash, saltfish and shepherd's pie.

Where to Shop

In Road Town, the shopping hub is located on Main Street, starting at the **Sir Olva Georges Plaza**. Unfortunately there is no duty-free shopping, and you must sift through imported goods from Great Britain to find any bargains. **Pusser's Rum** (the "official drink of the British Royal Navy"), is one of the big island buys, available at the company store on Main Street. An aromatic excursion to the **Sunny Caribee and Spice Company** won't be time wasted, especially if you want to pick from the best selection of Caribbean spices and handicrafts on the island. Stop next door at the **Sunny Caribee Gallery**, which features fine artwork by islanders as well as handpainted furniture and wood carvings. If you need to supplant your vacation wardrobe, there are several boutiques including **Sea Urchin** in the Abbot Building, and **Kids in De Sun**, also in the Abbot Building, which specializes in tropical attire for children.

Resort Islands Near Tortola

It will take an extra effort to get to these resorts (private ferry, boat taxi or private plane), but all you need do is ask the management when you make the reservation. What you get in return are resorts that take full advantage of the natural surroundings; sometimes you won't even have a phone, TV or road to remind you of civilization. Best nature walks (though strenuous) are found at the **Guana Island Club**, north of Tortola's east end, which has been designated as a nature sanctuary. The luxury property is the **Peter Island Resort and Yacht Harbour**, which attracts wealthy yacht-owners to its attractive pool and tennis courts, as well as families who can take advantage of the two-bedroom villas.

Anegada

Only 290 people live on Anegada, mostly in the community called The Settlement. They share this seven-mile curve of coral with some very large iguanas and about 16 flamingos that were released into the ponds in 1992. Hawksbill and green turtles nest along the northshore. The fishing here is excellent and enough vessels have crashed against the craggy coral reefs to make wreck diving a spectacular sport. Even snorkelers can find deep satisfaction exploring caverns and ledges just off the shore in the coral reefs, where they will see shoals of neon-colored fish, nurse sharks, rays, turtles, and barracudas. Lobloy Bay has a small beach bar and sun shelters. Over the years Anegadians have been the victims of several development schemes that have left them suspicious, not to mention poorer, but they remain friendly to the selected tourists who risk the small planes to arrive. Although there is no regular boat ferry, day trips to the island are available. (Note that only qualified crew are allowed to navigate the route to Anegada because of the dangerous reef system.)

Where to Stay

Hotels and Resorts

Anegada Reef Hotel   **$130–$230**   ★★

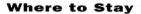

Setting Point, ☎ (809) 495-8002, FAX (809) 495-9362.
Single: $130–$170. Double: $165–$230.
Located in a rural setting on rural Anegada, this small hotel appeals to those who truly want to get away from it all, and don't mind a lack of amenities and extras. Accommodations are very simple, but clean and comfortable, and the family that runs the place goes out of their way to please. The hotel owns its own fishing boat for deep-sea excursions. The rates are a bit high for what you get, but lots of people

come again and again, lured by the laid-back tranquility of this spot. Three meals a day are included with room rate.

Where to Eat

Anegada Reef Hotel $$$ ★★

Setting Point, ☎ (809) 495-8002.
International cuisine. Specialties: Lobster.
Lunch: 8:30 a.m.–4 p.m., entrees $17–$30.
Dinner: 4–9:30 p.m., entrees $17–$30.
Visions of lobster barbecuing on the beach at this low-key resort (the only one on Anegada) draw day-trippers to experience a very informal (if pricey) crustacean feast served on picnic tables. Sides usually include caesar salad and garlic bread. To dine here, reserve by 4 p.m., and if you are flying in, the hotel will meet you with a private bus.

Del's Restaurant and Bar $$ ★★

The Settlement, ☎ (809) 495-8014.
Seafood cuisine. Specialties: Cracked conch.
Lunch: Noon–3 p.m., entrees $7–$10.
Dinner: 7:30 p.m.–midnight, entrees $10–$20.
Del's is one of a small number of beach bars and restaurants serving local food on this tiny coral atoll with only one hotel, a campground and lots of beautiful sand. Naturally, it's West Indian, rounded out with sandwiches and seafood served three times a day. It's a great way to start or end a day trip to Anegada, which can be reached by air or boat.

Guana Island

Where to Stay

Guana Island $485–$635 ★★★★★

Guana Island, ☎ (800) 544-8262, (809) 494-2354, FAX (809) 495-2900.
Single: $485–$585. Double: $485–$635.
Situated on a pristine 850-acre island, this hideaway resort was formerly a sugarcane plantation and is now a nature sanctuary. Accommodations are in white stone cottages arranged along a hilltop with smashing views of neighboring islands. The rooms are simple but lovely and lack real-world distractions like phones, televisions and air conditioners. Groups of 30 can rent the entire island—the perfect spot for a family reunion of jet-setters. Great hiking and bird watching, as well as tennis and watersports. Tranquil and lovely.

Jost Van Dyke

Jost Van Dyke (pronounced "yost") is that perfect island for Robinson Crusoe fans who want to get away from it all. No markets, no electricity, though there are some spiffy bars and restaurants where you can meet international yacht owners who cruise up in their multimillion-dollar schooners. **White Bay Beach** is most easily reached by boat and has a beautiful sandy beach, small hotel, and restaurant. **Sandy Cay**, an uninhabited islet off Jost Van Dyke, boasts a lovely white stretch of sand—and nothing else. Windsurfing and snorkeling are considered excellent. The BVI have established campgrounds on Jost Van Dyke—about fifteen campsites, with a small restaurant, or snack bar and grocery. The camp is directly next to the ferry landing, a fortunate choice since the islands have no taxis or cars for hire. Bring your own bedding and cooking supplies; a few erected tents are available, but most are bare sites. Write ahead to reserve a space, because the idea has caught on with great popularity lately. Each campsite has its own prices. For more information, write the **British Virgin Islands Tourist Board**, *1686 Union St. Ste 305, San Francisco, CA. 94123* ☎ *(800) 835-8530.*

Where to Stay

Hotels and Resorts

Sandcastle   **$225–$295**   ★

White Bay, ☎ *(809) 771-1611, FAX (809) 775-5262.*
Single: $225–$295. Double: $240–$295.
This tiny resort consists of four octagonal cottages set among tropical gardens. This place is not for everyone—there's no electricity and just limited hot water—but those who don't mind roughing it love the peace and serenity. Dinner by candlelight is a romantic affair.

Apartments and Condominiums

Sandy Ground Estates   **$740–$1200 per wk.**   ★ ★

P.O. Box 594, West End, White Bay, ☎ *(809) 494-3391, FAX (809) 495-9379.*
Rack rate Per Week: $740–$1200.
This tropical isolated retreat consists of eight houses with simple, casual furnishings and full kitchens. Each house looks different and is individually furnished. Arrange to have your refrigerator stocked prior to arrival. Rates are $740 to $1200 for a week; the larger houses sleep eight.

Where to Eat

Abe's By The Sea   **$$$**   ★ ★

Little Harbour, ☎ *(809) 495-9329.*
Seafood cuisine. Specialties: Fresh lobster with lime and butter sauce, pig roast.
Lunch: 11:30 a.m.–3 p.m., entrees $8–$25.
Dinner: 7–9:30 p.m., entrees $12–$30.
Abe's is a swinging place to try fresh fish, lobster and conch on a waterfront terrace in Jost Van Dyke's Little Harbour. Bright coral and fish nets decorate this popular hangout for yachtspeople and tourists who drop in morning, noon and night. An American breakfast with sausage, ham, bacon and eggs and juice is a good buy for $5. Lunches and dinners are substantial and served with rice and peas, coleslaw or green salad and corn on the cob; sandwiches are also available. There's a traditional pig roast Wednesdays.

Club Paradise   **$$$**   ★★
Great Harbour, ☎ *(809) 495-9267.*
Seafood cuisine. Specialties: Sauteed grouper, flying fish sandwich.
Lunch: 11 a.m.–3 p.m., entrees $4–$8.
Dinner: 7–10 p.m., entrees $15–$25.
There are many nice touches that make this simple open-air restaurant in Great Harbour a good place to stop. There's a delicious Barbados-style flying fish sandwich available for lunch for $5, served on home-baked bread. At dinner, patrons can pick a lobster from the tank. On Wednesdays there's a pig roast, and live entertainment is a regular feature. Cheeseburgers on fresh-baked bread, a whole cornish hen with honey-glazed carrots and garlic, and sauteed grouper can also be enjoyed here on a regular basis.

Foxy's Tamarind   **$$$**   ★★
Great Harbour, ☎ *(809) 495-9258.*
American cuisine. Specialties: Filet mignon, rotis, painkiller punch.
Lunch: Noon- 2:30 p.m., entrees $6–$9.
Dinner: 6:30–9 p.m., entrees $15–$30.
Don't expect luxury at this famous beach bar presided over by the magical Philicianno "Foxy" Callwood—only unabashed camaraderie and excellent grilled meat and seafood. An institution for close to 30 years, Foxy's Tamarind Bar draws an amazing yachting crowd for New Years' Eve, overwhelming Great Harbour with an overflow of boats and frenzied folks. The rest of the year it's calypso, reggae or soca (soul and calypso) music with burgers, rotis and killer rum punches. Foxy's is open from 9 a.m. until closing time, which varies.

Sandcastle   **$$$**   ★★
☎ *(809) 775-5262.*
International cuisine. Specialties: Boneless chicken breast, New York steak, fresh fish.
Lunch: 11 a.m.–3:30 p.m., prix fixe $18–$25.
Dinner: 7:30–11 p.m., prix fixe $30–$35.
Arrive in your own boat or arrange to be picked up by the Sandcastle's private motor launch from Tortola to dine simply and by candlelight (there's no electricity). The five-course prix fixe meal includes a basket of fresh bread, soup, a garden salad, an entree (depending on what's fresh) and dessert. Reservations should be made by 4 p.m. for dinner, and patrons usually call from a VHF radio to relay their meal choices with Chef Bill, who caters to special dietary needs. Seafood and shellfish choices are seasonal, but there's usually chicken breast and steak.

Mosquito Island

Privately owned by Drake's Anchorage resort, Mosquito Island has drop-dead views over North Sound to Virgin Gorda and Prickly Pear. The only way to get there is by boat. If you've got the dough, why not rent the whole island and let your friends come over? The beach at South Bay is extremely pleasant, dotted with huge boulders and quiet sandy coves.

Where to Stay

Drake's Anchorage $223–$600 ★ ★ ★ ★

Mosquito Island, ☎ (800) 624-6651, (809) 494-2254, FAX (617) 959-5147.
Single: $223–$600. Double: $316–$600.

Located on a private island just off Virgin Gorda, this resort has four beaches, with one just big enough for a snuggling couple. The recently redone accommodations are in three separate cottages lining a narrow beach and feature Haitian art, red-tile floors and modern baths; ceiling fans keep things cool. There are also two luxurious villas set off a bit. Three excellent restaurants give guests dining choices, and all the usual watersports are available. Life is laid-back at this peaceful and unpretentious spot. You'll hate to leave.

Necker Island

Got $10,000 per day to spend on a Caribbean vacation? (Hey, meals included!) The hefty price tag at the incredible Necker Island includes everything, even the whole private island, which accommodates one group of up to 24 people at a time. Upon landing in St. Thomas, you're whisked away by helicopter to a tiny land mass—74 lush green acres covered with brilliantly red bougainvillea atop of which is a Bali-like tropical mansion that has brought ooh's and aah's to the lips of Princess Diana, Steven Spielberg, Oprah Winfrey, Robert Redford, etc. Created by British entrepreneur Richard Branson of Virgin Atlantic Airways and Virgin Records, the open-air house sports a living room with a 360-degree view of the sea. There are two guesthouses, besides the main 10-bedroom, eight-bathroom house, several freshwater pools, and a cheerful staff who can cook for you or assist you in cooking your own. In the main house, the 24-foot long dining table is bordered by 22 chairs, complete with beautiful settings, elegant placemats, gleaming silver, etc. Food is luscious, endless and irresistible, everything from nonstop desserts to the potpourri of freshly caught fish. Activities are endless, from tennis, snorkeling, waterskiing, swimming, banana boating, windsurfing, power boating and hiking, to just lazing about on the beach.

Where to Stay

Apartments and Condominiums

Necker Island $5500–$10,900 per day ★ ★ ★ ★ ★

Necker Island, ☎ (800) 225-4255, (809) 494-4492.
Rack rate Per Day: $5500–$10900.

Got $5500 burning a hole in your pocket? Need room to spread out? Try this private house—mansion is more like it—on its own 74-acre estate. The hilltop house has 10 bedrooms, six with their own bath, a Jacuzzi in the master bedroom, and its own pool, tennis court and watersports. The rates (which only start at $5500 and go all the way up to $10,900—per day) include three maids, two gardeners, a couple to cook your meals and a boatman to whisk you off to neighboring islands. Who says money can't buy happiness?

Peter Island

Where to Stay

Hotels and Resorts

Peter Island Resort $195–$3900 ★★★★★

Peter Island, ☎ (800) 346-4451, (809) 494-2561, FAX (809) 949-2313.
Single: $195–$480. Double: $195–$3900.

Located on its own private island south of Tortola, this smashing resort shuttles guests over by boat or helicopter. Everything is quite luxurious, and the beaches are to die for. Accommodations are beautifully done and include standard guest rooms and villas with two to four bedrooms. The extensive grounds (the resort takes up about half of the 1800-acre island) include a gorgeous free-form pool, four tennis courts with a pro, a yachting marina and extensive trails for walking or mountain biking. The food is great and the service impeccable. Lovers can spend the day at their own private beach with a picnic lunch for a very reasonable price. Bravo!

Where to Eat

The Tradewinds Restaurant $$$ ★★★★

Peter Island, ☎ (809) 494-2561.
International cuisine. Specialties: Tortola seafood soup, crab-stuffed island chicken.
Dinner: 7–9 p.m., entrees $18–$36.

Glide onto the Peter Island ferry (after reservations are made, of course) for a short ride to this beautiful private island and its attached resort. The Tradewinds, the island's main dining room, is known for expensive but five-star gourmet dinners served year-round. A memorable meal consists of an appetizer of grilled honey-glazed quail, followed by Caribbean pepperpot soup, caesar salad, lemon-poached shrimp with shrimp mousse, and strawberries Romanoff. Afterwards, dance with your partner under a starlit sky.

Salt Island

What to See

Parks and Gardens

Rhone National Marine Park ★★★★

Salt Island, Salt Island.

One of the Caribbean's best diving spots, the underwater scenes in the movie *The Deep* were filmed here. The chief attraction is the wreck of the RMS *Rhone*, a 310-foot British steamer that sank in a hurricane in 1867. Pieces of the boat rest from 20 to 80 feet deep and make for fascinating viewing.

Virgin Gorda

Huge boulders form a natural swimming pool and underwater caves known as The Baths of Virgin Gorda.

The most chic resorts of the BVI are located on Virgin Gorda, an eight-square-mile slab of scrub and cactus whose shape some say resembles a "fat virgin"—hence its name. Notwithstanding a brief gold rush in the 17th century, the idyllic island lay undiscovered until Laurence Rockefeller cruised the bay and decided to build his Little Dix Bay Hotel. Boats from Tortola regularly dock at the southern settlement of Spanish Town, where most of the 1500 islanders live. The best beaches lay south of Spanish Town, and in the extreme southeast you can find ruins of an old 19th-century copper mine. The road to the north of the island passes through Savannah Bay and Pond Bay before reaching Virgin Gorda's second town, Gun Creek. Below is North Sound, where two fine resorts are located.

The big attraction on Virgin Gorda is a spectacular series of massive granite boulders, the Baths, whose jumbled piles are backed by coconut palms. The stones, made of a granite that is not common to the Caribbean, are thought to have been carried there by glacial movement during the Ice Age. "Having nothing to do" is one of the major pastimes here, but if you say you're bored while staying at Little Dix Bay, they will scurry you off along the coast to a secluded beach, deposit you with drinking water, a picnic and an umbrella, and pick you up later.

Arrival

Most folks take the easy route and take a frog-jumper's flight with American Eagle or Sunair. Boats can also be chartered from Road Town, Tortola, or from St. Thomas in the USVI. Nothing seems to run on schedule here, which is okay, because there's no place to rush to.

Treks and Beaches

Virgin Gorda looks like two different islands north to south. The northern tip is mountainous, while the south is flat, with boulders blocking every curve. Everything above a thousand feet on Virgin Gorda is considered a national park. You'll find a self-guided trail at the 265-acre park at the forested peak near the island's center; it leads to an observation point. The lookout is the end of a paved road leading to Little Dix Bay resort. The first place most people head to are **The Baths**, where snorkeling in the limpid pools created by the pattern of the huge boulders is considered to be superb. (These days you may have to fight for space among the many cruise passengers who alight here; ask your hotel what their arrival schedule is.) Some hearty souls actually climb the island's tallest mount, the 1370-foot **Gorda Peak**; the trail boasts some unusual flora, including tropical orchids. Great treks can be made through **Devil's Bay National Park**; a 15-minute trail through a natural garden of native vegetation and massive boulders will take you to a fine secluded beach. Other beaches noted for their beauty include **Trunk Bay**, wide and sandy and reachable by boat or along a rough path from Spring Bay, a sandy beach north of Yacht Harbour. There is also **Mahoe Bay**, at Mango Bay Resort, with its gently curving beach and vivid blue water.

The greatest adventure in Virgin Gorda is to just get on a boat and explore the numerous other islands, such as **Necker**, **Mosquito**, **Jost Van Dyke** and **Anegada**. You'll usually find at least one resort on these islands, where you can have a fabulous lunch.

City Celebrations

Virgin Gorda Tours Association ★★★

Fischers Cove Beach Hotel, South Sound, ☎ *(809) 495-5252.*

Want to see the island but lack your own wheels? They'll shuttle you about, taking in all the high points, for $50. Two tours are offered daily; call for a schedule.

Parks and Gardens

Virgin Gorda Peak

South Sound.

The "peak" in the name rises some 1500 feet, making it the island's highest point. This 265-acre preserve is home to indigenous and exotic plants and has been reforested with mahogany trees. Hike to the top, then catch your breath at the observation tower, though foliage obscures the view.

Tours

The Baths   ★

Lee Road, South Sound.

Gigantic house-size boulders strewn about have formed saltwater grottoes and small pools great for snorkeling. A new step and ladder system and a protected swimming area are welcome additions to this must-see natural wonder. This is by far the island's most-visited spot, so come early in the morning or late in the afternoon to avoid the crowds.

Sports

Beyond a tennis court at the Little Dix Bay resort, all other sports take advantage of the glorious seas. Most hotels will arrange diving, sailing expeditions, and deep-sea fishing; you can also find agencies at the Yacht Harbour or negotiate directly with crew members lolling about. At **Kilbrides Underwater Tours**, you can speed out to underwater caves, wrecks and coral forests in two 42-foot dive boats under the able direction of Bert Kilbride, considered a true pro in the area. Certification courses run about $60 and you can even get a video made of your dive. If you are interested in chartering a yacht, there are a couple of agencies beside the Little Dix Bay Resort. Both one-day trips and longer excursions can be arranged.

Where to Stay

There are fabulous resorts here, as well as other options, from inns to bargain alternatives that should be scoped out in person.

Hotels and Resorts

Little Dix Bay still remains the premier luxury resort, with enough activities to keep you exhausted. Special packages throughout the year are well worth taking advantage of. **Biras Creek** comes in a close second, an 150-acre estate that even houses a bird sanctuary. The beach at Leverick Bay Hotel can often seem overrun by cruise passengers.

Biras Creek Hotel   **$340–$840**   ★★★★

North Sound, ☎ *(800) 223-1108, (809) 494-3555, FAX (809) 494-3557.*
Single: $340–$670. Double: $340–$840.

Located on a 150-acre estate and accessible only by boat, all accommodations at this tropical retreat are in suites with pleasant decor and, best of all, open-walled private showers. The beach is rather grassy, so most guests opt for sunning at the pool. Surrounded by water on three sides, this is a true escape, and guests are appropriately pampered. The rates include most watersports (skiing and diving costs extra) and tennis on two courts. The restaurant is highly regarded, and the beach barbeques are themselves worth the trip.

Bitter End Yacht Club   **$295–$405**   ★★★

North Sound, ☎ *(800) 872-2392, (809) 494-2746, FAX (809) 494-2745.*
Single: $295–$405. Double: $295–$405.

This lively yacht club and cottage colony houses guests in hillside or beachfront villas with tropical decor and small porches. Visitors can also opt to stay in eight Freedom sailboats. There's lots going on at all times; those seeking an island hideaway will be happier elsewhere. All kinds of watersports are for the taking, and the sailing school is highly touted as among the Caribbean's best. A fun spot for both sailors and landlubbers.

Fischer's Cove Beach $95–$270 ★★

North Sound, ☎ *(800) 621-1270, (809) 495-5252.*
Single: $95–$270. Double: $105–$270.
This cottage enclave overlooks St. Thomas Bay. Accommodations are in stone cottages with one or two bedrooms and a kitchenette. The property includes two bars and two restaurants, but little else in the way of diversions. Great local food.

Little Dix Bay Hotel $225–$1000 ★★★★

Little Dix Bay, North Sound, ☎ *(800) 928-3000, (809) 495-5555, FAX (214) 871-5444.*
Single: $225–$755. Double: $225–$1000.
Lots of couples at this luxury resort, which was completely redone in late 1993. Set on a private bay on a 500-acre estate, Little Dix has a lovely crescent beach, formal gardens, seven tennis courts and a fleet of boats to take you to the beach of your choice. Accommodations are in wood cottages with natural tropical decor; about half have air conditioning. The service is so good you'll be spoiled for life, but some consider this spot a tad pretentious.

Apartments and Condominiums

Self-catering cottages and villas are available, though you should probably bring most staples from home. **Guavaberry-Spring Bay Vacation Homes** is close to the Baths, one of the island's main attractions.

Guavaberry Spring Bay $90–$195 ★★

North Sound, ☎ *(809) 495-5227.*
Single: $90–$195. Double: $90–$195.
Unique hexagonal or round cottages, perched on stilts, are simply furnished with one or two bedrooms, a sitting room, modern bath and kitchen. Great views of Sir Francis Drake's Passage and neighboring islands. The helpful management will shuttle you about, but you'll still want a car for mobility. This nice spot is enhanced by the friendly service.

Leverick Bay Resort $96–$255 ★★

North Sound, ☎ *(800) 848-7081, (809) 495-7421, FAX (809) 495-7363.*
Single: $96–$120. Double: $96–$255.
A hillside villa complex with standard guest rooms, two-bedroom condos and one-to four-bedroom villas with kitchens. There's an outdoor pool and 44-slip marina, as well as tennis, a dive shop, beauty salon and restaurant. The resort gets crowded with day-trippers when cruise ships are in port.

Mango Bay Resort $105–$320 ★★

North Sound, ☎ *(800) 223-6510, (809) 495-5672, FAX (809) 495-5674.*
Single: $105–$320. Double: $140–$320.
Located on a gorgeous stretch of beach overlooking Sir Frances Drake Channel, this simple resort houses guests in attractive one- to four-bedroom villas, each with

kitchen, private patio and daily maid service. Cooks are available on request. The grounds include watersports (great snorkeling), but you'll have to cook in or venture elsewhere for meals.

Inns

There's only one inn on the island, managed by the owner. The style is casual, the furnishings nothing to write home about. You'll have close contact with the other guests.

Olde Yard Inn   **$85–$180**   ★★★

The Valley, ☎ *(800) 633-7411, (809) 495-5544, FAX (809) 495-5986.*
Single: $85–$180. Double: $100–$180.

Situated in a garden setting overlooking Handsome Bay, this charming inn puts guests up in two-story buildings (great views from the upper floors) with simple island furniture, tile floors and roomy baths. Four rooms are air-conditioned. A reading and film library keeps visitors contented, and the staff happily accommodates those with special interests, arranging sea sails and the like. New this year are a pool, Jacuzzi, poolside bar and exercise room. The restaurant draws raves.

Low Cost Lodging

Best bargains can be found after the winter season (starting in April-November). If you're game, take a day trip to the island and ask about for any rooms in private homes. Groups of travelers can also rent houses and bring down the per-person rate.

Where to Eat

For such a tiny island, the cuisine on Virgin Gorda can run to the superb, especially at the **Little Dix Bay Hotel** (the stupendous views from the dining terrace don't hurt either). At the **Biras Creek** hotel, dining is highly romantic, perched high on the hilltop, and the wine list is considered to be one of the best in the Caribbean. The best place to have Sunday brunch is **Pusser's Pub**, at Leverick Bay, on North Sound (good place for American-style hamburgers as well).

Biras Creek   **$$$**   ★★★★

☎ *(809) 494-3555.*
International cuisine. Specialties: Half lobster any style, stilton with port.
Dinner: 7:30–9 p.m., prix fixe $40.

Dine in a stone "castle keep" with all-encompassing views of the Caribbean and Atlantic from the airy and luxurious main dining room of the tony Biras Creek Resort. The four-course, prix-fixe dinner menu changes each evening, but fresh half-lobster served grilled or poached with lemon or garlic butter is always available if requested by 4 p.m., for an extra $5. The well-chosen menus combine local specialties like conch with spicy mango chutney or pumpkin soup with rum. For a "veddy" English touch, stilton and port arrive shortly after dessert.

Chez Michelle   **$$$**   ★★

The Valley, ☎ *(809) 495-5510.*
International cuisine. Specialties: Lobster remy, pastas.
Dinner: 6:30–9:30 p.m., entrees $16–$28.

An intimate Gallic spot amidst the surf and turf, Chez Michelle provides cozy, candlelit surroundings in a West Indian house near the Yacht Harbour. The specialty is local lobster, flambeed in cognac and served with a delicately rich mushroom sauce. Fresh pastas made in-house are justifiably popular, as is the rack of lamb.

Olde Yarde Inn $$$ ★★★

The Valley, ☎ *(809) 495-5544.*
International cuisine. Specialties: Seafood delight, fresh fish, grilled lamb chops.
Dinner: 6:30–8:30 p.m., entrees $18–$30.
The ambience is lovely at this garden restaurant in the Olde Yarde Inn, and the French-Continental food enhances the experience. Inn guests and others can dine here all day, starting with a breakfast menu that commences at 8 a.m. But the real draw is dinner, where classics like escargot with garlic butter or caesar salad for two can be paired with local fish of the day, or Caribbean lobster with lemon butter sauce. Desserts are all homemade and change frequently.

Pirate's Pub & Grill $ ★★★

Saba Rock,
American cuisine. Specialties: Barbecue, sandwiches, dessert drinks.
Lunch: Noon–4 p.m., entrees $5–$7.
Dinner: 4–8 p.m., entrees $5–$7.
It can get wild and woolly here some nights when the booze flows, but this informal pub is (relatively) kind to the pocketbook, serving a small menu of hefty sandwiches, ribs and chicken with all the trimmings for under $10, although a side order of potato salad at $2.50 is a tad much. Patrons are expected to drink their desserts here, downing such delights as raspberry pound cake and strawberry short cake blended at the bar. Entertainment is in the form of darts, or impromptu jam sessions with whomever washes up on the beach.

Pusser's Leverick Bay $$$ ★★★

Leverick Bay, ☎ *(809) 495-7369.*
American cuisine. Specialties: Filet of beef Wellington, mud pie.
Lunch: 11:30 a.m.–4:30 p.m., entrees $6–$10.
Dinner: 6–10 p.m., entrees $13–$24.
The Virgin Gorda branch of the popular Pusser's chain is located in a boisterously colored Victorian house, where familiar and tasty stateside favorites like nachos with guacamole and jalapeño pepper and cheddar fries are served with drinks. The chain's filet of beef Wellington is a specialty, served with fresh mushrooms and encased in pastry. There's also lobster, and pasta with vegetables. Desserts are huge and sweet, like mud pie with mocha ice cream and cookie crust, or the Mud Head, a chocolate and Pusser's rum concoction with gooey cream on top.

Teacher Ilma's $$$ ★★★

The Valley, ☎ *(809) 495-5355.*
Latin American cuisine. Specialties: Calalloo, grouper.
Lunch: 11 a.m.–1:30 p.m., entrees $3–$10.
Dinner: 7–9:30 p.m., prix fixe $18–$25.
Teacher Ilma is Mrs. Ilma O'Neal, a veteran schoolmistress and now kitchen doyenne serving full-course dinners each night and lighter repasts at lunch. Located in

her own home at Princess Quarters, Teacher presents genuine island favorites like conch, callaloo soup and roast pork to an appreciative culinary audience. Desserts might include pies and cakes made with exotic local fruits and nuts.

The Bath and Turtle Pub $$$ ★ ★ ★

The Yacht Harbour, ☎ *(809) 495-5239.*
International cuisine. Specialties: Fried shrimp in coconut batter, specialty pizzas.
Lunch: 11:30 a.m.–5 p.m., entrees $7–$15.
Dinner: 6:30–9:30 p.m., entrees $11–$30.

A convivial bar-tavern, The Bath and Turtle has two happy hours a day, one mid-morning, and another one before sundown. Drinks are usually fruity and tropical, accompanied by good pizzas (Mexican crabmeat, veggie and special of the day), a West Indian chicken sandwich with spicy local seasonings, filet mignon, lobster and burgers. The location is fine too, next to a shopping center and the local lending library. The Pub is open for breakfast from 8 a.m. and usually stays open until 9 p.m.

The Crab Hole $$ ★ ★ ★

South Valley, ☎ *(809) 495-5307.*
Latin American cuisine. Specialties: Calalloo soup, stewed goat, rotis.
Lunch: 11 a.m.–3 p.m., entrees $6–$12.
Dinner: 6:30–9 p.m., entrees $10–$15.

One of a growing handful of West Indian restaurants in Virgin Gorda, The Crab Hole draws locals who come to chow down on home-cooking, island style, be it callaloo (local spinach) soup, spicy chicken curried rotis or plantains and rice and peas. There's lively entertainment as well on Friday and Saturday nights.

Where to Shop

The British Virgin Islands don't give American citizens the same duty-free break as do the U.S. Virgin Islands. There's not much to rave about here in terms of quality. Boutiques at Little Dix Bay and the Bitter End resorts carry the proverbial casual wear and souvenir merchandise. Along the Yacht Harbour you'll find another bevy of shops, including a few handicraft stores. Most of the work is imported from other islands, though you can find interesting buys on homemade preserves and spices.

British Virgin Islands Directory

ARRIVAL AND DEPARTURE

Travel to and from Tortola and the BVI requires an extra step. There is no airport in the country big enough to handle large jets, so most visitors transfer in San Juan, St. Thomas or St. Maarten and arrive via a smaller island hopper (which should give you the idea to include those other stops in your itinerary.) American Eagle makes seven flights a day from San Juan to Beef Island/Tortola. In the U.S., call ☎ *(800) 433-7300*. Sunaire also has daily service to Tortola from St. Thomas and St. Croix. LIAT flies from Antigua, St. Kitts, St. Maarten, St. Thomas and San Juan, but the planes are very small and they are rarely on time. The departure tax per airline passenger is $5.

St. Thomas can also be reached by boat from Tortola, a 45-minute trip on public ferry. You can buy tickets from several companies, including **Smith's Ferry Service** ☎ *(809) 494-4495* and **Native Son** ☎ *(809) 495-4617*. The departure tax for sea passengers is $4.

Because government regulation forbids anyone to rent a car at the airport, taxis are omnipresent whenever a plane arrives. Your hotel can also arrange for a taxi to meet you.

BUSINESS HOURS

Stores open Monday–Saturday 9 a.m.–5 p.m. Banks open Monday–Thursday 9 a.m.–2:30 p.m. and Friday 9 a.m.–2:30 p.m. and 4:30–6 p.m.

CLIMATE

Little rain falls on this nearly-perfect temperate island, with temperatures hovering between 75 degrees F and 85 degrees F year-round. The constant tradewinds keep the humidity low. Even during the rainy season, rain usually arrives in 10-minute bursts that stop as fast they start.

CRUISES

BVI has become a ready port of call for many cruise liners. Many stop at Tortola and bring passengers aboard on small ships.

DOCUMENTS

Customs officials prefer visitors bring passports, but will accept proof of citizenship (birth certificate, voter's registration card, plus a photo ID). Travelers must also show an ongoing or return ticket. Departure tax by air is $5; by sea $4.

ELECTRICITY

Current runs 110 volts, 60 cycles, as in the U.S.

GETTING AROUND

Private ferry service between Caneel Bay and Little Dix Bay is provided by the island resorts three times a week. Or your concierge can arrange a private water taxi—a fast twin-engined outboard catamaran for $275 one way. Public ferries are also available. They run Thursday and Sunday, between Cruz Bay and Spanish Town on Virgin Gorda. Call **Transportation Services** on St. Thomas, for information ☎ *776-6282l*, $22 one way. A passport is required for travel between the American and British Virgin Islands.

Public ferries also make the 45-minute voyage from St. Thomas (Charlotte Amalie) to Road Town and West End on Tortola. Companies providing this service include **Smith's Ferry Service** ☎ *(809) 494-4495* and **Native Son** ☎ *(809) 495-4617*.

Transportation on Virgin Gorda is mainly by boat, often in the form of one of Little Dix's handy Boston Whalers.

Pick up a copy of the BVI "Welcome Tourist Guide," which gives an extensive list of yachts, sloops, trimarans and Carib runabouts that may be charted on Tortola and Virgin Gorda. Prices per day range from U.S. $60 to U.S. $19,000 per week.

Car rental prices can be exorbitant during high season because the demand is so high. As such, it's best to reserve a car before you arrive. Rates seems to change daily, so verify any last-minute adjustments at least two days before your expected pickup. Narrow dirt roads that are often not well lighted require sturdy wheels such as gurghels or jeeps. To rent a car, you must obtain a BVI license by presenting your valid hometown driver's license and shelling out $10. Though there are numerous local agencies, the best security is to stay with U.S.-based agencies that can verify mistakes in billing, etc. Among the best are **Avis** ☎ *(809) 494-3322*, **National** ☎ *(809) 494-3197*, **Hertz** ☎ *(809) 495-4405* or toll-free *800-654-3001* in the United States.

LANGUAGE

British English is spoken with a West Indian accent.

MEDICAL EMERGENCIES

The Peebles Hospital, Porter Road, Road Town; ☎ *(809) 494-3497* is a fully functioning facility with lab and X-ray machines. Hotels usually have a list of doctors on-call in Tortola.

MONEY

The American dollar is used exclusively.

TELEPHONE

To reach BVI from the U.S., dial *809* (area code) + *49* (country code) + local number. Area code is *809*.

TIME

Atlantic Standard Time throughout the year.

TIPPING

Hotels customarily add a 10–15 percent service charge to the bill; feel free to tip more for special service. Waiters and taxi drivers both expect to be tipped 10–15 percent.

TOURIST INFORMATION

The **British Virgin Islands Tourist Board** on Tortola is located in the *Joseph Josiah Smith Social Security Building, Waterfront Drive, Road Town;* ☎ *(809) 49-43134,* FAX *(809) 49-43866.* Few hotels have phones in the room, so do ask in advance if you need one. Calls can be made with phone cards purchased from the Cable & Wireless company. In the United States call ☎ *(800) 538-8530.*

WHEN TO GO

The BVI Summer Festival in August is one of the island's biggest events, which includes two weeks of festivities, song, dance and parades. Also in August, fish enthusiasts can also attend the International Marlin Tournament at the Birch Creek resort. In November hop a ferry to Virgin Gorda's Bitter End Yacht Club when the Pro-Am Regatta sets sail. The annual Spring Regatta is a Caribbean-wide yacht race, featuring outdoor music and street fairs. For a schedule, call ☎ *(800) 835-8530* in the U.S. Easter is celebrated by a three-day festival in Virgin Gorda.

BRITISH VIRGIN ISLANDS HOTELS		RMS	RATES	PHONE	CR. CARDS
Anegada					
Setting Point					
★★	**Anegada Reef Hotel**	16	$130–$230	(809) 495-8002	None
Guana Island					
★★★★★	**Guana Island**	15	$485–$635	(800) 544-8262	None
Jost Van Dyke					
White Bay					
★★	**Sandy Ground Estates**	8	$780–$1200	(809) 494-3391	MC, V
★	**Sandcastle**	4	$225–$295	(809) 771-1611	MC, V
Mosquito Island					
★★★★	**Drake's Anchorage**	12	$223–$600	(800) 624-6651	A, MC, V
Necker Island					
★★★★★	**Necker Island**			(800) 225-4255	None
Peter Island					
★★★★★	**Peter Island Resort**	50	$195–$3900	(800) 346-4451	A, DC, MC, V

BRITISH VIRGIN ISLANDS HOTELS		RMS	RATES	PHONE	CR. CARDS
Tortola					

Road Town

★★★	Long Bay Beach Hotel	80	$55–$295	(800) 729-9599	A, D, MC, V
★★★	Prospect Reef Resort	131	$91–$279	(800) 356-8937	A, MC, V
★★★	Sugar Mill Hotel	21	$115–$320	(800) 462-8834	A, MC, V
★★★	Treasure Isle Hotel	43	$85–$230	(800) 334-2435	A, D, MC, V
★★	Admiralty Estate Resort	30	$110–$275	(809) 494-0014	A, MC, V
★★	Fort Burt Hotel	8	$60–$95	(809) 494-2587	A, D, MC, V
★★	Fort Recovery Estates	10	$125–$295	(800) 367-8455	A, MC, V
★★	Frenchman's Cay Resort	9	$107–$270	(800) 235-4077	A, D, MC, V
★★	Moorings-Mariner Inn	40	$80–$165	(800) 535-7289	A, MC, V
★★	Nanny Cay Resort	42	$50–$195	(809) 494-2512	A, MC, V
★★	Rockview Holiday Homes	20	$100–$755	(800) 621-1270	A, MC, V
★★	Village Cay Marina Hotel	19	$115–$330	(809) 494-2771	A, D, MC, V
★	Sebastian's on the Beach	26	$75–$190	(800) 336-4870	A, D, MC, V

Virgin Gorda

North Sound

★★★★	Biras Creek Hotel	33	$340–$840	(800) 223-1108	A, D, MC, V
★★★★	Little Dix Bay Hotel	98	$225–$1000	(800) 928-3000	A, DC, MC, V
★★★	Bitter End Yacht Club	94	$295–$405	(800) 872-2392	A, DC, MC, V
★★★	Olde Yard Inn	14	$85–$180	(800) 633-7411	A, MC, V
★★	Fischer's Cove Beach	20	$95–$270	(800) 621-1270	A, MC, V
★★	Guavaberry Spring Bay	16	$90–$195	(809) 495-5227	None
★★	Leverick Bay Resort	16	$96–$255	(800) 848-7081	A, MC, V
★★	Mango Bay Resort	8	$105–$320	(800) 223-6510	None

BRITISH VIRGIN ISLANDS RESTAURANTS	PHONE	ENTREE	CR. CARDS

Anegada

Setting Point

	International		
★★ Anegada Reef Hotel	(809) 495-8002	$17–$30	MC, V
	Seafood		
★★ Del's Restaurant and Bar	(809) 495-8014	$7–$20	MC, V

Jost Van Dyke

White Bay

	American		
★★ Foxy's Tamarind	(809) 495-9258	$6–$30	MC, V
	International		
★★ Sandcastle	(809) 775-5262	$18–$35	MC, V
	Seafood		
★★ Abe's By The Sea	(809) 495-9329	$8–$30	MC, V
★★ Club Paradise	(809) 495-9267	$4–$25	A, MC, V

Peter Island

	International		
★★★★ The Tradewinds Restaurant	(809) 494-2561	$18–$36••	A, MC, V

Tortola

Road Town

	Asian		
★★ Chopsticks	(809) 494-3616	$10–$20	A, MC, V
	English		
★★★ Virgin Queen	(809) 494-2310	$7–$16	None
	Indian		
★★★ Mrs. Scatliffe's	(809) 495-4556	$0–$0•	None
★★★ The Apple	(809) 495-4437	$15–$35••	A, MC, V
★★ Bing's Drop Inn	(809) 495-2627	$10–$20••	A, MC, V
	International		
★★★★ Skyworld	(809) 494-3567	$7–$40	A, MC, V

BRITISH VIRGIN ISLANDS RESTAURANTS	PHONE	ENTREE	CR. CARDS
★★★★ The Upstairs	(809) 494-2228	$10–$27	A, MC, V
★★★ Sugar Mill	(809) 495-4355	$6–$28	A, MC, V
★★ Pusser's Landing	(809) 495-4554	$5–$25	A, D, MC, V
★★ Pusser's Outpost and Pub	(809) 494-4199	$7–$25	A, MC, V

Italian

★★★★ Brandywine Bay	(809) 495-2301	$20–$28••	A, MC, V
★★★★ Capriccio di Mare	(809) 494-5369	$8–$15	A, D, MC, V
★★ Spaghetti Junction	(809) 494-4880	$10–$25••	None

Seafood

★★★ The Fish Trap	(809) 494-3626	$8–$25	A, MC, V

Virgin Gorda

North Sound

American

★★★ Pirate's Pub & Grill		$5–$7	A, MC, V
★★★ Pusser's Leverick Bay	(809) 495-7369	$6–$24	A, MC, V

International

★★★★ Biras Creek	(809) 494-3555	$40–$40••	A, MC, V
★★★ Olde Yarde Inn	(809) 495-5544	$18–$30••	A, MC, V
★★★ The Bath and Turtle Pub	(809) 495-5239	$7–$30	A, MC, V
★★ Chez Michelle	(809) 495-5510	$16–$28••	MC, V

Latin American

★★★ Teacher Ilma's	(809) 495-5355	$3–$25	None
★★★ The Crab Hole	(809) 495-5307	$6–$15	None

Note: • Lunch Only

        •• Dinner Only

DOMINICA

Bananas, coconuts, grapefruit, limes and passionfruit are important to Dominica's economy.

Home to one of the finest primal rain forests in the world, Dominica has changed little since Columbus set foot on its shore some 500 years ago. Just as it was in 1493, there are still no sugar-white beaches, no resorts, no McDonald's, no duty-free stores and little nightlife. What Dominica does have is one of the world's last ocean rain forests, a flooded fumarole said to be the largest in the world, a lake covered with purple hyacinths, and so many species of trees that one of them is even named "no-name." Here is an earth of boiling lakes and mountain cascades, of desolate lava-ravaged landscapes, of forests dense with bromeliads and lianas, chataigniers and gommiers, of landscapes so dazzlingly accented with helicnia and anthurium blossoms that you could easily believe you're in the Garden of Eden. (The island receives so much rain—400 inches a year—that it may be the only nation in the world that exports water, but there is so much mist from the morning and evening showers that rainbows are as predictable as the sun.) Days on Dominica simply take on a different dimension than on other Caribbean islands. The Dominica experience is about fighting your way up treacherous mountain paths, shading yourself beneath chatannyé and mang blanc trees, boiling your body in hot sulfur springs, and tracking the two-note song of the sifflé montang. Quite frankly, Dominica is not for the faint-hearted or the out-of-shape tourist. Divers best know how to exploit a real surf-and-turf vacation—most take a two-hour tank dive in the morning, followed by some equally daunting land excursion in the afternoon. Simply, come to Dominica and expect yourself to be taxed to the max—you may need another Caribbean isle on which to recover.

 Note: *Wide Sargasso Sea*, a darkly romantic novel by Jean Rhyss, took place on a plantation in Dominica. Made into a fiercely erotic movie, it is now available on video.

Bird's Eye View

Dominica's small Emerald Pool waterfall attracts hordes of tourists.

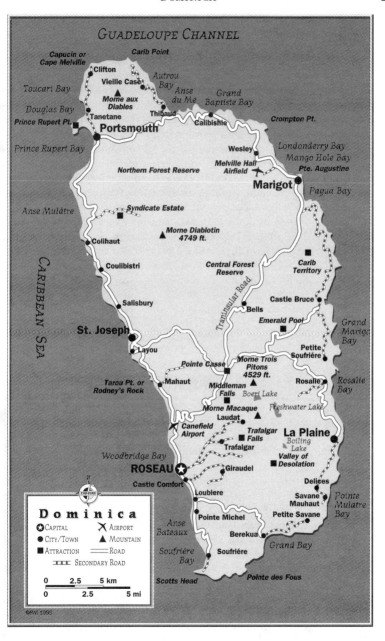

GUADELOUPE CHANNEL

Capucin or
Cape Melville
Carib Point
Clifton
Vieille Case
Autrou
Bay
Anse
du Me
Toucari Bay
Morne aux
Diables
Grand
Baptiste Bay
Douglas Bay
Thibaud
Prince Rupert Pt.
Tanetane
Calibishie
Crompton Pt.
Portsmouth
Prince Rupert Bay
Wesley
Londonderry Bay
Mango Hole Bay
Melville Hall
Airfield
Pte. Augustine
Northern Forest Reserve
Marigot
Pagua Bay

Anse Mulâtre
Syndicate Estate
Colihaut
Morne Diablotin
4749 ft.
Carib
Territory
Coulibistri
Central Forest
Reserve
CARIBBEAN SEA
Salisbury
Castle Bruce
St. Joseph
Bells
Emerald Pool
Grand
Marigot
Bay
Layou
Pointe Casse
Morne Trois
Pitons
4529 ft.
Petite
Soufrière
Tarou Pt. or
Rodney's Rock
Mahaut
Middleman
Falls
Rosalie
Rosalie
Bay
Boeri Lake
Morne Macaque
Freshwater Lake
Canefield
Airport
Laudat
Trafalgar
Falls
La Plaine
Boiling
Lake
Trafalgar
Valley of
Desolation
Woodbridge Bay
ROSEAU
Giraudel
Delices
Castle Comfort
Savane
Mauhaut
Pointe
Mulatre
Bay
Loubiere
Anse
Bateaux
Pointe Michel
Petite Savane
Berekua
Grand Bay
Soufrière
Bay
Soufrière
Scotts Head
Pointe des Fous

Dominica
★ CAPITAL   ✕ AIRPORT
● CITY/TOWN   ▲ MOUNTAIN
■ ATTRACTION   ═══ ROAD
▥ SECONDARY ROAD

0   2.5   5 km
0   2.5   5 mi

©RV 1995

Not to be confused with the Dominican Republic, Dominica sprawls over a 29-mile by 16-mile rocky terrain, lying between Guadeloupe to the north and Martinique to the south. The island is part of the Caribbean Rim of Fire, those jagged terrains born of the violence of volcanic eruptions (Dominica was in fact formed by 15 such eruptions). Verdant-green mountains, some scaling up to 4700 feet, reach to the edge of the sea, as valleys actually dip under the sea, making for spectacular diving conditions as well as hot springs that provide natural spas. There is virgin rain forest with trees as straight as chimneys and tall as cathedrals growing in a tangle of ferns and epiphytes. Offshore, underwater pinnacles reflect the mountainous terrain above. A coral reef stretches along the south coast, attracting many species of tropical fish. In the interior, often cloaked by clouds of vapor, is **Boiling Lake**, near the Valley of Desolation in the 16,000-acre **Morne Trois Pitons National Park**. The lake is the second largest in the world, with temperatures that hover between 180-197 degrees F. In the lake basin, rainfall and water from two small streams seep through the lake's porous bottom to the lava, where it is heated to a boiling point. The small, beautiful Emerald Point and waterfall, in a forest grotto about 45 minutes from Roseau, is a 10- or 15-minute walk from the main Castle Bruce road.

History

Dominica was first settled by Arawaks and then Carib Indians, the latter who dubbed the island "Tall Is Her Body." During the 17th and 18th centuries, control for the island was hotly contested between the British, the French and the native tribes. The British finally prevailed and Dominica formed part of the Leeward Islands federation until 1939. In 1940 it was transferred to the Windward Islands and remained attached to that group until the federal arrangement was ended in December 1959. Under a new constitution, effective from January 1960, Dominica achieved a separate status with its own administrator and an enlarged legislative council. In 1967, it became one of the West Indies Associated States, gaining full autonomy in internal affairs with the United Kingdom retaining responsibility for defense and foreign relations. Following a decision in 1975 by the Associated States to seek independence separately, Dominica became an independent republic within the Commonwealth on Nov. 3, 1978. A program instigated in August 1991, granting Dominican citizenship to foreigners in return for a minimum of U.S. $35,000 in the country, caused considerable controversy, but by July 1992, the amount had been reduced and a quota set. By mid-1993, 466 people had taken advantage of the program, however, mostly Taiwanese. In foreign policy, Dominica has close links both with France and the U.S. As a member of the Organization of the Eastern Caribbean States, it contributed assistance to the U.S. intervention in Grenada.

People

Almost all of the people on the island of Dominica profess Christianity, and about 80 percent are Roman Catholics. There is a small community of Carib Indians on the east coast. The tourist industry is small and farming is the principal industry, heavily dependent on the banana, which is very vulnerable to weather conditions. In 1989 the island and its residents suffered greatly from Hurricane Hugo, but have now recovered. Much effort in the past several five years has made Dominica into one of the most active promoters of tourism in the Caribbean. As such, what hotels and restaurants may lack in efficiency is made up by a friendly, generous nature.

Beaches

Dominica has only a few beaches of any worth; the best bathing is done in rivers. The west coast does have some admirable strands, directly south of Prince Rupert Bay in the **Picard** area. On the Caribbean coast, the sand is black, as at Mero, where the Castaways Hotel is located. The closest beach to the city of Roseau is Scott's Head, a 20-minute bus ride away. White beaches best suited to swimming are located on the northeast coast, such as **Woodford Hill** (near Melville Hall airport) and **Hampstead**. The sand is a beautiful golden color at **Pointe Baptiste**. Most of the beaches, however, consist of black volcanic sand.

Underwater

Diving on Dominica was an insider's secret only a few years ago, but the island has quietly emerged as one of the four or five best dive locations in the Eastern Caribbean. The terrain under water looks much like the mountains above: walls drop for hundreds of feet but are still manageable for beginning-to-intermediate divers. Visibility, despite frequent rain run-off, averages a respectable 75 feet; sediment is quickly carried to plunging depths (the mountain soil actually contributes to the underwater scene far more than it detracts by supplying nutrients to the reef's many filter feeders). Most of the diving is concentrated in **Soufriere Bay**, a submerged volcanic crater, a mile across, that drops to nearly a thousand feet in its center; pinnacles are scattered liberally along the sheer lip and invertebrate life is superbly displayed. There is also good diving in **Douglas Bay** just north of Portsmouth, and in **Castle Comfort**, the rocky cove immediately south of Roseau. Snorkelers will enjoy the inside of Scott's Head and should not miss the singular sparkle of Champagne.

Canefield Wrecks

The primary site is a 60-foot tugboat, sitting upright and intact, 90 feet down. It was sunk only a few years ago and is now beginning to develop coral growth which invites schools of squirrelfish and occasional barracuda; sharp eyes may glimpse seahorses. One small catch: the tug lies near the stream runoff from a stone-crushing plant which limits adequate visibility to Sundays (when the business is closed). Another wreck, a barge at 40 feet, is less interesting, but makes a suitable sight for snorkeling. The wrecks are located just off shore from the airport north of Roseau.

Champagne

Dominica's most unique underwater attraction is an easy dive or snorkel (to 10 feet) which navigates shallow coral and boulders. The dive continues to bubbling steam vents that sparkle effervescently, the bottom warm to the touch. A 50-foot shrimping boat was put down nearby in 1994 as an artificial reef; the site makes a scintillating night dive.

Dangleben's Pinnacles

Five spires reaching to within 30 feet of the surface, the outstanding Dangleben's Pinnacles lie on the north rim of Soufriere Bay and plunge spectacularly to a depth approaching 1000 feet. The pinnacles are littered with colorful growth, including black coral, massive sponges and crinoids.

Des Fous

A pair of opposing walls which connect at a sharp corner below Point des Fous, this is a very advanced dive for those seeking the bigger fish of the rugged Atlantic. The shelf above runs 25–40 feet, while the wall drops to 150 feet, drawing barracuda and nurse sharks.

Scotts Head Dropoff

Perhaps the island's best wall, located inside the south rim of the eroding crater, this area is packed with the smaller life common to Dominica, including cleaner shrimp, yellow line arrow crabs, bristle worms, sea horses and frog fish. The wall drops down almost 200 feet and makes an exciting dive for novices.

Scotts Head Pinnacle

A needle rising to within ten feet of the surface off the tip of Scotts Head, this site drops to 170 feet and features tunnels crowded with French grunts and blackbar soldierfish, while schools of vivid red fish accent the palette. A touch of the Atlantic flows through the area which keeps marine life abundant and varied. Rough ocean conditions can make this a difficult, if spectacular, plunge for advanced divers.

Dive Shops

Anchorage Hotel and Dive Center

Castle Comfort; ☎ *(809) 448-2638.*
PADI outfit open since 1987 with courses to the Divemaster level; uses small groups under eight. Two-tank dive $65. Whale-watching trips, with a proclaimed 95 percent success rate spotting pilot and sperm whales (up to 65 feet) off the western coast November through March; a recent law now bans divers from swimming with the creatures.

Dive Dominica

Castle Comfort; ☎ *(809) 448-2188.*
The island's oldest outfit (established in 1984), PADI and NAUI affiliated, this shop features three boats including a huge 47-foot catamaran (accommodating up to 60 snorkelers when cruise ships dock) but keeps dive groups to 8 or 10. Two tank dive $70. Resort course, $80. Also schedules whale-watching trips.

Nature Island Dive

Soufriere; ☎ *(809) 449-8181.*
Newer outfit in advantageous Soufriere Bay location overlooks island's best dive spots. Two tank dive $63. Resort course, $84. Also sea kayak rentals ($42 full day, $26 half day; stick to the coast rather than heading straight out) and mountain bikes (see "By Pedal").

On Foot

Waterfalls tumbling past wild orchids, slender ridges leading to mist-blown peaks, and three crater lakes—cool or boiling, take your pick. If there's a better adventure destination in the Caribbean than Dominica, step forward now. The self-proclaimed "nature island" has guarded its precious wild assets with remarkable foresight for an island of such fragile economic resources. In 1995 the government was investigating the novel, if risky policy of instituting a fee to visit some of the island's special sights. Time will tell if such a surcharge is supported by tourists, or if the moneys generated will in turn be spent wisely maintaining the island's considerable National Park and Forest Reserve areas. But why wait and see? Your visit to the verdant forests and volcanic innards of this out-of-the-way destination will be nothing less than memorable.

Guides are available for all excursions, but are not absolutely necessary for experienced hikers tackling the Freshwater and Boeri Lakes, Middleham or Trafalgar Falls trails listed below. Visitors do become lost, however, and the trek to the Boiling Lake should not be attempted without a guide. Dominica's regular and heavy rainfall works against trails in two ways: paths become washed out or engulfed with mud, and the forest never stops growing, enveloping the trails in green with lightning speed. Guides almost always carry a machete and can frequently be seen maintaining trails even when they're not leading hikes. In addition to the outfits listed below, guides of varying ability are available at many trailheads, or the management of Papillote (see "Where to Stay") can help set you up. Two other worthy treks are not discussed here: **Morne Diablotin**, the country's highest point and home to the endangered Sisserou parrot, and **Morne Trois Pitons**, where heavy rain inspires ribbons of water to cascade from its sheer north face; neither are long trips, but both require the services of a qualified guide.

The Boiling Lake

This hike has developed a global reputation over the past decade as the most intense and spectacular trek in the entire Caribbean basin. Amazingly, it still justifies its celebrity. The trail begins near the village of Laudat and ascends two substantial ridges on the slopes north of Morne Watt before dropping down into the **Valley of Desolation**, a canyon eerily alive with hot springs, mud pots, sulfur vents and a stream rendered milky blue from the abundant minerals which trickle, ooze and sputter into its path. The valley was once a forest, but was wiped out by an 1880 eruption. A final short hill leads to a crater containing the Boiling Lake, which is usually deep gray in color and kept tumbling briskly by the magma reservoir deep beneath the island.

Wear old clothes to soak up the ample layer of mud you'll accumulate, and make sure to wade up the narrow **Titou Gorge**, where a waterfall rinse provides a memorable conclusion for the trip. Although the five-mile trail is well-traveled and under regular maintenance it's easy to get off the main track, and the area's geology is continuing to evolve; stepping off the trail could mean injury if you break through the brittle, steaming crust. In short, hire a guide. Allow six-to-seven hours, round-trip, for this muscle-pounding expedition.

Freshwater Lake and Boeri Lake

The island's largest lake, Freshwater, is reached by walking or driving a well-worn two mile jeep trail originating near the village of Laudat. A ridge east of the lake (actually the lip of a crater) yields spectacular views of Dominica's volcanic crest. From Freshwater, a moderate, but sometimes slippery trail leads left (north) through giant fern trees, abandoned gardens, montane forest and elfin woodlands to reach Boeri Lake (elevation 2800 feet). Like Freshwater, Boeri fills a crater nestled beneath **Morne Trois Pitons**, Dominica's second-highest summit. Allow two hours round-trip from Freshwater to Boeri Lake, or at least three hours if beginning the trip at Laudat. From the parking lot at Freshwater, another trail heads east down the mountain to the coastal village of **Rosalie** while an alternate track to the **Boiling Lake** branches to the south; though easier than the standard route, it still requires a guide, and it bypasses the spectacular Valley of Desolation.

Middleham Trails

A group of trails lie on the slopes beneath and southwest of Morne Trois Pitons and filter through some of Dominica's lushest forests (by now, you know that's saying a lot). The trails can be accessed out of the village of Cochrane, but the preferred route begins at Providence, below Laudat, and quickly deposits you into dense rainforest. After a half-hour or so, you'll arrive at a junction; take the left branch, and soon after, another intersection leads left to splendid **Middleham Falls**, which plunges 150 feet into a pool of deep blue. Return to the main trail, passing a shelter on the left and cross several streams (a consideration in the rainy season) to another junction. Bear left again to encounter **Tou Santi**, a crumpled lava tube which is home to numerous bats; a hot air fissure heats their guano and provides the name, which translates to "stinking hole" in the local patois. The trail continues a little further through estate lands and cultivated fields before reaching Cochrane. Allow about three hours for this routing, though there are also variations which will create an appealing loop trip, and return you to your starting point (allow four to five hours). If you don't have a guide, a map and a good sense of direction is a prerequisite.

Trafalgar Falls

For visitors not up for the "big" treks, an easy 10-minute stroll follows a well-defined path through dense vegetation to the base of Dominica's beautiful twin waterfalls, sometimes referred to as the "father" and "mother" falls (one is tall and slender, the other shorter and broad-lipped). The hike traverses the steep western slopes of Morne Macaque, beginning at Papillote Wilderness Retreat, a mile past the village of Trafalgar. This short excursion does not require a guide, although exploring the hot springs at the base of the upper falls is recommended only for the sure-footed (a guide is helpful); also use caution during heavy rainfall which can cause flash floods.

Victoria Falls

Few tourists travel to the remote southeast part of Dominica, where the Atlantic pounds the coastline fervently. Victoria Falls can be seen from the end of the road near Delices, or you can hire a guide in town to take you up the slippery paths to its base. Another waterfall, the Sam Sari, tumbles into the ocean at nearby Savane Mahaut; this is a popular picnic area for locals on weekends. Be very cautious at both falls in periods immediately following heavy rain.

Trekking Tours

Ken's Hinterland Adventure Tours

Roseau; ☎ (809) 448-4850.

Van and hiking tours; guide for group of up to four people to Boiling Lake or Morne Diablotin, $120.

Insider Tip:

Dress right for trekking: sturdy shoes with good ankle supports and loose-fitting, lightweight clothes. Take your own water supply and make sure you use sunscreen, even if there seems to be no light filtering through the treetops.

By Pedal

Biking on Dominica is not for the faint-hearted. Yet those who are up to its steep and winding roads will discover numerous possibilities. One demanding all-day trip laced with spectacular views of Morne Trois Pitons through the mists totals about 25 miles and heads north out of Roseau to take in the western coastline, turning inland at Layou River. Where the main road splits a couple miles later, take the right branch which climbs steadily toward Pont Casse before heading down the precipitate main artery into Roseau. The route around the island's perimeter is strictly for Tour de France types: 55 dizzying, thigh-busting miles.

Bike Rental Shops

Nature Island Dive

Soufriere; ☎ *(809) 449-8181.*

Only six mountain bikes on hand, but they plan to add to their collection as demand builds. Full day rental, $32; half day (four hours), $21. Offers three excellent tours of reasonably challenging difficulty, each of which start at Pont Casse (elevation: 2000 feet) and head mostly downhill through scenic and less-visited areas. $84 per person for a group of two or three, $68 each for four or five, including transport, bike rental and lunch.

What Else to See

Roseau, Dominica's capital, has made Old Market Plaza a pedestrian area.

In Roseau, all the sights are within walking distance; don't miss the **Botanic Gardens** and especially the **Dawbiney Market Plaza**, which is chock full of art exhibits and local fruits and vegetable stands. You'll also find tourist information centers here. By the time you arrive, there may even be handicraft vendors.

Save a whole other day for a **circuit of the island**—north to Portsmouth and Fort Shirley, down the Atlantic coast, and through the Carib Indian reservation, with a stop for lunch at Calibishie or Castle Bruce. Many people visit the Carib reservation in the northeast of the island where some interesting woven handicrafts, including authentic native baskets, are for sale. Also interesting is **The Point Cabrits National Park**, a double-peaked peninsula defining the northern edge of Prince Rupert Bay and the southern edge of Douglas Bay. It's home to **Fort Shirley** (originally named Prince Rupert's Garrison), a British fort dating back to the mid-1700s. Most fascinating is the series of crisscrossing paths from the sentry post to the armory to the garrison.

Parks and Gardens

Cabrits National Park   ★ ★ ★ ★ ★

Portsmouth, ☎ (809) 448-2401.

Located on the northwestern coast, this gorgeous spot encompasses 1313 acres of tropical forests, swampland, beaches, coral reefs and various ruins. The best preserved is Fort Shirley, a 1770 military complex, which includes a small museum. Good for birding.

Morne Trios Pitons National Park   ★ ★ ★ ★ ★

South-central region, Roseau, ☎ (809) 448-2733.

The 25-square-mile slice of nature is a primordial rainforest complete with famous Trafalgar Falls, reached by an easy 15-minute hike. There are some other great sights to see here, including a lake nestled in the crater of an extinct volcano, and Boiling Lake, a bubbling mass of mud that's seen only by the hardy—it takes four strenuous hours to trek there. The Emerald Pool Nature Trail is for more moderate hikers.

Tours

Guided Tours   ★ ★ ★

Various locations, Roseau.

A number of outfits will take you around Dominica, from the city sights of Roseau to the rainforest, Traflagar Falls to Portmouth: **Wilderness Adventure Tours** (☎ 448-2198), **Rainbow Rover Tours** (☎ 448-8650), **Dominica Tours** (☎ 448-2638), **Emerald Safaris** (☎ 448-4545), **Ken's Hinterland Adventures** (☎ 448-4850), and **Sun Link Tours** (☎ 448-2552), which also offers sea excursions. Prices are generally in the $20 to $30 range.

BEST VIEW:

Stop for a pick-me-up drink at the Picard Beach Cottages and enjoy a spectacular view of Prince Rupert's Bay.

Sports

Sailing, windsurfing and deep-sea fishing are popular pastimes in Dominica.

Although hiking predominates, Dominica also offers tennis, waterskiing, windsurfing and snorkeling. Scuba diving along walls plunging hundreds of feet and even in hot springs is especially popular. Two dive shops are **Waitikubuli** ☎ *(809) 44-82638* and **Dive Dominica** ☎ *(809) 44-82188*.

Scuba Diving

Various locations, Roseau.

If your hotel can't help you arrange a diving excursion, try one of these: **Castaways Hotel Dive Center** *(☎ 449-6244)*, **Dominica Dive Resorts** *(☎ 448-2638)*, and **Nature Island Dive** *(☎ 449-8181)*. All offer classes and dive trips. Prices are generally about $65 for a two-tank dive, $90 for a resort course. They also rent equipment to snorkelers.

Where to Stay

Fielding's Highest Rated Hotels in Dominica

★★★★★	**Fort Young Hotel**	$105–$135
★★★★	**Evergreen Hotel**	$75–$165
★★★★	**Lauro Club**	$73–$140

Fielding's Most Romantic Hotels in Dominica

★★★★	**Lauro Club**	$73–$140
★★	**Picard Beach Cottages**	$120–$145

Fielding's Budget Hotels in Dominica

★	**Continental Inn**	$45–$55
★★	**Springfield Plantation**	$45–$90
★	**Layou Valley Inn**	$55–$85
★	**Coconut Beach Hotel**	$60–$90
★★	**Layou River Hotel**	$50–$100

The low price of hotels and guest houses will astound you on Dominica if you are used to inflated ones on other Caribbean islands. Most hotels are small (fewer than 40 rooms) and most are locally owned. You can choose to stay on the beach or on the hillsides, but since you're here in the middle of a volcano, why not immerse yourself in nature and stay 1000 feet up in the foliage at the **Papilotte Wilderness Retreat**, where the 10 simple rooms are decorated with handpainted representations of lianas and greenery and you wake up not knowing whether you are outdoors or in. For a complete list of hotels with the most recent prices, contact the **National Development Corporation**, *P.O. Box 73, Roseau, Dominica, West Indies;* ☎ *(809) 448-2351.*

Hotels and Resorts

Fort Young Hotel, on the site of the former fort, gets A-plus for historical value and civilized service. **Anchorage** is a companionable property run congenially by an entire family—from the reception to the dive facilities. **Layou River Hotel** is for those who can't get enough of the great outdoors.

Anchorage Hotel $65–$140 ★★

Castle Comfort, Roseau, ☎ (809) 448-2638.
Single: $65–$80. Double: $85–$140.
Located about a mile south of Roseau, this casual hotel appeals mainly to divers. Accommodations are basic, and the older rooms need refurbishment, so be sure to book one of the newer units. There's a pool, good restaurant, dive center and watersports, which cost extra. Though it's located on the water, there is no beach to speak of, but this spot remains popular for its friendly, family-run service.

Castaways Beach Hotel $75–$110 ★★

Mero Beach, ☎ (800) 322-2223, (809) 449-6244, FAX (809) 449-6246.
Single: $75–$101. Double: $101–$110.
Situated between a rain forest and a long gray-sand beach, the Castaways is Dominica's major beach resort. Accommodations are in a two-story wing running along the beach; only a few have air conditioning, but all are pleasant and comfortable. Recreational pursuits include a dive shop, tennis, pool and watersports. A nice property, but if you're looking for a truly wonderful beach resort, pick another island.

Evergreen Hotel $75–$165 ★★★★

Castle Comfort Street, ☎ (809) 448-3288, FAX (809) 448-6800.
Single: $75–$85. Double: $100–$165.
Plenty of island character at this small, family-run hotel near Roseau. The converted two-story house is complimented by a lovely, lush garden that separates the property from a rocky beach. Accommodations are comfortable and bright and have air conditioning; the newer units are better, though the original rooms have more character. There's a pool and restaurant, and they'll help arrange watersports.

Fort Young Hotel $105–$135 ★★★★★

Victoria Street, Roseau, ☎ (809) 448-5000, FAX (809) 448-5006.
Single: $105–$115. Double: $125–$135.
Built within the ruins of old Fort Young, which dates back to the 1720s, this is Dominica's best property, though it draws mainly business travelers. Nicely accented with antique art, rooms are air-conditioned and look out over the harbor. The three suites are beautifully done, filled with antiques, and well worth the extra splurge. The pool is decent, too. A great in-town spot.

Layou River Hotel $50–$100 ★★

Clark Hill Estate, ☎ (800) 776-7256, (809) 449-6281, FAX (809) 449-6713.
Single: $50–$70. Double: $60–$100.
Set beside a beautiful river that is cold but swimmable, this modern hotel houses guests in standard air-conditioned rooms. Futuristic structures house a restaurant (the Sunday buffet is popular) and a small boutique. There are two pools for cooling off, and a free shuttle transports guests to the beach, about five minutes away. A neat spot for families.

Portsmouth Beach Hotel $35–$145 ★

Picard/Portsmouth, FAX (809) 445-5599.

Single: $35–$145. Double: $45–$145.

Located near Cabrits National Park and on the beach, this casual spot has simple, motel-like rooms that rely on ceiling fans to keep things cool. There are also eight cottages that offer more room to spread out. There's a pool and watersports, and a dive center is nearby. Weekly entertainment is a plus.

Reigate Hall Hotel   **$75–$180**   ★ ★

Reigate Street, ☎ (809) 448-4031, FAX (809) 448-4034.
Single: $75–$100. Double: $95–$180.

Set high on a hill overlooking Roseau, this stylish hotel is adorned with lots of antiques and artwork. Accommodations are nicely done with air conditioning, heavy wood furnishings, antique four-poster beds and balconies. The dining room chandelier hangs from the ceiling via a heavy chain. The beach is 2.5 miles away; a gym, sauna, pool and tennis court keep guest occupied. One of Dominica's better hotels.

Reigate Waterfront Hotel   **$55–$95**   ★

Castle Comfort, ☎ (809) 448-3111, FAX (809) 448-3112.
Single: $55–$70. Double: $80–$95.

Located a mile south of Roseau and overlooking the sea, this motel-like property offers basic rooms that let you sleep in air-conditioned comfort. There's a pool, and diving and watersports can be arranged. Besides a weekly barbecue, not much happens here.

Apartments and Condominiums

Dominica has a handful of places for rent, but don't expect to find modern shopping facilities, and if you have any favorites you can't live without, you better bring them from home. If you want to stay long-term, come to the island first and then snoop around for what you want. Prices could be negotiable, depending on the length of your stay.

Coconut Beach Hotel   **$60–$90**   ★

Picard Beach, ☎ (809) 445-5393, FAX (809) 445-5693.
Single: $60–$80. Double: $65–$90.

Located on one of the island's better beaches, this is an enclave of cottages and apartments that lack air conditioning but include kitchenettes; furnishings are simple and basic. There's also a restaurant on site if you're not up to cooking. Activities include watersports, river tours and hiking; there's no pool. Populated mainly with European tourists.

Lauro Club   **$73–$140**   ★ ★ ★ ★

Salisbury, ☎ (809) 449-6602, FAX (809) 449-6603.
Single: $73–$91. Double: $105–$140.

Situated on a cliff and bordered by two beaches, this rustic villa complex offers separate living rooms and kitchens on a large veranda—but no air conditioning. A long staircase takes you to the beach; if you're feeling lazy, just hang by the pool. The restaurant is a nice spot to escape kitchen duties; a tennis court rounds out the facilities. You'll want to rent a car as this spot is rather remote.

Picard Beach Cottages   **$120–$145**   ★ ★

Prince Rupert Bay, ☎ (809) 445-5131, FAX (809) 445-5599.

Single: $120–$125. Double: $140–$145.

Set on the northwest coast on a former coconut plantation at the foot of Morne Diablotin, the island's highest mountain, the cottages here are designed in 18th-century Dominican-style architecture. Each has a kitchenette and veranda; ceiling fans help cool things off. There's a bar and restaurant, and guests can use the pool at a hotel next door. Decent, but a tad pricey for what you get.

Inns

Papilotte has the best inn feel, but **Chez Ophelia**, with its five lovely cottages, and **Layou Valley Inn**, have their own distinct personalities. The latter is great for hikers who just want to find the trail outside their door.

Layou Valley Inn $55–$85   ★

Layou Valley, ☎ (809) 449-6203, FAX (809) 449-6713.
Single: $55–$85. Double: $65–$85.

Perfect for nature lovers, this appealing inn is situated in the foothills of Morne Trios Pitos, seven miles from the beach. Overlooking a primordial forest with great views, the inn has comfortable rooms with private baths but no air. A good jumping-off spot for hiking and rafting.

Papillotte Retreat $50–$125   ★

Trafalgar Falls Road, ☎ (809) 448-2287, FAX (809) 448-2285.
Single: $50–$125. Double: $55–$125.

This small family-owned inn is set right in the rain forest, some 20 minutes from Roseau, in a lush valley amid mineral pools, gardens and waterfalls. Standard rooms are simple and basic and lack air conditioning; there's also a two-bedroom, two-bath cottage with a kitchen. Meals are served outdoors with lots of fresh fruits and vegetables. Come prepared for the eventuality of rain—this is, after all, the rain forest, but if you don't mind that, this is a very special place far removed from city life.

Springfield Plantation $45–$90   ★★

Springfield, ☎ (809) 449-1401, FAX (809) 449-2160.
Single: $45–$70. Double: $65–$90.

This mountain inn dates back to 1940. Accommodations are beautifully done with antique four-poster beds complete with mosquito netting, huge wooden armoires and other antiques. There are also several cottages available for monthly rental. There's a protected river pool for splashing about, nature trails for hiking and safari tours for exploring. Nature lovers love it here, but those into a resort atmosphere will be happier at a more commercial establishment.

Low Cost Lodging

Since rates are not expensive on Dominica, budget opportunities are easy to find. You sacrifice any hope of furnishings other than West-Indian basic. You will be lucky to find air-conditioning (Continental Inn has it).

Castle Comfort Lodge $85–$120   ★★

Castle Comfort Street, ☎ (800) 544-7631, (809) 448-2188, FAX (809) 448-6088.
Single: $85. Double: $120.

Located three miles from the beach, this small lodge attracts primarily divers. The rooms are basic but at least air-conditioned. The owners arrange dive trips and nature walks. There's a restaurant, but little else in the way of amenities.

Continental Inn   **$45–$55**   ★

37 Queen Mary Street, Roseau, ☎ *(809) 448-2215, FAX (809) 448-7022.*
Single: $45. Double: $50–$55.

This small hotel in the heart of Roseau has air-conditioned rooms, but only some have a private bath. The restaurant serves Creole dishes. Mainly used by business travelers.

Where to Eat

Fielding's Highest Rated Restaurants in Dominica

★★★★★	La Robe Creole	$7–$27
★★★★	Evergreen	$17–$20
★★★★	Guiyave	$8–$19
★★★★	World of Food	$2–$15
★★★	Almond Beach Restaurant	$8–$15
★★★	Balisier	$9–$22
★★★	Callaloo Restaurant	$6–$14
★★★	Coconut Beach	$10–$25
★★★	De Bouille	$5–$30
★★★	Floral Gardens	$14–$25

Fielding's Special Restaurants in Dominica

★★★★★	La Robe Creole	$7–$27
★★★★	World of Food	$2–$15
★★★	De Bouille	$5–$30
★★★	Floral Gardens	$14–$25
★★★	Papillotte	$8–$19

Fielding's Budget Restaurants in Dominica

★★	The Mouse Hole	$6–$10
★★	Le Flambeau	$4–$13
★★★★	World of Food	$2–$15
★★★	Callaloo Restaurant	$6–$14
★★★	Orchard Restaurant	$4–$17

Although Dominica is sandwiched between Guadeloupe and Martinique, a French style of cooking has not invaded the island. Flavors tend to lean toward the English (meaning basic and sometimes boring). Most people are too tired after hiking to care about anything but quantity. The best place to find a good meal is at a hotel; the tastiest are the ones at **Papillote** and **Springfield Plantation**. Freshly caught fish is the smartest way to go, as well as local fruits and vegetables; the local pawpaw (or papaya) and christophine (Caribbean squash) are delicious. Beware when you see mountain chicken on the menu—here in Dominica, it isn't chicken at all, but the legs of huge frogs that burrow into the woods.

Almond Beach Restaurant $$ ★★★

Calibishi, Roseau, ☎ *(809) 445-7783.*
Latin American cuisine. Specialties: Callaloo, chicken palau.
Lunch: Noon–2 p.m., entrees $8–$15.
Dinner: 6–8 p.m., entrees $8–$15.

A convenient village restaurant on the east coast, Almond Beach is a cool spot to stop for refreshing and exotic fruit and spice beverages made with anise or ginger. The view of the sea is just ahead, and meals include a savory chicken and rice dish, lobster or callaloo (dasheen) soup.

Balisier $$$ ★★★

Place Heritage, Roseau,
International cuisine. Specialties: Chicken garraway.
Lunch: 12:30–3 p.m., prix fixe $9–$17.
Dinner: 7–10:30 p.m., entrees $13–$22.

Located in a modern, newish hotel on the oceanfront in Roseau, the Balisier is a view restaurant on the first floor, serving competently prepared local fish, curries and a specialty, Chicken Garraway, a moist breast rolled around a local banana and exotic spices. Pies are home-baked and tasty.

Callaloo Restaurant $$ ★★★

63 King George Street, Roseau, ☎ *(809) 448-3386.*
Latin American cuisine. Specialties: Curried conch, callaloo.
Lunch: 11:30 a.m.–2:30 p.m., entrees $6–$14.
Dinner: 6:30–10:30 p.m., entrees $6–$14.

Chefs at Callaloo present home-style cooking on a terrace overlooking downtown Roseau. Like its namesake, the hearty soup made from the omnipresent dasheen (a spinach-like green) is made from scratch daily. There are daily specials, which often include conch prepared in a number of different ways.

Castaways Beach Hotel $$ ★★

Mero Beach, Mero, ☎ *(809) 449-6244.*
Latin American cuisine.
Lunch: Noon–2 p.m., entrees $12–$18.
Dinner: 7–9 p.m., entrees $12–$18.

Dine informally by the ocean at this hotel restaurant popular for good breakfasts, tropical rum punches and the ubiquitous national dish of crapaud, or frog legs.

Sometimes there is crab and conch, and although most of the food is freshly prepared, it varies in quality.

Coconut Beach $$$ ★ ★ ★

Picard Beach, Portsmouth, ☎ *(809) 445-5393.*
Seafood cuisine.
Lunch: Noon–2:30 p.m., entrees $10–$15.
Dinner: 6:30–10:30 p.m., entrees $10–$25.
A casual sandwich and seafood eatery right on the beach located south of Portsmouth, the Coconut Beach serves as a yacht and boat stop as well as a watering hole for daytrippers passing through the island's second-largest town. It's also a good place to try rotis, or flatbread rolled around curried meat or vegetables.

De Bouille $$$ ★ ★ ★

Victoria Street, Roseau, ☎ *(809) 448-5000.*
International cuisine. Specialties: Pumpkin soup, lobster.
Lunch: Noon–2:30 p.m., entrees $5–$14.
Dinner: 7–10 p.m., entrees $14–$30.
A baronial and stately restaurant serving a varied cuisine, De Bouille is ensconced in an old fort, now one of Roseau's finest hotels. Diners can feel history in the stone walls, which add plenty of atmosphere to go along with the pumpkin soup, seafood and steaks served here. A good place to spot local movers and shakers.

Evergreen $$$ ★ ★ ★ ★

Castle Comfort, Roseau, ☎ *(809) 448-3288.*
International cuisine. Specialties: Frogs' legs, crab.
Lunch: 1 p.m.–2 p.m., prix fixe $17.
Dinner: 6–10 p.m., prix fixe $20.
One of the island's most convivial spots, the Evergreen Hotel's dining room is open to non-guests for a prix-fixe five-course meal with a choice of soup and salad; entrees of chicken, frogs' legs and lamb; side dishes, relishes and homemade desserts. The owners, the Winston family, run a very tight ship, with excellent service all around.

Floral Gardens $$$ ★ ★ ★

Concord Valley, Concord, ☎ *(809) 445-7636.*
Latin American cuisine.
Lunch: 11 a.m.–3 p.m., entrees $14–$25.
Dinner: 7 p.m.–midnight, entrees $14–$25.
The name of this restaurant near the Carib Territory couldn't be more apt—the grounds are surrounded by amazingly fertile plants and flowers. Owned by a former prime minister and his wife, Floral Gardens serves creole and international specialties in a room overlooking the Pagwa River. Tour groups often stop here for refreshments, so service can be slow.

Guiyave $$ ★ ★ ★ ★

15 Cork Street, Roseau, ☎ *(809) 448-2930.*
Latin American cuisine. Specialties: Goat water, rotis.
Lunch: 8 a.m.–2 p.m., entrees $8–$19.
Dinner: 2–5 p.m., entrees $8–$19.

This informal eatery is a popular breakfast and lunch spot serving ham and eggs, French toast, and sandwiches during the week. Saturday's home-cooked creole food is a tradition, and that may involve goat water (a spicy meat stew), blood pudding, calalloo, pumpkin soup, and rotis. Guiyave is also THE local juice bar, squeezing out whatever's fresh that day, including tamarind, mango, or soursop, a tangy citrus fruit.

La Robe Creole $$$ ★★★★★

3 Victoria Street, Roseau, ☎ (809) 448-2896.
Latin American cuisine. Specialties: Mountain chicken, calalloo.
Lunch: 10 a.m.–3:30 p.m., entrees $7–$27.
Dinner: 3:30–9:30 p.m., entrees $7–$27.
Regarded as Dominica's fanciest restaurant, La Robe Creole, named after the native madras costume, serves a sublime callaloo soup with coconut and crab and an unforgettable rum punch. There's also pizza and chicken and tropical fruit and coconut pies. Patrons are prominent citizens who come to see and be seen in air-conditioned luxury, but as sometimes happens on this relaxed isle, service can be very slow.

Le Flambeau $$ ★★

Prince Rupert Bay, Portsmouth, ☎ (809) 449-5131.
International cuisine. Specialties: Creole pork chops, homemade ice cream.
Lunch: 7 a.m.–4 p.m., entrees $4–$6.
Dinner: 4–11 p.m., entrees $9–$13.
A pleasing change from exotic Creole specialties, Le Flambeau, located on the sand at the Picard Beach Cottage Resort, flips omelettes, pancakes and French toast to an appreciative crowd at breakfast. The rest of the day and well into the evening, pork chops and vegetarian specialties are available, and the fresh fruit ice creams are delightful.

Orchard Restaurant $$ ★★★

31 King George Street, Roseau, ☎ (809) 448-3051.
Latin American cuisine. Specialties: Callaloo, conch.
Lunch: 11:30 a.m.–4 p.m., prix fixe $4–$17.
Dinner: 7–9 p.m., prix fixe $4–$17.
Hearty, complete meals for under $20 draw patrons to this informal downtown eatery, which also has a popular bar. Entrees like conch (called *lambi* here) are served with trimmings, which in this case involve rice, relishes, salads and whatever the chef has on hand. Those wishing to eat lighter can order a la carte sandwiches and soups, or get food to go. No dinner is served on Saturdays.

Papillotte $$ ★★★

Trafalgar Falls Road, Trafalgar, ☎ (809) 448-2287.
Latin American cuisine. Specialties: Flying fish, callaloo soup.
Lunch: Noon–3 p.m., entrees $8–$19.
Paradise awaits in this garden of Eden near Trafalgar Falls, a haven for nature lovers; amateur botanists will be in seventh heaven. The Retreat's restaurant is only open to nonguests for lunch, but some selections from the small menu, like river shrimp and flying fish, are rarely available elsewhere. There's a hot springs pool on the premises where daytrippers can dip before or after meals.

Reigate Hall   **$$**   ★★
> *Mountain Road, Reigate,* ☎ *(809) 448-4031.*
> *French cuisine. Specialties: Mountain Chicken.*
> *Lunch: 12:30–2:30 p.m., entrees $7–$12.*
> *Dinner: 7–10 p.m., entrees $7–$15.*
> High up on King's Hill near Trafalgar Falls is the Reigate Hall Hotel, a refurbished plantation home with an attached restaurant serving French and Creole specialties. Not unlike eating in a castle, guests enjoy coq au vin, scampi or mountain chicken in a formal atmosphere, but the waitstaff can be less than alert on occasion.

The Mouse Hole   **$**   ★★
> *3 Victoria Street, Roseau,* ☎ *(809) 448-2896.*
> *Latin American cuisine. Specialties: Rotis, pastries.*
> *Lunch: 10 a.m.–2:30 p.m., entrees $6–$10.*
> *Dinner: 2:30–9:30 p.m., entrees $6–$10.*
> The cutely monikered Mouse Hole serves as the takeout-short order adjunct to its big sister, La Robe Creole, which holds court upstairs. There is a counter for sit-down service, but most patrons order rotis of curried chicken, sandwiches, pastries and small meals to go.

World of Food   **$**   ★★★★
> *48 Cork Street, Roseau,* ☎ *(809) 448-3286.*
> *Latin American cuisine. Specialties: Fresh fish, lambi (conch).*
> *Lunch: Noon–3 p.m., entrees $2–$15.*
> *Dinner: 6–10:30 p.m., entrees $2–$15.*
> Literary lions will delight in the fact that this restaurant is located at the site of author Jean Rhys' birthplace. Owner Vena McDougal has turned it into a patio restaurant that brims with office workers at cocktail hour. Diners can sit under a spreading fruit tree and partake of local fish cakes, souse (black pudding) or reasonably priced sandwiches and soups.

Where to Shop

Martinique—Dominica isn't. There are no fancy imports or duty-free stores. Instead, you will have to scope out handicraft shops which, ironically enough, will render you some of the most fantastic souvenirs of your days in the Caribbean.

Dominica Directory

ARRIVAL AND DEPARTURE

Dominica cannot be reached directly by air from the United States but through such island gateways as Antigua, Puerto Rico, St. Maarten, Guadeloupe, Martinique, St. Lucia and Barbados. From those islands, passengers have to switch to a small regional plane such as those on Air Guadeloupe, LIAT or WINAIR, all of which fly into Dominica. There are two small airports on the island: Melville Hall is almost a one-hour drive from Roseau, where most hotels are situated. Canefield is about five minutes from the capital.

BUSINESS HOURS

Stores open weekdays 8 a.m.–1 p.m. and 2–4 p.m. and Saturday 8 a.m.–1 p.m. Banks open Monday–Thursday 8 a.m.–3 p.m. and Friday 8 a.m.–5 p.m.

CLIMATE

Climate is tropical, though tempered by the sea winds that sometimes reach hurricane force, especially from July-September. Average temperature is 80 degrees F., with little seasonal variation. Rainfall is heavy especially in the mountainous areas, where the annual average is 250 inches compared with 70 inches along the coast.

DOCUMENTS

Visitors will need a passport or proof of citizenship in conjunction with a photo ID as well as a return or ongoing ticket.

ELECTRICITY

The current is 220 volts/50 cycles, which means you must have a transformer with the proper plug adapters. Rechargeable strobes and lights should be charged on the stabilized lines most dive operators have available for his purpose.

GETTING AROUND

Taxis and buses are inexpensive and plentiful. Car rentals are available, but driving is on the left and the roads are narrow and twisting, often with a steep drop on one side and a steep rain gutter on the other.

LANGUAGE

English is the official language, but a local French patoi, or Creole is widely spoken. In part of the Northeast, an English dialect known as Cocoy, is spoken by the descendants of the Antiguan settlers.

MEDICAL EMERGENCIES

There are two main hospitals at Roseau and Portsmouth, with 242 and 50 beds, respectively.

MONEY

The official currency is the Eastern Caribbean dollar, but the U.S. dollar is accepted virtually everywhere.

TELEPHONE

The area code is *809*. To call Dominica from the U.S., dial *011* (international code)+*809* (country Code)+*44* (local access) +five-digit number. If you want to save money, head for the Cable & Wireless (West Indies) Ltd. company where you can make international calls, send faxes, telexes, teletypes and telegrams. You can also purchase phone cards here which can be used in pay phones. You can make both local and international calls from pay phones. (Avoid making long-distance calls from your room —if your room indeed even has a phone—as hotel surcharges and operator assistance can raise the bill even higher than the room rate.)

TIME

Atlantic Standard Time, one hour later than New York.

TIPPING AND TAXES

Hotels collect a five percent government tax; restaurants a three percent charge. A 10 percent service charge is added to your bill by most hotels and restaurants. In addition, there is another three percent sales tax. If you feel inclined to leave more for service, do so.

TOURIST INFORMATION

For more information write to the **Dominica Division of Tourism** *(Box 293, Roseau, Dominica, WI;* ☎ *(809) 448-2186, FAX (809) 448-5840).* Mail from the States takes about two weeks to arrive.

WHEN TO GO

Carnival takes place the Monday and Tuesday preceding Ash Wednesday.

Labor Day is May 1. Independence Day is Nov. 1.

DOMINICA HOTELS	RMS	RATES	PHONE	CR. CARDS
Bagatelle				
★★★★★ **Fort Young Hotel**	33	$105–$135	(809) 448-5000	A, MC, V
★★★★ **Evergreen Hotel**	16	$75–$165	(809) 448-3288	A, D, MC, V
★★★★ **Lauro Club**	10	$73–$140	(809) 449-6602	A, DC, MC, V
★★ **Anchorage Hotel**	32	$65–$140	(809) 448-2638	A, D, DC, MC, V
★★ **Castaways Beach Hotel**	26	$75–$110	(800) 322-2223	A, MC, V
★★ **Castle Comfort Lodge**	11	$85–$120	(800) 544-7631	A, MC, V
★★ **Layou River Hotel**	36	$50–$100	(800) 776-7256	A, D, MC, V
★★ **Picard Beach Cottages**	8	$120–$145	(809) 445-5131	A, D, MC, V
★★ **Reigate Hall Hotel**	25	$75–$180	(809) 448-4031	A, MC, V
★★ **Springfield Plantation**	12	$45–$90	(809) 449-1401	
★ **Coconut Beach Hotel**	22	$60–$90	(809) 445-5393	A, D, MC, V

DOMINICA HOTELS		RMS	RATES	PHONE	CR. CARDS
★	Continental Inn	11	$45–$55	(809) 448-2215	A, MC, V
★	Layou Valley Inn	8	$55–$85	(809) 449-6203	A, DC, MC, V
★	Papilotte Retreat	8	$50–$125	(809) 448-2287	A, D, MC, V
★	Portsmouth Beach Hotel	104	$35–$145	(809) 445-5142	A, D, MC, V
★	Reigate Waterfront Hotel	25	$55–$95	(809) 448-3111	A, MC, V

DOMINICA RESTAURANTS		PHONE	ENTREE	CR. CARDS
Bagatelle				
French				
★★	Reigate Hall	(809) 448-4031	$7–$15	A, MC, V
International				
★★★★	Evergreen	(809) 448-3288	$17–$20	A, MC, V
★★★	Balisier		$9–$22	MC, V
★★★	De Bouille	(809) 448-5000	$5–$30	A, MC, V
★★	Le Flambeau	(809) 449-5131	$4–$13	A, DC, MC, V
Latin American				
★★★★★	La Robe Creole	(809) 448-2896	$7–$27	D, MC, V
★★★★	Guiyave	(809) 448-2930	$8–$19	A, MC, V
★★★★	World of Food	(809) 448-3286	$2–$15	None
★★★	Almond Beach Restaurant	(809) 445-7783	$8–$15	D, MC, V
★★★	Callaloo Restaurant	(809) 448-3386	$6–$14	None
★★★	Floral Gardens	(809) 445-7636	$14–$25	A, D, DC, MC, V
★★★	Orchard Restaurant	(809) 448-3051	$4–$17	A, MC, V
★★★	Papilotte	(809) 448-2287	$8–$19•	A, MC, V
★★	Castaways Beach Hotel	(809) 449-6244	$12–$18	MC, V
★★	The Mouse Hole	(809) 448-2896	$6–$10	A, MC, V
Seafood				
★★★	Coconut Beach	(809) 445-5393	$10–$25	A, DC, MC, V

Note: • Lunch Only

•• Dinner Only

GRENADA

Horseback riding is fun for adults and children on Grenada's beaches.

Grenada isn't called The Spice Island for nothing. Walk along The Carenage, the island's bustling waterfront, and you'll see dozens of turbaned black ladies selling their fragrant cloves, allspice, cinnamon and nutmeg with a merry song and a spiel. Aroma, it seems, takes on a seductive, almost musical quality on this tiny island, whose stunning natural wonders—lush mountain forests, cascading waterfalls and secret beaches—complete a delightful package that tourists are now discovering 12 years after U.S. troops quelled the Marxist-based coup. From rum shop to fishing village to market square, Grenada preserves the Caribbean the way it *was*, long before the American cultural intervention of Big Macs and Coke; best of all, tourist development, though viable, has been kept to a reasonable scale. It's here on

Grenada that you can still glimpse women scrubbing laundry in the streets, goats and chickens vying with traffic and old native ladies wearing baskets of bananas on their heads. Beyond Grenada's 45-plus beaches, travelers can hike rain forest trails riddled with cascading rivers, seek out more than 450 flowering plant species and 150 varieties of birds, or just discover a new dive site. For refreshment, there's elegant dining in old plantation houses, where the delicious callaloo soup can be sampled in a hundred different ways, and for adventure, a few hours lost in the ramparts and tunnels of forts that the French and British built during their 100-year-old custody battle.

Bird's Eye View

In Grand Anse, no development may be taller than a coconut palm.

Sixty miles southwest of St. Vincent and 90 miles north of Trinidad, Grenada lies in the southernmost part of the Windward Islands, the smallest independent nation in the Western hemisphere. Egg-shaped, the island is 12 by 21 miles, volcanic in origin, with vegetation so thickly clad that it looks as if it is upholstered in deep green velvet. Its fertile volcanic soil springs forth a bounty of tropical fruits and vegetables and grows more species per square mile than anywhere else on the planet. In fact, the landscape is so lush that Grenada's residents regularly carry machetes as if the path they cleared today

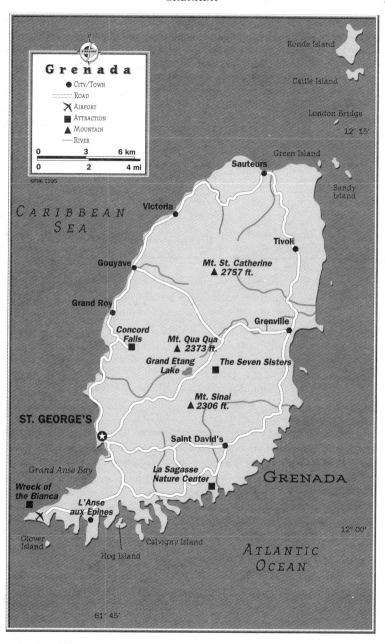

will be overgrown with green tangles tomorrow. The capital of St. George is one of the prettiest harbors in the Caribbean, with a pedestrian walk, The Carenage, which hugs the horseshoe-shaped harbor, inviting you for a stroll beside the sea. Several lofty lookouts—Fort George with cannons aimed seaward, Fort Frederick and Cemetery Hill—present splendid views of the town clambering up the slopes from the waterfront. The island, once a British Crown Colony, but now independent, also includes two other islands—Carriacou, with a very slight infrastructure, and Petite Martinique, famous as a pirate's haunt.

History

Grenada was discovered by Columbus on his third voyage in 1498. The French built Grenada's first settlement, first appeasing and then battling the native Carib Indians, the last of whom leaped to their death from Morne de Sauteurs, a rock promontory in the island's north coast, in 1651. Over the next century, Grenada was a battlefield between the French and British until the island was declared British under the Treaty of Versailles in 1783. Soon after, the island experienced the first rebellion led by a French plantocrat, Julien Fedon, resulting in the murder of 51 British colonists. (Fedon, who was never captured, remains a legend today in Grenada.) In 1838, the Emancipation Act freed Grenada's African slaves, forcing plantation owners to import indentured laborers from India, Malta and Madera. The descendants of this cultural stew live on today in the multiethnic cuisine, the French-African lilt to the language, and the British and French village names. Until 1958, the island remained a British colony, when it joined the abortive Federation of the West Indies. In 1967 it became a member of the West Indies Associated States, with Britain retaining responsibility. Many Grenadians were opposed to self-rule under Eric Gairy, the first Prime Minister, who was often compared to Haiti's Papa Doc Duvalier. Nevertheless, Gairy became a champion of the poor overnight, though he gained an irreverent reputation for some strange actions—for example, marching a steel band through an opponent's meeting and lecturing the U.N. about UFOs. In the early '70s, Maurice Bishop, a charismatic lawyer, just back from his studies in England, earned popular support as a human-rights activist when his New Jewel Movement convicted Gairy of 27 crimes in a mock trial that

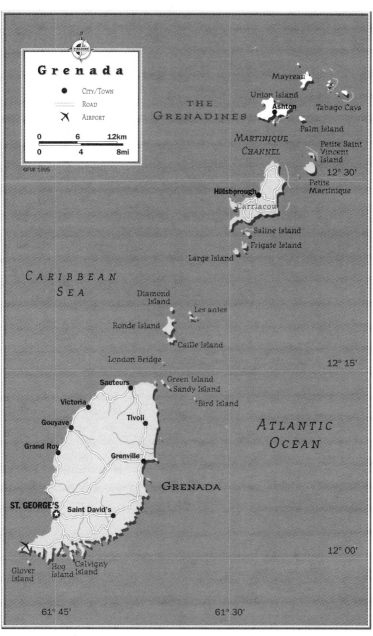

Grenada

● CITY/TOWN

---- ROAD

✈ AIRPORT

0   6   12km
0   4   8mi

©FWI 1995

THE
GRENADINES

Mayreau

Union Island

Ashton

Tabago Cays

Palm Island

MARTINIQUE
CHANNEL

Petite Saint
Vincent
Island

12° 30'

Petite
Martinique

Hillsborough

Carriacou

Saline Island

Frigate Island

Large Island

C A R I B B E A N
S E A

Diamond
Island

Les antes

Ronde Island

Caille Island

London Bridge

12° 15'

Green Island

Sandy Island

Bird Island

Sauteurs

Victoria

Tivoli

Gouyave

A T L A N T I C
O C E A N

Grand Roy

Grenville

GRENADA

ST. GEORGE'S

Saint David's

12° 00'

Glover
Island

Hog
Island

Calvigny
Island

61° 45'

61° 30'

called for his resignation. Bishop, along with other members of his party, was mercilessly beaten by Gairy's police and thrown into jail for the night.

Such was the climate when Grenada (and its two dependencies, Carriacou and Petite Martinique) gained its independence from the British Commonwealth on Feb. 7, 1974. That very day management of the Holiday Inn pulled out, leaving an entire independence banquet in the hands of one pastry chef. By the late'70s, Gairy's economy was a shambles and his support diminished, even among the poor. On March 13,1979, Bishop staged the first modern coup in the English-speaking Caribbean while Gairy was off-island. The economy improved early in his tenure and countries around the world accepted Bishop and the new Jewel Movement as a governing force. Still, free elections were never held. Bishop fostered ties with Cuba and the Eastern Bloc countries, and as his friend Fidel Castro granted Grenada aid and labor to build a larger airport at Port Salines in the south, U.S. ties began to unravel. In 1983 Bishop was ousted by a more Marxist/Leninist member of his own party, Bernard Coard, who placed Bishop under house arrest and imprisoned some of his followers. At a rally to support the release of Bishop, members of the People's Revolutionary Army fired into the throng; today no one is sure how many men, women and children were killed. The U.S. government, using the subsequent brutal execution of Bishop as pretext, landed 7000 troops on Oct. 26, 1983, on the shores of Grenada, accompanied by the military forces of other neighboring islands—ostensibly to protect democracy and defend the lives of some 1000 Americans residing there, mostly medical students at St. George's University. The American troops were welcomed with open arms by most Grenadians who called the mission not an invasion, but an "intervention."

The aftermath of what has been considered a bad dream by Grenadians has been a stars-and stripes p.r. blitz—new bridges, a retrained police force, and a renewed sense of democracy. The Americans put the finishing touches on the airport, and in 1990 American Airlines began its daily run. Today Grenada holds democratic elections every five years, with five major political parties vying for votes. Among these are the Maurice Bishop Patriotic movement and Gairy's GULP. The once-exiled Gairy, well into his 70s, and virtually blind, promises that if he's elected, the Almighty will restore his vision.

People

Like other recently created Caribbean countries freed from colonial ties, Grenada must constantly test the political waters—a fact that explains why Grenadians seem so politically aware and fascinated by foreigners. Warm and witty, Grenadians are insatiably curious, often quizzing tourists on Clintonomics or the latest word on Michael Jackson. About 75 percent of residents are black, the balance being largely mulatto. Although most of the 91,000 residents live off the land, unemployment is a huge problem (estimated to be about 30 percent in 1990). As a result, crime, especially in the lagoon area between St. George's and Grand Anse beach, has increased; hoteliers warn guests not to walk on that beach after dark, but to take the lighted service road instead. Grenadians are very pro-American, however, and still grateful to the U.S. for the military invention 13 years ago. In fact, graffiti on the island still sings praises and thank-you's to "our saviour Ronald Reagan." Although there are no longer American troops on Grenada, you will run into lots of American students studying under palm trees at St. George's Medical School on the Grand Anse campus.

Beaches

Grenada claims 45 beaches, all free of charge to the public. All have fine white sand. The most famous is long and stunning **Grand Anse**, home to many of the island's resorts and hotels. Also in the south are **Calabash** and **Horseshoe**. If you are looking to pack a picnic lunch, head for **Levera Beach** on the northeastern shore, where you will find swaying palms and deserted stretches. Other good beaches are near Lance aux Epines. This is where the Atlantic and the Caribbean meet. The best beaches in Carriacou are **Paradise** and **Sandy Island**.

Underwater

Diving is a low-key, comfortable pursuit in Grenada, free of much of the hustle and crowding prevalent at better-established locations. Part of this can simply be attributed to the newness of the sport here. In the rush to attract visitors and develop a tourism infrastructure in the years following the excitement of 1983, it took awhile to recognize that the island boasted attractive dive sights. Most are located at **Moliniere Point**, a 10-to-15 minute boat ride north from the Grand Anse area, where the dive shops are based. The *Bianca C*, easily the Caribbean's largest wreck, is a very dramatic dive which will thrill sunken ship enthusiasts. Farther afield, the pristine area off Carriacou should not be overlooked. Snorkelers looking for shore dives should check out the cliffs at the south end of **Grand Anse** or nearby **Point Salines**; boat trips will take snorkelers to Moliniere or to Boss Reef off Grand Anse Bay.

Boss Reef

Grenada's largest reef runs from St. George's harbor southwest to Point Salines; the harbor end is heavily silted while the Salines end is largely dead. But the central section offers at least three prime sights with a banquet of colorful reef activity. Watch for rainbow runners, Spanish hog fish, nurse sharks and, at The Hole, elusive green morays.

Kick Em Jenny

Named after the sporadically active volcano which (at this writing) is still about 500 feet below sea level, this location encompasses several sights featuring excellent visibility in the area surrounding Isle de Ronde near Carriacou. In addition to excellent coral and marine life, the site includes an underwater cave that leads to an open-air passage.

Moliniere Point

Several dives, ranging from beginner to advanced are possible on this formation just north of St. George's. The reef averages 25 to 35 feet with sand channels slicing through the coral running perpendicular to the coast; small tropicals swarm the reef, including spotted drums as well as yellow-headed and mottled jaw fish. A wall drops down to 80 feet and leads to lobster and spotted morays, and to the *Buccaneer*, a 42-foot two-masted sloop sitting on its side, 75 feet down. A second wreck, a cabin cruiser, the *Don Juan*, went down nearby in 1995.

Sister Rocks

Just off Carriacou's Point Cistern, this intermediate-to-advanced dive off a pair of rock outcrops visits a nice selection of hard and soft coral formations frequented by turtles, barracudas, nurse sharks and, if you're lucky, sting rays. The wall here drops from 35 to 130 feet.

Wreck of the *Bianca C*

A mammoth cruise ship that caught fire after a boiler exploded in 1961, the 584-foot *Bianca C* is justly termed "The Titanic of the Caribbean." Fortunately, only two crew members died in the accident; Grenadans assisted in the evacuation of the ship and welcomed its passengers into their homes. Although the explosion occurred while the ship was anchored at St. Georges, the *Bianca C* was towed out of the harbor as a safety precaution and began to sink just off Point Saline. Dive boats tie-off on the ship's now-submerged swimming pool; after the quick sink from the turbulent surface, watch for giant turtles, spotted eagle rays and a huge grouper that calls one of the smokestacks home. Although it is split in two, most of *Bianca's* crumbling innards are difficult to navigate due to whiteouts, but the exterior, covered in huge black coral trees, will keep you sufficiently awed. Listing sharply and situated eerily on a bank 165 feet down in open seas, this wreck is a serious destination for advanced divers only; all local shops will verify your abilities on a checkout dive before taking you down.

Dive Shops

Dive Grenada

Grand Anse; ☎ *(800) 329-8388, (809) 444-1092.*

Grenada's first dive shop opened in 1989. Believes scuba should be a low-impact sport and attempts to locate drift dives whenever possible. PADI courses (up to Assistant Instructor). Two-tank dive, $50.

Grand Anse Aquatics

Grand Anse; ☎ *(809) 444-1046.*

New retail store makes this a PADI five-star facility. Single-tank dives, $40. Weekly runs up to Isle de Ronde; two dives, $90, including lunch.

Scuba World

Grand Anse; ☎ *(809) 444-4371.*

Friendly staff and new equipment as of 1995; PADI courses up through Divemaster. Separate location at the Rex Grenadian on Point Salines. Two-tank dive, $65, or an all day trip (with lunch) to north coast areas, $110. Snorkeling trips.

Silver Beach Diving

Carriacou; ☎ *(809) 443-7337.*

An independent operator, the only one based on Carriacou. PADI facility with courses to Assistant Instructor on request. Single tank dive, $40. Also offers half-day snorkel trips to Sandy Island and Anse La Roche, $23.

On Foot

For a bantam destination, the rumpled topography of Grenada provide
splendid hiking opportunities, making the island one of the best walking
destinations in the Eastern Caribbean. As you walk through Grenada's gen
tle range of mountains amid wafts of the local nutmeg and cloves, the term
"spice island" will float through your senses. Many fruits and vegetables ar
grown here and contribute to this lovely island's interior appeal. Thoug
some may tell you they are three separate hikes, the truly ambitious can com
bine **Mount Qua Qua**, **Fedon's Camp** and **Concord Falls**, which are relativel
close to each other, for a vivid all-day trek. Less grandiose ambitions can b
sated in the coves and hills surrounding **La Sagesse Nature Center**; the pleas
ant owners will eagerly point you toward several lovely trails, particularly i
you stay for lunch. Several of the island's longer hikes invite a guide's fami
iarity for uncomplicated navigation. But it's worth noting that escorts ar
available for anything harder than getting out of your car, which means yo
are in the awkward position of evaluating your physical stamina and Carib
bean route-finding abilities—always carry the *Ordnance Survey* map—vs. th
leadership and amiable banter of a knowledgable tour guide. If in doub
spring for the local help; but it helps knowing that, although tracks divide
cross and converge with maddening frequency, it's hard to get lost for lon
on this cozy island.

Concord Falls

Although the lower falls are approached by road, few visitors take the obvious trai
to the second drop, which is reached after about 30 minutes of stream fordings. The
plunge is only about 40 feet, but this is an idyllic location for a swimming hole and
it provides a quick respite from touring. Guides will make themselves well known
but really aren't necessary if you are reasonably sure-footed.

Fedon's Camp

This is the outpost used by rebel Julian Fedon, a French plantation owner who
staged an insurrection against the British in 1795, killing the island's governor and
47 others. The hike starts at the Concord Falls trailhead, and continues past the sec
ond falls along a steep valley which gradually levels as it enters the forest reserve
This section can be hard to follow in places, but you'll eventually arrive at a shallow
cave which served as Fedon's hideout and is now a Historical Landmark. Allow six
to-eight hours for the roundtrip from Concord to Fedon and back. Or, continue or
to nearby Mount Qua Qua and descend to Grand Etang; beginning the one-way

trek from Grand Etang allows you to start at a higher elevation and descend to Concord Falls.

Grand Etang Circuit

Grenada's volcanic crater lake is photographed from the nearby road by many, but this relatively easy path around the water is worthy for its eclectic mix of wildlife. A small pond before you reach the lake is home to freshwater lobster and crayfish; mona monkeys (imported from Africa by slave traders) hover in the stands of bamboo, cattle egrets and blue herons troll the etang, while orchids dangle from many of the trees. A lovely hour-and-a-half walk.

Morne La Baye Trail

A short interpretive trail ascends the small hill that lies just behind the visitor center overlooking Grand Etang. Marouba trees tower above, orange heliconias color the path and the endemic grand etang fern blankets the ground. The self-guided walk takes about 20 minutes.

Mount St. Catherine

Grenada's highest point (2757 feet) is a moderately difficult hike with a number of routing possibilities. The easiest takes off from the road which dead-ends at the tiny town of Mount Hope, four miles northwest of Grenville. From the end of the road, you are less than one steep mile from the summit, although you'll need to ask specific directions from one of the townspeople. Another, longer trail can be attempted from the other side, from the village of Mount Nelson (above Victoria); this route is probably more interesting, but even less maintained, and requires a solid half-day. If in doubt, hire a guide, the standard method of ascent.

Mount Sinai

This 2306-foot peak is approached not from the Grand Etang area (which the summit overlooks), but from the tiny village of Petit Etang nestled amid banana fields; the trailhead is reached by a side-road which climbs into the hills from the town of Providence. The path is faint and ill-maintained, but heads generally northwest toward the top where it steepens, then yields lovely views of the south coast. Allow two hours round-trip.

Mount Qua Qua

From Grand Etang, the marked trail to the summit of 2373-foot Mount Qua Qua ascends a slippery, sometimes narrow ridge of red clay. As you rise above the lake, the foliage evolves into elfin woodland (smaller trees sculpted by the wind), the angle increasing as you approach the top. The summit offers excellent views on clear days, but hikers should be prepared for rain, which can top 150 inches annually. Allow one-and-a-half hours to the top, slightly less for the return.

The Seven Sisters

Perhaps Grenada's nicest adventure, and the trek for which guides are most regularly hired, the Seven Sisters is a series of waterfalls that tumble into plush pools a mile northeast of Grand Etang. The hike can be done several ways, but ideally your guide should take you to the top of the falls (if you're up for it) and on to the Park Center above Grand Etang. Allow a half-day and bring a swimsuit.

Trekking Tours

Henry's Safari Tours

St. George's; ☎ *(809) 444-5313.*

The very pleasant Denis Henry manages a group of guides who handle the island's hikes as well as driving tours. The trek to the Seven Sisters is $70 for a solo traveler, $45 each for a pair.

FIELDING'S CHOICE:

Prepare yourself first for dodging chickens, bikes and pedestrians, but rent a car and go north along the coastline, turning inward at Halifax Harbour toward the central mountain range, leading to Grand Etang Lake, a 36-acre volcanic crater whose glassy waters shimmer in the shadow of 2373-foot Mount Qua Qua. Add to that a boisterous hike around the lake or a heroic trek along a five-hour trail from Concord Falls deep in the central mountains, where the Concord River plummets down a series of rocky ravines.

By Pedal

Pick up a copy of the detailed *Ordnance Survey* map and you'll discover an intricate maze of roads and paths covering the entire island. Those looking for a casual spin should stick to the gentle hills south of St. George's, but stay alert; traffic is at its thickest in this area. Also worthy of caution is the beautiful but steep, twisting road between St. George's and Grenville; minibus drivers assault this as though they can drive blindfolded. Circling the island by bicycle is a serious, but memorable workout: from St. George's, take the main coastal road north to Gouyave and turn inland at Duquesne Bay, which leads to Sauteur. Then head south through sugarcane fields to Grenville where you'll veer west and ascend the lush road to Grand Etang, followed by a sharp drop back to St. George's (heading the other direction through Grand Etang is well-nigh impossible on a bike without dismounting at several points). The entire route will take a strong rider about six hours, but allow the whole day to incorporate sightseeing. If off-roading is your pleasure, there are ample possibilities leading down from Grand Etang to the eastern shores, but be sure to carry a patch kit for the inevitable bramble bushes.

Bike Rental Shops

Ride Grenada

Grand Anse (inside Green Grocer next to banks); ☎ *(809) 444-1157.*
Raleigh 15- and 18-speeds, $10 per day. With just 12 bikes on hand, amiable Dexter Yawching runs a strictly low-key operation.

What Else to See

Grenada is full of natural wonders, but a stroll through the narrow streets and cobbled alleys of **St. George's**, the capital, should be a priority on your itinerary. There are centuries-old churches to explore and the **National Museum**, once a French garrison, where an antique rum still, wildlife specimens and even the personal effects of Josephine Bonaparte—including the marble tub she used as a child—are kept. The ramparts of Fort George tower over the Carenage and look out to sea—today it is the police headquarters. On Richmond Hill, marvel at the 18th-century military construction of Fort Frederick and drink in the view of the capital with a rum punch at the nearby Hotel Balisier. The best day to visit St. George's Market Square is on Saturday, when the plaza bustles with the brightest aromas and colors of the Caribbean. For a few dollars you can come home laden with baskets of cocoa balls (to make coca tea), sorrel, tannia, yams, limes, mangoes and luscious papayas. A tour of the **Doug Laldston Estate** near Gouyave will give you a glimpse into the secrets of nutmeg cultivation. Afterward, a dollar will get you into the Nutmeg Processing Station, where nuts and mace are separated and graded by hand, then stored in huge burlap bags.

Historical Sites

Fort George ★★★

Church Street, St. George's.
Built by the French in 1705 on a promontory to guard the entrance to the harbor, this old fort has lots of small rooms and four-inch-thick walls.

Museums and Exhibits

Grenada National Museum ★★★

Monckton Street, St. George's, ☎ *(809) 440-3725.*
Hours open: 9 a.m.–4:30 p.m.
Set in the foundations of an old French army barracks and prison dating back to 1704, this small museum has some interesting exhibits on the island's natural and historical past. Don't miss Josephine Bonaparte's marble bathtub!

Parks and Gardens

Annandale Falls ★★★★★

Main Interior Road, St. George's, ☎ *(809) 440-2452.*
Hours open: 8 a.m.–4 p.m.

Bring a picnic and your swimsuit (changing rooms are available) to this pretty spot, where water cascades down some 50 feet into a pool perfect for dips. There's a good gift shop on site with handicrafts and species native to the island.

Grand Etang National Park ★★★★★

Main Interior Road, St. George's, ☎ *(809) 442-7425.*
Hours open: 8:30 a.m.–4 p.m.

This rainforest and bird sanctuary, located in the island's interior between St. George's and Grenville, has lots of gorgeous, unspoiled scenery. Several trails wind throughout for easy to difficult treks. Don't miss Grand Etang Lake, whose 13 acres of cobalt blue waters are nestled in the crater of an extinct volcano.

Tours

Nutmeg Processing Plant ★★

Gouyave.

You'll never again take this little spice for granted after a half-hour tour of the processing plant. Nutmeg is Grenada's largest export and smells sweet, too.

FIELDING'S CHOICE:

The Tower was a fabulous plantation house built in 1917 by a Grenadian lawyer to please his bride. Today, the owners, Paul Slinger and his wife, Victoria, open their historic home to visitors for a $10 tour every Thursday. The Tower is full of antiques, including Hogarth prints collected by Paul's grandfather (who commanded the West Indian regiment in World War I). Situated on nine acres of land, the property is a veritable plantation of tropical fruits, samples of which are served during your tour along with a fruit punch.

Sports

Sailing is the premier sport on Grenada, particularly through the islands of the Grenadines, where the conditions are said to be some of the best in the world. Seagoing travelers always come back with great tales of derring-do, hidden coves and an occasional disaster. St. George has excellent equipment for rent, including Hobie Cats, Sailfish and Sunfish for short excursions. Numerous charter operations can arrange programs for any length or vessel (rates are about 20 percent lower in off-season). Sometimes the easiest thing is to hop a fishing boat to the nearby Hog Island or Calivigny. The Carriacou's Regatta, held in the first weekend of August, attracts classic seamen from all over the world who thrive on the ferocious competition.

Sportfishing is excellent November -May; several operators offer four-hour or longer charters. Several hotels have tennis courts, including Calabash, Coral Cove, Secret Harbor, Spice Island Inn and the Grenada Renaissance.

Grenada Golf Club

Frand Anse, St. George's, ☎ *(809) 444-4128.*
Not the greatest golf in the world, but since it's the only one on the island, it'll do. The nine-hole course has some nice views. Greens fees are a reasonable $20.

Watersports

Various locations, St. George's.
Your hotel will probably offer watersports for free or a nominal fee, or checkout one of these outfits. Scuba diving and snorkeling: **Grenada Aquatics** *(*☎ *444-4129)*, and **Dive Grenada** *(*☎ *444-4371).* Boating: **Seabreeze Yacht Charters** *(*☎ *444-4924)*, and **The Moorings** *(*☎ *444-4548).* Cruises: **Best of Grenada** *(*☎ *440-2198).* Deep-sea fishing: **Dive Grenada** *(*☎ *444-4371)*, and the **Best of Grenada** *(*☎ *440-2198).* A major fishing tournament is held each January. On Carriacou, contact **Dive Paradise** at the Silver Beach Resort *(*☎ *443-7337)* for watersports.

FIELDING"S CHOICE:

Every other Saturday a bunch of Grenadians known as the Hash House Harriers get together, split into teams, and set off on chases through glorious countryside on trails that always end up at Rudolf's, a bar next to the Carenage in St. George's. It's a great way to meet and mingle with those Grenadians not in good enough shape for the triathlon.

Where to Stay

	Fielding's Highest Rated Hotels in Grenada	
★★★★★	Calabash Hotel	$170–$495
★★★★★	La Source	$250–$590
★★★★★	Spice Island Inn	$270–$475
★★★★	Rex Grenadian	$115–$360
★★★★	Secret Harbour Hotel	$100–$225
★★★	Blue Horizons Cottages	$100–$165
★★★	Coyaba Beach Resort	$75–$165
★★★	Grenada Renaissance Hotel	$120–$170
★★★	Silver Beach Resort	$80–$95
★★★	Twelve Degrees North	$130–$285

	Fielding's Most Romantic Hotels in Grenada	
★	La Sagesse Nature Center	$40–$90
★★★★	Secret Harbour Hotel	$100–$225
★★★★★	Spice Island Inn	$270–$475

	Fielding's Budget Hotels in Grenada	
★	Villamar Holiday Resort	$42–$62
★	South Winds Holiday	$40–$80
★	La Sagesse Nature Center	$40–$90
★★	No Problem Apartments	$55–$85
★	Maffiken Apartments	$60–$85

More than 85 percent of Grenada's hotels are owned by Grenadians; their stake in tourism accounts for the pride they show in personal touches that make their guests feel very special. A doubling of hotels is expected in 1996, but a happy medium in new construction is being pursued to appease ecologists. Many of the island's finest resorts are located on the idyllic strip of sand called **Grand Anse Beach**; these are not high-rise hotels but small intimate inns and guest houses. (By law no hotel in Grenada can be higher than a palm tree or more than three stories tall.) Other options on Grenada include apartments, yachts or the proverbial cottage.

Hotels and Resorts

Not only new construction but renovations and additions have kept the hotel trade busy in the last year. At the **Calabash Hotel** six of the eight existing suites have been replaced by new units, complete with whirlpools, lounge areas and minibars, as well as a new fitness center, new boutique, and beach kitchen for hot lunches. At **Magonay Run**, a multi-million-dollar restaurant, bar and 36 superior rooms with gardens was to have been completed by the end of 1995. **Spice Island Inn**, the romantic 36-room property on Grand Anse, has totally renovated eight whirlpool beach suites and extended both bathrooms and bedrooms. The newest addition is **La Source**, an all-inclusive 100-room resort with a spa and nine-hole golf course, and the **Rex Grenadian**, the island's largest hotel on a three-acre lake; both hotels are situated on expansive white sand beaches on the southwest coast.

Calabash Hotel   **$170–$495**   ★ ★ ★ ★ ★

L'Anse aux Epines, St. George's, ☎ *(800) 528-5835, (809) 444-4334, FAX (809) 444-5050.*

Single: $170–$465. Double: $205–$495.

Set among coconut groves and gardens on an eight-acre estate, all accommodations are suites housed in stone and wood cottages at this very fine resort. Some have private pools, others kitchens, others Jacuzzis and all are bright and cheery. There are three bars and a restaurant, watersports and tennis, frequent live entertainment and wonderful, attentive service. A great choice.

Coyaba Beach Resort   **$75–$165**   ★ ★ ★

Grand Anse, St. George's, ☎ *(809) 444-4129, FAX (809) 444-4808.*
Single: $75–$115. Double: $95–$165.

Set on the site of an ancient Arawak Indian village, this family-run resort puts guests up in tropically decorated rooms with bright island artwork. The pool has a swim-up bar, perfect for cooling off after a set or two on the tennis court. The restaurant and cafe are open-air. The beach is a short stroll from the rooms.

Flamboyant Hotel   **$70–$220**   ★ ★

Grand Anse Beach, St. George's, ☎ *(800) 223-9815, (809) 444-4247, FAX (809) 444-1234.*
Single: $70–$215. Double: $85–$220.

Set on a hillside that slopes gently to the beach, this complex offers standard guest rooms and 23 suites with kitchenettes, most with sweeping views. The good location makes this a relative bargain, and the friendly staff keeps guests happy. There's a restaurant, pool and free snorkel equipment.

Grenada Renaissance Hotel   **$120–$170**   ★★★

Grande Anse Beach, St. George's, ☎ (800) 228-9898, (809) 444-4371, FAX (809) 444-4800.

Single: $120–$170. Double: $120–$170.

This handsome complex has a nice location—right on the beach and across from a good shopping complex—but lacks island flavor. Accommodations are comfortable but on the small side, and the motel-like furnishings are generic. On the plus side, the hotel offers a complete range of amenities, from watersports to tennis courts to yacht charters, and attracts families with its supervised children's programs (on holidays). A lively night scene, too.

Hibiscus Hotel   **$60–$125**   ★

Grand Anse, St. George's, ☎ (809) 444-4233, FAX (809) 444-2873.

Single: $60–$125. Double: $80–$125.

This small hotel is 300 yards from Grand Anse Beach. Accommodations are in air-conditioned duplex cottages with patios. There's a restaurant and pool on site.

Horse Shoe Beach Hotel   **$70–$155**   ★★

L'Anne Aux Epines, St. George's, ☎ (809) 444-4244, FAX (809) 444-4844.

Single: $70–$130. Double: $80–$155.

Set on a hillside overlooking the bay, this hotel puts up guests in cottages with air conditioning, period furnishings and patios; some also have four-poster beds. Each two units share a kitchen. The six suites in the main building are the best choice. Nicely landscaped grounds hold a pool and beach, with watersports nearby.

La Source   **$250–$590**   ★★★★★

Pink Gin Beach, St. George's, ☎ (800) 544-2883, (809) 444-2556, FAX (809) 444-2561.

Single: $250–$345. Double: $420–$590.

Opened in late 1993, this all-inclusive resort is situated on two beaches on Grenada's southwest tip. The price is steep, but includes all meals, drinks, watersports and—best of all—pampering treatments in the excellent spa. Accommodations are simply gorgeous, with Persian rugs, mahogany furniture, four-poster beds and Asian artwork. When you're not being spoiled in the spa, you can play tennis or nine holes of golf, swim in the two-level pool or enjoy a good array of watersports. Simply fabulous.

Rex Grenadian   **$115–$360**   ★★★★

Magazine Beach, St. George's, ☎ (800) 255-5859, (809) 444-3333, FAX (809) 444-1111.

Single: $115–$360. Double: $115–$360.

This large property offers all the bells and whistles resort lovers expect. Set on 12 acres that open onto two beaches, the hotel houses guests in nicely done standard rooms; you'll pay a bit extra for air conditioning and a bigger bathroom. A couple of neat restaurants give guests dining choices, and the typical watersports, fitness center and tennis prevail. There's even a man-made lake stretching over two acres. Nice, but expect a lot of business groups.

Secret Harbour Hotel   **$100–$225**   ★★★★

L'Anse aux Epines, St. George's, ☎ (800) 334-2435, (809) 444-4548, FAX (813) 530-9747.

Single: $100–$213. Double: $100–$225.

Overlooking Mount Hartman Bay on Grenada's southernmost tip, this elegant property consists of Mediterranean-style villas in which each unit is a suite. They're nicely decorated with four-poster beds, local art, trouser presses, large balconies and baths with Roman tubs. The grounds are lovely and the views breathtaking. The small beach offers all the usual watersports. Special packages allow guests to spend a few nights aboard one of their many yachts. Nice!

Siesta Hotel   **$55–$140**   ★★

Grand Anse, St. George's, ☎ (809) 444-4645, FAX (809) 444-4647.

Single: $55–$110. Double: $60–$140.

Located slightly inland from the beach, this small hotel has air-conditioned rooms with comfortable furnishings; some have kitchens. There's a restaurant and pool, but not much else in the way of extras.

Spice Island Inn   **$270–$475**   ★★★★★

Grand Anse Beach, St. George's, ☎ (809) 444-4258, FAX (809) 444-4807.

Single: $270–$425. Double: $320–$475.

Set on eight tropical acres on a gorgeous stretch of Grand Anse Beach, all accom-modations at this very fine resort are in suites. Some have whirlpools (and even private dip pools), and all are simply but comfortably furnished with huge, pampering bathrooms. The grounds are nicely done with lots of flowers, and there's a gym and tennis court for the active set. Others are happy just lounging on the picturesque beach. Great food and service, too. Simply charming.

Apartments and Condominiums

Grenadians are leaders in the Caribbean self-catering business. Don't be shy about bringing food from home, though fresh tropical fruits and vegetables can be easily bought at the markets. The best views are to be found at the **Cinnamon Hill**, which looks out onto the bay at Grand Anse Beach, but **Twelve Degrees North** also has excellent sea views. At Mahogany Run, Maffiken Apartments, Gem Holiday Beach resort, South Winds and Villamar, you will need to rent a car.

Blue Horizons Cottages   **$100–$165**   ★★★

Grand Anse, St. George's, ☎ (809) 444-4592, FAX (809) 444-2815.

Single: $100–$155. Double: $110–$165.

Set on a terraced hillside some 300 yards from Grand Anse Beach, accommodations are in one-bedroom cottages and duplex suites, each air-conditioned and sporting kitchens. There's a restaurant and two bars on hand, as well as a pool and Jacuzzi. Watersports take place at nearby sister property, the Spice Island Inn. Good value.

Cinnamon Hill Hotel   **$85–$153**   ★★

Grand Anse Beach, St. George's, ☎ (809) 444-4301, FAX (809) 444-2874.

Single: $85–$130. Double: $114–$153.

This Spanish-style hotel village consists of several buildings scattered over a hillside overlooking Grand Anse Beach; it's steep going so those with mobility problems should look elsewhere. Accommodations are in one- and two-bedroom apartments with kitchens and balconies. There's a restaurant and pool on-site, with all water-sports available on the public beach.

Coral Cove Cottages $65–$120 ★

Coral Cove Beach, ☎ (809) 444-4422, FAX (809) 444-4718.
Single: $65–$120. Double: $65–$120.
Situated on a peaceful cove with nice views six miles from St. George's, this complex offers Spanish-style apartments and cottages with kitchenettes and terraces. There's a tennis court and small pool, but no dining facilities.

Gem Holiday Beach Resort $55–$140 ★

Morne Rouge Bay, ☎ (800) 223-9815, (809) 444-1189.
Single: $55–$120. Double: $65–$140.
Located on the beach some six miles from St. George's, this apartment hotel houses guests in one- and two-bedroom units that are air-conditioned and have full kitchens. There's a restaurant and bar if you'd rather leave the cooking to someone else, and a lively disco. You'll probably want a rental car to get around.

Holiday Haven $60–$145 ★

L'Anse aux Epines, St. George's, ☎ (809) 440-2606.
Single: $60–$145. Double: $65–$145.
This basic complex offers one- to three-bedroom apartments with full kitchens and verandas; most have two bathrooms. Maids keep everything looking spiffy. Nothing extra in the way of facilities, so you'll have to venture out. Three Cottages.

La Sagesse Nature Center $40–$90 ★

St. David's, ☎ (809) 444-6458, FAX (809) 444-6458.
Single: $40–$75. Double: $65–$90.
Located in a remote setting 10 miles from the airport, this small, family-run operation has six apartments in a guesthouse with full kitchens and ceiling fans to keep things cool. The surrounding grounds are really pretty, with lots of hiking and bird-watching opportunities. Really appealing for nature lovers.

Maffiken Apartments $60–$85 ★

Grand Anse, St. George's, ☎ (809) 444-4255, FAX (809) 444-2832.
Single: $60–$70. Double: $70–$85.
Set on a hillside overlooking Grand Anse Beach a short stroll away, this small stucco hotel houses one- and two-bedroom apartments with air conditioning, kitchenettes and maid service. No recreational facilities, but restaurants and shopping are nearby.

No Problem Apartments $55–$85 ★★

True Blue, St. George's, ☎ (809) 444-4634, FAX (809) 444-2803.
Single: $55–$75. Double: $65–$85.
Located near the airport on the outskirts of town, this Mediterranean-style complex has air-conditioned suites with full kitchens. A free shuttle takes you to town and Grand Anse Beach, so you won't need a rental car as with most other apartment hotels. There's a restaurant and pool and a fleet of bicycles for the asking. Decent.

South Winds Holiday $40–$80 ★

Grand Anse, St. George's, ☎ (809) 444-4310, FAX (800) 233-9815.

Single: $40–$80. Double: $40–$80.
Grand Anse Beach is about 500 yards from this complex of cottages and apartments, all with kitchens and most with air conditioning. Popular with families, there's maid service, but little else in the way of extras. Good rates for the location, though.

True Blue Inn $65–$110   ★★

St. George's, ☎ (800) 742-4276, (809) 444-2000, FAX (809) 444-1247.
Single: $65–$95. Double: $75–$110.
Accommodations at this south coast property are in one-bedroom apartments and two-bedroom cottages, all with air conditioning and full kitchens. There's maid service, a sailing school for both adults and children, a pool and bicycles for tooling about. A nice, friendly atmosphere.

Twelve Degrees North $130–$285   ★★★

St. George's, ☎ (800) 322-1753, (809) 444-4580.
Single: $130–$285. Double: $130–$285.
Located on the southeast coast and facing the sea, this small property has one- and two-bedroom apartments with kitchens and—what a plus!— a housekeeper who cooks, cleans and even does laundry. No air conditioning, but ceiling fans do the job nicely. The grounds include a lot for an apartment complex, with a pool, tennis court, private beach and watersports. No kids under 12.

Villamar Holiday Resort $42–$62   ★

L'anse aux Epines, St. George's, ☎ (809) 444-1614, FAX (809) 444-1341.
Single: $42–$52. Double: $52–$62.
Located in a remote spot two minutes from Grand Anse Beach, this complex has one- and two-bedroom suites with air conditioning, kitchens and private balconies. There's a bar, restaurant and pool, and they'll help arrange watersports and golf.

Wave Crest Holiday Apts. $75–$95   ★

Grand Anse, St. George's, ☎ (809) 444-4116.
Single: $75–$95. Double: $75–$95.
Grand Anse Beach is a five-minute walk from this small property, where you can choose from standard guest rooms and one- and two-bedroom apartments with air conditioning, verandas and kitchens. There's a bar, but not much else.

Inns

Grenada's inns are run and owned by devoted families who make their unique personalities known in every detail. Peace and quiet relaxation is the business at **Morne Fendue**, the private home of a longtime resident still full of her family antiques. **Hibiscus Hotel** gives the feeling of a tiny village with its five small cottages situated near a common pool. **True Blue Inn** is commendable for its modern kitchen facilities in the one-bedroom apartments and cottages, and the attractive seaside restaurant.

Low Cost Lodging

To save lots of money on Grenada, you will either have to share a bathroom, stuff a lot of people into an apartment or cottage, or go in off-season. You might also ask the tourist board if anyone rents rooms in private homes.

Where to Eat

Fielding's Highest Rated Restaurants in Grenada

★★★★★	La Belle Creole	$22–$30
★★★★★	Morne Fendue	$17–$17
★★★★	Canbouley	$10–$30
★★★★	Coconut's Beach	$6–$26
★★★★	Nutmeg, The	$5–$20
★★★	La Source	$45

Fielding's Special Restaurants in Grenada

★★★★★	La Belle Creole	$22–$30
★★★★★	Morne Fendue	$17–$17
★★★★	Canbouley	$10–$30
★★★★	Coconut's Beach	$6–$26
★★	Mamma's	$19–$19

Fielding's Budget Restaurants in Grenada

★	La Sagesse	$6–$12
★	Rudolf's	$8–$15
★★★★	Nutmeg, The	$5–$20
★	Portofino	$6–$22
★★★★	Coconut's Beach	$6–$26

Few West Indians have mastered the art of adapting local fruits, vegetables, seafood and spices to Continental-style recipes as well as Grenadians have. The restaurant scene in Grenada, which traditionally centered around the major hotels, now includes newcomers that have added not only spice but variety to the island cuisine. The national dish, "oil down," concocted with readfruit and salt pork wrapped in dasheen leaves and steamed in coconut milk, is delicious, but also don't miss tasting callaloo soup (made with the spinachlike leaves of the dasheen), christophine au gratni, pepperpot stew, and nutmeg ice cream (nutmeg is the main spice import of Grenada). All dining options are available, however, whether you choose to dine on possum and armadillo at the tin-roofed **Mama's** or eat international cuisine in the elegant **Canboulay**, overlooking the Grand Anse beach. American medical students from St. George's Medical School hang at **Red Crab**, a legendary fish-and-chips, beer-belly pub just outside the gates of the Calabash Hotel. Don't miss sampling a proper Grenadian rum punch, or a local candy called nutmeg cheese.

Bird's Nest   **$$$**   ★

Grand Anse Beach, Grand Anse, ☎ *(809) 444-4264.*
Chinese cuisine.
Lunch: 10:30 a.m.–2 p.m., entrees $11–$24.
Dinner: 2–11 p.m., entrees $11–$24.
A no-surprises, pleasant Chinese restaurant that also serves good sandwiches for lunch, Bird's Nest roosts near the airport and several hotels in Grand Anse. Specialties include sweet and sour chicken or fish, served with tasty fried rice. The restaurant is open on Sunday for dinner only, from 6 p.m. to 11 p.m.

Canbouley   **$$$**   ★★★★

Morne Rouge, ☎ *(809) 444-4401.*
International cuisine.
Lunch: 11:30 a.m.–2:30 p.m., entrees $10–$20.
Dinner: 6:30–10 p.m, entrees $20–$30.

For a grand night out in exotic surroundings, most visitors choose this festive restaurant with a view of the lights of the capital across the bay. The decor and the tropical-Asian cuisine reflect the heritage of Trinidad-born owners Erik and Gina-lee Johnson, where spices, heady scents and Carnival are a way of life. The Johnsons really shine with shrimp prepared in interesting ways, including an Indonesian peanut and fruit satay. Desserts are memorable, especially a chocolate-orange mousse and a custard-filled coconut cake called "Oh Goood!"

Coconut's Beach   **$$$**   ★★★★

Grand Anse Beach, ☎ *(809) 444-4644.*
French cuisine. Specialties: Lobster, conch.
Lunch: 10 a.m.–6 p.m., entrees $6–$13.
Dinner: 7–10 p.m., entrees $13–$26.
As the name implies, guests can eat right on the beach in high style under palm-frond shelters, or in the dining room of a spiffy, native house with an open kitchen where the chefs deftly saute the catch of the day in gleaming cookware. Lobster with various butter sauces or lambi (conch) curry are mouth-watering choices, as are ribs, chicken or steak. A good lunch menu of crepes, salads or sandwiches offers most dishes for under $10.

Cot Bam   **$$$**   ★

Grand Anse Beach, Grand Anse, ☎ (809) 444-2050.
American cuisine.
Lunch: 9 a.m.–2 p.m., entrees $6–$30.
Dinner: 2–11 p.m., entrees $6–$30.

Savory, quick meals and a cold brew draw guests to this convivial bar and grill after a hard day at the beach. Since it's within strolling distance of all hotels on Grand Anse, why settle for room service? Snacks and plate meals include West Indian rotis, salads, shrimp and chips, etc.

Delicious Landing   **$$$**   ★

The Carenage,
Seafood cuisine.
Lunch: 10:30 a.m.–2 p.m., entrees $17–$24.
Dinner: 6:30–11:30 p.m., entrees $17–$24.

Although many eating establishments on this island boast enviable views, Delicious Landing may have the best one of all, situated right on the water's edge near St. George's Harbor. Decently prepared seafood and fish is featured, but the sea vistas, breezes and excellent tropical drinks are the main reason to linger here.

La Belle Creole   **$$$**   ★★★★★

Grand Anse Beach, Grand Anse, ☎ (809) 444-4316.
Seafood cuisine. Specialties: Callaloo quiche.
Lunch: 12:30–2:30 p.m., entrees $22–$28.
Dinner: 7–9 p.m., entrees $25–$30.

Some of the most creative West Indian food is served in this airy terrace restaurant on the grounds of the Blue Horizons Cottages. For many years "Mamma" Audrey Hopkin earned a deserved reputation as the best Creole home chef in town, and now her sons have carried the torch with admirable results. Real men (and women) eat quiche here, which is an unusual combo of callaloo (dasheen leaf) and lobster or shrimp; there's also a veal roulade with crab and a tasty fish mousse. Desserts are equally imaginative—try the unique farine pudding, a custard made from cassava. An ever-changing fixed-price dinner of up to five courses, including dessert, is available nightly for $40. The service is as good as the food, and the atmosphere is perfect for lovers.

La Sagesse   **$$**   ★

Eastern Main Road, St. David, ☎ (809) 444-6458.
American cuisine.
Lunch: 11 a.m.–3:30 p.m., entrees $6–$11.
Dinner: 6:30–9 p.m., entrees $8–$12.

This small restaurant by the sea is part of the La Sagesse Nature Center, formerly the home of a cousin of Queen Elizabeth, now an inn and banana plantation. Fittingly, patrons can get a nice organic vegetarian platter or blended tropical fruit drinks. Other dishes include seafood, sandwiches and burgers. The calm waters here are only eight minutes away from the capital.

La Source   **$$$**   ★★★

Pink Gin Beach, ☎ (809) 444-2556.

Spa cuisine.
Dinner: 7:30–9:30 p.m., prix fixe $45.
Chef Richard Lovett gives new meaning to spa food at this tasty restaurant at the all-inclusive La Source. Thanks to wonderful entrees like vegetable cutlets coated with parmesan cheese and crab-stuffed chicken, you can pig out without an ounce of guilt. There's even a selection of low-fat desserts. Items like braised shank of lamb are also featured for those not watching their waistline. The prix-fixe dinner includes drinks and wine, appetizer, entree and dessert.

Le Karacoli   **$$$**   ★★

Grande-Anse Beach, Grand-Anse, ☎ (590) 28-41-17.
French cuisine.
Dinner: entrees $8–$25.
This bustling beachfront restaurant with an unlikely name (the snail) offers reasonably priced creole dishes (mostly seafood) to locals and the numerous tourists who have discovered the place. Try the crab backs stuffed with shrimp or enjoy a full-course meal with yams and vegetable accompaniments for $14. Service is gracious even during peak times.

Mamma's   **$$$**   ★★

Lagoon Road, ☎ (809) 440-1459.
Latin American cuisine. Specialties: Oil down, exotic small game.
Lunch: 8 a.m.–1:30 p.m., prix fixe $19.
Dinner: 7:30–11 p.m., prix fixe $19.
Yes, eating here is like Sunday dinner at Mamma's—if she was West Indian. But no one has to wait until the end of the week to dine here; Mamma's daughter Cleo and other family members set out a groaning buffet of some 20 local dishes in a friendly, boardinghouse atmosphere every day of the week. The menu features the overwhelming bounty of this verdant isle, including the pear-shaped christophene vegetable stuffed with crab, oil down (breadfruit, meats, callaloo in coconut milk) and curries. The daring can call ahead for a taste of stewed armadillo or iguana.

Morne Fendue   **$$$**   ★★★★★

St. Patrick's, St. Patrick's Parish, ☎ (809) 442-9330.
Latin American cuisine. Specialties: Pepper pot.
Lunch: 12:30–3 p.m., prix fixe $17.
Lunch at this history-laden plantation house may soon be a thing of the past, as owner Betty Mascoll, who has been holding court here for many years, is well into her 80s. So while you can, reserve a place at this traditional West Indian buffet and make friends with the repeat visitors and a faithful staff that prepares a mean pepper pot stew, peas and rice, stewed chicken and island vegetables every afternoon except Sunday. The house itself, built of native stone and decorated with family keepsakes, is a national treasure.

Nutmeg, The   **$$**   ★★★★

The Carenage, ☎ (809) 440-2539.
Seafood cuisine. Specialties: Nutmeg ice cream, conch.
Lunch: 9 a.m.–4 p.m., entrees $5–$15.
Dinner: 4–11 p.m., entrees $9–$20.

This well-known and widely visited restaurant with a view of seagoing vessels in St. George's Harbor features its heady namesake spice in a few specialties, including a nutmeg ice cream and rum punch. Otherwise, for a few dollars, sample local dishes like callaloo soup, lambi curry or fish sandwiches and fries, washed down with the locally brewed Carib beer.

Portofino   **$$**   ★

The Carenage, ☎ *(809) 440-3986.*
Italian cuisine. Specialties: Pizza, Pastas.
Lunch: 11 a.m.–2 p.m., entrees $6–$22.
Dinner: 2–11 p.m., entrees $6–$22.

A comforting plate of pasta plus a harbor view make this upper-level Italian charmer an unbeatable draw. Jazz often plays in the background, putting everyone in a relaxed mood. It's also a good place for the kids, who can choose from a wide variety of their favorite food: pizza. Lobster and veal dishes are also available.

Red Crab, The   **$$$**   ★

L'Anse aux Epines, Grand Anse, ☎ *(809) 444-4424.*
International cuisine. Specialties: Steak.
Lunch: 11 a.m.–2 p.m., entrees $10–$31.
Dinner: 6–11 p.m., entrees $10–$31.

This place should have been named the Plush Cow, because although it serves seafood, old-timers roll in here for the beefsteaks, which are the best on the island. It's located in the posh southern point of the island, in one of Grenada's original tourist developments. Travelers staying in the Grand Anse area can get here by car in five minutes.

Rudolf's   **$$**   ★

The Carenage, ☎ *(809) 440-2241.*
International cuisine. Specialties: Conch.
Lunch: 10 a.m.–2 p.m., entrees $8–$15.
Dinner: 2 p.m.–midnight, entrees $8–$15.

Although it's got a humming bar scene, Rudolf's features a large selection of seafood and steak dishes for those who want to eat here. It also helps that this pub eatery with a harbor view has some of the best prices in town—many dishes are under $10. There are daily specials, usually lobster or conch (highly recommended), as well as sandwiches, salads and fish and chips.

Where to Shop

Shopping isn't duty free on Grenada, but sometimes bargains can get you very close. Special buys to bring home are spice baskets full of native-grown nutmeg, cinnamon, cloves, ground coriander, and others—perfect for Christmas gifts or for spiking the eggnog. At the **Grand Anse Shopping Center** (closest to the hotels) there are even spice vendors who stroll up and down the streets barking their prices (don't be shy about bargaining). Imported china can be found at prices 60 percent cheaper than in the States. You can find other shopping centers on the **Esplanade side of Fort George** and on **Melville Street**, facing the harbor. A good bakery and coffee shop is located in the **Le Marquis Complex**, in the Grand Anse district. Grenada shops open and close with their own schedules, but usually cater hours to cruise ships. Best time to visit the Granby Street food market on Market Square is Saturday.

Carriacou

Carriacou (Carry-a-COO) is a 14 -square mile island lying 40 miles north-east of St. George's, reachable by daily 10-minute flights in very small planes. Although administered by its own staff, the island is under the government of Grenada. The capital is Hillsborough and home to 4600. A postage-stamp paradise untouched by large-scale development, it boasts only 11 inns and guest houses with no more than 20 rooms in the largest. **Gramma's Place** on Main Street, an unofficial meeting place, serves breakfast and snacks. For dinner the **Callaloo Restaurant** is a find. The tiny museum was once a cotton ginnery, and the hillside cemetery is notable as a place where young girls tend their goats. The Scottish influence can be seen in the wooden schoo-ners of local white cedar, while strong African roots vibrate in the drum song and dance unique to the island.

To get there, take a small plane from Port Salines International Airport in Grenada on inter-island flights from St. Vincent or from Barbados. You can also catch a ride on the mailboat or fishing boat or charter a private yacht. Everyone on Carriacou will be clamoring for American dollars, so don't worry about exchanging any.

Where to Stay

Lodging is humble on Carriacou, but not without grace. The best are the cottages at the Caribbee Inn, easy accessible to the shore, and the seaview rooms at Silver Beach. More properties will be opening up in the future, so check with the tourist board.

Hotels and Resorts

Cassada Bay Resort   **$80–$125**   ★ ★

Belmont, Hillsborough, ☎ *(809) 443-7494.*
Single: $80–$95. Double: $95–$125.
Accommodations are in simple cabins with ceiling fans set on a hillside sloping down to the beach. Wonderful views and lots of watersports, plus free ferry rides to neighboring islands. Good bird-watching possibilities.

Silver Beach Resort   **$80–$95**   ★★★

Hillsborough, ☎ *(809) 443-7337, FAX (809) 443-7165.*
Single: $80–$90. Double: $85–$95.

Set on a quiet beach, this family-run hotel has comfortable rooms with ceiling fans; eight cottages offer more room to spread out and full kitchens. Activites include fishing and boating to nearby islands, and all the usual watersports, including good scuba.

Hillsborough

Caribbee Inn   **$95–$135**   ★★

Prospect, Hillsborough, ☎ *(809) 443-8142.*
Single: $95–$135. Double: $95–$135.

All accommodations are in cottages on a hillside, with the beach a short stroll away. Ceiling fans keep things cool. Tasty dinners are served from a prix fixe menu. Great views of neighboring islands at this pleasant spot.

Petite Martinique

A tiny burp in the sea is this third island in Grenada's troika. Fishermer know exactly where it is. To get here, best to hop a ride on a mail boat.

Grenada Directory

ARRIVAL

American Airlines provides daily service to Grenada from its San Juan hub while BWIA offers two direct flights a week from New York and connections from Miami and Toronto via Trinidad and other Caribbean islands. LIAT also serves Grenada several times a day from Barbados, Trinidad and Venezuela.

If you feel comfortable driving on the left and sharing the island's twisting roads with goats and peds, rent a car. A standard car at **Spice Island Retreats** which represent **Avis** ☎ *(809) 440-3926* and **MCR Car Rentals** ☎ *(809) 440-2832* or pager *411-8235* is about $50–60 a day.

Alternately, taxi companies and tour operators excel at showing off Grenada's greatest assets.

BUSINESS HOURS

Stores open weekdays 8:30 a.m.–noon and 2:30–6 p.m. Banks open weekdays 8 a.m.–noon and 2–4 p.m., but during the summer, hours are generally 8 a.m.–3 p.m.

CLIMATE

A dry and rainy season dominate Grenada's climate. April–December is the dry season; May–January the rainy, though showers are brief. Temperatures hover around 80 degrees F. There is blissfully little humidity because of the constant trade winds.

DOCUMENTS

U.S. citizens must present a valid passport or proof of citizenship (birth certificate or voter's registration card), plus a photo ID) and an ongoing or return ticket. All visitors pay a departure tax of $14.

ELECTRICITY

The official current is 230 volts, 50 cycles AC, so you must bring an adapter.

GETTING AROUND

Driving on the left, but risky for the twisting and sometimes poor roads over rough terrain. Instead, do as residents do, and get around on so-called buses, really vans that accommodate up to 14 in very cozy quarters. To make a sightseeing tour, hire a taxi and driver for a day, and head out to the forest reserve, waterfalls, small fishing village and great views.

Grenanda's sister island of Carriacou is now accessible by air after dark with the addition of night landing facilities to the island's Lauriston Airport.

LANGUAGE

Since Grenada was formerly under the British throne, natives speak English with a beautiful lilt. A local dialect mixes French with African slang.

MEDICAL EMERGENCIES

The General Hospital in St. George has limited facilities; you might find better advice at the Grenada University School of medicine ☎ *(809) 444-4271*, a privately owned, U.S.-managed school on Grand Anse Beach.

MONEY

The official currency is the Eastern Caribbean dollar (EC). Make sure you know which dollar is being quoted to you by a shopkeeper or taxi driver. Traveler's checks and major credits are also widely accepted. If you exchange at the local bank, you may end up in endless lines. If you pay big bills in dollars, the exchange rate will probably not be calculated in your favor.

TELEPHONE

Area code is *809*. To save money, head for the Grenada Telecommunications, Ltd., in St. George or use a special phone card on other telephones. Cellular phone service can be purchased through Boatphone ☎ *(800) 567-8336*.

TIME

Atlantic Standard Time, which is one hour later than New York time.

TIPPING

Expect a 10 percent service charge; no need to tip help further. At eateries not connected to your hotel, leave a 10–15 percent tip. Only tip a taxi driver if he carries your bags.

TOURIST INFORMATION

Grenada Board of Tourism is located at The Carenage, St. George's ☎ *(809) 440-2001* and will answer questions, offer brochures and maps. Stop here if you are traveling on to other Grenadine islands. **Grenada Hotel Association Ross Point Inn, Lagoon Road, St. George's** ☎ *(809) 444-1353.* In the United States call ☎ *(800) 927-9554.*

WHEN TO GO

Don't miss Grenada's Carnival in early August, a four-day-to-night blowout of calypso songs and steel bands, and the traditional "jump-up" parades. Carriacou comes alive in early August for its annual Regatta. Also check out the ninth annual International Triathlon, usually held in January. Competitors come from as far away as Australia and Norway and it takes place along and near Grand Anse Beach.

GRENADA HOTELS	RMS	RATES	PHONE	CR. CARDS
Carriacou				
Hillsborough				
★★★ Silver Beach Resort	16	$80–$95	(809) 443-7337	A, DC, MC, V
★★ Caribbee Inn	10	$95–$135	(809) 443-8142	A
★★ Cassada Bay Resort	16	$80–$125	(809) 443-7494	A, MC, V
Grenada				
St. George's				
★★★★★ Calabash Hotel	28	$170–$495	(800) 528-5835	A, MC, V
★★★★★ La Source	100	$250–$590	(800) 544-2883	A, MC, V
★★★★★ Spice Island Inn	56	$270–$475	(809) 444-4258	A, D, DC, MC, V
★★★★ Rex Grenadian	212	$115–$360	(800) 255-5859	A, MC, V
★★★★ Secret Harbour Hotel	20	$100–$225	(809) 334-2435	A, MC, V
★★★ Blue Horizons Cottages	32	$100–$165	(809) 444-4592	A, D, DC, MC, V
★★★ Coyaba Beach Resort	40	$75–$165	(809) 444-4129	A, D, DC, MC, V
★★★ Grenada Renaissance Hotel	186	$120–$170	(800) 228-9898	A, D, DC, MC, V
★★★ Twelve Degrees North	8	$130–$285	(800) 322-1753	None
★★ Cinnamon Hill Hotel	20	$85–$153	(809) 444-4301	A, D, MC, V
★★ Flamboyant Hotel	39	$70–$220	(800) 223-9815	A, D, DC, MC, V

GRENADA HOTELS		RMS	RATES	PHONE	CR. CARDS
★★	Horse Shoe Beach Hotel	22	$70–$155	(809) 444-4244	A, D, MC, V
★★	No Problem Apartments	20	$55–$85	(809) 444-4634	A, D, MC, V
★★	Siesta Hotel	37	$55–$140	(809) 444-4645	A, D, MC, V
★★	True Blue Inn	7	$65–$110	(800) 742-4276	A, D, DC, MC, V
★	Coral Cove Cottages	11	$65–$120	(809) 444-4422	D, MC, V
★	Gem Holiday Beach Resort	23	$55–$140	(800) 223-9815	A, D, DC, MC, V
★	Hibiscus Hotel	10	$60–$125	(809) 444-4233	A, D, MC, V
★	Holiday Haven	12	$60–$145	(809) 440-2606	
★	La Sagesse Nature Center	6	$40–$90	(809) 444-6458	A, MC, V
★	Maffiken Apartments	12	$60–$85	(809) 444-4255	A, MC, V
★	South Winds Holiday	19	$40–$80	(809) 444-4310	A, D, DC, MC, V
★	Villamar Holiday Resort	20	$42–$62	(809) 444-1614	A, MC, V
★	Wave Crest Holiday Apts.	20	$75–$95	(809) 444-4116	A, D, MC, V

GRENADA RESTAURANTS	PHONE	ENTREE	CR. CARDS

Grenada

St. George's

American			
★ Cot Bam	(809) 444-2050	$6–$30	A, D, MC, V
★ La Sagesse	(809) 444-6458	$6–$12	A, MC, V
Chinese			
★ Bird's Nest	(809) 444-4264	$11–$24	A, D, MC, V
French			
★★★★ Coconut's Beach	(809) 444-4644	$6–$26	MC, V
★★ Le Karacoli	(809) 444-4117	$8–$25••	MC, V
International			
★★★★ Canbouley	(809) 444-4401	$10–$36	A, MC, V
★ Red Crab, The	(809) 444-4424	$10–$31	A, D, MC, V
★ Rudolf's	(809) 440-2241	$8–$15	MC, V
Italian			
★ Portofino	(809) 440-3986	$6–$22	A, MC, V

GRENADA RESTAURANTS	PHONE	ENTREE	CR. CARDS
Latin American			
★★★★★ **Morne Fendue**	(809) 442-9330	$17–$17•	None
★★ **Mamma's**	(809) 440-1459	$19–$19	None
Seafood			
★★★★★ **La Belle Creole**	(809) 444-4316	$22–$30	A, D, DC, MC, V
★★★★ **Nutmeg, The**	(809) 440-2539	$5–$20	A, D, MC, V
★ **Delicious Landing**		$17–$24	None

Note: • Lunch Only

•• Dinner Only

GUADELOUPE

Guadeloupe's Ste.-Anne offers white sand beaches and crystal clear water.

Guadeloupe is an island with split personalities. Beaches wash up against volcanoes, sugarcane sprouts next to mangrove swamps, the most luxurious hotels vie for competition with mere wooden huts. Even its population is divided among French apologists and African militants, plus a growing new sector clamoring for a united Carib identity. Guadeloupe's terrain is shaped like a two-winged butterfly, one side verdant mountains, the other rocky and ringed with white beaches. These days Guadeloupe is a paradise for those eco-adventurers who want to challenge themselves to the max. Diving is a matter of fierce honor among the French-operated industry, and certification courses are considered to be some of the toughest. An entire vacation could be spent trekking over 6000 acres within the national park. But the latest craze in Guadeloupe—a sport for which you need stamina, grit—and a big dose of humor—is cycling. The island terrain is perfect for the two-wheeler activity, which not only lets you see the countryside close up but permits the opportunity to compete with crazy French drivers—an experience that will leave you thankful to be alive.

Bird's Eye View

Guadeloupe is the most northerly of the Windward Islands group in the West Indies. Dominica lies to the south and Antigua and Montserrat to the northwest. A 659-square-mile archipelago, Guadeloupe is formed by two large islands, Grande-Terre and Basse-Terre, separated by the Riviere Salé, a narrow four-mile sea channel (but linked by a bridge) with a smaller island, Marie Galante, to the southeast, and another La Désirade, to the east. At 312 square miles, Basse-Terre (which means lowland) lies on the leeward side of the island, where the winds are calmer. The smaller, less mountainous Grande-Terre received the more dramatic waves and air currents typical to the windward side. There are also a number of small dependencies, mainly Saint Bart and the northern half of St. Martin.

History

Christopher Columbus stumbled upon Guadeloupe during his 1493 excursions, dubbing it Santa Maria de Guadeloupe de Estremadura in honor of a Spanish monastery with which he had close ties. Some 143 years later, the French landed, peopling the island with settlers who had to work in indentured conditions for three years to pay off their sea passage from France. Unfortunately, many proved to be unskilled and unacquainted with tropical farming, and the island soon fell into disrepair while nearby Martinique continued to prosper. The French Revolution inspired the settlers to revolt; they eventually declared themselves independent and even solicited the help of the British enemy. In response, the French government sent more than a thousand soldiers to whip the settlers into shape, expelling the British and

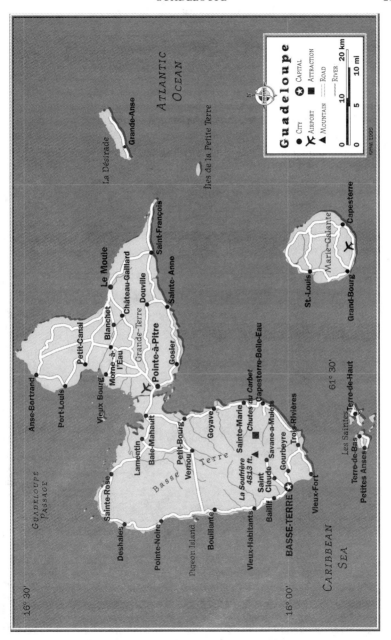

executing more than 4000 Guadeloupian rebels on guillotines set up in the main squares. Under the Napoleonic reign, slavery was reinstated. In 1810 the British successfully reinvaded the island, handing it over to Louis XVIII during the Restoration, and returning when Napoleon came to power; the Brits finally surrendered the island for the last time when the French emperor was exiled to St. Helena in 1815. Since then, Guadeloupe has retained its distinct French flavor combined with a spicy West Indian allure. In September 1989, Hurricane Hugo struck the islands, causing widespread devastation and leaving about 12,000 people homeless. But by the mid-1990s the banana industry and the tourist industry had recovered and the majority are looking forward to prosperous years.

People

Bananas are the largest export for Guadeloupe.

The proximity of rugged natural resources has bred a spiritual people highly attuned to nature. The medicinal uses of plants and their spiritual properties is common knowledge, particularly among the older residents, but it takes some convincing to induce them to part with the secrets. What most characterizes the people of Guadeloupe, however, is a love of music. In recent years, beats born in Guadeloupe have taken flight onto the international scene, bringing forth a new generation of musicians who are being recognized on the world market. Influenced by black American radicalism in the 1960s, Guadeloupe artists began to redefine their relationship to *gqoka*, or slave music, thus transcending any negative connotations. Infusing the beat with a new political message, a new African-based identity was affirmed. For years a struggle between two musical factions divided musical techniques; one favoring heavy Afro-oriented drum beat while the other favored beguines played on European instruments. The group Kassav suddenly bolted into prominence in the '80s, uniting the two factions by using all matters of instruments and rocking the dance clubs of New York, Paris and Amsterdam. In their wake, many younger groups have been inspired. (For more information about the music of Guadeloupe, see the chapter "Caribbean Culture.")

Most of the locals of Guadeloupe profess Christianity and many are Roman Catholics. There is a segment of the population which is East Indian, but like their fellow islanders from Africa, they have lost the use of their language and speak only Creole. Most women don't even know how to tie a sari anymore. But Hindu worship still continues in the privacy of their homes. Offsetting the multiracial mixture is a small but significant group of whites called Blancs-Matignons, who steadfastly cling to racist attitudes.

Beaches

Most of Guadeloupe's beaches are lovely white strand open to the public at no extra charge. Hotels sometimes charge minimal fees for nonguests to utilize the resources of their changing facilities, including beach chairs and towels. Some of the best beaches, with long white stretches, are to be found in Grande-Terre. Gray volcanic sand characterizes the beaches in the southern tip of Basse-Terre; the color is gloriously golden as you move toward the northwest coast. Beaches on the windward (Atlantic side) are simply too rough for swimming; divers who use the water should be exceptionally skilled in maneuvering strong currents. Beaches are generally accessible by roads, paved and otherwise. The exception is Islet du Gosier, which is a blip off the shore of Gosier that welcomes nude bathers. It's a great place to plop yourself for a daylong picnic, and arrangements for watersports can be made through the Creole Beach hotel in Gosier.

Caravelle Beach probably wins the award for the most stunning in Guade-loupe—tropical beauty with an immense strand. The sand is exceedingly powdery. Reefs surrounding the beach make excellent conditions for snor-keling. **Club Med** makes use of one end of the beach, but the **Hotel La Toubana** in the hills above has snorkeling equipment for rent. Le Meridien Hotel also sports a fine beach at Raisin-Clairs, where equipment for water sports can be hired. Most popular with the weekend crowd—best to go during the week if you want seclusion—is **Anse de la Gourde**; you will find a restaurant and snack bar there. Lots of nude bathers head for **Tarare**, a private strand just before the tip of Pointe des Châteaux Another popular nude beach is **Place Crawen**.

Les'Saintes' placid half-mile strand on Terre-de-Haut. Changing facilities are available a five-minute walk away at **Bois Joli Hotel**. A lovely "feet in the water" restaurant can be found on **La Grande Anse**, just outside of Dashaies, on the northwest coast of Basse-Terre. the Creole cuisine is excellent at the **Karacoli Restaurant**. Along the western shore, you'll find lots of beaches in miniature, including the gray sands of **Pigeon Beach** and the blackish ones farther south. **Petit-Anse**, on Marie-Galante, is a beautiful large beach with gleaming gold sand that fills up fast on the weekends.

Underwater

When Jacques Cousteau names a destination one of the top ten dive spots in the world, you can expect that a sizable industry will spring up around it. In reality, Cousteau placed **Pigeon Island** on his top ten list some years ago, when many areas of the undersea world were still waiting to be explored, so the designation is of a qualified nature today. Still, the locally-named **Reserve du Commandant Cousteau** at Pigeon Island is a marvelous dive location, and at least one Guadeloupe operator paves the way for American visitors to expe-rience its lush depths. Beginners will find a number of easier sites surround-ing Pigeon, although one must remember that French dive tables and apparatus are different from those used by most American-run operations. Visibility off Pigeon often exceeds 100 feet, although showers will carry mountain silt down to the reefs surrounding Basse-Terre; usually this settles in a matter of hours. Unfortunately, crowded boats are a common complaint from many visitors at this busy location, and avid divers should also try to ex-plore other portions of the expansive west coast, sometimes referred to as "the Kingdom of Sponges." It's worth noting that, unlike most other Car-

bean islands, Guadeloupe dive shops price their dives based on the distance
traveled from shore, creating a more diverse price structure than we can de-
ail here. The **Iles des Saintes** also offer pristine diving, centered around the
sland's reef plateau which offers relatively shallow depths. In addition to the
western face of Pigeon Island, snorkeling is good in the coral garden below
the bluffs just north of the harbor at **Deshaies**, off the **Ilet du Gosier** (the tiny
sland with a lighthouse facing Gosier), at **Anse a la Barque** (small cove six
miles north of Basse Terre), and in the reefs surrounding **Ilet a Fajou** (north
of the Riviere Salee).

es Alizes

A favorite dive located on the Atlantic side of the island, noted for its quantity of
large sponges. The site is regularly visited by nurse sharks, turtles, rays and angelfish,
while lobsters play hide and seek in the cracks and cuts. The easy slope makes Les
Alizes great for beginners (to 60 feet).

e Sec Pate

The most popular dive off Les Saintes, Le Sec Pate surrounds a rock sea mount
which rises 50 feet above water, descending 100 feet below. The impressive site is
blanketed in colorful corals (including huge, rare pink corals) and yields casual diving among numerous big angels and other reef fish.

Pigeon Island

Cousteau's reserve offers several possible dives, particularly on its northern and
western sides. The northeast face offers a wall which descends from 40 feet to a
ledge, and then becomes increasingly vertical to 140 feet. On the sloping northern
reef, tube sponges grow to six feet or more, while green and purple sea fans are juxtaposed against the island's drop-off, accentuated by a labyrinth of channels and
coral buttresses. The popular west side of Pigeon reveals a dramatic landscape with
large heads of brain coral, orange sponges and soft corals. The marine life in the area
displays the greatest diversity on Guadeloupe, featuring angels, butterfly fish, barracudas, tazar, parrotfish and tame gray snappers.

Wreck of *La Gustave*

One of the casualties of Hurricane Hugo in 1989, the Gustave is a 160-foot cargo
ship, lying on a floor, 130 feet down off Pigeon Island. The wreck is suitable for
intermediate divers and can be penetrated in some parts.

Dive Shops

Aqua-Fari Club

Gosier; ☎ *(590) 842-626.*
Convenient to the main resort area, Aqua-Fari dives the Ilet du Gosier as well as the
Ilet a Fajou (in the northern bay between Grande- and Basse-Terre). Single-tank
dive in the Gosier area, $37; more for longer trips, which includes Pigeon Island
(one hour by car from Gosier).

Les Heures Saines

Bouillante; ☎ *(590) 98-86-63.*

The oldest, and perhaps biggest, operator on the island; Les Heures Saines offer "baptisms" and some of their instructors speak English. Uses PADI, NAUI and a European dive systems, including CEDIP. Four divers per moniteur, with a maximum dive group of 25. One-tank dive $43; Baptism, $48. Snorkeling, $21 for two hour trip. Night dives on Fridays, wreck dive Sunday mornings.

Plongee Club De L'autre Bord

Moule; ☎ *(590) 93-97-10.*

Very small operation (maximum number of divers, four), concentrates on "the other beach," the north coast area. PADI affiliated, with most sites close to shore; beginner dives conducted in the lagoon. $41 for a single-tank dive. Small size allow flexible schedule and operation.

Centre Nautique Des Saintes

Terre-de-Haut; ☎ *(590) 99-54-25.*

Only dive shop in Les Saintes, 10 years in existence. $41 for a one-tank dive; $52 to Le Sec Pate. Handles PADI and NAUI referrals. Two boats, accommodating groups of up to 30 divers; all sites are within 20 minutes. Snorkeling trips organized on request. English speaking staff.

On Foot

Guadeloupe is second only to Martinique for maintaining the best and most extensive trail system in the Caribbean. From easy walks approaching tall waterfalls to a fierce traverse of the island's volcanic spine, there is no shortage of trails to keep active travelers engaged. The island's geologic focus, Soufriere in the vast **Parc National**, is one of the region's more recently troubled summits—a series of eruptions in 1976–1977 were exciting enough to occasion the evacuation of Basse-Terre—and, ironically, it's probably the most visited. Almost every day, dozens of hikers gamely ascend the moderate path to its moonlike crown, the highest in the Eastern Caribbean. Because island trails are so well-maintained, guides are generally unnecessary. The hikes outlined below, all of which are on Basse-Terre, are but a small sample of several dozen available (hiking on Grande-Terre is limited to beach and country strolls). A guidebook containing additional routes within the Parc National is available from the **Organization des Guides de Montagne** in Basse-Terre *(☎ (590) 814-579);* they also conduct guided walks in English.

Chutes Du Carbet

Guadeloupe's most popular hiking region lies in the rumpled valleys above the village of St. Sauveur, where a series of three impressive waterfalls pour down the slopes from Soufriere. At the road-end a trail leads down one-and-a-half miles to the lowest set of falls which, at 70 feet, are the shortest plunge, but also contain the greatest volume of water. From the same road-end, the 20-minute climb to the 360-foot second set of falls is reasonably easy and you will likely encounter bathers enjoying the water. A steep, muddy trail continues from here to the base of the 370-foot Premiere Chute du Carbet, the most spectacular falls, which features soaring views down the canyon. Allow two hours from the parking lot to the base of the upper falls. It is also possible to continue, from a point near the upper falls, toward the Soufriere summit, a very demanding trek.

Chutes Du Galion and La Citerne

This trail begins just south of Savane-a-Mulets, leading away from the Soufriere trail, and descends the slope to a fork. Take the path on the left, passing excellent views on the way down to the Citerne River, just below the Galion Falls. From here, you may bound up the slippery riverbed to the base of the 130-foot falls or cross the river to a path that takes you to an overlook of Galion. Allow three hours down and return.

The Soufriere Hike

On clear days, a steam plume wafting from the gullet of Soufriere is visible from Grande-Terre's southern coast, seducing would-be adventurers on a memorable trek up an active volcano. Drive up the steep road out of Basse-Terre to the parking lot at Savane-a-Mulets (stop at the nearby Volcano Museum en route which provides a geologic history of the area). Although the 4813-foot volcanic cone looks imposing from here, you're already high on the hill and the ascent is not difficult, requiring about 90 minutes of steady climbing on a well-defined path. After circling from the green, but treeless western slopes around to the eastern face about two-thirds of the way up, you'll enter a ravine where the path splits; take the right-hand passage toward the top. You may expect a bowl-shaped crater at the summit, but instead you'll encounter a misty, lunar landscape featuring mounds of gray and black rock accented by tufts of green grass and the smell of sulfur permeating the crisp mountain air. If you're lucky to be on top on a clear day, you'll glimpse Dominica to the south. On the way down, turn right at the ravine junction, which takes you around the summit via its southern slopes and crosses the area of the most recent activity. This route returns to the main road about a quarter-mile past the parking lot where you began, allowing you to climb and circle the entire cone in about three hours. One of the Caribbean's don't-miss hikes, but come prepared for some of the 400-plus inches of rain the summit area receives annually.

The Victor Hugues Trail

Possibly the longest trek in the Eastern Caribbean, this spectacular trail accesses the volcanic spine of Guadeloupe. Its length (allow eight hours, one way) and the rugged mountains it traverses, makes it for advanced hikers only. From Petit-Bourg, follow the N1 two miles south to a road leading to Montebello; where the road splits, stay to the left and proceed to the end to a banana plantation. The trail begins here and crosses the banana field on its way up a long, steep valley to a ridge where it meets the Merwat Trail (see below). Turn left (south) at the crest, passing a shelter and ramble along this airy passage toward Soufriere; the views are staggering. At the junction with the Carmichael Trail, bear right to descend to the village of Matouba and the end of the hike. This is a serious expedition requiring strong legs and fortitude; inquire with the Parc National for the latest trail conditions before embarking, and carry ample water and rain gear (you may want to consider hiring a guide). Be sure to arrange for a pickup at the end of the hike. NOTE: The Trace Merwat is a well-known alternate route that starts instead near the tiny village of Vernou, just off the Route de la Traversee, also at a banana plantation. This path ascends Morne Merwat before joining the better-maintained Hugues trail, but should not be considered a shorter variation.

By Pedal

A winter home to French racers, Guadeloupe is well-established as one of the Caribbean's leading cycling destinations. Bringing your own bike from home is a reasonable option (repair shops are sprinkled island-wide), while rental outfits can be found in Pointe-a-Pitre and most major towns. Guadeloupe boasts a well-maintained road system covering more than 1200 miles. Navigating the island's busier roads can be a challenge in itself. In particular, use caution on the fast N4 that plows east from Pointe-a-Pitre along the developed southern coastline of **Grande-Terre** (it quiets down east of St. Francois) and on the busy N1, which is the main route between Pointe-a-Pitre and the capital of **Basse-Terre**. Otherwise, Guadeloupe's eastern wing offers some of the Caribbean's most pleasant riding, over rolling hills and through green sugarcane fields. Head north from any of the south-coast resort areas for a delightful tour of the French countryside, Caribbean-style. The seven-mile stretch from **St. Francois** to **Pointe des Chateaux** is lovely and easy. On Guadeloupe's other wing, exacting rides rule the day. Basse-Terre's mountainous interior frequently extends right to its busy coastline, providing little relief for riders but plenty of challenges for the fit. The beautiful **Route de la Traversee** is a real thigh-buster, while the hilly coastline north of **Pigeon Island** accesses quieter beaches and villages that happily proffer *croissant* and *cafe au lait* for early morning cyclists. The islands of **Terre-de-Haut** and **Marie-Galante**

oth considerably easier (or smaller, anyway) to conquer than Guadeloupe,
ffer mountain bike rentals at some scooter and motorcycle outlets.

Bike Rental Shops

le Rolle
Rue Frevault, Pointe-a-Pitre; ☎ *(590) 83-15-74.*
A reliable repair shop servicing road and mountain bikes.

quateur Moto
Gosier; ☎ *(590) 84-59-94.*
Peugeot and MBK mountain bikes. One day rental, $18; weekly rate, $109.

What Else to See

Point-a-Pitre is the Caribbean in double time. The city of some 100,000
people moves at a faster pace than probably any other Caribbean city, a maze
of narrow streets, traffic pileups and honking horns. The city has paid its
dues over the years, a victim of various hurricanes, earthquakes and other
natural disasters, the last being Hurricane Hugo in 1989. Some French colonial structures still remain, but downtown has been recently renovated,
and the new cruise terminal called Centre St. John Perse has brought a lively
commercial feel with its numerous boutiques and restaurants.

First stop in the city should be at the **Tourist Office in Place de la Victire,** to
pick up maps and brochures. Even outside the door you'll find lots of lively
locals hawking anything from pots and pans to underwear. Fruits and vegetables can be bought from a bevy of women dressed in brightly colored costumes near the port. The local Marketplace, between the streets of St.John
Perse, Freebault, Schoelchen and Peynier, is a beehive of activity for the purchase of the latest crops from the fields. Take time to meet the ladies of the
market, whose beautiful smiles could light up anybody's day. Due to the
presence of crowds, give attention to your handbag as you stroll through.

Two museums are worth a look. The **Musee St. John Perse** in a restored colonial house is a tribute to the 1960 Nobel Prize winner in literature, where
you can read works of his poetry. Also check out the **Musée Schoelcher**, a memorial to Victor Schoelcher, a 19th-century Alsataon freedomfighter who
was responsible for emancipation in the French West Indies.

The capital of the island, **Basse-Terre,** is significant for its port and its market, both situated along boulevard General de Gaulle. A fine colonial square
houses several old structures at Champ d'Arbaud. A few beautiful hours can

be spent strolling the gardens at **Jardin Pichon**. A short stop can be made t
the 17th-century fort St. Charles and the Cathedral of our Lady of Guade
loupe. A look at the volcano in this area can be made from any number c
picnic tables in the suburb of **St. Clade**. (For information on how to scale th
mountain, see under "Treks" above.) Near the ferry landing for Les Sainte
the **Parc Archéologique des Roches Gravees** contains a collection of pre-Co
lumbian rock engravings. Exhibits explain the engravings of folk and faun
symbols on the petroglyphs. The park, inside a handsome botanical garder
is a quiet haven for tourists who need to escape the bustle of Pointe-a-Pitre

Take time to visit the islands lying directly offshore the mainland. Ferric
run regularly to Marie-Galante, Desirade and Terre-Haut (see below fc
more information, after "Where to Shop"). Ferry schedules, however, ca
never be counted on, but check with the tourist office to find out the lates
pseudo-itinerary. If you plan to spend time on some of these outposts,
good handle on French is necessary because you will be hard put to find any
one who speaks English. Most of your simple needs can be met with a finge
pointed to your mouth or the word "toilette" (pronounced twa-lette
There's no need to carry much with you; in fact you can wear your bathin
suit under your outer clothes, but you should bring a towel. The island c
Dominica is just a short hop away on an airplane. The trip can be done in
day and excursions can be arranged ahead of time to save you wasting tim
on the island itself.

Historical Sites

Parc Archeologique des Roches   ★★★
> *Trois-Rivieres.*
> *Hours open: 9 a.m.–5 p.m.*
> At this peaceful spot near the wharf, displays interpret the rock engravings by Carib
> Indians that date back to A.D. 300.

Museums and Exhibits

Edgar Clerc Archaeological Museum   ★★★
> *La Rosete, Moule.*
> This small museum displays artifacts from the Carib and Arawak Indians found on
> the islands of the Eastern Caribbean. Closed Wednesday afternoons and Tuesdays.

Musee Schoelcher   ★★
> *24 Rue Peynier, Pointe-a-Pitre.*
> Displays highlight the personal papers and belongings of Victor Schoelcher, who, in
> the 19th century, worked to abolish slavery in the French West Indies.

Musee du Rhum   ★★★
> *Bellevue, Sainte-Rose, Basse-Terre.*
> *Hours open: 9 a.m.–5 p.m.*
> The Rum Museum showcases three centuries in the making of the quaff, which is
> produced with sugarcane. After a guided tour, you get to taste the potable, and, of
> course, buy some to take home. But perhaps the best reason to come here is to

check out "la Galerie des Plus Beaux Insectes du Monde," where you can marvel at more than 5000 (safely dead) critters—from beautiful butterflies to spine-tingling spiders, roaches, and other huge creepy-crawlies. Those interested in the rum-making process should also check out the **Domaine de Severin in Sainte-Rose** (northern Basse-Terre, ☎ *590-28-91-86*). This distillery still functions with a paddle wheel; a guided tour takes you through each step of production. It's open daily from 8 a.m.– 1 p.m. and from 2-6 p.m., and from 9 a.m.–noon on Sundays.

Musee St. John Perse ★★

Achille Rene-Boisneuf Rue, Pointe-a-Pitre.
Hours Open: 9 a.m.–5 p.m.
This museum in a restored colonial house contains the works of St. John Perse, a local boy made good who won the Nobel Prize in Literature in 1960.

Parks and Gardens

Floral Park ★★

Cabout, Petit-Bourg, Basse-Terre.
Hours open: 9 a.m.–5 p.m.
Le Domaine de Valombreuse is the official name of this Eden-like spot on the east coast of Basse-Terre. Numerous shady valleys house 300 species and 200 subspecies of flowers and a slew of exotic birds. The Park Restaurant is open daily for lunch, and there's a playground on site for little tykes. Admission is $5.00 for kids under 12.

Parc Naturel de la Guadeloupe ★★★★★

Route de la Traversee, Trois-Rivieres.
Covering 74,000 acres with 200 miles of trails, this national park has something for everyone: waterfalls, thick vegetation, nature walks and the centerpiece, La Soufriere, a smoldering volcano that last erupted in 1975. Stop by the Maison de la Foret for a look at the park's history (only, alas, in French) and a booklet on hiking trails. Wear rain gear, as this area gets some 250 inches per year. If you're interested in a guided hike tailored to your level, contact the **Organisation des Guides de Montagne de Caraibe** at ☎ *80-05-79*.

Zoological and Botanical Park ★★★

Route de la Traversee, Bouillante, Basse-Terre.
Hours open: 9 a.m.–4:30 p.m.
Located high in the hills of Basse-Terre, this reserve is home to myriad trees, bushes and creepers that lots of little critters like mongoose, iguana, land turtle, and raccoon (called ti-raccoon here) call home. Great views abound at Le Ti-Raccoon restaurant (open daily for lunch except Mondays), which serves up authentic creole cuisine. Admission for children is $3.00.

Tours

Aquarium de la Guadeloupe ★★★★★

Place Creole, Marina Bas-du-Fort.
Hours open: 9 a.m.–7 p.m.
This is the Caribbean's largest aquarium and considered to be France's third most important. Good exhibits feature everything from tiny fishes to giant sharks. While

in the area, check out the 18th-century Fort Fleur d'Epee, complete with dungeons and spectacular views.

Sports

Strong currents and good winds make yachting a popular sport in Guadeloupe. Safe anchorages can be found at the offshore isles of Marie-Galante and Les Saintes—many people go here on day excursions. In the harbor are yachts of all shapes and sizes, which can be hired, chartered, crewed or bareboat, for any length of time. You can, through the services of **Le Boat**, a unique service, take one boat to an island and leave it there (ask the Tourist Office for more information). Windsurfing is also popular and lessons and equipment can be arranged through all the seaside hotels. Hotels also assist in arrangements for deep-sea fishing from boats based at the **Port de Plaisance Marina in Bas du Fort** ☎ *(590) 82-74-94.* Marlin and tuna are profuse in the waters off the west coast of Basse-Terre at Pigeon Island. The season for barracuda and kingfish is January to May. Horseback riding can also be arranged through **Le Criolo**, a riding school at St. Félix near Gosier. (For diving, trekking and cycling, see under the appropriate sections above.)

Golf Municipal Saint-Francois

St.-Francois.

The island's only golf course features 18 holes designed by Robert Trent Jones and an English-speaking pro. Greens fees for the par-71 course are $45.

Holywind

Pointe de la Verdure, Gosier.

Feeling daring? Fly along the coastline in an Ultra Leger Motorise, a lightweight seaplane.

Watersports

Various locations, Pointe-a-Pitre.

Your hotel probably has enough watersports to keep you happy. If not, check out one of the following. Scuba diving: **Chez Guy et Christian** *(☎ 98-82-43),* **Aqua-Fari** *(☎ 84-26-26),* and **Nauticase** *(☎ 84-22-22).* On Isle des Saintes, **Centre Nautique des Saintes** *(☎ 99-54-25).* Windsurfing: **Callinago** *(☎ 84-25-25)* and **UCPA Hotel Club** *(☎ 88-64-80).* Deep-sea fishing: **Caraibe Peche** *(☎ 90-97-51),* **La Rocher de Malendere** *(☎ 98-70-84),* **Evasion Exotic** *(☎ 90-94-17),* and **Fishing Club Antilles** *(☎ 86-73-77).* Boat rentals: **Soleil et Voile** *(☎ 90-81-81),* **Vacances Yachting Antilles** *(☎ 90-82-95),* and **Locaraibes** *(☎ 90-82-80).*

Where to Stay

	Fielding's Highest Rated Hotels in Guadeloupe	
★★★★★	Auberge de la Vieille Tour	$118–$231
★★★★★	Le Meridien St. Francois	$199–$285
★★★★★	Le Meridien la Cocoteraie	$160–$680
★★★★	Fleur d'Epee Novotel	$123–$213
★★★★	Hotel Hamak Beach	$175–$255
★★★★	La Creole Beach Hotel	$60–$550
★★★★	PLM Azur Marissol Hotel	$94–$185
★★★★	Villa Creole Hotel	$71–$115
★★★	Canella Beach Residence	$87–$230
★★★	Tropical Club Hotel	$92–$192

	Fielding's Most Romantic Hotels in Guadeloupe	
★★★★	Auberge les Petits Saints	$65–$130
★★★★	Hotel Hamak Beach	$175–$255
★★	Village Creole	

	Fielding's Budget Hotels in Guadeloupe	
★★	Auberge de l'Arbre a Pain	$40–$50
★★★	Relais Grand Soufriere	$49–$93
★★	Sucrerie du Comte	$50–$100
★★★	Village de Menard	$60–$100
★	Kaliko Beach Club	$80–$99

Most of Guadeloupe's hotels and resorts predictably hug the coast and the sandy coves. Despite the French presence on the island, service is not the best in the Caribbean, but it is generally friendly. Simply, stiff formalities are not practiced here, and you are more likely to have to wait a while for a request to be fulfilled; enjoy the time relaxing. **Gosier**, once a sleepy town, is now the hub of tourism; there are several resorts to pick from as well as more intimate guest houses. **L'Anse Bertrans** on the northern coast of Grande-Terre is just now becoming developed. One of the most attractive newer areas is **Bas du Fort**, between Pointe-a-Pitre and Gosier; the apartments here are particularly serviceable and restaurants are conveniently located. About a half-hour drive from Pointe-a-Pitre is **Saint François**, where you can choose among several sailing options at the harbor.

Hotels and Resorts

It's hard to believe, but on Guadeloupe room service is hard to obtain, even in the finest hotels. **Club Med** remains a winner on Guadeloupe, the all-inclusive regime attracting a lot of French and Americans.

Basse-Terre

Sucrerie du Comte   **$50–$100**   ★★

Sainte Rose, ☎ *(590) 28-60-17, FAX (590) 28-65-63.*
Single: $50–$100. Double: $50–$100.
Built on the grounds of an old sugarcane factory, this peaceful spot opened in 1994. Many ruins of the factory remain, including an 18th-century aqueduct and a large processing plant that was ruined in a 1966 hurricane. Guestrooms are very small and simple, furnished with twin or queen beds, tile floors, and telephones. Each has air conditioning, ceiling fans, and a small, shower-only bath. The grounds include a small but pretty pool, one tennis court, a fabulous restaurant, and a wonderfully atmospheric bar where you'll find the only TV on-site. The beach is a five-minute walk through grounds dotted with papaya, orange, mango, and fruit trees. Recommended for nature lovers as opposed to resort seekers.

Village Creole Hotel   **$71–$115**   ★★★★

Petionville, Soufriere, ☎ *(590) 45-62-41.*
Single: $71–$115. Double: $83–$115.
Set high on the hills and surrounded by a forest, this comfortable, family-run hotel has a loyal following. The spacious guest rooms are air-conditioned and accented with Haitian furniture. There's a free-form pool in a nicely landscaped garden and lots of interesting local art in the public areas. Two tennis courts await the athletic set. A nice property with lots of island flavor.

Grande-Terre

Auberge de la Vieille Tour   **$118–$231**   ★★★★★

Point a Pitre, Gosier, ☎ *(800) 221-4542, (590) 84-23-23, FAX (590) 8-43343.*
Single: $118–$208. Double: $128–$231.
Set on a 15-acre estate overlooking the Caribbean Sea, this posh property includes the tower of an 18th-century sugar mill. Accommodations are nicely done with expensive furnishings and lots of amenities; request one of the newer ones, added a few years ago and situated in townhouses. There's two tennis courts and a pool, with watersports available nearby. The small beach can get crowded.

Callinago Hotel & Village $102–$216

Pointe de la Verdure, Gosier, ☎ (590) 84-25-25, FAX (590) 84-24-90.
Single: $102–$166. Double: $121–$216.

This complex comprises a 40-room hotel on a hill and a 115-unit apartment building on the beach. All units are nicely done with European baths; the apartments have kitchens, too. There are two restaurants, a pool and watersports, with a casino adjacent. A popular spot, especially with families.

Canella Beach Residence $87–$230

Pointe de la Verdure, Gosier, Gosier, ☎ (590) 90-44-00.
Single: $87–$230. Double: $109–$230.

Set in the heart of Gosier's hotel scene, this hotel has small but adequate air-conditioned guestrooms and suites. All have a simple kitchenette on the terrace with cheap cooking utensils and dishware. The beach consists of gray sand, the no-see-ums are everywhere, and the ocean is downright dirty—so look elsewhere if you're intent on a tropical paradise. On the plus side, there are all the usual resort diversions at this busy property and lots within an easy walk, including one of Guadeloupe's few casinos. Parents can stash the kids in supervised programs during high season. The staff is friendly and eager to practice their English—a definite plus on this French-speaking island.

Club Med Caravelle $784–$1685 per week

Ste. Anne, ☎ (800) 258-2633, (590) 88-21-00.

Encompassing 45 acres with a wonderful mile-long private beach, this Club Med appeals mainly to tourists from France, so much so that many activities are held in French. (A good chance to learn the language, and they have labs to help you do just that.) The all-inclusive rates cover just about everything. All the resort amenities are here, from tennis to watersports to a lively night scene—but while nice, this is not one of the better Club Meds.

Cottage Hotel $112–$220

Le Moule, ☎ (590) 23-78-38, FAX (590) 23-78-39.
Single: $112–$194. Double: $142–$220.

Just opened in early 1995, this friendly property accommodates guests in a pretty building in yellow and blues with fanciful gingerbread trim. Lodgings are in nicely done duplexes with high ceilings, two sofa beds in the living room, one and a half baths, a kitchenette on the balcony, and a small loft bedroom. Excellent for families, each unit has a TV, telephone and air conditioning. The balconies overlook a parking lot and the sea; it's just a minute or two stroll to the beach. Guests can use the pool, restaurants, and watersports facilities at the adjacent Tropical Club Hotel.

Domaine de l'Anse des Rochers $80–$220

Sainte-Francois, ☎ (590) 93-90-00, FAX (590) 93-91-00.
Single: $80–$220. Double: $80–$220.

An immaculate collection of pastel-colored creole buildings trimmed with white gingerbread is the core of this upscale resort near Sainte-Francois. Guests are accommodated in nicely decorated rooms or in 34 villas on the hillside. Each room is air conditioned and has a furnished terrace, modern bath, radio, refrigerator and direct-dial telephone. The expansive grounds include several restaurants, the largest natural lagoon pool in the Caribbean, a gorgeous swimming pool, tennis and two reef-protected beaches. There's a disco on-site and various theme evenings each week.

Ecotel Guadeloupe $60–$130   ★★

Montauban, Gosier, ☎ *(590) 90-60-00, FAX (590) 90-60-60.*
Single: $60–$95. Double: $85–$130.
Located less than half a mile from the beach and a mile from Gosier Village, this motel-like operation is a hotel school, so you can count on professional, enthusiastic service. Rooms are comfortable and air-conditioned, but nothing too exciting. There are two restaurant and a pool, but not much else. A good bargain though, with a mostly European clientele.

Fleur d'Epee Novotel $123–$213   ★★★★

Bas du Fort, ☎ *(800) 221-4542, (590) 90-40-00, FAX (590) 9-09907.*
Single: $123–$182. Double: $142–$213.
Set on a peninsula near a fine sandy beach, this Y-shaped hotel is informal and friendly, attracting laid-back types who enjoy a range of activities from watersports to tennis to bridge. Guest rooms are air-conditioned and most have sea views from the balconies. Supervised programs keep kids busy while their parents laze at the pool or beach. Lots of young Europeans like this spot.

Hotel Arawak $130–$240   ★★

Pointe de la Verdure, Gosier, ☎ *(590) 84-24-24, FAX (590) 84-38-45.*
Single: $130–$200. Double: $150–$240.
Catering to a mostly European and Canadian clientele, this 10-story complex has bright and comfortable guest rooms, most with a nice ocean view and balcony. Three tennis courts, a pool, casino, watersports and a fitness center keep guests busy. The top-floor suites are enormous and worth the splurge. The beach is lively and topless.

Hotel Hamak Beach $175–$255   ★★★★

St. Francois, ☎ *(590) 88-59-59.*
Single: $175–$225. Double: $205–$255.

Set on 200 secluded acres bordering a reef-protected lagoon, this lushly landscaped property is elegant and exclusive. Accommodations are in air-conditioned bungalows with one or two bedrooms, kitchenettes and outdoor showers. There's an 18-hole golf course across the street, and tennis, air-charter tours (they have their own landing strip) and three small private beaches on site. Excellent service and a well-heeled atmosphere make this one of Guadeloupe's finest resorts.

Hotel Toubana $105–$230   ★★★

Fonds Thezan, Ste. Anne, ☎ *(590) 88-25-78, FAX (590) 88-38-90.*
Single: $105–$170. Double: $130–$230.
Set on a hill overlooking the south shore of Grande Terre, this charming complex boasts magnificent views of the raging sea. Guests stay in air-conditioned bungalows with kitchenettes and private gardens. The grounds include a pool, tennis

court, bar and restaurant. The beach is a short stroll down a very steep hill, where watersports await. Not bad.

Kaliko Beach Club $80–$99 ★

La Gonave Bay, Montrouis, ☎ (590) 22-80-40.
Single: $80. Double: $99.
Situated on 15 acres in the Arcahaie beach area, this complex houses guests in circular stone bungalows nicely furnished and air-conditioned. The beach is quite nice and affords all the usual watersports, plus a good diving center. There's also a pool and tennis on two courts.

La Creole Beach Hotel $60–$550 ★★★★

Point de la Verdure, Gosier, ☎ (590) 90-46-46, FAX (590) 90-46-00.
Single: $60–$550. Double: $151–$550.
Located on a 10-acre estate on Pointe de la Verdure Beach, this resort offers large and modern air-conditioned guest rooms. Entertainment nightly under the stars is a nice touch. The wide beach offers up all watersports, including free scuba lessons, and there are also a pool, two tennis courts, and a gym. The casino is nearby.

Le Meridien St. Francois $199–$285 ★★★★★

St. Francois, ☎ (800) 543-4300, (590) 88-51-00, FAX (590) 88-40-71.
Single: $199–$285. Double: $199–$285.
Located on the southern shore of Grand Terre, this contemporary resort sits on 150 acres fronting one of the best beaches in the country. The European-style resort is self-contained, with lots going on in the protected lagoon and on the tennis courts, in the marina and on the archery range. Guest rooms are on the plain side, but have comfortable tropical furnishings and English-language stations on the TV. A casino and the municipal golf course are nearby. Tres chic, and one of the few resorts where North Americans won't feel out of place.

Le Meridien la Cocoteraie $160–$680 ★★★★★

Avenue de L'Europe, Saint Francois, ☎ (590) 88-79-81, FAX (590) 88-78-33.
Single: $160–$335. Double: $335–$680.
Mostly well-heeled Europeans visit this resort, where every room is a nicely furnished suite. The beach is quite small and there are two tennis courts and a restaurant. All other facilities are found next door, at the Meridien St. Francois, including a marina and watersports. Elegant, but English speakers may feel out of place (and out of touch).

Mini Beach Hotel $70–$150 ★★★

Plage de Sainte-Anne, ☎ (590) 88-21-13, FAX (590) 88-19-29.
Single: $70–$150. Double: $70–$150.
This small spot is set right on Sainte-Anne's pretty beach. Accommodations are in air-conditioned guestrooms with colonial-style decor. There are also three bungalows for those desiring more room. The on-site restaurant serves up tasty creole and French fare daily except Wednesdays, and breakfast is included in the room rate. Watersports are nearby.

PLM Azur Marissol Hotel $94–$185 ★★★★

Bas du Fort, ☎ (590) 90-84-44, FAX (590) 9-08332.

Single: $94–$139. Double: $111–$185.

Facing the bay of Point-a-Pitre, this resort complex shares its fine beach with the Fleur d'Epee Novotel. Accommodations range from standard guest rooms to bungalows, all air-conditioned and sporting balconies. Pampering treatments await in the spa. A few restaurants, large pool and watersports provide other diversions. There's also tennis on site and a marina nearby. Like many of its competitors, this one attracts mostly young and casual Europeans.

Plantation Ste. Marthe $157–$315   ★★★

Sainte-Francois, St. Francois, ☎ *(800) 333-1970, (590) 88-72-46, FAX (590) 88-72-47.*
Single: $157–$315. Double: $181–$315.

Sitting high on a hill with sweeping views and surrounded by 15 acres of fields and gardens, this great choice puts up guests in Louisiana-style buildings housing very nice guest rooms and duplexes, all with air conditioning and extras like room service, mini bars, and hair dryers. Shuttles transport beach lovers to the sand. There's a pool and fitness center on-site, while 18 holes of golf are nearby. The hotel's French creole restaurant is highly regarded. Very pleasant, if you don't mind the off-beach location.

Tropical Club Hotel $92–$192   ★★★

Le Moule, ☎ *(590) 23-78-38, FAX (590) 23-78-39.*
Single: $92–$168. Double: $114–$192.

Built up against an untamed cliff lush with yucca trees, this family-friendly hotel has rooms with a queen bed and in a small alcove, bunk beds for the little tykes. The pretty blonde furnishings are enhanced by gaily colored fabrics. Other features include a kitchenette on the terrace, air conditioning and ceiling fans, TV, telephones, and small shower-only baths. Request a unit on the second or third floor for the best sea views. The grounds include a nice pool area, a fitness room, several restaurants, a watersports center with diving facilities, a beach bar, and a long, reef-protected beach great for windsurfing. The rates include breakfast and a free diving or windsurf lesson; an extra $224 per person per week buys dinner nightly. This is one of the few hotels favored by Hurricane Hugo's devestation—prior to the storm, the beach was so full of coconut trees it was hard to get a decent tan!

Apartments and Condominiums

Since eating out is an art in Guadeloupe, cooking on the island in your own facilities may seem superfluous or beside the point. However, it's nice to know you can whip up your own breakfast, and maybe picnic lunch, then apply the savings to fabulous dinners. Many French ex-pats rent out their fashionable villas and apartments during high season, however, some of the digs don't even have hot running water. Do your best to find out all facts before shacking up with a rental; some clients have been shocked at the results. Most rental operators don't speak English, so your French should be superb, particularly to verify any "small print" on your contract. Rentals can be arranged for one week (usually the minimum) to longer stays. Some beautiful seaside homes are among the prize of the lot. Specify your exact needs (location, sea view, distance to the beach, proximity to shopping, restaurants, etc.).

Grande-Terre

Relais du Moulin   **$105–$156**   ★★

Chateaubrun, Ste. Anne, ☎ *(590) 88-23-96, FAX (590) 88-03-92.*
Single: $105–$129. Double: $128–$156.

Located on an old sugar plantation amid tropical gardens, this complex is somewhat isolated, set in the remote, though scenic, countryside. Accommodations are in air-conditioned bungalows with kitchenettes and patios complete with hammocks. Tennis, archery and a swimming pool await. The beach is not too far a walk. Great views reward those who climb the beautifully preserved windmill.

Residence du Parc   **$382–$868**   ★★

Le Moule, ☎ *(590) 23-78-50, FAX (590) 23-78-39.*
Single: $382–$868. Double: $382–$868.

Self-caterers will find all they need at this complex of studios and one- and two-bedroom apartments adjacent to the Tropical Club Hotel. Bedrooms are on the small side and plainly furnished, but pleasant enough. Each unit has ceiling fans (but no air conditioning), complete kitchens on large balconies overlooking the sea, pretty fabrics, shower-only baths, and less-than-desirable plastic dining tables and chairs. Maid service is optional. Guests can use all the facilities at the Tropical Club, including a pool, watersports center, and several restaurants. Note that the price quoted above is per week.

Inns

Inns on Guadeloupe are often defined as a lodging with fewer than 50 rooms. Such accommodations are handled through a local association of hotels called **Relais Créoles**. Membership in the association does not ensure quality, so make sure you acquire as much information as possible. The best inns, like **Relais de Grand Soufriere**, combine the elegance of high ceilings and mansionlike elegance with the tropical breeziness. The smaller the hotel, the more necessary it is to speak French well; although hosts can be congenial, don't expect too much in the way of room service. **Auberge du Grand Large** boasts excellent creole food for both lunch and dinner.

Basse-Terre

L'Auberge de Distillerie   **$105–$125**   ★★★

Route de Versailles, Deshaies, ☎ *(590) 94-25-91, FAX (590) 9-41191.*
Single: $105–$125. Double: $105–$125.

This French-style country inn in a residential area near the national park appeals to nature lovers. Guest rooms are simple but comfortable with air conditioning and television sets. The Creole restaurant and bar are popular with locals. There's also a pool on site. You may feel left out if vous ne parlez pas francais.

Relais Grand Soufriere   **$49–$93**   ★★★

St. Claude, Deshaies, ☎ *(590) 80-01-27.*
Single: $49–$76. Double: $49–$93.

This historic inn dates back to 1859 and reopened in 1986 after extensive renovations. The lovely hillside grounds include a pool. Accommodations are in a mansion, once a private residence, and are elegant and quite comfortable.

Grande-Terre

Auberge du Grand Large   **$100–$105**   ★★

Route de la Plage, Ste. Anne, ☎ *(590) 88-20-06.*
Single: $100–$105. Double: $100–$105.

Located on Ste. Anne Beach, a nice stretch frequented by locals, this casual spot places guests in air-conditioned bungalows. Besides a bar and Creole restaurant, there's not much in the way of extras, but the rates are reasonable.

Low Cost Lodging

Considerable discounts can be arranged from mid-April to November, when the season moves into low status. Rates may vary with current fluctuations. **Relais Bleus de Raizet** is a motel whose chief virtue is that it is a 10-minute ride from the airport. Rooms are minuscule and the air-conditioning could keep you up all night, but it's cheap.

Where to Eat

Fielding's Highest Rated Restaurants in Guadeloupe

★★★★★	Auberge de la Vielle Tour	$23–$39
★★★★★	La Canne A Sucre	$18–$32
★★★★★	La Plantation	$14–$54
★★★★★	Le Chateau de Feuilles	$18–$29
★★★★	La Rocher de Malendure	$8–$18
★★★★	Nilce's Bar	$4–$15
★★★	La Louisiane	$22–$30
★★★	Le Poisson d'Or	$14–$27
★★★	Le Restaurant	$25–$40
★★★	Sucrerie du Comte	$13–$35

Fielding's Special Restaurants in Guadeloupe

★★★★★	Auberge de la Vielle Tour	$23–$39
★★★★★	Le Chateau de Feuilles	$18–$29
★★★★	Nilce's Bar	$4–$15
★★★	Sucrerie du Comte	$13–$35
★	La Braise Marine	$8–$30

Fielding's Budget Restaurants in Guadeloupe

★★	Le Jardin Creole	$4–$14
★★★★	La Rocher de Malendure	$8–$18
★★	La Saladerie	$7–$19
★★	Le Amandiers	$12–$16
★★★	Chez Paul de Matouba	$12–$18

Guadeloupe boasts some of the best creole cuisine in the Caribbean, and chefs care for their food with pride and love. Trust places that specialize in local foods—typically they'll say *cuisine créole*—and they reflect the obvious pride in creole style, the way a place would look in the French countryside if France were the Caribbean—which is precisely the case in Guadeloupe. Court bouillon is a lively fish soup, which makes a good starter. Rice and beans are often prepared in coconut water. Of the more than two dozen creole restaurants that thrive on the islands, there are a few that are considered out of this world. Among the best are **La Canne a Sucre**, in an elegant new location in the modern Centre St.-John Perse at the edge of the water (the brasserie down below is cheaper than the restaurant, which features red snapper with passion fruit mousse). **La Créole Chez Violetta** is also highly recommended. A voluptuous beachside lunch can be had at **Le Karacolo** restaurant in Deshaies (For more information, see the chapter "Caribbean Culture" under the heading Culinary Arts.

Basse-Terre

Chez Clara   **$$$**   ★★★

Ste. Rose, Ste. Rose, ☎ (590) 28-72-99.
Latin American cuisine.
Lunch: Noon–2:30 p.m., entrees $9–$27.
Dinner: 7–10 p.m., entrees $9–$27.
Like the jazz she once danced to, native chef Clara Lesueur's culinary improvisations are realized by years of perfecting basic techniques. Guests that patronize Clara's chez on Ste. Rose's seafront are fans of long-standing, guaranteeing a bit of a wait, but the refreshing rum drinks at the bar help ease the pain. Go easy on the cocktails so you can enjoy the Creole specials of lambi with lime and peppers, crayfish and crab backs. No dinner is served Sundays.

Chez Paul de Matouba   **$$**   ★★★

Riviere Rouge, ☎ (590) 80-29-20.
International cuisine.
Dinner: entrees $12–$18.
Enjoy a refreshing country lunch in this Creole restaurant in Matouba, formerly a Hindu settlement, in the mountains above Basse-Terre. The ambience here is similar to a fishing lodge, where diners enjoy a veritable marketplace of local greens and fresh seafood while a river runs outside. Specialties include *accras* (codfish fritters) with an incendiary sauce, or grilled *ouassous* (crayfish). Fixed-price meals under $20 are available.

La Rocher de Malendure   **$$**   ★★★★

Malendure Beach, Bouillante, ☎ (590) 98-70-84.
French cuisine.
Dinner: entrees $8–$18.
The vista from this upscale eatery perched on a bluff above Malendure Beach is Pigeon Island, a top diving locale and underwater reserve. If you can keep your eyes from the scenery, you'll be drawn to the the delectable creole treats on the fixed-

price lunch that runs under $20—accras, barbecued chicken, crayfish in sauce and a beverage. Dinners are served Fridays and Saturdays only.

Grande-Terre

Auberge de la Vielle Tour   **$$$**   ★ ★ ★ ★ ★

Montauban, Gosier, ☎ *(590) 84-23-23.*
French cuisine.
Dinner: 7–10 p.m., entrees $23–$39.
Possibly the finest cuisine in Gosier can be found in the main dining room of the Pullman Auberge de la Vielle Tour. The view alone, of the Ilet du Gosier and its lighthouse in the distance, is worth the high tariff. Tables facing the wrap-around windows are, naturally, the most sought after, so request one way in advance. A la carte offerings include red snapper or catch of the day served with exotic fruit butters, or lamb loin roasted with herbs. A prix-fixe menu ($45) is also available.

Chez Violetta   **$$$**   ★ ★ ★

Perinette Gosier, Gosier Village, ☎ *(590) 84-10-34.*
French cuisine.
Lunch: Noon–3:30 p.m., entrees $11–$25.
Dinner: 7:30–11 p.m., entrees $11–$25.
One of the best-known tourist establishments in the islands is this restaurant serving traditional Creole specials in a room resplendent with baroque trappings. This mecca for delicacies like *accra* (cod fritters) and *lambi* (conch) is still going strong, even after the death of its creator Violetta Chaville. Service is by women in traditional dress. This is an excellent visual and culinary experience for first-time visitors.

Folie Plage   **$$$**   ★ ★

Anse Laborde, Anse Laborde, ☎ *(590) 22-11-17.*
French cuisine.
Lunch: Noon–3 p.m., entrees $14–$18.
Dinner: 7–10 p.m., entrees $14–$18.
Local families flock to this restaurant/guesthouse in Anse Laborde on the north coast of Grand-Terre, especially on weekends, for a combination of beach-combing and grilled fish, court bouillon and chicken curry. If you're so inclined, rent a simple room from Madame Marcelin for under $50.

La Canne A Sucre   **$$$**   ★ ★ ★ ★ ★

Quai No. 1, Point-a-Pitre, ☎ *(590) 82-10-19.*
French cuisine.
Lunch: Noon–2:30 p.m., entrees $18–$32.
Dinner: 7:30–10 p.m., entrees $18–$32.
This fine restaurant in Pointe-a-Pitre's port of Centre Saint-John Perse has a seagull's eye view of arriving ships, with a location on the quay. Patrons have a choice of dining in a ground floor brasserie on grilled lamb and mixed seafood platters, or upstairs in a tony, rose-hued chamber. Chef Gerard Virginius is fond of enhancing the finest seafood and poultry available locally with soursop and starfruit-infused vinegars and wine sauces.

La Louisiane   **$$$**   ★ ★ ★

Quartier Ste. Marthe, St. Francois, ☎ *(590) 88-44-34.*

French cuisine.
Lunch: Noon–2 p.m., entrees $22–$30.
Dinner: 7–10 p.m., entrees $22–$30.

Located a few miles from the chic resort of St. Francois in Sainte Marthe, this bloom-filled hillside house has an established reputation for creative French-Antillean cuisine. Dinner for two can get pricey, but the experience is worth the splurge—specialties include shark prepared in a saffron sauce and pate of sea urchin roe.

La Plantation $$$ ★★★★★

Galerie Commerciale, Bas du Fort, ☎ *(590) 90-84-83.*
French cuisine.
Lunch: Noon–2:30 p.m., entrees $14–$54.
Dinner: 7–10:30 p.m., entrees $14–$54.

Guadeloupe's largest marina also boasts this well-known four-star establishment housed in two rosy, intimate dining rooms. La Plantation presents French classic cuisine with an emphasis on natural ingredients. Crayfish is a specialty, prepared in myriad ways—sometimes in a salad with foie gras, an unusual combination that works.

Le Chateau de Feuilles $$$ ★★★★★

Campeche, Anse Bertrand, ☎ *(590) 22-30-30.*
French cuisine.
Lunch: 11a.m.–3 p.m., entrees $18–$29.
Dinner: entrees $18–$29.

If you pass the remains of a crumbling old sugar mill in off-the-beaten-path Anse Bertrand, you're close to your goal—a four-star culinary landmark in an unlikely location—of a farm owned by chef-hosts Jean-Pierre and Martine Dubost. The atmosphere is like a house party, with a pool to swim in after lunch and a breathtaking choice of 20 flavors of rum, like a sophisticated Baskin-Robbins for adults. If you had a hard time finding the restaurant, don't indulge too much or you may never make it home. Dinner is served on Fridays and Saturdays, for a minimum of 10 people.

Le Poisson d'Or $$$ ★★★

Rue Sadi-Carnot 2, Port Louis, ☎ *(590) 22-88-63.*
Latin American cuisine.
Lunch: 9:30 a.m.–4:30 p.m., entrees $14–$27.
Dinner: 6–9 p.m., entrees $14–$27.

The pride of the quiet fishing town of St. Louis is this cozy spot serving Creole specialties and seafood in a homey atmosphere. Specials change frequently, but usually feature crab farcis with spicy stuffing and homemade ice cream.

Le Restaurant $$$ ★★★

Chateaubrun, Ste. Anne, ☎ *(590) 88-23-96.*
French cuisine.
Lunch: 12:30–2:30 p.m., entrees $25–$40.
Dinner: 7:30–9:30 p.m., entrees $25–$40.

Le Restaurant at the tropical village-style Le Relais du Moulin serves the usual Antillean-French dishes with some flair in an elegant dining room facing the resort's pool. Fixed price meals for $40 and a la carte offerings include grilled langoustes with herbs, blaff (fresh seafood in a spicy infusion) and lobster. After dinner, stroll the grounds; an old mill (moulin) dating back to the inn's plantation days makes a picturesque photo opportunity.

Les Oiseaux $$$ ★★★

Anse des Rochers, St. Francois, ☎ *(501) 88-56-92.*
French cuisine.
Lunch: Noon–3 p.m., entrees $14–$29.
Dinner: 5–10:30 p.m., entrees $14–$29.

It's easy to imagine that you're in the South of France while dining on the terrace of this stone structure facing the sea, located a few miles south of St. Francois. The talented chef is a whiz with seafood, attesting to the popularity of his cassoulet de fruits de mer, and a cheeseless fondue of various fish and shellfish cooked with aromatic oils.

Sucrerie du Comte $$$ ★★★

Comte de Loheac, Sainte-Rose, ☎ *(590) 28-60-17.*
cuisine.
Lunch: Noon–3 p.m., entrees $13–$35.
Dinner: 7–9:30 p.m., entrees $13–$35.

This pretty open-air restaurant, built of Brazilian woods and volcanic rock, is on the site of a former sugarcane factory and a small hotel that bears the same name. It's open all day for salads and sandwiches and offers such evening specialties as Tahitian fish with coconut milk, fish stew, mahimahi in parchment paper, and fresh fruit crepes. A good wine list accompanies the tasty dishes, many accented with local spices. On Sundays, the menu features traditional Creole dishes.

Victoria $$$ ★★★

Cottage and Troical Club hotels, Le Moule, ☎ *(590) 23-78-38.*
French cuisine.
Lunch: 11:30 a.m.–2:30 p.m., entrees $7–$30.
Dinner: 7–10 p.m., entrees $10–$37.

Ceiling fans, coral-colored walls, and rattan furniture with blue seat cushions is the pleasing decor at this pretty open-air cafe across from the beach at la Moule. Choose from imaginative meat, chicken, and fish dishes with traditional heavy creams; the goat cheese salad is to die for. Besides the tasty food and fine wine list, a big plus is the fact they speak fluent English here—a rare find on Guadeloupe. Also open for breakfast from 7:00-9:30 a.m. daily; lunch hours can vary, so call first.

Where to Shop

The market at Pointe-a-Pitre is a bonanza of straw hats.

Guadeloupe is not a shopper's paradise—better to go to Martinique. What Guadeloupe lacks in merchandise, it more than makes up for in fun, however-er. Head for the street stalls around the harbor quay, in front of the tourist office and at the open-air market. The **Juan Perse Cruise Terminal** caters to the more sophisticated, and expensive tastes of cruise passengers; here you'll find a spanking new mall with about 24 shops. Avoid days when cruise ships are in port and start shopping early in the morning, before the noonday sun gets too hot.

Paying with traveler's checks and/or credit cards can sometimes reap you a 20 percent discount. French products, from crystal to cosmetics, perfume and fashions, are often less expensive than stateside, but if you are interested in brand names, check the prices at home before coming. Native craftwork can run from the junky to the intriguing; the best buys are salako hats made of split bamboo, straw baskets and hats, and wood carvings. Table linens made from madras are particularly fine. Even if you don't drink, bring back at least one bottle of Guadeloupe rum; there's sure to be someone back home who will love it. Best shops for rum are **Delice Shop** in Pointe-a-Pitre and **Ets Azincourt**.

In Pointe-a-Pitre, the main shopping streets are **rue Frébault**, **rue de Nozieres** and **rue Schoelcher**. Bas-du-Fort's two shopping districts are the **Mammoth Shopping Center** and the **Marina**, where you will find a good supply of both boutiques and restaurants. This is the place to come if you are in need of resort-wear fast. Duty-free shops can be found at the **Raizet Airport**.

Lles des Saintes

The sailing school at Petite Anse, Terre-de-Haut, offers half or full day windsurfing courses.

Terre-de-Haut is the largest island in an archipelago of eight islands called Les Saintes, off the south coast of Guadeloupe. The 35-minute ferry ride to reach there from Trois-Rivieres or 60-minute ride from Pointe-a-Pitre can be torturous due to choppy waves; take motion sickness pills if you are susceptible. Terre-de-Haut has but 1500 residents on its five-square-mile terrain; its largest city is Bourg with seerla boutiques, restaurants and gingerbread houses hugging the hillsides. Daring explorers can scope out secluded coves; there's even a nude beach at Anse Crawen, which has been compared to Rio de Janeiro for its beauty. A third of the island's economy is dedicated to tourism, so expect locals to be generous and friendly. Among the most important sites (there really aren't that many) is **Fort Napoléon**, leftover from the days when the English warred with the native population, and a nearby museum that houses a modern collection of paintings.

The real reason to come to Terre-de-Haut is to revel in its tranquil, laid back charms. The quaint European-style village is a treat with its pastel wooden buildings (resist peeking in—many are private residences), friendly locals (who speak little English but are patient as tourists butcher their native French), decent restaurants, and limited shopping (note that virtually all stores close from noon to 2 or 3—or even 4 p.m.—for siesta). Don't miss the old Catholic Church at town center with its marble floor and high wooden ceiling; for five francs (about $1), you can light a candle in memory of a loved one. Then stroll up the street to **Chicken George's**, a local character who makes unforgettable (unless you drink too many) local punches. Also be on the lookout for **Kaz an Nou** ☎ *(590) 99-52-29* , where artisans make traditional wooden creole facades, the perfect souvenir to take home. While most of the island's beaches are not the greatest, the water is wonderfully clear and inviting. Be sure to check out Grande-Anse Beach on the Atlantic side, a lovely, lonely stretch you'll probably have all to yourself. The tide is much too strong for safe swimming (and signs forbid it), but it's the perfect spot for a picnic lunch.

The entire island has only about 30 cars; tourists get around on foot (easily done, though the trek up to Fort Napoléon is quite steep) or rent a motor scooter. You can arrange this just as you get off the ferry; expect to pay about $30 per day, including gas and insurance. You may plan to come just for the day, but just in case, pack an overnight bag. **Les Saintes** is magical, especially in the evening as the children play in the ferry square, locals emerge sleepily from their afternoon siestas, and atmospheric cafes prepare creole dinners you'll be hard-pressed to bid au revoir to this enchanted isle.

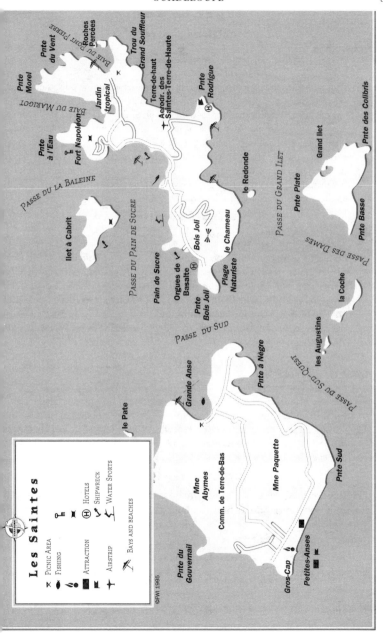

Les Saintes

PICNIC AREA
FISHING
ATTRACTION
AIRSTRIP

HOTELS
SHIPWRECK
WATER SPORTS
BAYS AND BEACHES

©FWI 1995

Pnte du Vent
Pnte Morel
Roches Percées
Baie du Pont Pierre
Trou du Grand Souffleur
Terre-de-haut
Aérodr. des Saintes-Terre-de-Haute
Pnte Rodrigue
Pnte des Colibris
Baie du Marigot
Jardin tropical
Fort Napoléon
Pnte à l'Eau
Grand Ilet
le Redonde
Pnte Plate
Passe du Grand Ilet
Passe de la Baleine
Pnte Basse
Ilet à Cabrit
Passe du Pain de Sucre
Pain de Sucre
Bois Joli
le Chameau
Passe des Dames
Orgues de Basalte
Pnte Bois Joli
Plage Naturiste
la Coche
Passe du Sud
les Augustins
le Pate
Passe du Sud-Ouest
Grande Anse
Pnte à Nègre
Mne Abymes
Comm. de Terre-de-Bas
Mne Paquette
Pnte Sud
Pnte du Gouvernail
Gros-Cap
Petites-Anses

What to See

Historical Sites

Fort Napoleon   ★★★★

Bourg, Les Saintes.
Hours open: 9 a.m.–12:30 p.m.

This old French fort, wherein you can survey barracks and prison cells, is quite well
preserved and a nice place to while away a few hours. All signage is in French, but
you can buy an English brochure for $5.00—a bit of a rip-off after the $4.00 admission fee. Still, it's a nice spot, with many interesting exhibits inside—huge model
ships, massive oil paintings depicting sea battles, and, oddly enough, a modern art
museum—and breathtaking views and lovely botanical gardens outside. Look
closely among the many varieties of cacti and you're sure to spot an iguana or two.
Wear sturdy shoes as the ground is uneven, and bring lots of water if you plan to
hike up the very steep road to the fort.

Sports/Recreation

Watersports in Les Saintes

Les Saintes.

Les Saintes may not have the most beautiful beaches in the Caribbean, but its crystal-clear waters beckon to be explored. For sailing excursions, try **Paradoxe Croi-
sieres** (☎ *590-88-41-73*) and **Atlantis** (☎ *590-99-50-56*). For general
watersports and diving, try **UPCA** (☎ *590-99-54-94*), Diving **Nautique des Saintes**
(☎ *590-99-54-25*), **Land Maidonneuvre Guy** (☎ *590-99-53-13*). For pedal boat
and canoe rentals, call **Lognos Paul** (☎ *590-99-54-08*) and **Deher Daniel** (☎ *590-
99-52-42*).

Tours

Guided Tours in Les Saintes

Les Saintes.

Terre de Haut is easily explored by foot or motorscooter—you can't rent a car. If
you'd rather leave the navigating to someone else, try one of these operators, who
provide island tours in small buses: **Procida** (☎ *590-99-55-13*), **Emilien Pineau**
(☎ *590-99-51-42*), **Rose Rosette** (☎ *590-99-50-61*), **Sigiscar** (☎ *590-99-53-
08*), and **Ch. Henri Vincent** (☎ *590-99-51-79*).

Where to Stay

Hotels are small here, with the general atmosphere of a West Indian inn
Service is congenial, and at times so familiar you'll feel as if you are renting
from your own family. Now is the time to visit the island before it succumb
to more commercial enterprises.

Hotels and Resorts

Auberge les Petits Saints   **$65–$130**   ★★★★

La Savane, ☎ *(590) 99-50-99, FAX (590) 99-54-51.*
Single: $65–$120. Double: $74–$130.

Enjoy lovely views from this elegant and eccentric hotel, perched on a hill about a
15-minute walk from the village. You could easily spend your entire holiday poking

through the whimsically crammed lobby, a glorious hodge-podge of antiques from around the world, including my favorite: a huge ornamental birdcage (more like a mansion) from Asia. Many of the items are for sale, so bring your checkbook! Four guestrooms share bathing facilities but have private toilets across the hall; the rest have connected private baths. All rooms are air conditioned and individually decorated with antiques and interesting artwork; the overall look is simple, yet clean and pleasant. My favorite is Room 12, which is outside the main house and has a large stone wall, queen bed and large balcony.The grounds include an excellent seafood restaurant, a small but pretty pool and a sauna. This unique spot is a real winner, provided you don't mind the steep walks into town and the beach.

Hotel Bois Joli	**$98–$192**	★★★

Lles des Saintes, ☎ *(590) 99-52-53, FAX (590) 99-55-05.*
Single: $98–$139. Double: $130–$192.

Set in a pretty location with great views, this decent hotel is the island's oldest, dating back to the 1960s. Guestrooms are simply furnished, and only some have air conditioning and private baths. The new bungalows are a better bet; each comes with white wooden furniture, twin beds in the master bedroom, bunk beds in the second bedroom, modern baths, refrigerators and a large patio overlooking the sea. There's a nice restaurant and bar on-site as well. With its cute bridge adding a touch of atmosphere, the pool is quite pleasant. Watersports await on the beach for an extra charge. This is one of Les Sainte's few full-service hotels, but its remote location—two miles from the village—is a definite drawback. You'll need to rent scooters to get around.

Apartments and Condominiums

Village Creole	**$80–$168**	★★★★

Pointe Coquelet, ☎ *(590) 99-53-83, FAX (590) 99-55-55.*
Double: $80–$168.

This charming spot perched on the Caribbean Sea, far below Fort Napoleon, offers oceanfront or garden duplexes just perfect for self-catering holidays. Each duplex is nicely decorated with a large living and dining area, a full bathroom, a complete and modern kitchen with high-quality cooking and dishware, and a patio on the first floor. Up the pine spiral staircase you'll find two bedrooms and another full bath; both have French-style hand-held showers. Bedrooms are air conditioned while the common areas rely on sea breezes to keep things cool. The rates include maid service and transportation from the ferry or airport. The beach and lovely village of Terre de Haut with its myriad restaurants are a short stroll away. French-born owner Ghyslain Laps is the consumate host, making sure his guests are kept happy and pampered. He's also a whiz at languages, speaking enough English, German, Swedish, and Italian to keep the lines of communication humming. Like all hotels on Les Saites, rates rise sharply during the Christmas and Carnival seasons (mid-Feburary to mid-March); expect to pay from $228 to $288 then. Very highly recommended.

Where to Eat

La Saladerie   **$$**   ★★

Anse Marie, Terre de Haute, ☎ *(590) 99-50-92.*
International cuisine.
Lunch: Noon–2 p.m., entrees $7–$19.
Dinner: 7–9 p.m., entrees $7–$19.

As the name implies, guests can get a good green salad as well as seafood lightly grilled with fresh vegetables on the side at this lovely little oasis filled with plants and good music from owner Edward's eclectic CD collection. Prices are very reasonable for the great sea views, the high quality of the food, and the very gracious service. Save room for the luscious desserts, especially the fresh fruit sorbets. Highly recommended!

Le Amandiers   **$$**   ★★

Placc de la Mairie, Terre de Haute, ☎ *(590) 99-50-06.*
Latin American cuisine.
Lunch: 11a.m.–2:30 p.m., entrees $12–$16.
Dinner: 7–11 p.m., entrees $12–$16.

This casual bistro is a superb base from which to while away the hours in the quaint Norman-flavored town of Bourg de Saintes, with its location right on the central square. A set-price lunch of local vegetables, salads, cod fritters and dessert is a bargain at $10. At dinner, sea-fresh selections like conch and crayfish keep visitors coming back for more.

Le Jardin Creole   **$**   ★★

Place du Debarcadere (the ferry pier), ☎ *(590) 99-55-08.*
Seafood cuisine.
Lunch: 9 a.m.–2 p.m., entrees $4–$14.
Dinner: 7–10 p.m., entrees $4–$14.

This casual spot is perfect for grabbing a quick bite before or after the ferry—or anytime, for that matter. Inside is rather plain, but outside, on the patio, patrons have a bird's-eye view of the goings-on below in the square; it's especially charming at night, when the children come out to play (and happily ignore the restaurant owner's pleas of "silence, si vous plait!") The menu offers up a large selection of crepes, steaks, mussels and smoked fish; I particularly liked the hardy fish pie with its golden, flaky crust. An added bonus: the owner speaks excellent English.

Nilce's Bar   **$**   ★★★★

Place du Debarcadere (ferry pier), ☎ *(590) 99-56-80.*
International cuisine.

This place debuted in June 1995 to instant success—I was there just three days after the grand opening, and it was mobbed! With good reason, too. Nilce, a beautiful Brazilian-born singer married to the owner of Village Creole (see Hotels), wows the crowd as she and an incredibly talented keyboardist belt out tunes from 6:00 p.m. nightly. The atmosphere is unmistakingly French—even the furniture came from an old French bistro—and depending on the crowd, there'll be local musicians jamming, abandoned dancing, and a hell of a good time for all. Set in an old house, the cafe serves American and French breakfasts and a tapas menu for lunch and dinner.

Look for the old white building with fresh green trim and prepare for an evening of new friends and general merriment.

La Désirade

La Désirade, five miles east of Guadeloupe, was coveted by Columbus when he spotted the island on Nov. 3, 1493. The name he chose, which means "desired land" showed his true feelings about the exotic nature of the terrain. Ironically, the island became a leper colony for several years. Today it is a perfect place to escape with a picnic to one of the more beautiful beaches of **Souffleur** and **Baie Mahault**. Presently, the island is nearly pristine. In the main village of Grand Anse, there is a charming old church to visit and a hotel called **La Guitone**, where you can get a fine fish meal.

Marie-Galante

At 60 square miles, Marie-Galante is the largest of Guadeloupe's islands. The Caribs retreated here when they were driven from the mainland by the French; centuries later it's become a favorite haven for tourists, both local and foreign, who find the beach at Petit-Anse particularly charming. The island is the epitome of laid-back, though back in the 1800s it had a thriving sugar plantation industry. Ruins of sugar mills can be found all over the island. To get here, take the ferry from Pointe-a-Pitre, which drops you off at Grand Bourg, its largest city with a population of 8000, or one of the numerous short flights offered from Pointe-a-Pitre.

What to See

Museums and Exhibits

Chateau Murat ★★

Near Grand-Bourg, Marie-Galante.
After being destroyed by an earthquake in 1843, this 18th-century sugar plantation has been faithfully restored to its former glory. The mill is constructed of handhewn stone and houses the Ecomusee, an arts and traditions museum on island life. The adjoining botanic garden produces many of the medicinal herbs used on Marie-Galante.

Rhum Magaalda

Domaine de Bellevue, Capesterre, Marie-Galante.
This rum factory, located on the Bellevue property, dates back to 1821 and was completely rebuilt after being felled by a hurricane in 1928. The hospitable elderly owners welcome the public for impromptu tours—"just drop by and knock"—but come with a French phrase book, as they don't speak much English. Also bring lots of insect repellant—this place is charming, but crawling with mosquitos.

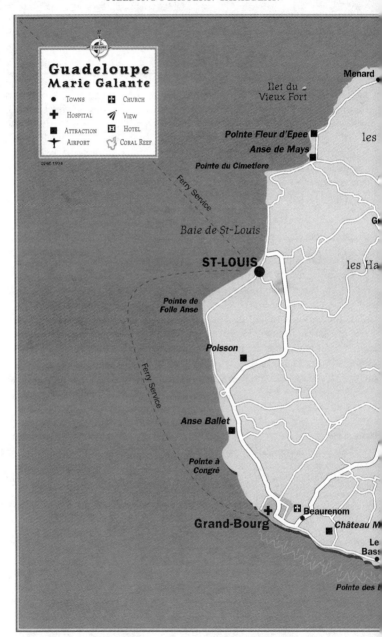

Guadeloupe
Marie Galante

- ● TOWNS
- ✚ HOSPITAL
- ■ ATTRACTION
- ✈ AIRPORT
- ✚ CHURCH
- ✈ VIEW
- H HOTEL
- 🪸 CORAL REEF

Ilet du
Vieux Fort

Menard

Pointe Fleur d'Epee ■

Anse de Mays ■

Pointe du Cimetiere

Ferry Service

les

Baie de St-Louis

ST-LOUIS ●

les Ha

G

*Pointe de
Folle Anse*

Poisson ■

Ferry Service

Anse Ballet ■

*Pointe à
Congrè*

✚ ✚ **Beaurenom** ●

Grand-Bourg

Château M

■

Le
Bass

Pointe des

se Pointe

Gueule Grand Gouffre

nbrai

Maletie

Caye Plante

Anse Bois d'Inde

Anse Chapelle

Anse Piton

Borée

le Trou au Diable (Cave)

on
uth

Ste. Croix

elle

Robert

St Anne

Capesterre

Petite Anse

Aérodrome. de Marie-Galante

Sports/Recreation

Guided Tours of Marie-Galante

Marie-Galante.

The island is best explored by rental car, which costs about $50.00 per day. If you'd rather leave the driving to someone else, call one of the following: **Bavarday Philippe** ☎ *(590) 97-81-97*, **Jernival Roseline** ☎ *(590) 97-73-14*, **Glovert Gino** ☎ *(590) 97-34-18*, **Moysan Eugene** ☎ *(590) 97-31-05*, **Leveille Etiene** ☎ *(590) 97-72-97*, **El Rancho** ☎ *(590) 97-81-60*, and **Goram Frederic** ☎ *(590) 97-09-89*.

Watersports on Marie-Galante

Marie-Galante.

Take advantage of Marie-Galante's lovely beaches and inviting sea. For windsurfing, try **Fun Evasion** *(Capesterre,* ☎ *(590) 97-35-21)*; for diving, call **Maison Poullet Section Murat** *(Grand-Bourg,* ☎ *(590) 97-75-24)*.

Tours

Bezard ★★★

Between Etang-Noir and Grand Case, Marie-Galante.

This spot was still under construction when I passed though in the summer of 1995, but it should be open for 1996. It features a newly renovated windmill that will demonstrate how sugarcane is crushed, and re-created slave huts made from straw and goelette wood that will house boutiques. Worth a stop if you're in the area.

Sea Arch at Gueule ★★★★

The islands's northern tip, Marie-Galante.

It's well worth the scenic drive to reach this stunning sea arch at Gueule. Bring lots of film and beware of climbing past the fenceline. If you're heading back south toward Capesterre, be on the lookout for the island's oldest house, an unmarked shack made from cane. It's between Caye Plate and Pointe Pisiou, on the left.

Where to Stay

Hotels and Resorts

Auberge de l'Arbre a Pain $40–$50 ★★★

Rue Jeanne d'Arc, Grand-Bourg, ☎ *(590) 97-73-69.*
Single: $40. Double: $50.

This small and pleasant spot is located near the harbor within an easy walk to the beach. Rooms are simple but clean, air conditioned, and have private baths. The creole restaurant is open for three meals daily.

Le Salut $34–$50 ★

Saint-Louis, ☎ *(590) 97-02-67.*
Double: $34–$50.

Recommended only if you're watching every dollar (or actually, franc), this low-frills hotel has basic rooms with or without air conditioning and private bath. There's a bar/restaurant on-site, but no pool, and the beach is a walk.

Village de Menard $60–$100 ★★★

Menard, Saint-Louis, ☎ *(590) 97-77-02, FAX (590) 97-76-89.*
Single: $60–$100. Double: $60–$100.

This peaceful spot is located on the site of an old rum factory, with some stone ruins dotting the grounds. Accommodations are in bungalows with one or two bedrooms (the second one has bunk beds and a twin) and complete kitchenettes. The more deluxe units are well worth the small bump in price and feature tile floors, high beamed ceilings, telephones and TV. In all units, air conditioning is available only in the bedrooms. Save for an inviting pool, there's nothing on-site and not much in the immediate area, so you'll definitely want to rent a car. The beach is a 15-minute walk. A new package is a great deal: $200 per person per day (at a minimum of seven nights) includes roundtrip air from Pointe-A-Pitre to Marie-Galante, accommodations, bicycles, three meals a day (via coupons at area restaurants), and a car. Add $120 per day for each additional person.

Where to Eat

Auberge de la Roche d'Or   **$$$**   ★ ★

Capesterre, ☎ (590) 97-37-42.
International cuisine.
Dinner: 7:30–9:30 p.m., entrees $20–$30.
This inviting spot offers up pleasing specialties like conch pannes, breadfruit gratin, and iced pineapple flambe. You'll also find red snapper, local river shrimp, and other treats from la mer. Closed each May and Wednesday and Sunday for dinner year-round.

L'Auberge L'Arbre a Pain   **$$$**   ★ ★

Rue Jeanne d'Arc, Marie-Galante, ☎ (590) 97-73-69.
International cuisine.
Lunch: entrees $10–$30.
Dinner: entrees $10–$30.
It may help if you have a working knowledge of French in order to stay or eat at this small (seven room) inn located in Grand-Bourg, the civic center of Marie-Galante. But most visitors to this rural outpost are drawn to the simple country ways and lack of development that make this destination choice. Guests who fly down for the day can enjoy unique seafood dishes here, like octopus, or a more familiar grilled conch or seafood platter. There's also a five-course meal for $30.

La Braise Marine   **$$$**   ★

Face Plage de la Ferriere, Capesterre, ☎ (590) 97-42-57.
International cuisine.
Lunch: 11:30 a.m.–3:30 p.m., entrees $8–$30.
Dinner: 7–11 p.m., entrees $8–$30.
The menu changes daily at this casual eatery right across the street from one of Marie-Galante's most beautiful beaches. Expect to see sea urchin fritters, grilled fish, and creole blood sausages. If ouassou is offered, grab it. This large prawn-like delicacy, unique to the rivers of Guadeloupe and its islands, tastes like lobster and is just fabulous!

Guadeloupe Directory

ARRIVAL AND DEPARTURE

American Airlines makes year-round flights to Guadeloupe from more than 100 cities direct to San Juan, with nonstop connections to Guadeloupe via American Eagle. Minerve Airlines, a French charter carrier, has flights Friday-Sunday from New York during December-March peak season. Air Canada flies nonstop from Paris and Fort-de-France and has direct service from Miami, San Juan and Port-au-Prince. Air Guadeloupe flies daily from St. Martin and St. Maarten, St. Barts, Marie-Galante, La Desirade, and Les Saintes. LIAT flies from St. Croix, Antigua and St. Maarten.

All flights arrive at La Raizet International Airport, 2.5 miles from Pointe-a-Pitre. It's easy to hire a cab, from the many lined up at the airport. Cars can be rented at the airport.

BUSINESS HOURS

Stores open weekdays 9 a.m.–1 p.m. and 3–6 p.m. Banks open weekdays 8 a.m.–noon and 2–4 p.m. Some shops and banks are also open Saturday mornings.

CLIMATE

The climate is tropical with an average temperature of 79 degrees F. The more humid and wet season runs between June and November.

DOCUMENTS

If you're only staying up to three weeks, you need show only a current or expired passport (five years old or less) or proof of citizenship (voter's registration, birth certificate and official photo ID), as well as an ongoing or return ticket. Longer stays require a valid passport.

ELECTRICITY

Current is 220 volts, AC, 50 cycles. Adapters for U.S. appliances are needed.

GETTING AROUND

Taxis are plentiful and fares are set by the government. Between 9 p.m. and 7 a.m., fares increase 40 percent. You will have to be able to speak French to hire radio cabs.

Buses throughout the island run from 5:30 a.m.–7:30 p.m., and connect the island's major towns to Pointe-a-Pitre. Conditions are modern. Bus stops are included along the road and in shelters marked arrêtbus, but buses will often stop if you flag them down. Fares are inexpensive but the schedules are not reliable and they are often too crowded for comfort. Avoid riding them before and after school.

Since biking is a major sport here, you won't feel alone if you rent one. Bike rentals average about $10 a day, somewhat more for mountain bikes. Vespas are also good vehicles to rent, costing about $40 a day, plus a $200 deposit or a major credit card.

Cars are easy to rent on Guadeloupe. You may use your own driver's license up to 20 days; after that you need to obtain an international driver's permit. Roads are excellent here (more than 1225 miles), though the hairpins on Basse-Terre will take some careful negotiating. Natives drive well but fast, so be aware of passers. Stick with the top names like Hertz, Budget and Avis, in case there is trouble with your bill once you return home. In general, rentals here, about $60 a day, are a bit higher than on other islands. Check with your travel agent to see if prearranged rentals will save you money.

For some reason known only to Guadeloupeons (and even they're not too sure why), the three ferries that service Marie-Galante, Les Saintes, and La Desirade all offer virtually the same schedule. It's quite an amusing sight as they all pull into Point-a-Pitre at the exact same time and vie for passengers. Each leaves Pointe-a-Pitre at about 8 a.m. and departs for the return at about 4 p.m. Depending on the weather, the ferry ride can be quite rough, so take motion-sickness pills if you don't have great sea legs. Other times, it can be a smooth and exhilarating ride, especially if you sit on top in the open air. Call for information. **ATE** ☎ *(590) 95-13-43*, **Brudey Freres** ☎ *(590) 90-04-48*, and **Princess Caroline** ☎ *(590) 99-53-79*.

LANGUAGE

The official language is French. The African-influenced Creole is spoken by nearly everyone. Only some people speak English, so bring a French phrase book.

MEDICAL EMERGENCIES

There are five hospitals and 23 clinics in Guadeloupe. Your hotel or the tourist office can assist you in finding an English-speaking physician.

MONEY

The official currency is the French franc. The best exchange rate is to be found at banks or bureau de change; to convert francs back to dollars, you must go to a bank. For some reason, paying for purchases with dollar-denomination traveler's checks or credit cards may get you the best exchange rate.

TELEPHONE

The area code is *590*. To phone from Guadeloupe, buy a "telecarte," a plastic credit card sold at post offices and other outlets marked "Teleporte en Vente Ici." Use these cards on phones marked "Telecom." Operator-assisted calls and those made from your hotel room are much more expensive.

TIME

Guadeloupe is one hour later than Eastern Standard Time.

TIPPING

Restaurants and bars are required by law to add a 15 percent service charge. Most taxi drivers don't expect tips, especially if they own their own cars. Room maids should be tipped $1–$2, bellboys 50 cents–$1 a bag.

TOURIST INFORMATION

Brochures, maps and advice can be found at the Office Départemental du Tourisme de la Guadeloupe located near the waterfront in *Pointe-á-Pitre at 5 Pl. de la Banque;* ☎ *(590) 82-09-30.* The office is open Monday–Saturday. In the U.S. call ☎ *(213) 658-7462.*

WHEN TO GO

Between December and May. June–November is the humid and wet season.

GUADELOUPE HOTELS	RMS	RATES	PHONE	CR. CARDS
Basse-Terre				
Basse-Terre				
★★★★ Village Creole Hotel	72	$71–$115	(590) 45-62-41	A, MC, V
★★★ L'Auberge de Distillerie	15	$105–$125	(590) 94-25-91	A, DC, MC, V
★★★ Relais Grand Soufriere	21	$49–$93	(590) 80-01-27	A, DC, MC, V
★★★ Sucrerie du Comte	50	$50–$100	(590) 28-60-17	MC
Grande-Terre				
Pointe-a-Pitre				
★★★★★ Auberge de la Vieille Tour	153	$118–$231	(800) 221-4542	A, MC, V
★★★★★ Le Meridien la Cocoteraie	50	$160–$680	(590) 88-79-81	A, DC, MC, V
★★★★★ Le Meridien St. Francois	265	$199–$285	(800) 543-4300	A, MC, V
★★★★ Club Med Caravelle	310		(800) 258-2633	A
★★★★ Fleur d'Epee Novotel	190	$123–$213	(800) 221-4542	A, DC, MC, V
★★★★ Hotel Hamak Beach	56	$175–$255	(590) 88-59-59	A, CB, MC
★★★★ La Creole Beach Hotel	321	$60–$550	(590) 90-46-46	A, DC, MC, V
★★★★ PLM Azur Marissol Hotel	200	$94–$185	(590) 90-84-44	A, DC, MC, V
★★★★ Tropical Club Hotel	84	$92–$192	(590) 23-78-38	A, MC, V
★★★ Canella Beach Residence	146	$87–$230	(590) 90-44-00	A, DC, MC, V
★★★ Hotel Toubana	32	$105–$230	(590) 88-25-78	
★★★ Plantation Ste. Marthe	120	$157–$315	(590) 88-72-46	MC, V
★★★ Residence du Parc		$382–$868	(590) 23-78-50	A, MC, V

GUADELOUPE HOTELS		RMS	RATES	PHONE	CR. CARDS
★★	Auberge du Grand Large	10	$100–$105	(590) 88-20-06	A, MC, V
★★	Cottage Hotel	24	$112–$220	(590) 23-78-38	A, MC, V
★★	Domaine de l'Anse des Rochers	356	$80–$220	(590) 93-90-00	MC, V
★★	Ecotel Guadeloupe	44	$60–$130	(590) 90-60-00	A, DC, MC, V
★★	Hotel Arawak	154	$130–$240	(590) 84-24-24	A, DC, MC, V
★	Callinago Hotel & Village	110	$102–$216	(590) 84-25-25	A, DC, MC, V
★	Kaliko Beach Club	40	$80–$99	(590) 22-80-40	A, MC, V
★	Relais du Moulin	40	$105–$156	(590) 88-23-96	A, DC, MC, V

Sainte-Anne

★★★	Relais du Moulin	40	$105–$156	(590) 88-23-96	A, DC, MC, V
★★	Mini Beach Hotel	9	$70–$150	(590) 88-21-13	MC, V

Lles des Saintes

Terre-de-Haut

★★★★	Auberge les Petits Saints	10	$65–$130	(590) 99-50-99	MC, V
★★★	Hotel Bois Joli	29	$98–$233	(590) 99-52-53	MC, V

Marie-Galante

★★★	Village de Menard	5	$60–$100	(590) 97-77-02	MC, V
★★	Auberge de l'Arbre a Pain	7	$40–$50	(590) 97-73-69	
★	Le Salut	15	$34–$50	(590) 97-02-67	

GUADELOUPE RESTAURANTS		PHONE	ENTREE	CR. CARDS

Basse-Terre

Basse-Terre

	French			
★★★★	La Rocher de Malendure	(590) 98-70-84	$8–$18••	DC, MC, V
	International			
★★★	Chez Paul de Matouba	(590) 80-29-20	$12–$18••	MC, V
	Latin American			
★★★	Chez Clara	(590) 28-72-99	$9–$27	MC, V

GUADELOUPE RESTAURANTS	PHONE	ENTREE	CR. CARDS
Grande-Terre			
Pointe-a-Pitre			
French			
★★★★★ Auberge de la Vielle Tour	(590) 84-23-23	$23–$39••	A, DC, MC, V
★★★★★ La Canne A Sucre	(590) 82-10-19	$18–$32	A, MC, V
★★★★★ La Plantation	(590) 90-84-83	$14–$54	A, DC, MC, V
★★★★★ Le Chateau de Feuilles	(590) 22-30-30	$18–$29	MC, V
★★★ Chez Violetta	(590) 84-10-34	$11–$25	A, DC, MC, V
★★★ La Louisiane	(590) 88-44-34	$22–$30	MC, V
★★★ Le Restaurant	(590) 88-23-96	$25–$40	A, DC, MC, V
★★★ Les Oiseaux	(501) 88-56-92	$14–$29	V
★★ Folie Plage	(590) 22-11-17	$14–$18	A, DC, V
Latin American			
★★★ Le Poisson d'Or	(590) 22-88-63	$14–$27	MC, V
Terre-de-Haute			
Terre de Haute			
International			
★★ La Saladerie	(590) 99-50-92	$8–$18	MC, V
Latin American			
★★ Le Amandiers	(590) 99-50-06	$12–$16	A, MC, V
Marie-Galante			
Marie-Galante			
International			
★★ L'Auberge L'Arbre a Pain	(590) 97-73-69	$10–$30	V

Note: • Lunch Only;

•• Dinner Only

MARTINIQUE

Martinique is the best place for bargains on French imports from perfume to clothes and crystal.

Martinique is a little bit of foie gras in the middle of the Caribbean. From the cuisine to the chic style of the women, to the lilt of the language, Martinique exudes the charm of its mother country—France. But add to that a decidedly West Indian cachet and shopping values that would make a Parisian's jaw drop open, and you have a tiny island nation waiting to be loved. Rising from beaches to rain forest to the heights of a volcanic mountain that wiped out an entire city in 1902, Martinique is rife with opportunities to dive, trek, sail, surf, parasail and about any other sport imaginable—from mountain biking to deep-sea fishing in some of the clearest waters in the Caribbean. The island has stayed ecologically pure enough to still boast good sightings of many birds in the mangroves, including the yellow-breasted sandbird, a symbol of the island. Best of all, tourism is just beginning to snap at the heels of this nearly forgotten island and locals are still green enough—business-wise—to have escaped becoming jaded. Of course, on an island such as this one, there will always be a few cases of French snoots, but try to ignore them and concentrate on the natural beauties.

Bird's Eye View

Fifty miles long and 22 miles long, Martinique covers 425 square miles. Of its neighboring islands, Dominica lies to the north and St. Lucia to the south; Miami is 1470 miles away. Martinique comes from volcanic origins, and today the 4575-ft. Mount Pelé in the Parc Naturel Regional de la Martinique is the only active volcano, situated in the northwest island. Most of the island is mountainous. In the center of the island lie the Pitons de Carbet and the Montagne du Vauclin is in the south. These mountains are linked by hills, and the airport is situated in the central plains area. The north of the island is covered by an enormous rain forest; banana and pineapples are cultivated there, while sugarcane dominates the rest of the island. Black sandy coves are found throughout the south and along the rugged coast open to the Atlantic, white and gray sands characterize the beaches facing the Caribbean and in the south. On the east coast, the peninsula of Caravelle, the oldest volcanic formation of the island, stretches into the rough Atlantic, boasting a mangrove swamp lined with a coral reef. The capital, Fort-de-France, is situated on the Baie des Flamandes on the western coast, while the burgeoning town of Lamentin is slightly more inland.

History

Columbus was stunned when he chanced upon Martinique—historians can't decide whether it was 1493 or 1502—but phrases like "the most fertile, the softest...the most charming place in the world" leave no doubt regarding his true feelings. Carib Indians were the resident locals on

MARTINIQUE PASSAGE

61° W

ATLANTIC OCEAN

Grand' Rivière

Basse-Pointe

Les Gorges de la Falaise

Montagne Pelée 4467 ft.

Marigot

Le Prêcheur

Le Morne Rouge

Caravelle Peninsula

Saint-Pierre

Canal de Beauregard

La Trinité

Baie du Galion

Gros-Morne

Le Carbet

Piton du Carbet 3890 ft.

Saint Joseph

Le Robert

Havre du Robert

Bellefontaine

Le Lamentin

FORT-DE-FRANCE

Le François

BAIE DE FORT-DE-FRANCE

Le Lamentin Airport

Ducos

Le Saint-Esprit

Montagne du Vauclin 1954 ft.

Les Trois-Îlets

Rivière-Salée

Le Vauclin

14° 30'N

Grand Anse

Les Anses-d'Arlets

Le Diamant

Rivière-Pilote

CARIBBEAN SEA

Ste. Luce

Le Marin

Ste. Anne

N

SAINT LUCIA CHANNEL

Martinique

▲ MOUNTAIN
● CITY
✕ AIRPORT

═══ ROAD
─── TRAIL
∼∼∼ RIVER

0   5   10 km
0   2.5   5 mi

©PM 1995

Martinique when Columbus happened by. Martinica was the name Columbus bestowed on the volcanic island, in honor of St. Martin. The Caribs called it Madinina, meaning "island of flowers." The Caribs proved too hostile for the Spaniards who moved on to other shores, but they continued to fight the French who settled on the island in 1635. Twenty-five years later the French signed a treaty with the Caribs who agreed to stay on the Atlantic side of the island; nevertheless, they were soon exterminated. The next 200 years was a struggle between the Brits and the French. In 1762 the Brits took control, only to pass it over in exchange for Canada, Senegal, the Grenadines, St. Vincent and Tobago. France remained with Guadeloupe and Martinique because they were knee-deep in the sugarcane. The English took over again between 1794-1802, at the request of plantation owners who needed assistance in the face of growing dissent among slaves. Slavery was abolished in 1848 by the French but not before a major slave rebellion occurred in 1879, encouraged by the French Revolution. Eventually, a new wave of immigrant workers from India began to change the dominant color of skin in the island's population. Martinique finally became a French Department in 1946 and a region in 1974.

People

There are about 369,000 people in Martinique, about half of which are living in the capital of Fort-de-France. A racially mixed batch of Africans, East Indians, whites and others, they are all considered citizens of France, and governed by a Prefect, appointed by the French Government. Unemployment is quite high, about a third of the people have no jobs. About a quarter of those employed are in tourism. To get a good glimpse of social life, hang out in the Savane, a 12-acre park of lawn, shade trees, footpaths and benches where families relax and children play, and old men play serious games of dominoes. Locals are called Martiniquaises.

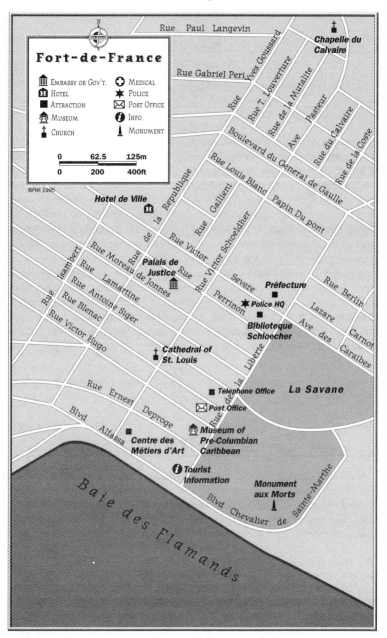

Rue Paul Langevin

Chapelle du Calvaire

Rue Gabriel Peri

Rue Yves Coussard

Rue T. Louverture

Rue de la Mutalité

Pasteur

Rue du Calvaire

Rue de la Coste

Ave.

Boulevard du General de Gaulle

Fort-de-France

🏛 EMBASSY OR GOV'T.   ✚ MEDICAL
🏨 HOTEL   ✦ POLICE
■ ATTRACTION   ✉ POST OFFICE
🏛 MUSEUM   ℹ INFO
✝ CHURCH   ⬍ MONUMENT

0   62.5   125m
0   200   400ft

©FWI 1995

Rue Louis Blanc

Papin Du pont

Hotel de Ville 🏨

Rue de la Republique

Rue Gallieni

Rue Victor

Rue Moreau de Jonnes

Rue de la

Palais de Justice 🏛

Rue Victor Schoeldher

Severe

Préfecture ■

Rue Berlin

Rue Isamberti

Rue Lamartine

Rue Antoine Siger

Rue Blenac

Perrinon

✦ **Police HQ**

Lazare

Ave. des

Carnot

Rue Victor Hugo

✝ **Cathedral of St. Louis**

Biblioteque Schloecher ■

Rue de la Liberté

Caraibes

Rue Ernest Deproge

■ **Telephone Office**

La Savane

Blvd Alfassa

✉ **Post Office**

■ **Centre des Métiers d'Art**

🏛 **Museum of Pre-Columbian Caribbean**

ℹ **Tourist Information**

Monument aux Morts ⬍

Rue de Sainte-Marthe

Blvd Chevalier de

Baie des Flamands

Beaches

You can find a magnificent beach at **Grand Anse** in South Martinique. It is less visited by tourists than the beaches at Pointe du Bout, although it can get more crowded on weekends. Nearby is the petite pretty village of **Anse d'Arlets**. **Diamant Beach**, just south of Ande d'Arlets, is a paradisiacal stretch of 2.5 miles along the south coast dominated by the **Diamond Rock**, a famous volcanic rock that stands about a mile out to sea where the English stationed cannons in the 18th century (British ships still passing it salute her Majesty's "Ship Diamond Rock"). The beach is nearly deserted and fringed with coconut palms and almond trees. It is not advised for swimming since the currents are strong. From the town of Le Marin south, you'll find long white sand beaches fringed with palms trees and calm, clear seas. **Ste. Anne**, where the Club Med is, has its own fine beach, adjacent to the public one, where you can see a terrific view of the southwest coast. There are many places for shade on Ste. Anne under trees that sometimes overhang into the sea. There are lots of bars and restaurants here. There's a family beach on the road heading east from Marin called Cap Chevalier.

Underwater

Walls and caves, reefs and wrecks, Martinique offers a little of everything for divers. Sites are situated along the western coast, north and south of Fort-de-France, with the scalloped coastline between Pointe du Bout and Le Diamant noteworthy for its abundance of smaller reef fish and colorful coral life, particularly Cap Salomon and nearby Les Anses d'Arlets. Because the island is so densely populated, many of the reefs are overfished and some of the coral is damaged. However, the bay off St. Pierre provides one of the Caribbean's most unusual wreck sites, a veritable graveyard created by the eruption of Mt. Pelee in 1902. There are over a dozen dive companies on Martinique, and most of them provide the French "baptism" dive for first-timers, priced only slightly more than a single-tank dive; many resorts also provide underwater initiation in a hotel pool at no charge. Two-tank boat trips are not generally offered in the French West Indies; it is *de rigueur* to share a casual meal between dives. A medical certificate must be produced before diving, and although PADI and NAUI instructors can be found, it's helpful to be familiar with the French dive standards before heading out on a boat.

Diamond Rock

Sometimes referred to as the "Caribbean Gibraltar," this landmark spire breaks the surface of the water just south of the village of Le Diamant. An advanced dive surrounding the island visits caverns sliced deep into the monolith's steep walls (to 85 feet). Difficult surface conditions are not unusual, but this creates the location's excellent visibility; vast schools of small fish, colorful coral growth and sponges, and even a pair of canons are among the sights.

La Perle

This tiny islet lies just off the end of the west-coast road, below the lush flanks of Mt. Pelee, and offers a rich setting for more advanced divers when the water is calm. A highlight is the exciting tunnel filled with sponges and coral, and patrolled by schools of reef fish. Angels, grouper, snapper, soldierfish, and a long black-and-white creature known locally as "Monsieur l'Abbe" fill out the roster.

St. Pierre

At least a dozen ships anchored in St. Pierre's harbor on the morning of May 8, 1902 have been located, providing a most unusual dive site, an underwater memorial to some of St. Pierre's 30,000 residents who lost their lives when Mt. Pelee erupted fiercely. The three-masted *Tamaya* is situated spectacularly on its side, 280 feet down, too deep for recreational diving (but within reach of the tourist sub ride), while the 328-foot *Roraima* can be perused from above by advanced divers; the *Roraima* sits 150 to 200 feet down. Among the other relics are cargo vessels, a tug and an Italian yacht, each beautifully encrusted and teeming with fish life.

Espace De Plongee Meridien

Pointe du Bout; ☎ *(596) 66-01-79.*

Primarily serves clientele of the Meridien Hotel, but welcomes non-guests. Groups limited to 15; there is one PADI instructor on staff, as well as some English-speaking staff. One tank dive, $41; Baptism, $52. Half-day snorkeling trips on the dive boats, $10.

Tropicasub

St. Pierre; ☎ *(596) 78-38-03.*

Lionel and Francoise Lafont have been operating this shop for ten years. Two dives daily, 9:30 and 3:00; closed Monday. One tank dive $41; Baptism, $45. Maximum group size, 10, including crew/instructors. Snorkel trips available. English language staff.

On Foot

Showcasing a variety of trails through a surprisingly diverse selection of landscapes and climate regions, Martinique is truly a hiker's paradise. All of this coexists in relatively close proximity to the island's fast-paced and cosmopolitan lifestyle, creating a breathtaking juxtaposition, even by Caribbean standards, where contrasting environments are the spice of life. The island's population and tourist center is heavily concentrated in and around Fort-de-France, leaving Martinique's outlying forests well-visited, but comparatively unscathed by development. Hikers must beware the rare fer de lance, a poisonous snake found predominantly in the drier areas to the south (see "On Foot" introductory chapter). The hikes listed below are merely the *creme de la creme* of a rich and impressive lot. An excellent trail guidebook, *Guide des Sentiers Pedestres a la Martinique*, (in French) is available in local bookstores, and the tourist maps of the island mark many of the major trails.

Canal de Beauregard

This delightful excursion parallels a 200-year-old canal that was used to supply water to sugar mills in the Carbet River Valley. From a point about an hour north of Fort-de-France on the Route de la Trace, turn left on the D-1 toward Fond-St-Denis; take another left immediately after entering town and drop down a short hill to the Canal de Beauregard where the path begins. The narrow trail stays on the hillside above the canal and, at some points, makes an airy traverse several hundred feet above the Carbet River. The evolving views of the grand Pitons are spectacular; allow three hours round-trip.

Les Gorges de La Falaise

Just outside the town of Ajoupa-Bouillon, the Falaise River has slowly carved out one of Martinique's most beautiful settings, a series of gorges and waterfalls pouring down from the eastern slope of Mount Pelee. The trail is marked and quickly descends to the river and into the gorge upstream; you'll probably find yourself navigating the riverbed more than the hillside path. The gorge narrows to about six feet across at one point, and you may need to swim around one bend to reach the 40-foot cascade marking the trail's conclusion. For obvious reasons, a camera is not advised. Avoid the trail after heavy rain runoff and allow an hour-and-a-half round-trip. This is a relatively easy hike visiting lush and uninhabited forests and is a highly recommended escape.

Le Precheur to Grand-riviere

It was once possible to drive all the way around the northern tip of Martinique, but the road which follows this coastline has not been maintained for many years and now makes a wonderful, albeit long, trek. The 11-mile trail starts at Anse Couleuvre, three miles north of Le Precheur, and will seem briefly discouraging on the hot concrete until one reaches the forested area, where vegetation and isolation begin to take over. Orchards and old plantations are soon replaced by virgin forests and savanna, and seemingly untouched beaches appear around several bends. Although there are small hills to surmount, the trail is not difficult, outside its length, which will require five-to-six hours, one way. It is also possible to join the guided hike offered by the **Syndicat d'Initiative** in Grand-Riviere (☎ *(596) 55-72-74)*, which does the trail in the opposite direction and returns by boat every other Sunday.

Mount Pelee

The site of the most violent volcanic eruption in recorded Caribbean history, Mount Pelee roared to life on May 8, 1902, sending a torrent of hot ash and gas—a fireball termed *nuee ardente*—down its slope to consume St. Pierre and its 30,000 residents in mere minutes; the only known survivors were a prisoner, locked deep in an underground cell, and someone on a nearby ship. Aside from some rumbling in 1929–1932, the mountain has stayed relatively calm for the balance of the century, and now stirs hikers' hearts and minds in heated pursuit of its striking summit.

Three separate trails climb Mount Pelee, but the most popular is the shortest and steepest, a path ascending the southeast slope above the village of Morne Rouge. The hike is straightforward, and difficult at the start, but climbs to easier slopes along a ridge before making a final push to the lower lip of the crater. Clouds may conceal it, but the primary cone (4462 feet) is a little farther and higher, denoted by a shelter; while Pelee's actual summit (4584 feet) is farther still, and obtained using a slippery, overgrown path. On clear days, this northernmost peak produces splendid views of Dominica. Allow four hours for the round-trip.

The western route, named the Grand Savane Trail, follows an exposed, dry and brushy slope through vegetable fields, to a ridge bordered by tree ferns which leads to the summit area. A marked dirt road (bearing east from the main road heading into Le Precheur) accesses the trailhead; the hike is longer than the traditional route, and has a greater elevation change, but is actually easier in some respects (allow five hours round-trip). A third route begins from one of two points between Grand Riviere and Macouba (the trails merge higher up) and ascends the long northern slope of the mountain. The terrain is more difficult, and the hike is longer again, but it provides entry to one of Martinique's most remote areas; allow at least six hours round-trip. Of course, if you coordinate transportation in advance, a trip utilizing two of these trails is easy to conceive.

Le Pitons Du Carbet Circuit

Martinique's most ambitious trek is also probably its most rewarding, surmounting the "Alps" of the Caribbean, a ridge of six peaks, each topping 3500 feet. The Pitons du Carbet trail may be accessed from either the tiny village of Colson, or the

Plateau Boucher, both about an hour north of Fort de France on the Route de la Trace. The main ridge runs northeast-southwest, sometimes supporting nothing more than a knife-edge path plunging precipitously to the valleys on either side below. From the Plateau Boucher, climb a fierce slope through dense tropical rain forest which soon evolves into stunted and windblown elfin woodland; in this first hour of hiking, you'll ascend over 1300 feet. The first peak you top is that of Piton Boucher (3511 feet), which yields eye-filling views, down to the Route de la Trace and southwest to Piton Lacroix (3924 feet, the highest of the range, and even better views). Your route follows the ridge between these two peaks, with optional short climbs to Morne Piquet and Piton Daumaze before descending steeply to Colson. The trail is well-marked and not as complex as it sounds, but should not be under-estimated. The hiking is hard, sheer and slippery; allow six hours, one way.

Trekking Tours

Parc Naturel Regional de La Martinique
Fort-de-France; (596-64-42-59).
Provides an assortment of guided hiking tours within the park. $12 per person. They also sell a fine guide to the best hikes, *Les Plus Belles Balades de la Martinique*. (in French); $38.

By Pedal

The unofficial national sport of the French West Indies, cycling is officially celebrated with the annual "Tour de la Martinique," which takes place mid-July. You'll find a number of locals on bikes on weekends, while the **Parc Naturel Regional de la Martinique** has worked with local biking organizations to identify mountain trails and routes of interest *(☎ 596) 64-42-59)*. A beautiful route for less advanced riders circumnavigates the island's tiny southernmost tip on dirt and secondary roads; the tour visits the Petrified Forest and lovely Grande Anse des Salines. The bigger peninsula bordered by Trois-Ilets and Le Diamant offers slightly more difficult riding, while heading into the mountains of Martinique's northern half will present clear challenges and inspiring riding. Also appealing is the coastal road between Fort-de-France and St. Pierre.

Bike Rental Shops

V.T. Tilt
Trois Ilets; ☎ *(596) 68-16-75.*
Prefers not to rent their collection of 40 Giant and Specialized bikes, using them instead for tours which take in the natural environment and culture of Martinique.

Rates range from $45 for a half-day trip to $1090 for a seven-day camping tour. Friendly, English-fluent staff; leads rides at all levels of ability and for all age groups.

What Else to See

The Fort-de-France market in Martinique has a plethora of fruits.

The capital of Martinique, **Fort-de-France**, is one of the most charming cities in the Caribbean to see on foot. Among the first sites to check out is the city's architectural pride and joy, the **Bibliotheque Schoelcher**, or Schoelcher Library, a Romanesque Byzantine treasure constructed a century ago for the Paris Exposition of 1889, then dismantled and shipped to Martinique piece by piece. It sits close to **Savane**, the city's central park, full of exotic flora; it's a lovely place to stroll and eavesdrop on locals. Narrow streets with beautiful balconies overhanging sidewalks filled with shops and restaurants lead you to another must-see: the **Cathedral of Saint-Louis**. Nearby is the Palais de Justice with its statue of Victor Schoelcher. The Musée Departemental de la Martinique presents archaeological finds from prehistoric Martinique. The **Jardin de Balata** (Balata gardens) is a tropical botanical park around a restored Creole house. It's a lovely place for browsing and relaxing. By the Riviere Madame (Madame River) you'll find the bustling fish markets. If you want a guided tour, you can find excellent ones offered by **Azimut** ☎ *(596) 60-16-59.*

Time should also be carved out on your itinerary for travels outside the city of Martinique.

North along the coast, you'll discover **St. Pierre**, considered the "Paris of the West Indies" until 1902 when Mount Pelé Volcano erupted and flowed lava Pompeii-style all over it. You can see the full extent of the tragedy in the exhibits of the museum there. To get there with style, take the little train called **Cyparis Express**, which presents one-hour tours during the week and half-hour tours on the weekend. The drive from Fort-de-France is less than an hour, but make time to stop at such atmospheric fishing villages as **Case-Pilote** and **Bellefontaine**, as well as **Carbet**, where Columbus landed in 1502; Gauguin lived and painted there in 1887. A museum featuring his work is found in Carbet.

In the north, a dazzling route through the rain forest, called **La Trace**, is lush with banana and pineapple plantations, avocado groves, cane fields and lovely inns such as **Leyritz** and **Habitation Lagrange**. Le Précheur, the last village along the northern Caribbean coast, is known for hot springs of volcanic origin as well as the **Tomb of the Carib Indians**. Ajoupa Bouillon is an enchanting flower-lined town with a nature trail called **Les Ombrages**.

Rum is king on Martinique and most visitors enjoy sampling the island-brewed wares at distilleries. The St. James Distillery at Sainte-Marie in the north operates the **Musée du Rhum**. Nearby is a straw-weaving center called **Horne des Esses**. The **Fonds Saint Jacques**, a historically important 17th-century sugar estate in the north, attracts visitors with its museum, Musée du Pere Labat. A modern museum devoted to sugar and rum, called **Maison de la Canne**, is just outside Trois Ilets. Also near Trois Ilets is Joséphone Bonaparte's birthplace, **La Pagerie**, which has a museum chock full of her mementos.

Martinique is often known as the "Ilse of Flowers" and there are numerous floral gardens that are lovely to visit. Nearby La Pagerie is **Parc des Floralies**, a peaceful and pretty botanical park. One of the most beautiful is the **Jardin de Balata** on the Route de La Trace in the suburbs north of the capital. A short drive from here is the Sacré Coeur de Balata, a replica of the well-known basilica that dominates Montmarte in Paris. Other attractions south of Martinique include the H.M.S. *Diamond Rock*, a kind of Rock of Gibralter Caribbean-style rising 600 feet from the sea as used by the British in 1804 as a sloop of war. Anyone not venturing into the depths of the sea with a dive tank should really take a ride on the thrilling **Aquascope**, a semi-submersible craft that makes about an hour tour. One is located at the Marina Pointe du Bout and the other at Le Marin.

Museums and Exhibits

Maison de la Canne ★★★

Trois-Ilets, Fort-de-France.
Hours open: 9 a.m.–5:30 p.m.

You've probably always taken sugar for granted, but won't anymore after touring this museum dedicated to the history and production of sugarcane. Signage is in both French and English. Really quite interesting

Musee Departementale de Martin ★★★

9 Rue de la Liberte, Fort-de-France.

Decent exhibits on the history of slavery, clothing and furniture from the colonial period and artifacts from the pre-Columbian eras of the Arawak and the Carib indians.

Musee Paul Gauguin ★★★

Anse-Turin, Le Carbet.
Hours open: 10 a.m.–5 p.m.

Famed artist Paul Gauguin lived in Martinique in 1887. This museum pays homage to that period, with reproductions of works he created while here, letters and other memorabilia pertaining to his life. The museum also displays the works of other noted artists and changing displays by local artists.

Musee Vulcanologique ★★★★

St. Pierre, Fort-de-France.
Hours open: 9 a.m.–5 p.m.

American Frank Perrot established this museum in 1932, an homage to St. Pierre, the island's oldest city and a bustling one at that, until a devastating eruption of volcano Mt. Pelee on May 8, 1902. The entire town was buried in minutes and some 30,000 residents perished, all except for a prisoner whose underground cell saved him. (He later joined Barnum and Bailey's circus as a sideshow oddity.) Residents had been warned of the imminent danger but city fathers played it down because of an upcoming election. St. Pierre today is a modest village, but you can get a feel for its former glory days at the museum, which exhibits photographs and documents from the period.

Musee de Poupees Vegetables ★★★

Leyritz Plantation, Basse-Pointe.
Hours open: 7 a.m.–5:30 p.m.

Certainly the only one of its kind in Martinique (or possibly the world for that matter), this small museum displays sculptures made entirely of leaves and plants, designed to look like famous women in French history. It is located at the scenic Leyritz Plantation, which is detailed in the lodging section.

Musee du Rhum ★★★

Ste. Matie, Fort-de-France.
Hours open: 9 a.m.–6 p.m.

The St. James Distillery owns this monument to rum, located on a sugar plantation in an old creole house. After a guided tour showing the history and production of rum, you can taste-test the product yourself.

Musee le la Pagerie ★★★★

Trois-Ilets, Fort-de-France.
Hours open: 9 a.m.–5 p.m.

Located on the grounds of the birthplace of Josephine, Napoleon's wife and empress of France from 1804-1809, this museum is housed in a stone building that was formerly the kitchen (the rest of the estate was destroyed by hurricane). Memorabilia of her life, her childhood bed, and a passionate love letter by Napoleon are among the interesting exhibits.

Parks and Gardens

Jardin de Balata ★★★

Rte de Balata, Balata.
Hours open: 9 a.m.–5 p.m.

This tropical park, located on a hillside some 1475 feet above sea level, has stunning views and more than a thousand varieties of trees, flowers and plants. A lovely spot to while away the afternoon exploring winding walkways, lily pond, and breathtaking overlooks.

Tours

Martinique Aquarium ★★★

Blvd. de Marne, Fort-de-France.
Hours open: 9 a.m.–7 p.m.

Ths large aquarium has more than 2000 fish and sea creatures representing some 250 species. Of special interest are the shark tank and piranha pool.

Zoo de Carbet ★★★

Le Coin, Le Carbet.
Hours open: 9 a.m.–6 p.m.

Also called the Amazona Zoo, this park showcases 70 species from the Amazon Basin, including birds and big cats.

Sports

Sailing, scuba, snorkeling, golf, deep-sea fishing, windsurfing, horseback riding, squash, tennis, cycling and motorbiking, hiking —the list of sports on Martinique is endless and depends only on your skill, passion and time. Consider touring the island by bike. For more information contact the **Parc Naturel Régional**; ☎ *(596) 60-25-72*, which has designed highly unusual itineraries. You can even rent your own plane (have a license from back home in order to get the French equivalent at the Lamentin Airport). Then contact local plane owners through the **Aero Club de la Martinique** ☎ *(596) 55-01-84.* As for sailing, an enormous combination of excursions can be made to neighboring islands, among them Antigua, Dominica, Barbados, St. Lucia, St. Vincent and the Grenadines, and Mystique among others. Look for the comprehensive bilingual yachting manual "Guide Trois Rivieres: A Cruising Guide to Martinique" available in local bookstores, about $35 or from *Edition Trois Riviere, B.P. 566, 97242 Fort-de-France* ☎ *(596) 75-07-07.* Spectator sports on the island are weird but exciting if you have a taste for blood: mongoose and snake fights, and cockfights seem to be national pastimes and can be seen December to the beginning of August at Pitt Ducos, **Quartier Brac** ☎ *(596) 56-05-60* and **Pitt Marceny**. Horse racing can be found at the Carere racetrack in Lamentin ☎ *(596) 51-25-09.*

Golf

Trois-Ilets, near Pointe du Bont.
Martinique's only course, the Golf de Imperatrice Josephine, was designed by Robert Trent Jones. The 18-hole, par-71 course covers 150 acres and is quite scenic. The grounds include a pro shop (with an English-speaking pro), restaurant and three tennis courts. Greens fees are about $45; guests in some hotels receive a discount, so be sure to ask.

Horseback Riding

Various locations, Martinique.
Several outfits offer trail rides: **La Cavale** *(76-22-94)*, **Ranch Jack** *(68-37-67)*, **Black Horse Ranch** *(68-37-80)*, and **Ranch Val d'Or** *(76-70-58)*.

Watersports

Various locations, Fort-de-France.
Most hotels offer watersports. If not, try one of following. Scuba diving: **Bathy's Club** *(Pointe du Bont 66-00-00)*, **Sud Diamant Rock** *(Le Diamant, 76-42-42)* **Cressmal** *(Fort-de-France, 61-34-36)*, **Planete Bleue** *(Trois-Ilets, 66-08-79)*, Oxygene Bleu *(Lamentin, 50-25-78)*, and **Tropic Alizes** *(Le Bateliere, 61-49-49)*. Boating and sailing: **Soleil et Voile** *(Pointe du Bont 66-09-14)*, **Captains Shop** *(Pointe du Bont, 66-06-77)*, **Ship Shop** *(Fort-de-France, 71-43-40)*, **Carib Charter** *(Schoelcher, 73-08-80)*, **Caraibes Nautique** *(Trois-Ilets 66-06-06)*, and **Cercle Nautique** *(Schoelcher, 61-15- 21)*. Snorkeling: **Aquarium** *(Fort-de-France, 61-49-49)*.

Where to Stay

Fielding's Highest Rated Hotels in Martinique

★★★★★	Sofitel Bakoua Hotel	$135–$270
★★★★	Habitation Lagrange	$325–$355
★★★★	Leyritz Plantation	$87–$147
★★★★	Meridien Martinique	$253–$779
★★★	Diamant Novotel	$167–$342
★★★	Fregate Bleue Inn	$125–$230
★★★	La Bateliere Hotel	$115–$275
★★★	St. Aubin Hotel	$58–$86

Fielding's Most Romantic Hotels in Martinique

★★★★	Habitation Lagrange	$325–$355
★★★★	Leyritz Plantation	$87–$147

Fielding's Budget Hotels in Martinique

★★	Martinique Cottages	$60–$65
★	le Balisier	$56–$77
★★	Victoria Hotel	$65–$76
★★★	St. Aubin Hotel	$58–$86
★★	Rivage Hotel	$75–$75

Accommodations on Martinique run from the 300-room resort to the inn with 10 rooms. You can choose between resorts happily ensconced on the seashore to guesthouses run by congenial families, part of the "Relais Creoles" organization. Prices range from expensive to modest. All of the larger hotels have sports facilities, a choice of restaurants and evening entertainment. All beachfront hotels offer a full watersports program. Some hotels have kitchenette studios.

Hotels and Resorts

Sofitel Bakoua Hotel, perched on a hillside, is the leading resort, retaining a distinct local feel in the historical plantation-style surroundings. **La Bateliere Hotel**, with its recent renovations, comes in a close second for style, service and location.

Alamanda $69–$115 ★★

Anse Mitan, ☎ (596) 66-13-72, FAX (596) 73-20-75.
Single: $69–$87. Double: $89–$115.
Located right in the heart of the tourist region and within walking distance to the beach, this small hotel accommodates guests in studios, some with kitchens. There's not much here in the way of diversions, but you'll find watersports, shopping and restaurants nearby.

Anchorage Hotel $135–$135 ★★

Domaine de Belford, ☎ (596) 76-92-32.
Single: $135. Double: $135.
This village-style resort is perched on a hillside overlooking the sea. Accommodations are in country French-style buildings, each with its own check-in and swimming pool. Rooms are very nicely done with good-quality furnishings, high ceilings and comfortable appointments. All have kitchenettes either inside or on the balcony. The beach at Salines is a 10-minute drive.

Diamant Novotel $167–$342 ★★★

Diamant, ☎ (800) 221-4542, (596) 76-42-42, FAX (596) 76-25-99.
Single: $167–$252. Double: $195–$342.
Bordered by white sand beaches near a fishing village, this hotel houses guests in comfortable rooms in three-story buildings. Most rooms have nice views of the sea. There's a pool, table tennis, a floating barge on which to sun, two tennis courts and supervised programs for children. A handful of bars and restaurants complete the scene. Popular with families.

Diamant les Bains Hotel $60–$120 ★★

Diamant, ☎ (596) 76-40-14, FAX (596) 76-27-00.
Single: $60–$95. Double: $73–$120.
Set on a sandy beach overlooking Diamond Rock, this small family-run property accommodates guests in the main house or in small, rustic bungalows with refrigerators. There's a pool and restaurant on-site, with watersports nearby. Service is cheerful and caring.

L'Imperatrice Village $78–$123 ★★

Anse Mitan, ☎ (596) 66-08-09, FAX (596) 72-66-30.
Single: $78–$103. Double: $98–$123.
Set on tropical grounds across the bay from Fort-de-France, this resort houses guests in standard rooms, studios, and bungalows with kitchens. All are on the modest side, but pleasant enough. A bit off the beaten path, so you'll want to rent a car. On-site features include a restaurant and bar, pool and games like billiards and ping-pong.

La Bateliere Hotel $115–$275 ★★★

Schoelcher, ☎ (596) 61-49-49, FAX (596) 61-70-57.

Single: $115–$185. Double: $200–$275.

Located on 6.5 acres on a bluff overlooking the sea, this five-story hotel opened as a Hilton. Guest rooms are spacious, with all the modern amenities. For recreation, there are eight lighted tennis courts and a pro, all watersports, a pool, excursions in a cabin cruiser, and a fine, sandy beach.

Several restaurants, a disco, and the island's first casino. Dependable service.

La Dunette   **$100–$125**   ★

Ste. Anne, ☎ (596) 76-73-90, FAX (596) 76-76-05.
Single: $100. Double: $120–$125.

Located in a fishing village, this three-story hotel offers simple rooms, some with balconies. Besides the bar and dining room, there is little in the way of extras.

Meridien Martinique   **$253–$779**   ★ ★ ★ ★

Point du Bont, ☎ (800) 543 4300, (596) 66-00-00, FAX (596) 66-00-74.
Single: $253–$779. Double: $305–$779.

Located across the harbor from Fort-de-France, this seven-story property shows its age, and attracts mainly convention groups. Rooms are small but comfortable. There's lots to do at this busy resort, including complimentary watersports, a pool, health club, two tennis courts and a 100-slip marina. The man-made beach is small and gets crowded. There's also a casino and nightly entertainment during high season. A ferry transports passengers to Fort-de-France. Decent for its wide range of facilities, but best suited to the group market.

PLM Azur Carayou Hotel   **$125–$243**   ★ ★

Pointe de Bout, ☎ (800) 221-4542, (596) 66-04-04, FAX (596) 66-00-41.
Single: $125–$243. Double: $130–$243.

Located on Fort-de-France Bay, this hotel caters mainly to groups. Accommodations are quite nice, with large, modern baths that include bidets. All units have a balcony. The small beach is found in a sheltered cove. There's also a large pool, two tennis courts, archery, a driving range and watersports. The disco is popular during high season.

PLM Azur Squash Hotel   **$77–$141**   ★ ★

3 Blvd. de la MArne, ☎ (596) 63-00-01, FAX (596) 78-92-44.
Single: $77–$141. Double: $92–$141.

Located in a residential neighborhood close to the center of town, this modern hotel is frequented by business travelers. Accommodations are clean, comfortable and tastefully decorated. There's live entertainment in the bar twice weekly. The well-equipped health club includes an exercise room, sauna, Jacuzzi and Turkish bath. There's also a pool and three squash courts. The beach is nearby.

PLM Azur la Pagerie   **$126–$175**   ★ ★

Pointe du Bout, ☎ (800) 221-4542, (596) 66-05-30, FAX (596) 66-00-41.
Single: $126–$136. Double: $155–$175.

This informal hotel faces the marina across the bay from Fort-de-France. Guest rooms are spacious with bidets in the bathrooms; some have kitchenettes while others have only refrigerators. Located in a high-density hotel area, there is a pool but little else on-site. Guests can use the facilities at the nearby PLM Azur Carayou, where they have restaurants, tennis and watersports.

Sofitel Bakoua Hotel $135–$270 ★★★★★

Pointe du Bout, ☎ *(800) 221-4542, (596) 66-02-02, FAX (596) 66-00-41.*
Single: $135–$270. Double: $135–$270.
Located in a garden setting on a bluff above a private beach, this deluxe hotel is one of Martinique's best. Accommodations are on the hillside or the beach; all quite nice but on the small side. There are two lighted tennis courts, a lovely pool, all watersports and a nearby golf course. The service is among the island's best, and most of the French staff speaks at least some English. The beach is fine. Worth the splurge.

le Balisier $56–$77 ★

21 Victor Hugo Street, ☎ *(596) 71-46-54, FAX (596) 71-46-54.*
Single: $56–$77. Double: $67–$77.
Set in the heart of Fort-de-France, this budget property offers small and simple rooms. There are also three apartments with kitchenettes. There are no dining or recreation facilities on-site, but many within walking distance.

Apartments and Condominiums

The **Villa Rental Service** of the Martinique Tourist Office ☎ *(596) 63-79-60* can arrange vacation home rentals. Among the choices are apartments, studios, or villas. Most of the properties are located in the southern sector, near good beaches. Rentals can be arranged for the week or month.

Les Ilets de l'Impératrice are two tiny islands off Le François on the windward coast, each with a 19th-century vacation house, beach, watersports, full-time maid and cook. Ilet Thierry's house has six double bedrooms; Ilet Oscar's has five. All-inclusive rates (airport pickup, lodging, food and drink, and sports, etc.) runs $200 per person per day year round. Contact Jean-Louis de Lucy ☎ *(596) 65-82-30,* FAX *(596) 63-18-22.*

Martinique Cottages $60–$65 ★★

Jean d'Arc, ☎ *(596) 50-16-08, FAX (596) 50-26-83.*
Single: $60. Double: $65.
Located in a residential area 15 minutes from Fort-de-France, this small operation is popular, especially with business travelers. Accommodations are in bungalows nestled among the trees. Each is nicely done with small kitchens and verandas. The beach is 15 minutes away; if that's too far, you can relax by the free-form pool. There's also a restaurant and bar. This family-owned spot is peaceful and pleasant.

Residence Grand Large $325–$395 per wk. ★★

Ste. Luce, FAX (596) 66-06-56.
Off on its own on the south shore of Ste. Luce, a fishing village, this small complex offers fully furnished studios with kitchens and ocean views. There's nothing on-site, so you'll need a car to get around. The rates are quite reasonable.

Rivage Hotel $75–$75 ★★

Anse Mitan, ☎ *(596) 66-00-53, FAX (596) 66-06-56.*
Single: $75. Double: $75.

This small, family-run operation is near the beach. All rooms have a kitchenette and balcony; if you want a TV, you'll pay extra. There's a bar and pool, and lots of diversions within walking distance.

Inns

Fregate Bleue Inn $125–$230

Le Francois, ☎ (800) 633-7411, (596) 54-54-66, FAX (803) 686-7411.
Double: $125–$230.

Set on a hillside overlooking the sea, this gingerbread-trimmed inn is postively charming. All accommodations are in spacious studios with kitchenettes, armoires, antiques and four-poster beds. Breakfast is complimentary each morning, but you'll have to cook in or venture off-site for other meals. There's a pool for those too relaxed to walk three minutes to the beach. Very elegant and gracious, this lovely inn is best suited to those not seeking a lot of action.

Habitation Lagrange $325–$355

Marigot, ☎ (800) 633-7411, (596) 53-60-60, FAX (803) 686-7411.
Single: $325–$355. Double: $325–$355.

This 18th-century creole mansion was refurbished and opened as an inn in 1991. Some guest rooms are in the great house, the former headquarters of a sugar and rum factory. Others are found in new two-story buildings. All are elegantly decorated with canopy beds, antique furnishings, VCRs and minibars, plus modern comforts like air conditioning. For recreation, there's a putting green, pool and tennis courts, plus exploring the ruins of the former plant. Charming and romantic.

Leyritz Plantation $87–$147

Basse-Point, ☎ (596) 78-53-92, FAX (596) 82-94-00.
Single: $87–$121. Double: $117–$147.

This inn is another charmer, though its remote location isn't for everyone. Set on the grounds of a 230-acre banana plantation, it accommodates guests in a converted 18th-century great house and in the former guardhouse and slave quarters, as well as in bamboo and stone cottages. All are air conditioned, antique filled, have four-poster beds and loads of charm. The most atmospheric rooms are in the main house with its high ceilings, dormer windows, and thick walls. The beach is a full half-hour away, but there's a pool on-site. There's also a tennis court, and you can spend hours exploring the former plant. A major drawback are the hordes of tourists on organized tours. Nonetheless, this picturesque spot is hard to leave.

St. Aubin Hotel $58–$86

Petite Riviere Salee, ☎ (596) 69-34-77.
Single: $58. Double: $73–$86.

This colonial-style inn, a former private residence, sits on a hillside with nice views of the surrounding area. An old-fashioned porch wraps around the building on two floors; you'll spend a lot of time on it reading or just taking in the view. Each room is individually decorated with modern amenities. The grounds include a pool and good dining room serving French and creole fare. You'll definitely need a car to explore beyond this remote spot.

Low Cost Lodging

Martinique has more than 200 **Gites de France** ☎ *(596) 73-67-92*, which are apartments, studios and guest rooms in private homes. **Logis Vacances Antilles** ☎ *(596) 63-12-91* also offers rooms in private homes, as well as holiday studios and houses. Camping can be done almost anywhere—in the mountains, forest, and on many beaches, although indiscriminate camping is not permitted. **Tropicamp** at Gros Raisins Plage, Ste. Luce ☎ *(596) 62-49-66* is one of several companies with full services, including hot showers. Other comfortable camps with showers and toilets are **Nid Tropical** at Anse-a-l'Ane near Trois Ilets ☎ *(596) 68-31-30*; one at **Vauclin** on the southeast Atlantic coast ☎ *(596) 74-45-88*; an another at **Pointe Marin** near the public beach of Ste. Anne ☎ *(596) 76-72-79*. A nominal fee is charged for facilities. For details, contact the **Office National des Dorês**, 3.5 km, route de Mouette, Fort-de-France; ☎ *(596) 71-34-50*.

The trend these days is to rent a camping car, which allows you opportunity to discover many of the treasures along Martinique's 300-mile roadway. One recommended camping-car operation is **West Indies Tours**, whose campers are outfitted with beds for four, refrigerator, shower, sink, 430-gallon water tank, dining table, stove and radio/cassette player. Contact **Michel Yula, West Indies Tours, Le François**; ☎ *(596) 54-50-71*; or **Wind Martinique, Anse Mitan**; ☎ *(596) 66-02-22*.

It's also possible to rent rooms in private houses, apartments, and houses in all price ranges with weekly or monthly rates. To rent a gîte as they as called, contact **Gîtes de France**, *Martinique, Maison du Tourisme Vert, 9 BD du Général-de-Gaulle, BP 1122, 97248 Fort-De-France*; ☎ *(596) 73-67-92*.

Auberge de l'Anse Mitan $65–$95   ★

Anse Mitan, ☎ *(596) 66-01-12, FAX (596) 66-01-05.*
Single: $65–$75. Double: $85–$95.
This casual French-style inn is within walking distance of the beach in Anse Mitan. Accommodations include standard rooms in the three-story main building and six studios with kitchenettes. All are air-conditioned and have private baths and telephones. There's a bar and restaurant serving French and creole fare, but little else in the way of extras. Friendly and cheerful service at this family-run establishment.

Caraibe Auberge $51–$110   ★

Anse Mitan, ☎ *(596) 66-03-19, FAX (596) 66-00-09.*
Single: $51–$82. Double: $70–$110.
This small beachfront hotel is in the center of the hotel resort action. Rooms are simple and fairly spartan, as reflected by the rates. There's a small pool on-site, but little else.

Victoria Hotel $65–$76

Rte de Didier, ☎ *(596) 60-56-78, FAX (596) 60-00-24.*
Single: $65–$70. Double: $70–$76.
Located on a hillside in a residential neighborhood with nice views, this colonial-style hotel offers good value for its reasonable rates, and attracts mainly business travelers. Accommodations are in comfortable rooms, some with TVs and others with kitchenettes. There's a French restaurant and a pool on site.

Where to Eat

Fielding's Highest Rated Restaurants in Martinique

★★★★	La Fontane	$30–$50
★★★★	Leyritz Plantation	$27–$50
★★★	Athanor	$11–$30
★★★	Aux Filets Bleus	$13–$30
★★★	Chez Mally Edjam	$11–$29
★★★	La Mouina	$15–$30
★★★	La Villa Creole	$14–$18
★★★	Le Colibri	$18–$27
★★★	Le Coq Hardi	$18–$36
★★★	Le Poisson d'Or	$25–$30

Fielding's Special Restaurants in Martinique

★★★★	La Fontane	$30–$50
★★★	Chez Mally Edjam	$11–$29
★★★	La Mouina	$15–$30
★★★	Le Colibri	$18–$27
★★	Yva Chez Vava	$18–$27

Fielding's Budget Restaurants in Martinique

★★★	Le Second Souffle	$8–$12
★★	La Dunette	$6–$20
★★★	La Villa Creole	$14–$18
★★	Le Cantonnais	$14–$20
★★	Diamant Les Bains	$16–$20

Perhaps it's the irrepressible French dedication to cuisine, but chefs in Martinique seem to take special care with their menus, overseeing both the preparation and the service. Throughout the island you will generally find one of two cuisines: traditional French or island Creole; many restaurants combine the two on their menus. Fresh seafood dishes are omnipresent, among the tastiest are *chatrou* (octopus), *langouste* (small clawless lobster), *lambi* (conch), and *cribiches* (large river shrimp). Red snapper is served in a variety of ways. *Coquille de lambi* (minced conch in creamy sauce served in a shell) is an island must; the *blaff de poisson* (steamed fish in local spices) is excellent at Le Mareyeur. Another island specialty, *pâté en pot*, is a thick creole soup made with mutton. A good afternoon drink to cool you off is *les planteurs*— a planter's punch in a sweet fruit juice base. Heart islanders tend to chug down *décollage*—aged herbal rum with a fruit juice chaser. Most restaurants have excellent selections of French wines. Prices per person for a three-course meal without wine range from $30–$45 and up. The French & English booklet *Ti Gourmet*, available from the Tourist Office, will give out more information about where and what to eat.

Fort-de-France

Diamant Les Bains   **$$$**   ★★

Le Diamant, 97223, Le Diamant,
Latin American cuisine. Specialties: Blaff, Coconut Flan.
Lunch: entrees $16–$20.
Dinner: entrees $16–$20.

Good local fare is served in a motel-like hostelry in Le Diamant, a cozy beach town whose claim to fame is the imposing Diamond Rock, majestically rising from the deep to an almost 600-foot height. The beach it fronts is nothing special, but it's a nice spot to dine on blaff fish (cooked with thyme, peppers, clove and other spices), boudin and coconut flan.

La Fontane   **$$$**   ★★★★

Km. 4 Rue de Balata, ☎ *(596) 64-65-89.*
French cuisine.
Lunch: entrees $30–$50.
Dinner: entrees $30–$50.

A highly-regarded French-creole restaurant, La Fontane is located in a restored gingerbread house surrounded by fruit trees. The service is formal, the interior is antique-filled and tasteful, with exotic carpets on the floors. Dishes have included crayfish salad with fruit, lamb and mango and red-snapper with a citrus sauce.

La Mouina   **$$$**   ★★★

route de Redoute, Redoute, ☎ *(596) 79-34-57.*
French cuisine. Specialties: Crab Farcis.
Lunch: Noon–4 p.m., entrees $15–$30.
Dinner: 7:30–9:30 p.m., entrees $15–$30.

This is suburbia Fort-de-France style—fine dining in a typical upper-class home in Redoute, high above the capital below. Guests are made welcome in a dining salon on a balcony with a garden view. The smart set likes to make La Mouina a regular stop for luncheons of stuffed crab backs, tournedos and crayfish. Dinners are served by candlelight.

La Villa Creole $$$ ★★★

Anse Mitan 97229, Anse Mitan,
Latin American cuisine.
Lunch: Noon–2 p.m., entrees $14–$18.
Dinner: 7–10 p.m., entrees $14–$18.

A friendly and warm atmosphere permeates this gingerbread house with tables set on a seaside terrace in Anse Mitan, a beach resort famed for low-key, moderately priced hotels. There are several prixe-fixe meals to choose from, from plain to fancy, but all feature a bevy of side dishes, vegetables and dessert. The owner sometimes gives impromptu song and dance performances.

Le Cantonnais $$$ ★★

La Marina,
Chinese cuisine.
Dinner: 6:30–11 p.m., prix fixe $14–$20.

Guests staying at the large resort hotels near the marina in Pointe du Bout can take a break from French-creole cuisine at this Chinese foodery serving a voluminous menu of unusual dishes including broiled shark's fin and bird's nest soup. Vegetarians also have a choice of several meatless entrees.

Le Colibri $$$ ★★★

allee du Colibri, Morne des Esses,
Latin American cuisine. Specialties: Colombo, Tourte aux Lambis, Flan au Coco.
Lunch: Noon–3 p.m., entrees $18–$27.
Dinner: 7–11 p.m., entrees $18–$27.

A family-run operation, Le Colibri (The Hummingbird), located in the northwestern side of the island, could be named for the friendly bustling about hither and tither of Mme Paladino and her daughters, who are busy serving scrumptious creole meals to weekenders from Fort-de-France. These denizens often fill the veranda of the house for conch pie, crayfish stew and a dreamy coconut flan. Come early to nab these choice seats or you'll be seated inside facing the open kitchen (not so bad an idea).

Le Coq Hardi $$$ ★★★

Rue Martin Luther King, ☎ *(596) 63-66-83.*
International cuisine. Specialties: Tournedos Rossini, Prime Rib.
Lunch: Noon–2 p.m., entrees $18–$36.
Dinner: 7–11 p.m., entrees $18–$36.

Red meat is god here, prepared *au bleu* (very rare) which is the French way. Master charcutier Alphonse Sintive regularly imports the choice cuts of T-Bone, filet mignon and entrecote from France. After you choose your own steak, it's cooked over an open wood fire. An old-fashioned tournedos rossini is prepared with foie gras and truffles, and is a favorite here. If you still have room after the huge portions served, there's still a wide selection of scrumptious desserts and sorbets.

Le Poisson d'Or $$$ ★ ★ ★

Anse Mitan, Anse Mitan,
Latin American cuisine.
Lunch: Noon–2:30 p.m., prix fixe $25–$30.
Dinner: 7–10 p.m., prix fixe $25–$30.

This is a casual roadside seafood eatery set between the beach cities of Anse Mitan and Pointe du Bout. Tropical greenery and a bamboo ceiling make you feel like you're dining on an isle in the South Seas. A fixed-price meal for $25 is a good buy for an array of creole specialties including a Conch appetizer and an elegant dessert.

Le Second Souffle $$ ★ ★ ★

27 Rue Blenac, ☎ (596) 63-44-11.
Latin American cuisine.
Lunch: Noon–3 p.m., entrees $8–$12.
Dinner: 7:30–10 p.m., entrees $8–$12.

A treat for the body and soul is a cleansing visit to this pleasant vegetarian restaurant after a tour of the Byzantine Saint Louis Cathedral nearby. Le Second Souffle (is there a first?) dishes up a salad of seasonal fruits with honey sauce, or a meatless plat du jour, which may include a christophene or callaloo souffle.

Leyritz Plantation $$$ ★ ★ ★ ★

Basse Pointe 97218, Leyritz, ☎ (596) 78-53-92.
Latin American cuisine.
Lunch: 12:30–2 p.m., entrees $27–$40.
Dinner: 7:30–9 p.m., entrees $36–$50.

Dining at one of Martinique's prime tourist attractions sounds like a recipe for disaster, but surprisingly, the Creole cuisine remains first rate. Guests also get a lot of food for their francs, especially a set luncheon of stuffed crab, blood pudding, an entree (sometimes conch), rice and vegetables and dessert. The million-dollar setting amidst an 18th century sugar plantation is a fond postcard memory. Although lunch is the preferred time, come for dinner when the tour bus pandemonium becomes practically nonexistent.

Basse Pointe

Athanor $$$ ★ ★ ★

Rue de Bord de Mer, Ste. Anne, ☎ (596) 76-72-93.
French cuisine. Specialties: Grilled Lobster.
Dinner: 7–10 p.m., entrees $11–$30.

This informal eatery located one block from the beach in Ste. Anne prepares tasty pizzas, salads and other casual meals from a large menu. Diners can choose a few fancier items including the specialty, grilled lobster, which is delicious. There's a choice of seating in a pretty garden behind the restaurant or in a greenery-draped dining room indoors.

Aux Filets Bleus $$$ ★ ★ ★

Point Marin, Ste. Anne, ☎ (596) 76-73-42.
Latin American cuisine. Specialties: Delices de la Mer, Turtle Soup, Court Bouillon.
Lunch: 12:30–2:30 p.m., entrees $13–$30.
Dinner: 7:30–9:30 p.m., entrees $13–$30.

A restaurant of many contrasts—although Aux Filets Bleus charges haute cuisine prices, the place is so casual you can come here in a beach cover-up after a swim in the briny which is in full view of the tables. Also, dishes are mostly hearty West Indian dishes like *chatrous* (octopus) with red beans and rice, hardly justifying the stiff tab. Still, what you're served is usually very good, and the ambience is friendly and intimate.

Chez Mally Edjam $$$ ★★★

Route de la Cote, ☎ *(596) 78-51-18.*
French cuisine. Specialties: Fruit Confitures, Colombo de Porc.
Dinner: entrees $11–$29.

It's a very pleasant drive to get to this home-style restaurant run by stellar cuisiniere Mally Edjam and her family. The surrounding landscape en route is dotted with pineapple plantations, and trees hung heavily with boughs of green bananas. That's just a prelude to the symphony of flavors on the fixed-price lunches served here, which may include *pork colombo* (local curry), conch and fabulous desserts. Don't miss the homemade preserves made from local fruits. Dinners may be arranged by appointment.

La Dunette $$ ★★

Sainte Anne, 97227, Ste. Anne, ☎ *(596) 76-73-90.*
Seafood cuisine.
Lunch: entrees $6–$20.
Dinner: entrees $6–$20.

La Dunette is like a lot of pleasant seaside restaurants on the island that serves seafood specialties. Dine inside or out in a tropical garden facing the sea on poached sea urchins, curries or grilled fish. Connected to a pleasant, intimate hotel where you might consider staying if you're in the area, which is noted for gorgeous beaches and fine weather.

Yva Chez Vava $$$ ★★

Boulevard de Gaulle, Grand Riviere, ☎ *(596) 55-72-55.*
French cuisine.
Dinner: entrees $18–$27.

This chez on the northern tip of the island is the domain of local legend Vava and her daughter Yva, who now continues the tradition of cooking family-style creole meals in their own residence near a river. As Grand Riviere is a fishing village, seafood appears prominently on the menu. Specialties include *accras* (cod fritters), *chicken colombo* and *z'habitants* (crayfish prepared Martinique style). After lunch, you might want to visit the fish market where your food originated, or stroll on the black sand beach.

Where to Shop

"Go French" is the password when trying to decode what to buy in Martinique, a place where you can find the best bargains among French imports—perfumes, cosmetics, clothes, china, and crystal—at prices 25-40 percent lower than in the U.S. If you pay in traveler's checks, you'll receive an additional 20 percent discount. You will never find these prices in France. Don't miss picking up a few bottles of Martinique-brewed rum. Craft buys range from folk-styled appliqué wall hangings to the Martiniquais doll dressed in the national costume, which can be seen in nearly every store and in every size imaginable. A conical bakoua straw hat does nicely as a sun-stopper. If you're interested in the bright gold Creole jewelry that seems to be around many women's necks, ears and wrists, you will be joining a long-standing cultural tradition. The special "convict's chain" called *chaîne forçat*, and the *tremblants*, gold brooches with special adornment, can be found in several stores, where you should be able to judge authenticity by the price. Among the most reputable are **Cadet Daniel**, **Bijouterie Onyx** and **Emile Mothie's** workshop in Trenelle. (The latter are for serious fans who want to observe his work.) For delicious French delicacies, wines, foie gras and chocolates, head for **Boutique Michel Montignac**. To pick up the latest in island music, try **Hit Parade** on Rue Lamartine. The latest Parisian fashions can be found at **l'Univers**.

Martinique Directory

ARRIVAL AND DEPARTURE

Direct flights are available from New York/JFK every Saturday on North American Airlines. You can also catch one of many regular flights American Airlines offers to San Juan (via many gateways in the U.S.) and a Sunday flight on Air France from Miami. Interisland connections to Martinique, from St. Martin, Antigua, Dominica, St. Lucia, Barbados, St. Vincent, Mustique and Union Island can be made on Air Martinique. LIAT flies to and from neighboring islands. From Guadeloupe, you can catch frequent daily flights on Réseau Aérien Francais des Caraibes, a French Caribbean airline consortium that includes Air Martinique, Air Guadeloupe and Air France.

Martinique can also be reached from other islands by the ultra-modern catamaran Emeraude Express. Contact **Caribbean Express** ☎ *(596) 63-12-11*, FAX *(596) 63-34-47*.

Many cruise ships pull into Martinique as a port of call. Some dock at the attractive Passenger Terminal located at the harbor port a few minutes' drive from the center of the city; others anchor in Fort-de-France Bay and transfer passengers by tender, a 10-minute ride.

There is no departure tax charged for visitors, except charter flights.

BUSINESS HOURS

Stores open weekdays 8:30 a.m.–6 p.m. and Saturday 8:30 a.m.–1 p.m. Banks have varied hours but are generally open weekdays 7:30–noon and 2:30–4 p.m.

CLIMATE

Martinique's temperatures stay temperate all year long, hovering around 79 degrees F, with only a five degree difference between seasons. The air is cooled by constant wind currents (east and northeast); trade winds are called *les alizés*.

DOCUMENTS

For stays up to three weeks, U.S. and Canadian citizens traveling as tourists must show proof of citizenship in the form of a valid passport, or a passport that expired no more than five years ago, or other proof in the form of a birth certificate or voter's registration card with a government-authorized photo ID. For stays of more than three weeks, or for nontourist visas, a valid passport is necessary. Resident aliens of the U.S. and Canada and other foreign nationals other than those in the Common Market must have a valid passport and visa. All passengers must show an ongoing or return ticket.

ELECTRICITY

Current is 220 AC, 50 cycles. American and Canadian appliances require a French plug, converter and transformers.

GETTING AROUND

Taxi stands are located at the airport, in downtown Fort-de-France, and at major hotels. Rates rise 60 percent between 8 p.m. and 6 a.m. Eighty percent of the taxis are Mercedes Benz. There are also collective taxis (eight-passenger limousines bearing the sign TC).

Car rentals are available at Lamentin Airport, though hours are dependent on international flights. A valid driver's license is required, the minimum age is 21. Other agencies can be found in Fort-de-France. Among the best are **Avis**, *4 rue Ernest Deproge* ☎ *(596) 70-11-60*; **Budget**, *12 rue Félix Eboué, Fort-de-France* ☎ *(596) 63-69-00*; and **Hertz**, *24 rue Ernest Deproge, Fort-de-France* ☎ *(596) 60-64-54*.

Ferries, called vedettes, link Fort-de-France with Pointe du Bout daily from early morning until after midnight, and with Anse Mitan, Anse-al'Ane, Grand Anse d'Arlet from early morning till late afternoon. All ferries leave and arrive at Quai d'Esnambuc.

LANGUAGE

The languages of the isle are French and Creole. You'll find English spoken in most hotels, restaurants and tourist facilities, but you'll be happy if you remember to bring along a French phase book and pocket dictionary.

MEDICAL EMERGENCIES

There are 20 hospitals and clinics on the island, many well equipped; the best is **La Meynard** ☎ *(596) 55-20-00*. Ask the Tourist Office to assist you in securing an English-speaking physician.

MONEY

The official currency is the French franc, but U.S. and Canadian dollars are accepted almost everywhere. The rate of exchange, approximately five francs to the dollar, can change due to currency fluctuation.

TELEPHONE

The area code is *596*. To direct-dial from the U.S., dial ☎ *011-596*, plus the local Martinique number for station to station, or *01-596* plus local number for person to person. The best way to make international calls in Martinique is to purchase a "Telecarte" (a one-minute call to the U.S. is about $2.10. These credit cards can be purchased at all post offices and other outlets marked "Telécarte en vente Ici."; the booths you use them in are marked "Telécom." To use the assistance of an operator or to make a call from a hotel room will raise the price enormously.

TIME

Martinique is one hour later than New York (Eastern Standard Time). Time is related on the 24-hour hour schedule; i.e., 1 p.m. is 13:00 hours.

TIPPING AND TAXES

Some hotels add a 10 percent service charge and/or 5 percent government tax to the bill. Check your bill carefully and avoid adding on an extra service charge. If there is no charge added, a 10–15 percent charge would be appreciated by waiters and waitresses.

TOURIST INFORMATION

The **Martinique Tourist Office** ☎ *(596) 63-79-60* is located in handsome quarters on the Boulevard Alfassa, which borders on the waterfront in Fort-de-France. Hours are Monday-Friday 7:30 a.m.–12:30 p.m. and 2:30–5:30 p.m., and Saturday 8 a.m.–noon. Pick up complimentary maps, magazines and information bulletins; the English-speaking staff is quite helpful. A tourist office information desk at Lamentin Airport is open daily until the last flight comes in. In the U.S. ☎ *(800) 391-4909*.

WHEN TO GO

Carnival begins on Jan. 7 for five days, a total-island experience with parties and parades. Ash Wednesday is a blowout affair on March 1, with jammed streets, flowing rum, wild dancing and a funeral cortege at La Savane, Fort-de-France. The Aqua Festival du Robert on April 15–22 is a sea extravaganza in this Atlantic coastal town with yawl races, regattas, and concerts. Jazz a la Plantation on June 2, for two weeks at Basse Pointe, is a New Orleans-meets-French Antilles affair, with concert jams, street bands, Creole nights, and jazz lectures and workshops. Images Caraibes, on June 2 for two weeks, is the 5th Caribbean Film Festival in Fort-de-France. Tour de la Martinique is July 7–16, a weeklong bicycle race throughout the island. The tenth Tour des Yoles Rondes on July 30–Aug. 6, is a race of rawls used by Martinique fishermen. The Semi-Marathon, on Nov. 19, is a large race contest. Christmas Eve is celebrated with a midnight mass followed by a sumptuous supper, called Le Réveillon. New Year's Eve is another huge bash celebrated at hotels and restaurants.

MARTINIQUE HOTELS

		RMS	RATES	PHONE	CR. CARDS
Fort-de-France					
★★★★★	Sofitel Bakoua Hotel	138	$135–$270	(800) 221-4542	A, CB, MC, V
★★★★	Habitation Lagrange	17	$325–$355	(800) 633-7411	A, MC
★★★★	Leyritz Plantation	70	$87–$147	(596) 78-53-92	A, MC
★★★★	Meridien Martinique	295	$253–$779	(800) 543-4300	A, CB, V
★★★	Diamant Novotel	181	$167–$342	(800) 221-4542	A, MC, V
★★★	Fregate Bleue Inn	7	$125–$230	(800) 633-7411	A, MC
★★★	La Bateliere Hotel	199	$115–$275	(596) 61-49-49	A, MC, V
★★★	Martinique Cottages	8	$60–$65	(596) 50-16-05	A, CB, D, DC, MC, V
★★★	St. Aubin Hotel	15	$58–$86	(596) 69-34-77	A, MC, V
★★	Alamanda	30	$69–$115	(596) 66-13-72	MC
★★	Anchorage Hotel	187	$135–$135	(596) 76-92-32	A, MC
★★	Diamant les Bains Hotel	26	$60–$120	(596) 76-40-14	MC, V
★★	L'Imperatrice Village	59	$78–$123	(596) 66-08-09	A, MC
★★	PLM Azur Carayou Hotel	197	$125–$243	(800) 221-4542	A, DC, V
★★	PLM Azur Squash Hotel	108	$77–$141	(596) 63-00-01	A, MC, V
★★	PLM Azur la Pagerie	98	$126–$175	(800) 221-4542	A, MC, V
★★	Residence Grand Large	18	$325–$395	(596) 63-79-60	A, CB, D, MC, V

MARTINIQUE HOTELS	RMS	RATES	PHONE	CR. CARDS
★★ Rivage Hotel	20	$75	(596) 66-00-53	MC, V
★★ Victoria Hotel	32	$65–$76	(596) 60-56-78	MC, V
★ Auberge de l'Anse Mitan	20	$65–$95	(596) 66-01-12	A, DC, MC, V
★ Caraibe Auberge	31	$51–$110	(596) 66-03-19	A, MC
★ La Dunette	18	$100–$125	(596) 76-73-90	MC, V
★ le Balisier	27	$56–$77	(596) 71-46-54	A, MC

MARTINIQUE RESTAURANTS	PHONE	ENTREE	CR. CARDS

Basse Pointe

French

	PHONE	ENTREE	CR. CARDS
★★★ Athanor	(596) 76-72-93	$11–$30••	MC, V
★★★ Chez Mally Edjam	(596) 78-51-18	$11–$29••	A, MC, V
★★ Yva Chez Vava	(596) 55-72-55	$18–$27••	None

Latin American

	PHONE	ENTREE	CR. CARDS
★★★ Aux Filets Bleus	(596) 76-73-42	$13–$30	MC, V

Seafood

	PHONE	ENTREE	CR. CARDS
★★ La Dunette	(596) 76-73-90	$6–$20	MC, V

Fort-de-France

French

	PHONE	ENTREE	CR. CARDS
★★★★ La Fontane	(596) 64-65-89	$30–$50	A
★★★ La Mouina	(596) 79-34-57	$15–$30	MC, V

International

	PHONE	ENTREE	CR. CARDS
★★★ Le Coq Hardi	(596) 63-66-83	$18–$36	A, MC, V

Latin American

	PHONE	ENTREE	CR. CARDS
★★★★ Leyritz Plantation	(596) 78-53-92	$27–$50	MC, V
★★★ Le Second Souffle	(596) 63-44-11	$8–$12	MC, V

MONTSERRAT

Montserrat boasts three mountain ranges and lush green terrain.

Montserrat is about the closest thing to a Caribbean moonwalk. A volcanic blip that burst out of the sea four million years ago, the island has been called one of the last perfect ecosystems in the world—its nickname is "Emerald Isle of the Caribbean." Propelled by tremendous planetary shifts, volcanic surges of lava have left the island so fertile that everyone from people to fish, to birds, to plants and cattle, have plenty to eat. Exuberant flora, such as yellow hibiscus, blood-red canna and gold allamanda snake up the cliffs and beside the winding roads. Craggy rock walls, stained with eons-old mineral deposits, glimmer with colors as luminescent as those of a rainbow. Beneath the rocks lie beaches so black that the one white beach, Rendezvous Bay, seems like a miracle when you finally cruise onto its shores. Simply, Montserrat is an island to lay back and admire. Despite what's been called "the fatal beauty of Montserrat," the island is brimming with culture, mainly in the form of a vibrant musicality. Especially during Carnival, but also all year round, some of the most talented stars of reggae, soca and calypso in the Caribbean can be found in Montserrat's bars. A few years back, thanks to the efforts of George Martin, the former manager of the Beatles, you might have even gotten the chance to rub shoulders with Sting, Paul McCartney and others international rockers, who piled into Montserrat to take advantage of the world-class recording studio Martin built a few years ago. Unfortunately, in 1989 Hurricane Hugo blew away the remains of Air Studios, but some Montserratians claim they're happy to see their island return to some sleepy normalcy after its celeb rock invasion. Today the washed-away wharf is being built up again and homes have been restored, though a few are still standing as skeletons, a reminder of the devastation Mother Nature can wreak in the Caribbean. These days most of the income on the island is in the form of moneys sent from overseas relatives, and the only things locally made are sea-island cotton, ceramics, tapestries and postage stamps. Montserrat never set out to attract mass tourism, which is exactly why you should go now, before the inevitable commercial takeovers occur. Thankfully, these days Montserrat is still an island where you can find a storefront sign proudly announcing: "We Sell Brake Fluid, Pig Snout and Pig Tail."

Author's Note

The national bird, the Montserrat oriole, can be found on no other place on earth except here. Although it lost half its 1200 population to Hurricane Hugo, the puffed up, yellow-breasted bird has managed to survive every single cataclysm that has hit the island.

Bird's Eye View

The British Crown Colony of Montserrat is a lushly landscaped, 39.5-square mile island, some 27 miles southeast of Antigua. The island is compact, only 11 miles long by seven miles across; it takes almost 20 minutes to drive from the mid-island Anglo community of Woodlands to Plymouth. Near the airport, the land is flat and scrubby, but soon turns into a brilliant green terrain. Three mountain ranges cross the island; the highest, **Soufriere Hills**, rises to 3002 feet at the summit of **Mount Chance**. Volcanic in origin,

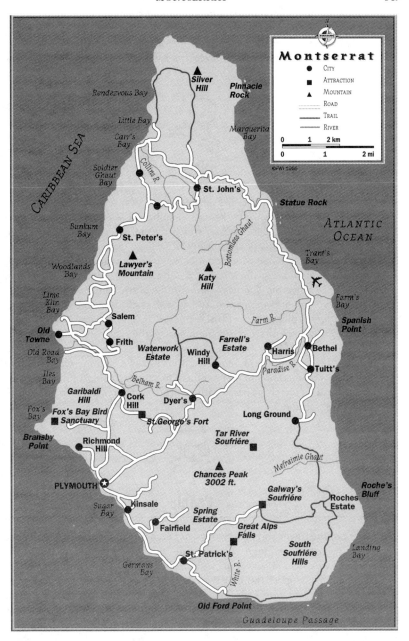

Silver Hill

Pinnacle Rock

Rendezvous Bay

Little Bay

Carr's Bay

Marguerita Bay

Soldier Ghaut Bay

Collins R.

St. John's

CARIBBEAN SEA

Statue Rock

Bunkum Bay

St. Peter's

ATLANTIC OCEAN

Woodlands Bay

Lawyer's Mountain

Katy Hill

Bottomless Ghaut

Trant's Bay

Lime Kiln Bay

Farm R.

Farm's Bay

Spanish Point

Salem

Old Towne

Old Road Bay

Frith

Waterwork Estate

Windy Hill

Farrell's Estate

Harris

Bethel

Iles Bay

Belham R.

Paradise R.

Tuitt's

Garibaldi Hill

Cork Hill

Dyer's

Fox's Bay

Fox's Bay Bird Sanctuary

St. George's Fort

Long Ground

Bransby Point

Richmond Hill

Tar River Soufrière

Mefraimie Ghaut

Roche's Bluff

PLYMOUTH

Chances Peak 3002 ft.

Galway's Soufrière

Roches Estate

Sugar Bay

Kinsale

Spring Estate

Great Alps Falls

South Soufrière Hills

Landing Bay

Fairfield

St. Patrick's

White R.

Germans Bay

Old Ford Point

Guadeloupe Passage

Montserrat

● CITY
■ ATTRACTION
▲ MOUNTAIN
ROAD
TRAIL
RIVER

0   1   2 km
0   1   2 mi

©FWI 1996

Montserrat boasts several active fumaroles and bubbling hot springs, an inactive volcano and sulphur spring. Most of the villages lie on the west coast, where they are connected by solid roads. **Plymouth**, the capital of the island, is compact but complete, with an excellent harbor, court, banks and government offices.

History

Ciboney Indians were the first inhabitants of Montserrat some 1500 years ago, later replaced by Arawaks and cannibalistic Caribs, the latter who dubbed the island "Alliouagana," which means either "island of the aloe plant" or "island of the prickly bush." In 1943, it was Christopher Columbus who gave the name Montserrat because of the island's resemblance to the luscious terrain near the Montserrat Monastery in Spain. Irish roots were laid in 1623 when Sir Thomas Warner, in St. Kitts, commanded rebellious Catholics to colonize the island. Today St. Patrick's Day is celebrated with glee and you'll still find lots of Irish names in the phonebook. After the slave trade began to support a sugarcane industry, the ratio between blacks and whites soared—10,000 blacks to 1300 whites in 1678. Emancipation arrived in 1834. Today, Montserrat remains a British Crown Colony, with a resident governor appointed by and representing Queen Elizabeth. At present, the island seems completely at peace with its protectorate relationship and shows no signs of rebelling,

People

Most of the towns and place names and even human names on Montserrat are of Irish origin, dating back to the mid-1600s when there were 1000 Irish families living here. Today, only a handful of full-blooded Irishmen still exist. The remaining are those of West African descent, whose ancestors were imported as plantation slaves from the 1660s to 1834. With such a small population (12,000), expect everyone in Montserrat to know each other (at least they make you think they do, so friendly are they). Also, everyone seems to know whenever and wherever a party is happening. Perhaps because of the devastating beauty of the island, locals tend to feel an intense connection to their land, and it's not surprising they have discovered numerous healing properties for native plants. Superstitions and belief in other-worldly things still run high, and many native-born carry not only their birth name but a "jumby" name as well—a magical name that protects them from spirits. Obeah, a voodoo-type religion with African roots, has been outlawed on the island, but expect to find a few hidden devotees amid the more Catholic masses. Most of the population is of African descent, but in recent years numerous wealthy Americans, Canadians and Britons, nicknamed "snow-birds," have bought retirement homes here. Consequently, much of the cultural life today in Montserrat, including the fine museum, is run by expats who have improved the quality of service, though a bit of genuine contact to folklore has been lost in the process.

Beaches

Montserrat is known for its black volcanic beaches, which in reality tend to mean sand that is a dark golden brown or silvery gray. Most of the "black" beaches are located in the northern tip of the island. Beaches with a bit whiter cast are located on the northwest coast; the most popular ones are **Rendezvous Bay**, **Little Bay** and **Carr's Bay**. The finest beach is **Woodlands**, with very limited facilities, where a delightful activity is swimming through caves. A rocky beach full of pebbles is **Fox's Bay**. Most beaches are reachable only by sailing, which can be arranged by the **Vue Pointe Hotel**.

Volcano Warning!

*Mother Nature knows how to keep tiny Montserrat on the map. The devasta-
tion from 1989's Hurricane Hugo that wiped out much of the island's greenery and many homes was all but forgotten when a fissure opened up on the
slopes of volcanic Chances Peak in July 1995 and spewed ash and smoke over
surprised Plymouth residents. Being the first signs of real activity on the
island in over six decades, it was dramatic enough to send vulcanologists
from the United States and England scurrying to the tiny outpost for evalu-
ation and monitoring. At press time, Plymouth and the southern half of the
island had been evacuated and tourist arrivals had slowed to a standstill.
Hopefully, the volcanic activity will have settled down by the time you read this and
the island's residents will be successfully putting the turmoil behind them. Before
planning your trip, call Montserrat's toll-free information line for the latest information:* ☎ *(800) 646-2002.*

Underwater

Virgin reefs featuring excellent soft coral growth and the relaxed charm of
an undiscovered island characterize diving on Montserrat, a fledgling activity
known to only a few so far. Most sites are spread along the length of the
western coastline, but plenty of others are waiting to be revealed. Visibility
approaches 100 feet on good days, particularly on the southern coast, and
shore dives are possible from several bays. There's a 200-foot pirate ship that
went down off the east coast in 1889 and is still partially intact while it awaits
excavation and preservation by the local National Trust. Snorkeling is feasible at **Woodlands Bay** and **Old Road**, and strong swimmers should investigate
the long reef between Little Bay and Rendezvous Bay.

O'Garrows

Situated off the southern coast, O'Garrows is an advanced dive amid unpredictable
currents that features a steep drop-off (45–90 feet) leading to heads of coral which
parallel the shore. The Atlantic brings loggerhead turtles, pelagics and barracuda

into the depths, while nurse, white-tip and sporadic hammerhead sharks plow these waters. The site showcases the island's healthiest coral growth and best visibility.

Pinnacle

Montserrat's best-known dive location, a seamount off Woodlands Bay, contains a coral garden of vast diversity and huge schools of barracuda. Suitable for strong intermediates, the dive averages 65 to 130 feet, but the west side of the pinnacle drops more than 300 feet, drawing sea turtles and pelagics and occasional surprises, like a six-foot kingfish spotted recently.

Shelia's Secret Spot

A circular patch reef 500 feet across reveals a dynamic variety of coral: brain, branched finger, staghorn, pillar and others, with large yellow and brown seahorses galloping through the forest. A lot of stingray action here, and queen conch lolling in the sea grass around the reef to round out the delightful mix. A huge concentration of fish must mean it's still a secret from local fishermen. Good for beginner-intermediates (45–65 feet).

Il Vaso Di Arianna

A beautiful sight off Rendezvous Bluff for intermediate-advanced divers (65–115 feet); barrel sponges up to six feet high, and pink and azure vase sponges are set among great star and stony corals. Fish life includes barracuda, mackerel, large snapper and stingrays.

Dive Shops

Aquatic Discoveries

Old Road Bay; ☎ *(809) 491-3474.*
A new operation based out of the Vue Pointe Hotel, centrally located in the middle of western coast. Two-tank dive, $65, including all equipment.

Sea Wolf Diving School

Plymouth; ☎ *(809) 491-7807.*
The island's three-year-old facility run by a friendly German couple, offers dives from kayaks and PADI training (up to Assistant Instructor). Two-tank dive $70, including all equipment.

On Foot

Montserrat's cozy dimensions do not deter hiking options and even allow for one full-blown trek through remote areas. A lattice of goat trails and old footpaths between the crumbling plantations appear on the detailed tourist map, and the underexplored northern tip of the island (behind and southeast of Rendezvous Bay) probably makes for splendid adventuring through a hot, near-desert environment. Guides are persistent and ever-present, but largely unnecessary for experienced hikers, with the possible exception of the paths in and out of Roches Estate.

The Bamboo Forest and Roches Estate

Beginning in the Galways Soufriere crater, an old donkey trail climbs out of the valley and over a small ridge into a lush canopy of bamboo towering 50 feet. The trail continues through the primordial South Soufriere Hills and down to Roches Estate, an abandoned plantation on a bluff overlooking Antigua and Guadeloupe. The track becomes a little more difficult to follow at this point, but continues north and drops into the Ghaut Mefraimie before finishing at Long Ground. Touring Montserrat's most isolated, least developed hillsides, this is a rewarding yet ambitious trail requiring five hours to complete; guides are available. Be sure to arrange for a pickup in Long Ground to avoid a formidable round-trip. NOTE: This hike concludes at a road-end less than one mile from the Tar River Soufriere, the epicenter of the 1995 volcanic activity. Check with local authorities before entering the area to verify that the trail is open and safe.

Chances Peak

At 3002 feet, Montserrat's attractive volcanic apex is a laudable goal, best assaulted in the early morning or late afternoon when temperatures are cooler and summit views less likely to be shrouded in clouds. The steep but straightforward hike begins at the end of the road rising above the villages south of Plymouth (locals can direct you to the trailhead). Beautiful montane and elfin forests envelope the path, while the crest rewards with splendid 360-degree views of St. Kitts, Nevis, Antigua and Guadeloupe. A tiny summit pond is rumored to be home to a mermaid, while just beyond, the intrepid can climb through dense vegetation and peer into the Chance's crater. Allow 90 minutes to the top.

Galway's Soufriere

From the parking lot a mile above Galway's Estate, a short path leads to a ledge overlooking Montserrat's previously most-famous soufriere (the Tar River Soufriere, on the other side of Chances Peak, is the location of the 1995 activity). The abundant sulfur and mineral deposits resemble a sloppy artist's palette, swathed in Day-Glo yellows and ocherous reds and browns. Guides are available to take you down into the steaming, marginally defined crater, but they're not necessary if you use caution amid the scalding fumaroles.

Great Alps Falls

Starting near sea level, a lovely trail ascends the verdant valley beneath Galways Soufriere. Scrambling over slick rocks (good footwear essential), the route crosses the White River several times and ends at a 70-foot cascade and pool, the Great Alps Falls, an idyllic setting in a gorge embroidered by elephant ear philodendrons and creeping vines. The path is hard to miss, but the guides who congregate at the trailhead likely will tell you differently.

Rendezvous Bay

Tour brochures refer to Rendezvous as Montserrat's only white-sand beach. Not to split hairs, but this quarter-mile-long cove is a lovely golden color, and its real claim to fame is not so much the sand's pigment but its secluded location. Boats are available out of Long Bay, or you can take this moderate, short hike. At the northern end of Long Bay, an obvious track climbs over Rendezvous Bluff passing cactus and scrub, then descends steeply to the isolated beach. Although easy to follow, the 30-minute hike requires sure footing; an easier, but slightly longer route leaves Long Bay from almost the same point but heads inland over gentler slopes. No water or facilities are available at Rendezvous.

By Pedal

Montserrat boasts more than 100 miles of paved roads and a determined bike rental outfit making the island ideal for cyclists seeking a relaxed, off-beat riding destination. A November "fat tire festival" has found its way onto regional biking calendars, and an Island Bikes training camp near Fox's Bay is scheduled to open in late 1995. The winding 28-mile road circumnavigating the island is an excellent half-day excursion, but requires healthy thighs for the numerous short, steep switchbacks; the parched area between Little Bay and the airport features dramatic scenery and almost no traffic. Easier trips can be undertaken in the coastal areas immediately north and, particularly, south of Plymouth. Off-roading possibilities are endless, but carry a patch kit for the ever-present stickers.

Bike Rental Shops

Island Bikes

Plymouth; ☎ *(809) 491-4696.*

Butch Miller and Susan Goldin are assertively promoting Montserrat as the mountain bike capital of the Caribbean. In addition to bike tours—a popular one carts bikes and riders in a van to Windy Hill for the delightful coast back into town—their well-stocked shop sells, rents and repairs more bikes than a number of larger islands. Rentals, $25 per day.

What Else to See

The first compelling sights on Montserrat are the natural ones, and you should schedule most of your vacation time around those. The city of Plymouth holds some very interesting old wooden buildings of various sizes and styles, and fortunately they were not destroyed by Hurricane Hugo. The grounds of the Victorian Government House may be toured weekdays, except Wednesday, on a green hill above Wapping Village. Historical buffs will enjoy the **Montserrat Museum**, ensconced in an old sugar mill at Richmond Hill in Plymouth. Some artifacts date back to the original native inhabitants, as far back as pre-Columbian history. Devoted philatelists should ask for the huge collection of stamps hidden in the bank vault. The harbor is somewhat quiet, but stop by the local market on Friday and Saturday when all the local vendors turn out. The Christmas season is the only time when nightlife in Plymouth can be described as anything beyond plebeian.

City Celebrations

Pilgrimage   ★★★★

Plymouth, ☎ *(809) 491-8288.*

This annual celebration takes place each August and runs over 10 days. Talk about something for everyone: Festivities include traditional street jump ups, African dance shows, fashion exhibitions, beach parties, barbecues, large markets, cultural concerts, bike races and tours, special hikes and cricket and domino tournaments with competitors from neighboring islands. The island also goes wild each St. Patrick's Day, which is not as incongruous as it first seems. The first European settlers on Montserrat were Irish, and on St. Patrick's Day, March 17, Montserrat slaves staged a revolt and marched on the Government House in 1768. Week-long events include a masquerade, jump-ups, street theater, Irish music and the Freedom Run Slave Fest.

Historical Sites

Galways Estate   ★★★

Near Plymouth, Plymouth.

A thriving sugar plantation for some 250 years, this estate dates back to the 1700s. It's now in ruins, but has been selected for renovation by the Smithsonian Institute under the auspices of the Montserrat National Trust. You can inspect the impressive sugar mill, great house, windmill tower and other structures.

Museums and Exhibits

Montserrat Museum　　　　　　　　　　★★★
Richmond Hill, Plymouth, ☎ *(809) 491-5443.*
Located in an old sugar mill, the country's national museum tells its history from
pre-Columbian times to the present. On display are old photographs, maps, natural
history exhibits and ancient artifacts. Donations are welcome.

Tours

Fox's Bay Bird Sanctuary　　　　　　　★★★
Grove Road, Richmond Estate.
This mangrove swamp and bog encompasses 15 acres and is home to lots of feath-
ered friends, including egrets and cuckoos. The nature trail leads to the beach.

Galway's Soufriere　　　　　　　　　　★★★
Near Upper Galway, south-central Montserrat.
A hike of 20 minutes or so up in the hills some 1700 feet above sea level takes you
to this volcanic field, complete with a bubbling crater and the overpowering stench
of sulfur.

Great Alps Waterfall　　　　　　　　★★★★
Shooters Hill Village, near St. Patrick's.
Stop in Shooters Hill Village to hire a guide for this quite strenuous hike through
verdant rainforest that takes at least 45 minutes. Your reward is the awesome falls,
which come from the White River and cascade down 70 feet into a shallow pool.

BEST VIEW:

*Panoramic seascapes are compelling from the top of the 18th-century Fort St.
George, 1184 feet above sea level. It's a 15-minute drive from Plymouth.*

Sports

Most of the island's activities are centered on scuba, snorkeling and sunbathing. (For diving sites, see above). Three tennis courts are available, asphalt ones at the Vue Pointe Hotel and the Montserrat Golf Club, and a
floodlit court at the Montserrat Springs Hotel. The Montserrat Golf Club's
18-hole course, carries a tremendous reputation in the Caribbean. Day sails
to Redonda, an island 16 miles northwest of Montserrat, can be arranged.
Other boat trips along the coast can be arranged through your hotel or directly with boat captains and dive operators in Plymouth. Horseback riding
is available at Sanford Farms for riders of all expertise and ages—over the

beach, through the countryside and on all-day picnic rides. Overnight expeditions for two or more riders can also be arranged in advance.

Montserrat Golf club

Old Town, Belham Valley.

This very hilly (and therefore rather challenging) course encompasses 100 acres. It has just 11 holes, but by playing some twice, you get a full 18. There's a bar and clubhouse in a converted cotton gin. Greens fees are about $23.

Watersports

Various locations, Plymouth.

Try these outfits for watersports: **Vue Point Hotel** (☎ *491-5210*) for general equipment, **Danny Water Sports** (☎ *491-5645*) for windsurfing and other equipment, **Sea Wolf Diving School** (☎ *491-7807*) for scuba excursions and instruction, **Aquatic Discoveries** (☎ *491-3474*) for scuba, whale watching, deep-sea fishing and snorkeling, and **Captain Martin** (☎ *491-5738*) for sailing and snorkeling.

Where to Stay

Fielding's Highest Rated Hotels in Montserrat

★★★★	Club Med Buccaneer's Creek	
★★★	Montserrat Springs Hotel	$85–$165
★★★	Villas of Montserrat	
★★★	Vue Pointe Hotel	$80–$160

Fielding's Most Romantic Hotels in Montserrat

★★	Providence Guest House	$45–$85
★★★	Vue Pointe Hotel	$80–$160

Fielding's Budget Hotels in Montserrat

★	Marie's Guest House	$35–$35
★	Lime Court Apartments	$30–$50
★★	Flora Fountain Hotel	$50–$80
★★	Providence Guest House	$45–$85
★	Oriole Plaza Hotel	$70–$70

The lodging options on Montserrat could fit into the palm of your hand. Take your pick from two resort hotels, one standard hotel, rental condos or guest house. Count on the trade winds to keep you cool, not air conditioning. Check your bill for any extra charges that you didn't make, but expect the 7–10 percent room tax to be added to the final tab.

Hotels and Resorts

Vue Pointe is the hub of island life, congenial owned and run by an island family—the West Indian barbecue on Wednesday nights attracts everyone around. Views are not great at the Flora Fountain, but its West Indian buffet breakfast is the only place to be on Saturday morning if you want to indulge in local delicacies. Montserrat Springs is 25 minutes by taxi from the airport and contains a pair of hot and cold baths since it is located in the site of natural springs.

Club Med Buccaneer's Creek   **$700–$1550 per wk.**   ★★★★

Pointe Marine, Ste. Anne, ☎ *(800) 258-2633, (596) 76-72-72.*

One of the Club Meds that still does the lion's share with singles, this village doesn't allow kids under 12. Very nicely designed, the resort covers 48 acres with lots of coconut groves and winding footpaths. The beach is one of Martinique's best, and there you'll find all the watersports anyone could hope for, though scuba diving costs extra. Other activities include golfing on a Robert Trent Jones course 45 minutes away (they'll take you there, and you will pay greens fees), seven tennis courts, exercise classes, softball, billiards, pingpong, and organized picnics and boat rides. Geared toward those who like group activity, this all-inclusive resort is best for singles looking for love (or at least lust) and outgoing couples. Accommodations are similar to other Club Meds: very simple and spartan, but also comfortable and clean. This year, the 4th Annual Club Med Bowl takes place here from April 1-8, with former Super Bowl champs on hand to sign autographs and conduct workshops. Rates are $700 to $1550 per week, double occupancy, plus $30 initiation fee and $50 annual fee.

Flora Fountain Hotel   **$50–$80**   ★★

Lower Dagenham Road, ☎ *(809) 491-6092, FAX (809) 491-2568.*
Single: $50–$65. Double: $65–$80.

This hotel in city center attracts mostly business travelers. Built around a circular courtyard with an impressive fountain, it offers basic rooms with twin beds and balconies. Good for those who want to be in the center of town, but sun lovers will be happier at a beach property, or at least a hotel with a pool.

Montserrat Springs Hotel   **$85–$165**   ★★★

Richmond Hill, ☎ *(809) 491-2481, FAX (809) 491-4070.*
Single: $85–$145. Double: $115–$165.

Set on a hillside with pretty sea views, this hotel has its own hot mineral springs, and guests can while away the hours soaking in a hot or cold whirlpool. Guest rooms, located in villas, are generally spacious and nicely done. There are also six suites with full kitchens. The steeply sloping grounds include a restaurant, two bars, a pool, two tennis courts, and the beach, where watersports await.

Vue Pointe Hotel   **$80–$160**   ★★★

Isles Bay Beach, ☎ *(800) 235-0709, (809) 491-5210, FAX (809) 491-4813.*
Single: $80–$150. Double: $105–$160.

Situated on a secluded hill above the beach, four miles from Plymouth, this property is Montserrat's best bet. Accommodations are housed in stucco buildings or hexagonal villas, all with Danish teak and rattan furnishings, twin beds and sitting areas. No air conditioning, but breezes help keep things cool. The grounds, which slope down to a black sand beach, include a pool, two tennis courts, a dining room with great food and two bars. Service is excellent.

Apartments and Condominiums

Lots of Americans and Canadians are building second homes in Montserrat, contributing to the building boom of condos and apartments. If you want to save money, you'll have to be satisfied with an out-of-the-way location, a bad view or small rooms. You can find luxurious apartments, but you'll have to add the cost of a car to your final bill. If you stay in a house around Vue Pointe, you'll be close to the supermarkets in Plymouth and the local vegetable market. Some of the best villas, rented in the owner's absence, are the ones at Villas of Montserrat.

Belham Valley Hotel   **$255–$480 per wk.**   ★

Old Towne, ☎ (809) 491-5553, FAX (809) 491-5283.

This small complex sits on a hill overlooking Belham Valley (hence the name) and its river, near the Montserrat Golf Course. The complex includes one studio apartment, one two-bedroom apartment and a studio cottage, all with fully equipped kitchens and stereos, but no air conditioning. The restaurant is highly regarded, but there's nothing else on-site. The beach can be walked to in under 10 minutes. Rates are $255 to $480 per week.

Lime Court Apartments   **$30–$50**   ★

☎ (809) 491-5069.
Single: $30–$50. Double: $30–$50.

Located in the center of town, this small apartment building sells out fast due to its very reasonable rates. Units range from studios to two-bedroom apartments, all with full kitchenettes and maid service. The penthouse unit is by far the best and well worth the few extra dollars. There's nothing on-site in the way of recreation or dining, but lots within walking distance, including the beach.

Shamrock Villas   **$630–$2000 per wk.**   ★ ★

☎ (809) 491-4660.

Located on a hillside near the Montserrat Springs Hotel, this complex consists of condominiums rented out in their owners' absence. Each is individually decorated and has a full kitchen and nice views. No air conditioning, though, and maid service costs extra. There's a pool on-site but little else. Shamrock also rents out villas located around the island, many with their own pool. Condos cost $430 to $670 per week, while villas run $630 to $2000.

Villas of Montserrat   **$1400–$2000 per wk.**   ★ ★ ★

☎ (809) 491-5513.

Located on a mountainside overlooking Isle Bay north of Plymouth, these three villas are quite luxurious, as they should be, since they cost a small fortune. Each has three bedrooms, three bathrooms (one with Jacuzzi), a living room, dining room, stereo, TV, and full kitchens with microwaves and dishwashers. Each also has maid service (only on weekdays) and their own pool. The services of a cook can be arranged. Rates are $1400 to $2000 per week; each villa sleeps six.

Inns

Providence Guest House   **$45–$85**   ★ ★

St. Peter's, ☎ (809) 491-6476.
Single: $45–$55. Double: $65–$85.

Located about 20 minutes from Plymouth in a country setting, this guesthouse has hosted the likes of Paul McCartney and Stevie Wonder. (Obviously, they rented out the whole house.) The old plantation house has been beautifully restored and has just two rooms for guests, both on the ground floor and very nicely decorated.

Wonderful views from the pool deck. There's a communal kitchenette, or you can arrange for the owners to make you dinner. Lovely, but a bit too off on its own for some tourists. You'll definitely want a car.

Low Cost Lodging

Do ask around for rooms in private homes—someone always knows someone. **Marie's Guest House** is for the young at heart who don't mind sharing a bathroom. Lots of West Indian businessmen stay at the **Oriole Plaza** hotel in the center of town.

Marie's Guest House   **$35–$35**   ★

☎ *(809) 419-2745.*
Single: $35. Double: $35.
This small inn in a garden setting near Plymouth offers simple but comfortable non-air-conditioned rooms at a price that's hard to beat. Guests share the kitchen, while each room has its own bath.

Oriole Plaza Hotel   **$70–$70**   ★

Parliament Street, ☎ *(809) 491-6982, FAX (809) 491-6690.*
Single: $70. Double: $70.
Appealing mainly to business travelers, this modest hotel is right in the center of town, about a five-minute walk to the beach. Rooms are simple and basic, and rely on ceiling fans to keep things cool. There's a bar and restaurant on-site, but little else.

Where to Eat

Fielding's Highest Rated Restaurants in Montserrat

★★★★★	**Belham Valley Restaurant**	$14–$23
★★★	**Blue Dolphin**	$9–$20
★★★	**Emerald Cafe**	$4–$20
★★★	**Montserrat Springs Hotel**	$4–$19
★★★	**Mrs. Morgan's**	$4–$5
★★★	**Niggy's Bistro**	$7–$17
★★★	**Vue Pointe Restaurant**	$13–$23

Fielding's Special Restaurants in Montserrat

★★★	**Mrs. Morgan's**	$4–$5
★★★	**Niggy's Bistro**	$7–$17
★★★	**Vue Pointe Restaurant**	$13–$23
★★	**The Village Place**	$5–$16

Fielding's Budget Restaurants in Montserrat

★★★	**Mrs. Morgan's**	$4–$5
★★	**The Attic**	$2–$10
★★	**Evergreen Cafe**	$2–$12
★★	**Golden Apple**	$5–$10
★★★	**Montserrat Springs Hotel**	$4–$19

The volcanic lava on the island allows an enormous variety of vegetables to grow with gusto, from cucumbers to breadfruit, tomatoes, pumpkin, cabbages, and the less-familiar West Indian squashlike Christophene. The two national dishes are goat-water, made of goat meat and flavored with scallions and thyme, called "herbs and chile," and mountain chicken, which is actually gigantic frog legs cooked in a variety of ways. Don't miss biting down into a Montserrat *pawpaw* (papaya); it's a memory most never forget. Great food and great island music can be had at **Niggy's**, in an old clapboard house in Kinsale, south of Plymouth. For elegance and top-class cuisine, try the **Vue Pointe Restaurant** at the hotel. **Emerald Cafe** is now considered an institution on the island since it was opened in 1988; recognizable food at a good price makes the floral ambiance even more pleasant. The **Blue Dolphin** restaurant is the prime spot to be initiated into the delicacy called "mountain chicken"— actually a large meaty frog that lives on the flanks of Mount Chance and is hunted after dark. Here it's served marinated in a spicy red sauce then deep fried in batter. Don't miss tasting *Ting*, a popular carbonated grapefruit drink that has migrated from St. Kitts.

Belham Valley Restaurant $$$ ★★★★★

Old Towne, Belham Valley, ☎ *(809) 491-5553.*
International cuisine. Specialties: Conch Fritters, Seafood Delight.
Lunch: Noon–2 p.m., entrees $14–$23.
Dinner: 6:30–11 p.m., entrees $14–$23.

This hotel dining room in a posh residential section of the island draws everyone in sooner or later for the serene views from an outdoor terrace and the chef's creative ways with fine local ingredients. The Seafood Delight, a trio of piscatorial pleasures (often including lobster) is blanketed with an herbed Vermouth sauce. The moderately-priced dinners often include a salad and fresh vegetables. When available, try the mango mousse or coconut cheesecake. Lunch is a viable option during the week in season.

Blue Dolphin $$ ★★★

Amersham, Amersham, ☎ *(809) 491-3263.*
International cuisine. Specialties: Mountain Chicken.
Lunch: Noon–2 p.m., entrees $9–$20.
Dinner: 6 p.m.–midnight, entrees $9–$20.

The interior of this West Indian restaurant in the Plymouth hills is nothing to brag about, but the mountain chicken (frog's legs) is the best in town, often prepared with a garlic sauce. Vegetarians won't feel slighted either, with a wide variety of fresh greens and starches available, including peas and rice and pumpkin soup.

Emerald Cafe $$ ★★★

Wapping Road, ☎ *(809) 491-3821.*
International cuisine.
Lunch: 8 a.m.–4 p.m., entrees $4–$20.
Dinner: 4 p.m.–midnight, entrees $4–$20.

There's something for everyone at this indoor-outdoor eatery located in a Plymouth suburb—burgers, crepes and West Indian blue plate specials. That often means mountain chicken, or fresh seafood served with rice and local vegetables. If you don't rate a table on the terrace under umbrellas, join a companionable group inside. This is also a good spot for a drink.

Evergreen Cafe $ ★★

Upper Marine Drive,
American cuisine.
Lunch: 7 a.m.–4 p.m., entrees $2–$12.
Dinner: 4–8 p.m., entrees $2–$12.

Folks needing a fast-food hit head on up to this no-frills cafe with a bakery attached. The burgers, pizzas and fried chicken dishes are relatively expensive for the surroundings ($5-12), but the quality is pretty good, and there's always a crowd. It might be a better idea to pick up a pastry here for breakfast or a tea time snack.

Golden Apple $ ★★

Cook Hill, Cook Hill, ☎ (809) 491-2187.
Latin American cuisine. Specialties: Goat Water.
Lunch: entrees $5–$10.
Dinner: entrees $5–$10.

This spacious local eatery is one of a growing number of weekend-only goat water pit stops. The bizarrely-named national dish of Montserrat is a heady brew of goat meat cooked until tender, with an infusion of cloves, spices and vegetables. Portions served are pretty hefty. Chicken and rice, conch and fish dishes are also available.

Montserrat Springs Hotel $$ ★★★

Richmond Hill, ☎ (809) 491-2481.
Latin American cuisine.
Lunch: 8 a.m.–3 p.m., entrees $4–$7.
Dinner: 3–11 p.m., entrees $11–$19.

The vista from the poolside restaurant of this upscale hotel is spectacular, encompassing Chance's Peak (the highest on the island) and the Caribbean Sea. Unfortunately, the cuisine is nothing to write home about, with sandwiches and such for lunch and surf and turf for dinner. A better bet is the Sunday barbecue served from noon to 3 p.m.—for under $25, you get grilled chicken, fish or meat, served with island vegies, a plethora of salads, and a choice of two homemade desserts.

Mrs. Morgan's $ ★★★

Airport Road, St. John's, ☎ (809) 491-5419.
Latin American cuisine. Specialties: Goat Water.
Lunch and Dinner: entrees $4–$5.

Visitors and residents return time and again for Mrs. Morgan's homemade goat water stew served only on Friday and Saturday. The humble hut, which serves as a bar the rest of the week, is located between the airport and Carr's Bay, a tiny fishing port. At these prices, a few bowls (bet you can eat only one) could feed a crowd. Call ahead to see what else she's preparing—it's a very informal operation. Usually open from 11:30 a.m. until the food runs out.

Niggy's Bistro $$ ★★★

Kinsale, ☎ (809) 491-7489.
International cuisine. Specialties: Beef Tenderloin with Bordelaise Sauce, Scampi.
Dinner: 6–10:30 p.m., entrees $7–$17.

Local politicos chew the fat (but not on the food) at this pension and restaurant in a pretty cottage in the suburb of Kinsale. The place is often abuzz with Hollywood talk (ex-actor Anthony Overman is the owner), music and fun. Diners eat outside on picnic benches, and the fare is often a melange of West Indian and international specialties served with pasta and salad. The bar, a converted boat, is a great gimmick.

Oasis $$ ★★

Wapping, ☎ *(809) 491-2328.*
International cuisine.
Lunch: Noon–1:30 p.m., entrees $5–$10.
Dinner: 6:30–10 p.m., entrees $5–$16.

This place, located in an old stone structure, has plenty of atmosphere, and is a cool spot on warm days. But most patrons opt for the airy patio to nosh on fish and chips and such—the owners are English. If you don't fancy fish, there's chicken, steak, red snapper, pizza and vegetarian platters; the possibilities are endless.

The Attic $ ★★

Upper Marine Drive, ☎ *(809) 491-2008.*
Latin American cuisine.
Lunch: 8 a.m.–3 p.m., entrees $2–$10.
Dinner: 6–9:30 p.m., entrees $2–$10.

It's not really in an attic, located on the second level of a nondescript building in Plymouth. But the small size and bustle give this place a cozy feel. The menu is basically a list of tasty West Indian and American dishes like rotis, burgers, fish and sometimes lobster and goat water. Tends to get crowded at times, but the line moves quickly.

The Village Place $$ ★★

Salem, north of Plymouth, ☎ *(809) 491-5202.*
American cuisine.
Dinner: 6 p.m.–midnight, entrees $5–$16.

This bar and restaurant (with an emphasis on bar) used to be the hangout of Jagger, Clapton and other visiting British rock greats when George Martin's Air Studios was up and running in the pre-Hurricane Hugo era. The Place is still popular with locals and other scenemakers who like the loud party atmosphere, the rum drinks and some of owner Andy Lawrence's thyme-marinated fried chicken. Since there's not much nightlife on this peaceful island, the Place, which stays open until at least midnight, should keep night owls pacified.

Vue Pointe Restaurant $$$ ★★★

Old Towne, north of, Belham Valley, ☎ *(809) 491-5211.*
Latin American cuisine.
Lunch: 12:30–2 p.m., entrees $13–$23.
Dinner: 7–9:30 p.m., entrees $13–$23.

Few people can resist the charms of this place—welcoming proprietors, a jumping Wednesday evening barbecue, stupendous views of a black sand beach below, and simple, but tasty cuisine. You can visit it for a simple lunch of seasonal fruit salads or sandwiches, a fixed-price ($25) dinner of mountain chicken and all the trimmings, or the aforementioned barbecue. If you opt for this event, get here early; it's popular. Otherwise, a more sedate barbecue is offered on Sundays around noon in the winter.

Where to Shop

Montserrat has a surprising number of crafts for a tiny island. Handwoven tapestries make excellent gifts, available from Montserrat Tapestries. Many island craftsmen work with wood, carving out fabulous furniture—chairs, beds, and tables can even be made custom-ordered. (Inquire first about shipping charges.) To see leather workers creating highly original designs, check out the studios at **Cultural Frontier** or **Productions Tannery**. Fine leather jewelry made by local artists can be found at **Carol's Corner**, as well as the Montserrat cookbook *Goatwater*. Locally handwoven cotton products are best bought at the **Montserrat Sea Island Cotton Company**.

Montserrat Directory

ARRIVAL AND DEPARTURE

LIAT provides several daily (18-minute) flights from Antigua, where you can catch a variety of other direct connections to the states (BWIA, Air Canada, British Airway and American). LIAT also flies from St. Thomas, via Sint Maarten and St. Kitts. WINAIR now provides two daily flights from Sint Maarten.

The departure tax is U.S. $6 for those over twelve years of age.

BUSINESS HOURS

Stores open Monday–Saturday 8 a.m.–5 p.m. Banks open Monday–Thursday 8 a.m.–3 p.m. and Friday 3–5 p.m.

CLIMATE

Temperate and tropical, temperatures average 73.5 degrees F to 86.5 degrees F., with very little variation from season to season. Humidity is blissfully low. Rain is most frequent in April and May, and July-September.

DOCUMENTS

U.S. and Canadian visitors need to show proof of citizenship (passport, birth certificate with photo ID), for stays up to six months. Those who do not show an ongoing or return ticket may be required to deposit a sum of money equivalent to that needed for repatriation.

ELECTRICITY

Current runs 220–230 volts AC, 60 cycles, so you will need an electrical transformer and an adapter.

GETTING AROUND

Taxi drivers are omnipresent whenever a flight arrives. Expect to pay about $11 from the airport to the town of Plymouth. Buses, another easy way to travel, cost about $1–$2 one day.

Car rental agencies are only local outfits. Toyotas, Jeeps and Daihatsus are available at the reliable **Pauline's Car Rentals**, on Church Road *(P.O. Box 171) in Plymouth* ☎ *(809) 491-2345*. Cars can be delivered to the airport or your hotel. Cards are accepted. To rent a car, you need to show a valid driver's license and pay $12. Ask the police officers at the Immigration Department at the airport for assistance.

LANGUAGE

Most everyone speaks English, though the lilt resembles a strong Irish brogue.

MEDICAL EMERGENCIES

Glendon Hospital in Plymouth ☎ *(809) 491-2552* has 68 beds and can provide adequate care for short-term cases. Serious emergencies should be flown to larger islands. Ask your hotel to suggest a doctor on call.

MONEY

The official currency is the Eastern Caribbean dollar. Some of the best exchange rates can be found at the Royal Bank of Canada.

TELEPHONE

The area code is *809*. Local numbers are four digits.

For international calls, skip calling from your room and head for the Cable and Wireless Ltd. on Houston Street, ☎ *2112*, open Monday-Thursday 7:30 a.m.–6 p.m., Friday 7:30 a.m.–10 p.m., and Saturday 7:30 a.m.–6 p.m. You'll find a new digital telephone system, faxes, telegraph, telex and data facilities. Phone cards (purchased there) and credit cards, toll-free service, and cellular phones can be used.

TIME

Atlantic Standard Time, one hour later than New York City.

TIPPING AND TAXES

Expect a 10 percent service charge to be added to all bills. Tipping a taxi driver will make him (or her) happy, but there is no expectation.

TOURIST INFORMATION

The Montserrat Tourist Board is located on Church Road in the Government Headquarters building. The mailing address is *P.O. Box 7, Plymouth;* ☎ *2230*, FAX *7430*. The office has produced a new brochure delineating a cross-section of restaurants and bars on the island. To call Montserrat from the U.S., dial area code 809 and access code 491 plus the local four-digit number.

MONTSERRAT HOTELS

		RMS	RATES	PHONE	CR. CARDS
Plymouth					
★★★★	**ClubMed Buccaneer's Creek**	300	$700–$1550	(800) 258-2633	A
★★★	**Montserrat Springs Hotel**	46	$85–$165	(800) 253-2134	A, D, MC, V
★★★	**Villas of Montserrat**	3	$1400–$2000	(809) 491-5513	None
★★★	**Vue Pointe Hotel**	40	$80–$160	(800) 235-0709	A, D, MC, V
★★	**Flora Fountain Hotel**	16	$50–$80	(809) 491-6092	A, D, MC, V
★★	**Providence Guest House**	2	$45–$85	(809) 491-6476	None
★★	**Shamrock Villas**	20	$530–$2000	(809) 491-4660	None
★	**Belham Valley Hotel**	3	$255–$480	(809) 491-5553	A, MC
★	**Lime Court Apartments**	8	$30–$50	(809) 491-5069	A, MC
★	**Marie's Guest House**	4	$35	(809) 419-2745	None
★	**Oriole Plaza Hotel**	12	$70	(809) 491-6982	A, MC

MONTSERRAT RESTAURANTS

		PHONE	ENTREE	CR. CARDS
Plymouth				
	American			
★★	**Evergreen Cafe**		$2–$12	None
★★	**The Village Place**	(809) 491-5202	$5–$16••	None
	International			
★★★★★	**Belham Valley Restaurant**	(809) 491-5553	$14–$23	A, MC, V
★★★	**Blue Dolphin**	(809) 491-3263	$9–$20	None
★★★	**Emerald Cafe**	(809) 491-3821	$4–$20	None
★★★	**Niggy's Bistro**	(809) 491-7489	$7–$17••	MC, V
★★	**Oasis**	(809) 491-2328	$5–$16	None
	Latin American			
★★★	**Montserrat Springs Hotel**	(809) 491-2481	$4–$19	A, D, MC, V
★★★	**Mrs. Morgan's**	(809) 491-5419	$4–$5••	None
★★★	**Vue Pointe Restaurant**	(809) 491-5211	$13–$23	A, MC, V
★★	**Golden Apple**	(809) 491-2187	$5–$10	None
★★	**The Attic**	(809) 491-2008	$2–$10	None

Note: • Lunch Only

•• Dinner Only

NEVIS

Nevis offers quiet, pastoral charm and friendly people.

With genteel plantations and scenic pastoral vistas, Nevis offers a taste of the old Caribbean. Sister to St. Kitts, Nevis is the quiet child, shunning the extravagant Kittian casinos for the leisure of a quiet drink on the veranda of a 200-year-old inn. To tell the truth, Nevis is no savvy island; sugar is sold for less than it costs to produce, and with the exception of the recent unfolding of the Four Seasons Resort on Pinney's Beach—one of the most beautiful strands in the Caribbean—nothing aggressive is much being done about tourism. Instead, what you find on Nevis are genuinely hospitable people, willing to share the quiet charm of their tiny island and the seemingly unlimited bank of their natural resources. No one seems to move faster than a ceiling fan in Nevis, and the dreams you might have, after a dinner of "hubcap

371

chicken" (yes, that's right, deep-fried in hubcaps) will be about the lusciou
array of tropical fruits that will grace your breakfast buffet in the morning
Despite the laid-back nature of the island, however, locals have not remaineo
lax in regard to ecology; in fact, Nevis boasts some of the strictest ecologica
laws in the world. For that reason, the hundred cruise liners that stopped ir
Nevis last year did little to upset the island's perfect ecological balance and
the island continues today to be a pristine environment.

Bird's Eye View

Six miles across and 18 miles around, Nevis is a little gumdrop-shaped vol
canic island separated from St. Kitts by the two-mile Narrows Channel. Eco
logically wilder than St. Kitts, Nevis has an exuberant rampage of trees
creepers and giant ferns that appear the moment you creep out of the sleepy
capital of Charlestown on the single round-island road. The highest point
Nevis Peak, is usually shrouded in clouds and mist, which inspired Colum
bus to name the island "Las Nieves." What were once huge plantations have
now returned to scrub punctuated by gardens lovingly cultivated by island
ers on the slopes of Mount Nevis.

Charlestown, the capital (population 1200), is a laconic sprawl of paste
walls, tin roofs and shady gardens, one of the most well-preserved in the Car
ibbean. As on St. Kitts, regulations prohibit any building taller than a palm
tree. One reason the island has remained so virginal is that the Brimstone
Hill Fortress of St. Kitts, perched like a sentinel high above the sea, was so
intimidating that ship captains often changed course rather than fall within
the range of its guns. Today the proverbial cannons have been replaced by
the residential community's commitment to ecological preservation—so
strong that the federal government has been inspired to initiate some of the
strictest building and marine regulations in the world. Hurricane Hugo
damaged Nevis badly, but today, most of the island has recovered. One o
the strangest but most wonderful facts about St. Kitts-Nevis is that there are
more monkeys than people on St. Kitts and Nevis combined (125,000 mon
keys vs. 46,000 humans).

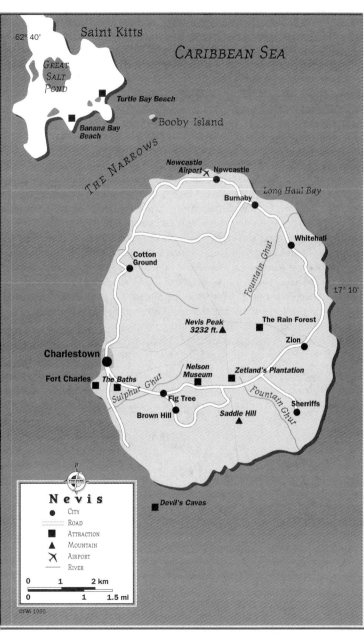

62° 40'

Saint Kitts

CARIBBEAN SEA

GREAT SALT POND

Turtle Bay Beach

Booby Island

Banana Bay Beach

THE NARROWS

Newcastle Airport

Newcastle

Burnaby

Long Haul Bay

Whitehall

Cotton Ground

Fountain Ghut

17° 10'

Nevis Peak 3232 ft. ▲

The Rain Forest

Zion

Charlestown

Fort Charles

The Baths

Sulphur Ghut

Nelson Museum

Zetland's Plantation

Fountain Ghut

Fig Tree

Brown Hill

Saddle Hill ▲

Sherriffs

Devil's Caves

Nevis

● CITY
⋯ ROAD
■ ATTRACTION
▲ MOUNTAIN
✕ AIRPORT
— RIVER

0   1   2 km
0   1   1.5 mi

©FWI 1996

History

Nevis has had a long history for such a small island. After spotting an island and naming it St.Christopher (later nicknamed St. Kitts) for his patron saint, Columbus spied a cloud-covered conic island rising out of the water during his second voyage, dubbing it "Nuestra Señora de las Nieves," or "Our lady of the Snows"—since it reminded him of the snow-capped Pyrenees—and promptly went on his way. British troops arrived in 1623, first joining forces with the French to conquer the Spanish and decimate the resident Carib Indian tribes, then later duking it out with the Gallic forces for the next 150 years. The British used St. Kitts as a base to colonize Nevis, Antigua, Barbuda, Tortola and Montserrat, while the French managed to dominate Martinique, St. Martin, Guadeloupe, St. Barts, La Désirade and Les Saintes. The Treaty of Versailles in 1783 ceded the islands to Britain. Known as the "Queen of the Carribbees" in the late 18th century for its thriving sugar trade, Nevis later saw its fortunes decline with the abolition of slavery in 1834. Almost 150 years later in 1983, Nevis, with St. Kitts, would become the Caribbean's newest independent country with the establishment of the federation of St. Kitts-Nevis in 1983.

People

The rhythm of life in Nevis is gentle and noninvasive, much quieter than St. Kitts. The local people are still imbued with age-old superstitions; door frames are painted blue to keep "jumby" spirits out in accordance with ancient obeah voodoo customs. Many still use herbal cures and some Nevisian retain their respect for the mystical powers of big fat toads called *crappos*. One of the most beguiling aromas you will smell throughout the island is that of *souse*, or pork stew. The local drink is *mauby*, made from the bark of a tree. A local phrase used commonly is "pocket o' mumps," which roughly means "in a good-spirited goof-off mood."

Nelson Spring on Nevis is one of the beautiful lagoons author James Michener visited while researching his novel Caribbean.

Beaches

Almost six miles of white sand, swaying palms and whispering surf make **Pinney's Beach** (on the leeward side) the longest. It's also the location of the

Four Seasons Resort, which boasts 196 luxurious rooms and suites, fine cui
sine, myriad activities and an abundance of watersports. There are severa
beach bars here. **Booby Island** in the middle of Narrows Channel is mostly in
habited by pelicans; the waters around there are good for diving. **White Ba**
Beach, down Hanleys Road on the Atlantic coast side, can get dangerous o
windy days, but generally is a lively alternative to the calmer surf at Pinney'
A reef farther out from here usually renders good fishing. A smaller beac
can be found at **Mosquito Bay** (live music and partying on Sunday afternoon:
and the waters under **Hurricane Hill** support good snorkeling. Snorkeling
good at a small beach called **Mosquito Bay**.

Consider chartered boat excursions to the beaches at St. Kitts. Dependin
on the wind, some windsurfers just let themselves drift from one island to
the other.

Underwater

With only one dive operator available (and no competition, keeping price
high), the waters off Nevis have yet to become a high-profile destination fo
divers. However, a diverse selection of interesting sites are available, includ
ing a unique ride through cool underwater lava tubes. The relative paucity o
dive business means that Nevis' reefs are in better shape than a number of i
lands visited by more divers; visibility averages 80 to 100 feet. The chann
between St. Kitts and Nevis, **The Narrows**, contains many of the best dives, in
cluding **Nags Head** (see "St. Kitts"); these sites are shared by the operators o
both islands. **Redonda Reef** off the remote southern coast offers a little-visite
wilderness where hammerheads and whales sometimes tarry (calm seas ar
required for diving). Many visiting divers inquire about the mysterious se
tlement of **James Town**, rumored to lie underwater off the island's west coas
One story goes that the village submerged dramatically as a result of a cat
clysmic earthquake, while others say a tidal wave or hurricane washed it ou
to sea. There are those who claim to have explored the actual site but, if so,
lies under a thick blanket of sand today. Consumed in myth and folklore, th
reality may be simply that the village was abandoned and/or overgrown b
marshland. No one knows the whole truth, and historical records are conve
niently contradictory, but local fishermen say that one can hear the churc
bells ringing as you near the ruins of James Town. Experienced snorkele
should head for **Longhaul Bay**, where a protected inner reef is hidden just pa

ne last jetty southeast of the main reef; novices will enjoy the shallows
round the jetty. Snorkeling also is reported to be good at the north end of
Oualie Beach near the rocks.

Monkey Shoals

Excellent visibility highlights this vast location that features several possible sites,
frequently dived from St. Kitts (it lies just west of the channel between the two
islands). Average depth is 50 feet, and visitors will find plentiful coral divided by
chutes of sand and crevices, and resting nurse sharks bedded down beneath overhangs. The delightful flying gurnard sometimes pops in to navigate purple and
green sea fans, elkhorn coral and slender sea whips.

Devil's Caves

A remarkable series of grottos formed by submerged lava tubes (maximum depth 40
feet), this site lies on the southwest coast of Nevis and is festooned with hard and
soft corals. Sea life includes schools of chub, large hawksbill turtles and spotted and
green moray eels. The tunnels are cozy in size—single file, please—and the surge
sometimes offers a free ride. The photogenic location is suitable for all levels of
divers and can even be visited by snorkelers.

Dive Shops

Scuba Safaris

Oualie Beach; ☎ *(809) 469-9518.*
Locally born Ellis Chaderton is Nevis' one dive operator who uses two 32-foot dive
boats to visit sites around Nevis and southern St. Kitts. Resort courses and PADI
certification through Divemaster. Two-tank dive, $80 (not including gear). Half-
day snorkel trips, $35.

On Foot

Life on Nevis is wrapped, literally, around an almost classically shaped vol-
anic cone. For adventurous visitors, hiking is, too. Or rather, ascending the
steep slopes of **Nevis Peak** is the main trek on the island, completed by relatively few intrepid outsiders, which leaves the trail overgrown and difficult to
follow in some sections. However, walking is really a way of life for islanders.
Nevis is small enough that many locals continue to use foot travel between
the small villages and vehicular traffic is light. Join them in their informal
method of transportation, even along the 20-mile main road circling the island, for an inviting glimpse into a slower Caribbean life-style.

Nevis Peak

It hasn't been active for more than 300 years, but soaring Nevis Peak still manage
to intimidate. The two-mile trail starts vaguely near the end of the road above th
Zetland Plantation and proceeds through clumpy meadows and fern forests. Whe
the angle and vegetation increases, watch for playful vervet monkeys. You'll soo
encounter a slippery combination of mud, vines and scrambling (mountain climb
ing, by Caribbean standards) before reaching the crater rim, which drops 800 fee
to its floor. The summit view is spectacular (if rare, owing to the frequency o
cloudy days), while indistinct paths lead around the rim of the steaming crater fo
further exploration. A guide is recommended for this demanding trek; mak
arrangements with the local tourist office.

Pinney's Beach Walk

One of the most seductive beaches in the region, the walk on Pinney's lazy curve c
soft, gray sand stretches four miles from Charleston, passing the massive, but sub
dued Four Seasons complex at midpoint. On either side of this resort, the narrov
sands are unfettered, peaceful and bordered by towering palms on one side an
views of mountainous St. Kitts on the other. Numerous paths connect the beac
with the main road, allowing you to construct an excursion of almost any length
Fort Ashby, just north of Cotton Ground, marks the end of Pinney's, and the sta
of another beach, Oualie. A lovely sunset walk.

The Rainforest Trail

The rainforested eastern slopes of Nevis Peak provide the backdrop for this popula
hike which begins at the Golden Rock Estate (which supplies guests with a trai
map). The path, starting near the parking lot cannons, is well-maintained an
ascends through white cedar into the heart of the rainforest, where vervet monkey
cavort, to a lookout, and eventually winds through ravines to a 70-foot-high ladde
the top of the ladder reveals The Source, the primary water supply for Nevis. Allo
three-to-four hours for the roundtrip. A shorter self-guided nature walk throug
rich flora is also available at the eco-sensitive Golden Rock Estate; late afternoo
strollers will encounter families of the vervet monkeys inhabiting the hillside (allo
30 minutes).

Saddle Hill and Nelson's Fort

Just beyond the Montpelier Guest House, where Admiral Nelson married Fann
Nisbet in 1787, is Saddle Hill and the ruins of a small fort where Nelson watche
for illegal shipping. A dirt road leads to the 1820-foot lookout, or you may follo
some of the goat paths that lace the hillside. The top surrenders excellent views c
Montserrat and uninhabited Redonda to the southeast, and to St. Kitts, St. Eusta
tius and, on a clear day, Saba in the northwest; an excellent option if you're not sur
of the journey up Nevis Peak.

By Pedal

Nevis' quiet perimeter road is ideal for pleasant, casual riding, although those seeking to conquer the entire 20-mile circuit should be advised that steep hills, climbing to over 900 feet above sea level, lie in the section between Fig Tree and Zion. Interesting off-road possibilities exist on the unsettled western coast south of Charlestown. If you want to spend more than a couple of days riding, consider taking a bike on the ferry over to St. Kitts, offering extensive possibilities along its length (see "St. Kitts").

Bike Rental Shops

Meadville Guest House

Off Craddock Road, outside Charlestown; ☎ *(809) 469-5235.*
Amiable Carlton Mead supplements his guest house operation by offering ten 18-speed mountain bikes at $12.50 per day.

What Else to See

The history of Nevis is buried behind the shutters and porches of its six great plantation houses, many of them now hotels. A taste of the leisure elegance of these times can still be experienced, especially if you head for one of them, such as the **Nisbet Plantation Inn**, for an afternoon drink on the veranda. **Charleston**, the capital of Nevis (pop. 1200) is a tropical rainbow of pastel storefronts, tin roofs and palm-shaded gardens—good for strolling and lingering. Anyone with a nautical interest should look into the new **Nelson Museum**, which offers fascinating displays of Nelsonia in the form of maps, model ships, mildweed prints, ornate costumes and other paraphernalia. You can also visit where Admiral Nelson married Fannie Nisbet in 1787—the St. John Fig Tree Church; his certificate of marriage is recorded there. In the city proper, a stop at the **Nevis Handicraft Coop** is *de rigeur*—particularly to pick up a few bottles of local fruit wines sold in old soda bottles; among the delicious flavors are sorrel, pawpaw, genip, gooseberry and homemade pepper sauce. Around the corner is the **Nevis Philatelic Bureau**, which does a brisk business selling first-edition Nevis stamps (different from St. Kitts). Saturday, the market of Charleston along the waterfront, brims with excitement as local farmers and vendors lay out their latest crops and crafts.

St. John's Fig Tree Church in Nevis contains interesting memorials to Admiral Nelson and his wife, Fanny Nisbet.

The **Eva Wilkin Gallery** on the Clay Ghaut Estate (an old stone plantation) commemorated the work of a now-deceased elderly lady artist whose evocative pastels and watercolors of Nevis life were beloved by the island. Today the gallery, which also shows contemporary Nevis art, is run by a Canadian couple and open to the public. Most will be surprised to discover that a Jewish community once thrived on Nevis, and you can see the restored cemetery and synagogue remains that date back to 1650 (perhaps the oldest in the Caribbean). In the last year a *mikvah*, or ritual bath used in Jewish practices, was also said to be discovered by historians.

Historical Sites

Eden Brown Estate

Near Huggins Bay, Charlestown.

This government-owned estate house was built in 1740. It is said to be haunted by the ghost of Julia Huggins, who was all set to get married in 1822. But the night before the wedding, the groom and best man got drunk, argued and ended up killing each other in a duel. Poor Julia became a recluse and is said to still hang around the house. The estate also includes stone ruins from other buildings on the plantation.

Museums and Exhibits

Alexander Hamilton Birthplace ★★★

Low Street, Charlestown.
Hours Open: 8 a.m.–4 p.m.

This Georgian-style house on the waterfront is actually a replica of Hamilton's childhood home, which was built in 1680 and destroyed by hurricane in the 19th century. Hamilton was born on Nevis in 1755, later emigrated to the fledgling United States, and was appointed by George Washington as the first secretary of the U.S. Treasury. He died in a duel with Aaron Burr. The building contains memorabilia of his life, as well as photographs and exhibits on the island's history. The Nevis House of Assembly is on the second floor.

Horatio Nelson Museum ★★★

Bath Road, Charlestown, ☎ *(809) 469- 408.*
Hours Open: 8 a.m.–4:30 p.m.

This small museum commemorates the life of Lord Nelson, who married local girl Frances Nisbet in the 1870s.

Tours

Bath Springs ★★★★

Near Grove Park, Charlestown.

You can soak in a tub of these mineral hot springs for $2 for 15 minutes (longer is not recommended). They are on the site of the once-glamorous Bath Hotel, built in 1778, closed about a century later, and now in ruins. In its heyday, the hotel attracted wealthy guests the world over, who came to soak in its rejuvenating waters and gamble in its casino.

Sports

Waterskiing, windsurfing, snorkeling and scuba are all prime activities on Nevis, and if your hotel can't arrange it, there are several agencies that will. Sport fishing takes advantage of a good supply of wahoo, tuna, kingfish and dorado. An 18-hole, Robert Trent Jones designed course has been built at the Four Seasons resort, though some complain that it straddles the island road with its electric carts. Several hotels have tennis courts, the Jack Tar has four (two lighted) and a pro. The Pro-Divers shop, which is the first PADI instruction center on the island, operates fully certified resort diving facilities out of Turtle Beach and from the Ocean Terrace Inn's Fisherman's Wharf restaurant, located not far from the hotel at water's edge in Pelican Cove. Half-day and full-day charters for cruising to other islands can be arranged through your hotel. (For more information on hiking, see "Treks" above.

The latest craze on Nevis is **horse racing**. Races are sponsored by the Nevis Turf & Jockey Club at the ramshackle track near White Bay at various times throughout the year. Races are generally held on holidays such as Boxing Day, New Year's Day, Tourism Week Sunday in February, Easter Monday, Culturama (the first Monday in August), Labor Day, and Independence Day. Admission is generally $4. The course follows the contour of the land, which means that it's a downhill race to the finish, tails and ears flying; the jockeys are often hard-put to stay astride. The setting is first-class, facing the sea on a rural tract known as Indian castle on the southeastern corner of the island, flanked by palm trees and volcanic mounds. To get to the racetrack, follow Hanley's Road south from Gingerland for two miles down to the sea. For more information call the **Hermitage Inn** ☎ *(809) 469-3477.*

For more information about diving and snorkeling, see "Dive Sites" above. Also see the chapter of St. Kitts for other activities.

Four Seasons Golf Course

Four Seasons Resort, Pinney's Beach, ☎ *(809) 469-1111.*
Designed by Robert Trent Jones, Jr., this is one of the Caribbean's most scenic and challenging courses. It encompasses 18 holes with tremendous views that made concentrating on your game a tad difficult. Greens fees are $95 for 18 holes if you are staying at the hotel, otherwise it is $110. Celebrate the 19th hole at one of this posh resort's watering holes.

Horseback Riding

Various locations, Charlestown.
You can hop on a horse and ride into the sunset at one of three outfits: **Nisbet Plantation** (☎ *469-9325* ($45 for two hours)), **Cane Gardens** (☎ *469-5648*), and **Gardner's Estate** (☎ *469-5528* ($35 for two hours)).

Watersports

Various locations, Charlestown.
A number of companies offer aqua activity. For general watersports equipment and boating, try **Newcastle Bay Marina** (☎ *469-9373*) and **Oualie Beach** (☎ *469-9518*). For deep-sea fishing, contact **The Lady James** (☎ *469-1989*) or **Jans Travel Agency** (☎ *469-5578*). For diving, try **Scuba Safaris** (☎ *468-9518*) or **Montpelier Plantation** (☎ *469-5462*). Windsurfing can be arranged through **Winston Cooke** (☎ *469-9615*).

Where to Stay

Fielding's Highest Rated Hotels in Nevis

★★★★★	Four Seasons Resort Nevis	$180–$555
★★★★	Montpelier Plantation Inn	$150–$280
★★★	Golden Rock Estate	$170–$245
★★★	Hermitage, The	$130–$425
★★★	Mt. Nevis Hotel	$170–$440
★★★	Nisbet Plantation	$180–$340

Fielding's Most Romantic Hotels in Nevis

★★★★★	Four Seasons Resort Nevis	$180–$555
★★★	Golden Rock Estate	$170–$245
★★★	Hermitage, The	$130–$425
★★★★	Montpelier Plantation Inn	$150–$280
★★★	Nisbet Plantation	$180–$340

Fielding's Budget Hotels in Nevis

★	Meadville Cottages	$50–$80
★	Pinney's Beach Hotel	$60–$185
★★	Croney's Old Manor Hotel	$85–$175
★★	Oualie Beach Hotel	$100–$205
★★★	Golden Rock Estate	$170–$245

Until the recent opening of the 350-acre Four Seasons Resort, considered one of the premier lodgings in the Caribbean and the Mt. Nevis Hotel and Beach Club, the island was known primarily for its intimate old plantation inns, most of which still flourish today despite the 1989 rampage of Hurricane Hugo. In general, the standards of rooms are as high as the cuisine, although at the inns, air conditioning is usually not available. Inn meal prices are usually about $10 per breakfast, $10 for lunch, and $30 for dinner (in American currency). Many of the inns offer free shuttles to beaches and recreational activities and have all their own swimming pools. Rates do not include a seven percent government tax or service charge, usually 10 percent.

The Bath Hotel, with its soothing hot springs, still draws more visitors than any other attraction on Nevis.

Hotels and Resorts

Pinney's Beach Hotel and the **Four Seasons Resort** are the only two properties located on the coconut palm-lined Pinney's Beach overlooking the narrow of St. Kitts.

Four Seasons Resort Nevis   **$180–$555**   ★ ★ ★ ★ ★

Pinney's Beach, ☎ (800) 332-3442, (809) 469-1111, FAX (809) 469-1112.
Single: $180–$555. Double: $180–$555.

You can always count on a Four Seasons property for the utmost in style and luxury, and this resort is no exception—in fact, it is one of the Caribbean's best hotels. Scattered over 350 acres opening right onto Nevis' best beach, low-rise buildings house two restaurants, three bars, a well-equipped health club, and air-conditioned guestrooms. Accommodations are lovely, with high-quality furnishings, Persian rugs, large baths, robes, and fresh plants and flowers. The choices range from standard guestrooms to the duplex-style Palm Grove Villas with two or three bedrooms; deluxe Mahogany Hill Estates, spacious privately owned homes, some with a private pool; and the brand-new Sunset Hill Estates, which also offer two or three bedrooms and private pools. These luxurious digs, which cost $600–$3,850 per night with a minimum five-night rental, are situated around the lovely championship golf course. The grounds also include 10 tennis courts, a large pool, and several restaurants. All watersports can be found on the very fine beach. Parents can relax after putting their kids in varied supervised programs. Simply fantastic in every aspect, but note that the atmosphere here is rather formal; you'll have to dress for dinner. Inquire about the myriad golf and tennis packages offered.

Mount Nevis Hotel & Beach Club $170–$440 ★★★

Shaws Road, Newcastle, ☎ (809) 469-9373, FAX (809) 469-9375.
Single: $170–$195. Double: $240–$440.

Located on the slopes of Mt. Nevis, this family-run property includes air-conditioned guest rooms with VCRs (videos are available to rent) and private patios with great views of St. Kitts. Studio units also have full kitchens. Facilities include a restaurant, bar, pool, and their own beach club on the sand, where watersports await. The hotel owns a ferry that takes guests on moonlight cruises.

Nisbet Plantation $180–$340 ★★★

Newcastle Beach, ☎ (800) 344-2049, (809) 469-9325, FAX (809) 469-9864.
Single: $180–$205. Double: $255–$340.

This well-run property combines the charm of an 18th-century coconut plantation with the amenities of a resort. Set on 35 acres fronting a mile-long beach, one of the island's best, this is the former home of Frances Nisbet, who married Lord Nelson. Accommodations are in air-conditioned cottages, all individually decorated and nicely done with screened-in porches. Facilities include two restaurants, two bars, a tennis court, a large pool, a small library, croquet and watersports. Complimentary laundry service and evening turndown are nice perks. The management will help arrange horseback riding and mountain climbing for the active set. A winner.

Oualie Beach Hotel $100–$205 ★★

Oualie Beach, ☎ (800) 255-9684, (809) 469-9735, FAX (809) 469-9176.
Single: $100–$155. Double: $130–$205.

Located right on the beach, this small property accommodates guests in gingerbread-style duplex cottages that are pleasant and comfortable. Only some have air conditioning and kitchens, but all sport screened porches with nice views of St. Kitts. There's a dive shop on-site that also handles most watersports. The restaurant is highly regarded. This is one of the few hotels without a pool if that's important to you.

Pinney's Beach Hotel $60–$185 ★

Pinney's Beach, ☎ (800) 742-4276, (809) 469-5207, FAX (809) 469-1088.
Single: $60–$70. Double: $75–$185.

This budget property sits right on the beach, which is just about all it has going for it. Rooms are air-conditioned but quite basic. The grounds include a pool, several bars and restaurants, and two tennis courts. Nothing to write home about.

Apartments and Condominiums

For grocery household needs, stop by the **Sunshine Shoppers** on Newcastle Airport Road, a one-stop mini-mart. **Nevis Bakery** on Happy Hill Drive in Charlestown features fresh breads, buns, pastries and cakes.

Hurricane Cove Bungalows $95–$400 ★★

Hurricane Bay, ☎ (809) 469-9462, FAX (809) 469-9462.
Single: $95–$145. Double: $155–$400.

Set on a steep hill with glorious views, this small complex consists of one- to three-bedroom bungalows with ceiling fans, complete kitchens and covered porches. There's a pool on-site, but little else. The beach is at the foot of the hill.

Meadville Cottages $50–$80   ★

Meadville Lane, ☎ *(809) 469-5235.*
Single: $50–$80. Double: $50–$80.

Located five minutes from Pinney's Beach, this small complex consists of modest cottages with one or two bedrooms, living/dining rooms, kitchenettes, and verandas. Maid service is available, but that's it for extras. You'll have to cook in or venture out for meals.

Inns

Golden Rock Estate $170–$245   ★★★

Gingerland, ☎ *(809) 469-3346, FAX (809) 469-2113.*
Single: $170–$200. Double: $185–$245.

This 18th-century sugar estate, set high up in the hills, encompasses some 100 acres. Run by the great-great-great granddaughter of the man who built the main house in 1815, it practically oozes charm. Accommodations are in a converted sugar mill or in cottages, all with antiques, island art, canopied king beds, large verandas and ceiling fans in lieu of air conditioning. The estate is surrounded by lush rain forest, with a good hiking trail starting at the property. The grounds include a spring-fed pool, tropical gardens, a tennis court, and free transportation to two beaches or into town. Really wonderful.

Hermitage, The $130–$425   ★★★

St. John's Parish, ☎ *(809) 469-3177, FAX (809) 469-2481.*
Single: $130–$315. Double: $210–$425.

Set on a 250-year-old plantation up in the hills, this property accommodates guests in restored cottages that are nicely done with Oriental rugs, pitched ceilings, canopied four-poster beds or twin beds, large verandas with hammocks and antiques. Some also have full kitchens. A gorgeous two-bedroom house set on two private acres with its own pool, oversized baths, full kitchen and antique canopy beds is also available, but quite expensive ($645–$690 nightly). The terraced grounds include stables for horseback riding, a pool, tennis and a plantation-style restaurant in an antique-filled room. The rates include a full American breakfast, afternoon tea and four-course dinner daily. Very nice.

Montpelier Plantation Inn $150–$280   ★★★★

St. John's Parish, ☎ *(800) 243-9420, (809) 469-3462, FAX (809) 469-2932.*
Single: $150–$225. Double: $180–$280.

Set on the slope of Mt. Nevis, this former sugar plantation encompasses 100 lovingly landscaped acres, including an organic garden and orchard that supplies ingredients for much of the excellent food. Accommodations are in cottages and of good size; all are nicely done with large private patios. Ceiling fans keep things cool. There's a pool and tennis court on-site, and they'll shuttle you to the beach, about 10 minutes away, where you can play with their speedboat.

Old Manor Estate ☎ **$85–$175** ★★★

Gingerland, ☎ (809) 469-3445, FAX (809) 469-3388.
Single: $85–$135. Double: $135–$175.

Perched high in the hills, this converted plantation house dates back to 1832. Many of the Georgian buildings on-site were made from lava rock. Guest rooms are nicely done and spacious, with marble floors, high ceilings, canopied king beds or twins with mosquito netting, verandas and ceiling fans (no air conditioning). Facilities include a bar, restaurant and pool. They'll shuttle you back and forth to the beach. Nice, but showing its age.

Where to Eat

Fielding's Highest Rated Restaurants in Nevis

★★★★★	Cooperage	$12–$20
★★★★★	Miss June's	$63–$63
★★★	Callaloo	$5–$7

Fielding's Special Restaurants in Nevis

★★★★★	Cooperage	$12–$20
★★★★★	Miss June's	$63–$63

Fielding's Budget Restaurants in Nevis

★★★	Callaloo	$5–$7
★★	Eddy's	$2–$12
★★	Cla-Cha-Del	$5–$15
★★	Muriel's Cuisine	$5–$16
★★	Caribbean Confections	$4–$20

Nevisian cuisine takes shape with such West Indian delicacies as jerked chicken, curried goat, salt-fish casserole, johnnycakes, breadfruit salad and piles of steamed squash and rice 'n' peas. While most guests tend to dine at their hotel—sometimes because the meals are included in the rates, most times because the cuisine is excellent—take the time to check out other locations. At the **Golden Rock Estate**, you can eat delicious West Indian buffet to the music of the Honey Bees String Band on Saturday nights. A sumptuous afternoon tea is served in the great house of the **Nisbet Plantation Beach Club**. For hearty breakfasts and light snacks, **Sea Spawn**, across from Pinney's Beach, is conveniently located and reasonably priced. Most dress is casual but the atmosphere in the plantation great houses should inspire romantic dressing.

Callaloo $ ★★★

Main Street, ☎ (809) 469-5389.
Latin American cuisine. Specialties: Grilled Kingfish, Burgers, French Pastries, Broasted Chicken.
Lunch: 10 a.m.–4 p.m., entrees $5–$7.
Dinner: 4–10 p.m., entrees $5–$7.

This unprepossessing place on Main Street in Charlestown is the place to come for fabulous, charbroiled burgers. West Indian specialties abound also, and you have a choice of seating either squeezed in at little tables on a sidewalk patio or in an air-conditioned dining room. Callaloo offers a wide variety of dishes from pizza to pastries.

Caribbean Confections $$$ ★★

Main Street, ☎ (809) 469-5685.
International cuisine. Specialties: Pumpkin Bread, Lamb Curry.
Lunch: 8 a.m.–3 p.m., entrees $4–$10.
Dinner: 5–11 p.m., entrees $12–$20.

As the name suggests, this popular downtown spot is known for fresh-from-the-oven pumpkin or ginger-infused sweets. Ferry passengers who alight near here come for the hearty breakfasts; others might drop in for lunch or dinner when the menu is either burgers, salads, curries or seafood specials. Dine indoors or in the tree-shaded garden restaurant known as the Courtyard Cafe.

Cla-Cha-Del $$ ★★

Shaw's Road, Newcastle, ☎ (809) 469-9640.
Latin American cuisine. Specialties: Goat Water, Conch, Lobster, Mutton.
Lunch: entrees $5–$9.
Dinner: 9–11 p.m., entrees $9–$15.

Newcastle, on the north coast of Nevis, boasts broad, white-sand beaches, roadside stands with tasteful handicrafts, and the Pinney family's authentic eatery, Cla-Cha-Del. Named after siblings Claudina, Charlie and Delroy, this West Indian dining spot showcases the family's ties to the local fishing industry. Try parrotfish, conch or lobster, or drop in on a weekend for goat water. Burgers, soups and sandwiches are also available.

Cooperage $$$ ★★★★★

Gingerland, ☎ (809) 469-3445.
International cuisine. Specialties: Provimi Veal, Jerk Pork or Chicken, Filet Mignon.
Dinner: 7–9:30 p.m., entrees $12–$20.

The historical setting and solidly good food help make a meal here well worth making a reservation for. Located in a restored, 17th-century plantation inn, the stone-walled dining room once reverberated with the sounds of coopers making barrels for the sugar mill. The cuisine, which is heavy on imported beef, veal or lamb, reflects the solid midwestern background of owner-hostess Vicki Knorr. For under $20 you can have filet mignon or veal scallopini. For a splurge, the green-pepper soup served with complete meals ($11 extra, includes dessert) is delicious.

Eddy's $$ ★★

Main Street, ☎ (809) 469-5958.

Latin American cuisine. Specialties: Flying Fish, Conch Fritters.

Lunch: Noon–3 p.m., entrees $2–$7.

Dinner: 7:30–9:30 p.m., entrees $9–$12.

Ever had a flying fish sandwich? Don't let it get away from you at this informal, second-story patio restaurant that's an ideal vantage point for tourist-watching. Inside the warmly decorated old wood townhouse, the crowd tends to be dominated by repeat visitors and permanent residents. Eddy's has a jumpin' bar with potent drinks and a well-attended Wednesday happy hour.

Miss June's $$$ ★★★★★

Stony Grove Plantation, ☎ *(809) 469-5330.*

Latin American cuisine. Specialties: All Inclusive West Indian Buffet.

Dinner: prix fixe $63.

Trinidadian Miss June Mestier serves a bountiful buffet groaning with delectable dishes (some 26 in all) several evenings a week, at one seating only, and strictly by reservation. Promptly at 7:30, guests assemble for a cocktail hour. Dinner begins at 8:30 with soup and fish, and then everyone is let loose at the buffet tables. After dinner, everyone adjourns to a parlor for aperitifs and anecdotes. Even if you have to eat dry toast and tea all week, this is a "don't miss" experience. Inquire about serving times when you make your reservation.

Muriel's Cuisine $$ ★★

Upper Happy Hill Drive, ☎ *(809) 469-5920.*

Latin American cuisine. Specialties: Curries, Seafood Rotis, Johnny Cakes.

Lunch: 8 a.m.–4 p.m., entrees $5–$7.

Dinner: 4–10 p.m., entrees $12–$16.

Miss Muriel's establishment is fast becoming a choice spot to dine in Charlestown, especially for her substantial Wednesday West Indian buffet lunches. This talented lady can't offer a sea view, but the food is rib stickin', especially the variety of curries (chicken, goat, sometimes seafood) served with local vegetables, which may include *christophene* (chayote), plantain and rice and peas.

Unella's $$ ★★

The Waterfront, ☎ *(809) 469-5574.*

Latin American cuisine.

Lunch: entrees $4–$10.

Dinner: entrees $5–$21.

If Eddy's nearby gets too crowded, give Unella's a try—it also has a second-floor patio, a more subdued atmosphere and luscious fresh lobster. Other fare includes scampi or conch, and Caribbean-style plate meals, although most of it is unexceptional. It's open from 9 a.m.

Where to Shop

Shopping is better in St. Kitts, but Nevis need not be ignored. Island Hopper carries the full line of Caribelle Batik fashions. Swimsuits and cotton handmade dresses can be picked up at **Amanda's Fashions**. An excellent array of souvenirs, crafts, guava jelly, soursop jam, banana chutney and gooseberry jam are available at **Nevis Handicraft Co-op**, a must stop. Stamp collectors will be delighted to know that the two islands are famous throughout the world for their issued stamps, and a philatelic bureau on each island issues totally different stamps. The commemorative stamps of Sept. 19,1993, which celebrate the 10th anniversary of the federation's independence, are considered instant collectibles. All photo needs can be served at **Rawlins Photo Color Lab & Studio**, located on Main Street in Charlestown, with one-hour processing.

Nevis Directory

ARRIVAL

American Eagle ☎ *(800) 43307300* offers daily connections to St. Kitts from the hub in San Juan, **LIAT** ☎ *(809) 465-2511* serves St. Kitts from either San Juan, Antigua or St. Maarten.

Short-hop flight on local airlines—like **Air St. Kitts-Nevis** ☎ *(809) 465-8571*, **Nevis Express** ☎ *(809) 469-3346* and St. Croix-based **Coastal Air Transport** ☎ *(809) 773-6862* provide regular on demand service to Nevis from St. Kitts and other islands. For a more unusual experience, take a 45-minute ferry from Basse-Terre, capital of St. Kitts to Charlestown (about $8 roundtrip); ☎ *(809) 469-5521*. Complimentary transportation is provided from St. Kitts for guests of the Four Season Resort Nevis.

Modestly priced taxis fares are available for all island destinations and three-hour island tours can be arranged from about $40. Try **All Seasons Streamline Tours** ☎ *(809) 469-1138)*, which has comfortable air-conditioned minibuses. Fares will usually be quoted in EC dollars.

Rental cars on Nevis start at $35 per day. Be sure to obtain a $12 driver's license and don't forget to drive on the left side of the road.

BUSINESS HOURS

Shops open Monday–Saturday 8 a.m.–noon and 1–4 p.m. Most close earlier on Thursday. Banks open Monday–Thursday 8 a.m.–3 p.m. and Friday 8 a.m.–5 p.m.

CLIMATE

As on St. Kitts, average temperatures hover between 78 and 85 degrees F, during the day; nighttime temperatures can drop to 68 degrees F. Trade winds keep it breezy, though the humidity can rise to uncomfortable levels during the summer. Downpours are quick but heavy between mid-June through mid-November, considered the rainy season.

DOCUMENTS

U.S. citizens need to present proof of citizenship (passport, voter's registration card or birth certificate), along with a return or ongoing ticket. There is a departure tax of $10.

ELECTRICITY

The current is 230 volts, though some hotels have 110 volts. Bring a transformer and adapter just in case.

GETTING AROUND

Inter-island flights are available with Nevis Express, a locally owned and operated airline, which uses 15-passenger Lyslander Tristars. The cost for the six-minute flight between St. Kitts and Nevis is U.S. $20

Carib Queen, the inter-island commuter ferry that links the two islands, makes multiple crossings every day. Other private ferries are operated by the Four Seasons Resort and Mt. Nevis hotel.

LANGUAGE

English is the official language, spoken with a rhythmic lilt. Natives also speak a local patois.

MEDICAL EMERGENCIES

Alexandra Hospital in Charlestown (☎ *(809) 469-5473*) operates a 24-hour emergency room service.

MONEY

Currency on both islands is the Eastern Caribbean dollar. In a pinch, shopkeepers and businesses will accept American and Canadian currency, but they have a hard time exchanging it.

TELEPHONE

The area code is *809*, for both St. Kitts and Nevis. Telegrams can be sent from the **Cable & Wireless office** on Main Street in Charlestown (☎ *469-5000*). You can also make international telephone calls from this office, which will save you a lot of money (do what you can to avoid making any international calls from your hotel room (if, indeed, your room even has a phone) since hotel surcharges will make the final bill outrageously expensive. The Cable & Wireless office is open from

Monday-Friday 8 a.m.–6 p.m., and on Saturday from 8 a.m.–noon. It is closed on Sunday and on public holidays.

TIME

Atlantic Standard Time, which is one hour later than New York time, except during Daylight Saving Time, when it is the same.

TIPPING AND TAXES

Expect your hotel to add a 10 percent service charge. Check restaurant bills before adding your own 10–15 percent service tip. If a taxi driver hasn't added the tip himself, do so (10–15 percent).

TOURIST INFORMATION

The **Nevis Tourist Office** is located on Main Street in Charlestown ☎ *(809) 469-1042*, FAX *(809) 469-1066*. You can pick up brochures, magazines, and a current list of hotel prices. It's open only Monday–Friday. In the U.S. ☎ *(212) 535-1234*.

WHEN TO GO

December is the month of Carnival, celebrated with blowout parties, costumed parades, and general merrymaking for days. Alexander Hamilton's Birthday is celebrated on Jan. 11. St. Kitts Horticultural Society holds an annual show usually in the last week of May featuring the work of local gardeners and nurserymen. The St. Kitts and Nevis Regatta of windsurfing and sunfish, an 11-mile race from Frigate Bay, is usually held in June. Culturama, a popular and festive event, celebrates the island's history, folklore and arts with presentations, talent shows, beauty pageants, calypso contests and West Indian delicacies.

NEVIS HOTELS		RMS	RATES	PHONE	CR. CARDS
Charlestown					
★★★★★	**Four Seasons Resort Nevis**	196	$180–$555	(800) 332-3442	A, CB, D, MC, V
★★★★	**Montpelier Plantation Inn**	17	$150–$280	(800) 243-9420	MC, V
★★★	**Golden Rock Estate**	15	$170–$245	(809) 469-3346	A, MC
★★★	**Hermitage, The**	14	$85–$690	(809) 469-3177	A, D, MC, V
★★★	**Mount Nevis Hotel & Beach Club**	32	$170–$440	(809) 469-9373	MC, V
★★★	**Nisbet Plantation**	38	$180–$340	(800) 344-2049	MC, V
★★★	**Old Manor Estate**	17	$85–$175	(809) 469-3445	A, D, MC, V
★★	**Hurricane Cove Bungalows**	10	$95–$400	(809) 469-9462	A, MC
★★	**Oualie Beach Hotel**	22	$100–$205	(800) 255-9684	A, D, MC, V
★	**Meadville Cottages**	10	$50–$80	(809) 469-5235	MC, V
★	**Pinney's Beach Hotel**	48	$60–$185	(800) 742-4276	NoneA, MC, V

NEVIS RESTAURANTS

	PHONE	ENTREE	CR. CARDS
Charlestown			
International			
★★★★★ **Cooperage**	(809) 469-3445	$12–$20••	A, MC, V
★★ **Caribbean Confections**	(809) 469-5685	$4–$20	A, MC, V
Latin American			
★★★★★ **Miss June's**	(809) 469-5330	$63–$63••	MC, V
★★★ **Callaloo**	(809) 469-5389	$5–$7	A, MC, V
★★ **Cia-Cha-Del**	(809) 469-9640	$5–$15	A, MC, V
★★ **Eddy's**	(809) 469-5958	$2–$12	A, MC, V
★★ **Muriel's Cuisine**	(809) 469-5920	$5–$16	A, MC, V
★★ **Unella's**	(809) 469-5574	$4–$21	D, MC, V

Note: • Lunch Only

       •• Dinner Only

SABA

Saba is lush with tropical vegetation and has 26 dive sites.

An isolated outpost of only 1200 islanders, Saba (pronounced Say-buh) sticks out of the water like a green gumdrop in the middle of the sea, its 2855-foot volcanic spiral clearly visible to neighboring isles. Until recently, this lava-encrusted Bali Hai was strictly for escapists contented with a well-thumbed paperback from their inn's library and their daily hike up the 1064 steps to the peak of Mount Scenery. But since divers started trickling in a few years ago, Saba has become a great little underwater destination. Encrusted with colorful coral and decorated with dramatic fingers of cooled lava that drop off 90–300 feet, Saba's sites are teeming with blue chromides, barracuda and marbled grouper. Today there are three dive shops (and a hyperbaric chamber donated by the Royal Netherlands Navy) to give you all the help

you need to reach the 26 unspoiled dive sites along the flanks of the volc
no—an area that the islanders had the foresight to protect as a marine par
back in 1967. So precipitously do the red-roofed gingerbread-trimme
houses perch on the rocky hillside 1000 feet and more above the sea, that
you have vertigo, you should probably stay home. There is only one roa
hand-built by islanders, and by the time you leave, you may have passed b
everyone on the island. Cool breezes and a crime-free life (what's there t
steal on a volcano?) have attracted some long-term visitors to Saba, but th
majority (save serious divers) stay only a few days. Committed divers, how
ever, thrill over the challenging dive sites, whose atmospheric names such a
Shark Shoal, Twilight Zone and Outer Limits should scare off the dile
tantes. If you're looking for one of the last frontiers in the Caribbean, yo
better get here before Winair increases its flights to 12 a day.

Bird's Eye View

Most of the houses on Saba are painted white with red roofs and green shutters.

The baby of the Netherlands Antilles, Saba lies 28 miles south of St
Maarten/St. Martin and 17 miles northwest of St. Eustatius. With virtuall
no flat ground, the island is literally an extinct volcano that protrudes out c
the sea, lush with tropical vegetation. The capital, ironically called The Bot

CARIBBEAN SEA

Diamond Rock

Great Point

Cave of Rum Bay

Green Island

Grey Hill

Juancho E. Yrausquin Airport ✈

Flat Point

Torrens Point

Torrens Bay

Sulphur Mines ■

Cove Bay

Mary's Point ■

Well's Bay

Mary's Point ▲ Mountain

Lower Hell's Gate

Spring Bay

Upper Hell's Gate ●

Middle Island ■

Mount ▲ Scenery 2855 ft.

Old Booby Hill

Ladder Bay

English Quarter

Ladder Point

The Gap ●

Core Gui Bay

THE BOTTOM ★

Windwardside ●

The ▲ Level 1716 ft.

Great Hill

Booby Hill ●

Thais Hill

St. John's Hill

St. John's Flat

Johnnies Ground

Corner Point

Tent Point

Fort Hill ●

Tent Bay

Fort Bay

Great Level Bay

CARIBBEAN SEA

Saba

- ● CITY
- PRIMARY ROAD
- TRAIL
- ■ ATTRACTION
- ▲ MOUNTAIN
- ✈ AIRPORT

0   .5   1 km

©FW 1995

tom, is halfway up the mountain. One tiny inlet acts as a dock, and unt
1943 there wasn't even one road, since the terrain was so rugged. (Toda
that serpentine road connects the pier, the airport and four villages.) Anoth
er town, Windwardside, is highly picturesque, a neat and tidy toy town c
red-iron roofs and white clapboard walls. Most visitors base themselve
there, where you can find the most natural air conditioning in the worl
The 1200-foot airport runway is half the length of many aircraft carriers, an
takeoff, if anything, is hairier than landing. Because the runway ends in mic
air (a crushing descent off a cliff to the sea down below), most people feel a
if they are still on it when the plane abruptly lifts up.

History

Columbus sighted the volcanic island in 1493, but it took another 12
years for some unlucky Englishman to shipwreck against the rocky coast. I
1665 the English privateer Thomas Morgan captured the island and threw
out the original Dutch settlers. Morgan's men stayed behind when he left,
fact that some locals use to claim their ancestors were pirates. Some histori
ans purport that Saba's original British settlers were actually Scottish refu
gees or exiles from the British civil wars in the 17th century. Until a pier wa
constructed in 1972, ships had to anchor in Fort Bay, where wooden long
boats would transfer people and products to shore in a very wet ride.

People

There are about 1200 Sabans living on the island today, equally split be
tween black and white. The blacks are descended from slaves who were im
ported to work the island's small farms and carry products up and down th
mountain. The whites claim various ancestry, many look Irish, and strangel
half the islanders, no matter which race, bear the Irish name Hassell (in 169
seven Hassells were listed in the census). There's one Chinese family on th
island, and they own the one Chinese restaurant. More than 100 Saban
served in the U.S. Navy during the first world war. A number of Sabans (par

icularly with the name Hassell) have distinguished themselves international-ly. After World War I there was a desperate need to seek work abroad and the male-female ratio became disastrously unbalanced. Today the men have returned, growing their own food and exporting fish to St. Martin. For centuries, Saban men have plied their trade on the sea, transporting prisoners from one island to the other, carrying all manner of cargo. For some yet-to-be-explained reason, the national greeting is "Howzzit? Howzzit?"

Beaches

Saba has only one fat sandy beach, accessible only by a hilly walk or a drive guaranteed to cause fibrillation. If you want to swim, it's best done in a hotel pool—Queens Gardens, Captain's Quarters, Willard's of Saba, Juliana's, Scout's Place (small) and Cranston's Antique Inn.

Underwater

It's no longer news that tiny Saba has emerged as one of the Caribbean's top dive locations. Part of the popularity is its unique underwater layout, which mirrors the above-water topography: sheer. Additionally, the island was one of the first in the Caribbean—close on the heels of ecosensitive Bonaire—to aggressively protect its marine environment through the use of permanent mooring buoys; the **Saba Marine Park** is currently the only self-supporting underwater reserve in the world. The increasing awareness of Saba's undersea paradise has ballooned the number of divers but, although the island is minute and dives are concentrated into a small area, you'll never feel crowded and the diving is still pristine. Saba remains a somewhat exotic destination, even by Caribbean standards, and the total number of divers visiting the island in 1994 was a mere 5165 (averaging five dives apiece).

The diving is centered off the island's west coast. Black sand covers the sea floor, keeping silt to a minimum and visibility sterling (approaching 125 feet in winter), while dramatic walls and substantial fish and coral life contribute to the vivid underwater environment. With the bottom dropping to more

than 1000 feet as close as a half-mile from shore, the diving is serious. It'
also a little more expensive here, but above-water costs tend to balance out
the difference; there is also a $2-per-dive fee to help support the Marine Park
(you'll save money by booking a dive package). Almost all of the island's 27
primary dive sites are within ten minutes of the boat dock at Fort Bay, and
permanent mooring buoys protect the reefs below. In winter, a north swell
will sometimes make snorkeling a little rocky, but a dynamic underwater trail
featuring an alley through the rocks is available at **Torren's Point**; a moderate
swim will take snorkelers from Well's Bay to the Torren's trail. Weather permitting, **Cove Bay**, near the airport, can also be a good location for snorkeling
from shore. Saba has the only recompression chamber in this section of the
Caribbean.

Diamond Rock

The notable 80-foot tooth which rises from the water off Torrens Point is usually
topped with magnificent frigatebirds, while down below (35-80 feet) schools of
horse-eye jack tour the depths. The actual rock is covered with soft corals,
sponges—abundant pink-tipped anemones will warm your heart—while the sandy
bottom is placid home to stingrays and turtles. Great for beginners or experts.

Man Of War Shoals

Just a few hundred feet from the Diamond Rock dive, this site tours a similar pinnacle, but one that is completely submerged. Two hills rise from the flat of sand at
70 feet to within 15 feet of the surface, containing caves richly covered in vivid
sponges and anemones; bull sharks patrol the depths occasionally.

Tent Reef

Three separate dives are possible but, by beginning at Tent Reef Deep, a relaxing
drift will usually glide you past all three areas (30-80 feet). Black sand provides shelter for garden eels while razorfish multiply on all sides. The reef is peppered with
gorgonians and barrel sponges while overhangs on the wall provide a startling drop-
off leading to yellow tube sponges and plush wire coral. On an island of superlatives,
this is probably Saba's best and most popular dive, a mere stone's throw from the
Fort Bay dock.

Third Encounter

Part of a horseshoe-shaped sea mount one mile west of Ladder Bay, Third Encounter is a sponge and coral-encrusted area featuring a spectacular 200-foot pinnacle,
the Eye of the Needle, around which black tip sharks cruise sternly. Big, tame groupers, stingrays and turtles frequent this and two adjacent locations, Twilight Zone
and Outer Limits; depths average 100 feet at this site suited for experienced divers.

Dive Shops

Saba Deep Dive Center

Fort Bay; ☎ *(011) 599-46-3347.*

The only shop located on the water, Saba Deep keeps groups under a dozen with three scheduled dives daily: deep, intermediate and shallow. A full PADI and NAUI training facility. Two-tank dive $80, including equipment.

Sea Saba Dive Center

Windwardside; ☎ *(011) 599-46-2246.*

Two ample 40-foot boats are limited to 12 divers; ask about drift and night dives. Half-day snorkeling trips to Torrens and another site, $25. Resort courses a specialty for the all-instructor staff, with courses continuing to Divemaster. Two-tank dive $80.

Wilson's Dive Shop

Windwardside; ☎ *(011) 599-46-2541.*

The first shop on the island (opened in 1973), Wilson McQueen was Saba's diving pioneer more than 20 years ago. PADI and NAUI affiliated. Two tank dives, $80, including transfers to harbor.

On Foot

Visitors are tempted to call Saba quaint—that is, until they climb the stair steps leading up **Mount Scenery**, the island's 2855-foot summit. On second thought, any hiker who spends a few moments observing Saba's sheer outline from an approaching plane or a neighboring island should know what they're getting into: the vacation equivalent of a stairmaster. Trails are discussed not in terms of mileage, but in number of steps (1064 to the top of Mount Scenery, the trailhead sign announces). Nonetheless, this is a walker's island, with a detailed lattice of paths snaking between the villages and peaks. Prior to 1943 when Saba's first (and only) road went into use, transportation was strictly on donkey or foot. But with the import of cars and construction of the airport in 1963, the trails fell into disrepair. In recent years, the tracks have found new fans among the more active tourists drawn to the island and the government now promotes hiking eagerly. A guide is not necessary for anyone reasonably fit, but the verdant valleys offer a diverse ecosystem and they'll hurdle from beautiful to fascinating with the assistance of a knowledgeable guide. Some trails cross private property; stay on the established paths. Stop by the tourist office to pick up a pamphlet outlining island hikes or the walking tour of Windwardside, one of the most charming villages in the region.

The Ladder

If climbing Mount Scenery sounds stimulating, so should the 524 stone steps that lead down 656 feet to Ladder Bay. The steps down the precipitate slope were constructed in 1934 to provide a more secure bad weather harbor than was available prior to enlarging the port at Fort Bay. The hike starts just past Nicholson's Market at a lookout named The Gap. Continue down the road through a residential area and look for the steps off to the left just before the pavement ends. Winter months bring flowers and there is a lovely picnic area overlooking Ladder Bay midway down. The descent is deceptively easy; take your time over the slippery steps and conserve your gams for the return.

Mount Scenery

Everyone who makes the trip to Saba finds a few hours to climb to the top of this beautiful peak, a spunky 2855 feet above sea level. The trail, which starts in Windwardside, enters a secondary rainforest about a third of the way up. Tree ferns, mountain palms and thickets of mountain raspberries line the stairs. Just before the top, you'll enter an elfin (or cloud) forest filled with mosses and tall mountain mahogany dripping with moisture while hummingbirds whir by. The summit is usually wrapped in clouds, but clear days reward with sumptuous views: St. Martin and St. Barts to the northeast; Statia, St. Kitts and sometimes Nevis to the southeast (be sure to continue to the left of the radio tower to reach the scenic lookout). Allow two to three hours round trip; the hike is not long, but it's very steep and should be undertaken with a windbreaker for the seemingly inevitable squalls (three rain shelters are provided along the way).

Sulphur Mine Track

Midway up the switchbacks on the road leading from the airport, a track heads north to the abrupt coastline overlooking Green Island and the remains of a sulphur mine and oven. The path through the dry scrub leads to splendid views, but the sheer, crumbling cliff should not be approached. Allow one hour round-trip.

Trekking Tours

James Johnson's Guide Service

The Bottom; ☎ *(599) 46-3307.*

Offers four-to-six-hour guided hikes to Mary's Point, Troy, and the Sulphur Mine on afternoons and weekends. $40–50 per person depending on itinerary selected.

What Else to See

Places worth visiting, other than the great natural wonders, are minuscule, limited to one charming museum and a small library. Ensconced in a sea cap-ain's house, the **Saba Museum** offers a look at the island's traditional furnish-ings, giving you a genuine feel of ye olden days. **Queen Wilhelmina Library** olds a special collection of studies on the flora and fauna of the island, as vell as a special section on West Indian science and history.

Museums and Exhibits

aba Museum ★★★

Behind the Captain's Quarters, Windwardside.
This small museum is found in the 19th-century home of a sea captain. It exhibits antiques from that era and pre-Columbian artifacts found around the island. Croquet matches are held the first Sunday of each month, a good chance to meet and greet the locals. Wear all white for that outing.

Tours

ount Scenery ★★★★

Mt. Scenery.
Pack a picnic lunch, catch your breath, then head up the 1064 steps that lead up 2855 feet to the top of Mount Scenery. Along the way you'll pass through gorgeous scenery, six ecosystems, all kinds of interesting flora and fauna (signs tell you what's what), and, the higher you climb, cooler temperatures. The summit has a mahogany grove and incredible views.

Sports

Sports on Saba are divided between trekking and diving. One of the great-st little hikes in the world is the ascent up to **Mount Scenery**, which takes you hrough the secondary rain forest to the mountain's peak. The most spectac-lar version is probably the one starting from Windwardside up a thousand-r-so steps to the crest, best done on a clear day or you will feel as if you are lisappearing in a cloud. No guide is needed; most people make it up the 000-foot crest in two hours. Another hearty trek is the climb down from he Bottom to **Ladder Bay**, the island's former "dock" for arriving boats be-ore the advent of the Fort Bay pier.

If you are a committed diver, buying a package deal saves you money and he time it takes to make arrangements. **Wilson's Dive Shop** Windwardside, ☎ *(599) 46-2544* offers a seven-night, 10-dive package that begins at $1490 or two divers, including hotel and breakfast. Lodgings are in simple hilltop nns. The **Sea Saba Dive Center** ☎ *(599) 46-2246* offers 10 dives and a week's tay at **Juliana's**, a white gingerbread compound high above the sea for $745. For more information about diving, see "Dive Sites" above.)

There is also a tennis court at the Sun Valley Youth Centre in The Bottom open to the public.

Watersports

Various locations, The Bottom.

Scuba diving is very good in Saba, which is dedicated to preserving its underwater treasures. The **Saba Marine Park** circles the entire island and has various zoned sections, including five recreational dive sites, where you'll see towering pinnacles, colorful coral and sponges, and tons of sea creatures. The **Harbor Office** *(☎ 63295)* in Fort Bay provides literature and offers occasional slide shows. The Marine Park also includes Saba's only harbor and its only beach, a tiny stretch of sand only existing in the late spring and summer, submerged by the tides in winter. The park charges $3 per person per dive, in addition to the fees charged by dive centers.

Where to Stay

Fielding's Highest Rated Hotel in Saba

★★★ **Captain's Quarters** $85–$130

Fielding's Most Romantic Hotel in Saba

★★★ **Captain's Quarters** $85–$130

Fielding's Budget Hotels in Saba

★	**Cranston's Antique Inn**	$40–$75
★	**Scout's Place**	$40–$105
★★	**Juliana's**	$65–$130
★★★	**Captain's Quarters**	$85–$130

Lodging in Saba might be called a hotel, but they all tend to look and feel like inns. One of the most charming is Captain's Quarters, in two houses (100 and 175 years old, respectively) with antique furniture and views from the terrace. **Scout's Place** is cheap, unpretentious and friendly, and the view is spectacular. **Queens Garden**, a premier luxury resort on Troy Hill, may be open by the time you read this. Give them a call ☎ *(599) 4-63339*, FAX *(599) 4-62450)*. You can find wood cottages that rent by the day, week or month. Contact the Tourist Board for information about kitchen-equipped apartments and furnished villas.

Hotels and Resorts

Juliana's **$65–$130** ★★

Windwardside, ☎ (599) 4-62389, FAX (599) 4-62389.
Single: $65. Double: $80–$130.

Guests can choose from a variety of accommodations at this small property. There are standard guestrooms, an apartment with a kitchenette, and a nearly 90-year-old cottage with two bedrooms, a kitchen and a porch. All are quite decent, and the daily fresh flowers are a nice touch. The rec room has a TV, VCR, games and books for whiling away the hours. There's also a pool and restaurant.

Apartments and Condominiums

Cottage rentals are a steal—$200–$300 per week—compared to prices on other is lands in the Caribbean. The charming, small, wooden Saban variety will make you feel a tucked in and cozy. The tourist office will have more complete listings.

Inns

Captain's Quarters　　　　　　　　　**$85–$130**　　　　　　　★ ★ ♦

> *Windwardside, ☎ (599) 4-62377, FAX (599) 4-62377.*
> *Single: $85–$100. Double: $100–$130.*
> This charming inn is Saba's best bet—not that there are a lot of choices, but thi place would get high marks anywhere. Set high on a hill with spectacular ocea views, this inn centers around an old wooden home, built by a sea captain in 1832 Four rooms are in this house, the rest in a newer wing. All are spacious and brigh and have private baths; some also boast antique four-poster beds. The grounds ar nicely landscaped with citrus trees and tropical blooms. The site includes a library swimming pool and a very good restaurant. Divine!

Cranston's Antique Inn　　　　　　　**$40–$75**　　　　　　　　　♦

> *The Bottom, ☎ (599) 4-63203, FAX (599) 4-63469.*
> *Single: $40–$60. Double: $63–$75.*
> This former government guest house dates back to 1830. Only one room has a pri vate bath, but all have antiques and four-poster beds. Some of the decor borders o the tacky and the whole place could use a re-do. There's a pool and decent dinin room on the premises, and the open-air bar is a locals' favorite. Ladder Bay is withi walking distance.

Scout's Place　　　　　　　　　　　　**$40–$105**　　　　　　　　♦

> *Windwardside, ☎ (599) 4-62388, FAX (599) 4-62388.*
> *Single: $40–$105. Double: $60–$105.*
> Great views from this casual inn, located some 1300 feet above the sea. Unles you're really into roughing it (or saving some bucks), reserve one of the newe rooms, which have private baths and hot water. (The original rooms have neither. There's also an apartment with kitchenette that sleeps five. Known locally for it very good food, this spot also has a small pool and a bar.

Low Cost Lodging

Rooms in private homes might be secured if you come in person and ask about. Cot tages listed above, especially packed with several people, can be quite reasonable.

Where to Eat

★★	Fielding's Highest Rated Restaurants in Saba	
★★	Brigadoon	$14–$17
★★	Captain's Quarters	$13–$22
★★	Corner Deli	$4–$10
★★	Guido's	$4–$10
★★	Lollipop's	$10–$26
★★	Saba Chinese Restaurant	$13–$19
★★	Scout's Place	$12–$25
★★	Tea House	$2–$7
★★	Tropics Cafe	$4–$10

★★	Fielding's Special Restaurants in Saba	
★★	Lollipop's	$10–$26
★★	Scout's Place	$12–$25

★★	Fielding's Budget Restaurants in Saba	
★★	Tea House	$2–$7
★★	Corner Deli	$4–$10
★★	Guido's	$4–$10
★★	Tropics Cafe	$4–$10
★★	Brigadoon	$14–$17

Most guests don't travel much farther than their own accommodations when the urge to eat strikes. When they do, they seem to congregate at **Scout's Place**, where you can get Caribbean fare such as stewed mutton or more appetizing dishes from the sea; the view is spectacular. Good pizza can be had at **Guido's**.

Brigadoon $$$

Windwardside, ☎ (599) 4-62380.
International cuisine. Specialties: Saba fish pot, lobster, peanut chicken.
Dinner: entrees $14–$17.

One of the newer eating establishments on the island, Brigadoon is developing
reputation for innovative seafood cuisine. Grilled fish with tomato sauce or a spic
local bouillabaisse are standouts. There are also plenty of chicken and beef dish
served with fresh vegetables. Lighter fare is also featured.

Captain's Quarters $$$ ★

Windwardside, ☎ (590) 4-62201.
International cuisine. Specialties: Grouper, lobster bisque.
Lunch: Noon-2 p.m., entrees $13–$22.
Dinner: 6:30-9 p.m., entrees $13–$22.

Guests dine comfortably in this pretty outdoor terrace restaurant on the grounds c
the historical Captain's Quarters hotel. There's plenty of greenery and fruit tree
providing shade. If you're staying here it's a nice spot for breakfast, but most non
guests come for lunch or hearty dinners. The menu changes often, but the chef i
known for her way with lobster.

Corner Deli $ ★

Windwardside,
American cuisine.
Dinner: 2-6 p.m., entrees $4–$10.

Homesick New Yorkers and others can pick up a thick sandwich on homemad
bread at this deli-market owned by a seasoned restaurateur. Specialty coffees, past
ries, and desserts can be sampled here or packaged for takeout. Stop by for picni
fixings on the way to Mt. Scenery.

Guido's $ ★

Windwardside,
Italian cuisine. Specialties: Pizza.
Dinner: entrees $4–$10.

Yes, there is nightlife on Saba, contrary to the rumors. It's here at Guido's, whic
masquerades as a burger and pizza joint during the week and dons a few sequins a
Mountain High Club and Disco on Saturday evenings. The food is okay, but it'
better for pool or darts and informal socializing.

Lollipop's $$$

St. John's, ☎ (599) 4-63330.
Seafood cuisine. Specialties: Stuffed crab.
Lunch: entrees $10–$15.
Dinner: prix fixe $26.

Lollipop, or Carmen Hassell (everyone in town is either a Hassell or a Johnson
offers free pickup to and from her outdoor eatery—and you're in good hands
because she moonlights as a cab driver. Located in the suburb of St. John's, abov
The Bottom, the dining area is on a patio with a view, and the food is basically Wes
Indian—curries, fish cakes, seafood, and goat.

aba Chinese Restaurant $$$ ★★

Windwardside, ☎ *(599) 4-62268.*
Chinese cuisine. Specialties: Conch chop suey, lobster cantonese.
Lunch: 11 a.m.-4 p.m., entrees $13–$19.
Dinner: 4 p.m.-midnight, entrees $13–$19.

This Chinese restaurant on the north side of Windwardside offers rather pricey Cantonese and Indonesian dishes. It seems to satisfy a lot of locals, who patronize it often. There's a wide variety of choices, including an old favorite, sweet and sour pork, and a more unusual conch chop suey.

cout's Place $$$ ★★

Windwardside, ☎ *(599) 4-62295.*
International cuisine. Specialties: Curried goat.
Lunch: 12:30-2 p.m., prix fixe $12.
Dinner: 7:30-10 p.m., prix fixe $17–$25.

Scout's is the creation of Ohioan Scout Thirlkield, who also turned the Captain's Quarters into a hotel-restaurant. He is still around, but has passed the mantle onto chef Dianna Medero. The outdoor restaurant, attached to the hotel of the same name, is a beloved local hangout. The fixed-price menu features fresh seafood, and a delicious curried goat often appears. There's also a bar and a snack shop in front for short-order meals, snacks and ice cream.

ea House $ ★★

Windwardside,
American cuisine. Specialties: Pastries.
Dinner: 9:30-6 p.m., entrees $2–$7.

After picking up some tips and brochures at the tourist office, stop at the Tea House right behind it for homemade, old-fashioned pastry treats like sticky cinnamon and raisin buns. There's a selection of soft drinks, coffees, teas and sandwiches.

ropics Cafe $ ★★

Windwardside, ☎ *(599) 4-63203.*
American cuisine.
Dinner: entrees $4–$10.

The Tropics is a no-frills eatery attached to Juliana's Apartments, located near Captain's Quarters. It's good to know about for the decently priced breakfasts, burgers and sandwiches for under $10. Get them to pack up a picnic basket for you.

Where to Shop

Saba lace is an extraordinary 125-year-old art that was introduced to the island by Mary Gertrude Johnson, who learned it at a convent school in Venzuela. Fine work can be purchased at the Community Center (in Hell's

Gate; lace-worked blouses, napkins and tablespreads are especially great buys). Silk-screening has also found a niche in Saba; try the Saba Artisan Foundation, which offers finely worked scarves, T-shirts, and beautiful dresses—they are not cheap.

Don't miss (or at least taste) the local brew called **Saba Spice**, a secret concoction unique to each brewer that's made with 151-proof cask rum, cinnamon, brown sugar and other spices. According to Queenie Simmons, who runs the Serving Spoon restaurant and offers her own highly regarded blend for sale, the final step of the brewing process is to "set a bit" and the "scratch a match and let it blaze off." You can enjoy the drink as a hot cider mixed with eggnog, or in any drink that has Kahlúa. As a summer drink, it refreshing in a colada blended with cream and shaved ice, served like a milk shake. Bottling traditions are quaint, and if made at home, the brew is usually put into whatever bottle is hanging around.

If you're interested in local art, stop by the **Breadfruit Gallery** in the Lambert Hassell Building in Windwardside.

Saba Directory

ARRIVAL

Because the runway is short, large planes cannot fly to Saba, nor can any plane land or take off in bad weather. **Winair** ☎ *(599) 4-62255*, the only scheduled airline, makes up to five daily 20-seater flights from St Maarten, 20 minutes away ($62 round trip). One or two flights are made from Eustatius. Flights with a stopover in St. Barts can be arranged ahead of time. Saba can sometimes be reached by boat; contact the **Great Bay Marina** in Sint Maarten ☎ *(599) 4-22167*. Cruise ship can call at a deep-water pier at Fort Bay.

The airport departure tax is U.S. $2 to the Netherland Antilles, U.S. $5 elsewhere.

BUSINESS HOURS

Stores generally open 8 a.m.–5 p.m. Bank (there's only one) open weekdays 8:30 a.m.–12:30 p.m.

CLIMATE

Temperatures average about 85 degrees F, but can dip as low as 65 degrees F on a cool night.

DOCUMENTS

U.S. and Canadian citizens need to show a current passport or one that expired less than five years ago, or other proof of citizenship (birth certificate or voter's registration plus a photo ID), as well as an ongoing or return ticket.

ELECTRICITY

The current is 100 volts, 60 cycles, the same as in the U.S.

GETTING AROUND

Numerous taxis are awaiting flights when they arrive, and drivers are usually the best guides on the island. Don't hesitate to ask one for a half-day tour or to stay with you the whole day until your flight leaves. If you want to join a group and save money, minibuses at the airport usually will make a 1.5 hour tour.

There are numerous agencies that will rent cars, although be forewarned; The Road, as it is called, is extremely difficult to navigate and the parking possibilities are limited. Hitchhiking is relatively safe.

LANGUAGE

The official language is English, though public signs are written in Dutch. English is the spoken language.

MEDICAL EMERGENCIES

Try not to get sick in Saba. Emergencies are flown to Sint Maarten; the clinic at The Bottom is limited in facilities. In cases of extreme illness, a chartered flight (one hour) should be arranged to San Juan, Puerto Rico. Saba has a decompression chamber, located at the Marine Park Hyperbaric Facility in Fort Bay ☎ *(599) 4-63205.*

MONEY

The official currency is the Netherlands Antilles florin, also called the guilder and abbreviated NAf. U.S. dollars are accepted by most businesses.

TELEPHONE

The country code is *5994.* If you are calling from another Caribbean country, the code might differ, so check with the operator. From the U.S. dial direct *011* (international access code)-*5994*-local number.

TIME

Atlantic Standard Time, one hour ahead of eastern standard time, and the same as Eastern Daylight Saving Time.

TIPPING AND TAXES

Most hotels, restaurants and bars add a 10–15 percent service charge; if they don't that's what you should leave. No porters at the airport to carry your bags, but taxi drivers expect $1 or $2 as tip.

TOURIST INFORMATION

The **Saba Tourist Bureau** is located in Windwardside, in the renovated Lambert Hassell Building ☎ *(599) 4-62231,* FAX *(599) 4-62350.* It's open only Monday-Friday. In the U.S. ☎ *(407) 394-8580, 1-800-722-2394.*

WHEN TO GO

The Queen's birthday on April 30 celebrates the life of Beatrix of Holland with festive fireworks, parades and sports competitions. The Saba

Summer Festival takes place in late July (10 days) with much merry-making, music (steel bands), dancing and games. Saba Days in December is a festival featuring maypole dancing, spearfishing and other games.

SABA HOTELS		RMS	RATES	PHONE	CR. CARDS
The Bottom					
★★★	Captain's Quarters	10	$85–$130	(599) 4-62377	A, D, MC
★★	Juliana's	10	$65–$130	(599) 4-62389	A, MC, V
★	Cranston's Antique Inn	6	$40–$75	(599) 4-63203	A
★	Scout's Place	15	$40–$105	(599) 4-62388	A, MC

SABA RESTAURANTS		PHONE	ENTREE	CR. CARDS
The Bottom				
American				
★★	Corner Deli	(599) 4-62517	$4–$10••	A, MC, V
★★	Tea House		$2–$7••	None
★★	Tropics Cafe	(599) 4-63203	$4–$10••	MC, V
Chinese				
★★	Saba Chinese Restaurant	(599) 4-62268	$13–$19	None
International				
★★	Brigadoon	(599) 4-62380	$14–$17••	A, DC, MC, V
★★	Captain's Quarters	(599) 4-62201	$13–$22	MC, V
★★	Scout's Place	(599) 4-62295	$12–$25	MC, V
Italian				
★★	Guido's	(599) 4-62230	$4–$10••	A, MC, V
Seafood				
★★	Lollipop's	(599) 4-63330	$10–$26	None

Note: • Lunch Only

•• Dinner Only

ST. BARTHÉLÉMY

Waterskiing is only permitted in Colombier Bay.

One local island guide says it all: No bums allowed on St. Barts. And strangely enough, there isn't even one. Once known by its long nomenclature, St. Barthélémy, this thumbprint-sized isle is simply the antithesis of the ramshackle outpost. In fact, it could be easily considered one of *the* hoity-toitiest places alive on the planet. Try as you might, you won't find the seedy smells of West Indian life or the frenzied street markets that define Carib life. Instead, on St. Barts what you'll discover is a subculture of wealth superimposed on a native lore that is slowly but surely sinking into the sea. Even though there exists gorgeous scenery, pristine beaches and a seaworthy harbor, St. Barts remains a place to snooze, to "cruise," to pick new husbands and discard old ones—in high season the island makes L.A. look limp. If you're the kind of person who feels happy paying for social comeuppance, then St. Barts will be your biggest fantasy isle.

Bird's Eye View

St. Barts boasts white sandy beaches surrounded by lush, volcanic hillsides.

Shaped like a soprano sax or a backwards check mark, St. Barts covers only 9.5 square miles, making it half the size of Manhattan. A ten-minute flight from St. Martin, it is 125 miles from Guadeloupe, of which it is a dependency. There are six large lagoons scattered over the island, and no hill rising over the 920 ft. **Morne Vitet**. More than 20 tiny isles dot the surrounding water, the largest of which is Fourchue.

The harbor town of **Gustavia** puts the word quaint in the dictionary—a storybook setting for a fairytale. The eerily romantic streets are a mix of French, Colonial Creole, and Swedish style, so pristine that there's not even one piece of garbage sighted. Taking a road marked **Lurin** you can head out in a southeasterly direction and find achingly beautiful landscape. Latanier palms, imported for the straw hat industry, line the road, along with so many flowers—hibiscus, bougainvillea, dwarf poincianas, shell ginger flowers, baby orchids, flowering African tulips, frangipani—that you may feel over-

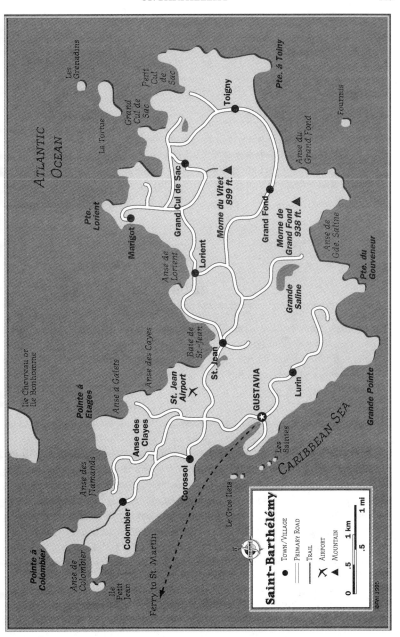

whelmed. With trees bent permanently out of shape by the strong trade winds, the eastern side of the island, known as **Grand Fond**, resembles something out of *Wuthering Heights*, as tall grass waves hypnotically and stone walls that were constructed over a century ago by French immigrants continue to crumble. It's on this side of the island, nearly deserted, that you'll find one lone house perched on the rocks at ocean's edge—once owned by Rudolph Nureyev. At **Lorient**, on the east, local fishermen work as they have for centuries. As you travel northward, more buildings appear, though it is still largely residential housing around the northeastern tip at Petit Cul-de-Sac. The larger **Grand Cul-de-Sac** is a tourist enclave right out of *Lifestyles of the Rich and Famous*. An enclave of million-dollar villas dot the rocky tip of **Pointe Milou**, where it's rumored some of Prince Andrew's clan have nested.

History

Some people believe Columbus discovered St. Barts, naming it after his brother, but the island didn't appear on any map until 1523, when a speck of dirt was labeled San Bartoleme by a Spanish cartographer. After being summarily ignored by both Carib Indians and European pirates, St. Barts was finally explored in 1637, eight years after St. Kitts was colonized, though some of the first Norman and British settlers were scalped by Carib Indians. Over time the island became a secret hiding place for pirates, while the island itself became tenaciously French. When Louis XVI traded the flagging island to the Swedes for some warehouse in Goteborg, the island magically flourished with new management (Thomas Jefferson himself declared the port free of all duties). By 1847, the island had been ravaged by hurricanes, trade competition, fires and piracy, leaving Gustavia, the capital, dirt poor—a fact that convinced the Swedes in 1878 to dump the island back in the lap of the French. Not until 1946 did the French government declare St. Barts a commune in the department of Guadeloupe in 1946. In 1947, aviator/hotelier Rémy de Haenen landed the first airplane here on the short, grassy pasture of St. Jean. With the construction of the airport and the island's first runway (called a STOL, i.e., short takeoff and landing), the floodgates of tourism were opened, with most visitors flocking to St. Jean, on the central point of the island.

People

As the actress Ann Magnuson once wrote, everybody on St. Barts looks related—to Olive Oyl. In truth, there are fewer than a hundred blacks on St. Barts since the island was too small to support a large import of slaves. Moreover, the rocky terrain of St. Barts was so inhospitable to growing sugarcane that the slave ships simply passed the island by, leaving the northern French farmers who settled here to follow their own Breton way of life. Today, the most traditional sect of the population are the fiercely independent grandmothers (or *grandmeres*)—tough old ladies, thoroughly Caucasian, West Indian by birth and French by heritage, who singlehandedly raised their huge families in the absence of husbands who had to frequently leave the island to make ends meet. (Today you can see them wearing their straw *caleches* pulled low over their brows, a type of peasant bonnet that served to shield their faces not only from the sun but from the staring eyes of passing sailors.) Sadly, with the influx of more than a 1000 ex-pats (many of them French) and thousands of high-class international tourists, the old traditions are slowly dying out as the middle-aged generation is caught in transition while their children are looking solidly into a modernized future.

Anyone looking for political struggles or racial tension simply won't find them on St. Barts. An uncommon feeling of unity exists here among locals. Crime is unheard of (unless you call land developers thieves), simply because the cost of living is too high to support a petty thief. Instead, everyone seems to be gainfully employed, from fishermen, to builders, to shopkeepers to hoteliers and restaurateurs; even the dogs look well fed. As such, many visitors hitchhike around to see the island, which is said to be a completely safe way of passage, not to mention a great way to make friends. Between the native Bartians and the Euro babes and dudes who arrive during high season, rumor has it that there are ten men to every woman on St. Barts—and most of them are straight and very handsome. One word of warning: although the "genuine" locals are polite, if not unduly humble, the French ex-pats who run many of the hotels have an attitude that simply should be shipped home to Paris. Come armed with ammunition.

Beaches

St. Barts is famous for its pristine, white beaches—at present count, 14.
Even during high season, they never become unbearably crowded, despite
being public and free of charge. The **Grand Saline** is the only official nude
beach, though stages of all levels of undress are seen throughout the island.
(Grand Saline has been dubbed Indochine Beach, after the Manhattan restaurant frequented by the terminally fabulous. The unstated seating rule: hip
and/or gay to the right side of the beach, conservative flanks to the left.
Both Grand Cul de Sac and St. Jean are the most developed beaches, with
several hotels, restaurants, and water sports activities readily available; the
two beaches are separated by the **Eden Rock** promontory. There is also a
smattering of small hotels and restaurants at Flamanda to the west, a classic
stretch of white sand fringed with lantana palms. For quiet seclusion, head
for **Marigot** and **Lorient** on the north shore, where you'll see many island families on Sunday. Total privacy can be found at Gouverneur in the south. If
you're walking, **Shell Beach** can be reached from Gustavia on foot; on the
other side of town. The public beach is near the commercial pier but is good
for a swim. The most difficult beach to reach is **Colombier**, a boat ride from
Gustavia. If you're driving, go as far as the village of Colombier; from there
you'll have a half-hour hike down a scenic path.

Underwater

Shallow reefs abound at this tony outpost, which makes snorkeling delightful and diving easy, bottoming out at about 80 feet. The best diving is on the
southwest coast and off the tiny islets decorating St. Barts outlying waters,
most of it no more than 10 or 15 minutes from the dock at Gustavia. Nearby
Ile Forchue is one such possibility, and **Les Petits Saints**, the three rock outcrops just outside the Gustavia harbor, features pompano and occasional
dolphins. Marigot Bay offers excellent snorkeling, and a narrow reef stretches into the channel toward the rock offshore, La Tortue ou l'Ecaille; winter

currents can make this area unsafe, however. The north side of **Anse de Colombier's** beautiful sands yield coral growth over the rocks, which are sprinkled with colorful reef fish and, in calm waters, one can snorkel the rocks past the south end, at Ile de la Pointe. Shell Beach, La Petite Anse and St. Jean Bay (northwest of Eden Rock) are other snorkeling possibilities.

Pointe A Colombier

The waters of the Atlantic and Caribbean meet at two 60-foot walls with numerous small caves featuring rays, eels and barracuda. Three dive spots have been identified around the reef, one in front, one in the middle and one behind Point a Colombier.

Wreck of the *Non-Stop*

A massive 210-foot power yacht that sank during 1989's Hurricane Hugo near Les Gros Ilets is now attracting life, particularly barracudas. The boat rests upside down, allowing divers to enter the swimming pool for a breath of fresh air.

La Baleine

The island's nicest reefs are a seamount (depth to 70 feet), located just outside Gustavia Harbor. Here, lobsters busy themselves amid a palette of corals, while nurse sharks, moray eels and barracuda explore nearby. Nearby Pain de Sucre offers separate dives, dropping to 60 feet and featuring a series of caverns and tunnels between colorful sponges and elkhorn coral.

Dive Shops

Club De Plongee - La Bulle

Gustavia; ☎ *(590) 27-62-25 or 27-68-93.*
Single tank dives, $50 off season, $60 mid-December through mid-April, including all equipment. Three scheduled dives daily, maximum 6 divers per trip. Not NAUI or PADI at present, but certified by the French Federation. Offers "baptisms," the French diving initiation in 15-20 feet of water, $70.

Marine Service.

Gustavia; ☎ *(590) 27-70-34.*
PADI affiliated with certification courses through open water and advanced. Aims for smaller groups of six to eight, and works with American (as well as French) equipment. Two-tank dive, $83, including gear. Also offers half-day snorkel/sailing tours to Ile Forchue, $60, or full-day, $100 (including lunch).

On Foot

Physically, St. Barts looks a little more impressive than it actually is. The island is tiny—just eight square miles—but appears larger due to the spunky

hills that rise to a pair of 900-foot peaks on the island's eastern side. The pre
ferred method of visitor transport is the ubiquitous Mini-Moke, but yo
needn't be hostage to these sputtering upstarts. See St. Barts' compact inte
rior of pastures and charming villages and its scalloped coastline on foot an
you'll be experiencing island over attitude. A few beaches hide in coves dif
ficult to reach on wheels, while an early morning stroll through Gustavia re
veals bold coffee, fresh croissants and a glimmer of the village that onc
was—St. Barts before being taken over by the chic set. Boats can be taken t
nearby **Ile Fourchue**, a half-sunk crater that rises to 340 feet off St. Barts
northwest tip and offers intriguing exploration on foot among cactus an
brush across a desert, rocky landscape.

Colombier Beach

One of St. Barts' very best beaches is accessible only by foot or boat, which means..
you won't have it to yourself. Visit the beautiful bay early in the morning or late ir
the afternoon for optimum solitude (and a cooler walk), avoiding the midday
onslaught. At the dead-end road above Petite Anse, the distinct trail winds and
drops for a half-mile or so through century plants and cactus. You may need to share
the rocky path with iguanas and goats. The entire bay and the house on the southern hill were once owned by the Rockefellers, but the current owners have been pre-
vented from developing the property, leaving visitors the winner. Bring water
saving some for the steep, hot ascent back to the road.

Lorient to Grand Fond

You'll follow the sparsely traveled main drag around the eastern tip of St. Barts, visiting teensy villages and some of the island's prettiest scenery on this delightful walk
From Lorient, head east to the coves of sand that begin with Marigot and end a
Anse du Petit Cul-de-Sac; come prepared, each of the four beaches are accessible.
and seductive. The main road curves to the south and follows the rocky coastline
(reminding some of the bluffs at Normandy), which draws surfers to the water
below. The road climbs between the island's two high points, Morne du Vitet on
the right, Morne du Grand Fond on the left (899 and 938 feet, respectively). It's
possible to arrange a pickup at Grand-Fond or you may continue on for another
hour back to your starting point at Lorient. Although a leisurely pace is encouraged,
bring water for the brief stretches between restaurants and set aside a half-day for
the entire circuit.

By Pedal

This is a pretty island, and bicycles should be an ideal way to experience it. Goat paths bisect the thorny countryside, providing ample exploration possibilities. But, although Rent Some Fun once offered mountain bikes, their customers found St. Barts too hot and hilly for enjoyable riding; bicycles are no longer available. Further, residents have collectively thumbed their noses at visiting bikers, letting them know that, on no uncertain terms, cyclists are not welcome on St. Barts. And these people call themselves French! No laws are in effect, yet, but with this kind of attitude, do you really want to lug your wheels on and off tiny planes to tool around in this environment?

What Else to See

St. Barts is blissfully free of tourist traps and boring museums. Anything worth finding will be your own special discovery, but a few hints will get you started. To find one of the last threads of traditional life, go to the once-isolated fishing village of Corossol on the southwestern coast, where you can still find old St. Bartian women weaving handicrafts from latanier palms. The wide-brimmed hats they're wearing, called *caleches,* may be hard to find, but you will find stalls of straw hats and baskets for sale. Second hint: Head for the northwest tip of the island, where the road dead-ends at Petite Anse. There's a goat path here that leads to **Anse de Colombier**. This rugged mountain trail is the sole land access to a beach that can otherwise only be enjoyed by island-hopping yachtsmen. A lizard-laden trail winds through the towering torch cacti and along the edge of a spectacular shoreline, ending up a paradise beach that is beyond description.

Museums and Exhibits

Municipal Museum   ★★★

Le Pointe, Gustavia.

This winsome little museum tells the island's history through costumes, antiques documents and artwork. It also has exhibits on St. Barth's vegetation and sea crea tures.

Sports

If you are interested in deep-sea fishing, head for the harbor at **Gustavia** where boat charters with fishing gear can be hired; hotels also will usuall make arrangements for you (you should expect them to, especially if you ar paying a mint for the room). As opposed to other Caribbean islands spearfishing is permitted, as long as the spearfisher is fully equipped in scub gear. Both diving and snorkeling equipment can be purchased in Gustavia Among the most popular fish anglers seek in St. Barts are dorado, bonit tuna, marlin, barracuda, amberjack, grouper and moray eel. Take time t talk to local fishermen and discover what are the best fish for the season an exactly which fish are edible—St. Barts has its own variety of edible fish Local fishermen can also be the source of fascinating yarns that go on fo hours, especially if they are inspired by a few beers.

Boating is more than a passion in St. Barts—it's a way of life, and sailors ar often judged socially by the make of their boat. The ideal location of S Barts—between Antigua and the Virgin Islands—gives sailors here a wide se lection of destinations to choose from. In Gustavia, there are docking facil ties and moorings for at least 40 vessels at one time. Other fine anchorage include **Colombier**, **Public** and **Corossol** bays. The calm winds of St.Jean an Grand Cul de Sac particularly take well to Sunfish; rentals are available there It's very easy to pick up a full-day picnic excursion, leaving from Gustavi and headed to nearby beaches and islets (up to six passengers, usually). Fu day sail to Ile Fourchue leaves the harbor at Gustavia at 9:30 a.m.

Surfing is terrific at **Lorient**. Always check the water conditions before yo go; it will save you time and money, and sometimes your life, if the waves ar too choppy. Most watersports facilities have boards for rent. Windsurfin equipment is also available at most facilities. Waterskiing is only authorize in Colombier Bay between 8:30 a.m. and 3 p.m.

Horseback Riding

Ranch des Flamands, Anse des Flamands.

Laure Nicolas is the person to see for trail rides and other excursions.

Watersports

Various locations, Gustavia.

La Marine Service *(☎ 27-70-34)* offers the island's most complete watersports center, with PADI-certified scuba diving, deep-sea fishing, snorkel excursions, and boat rides in the Aquascope from which you espy colorful coral, sea creatures, and a submerged yacht wreck. Also available are: **St. Barth Wind School** *(☎ 27-71-22)* and **Wind Wave Power** *(☎ 27-62-73)* for windsurfing instruction and rentals; **Club La Bulle** *(☎ 27-68-93)* and **Dive with Dan** *(☎ 27-64-78)* for scuba; and **La Maison de la Mer** *(☎ 27-81-00)* for deep-sea fishing.

Where to Stay

Fielding's Highest Rated Hotels in St. Barthélémy

★★★★★	Castelets	$100–$700
★★★★★	Guanahani	$110–$785
★★★★	Carl Gustaf Resort	$500
★★★★	Christopher Hotel	$195–$295
★★★★	Club la Banane	$130–$440
★★★★	Hotel St. Barth	$380–$705
★★★★	Hotel le Toiny	$394–$760
★★★★	Les Jardins de St. Jean	$60–$355
★★★★	Manapany Cottages	$125–$990
★★★	Emeraude Plage Hotel	$208–$500

Fielding's Most Romantic Hotels in St. Barthélémy

★★★★	Carl Gustaf Resort	$500–$1000
★★★★★	Castelets	$100–$700
★★★	Francois Plantation	$158–$405
★★★	Hostellerie Trois Forces	$80–$175
★★★★	Hotel le Toiny	$394–$760

Fielding's Budget Hotels in St. Barthélémy

★★	Normandie	$65–$80
★★★	St. Barth's Beach Club	$68–$115
★★	Le P'tit Morne	$67–$120
★★★	Hotel Baie des Flamands	$95–$135
★★★	Hostellerie Trois Forces	$80–$175

You don't come to St. Bart's without a gold card. Accommodations will be your biggest payout, unless you go crazy in the duty-free port. The trend in Bartian lodging leans toward the small, intimate and atmospheric—you won't see a high rise anywhere on the island. If you're intent on air-conditioning, ask in advance, because many properties depend on ceiling fans and the trade winds. Many people return to the same villa or inn year after year, having established a warm relationship with the owner. That's why reservations for the most popular properties should be made a year in advance, especially the villas, which go fast.

Hotels and Resorts

You'll find few big resorts on St. Barts. Most hotels have a homey feel; the final bill you receive will feel like nothing at home. Most of these hotels are environment-friendly, and take advantage of their luscious natural surroundings. The **Christopher Hotel** (a member of the Sofitel chain), and the **Grand Cul de Sac** are most typical of big hotels complete with modern facilities. More atmospheric are the villas of **Manapany**, tucked into a West Indian-type village, and the **St. Barth Isle de France**, where elegance prevails over efficiency. Namedroppers who want to run into other namedroppers tend to congregate at the **Guanahani**.

Baie des Agnes Hotel	$175–$230	★★

Baie des Flamands, ☎ (590) 27-63-61, FAX (590) 27-83-44.
Single: $175–$200. Double: $175–$230.
Located on a picturesque beach, this small hotel has air-conditioned rooms with private bath and terrace, as well as bungalows with kitchenettes. The restaurant serves breakfast only, but other eateries are nearby. No pool or other facilities at this basic spot.

Castelets	$100–$700	★★★★★

Mount Lurin, ☎ (590) 27-61-73.
Single: $100–$700. Double: $100–$700.
This exclusive villa resort is perched high on a mountain, with stunning views. Formerly called the Sapore Di Mare, it is now back to its original owner. Two rooms are in the main house, the rest in two-bedroom duplex villas furnished with fine antiques, very luxurious accoutrements, spacious living rooms, terraces and kitchens. The atmosphere is sophisticated and discreet, attracting many celebrities. The grounds include a small pool and excellent French restaurant. You'll want a car to get around; the beach is five minutes' driving time.

Christopher Hotel	$195–$295	★★★★

Pointe Milou, ☎ (590) 27-63-63, FAX (590) 27-92-92.
Single: $195–$270. Double: $220–$295.
French Colonial in design, this is St. Barth's newest hotel, opened in 1993 on the island's northern tip. The 40 rooms are stylish and quite comfortable, with high-quality furnishings, minibars, and great views from the terrace or balcony. The beach is 10 minutes away, so most guests hang by the enormous pool—the island's largest. The site also includes a full-service health spa (each guest gets a free mas-

sage!), two restaurants, three bars, and a concierge to arrange off-premises activities
Service at this Sofitel-managed hotel is fine.

### Club la Banane					$130–$440					★★★★

Quartier Lorient, ☎ *(590) 27-68-25, FAX (590) 27-68-44.*
Single: $130–$440. Double: $164–$440.
Located two miles from Gustavia, this small complex consists of nine inviting bun
galows, each individually decorated. All are quite nice, with antiques, local artwork
TVs with VCRs, private terraces, and ceiling fans in lieu of air conditioners. Lush
gardens surround the place. The restaurant is open only in the evenings. There's
pool on the premises and the beach is within walking distance. Nice.

### El Sereno Beach Hotel & Villas					$120–$340					★★★

Grand Cul de Sac, ☎ *(590) 27-64-80, FAX (590) 27-75-47.*
Single: $120–$275. Double: $120–$340.
Located on the beach five minutes from Gustavia, this small operation consists of
hotel and gingerbread-trimmed villas, each housing three one-bedroom suites with
full kitchens and lots of room. The standard hotel rooms are not as nice, but com
fortable enough. There's a small pool on the premises, as well as two restaurants
two bars and lush gardens. Watersports await nearby.

### Filao Beach Hotel					$210–$420					★★★

Baie de St. Jean, ☎ *(590) 27-64-84, FAX (590) 27-62-24.*
Single: $210–$420. Double: $210–$420.
Located right near the airport and on one of the island's better (and topless
beaches, this is a well-run operation. Guest rooms are in air-conditioned bungalows
with all the modern comforts. They are quite private, but most don't have ocean
views. Lovely perfumed gardens abound. There's also a large pool, windsurfing and
snorkeling, and a good bar and restaurant. Excellent service, too.

### Francois Plantation					$158–$405					★★★

Colombier, ☎ *(590) 27-78-82, FAX (590) 27 61 26.*
Single: $158–$404. Double: $205–$405.
Set on a hillside overlooking Baie des Flamands amid tropical gardens, this elegan
spot consists of 12 bungalows scattered about. All are very nicely done, with
mahogany furniture, four-poster beds, minibars, air conditioning, TVs, and terraces
with views of the ocean or gardens. The views everywhere are simply astounding
especially from the pool terrace, and the restaurant is quite good. The beach is a
five-minute drive.

### Grand Cul de Sac Hotel					$110–$335					★★

Grand Cul de Sac, ☎ *(590) 27-60-7, FAX (590) 27-75-57.*
Single: $110–$185. Double: $195–$335.
Half the rooms at this bungalow complex have beach views and kitchenettes, while
the other half have mountain views and refrigerators. All are air-conditioned and
basic but comfortable. There's a bar and restaurant on the premises, as well as a salt
water pool and gym. Guests can play tennis at sister property St. Barth's Beach
Hotel and Tennis Club.

uanahani $110–$785 ★★★★★

Grand Cul de Sac, ☎ *(590) 27-66-60, FAX (590) 27-70-70.*
Single: $110–$785. Double: $185–$785.
Located on seven beachfront acres at Cul de Sac, the romantic spot is especially popular with couples. Accommodations, in gingerbread-trimmed cottages, are deluxe. The higher-priced studios and one-bedroom suites have full kitchens, as well as whirlpools in the studios and plunge pools with the suites. The grounds include two restaurants, two tennis courts, a pool and watersports at the two beaches. Prepare for a lot of walking up and down the hillside. Nice.

ostellerie Trois Forces $80–$175 ★★★

Vitet, ☎ *(590) 27-61-25, FAX (590) 27 81 38.*
Single: $80–$175. Double: $80–$175.
When someone asks "what's your sign?" here it's not just the old come on—each cottage is individually decorated and designed to compliment the astrological sign after which it's named. Located up in the mountains, three miles from Gustavia, this peaceful retreat is run by the island's leading astrologer, who also happens to be a quite decent chef. The gingerbread-trimmed cottages are tiny but nicely done with handmade wooden furnishings and large terraces. Only four are air-conditioned, and none have phones or TV. There's a pool on-site, and this is probably the only hotel in the Caribbean where you can take yoga lessons, have your tarot cards read, and get your chart done. Very pleasant.

otel Baie des Flamands $95–$135 ★★★

Anse de Flamands, ☎ *(590) 27-64-85.*
Single: $95–$105. Double: $105–$135.
Set on a half-mile stretch of beach, one of the island's best, this small motel-like property is fairly isolated, so you'll want a rental car to get around. Accommodations are clean and basic, with the more expensive rooms offering a kitchenette on the patio. (The others come with a refrigerator.) The grounds include a very fine French restaurant, bar and saltwater pool. Good service at this family-run operation.

otel St. Barth $380–$705 ★★★★

Anse des Flamands, ☎ *(590) 27-61-8, FAX (590) 27-86-83.*
Single: $380–$705. Double: $380–$705.
Set along one of the island's best beaches, this newer property houses guests in cottages or a plantation-style house. All guest rooms are spacious and furnished with antiques, locally made pieces, expensive linens, large baths (some with whirlpool tubs), refrigerators, and patios or balconies. Facilities include an air-conditioned squash court, tennis court, two pools, and a fitness center. Very nice!

lanapany Cottages $125–$990 ★★★★

Anse des Cayes, ☎ *(590) 27-66-65, FAX (590) 27-75-28.*
Single: $125–$990. Double: $205–$990.
Set in a small cove on the north shore, this property consists of a complex of cottages along a hillside or the beach. Accommodations vary from standard guestrooms to suites with one or two bedrooms and full kitchens. All are fine, but not as luxurious as the rates suggest. The site incudes two restaurants, an exercise room,

pool and tennis court. The beach is pretty but tiny, and constantly windy. This operation is quite chic, but on the small side compared to other luxury resorts.

Normandie $65–$80   ★★

Loriet, Loriet, ☎ (590) 27-61-66, FAX (590) 27 98 83.
Single: $65–$80. Double: $65–$80.
This basic, family-run place offers some of St. Barts' cheapest accommodations. The rooms are decent for the rates—obviously quite basic, but clean and comfortable. Only two (the most expensive) have air conditioners; the rest rely on ceiling fans. There's a small pool but nothing else, so you'll want a car.

St. Barth's Beach Club $68–$115   ★★★

Grand Cul de Sac, ☎ (590) 27-60-70, FAX (590) 27-75-57.
Single: $68–$83. Double: $93–$115.
This two-story hotel is right on the beach. Though it calls itself a hotel and tennis club, it has only one court. Other facilities include a saltwater pool, gym and a wind-surfing school. Accommodations are modern; all have a balcony or patio, while some boast minibars and kitchens. You'll want a rental car, as this spot is fairly isolated.

Taiwana Hotel $955–$999   ★★★

Anse des Flamands, ☎ (590) 27-65-01, FAX (590) 27 68 82.
Single: $955–$999. Double: $955–$999.
Located on a secluded beach, this incredibly expensive spot houses its well-heeled guests in beautifully furnished and quite large suites loaded with antiques, modern furniture, handpainted tiles and enormous bathrooms, many with whirlpools. There are two pools (one for kids), tennis, and a restaurant. Watersports are available on the beach. The service can be sullen—not exactly what one has in mind when forking over $1000 for a night's stay. Unless you're turned on by paying exorbitant prices, try someplace else.

Tropical Hotel $97–$281   ★★★

Baie de St. Jean, Baie de St. Jean, ☎ (590) 27-64-87.
Single: $97–$207. Double: $125–$281.
Set some 25 yards from the beach on a hill overlooking St. Jean Bay, this small hotel centers around a ginderbread-trimmed building that houses the reception area, a lounge and bar. Guestrooms are light and airy, with comfortable trappings and furnished patios overlooking the ocean or lush gardens. There's also a restaurant and pool on-site. Pleasant.

Apartments and Condominiums

Self-catering in St. Barts is not "roughing it." Prices on villas with fully equipped kitchens can be exorbitant, but the surroundings are often worth it, such as the **Hotel Car Gustaf** near Shell Beach. Rental agencies are your best bet to secure the perfect accommodation for your needs. Decide ahead of time if you want to rent a car or whether you need a live-in staff. Snob-weary Americans should contact Sibarth, a real estate agency in Gustavia, run by Brook and Roger Lacour, a former U.S. citizen who married into the St. Barts life. Sibarth rents out villas that range from the modest to the luxurious. It also arranges sailing, snorkeling, diving, horseback riding, as well as transportation and restau

ant reservations. Call ☎ *(800) 932-3222*; villas start at $900 per week. One of the most
spectacular and celebrity-oozing rentals is dancer Mikhail Baryshnikov's two Mexican-
style villas superbly decorated by Billy du Mesnil, available December–April, for about
$4000 a week (each). (Contact ☎ *(590) 27-86-72* for more information.) For villa rent-
ers whose phone is restricted to local calls, a world-wide phone service, *Liaisons Mondi-
les*, allows off-island calls by dialing ☎ *27-79-91*. Find a copy of the *Vendôm Guide*, an
elegant, four-color publication which details villa rentals, hotels, restaurants and a variety
of island sports. It's in English and on sale through Sibarth on the island or through
VIMCO in Newport, RI.

| Carl Gustaf Resort | $500–$1000 | ★ ★ ★ ★ |

Rue des Normands, ☎ *(800) 948-7823, (590) 27-82-83, FAX (590) 27-82-37.*
Single: $500–$1000. Double: $500–$1000.
Named in honor of the king of Sweden, this all-suite hotel is situated on a hilltop
overlooking Gustavia harbor. Guests are housed in cottages of one or two bedrooms with wooden sundecks and tiny private plunge pools. The units are quite
stylishly done, with high ceilings, marble floors, luxurious furnishings, fax machines,
stereos, VCRs, and fully equipped kitchens. Two-bedroom suites have bunk beds
for kids. Facilities include a gourmet French restaurant, two bars, a fitness center, a
private cabin cruiser for sea and fishing excursions, and a botanical garden. Wonderful views abound everywhere at this sophisticated French-style resort. If you can
afford the rates, you won't be disappointed.

| Emeraude Plage Hotel | $208–$500 | ★ ★ ★ |

Baie St. Jean, ☎ *(590) 27-64-78, FAX (590) 27-83-08.*
Single: $208–$500. Double: $208–$500.
Situated right on the beach, this popular spot does a lot of repeat business, so book
early. Accommodations are in simple yet comfortable bungalows with all the modern conveniences, plus kitchenettes on the patios. Three units have two bedrooms,
and there's a beachside villa with two bedrooms, two baths and great views. All is
kept in tip-top shape by the very friendly staff. There's little in the way of extras, but
no one seems to mind. Guests get a discount on watersports at the nearby concession.

| Hotel le Toiny | $394–$760 | ★ ★ ★ ★ |

Anse de Toiny, ☎ *(590) 27-88-88, FAX (590) 27-89-30.*
Single: $394–$623. Double: $349–$760.
Set on a remote hillside on the southeastern coast, this newer hotel is set in a grove
of trees. Accommodations are lovely, consisting of suites in individual cottages with
quality furnishing and linens, four-poster beds, full kitchens, and TVs with VCRs—
plus a private pool for each. Spectacular views abound. There's an open-air French
restaurant and a large communal pool as well. The beach is a five-minute walk, but
you'll need a car to do any other exploring. Elegant.

| Le P'tit Morne | $67–$120 | ★ ★ |

Colombier, Colombier, ☎ *(590) 27-62-64, FAX (590) 27 84 63.*
Single: $67–$120. Double: $67–$120.

Set high up in the hills far from the madding crowds, this apartment hotel's rates are quite reasonable for expensive St. Barts. Units are air-conditioned studios with cable TV, minibars, fully equipped kitchens and decks. The premises include a pool and snack bar, which serves breakfast only. The beach is a five-minute drive down a twisting road.

Les Islets Fleuris Hotel Residence $70–$220   ★ ★

Hauts de Lorient, ☎ *(590) 27-64-22, FAX (590) 27-69-72.*
Single: $70–$220. Double: $100–$220.
This small complex has eight cottages set on the hillside. All are studios with full kitchens and large terraces that rely on ceiling fans for comfort. There's a pool on site, with restaurants nearby.

Les Jardins de St. Jean $60–$355   ★ ★ ★ ★

Rue Victor Maurasse, Baie de St. Jean, ☎ *(590) 27-70-19, FAX (590) 27-84-40.*
Single: $60–$255. Double: $88–$355.
This condominium hotel is located on a hillside, some 300 yards from the beach. Accommodations are in a cluster of two-story bungalows and run the gamut from studios to units with one or two bedrooms. All have full kitchens, private terraces and air conditioning. TV and radio are available for an extra charge. There's a large pool on the premises and much within walking distance.

Marigot Bay Club $80–$185   ★ ★ ★

Marigot Bay, ☎ *(590) 27-75-45, FAX (590) 27-90-04.*
Single: $80–$185. Double: $80–$185.
This small apartment hotel offers clean and basic units at a fair price. Set on a hillside overlooking the Atlantic, units are simply furnished and include full kitchens, private terraces, TVs and living rooms. Maids keep things tidy. There's a French restaurant on-site, but not much else. The beach is walkable.

Village St. Jean Hotel $85–$300   ★ ★ ★

Baie de St. Jean, ☎ *(590) 27-61-39, FAX (590) 27 77 96.*
Double: $85–$300.
Set on a hillside close to the beach, this property consists of 20 cottages with one or two bedrooms. Each is simply furnished but pleasant enough, with kitchens and private terraces. There are also standard hotel rooms with twin beds and small refrigerators. A restaurant, pool and Jacuzzi are on the premises, with lots within walking distance. This friendly, family-run operation is a good buy.

White Sand Beach Cottages $55–$205   ★ ★

Baie de Flamands, ☎ *(590) 27-82-08, FAX (590) 27 70 69.*
Single: $55–$145. Double: $85–$205.
This casual spot has eight cottages within walking distance of the beach and nearby resorts. The accommodations are simple yet pleasant, with kitchens and air conditioning. No facilities on-site.

Yuana Hotel $150–$355   ★ ★ ★

Quartier du Roy, ☎ *(590) 27-80-84, FAX (590) 27-78-45.*
Single: $150–$305. Double: $150–$355.

Set in a lush garden, this hillside hotel has great views. Guests are put up in spacious studios with full kitchenettes, TVs with VCRs, and comfortable furnishings. The restaurant serves breakfast only; you'll have to cook in or rent a car for other meals. There's a small pool for cooling off.

Inns

For more intimate lodgings, many tourists are flocking to the "inn scene," where the personal service and often remote locations create the profile of perfect hideaways. One of the grandest places, **Le Filao**, is a member of the Relais & Chateau clan, always a top name in lush surroundings and elegant cuisine. **Hotel Baie des Anges** is one of the few that offer kitchenettes in some rooms.

Low Cost Lodging

There are very few cheap lodgings on St. Barts, because frankly tourists without money are generally treated like lepers. You can save money by coming off-season, cramming a party the size of a small fraternity into a cottage or villa, and cooking your own food. At Presqui'ile, you should probably be able to speak French well, particularly since you will most likely have to share the bathroom. Hotel Le P'tit Morne is in the middle of nowhere, so you should have a car to get to the beach, unless you want to spend your St. Bart days near a pool. The best location is **Les Mouettes**, on the beach at Lorient.

Where to Eat

	Fielding's Highest Rated Restaurants in St. Barthélémy	
★★★★★	Le Toque Lyonnaise	$43–$61
★★★★	Ballahou	$15–$45
★★★★	Francois Plantation	$16–$50
★★★★	La Fregate	$10–$19
★★★★	Le Gaiac	$30–$60
★★★★	Le Sapotillier	$45–$60
★★★	Castelets	$25–$35
★★★	La Langouste	$23–$42
★★★	Marigot Bay Club & Art Gallery	$40–$50
★★★	Wall House	$30–$45

	Fielding's Special Restaurants in St. Barthélémy	
★★★★	Ballahou	$15–$45
★★★	Eddy's Ghetto	$15–$18
★★★	Le Select	$5–$10
★★★	Wall House	$30–$45

	Fielding's Budget Restaurants in St. Barthélémy	
★★★	Le Select	$5–$10
★★★★	La Fregate	$10–$19
★★	Santa Fe	$10–$21
★★★	Eddy's Ghetto	$15–$18
★★★	Pasta Paradise	$10–$25

The food in St. Barts has to be good enough to suit the persnickety jetsetters who arrive, plus locals have to have the attitude to endure them. Cuisine usually runs to the French, often using the spoils of the sea, such as *langouste* (lobster) and redfish, but you can find a few West Indian kitchens, such as the casual Topolino, on the road to Salines. The harborside **Chez Maya** is the hippest celebrity hangout, where the atmosphere is relaxed and the exotic cuisine—from French to Creole to Vietnamese—is superb. Best dining can be found at **la Cuisine de Michel**, a tiny roadside takeout place on the Grand Fond road; many locals stop by to pick up their Sunday meals here from the French chef Michel Brunet. **Eddy's Ghetto**, in Gustavia, is an open-air restaurant where everyone fits in, a funky lively joint where great meals come with good prices. When wallets get low, the village of Lorient proffers good hamburgers at **Chez Jo Jo**. Do your best to seek out the fresh-baked bread that a little old lady sells near the cemetery.

The club scene has slumped since the infamous club Au Tour de Rocher mysteriously burned down two years ago. Weekend nights at **Le Pélican** in St. Jean seem like a frat party. Every night except Wednesday is cabaret at **Club La Banane**, run by the French lady whose Parisian cabaret inspired "La Cage Aux Folles." Two of the favorite local bar hangouts—**Bar de l'Oubli** and **Le Sélect**—sit kitty-corner from each other on rue du Général de Gaulle in Gustavia, the busiest thoroughfare of the town, and are the places where you're most likely to meet new friends. If you are a young, drunken poet wannabe, drop in at **Chez Ginette S.O.S.**, and try the famous Punch Coco (a rum concoction whose ingredients are known only to owner Ginette). Wannabe sailors should try to get invited to dinner on one of the impressive yachts anchored in the match-box-size harbor—one even has the name *Octopussy*.

Adam	**$$$**	★★

Village St. Jean, St. Jean, ☎ *(590) 27-84-56.*
French cuisine.
Dinner: prix fixe $35.

On an island where fabulous eateries come and go, Adam prevails by proffering a seemingly infinite variety of three-course, prix-fixe dinners at a reasonable tariff. Entrees like filet mignon, lobster, or filet of pork with a coconut sauce are capped off with creme brulee or other heavenly desserts. The setting is also paradisiacal, high on a hillside with garden and lagoon views; there's art on the walls as well as on the plates.

Au Port	**$$$**	★★★

Rue Sadi-Carnot, ☎ *(590) 27-62-36.*
French cuisine.
Dinner: 6:30–10 p.m., entrees $19–$27.

Guests navigate a steep staircase to get to the second-floor dining room of this charming old house above the port of Gustavia. Cuisine is a fanciful blend of traditional French and creole—witness the popular colombo (Creole curry) of prawns or lamb served with seasoned rice. Ambience is understandably nautical.

Ballahou $$$ ★★★★

Anse des Cayes, Anse des Cayes, ☎ *(590) 27-66-55.*
French cuisine.
Lunch: 12:30–4 p.m., entrees $15–$30.
Dinner: 7:30–9:30 p.m., entrees $27–$45.

There's a lot of understandable ballyhoo (and hip-hooray) about this gorgeous restaurant in the sleek Hotel Manapany—architecturally, it seems to blend as one with the rim of the swimming pool. Specialties usually include seafood, but the menu changes often. Guests of the hotel and others dine here by candlelight only five months out of the year; it's closed in the warmer months. Manapany's Italian restaurant, Ouanalao, serves lunch and dinner all year round; try the gazpacho and risotto with prawns.

Castelets $$$ ★★★

Morne Lurin, ☎ *(590) 27-6173.*
French cuisine.
Dinner: 7–9 p.m., entrees $25–$35.

This long-established hotel went through a brief Italian phase as Sapore de Mare. Manager Genevieve Jouany returned and brought everything back to normal, including the chic dining salon presided over by two under-30s chefs (aren't they all?). These young wizards eschew heavy cream sauces in favor of fresh herbs and virgin olive oils. They also exhibit a propensity for wild morel and boletus mushrooms that show up frequently in pasta and seafood dishes.

Eddy's Ghetto $$$ ★★★

Rue du General de Gaulle,
French cuisine.
Dinner: 7–10 p.m., entrees $15–$18.

When locals go slumming they go to Eddy's for simple grills, salads, ribs, beef ragouts and island music. The yacht crowd often fills the wicker and plant-filled restaurant the moment it opens at 7 p.m., if the locals haven't gotten there first. The place fills the need for light meals and casual ambience not found in some of the pricier establishments in town. The owner is Eddy Stakelborough (a member of the clan that founded Le Select across the street), who oversees the action from a perch behind the bar.

Francois Plantation $$$ ★★★★

Colombier, Colombier, ☎ *(590) 27-7882.*
French cuisine.
Dinner: 6:30–10 p.m., entrees $16–$50.

No one doubts the serene beauty of this place—for exotic plantings, greenery and an interior boasting highly polished woods. But the food (lighter versions of traditional French favorites) and service have been slipping somewhat. It's hoped things will improve, as the innovativeness of the cuisine can't often be faulted.

Hostellerie Trois Forces $$$ ★★★

Vitet, Vitet, ☎ *(590) 27-6125.*

French cuisine.
Lunch: Noon–3 p.m., entrees $10–$50.
Dinner: 7–9:45 p.m., entrees $10–$50.

Tarot readings and fine food commingle nicely at this surprisingly unpretentious holistic, new age resort-restaurant in the small town of Vitet, east of Lorient. Chef and chief astrologer Hubert Delemotte and family serve creole/French meals with a nod to organic and vegetarian diners, although there is red meat on the menu. There's a three-course, prix-fixe dinner offering nightly. Ambience is low-key and pleasant.

Entrepont $$$ ★★

La Pointe, ☎ *(590) 27-9060.*
Italian cuisine.
Lunch: entrees $17–$25.
Dinner: entrees $25–$33.

Located in a newly fashionable area on the west side of Gustavia's harbor, this Italian restaurant owned by a Neapolitan family is renowned for unusual pizzas. Guests eat well in a garden setting that's open to the breezes. Other choices include beef carpaccio, pastas and veal.

Escale $$$ ★★★

La Pointe, ☎ *(590) 27-8106.*
Italian cuisine.
Dinner: 7 p.m.–midnight, entrees $14–$29.

This mostly Italian trattoria on the west side of the harbor has many faithful followers who clamor for the wide variety of pizzas (some say it's the best in town), or lasagna and seafood. Lately it's been facing some competition from other eateries in the area serving similar cuisine, although it swings at night, especially in the hip bar.

La Fregate $$ ★★★★

Flamandes Beach, Flamandes, ☎ *(590) 27-6651.*
French cuisine.
Lunch: Noon–3 p.m., entrees $10–$19.
Dinner: 7–9 p.m., entrees $10–$19.

Aim for an outside patio table at this excellent restaurant—if you still can. The word is out about the incredible edibles emerging from Jean-Pierre Crouzet's kitchen in a somewhat tacky beachfront motel in Baie des Flamandes. Island regulars know him from his past successes at Gustavia's La Sapotillier, where he was chef de cuisine. Here he continues to unleash a plethora of dishes utilizing the freshest local ingredients possible with a tried and true technique—although he is not yet 30, he has already worked his way through quite a few three-star establishments in France.

La Langouste $$$ ★★★

rue Bord-de-la-Mer, ☎ *(590) 27-69-47.*
Latin American cuisine. Specialties: Langouste.
Lunch: Noon–2 p.m., entrees $23–$42.
Dinner: 7–10 p.m., entrees $23–$42.

The island's national crustacean (a clawless lobster) is the star at this pleasant creole/French eatery owned by Annie Ange, a member of a St. Barts landowning family (St. Barth Beach Hotel). The delectable seafood is dependably fresh, and other finny offerings include stuffed crabs and accra de morue (cod fritters). It's located is a traditional Swedish-style dwelling near several public offices.

Le Gaiac $$$ ★★★★

Anse de Toiny, Anse de Toiny, ☎ *(590) 27-8888.*
French cuisine.
Lunch: entrees $30–$60.
Dinner: entrees $30–$60.

Nowadays, few great chefs stay in one place for long—Manapany's Jean Christophe Perrin has turned his talents to this small, very in spot at Le Toiny, a resort on a hilltop above a windward beach. It's very difficult to secure a seat in the 28-table outdoor restaurant (book way in advance) where such delights as conch cannelloni and rabbit with figs and pine nuts continue to dazzle guests.

Le Pelican $$$ ★★

Plage de St. Jean, Plage de St. Jean, ☎ *(590) 27-6464.*
Latin American cuisine.
Lunch: 11:30 a.m.–3 p.m., entrees $20–$40.
Dinner: 6:30–1 p.m., entrees $20–$40.

This pleasant restaurant located a few steps from St. Barts' most popular beach satisfies on many counts. At lunch it's perfect for casual meals and ocean and people watching from a vast, covered terrace. Later, for dinner, the large dining rooms are awash in candlelight while sounds of piano music grace the background. Cuisine is a melange of creole and French favorites. Closed for dinner on Sundays.

Le Sapotillier $$$ ★★★★

rue Sadi-Carnot, ☎ *(590) 27-6028.*
French cuisine. Specialties: Couscous with shrimp creole, fish mousse.
Dinner: prix fixe $45–$60.

Some fine chefs have emerged with an appreciative following from the kitchens of this memorable restaurant in a traditional old stone structure in Gustavia, including Le Fregate's Jean-Pierre Crouzette. La Sapotillier's reputation is still stellar, with classic French cuisine served with finesse in a small dining room or alfresco under the branches of a vast sapodilla tree.

Le Select $ ★★★

rue de la France, ☎ *(590) 27-86-87.*
International cuisine. Specialties: Burgers.
Lunch: 10 a.m.–4 p.m., entrees $5–$10.
Dinner: 4–11 p.m., entrees $5–$10.

This old favorite (circa 1950) provides a safe haven for ordinary folk seeking refuge from the high prices and sometimes over-stuffed, precious atmosphere of some island dining establishments. Besides serving what is probably the best cheeseburger in town (it's called cheeseburger in paradise), the scruffy, poster-festooned old warehouse is great for loud reggae, zouk, or soca music. Newcomers can't possibly miss it—just walk around Gustavia during the day and you'll bump into it; at night you hear it before you see it.

Le Toque Lyonnaise $$$ ★★★★★

Grand Cul-de-Sac, Grand Cul-de-Sac, ☎ *(590) 27-6480.*

French cuisine. Specialties: Grilled lobster with vanilla bean.
Dinner: 7–10 p.m., prix fixe $43–$61.

It's hard not to have a good meal here—chefs are from Lyon, which is the gourmet capital of France. This modern, oceanfront eatery, located a few miles out of Gustavia, boasts chefs who have trained with Paul Bocuse. Grilled seafood is the specialty, and the wine list is extensive and well-chosen. Closed June through October.

Marigot Bay Club & Art Gallery $$$

Marigot Bay, Marigot, ☎ *(590) 27-7545.*
French cuisine.
Lunch: entrees $40–$50.
Dinner: entrees $40–$50.

Two giant grilled langoustines appear on your plate here like creatures from Mars— yet they were freshly caught only this morning by a family of fisherfolk who own this popular restaurant at an intimate resort in the small bayside village of Marigot. You can have your crustacean plain or with a variety of sauces. Specialties rarely change, which is how most people who eat here like it. Closed for lunch on Monday and on Sundays from September through October.

Maya's $$$

Public Beach, Public, ☎ *(590) 27-7361.*
Latin American cuisine.
Dinner: 6–11 p.m., entrees $27–$35.

Maya from Martinique serves savory creole cuisine with some spicy touches to an appreciative crowd; it's one of the more popular eateries on the island. The restaurant has a waterfront location in Public (west of Gustavia) with tables on a plant-filled patio. The menu changes frequently, but the salads are a standout.

Pasta Paradise $$$

Rue de Roi, ☎ *(590) 27-8078.*
French cuisine.
Lunch: entrees $10–$25.
Dinner: entrees $10–$25.

French-inspired Italian food is served at this very popular restaurant in a traditional, historic building in Gustavia. Formerly the site of La Citronelle, the jolly exterior features gingerbread trim, white shutters, tangerine and white railings and a tropical mural. Guests can dine on several different daily pasta offerings in air-conditioned insularity or in a breeze-cooled patio. The menu also features lobster in saffron oil and beef filets. Closed for lunch on Sunday.

Santa Fe $$$ ★ ★

Morne Lurin,
American cuisine. Specialties: Burgers, steaks.
Lunch: Noon–2 p.m., entrees $10–$21.
Dinner: 5–10 p.m., entrees $10–$21.

Although the name evokes the American Southwest, the food served here is basically burgers (excellent), steak, and barbecue at American prices (reasonable). It's also a hangout for Anglais-speakers and sports fans of any stripe who come to watch their favorite teams play on wide-screen television, especially on Sundays. Located just a few miles east of Gustavia, it seems worlds away in atmosphere and in its isolation on a lofty hilltop. There's no ocean view; but that's not really necessary here. Closed for lunch on Sundays.

Wall House   **$$$**   ★★★

Gustavia Harbor, ☎ *(590) 27-71-33.*
French cuisine.
Lunch: entrees $30–$45.
Dinner: entrees $30–$45.

Almost every table in this whitewashed restaurant in the harbor has a lovely view; the wide picture windows in the dining room offer a panorama of swaying palms, small craft, azure waters, and a row of red tile-roofed, gingerbread-trimmed buildings. Diners can also sit outside to be closer to the action. The menu features lobster, rare lamb, duck breast, fabulous pates, and sinful desserts.

Where to Shop

To find one of the last threads of traditional life, go to the once-isolated fishing village of Corossol on the southwestern coast, where you can still find old St. Bartian women weaving handicrafts from latanier palms. The wide-brimmed hats called *caleches* may be hard to find atop their heads, but you will find stalls of straw hats and baskets.

Duty-free reigns in St. Barts, so if you're in the market for fine perfumes, china, crystal and liquor, you can find some of the best bargains in the Caribbean. Some French perfumes, like Chanel, are cheaper than they are in Paris. Due to the jetset crowd, a number of local crafts have found their way into international fashion magazines. Check around the small shops in Gustavia and in some of the outlying villages. **The Shell Shop** features unique jewelry, shells and coral found on the island. Yacht-owners and wannabes tend to congregate at **Loulou's Marine** in Gustavia, where everything you ever needed for a cruise is available—from clothes to rigs.

St. Barthélémy Directory

ARRIVAL

From the States, the principal gateway is Sint Maarten where you can make connections via inter-island carriers to St. Barts. Many flights are available daily. **Windward Islands Airways** offers a ten-minute flight from Juliana Airport on Sint Maarten ☎ *(590) 27-61-01* or **Air St**

Barthélémy ☎ *(590) 27-71-90*, which also has flights from San Juan, Guadeloupe, and Espérance Airport on French St. Martin. **Air Guadeloupe** ☎ *(590) 27-61-90* makes the flight from Espérance in 10 minutes and from Guadeloupe in one hour. Air Guadeloupe also flies from St. Thomas a few times a week. (To get to St. Thomas, take the 30-minute flight from San Juan, Puerto Rico, where **Air St. Thomas** ☎ *(590) 27-71-76* has connecting flights to St. Barts, a 45-minute ride.) If you have trouble making connections, you can always charter a flight through Windward Island Airways and Air St. Barthélémy.

St. Barts' airport has a short landing strip that can handle planes no larger than a 20-seat STOL aircraft. It is not equipped for night landing. Boutiques, bar and car rental agencies can be found at the airport, and a pharmacy and food market across the road in La Savane Commercial Center.

There is an airport departure tax of 10 francs (about $2) to the French side of St. Martin or Guadeloupe, and 15 francs ($3) to other destinations.

BUSINESS HOURS

Shops are open weekdays 8:30 a.m.–noon and 2–5 p.m. (some until 7 p.m.) and Saturday 8:30 a.m.–noon. Banks open weekdays 8 a.m.–noon and 2–3:30 p.m.

CLIMATE

St. Barts has an ideal dry climate and an average temperature of 72–86 degrees F.

DOCUMENTS

For stays of up to three weeks, U.S. and Canadian citizens traveling as tourists must have proof of citizenship in the form of a valid passport or that has expired not more than five years ago, or a birth certificate (original or copy) or voter's registration accompanied by a government authorized ID with photo.

For stays over three weeks, or for nontourist visits, a valid passport is necessary. Resident aliens of the U.S. and Canada, and visitors from countries other than those in the Common Market (E.E.C.) and Japan, must have a valid passport and visa. A return or onward ticket is also required of all visitors.

ELECTRICITY

Current runs at 220 AC, 60 cycles. American-made appliances require French plug converters and transformers.

GETTING AROUND

Car rentals are easy to secure on the island, but it is best to ask your hotel to reserve one for you in advance, especially during the winter season. Roads are hilly, steep, narrow and winding, and drivers must know how to use a stick shift; your best options are VW Beetles, little open Gurgels, and Mini-Mokes. You'll save money if you rent by the week —

daily rates go as high as $60 a day, which includes unlimited mileage collision damage insurance (first $500 deductible) and free delivery Gas costs about $3.25 a gallon. None of the two gas stations (near the airport and in Lorient) is open on Sunday. St. Barts' first all-night automatic gas station recently opened near the airport, requiring magnetically sensitized cards on sale at the station.

Some reliable agencies are: **Avis** at the airport ☎ *27-71-43*; **Budget** airport and town ☎ *27-67-43*; **Hertz** at the airport ☎ *27-71-14* or *27-60-21*. A few hotels have their own fleet of rentals, and may ask you to book through them because of limited parking.

Taxis stations (two) are located at the airport and one in Gustavia on rue de la République. To call a **taxi**, dial ☎ *27-66-31* on a local phone. For night taxis, call **Jean-Paul Janin** ☎ *27-61-86*, **Raymond Gréaux** ☎ *27-66-32*, or **Mathilde Laplace** ☎ *27-60-59*.

Motorbikes, mopeds, and scooters are easy to rent, but you must wear a helmet, required by law. You must also have a motorbike or driver's license. Rentals can be found at: **Denis Dufau's Rent Some Fun** ☎ *27-70-59*, which also carries 18-speed mountain bikes or **Fredéric Suligeau** ☎ *27-67-89*.

Sleek catamarans leave the marina on Dutch St. Maarten between 9:00 and 9:30 a.m. daily, arriving in Gustavia harbor less than 90 minutes later. One-way trips are possible, but the usual fare is one day round trips.

You can also arrive on St. Barts by ferryboats from St. Martin, such as the *St. Barth Express III*, which leaves at 7:30 a.m. and returns from Marina Porte La Royale in Mariot at 3:30 p.m. and Bobby's Marina in Philipsburg at 4:15 p.m., arriving in Gustavia 45 minutes later. To reserve, ☎ *(590) 27-77-24*, FAX *(590) 27-7723*. Two other ferryboats are the *Dauphin II* and the *Bateau Dakar*.

Private boat charters can be arranged through Sibarth in Gustavia ☎ *(590) 27-62-38* or its American affiliate WIMGO, Newport RI ☎ *(800) 932-3222* or *(410) 849-8012*.

LANGUAGE

French is the official language, spoken with a quaint Norman dialect. Most people speak English, but do plan to come loaded with an attitude to match that of the French employees at many hotels.

MEDICAL EMERGENCIES

Gustavia has a **hospital** ☎ *27-60-35*, eight resident doctors, three dentists, one gynecologist, and specialists in opthalmology, dermatology etc. There are pharmacies at **La Savane Commercial Center** ☎ *27-60-61* and in Gustavia ☎ *27-61-82*.

MONEY

The official currency is the French franc; the official exchange rate (Aug. 1995) was approximately 5 francs to the American dollar. The rate is subject to change due to currency fluctuations. Dollars are accepted everywhere and prices are often quoted in dollars.

TELEPHONE

The area code for St. Barts is *590*. To call from the U.S. dial *011* (international access code), then *590* plus the local number in St. Barts. To call St. Barts from Dutch St. Maarten, dial 6 plus St. Barts's local six-digit number. To call St. Barts from other F.W.I (Martinique, Guadeloupe, and French St. Martin), you can dial direct.

Public phones require the use of "Telecartes" that look like credit cards and can be easily purchased at the Gustavia, St. Jean and Lorient post offices and at the gas station near the airport. Both local and international calls can be made from these phones using the card.

TIME

St. Barts is one hour ahead of Eastern Standard Time. When it is nine o'clock in St. Barts, it is eight o'clock in New York. During daylight saving time, there is no time difference.

TIPPING AND TAXES

Most hotels include tax and service in their quoted room rates; others add 5–15 percent to the bill.

TOURIST INFORMATION

The Tourist Board, called the Office de Tourisme, is located in attractive quarters on the Quai Général de Gaulle, across from the Capitainerie in Gustavia, open Monday–Friday 8:30 a.m.–6:00 p.m., and Saturday 8:30 a.m.–noon. From May to November, hours are a bit shorter. When writing to the **St. Barts Tourist Office**, use the address: *B.P. 113, Gustavia, 97098 Cedex, St. Barthélémy, F.W.I.* In the U.S. ☎ *(213) 658-7462.*

For what's happening weekly, pick up a current issue of *St. Barth Magazine*, distributed throughout the island. There's also an English program at noon on Mondays and Thursdays called "This Week in St. Barts."

WHEN TO GO

Three Kings Day on January 8 is celebrated with special ephinany cakes served at festivals. The 11th Anniversary of the St. Barts Music Festival is held Jan. 8–22, with jazz, chamber music and guests from the Metropolitan Opera. Carnival is celebrated Feb. 24, with a school parade, Mardi Gras pageant and parade, and the burning of Vaval, King of Carnival at Shell Beach. The award-winning cookbook author and instructor Steven Raichlen presents a one-week class on Caribbean cuisine at Hotel Yuana. The Festival of Gustavia is celebrated on August 20, with dragnet fishing contests, dances and parties. The Festival of St. Barthélémy is a feast day of the island's patron saint, celebrated with the pealing of church bells, a regatta, public ball, fireworks and the blessing of boats. The Fête du Vent on August 26–27 is honored with dragnet

fishing contests, dances, fireworks and a lottery in the village of Lorien
The Swedish Marathon Race is held in December 6. The Réveillon d
la Saint Sylvestre, on New Year's Eve, is a grand gala at the island's ho
tels and restaurants.

ST. BARTHÉLÉMY HOTELS	RMS	RATES	PHONE	CR. CARDS
Gustavia				
★★★★★ Castelets	10	$100–$700	(590) 27-61-73	None
★★★★★ Guanahani	80	$110–$785	(590) 27-66-60	A, MC, V
★★★★ Carl Gustaf Resort	14	$500–$1000	(800) 948-7823	A, MC
★★★★ Christopher Hotel	40	$195–$295	(590) 27-63-63	A, MC, V
★★★★ Club la Banane	9	$130–$440	(590) 27-68-25	A, MC, V
★★★★ Hotel le Toiny	12	$394–$760	(590) 27-88-88	A, MC, V
★★★★ Hotel St. Barth	28	$380–$705	(590) 27-61-81	A, MC, V
★★★★ Les Jardins de St. Jean	22	$60–$355	(590) 27-70-19	A, MC
★★★★ Manapany Cottages	52	$125–$990	(590) 27-66-65	A, MC
★★★ El Sereno Beach Hotel & Villas	29	$120–$340	(590) 27-64-80	A, MC, V
★★★ Emeraude Plage Hotel	30	$208–$500	(590) 27-64-78	MC, V
★★★ Filao Beach Hotel	30	$210–$420	(590) 27-64-84	A, CB, D, DC, MC V
★★★ Francois Plantation	12	$158–$405	(590) 27-78-82	A, MC
★★★ Hostellerie Trois Forces	8	$80–$175	(590) 27-61-25	A, MC
★★★ Hotel Baie des Flamands	24	$95–$135	(590) 27-64-85	A, MC
★★★ Marigot Bay Club	6	$80–$185	(590) 27-75-45	A, MC
★★★ St. Barth's Beach Club	52	$68–$115	(590) 27-60-70	A, MC
★★★ Taiwana Hotel	9	$955–$999	(590) 27-65-01	None
★★★ Tropical Hotel	22	$97–$281	(590) 27-64-87	A, MC
★★★ Village St. Jean Hotel	20	$85–$300	(590) 27-61-39	A, MC
★★★ Yuana Hotel	12	$150–$355	(590) 27-80-84	A, MC
★★ Baie des Agnes Hotel	9	$175–$230	(590) 27-63-61	A, CB, MC, V
★★ Grand Cul de Sac Hotel	36	$110–$335	(590) 27-60-70	A, MC
★★ Le P'tit Morne	14	$67–$120	(590) 27-62-64	A, MC
★★ Les Islets Fleuris Hotel Residence	8	$70–$220	(590) 27-64-22	None

ST. BARTHÉLÉMY HOTELS	RMS	RATES	PHONE	CR. CARDS
★★ Normandie	8	$65–$80	(590) 27-61-66	None
★★ White Sand Beach Cottages	4	$55–$205	(590) 27-82-08	A, MC

ST. BARTHÉLÉMY RESTAURANTS	PHONE	ENTREE	CR. CARDS

Gustavia

American			
★★ Santa Fe		$10–$21	None
French			
★★★★★ Le Toque Lyonnaise	(590) 27-6480	$43–$61••	A, DC, MC, V
★★★★ Ballahou	(590) 27-66-55	$15–$45	A, DC, MC, V
★★★★ Francois Plantation	(590) 27-7882	$16–$50••	A, MC, V
★★★★ La Fregate	(590) 27-6651	$10–$19	A, MC, V
★★★★ Le Gaiac	(590) 27-8888	$30–$60	A, MC, V
★★★★ Le Sapotillier	(590) 27-6028	$45–$60••	MC, V
★★★ Au Port	(590) 27-62-36	$19–$27••	A
★★★ Castelets	(590) 27-6173	$25–$35••	A, MC, V
★★★ Eddy's Ghetto		$15–$18••	None
★★★ Hostellerie Trois Forces	(590) 27-6125	$10–$50	A, MC, V
★★★ Marigot Bay Club & Art Gallery	(590) 27-7545	$40–$50	A, V
★★★ Pasta Paradise	(590) 27-8078	$10–$25	MC, V
★★★ Wall House	(590) 27-71-33	$30–$45	MC, V
★★ Adam	(590) 27-84-56	$35–$35••	A
International			
★★★ Le Select	(590) 27-86-87	$5–$10	None
Italian			
★★★ L'Escale	(590) 27-8106	$14–$29••	MC, V
★★ L'Entrepont	(590) 27-9060	$17–$33	MC, V
Latin American			
★★★ La Langouste	(590) 27-69-47	$23–$42	MC, V
★★ Le Pelican	(590) 27-6464	$20–$40	A, V

ST. BARTHÉLÉMY RESTAURANTS	PHONE	ENTREE	CR. CARDS
★★ Maya's	(590) 27-7361	$27–$35••	A, MC, V

Note: • Lunch Only

•• Dinner Only

Hurricane Update

All hotels listed in the book were open at presstime or anticipated hurricane damage to be repaired by the end of the year, except those noted below.

Baie des Aignes

Closed indefinitely.

Castelets

Closed indefinitely.

Hotel Baiedes Flamands

Closed indefinitely.

Taiwana Hotel

Badly damaged. No reopening date set.

White Sand Beach Cottages

Closed indefinitely.

ST. CROIX

Straw hats of every style entice shoppers at the market in Christiansted.

If St. Thomas is the sophisticated cosmopolitan island of the United States Virgins Islands, and St. John is the nature island, then St. Croix is a cross between the two, a rustic environment with tinges of elegance. Columbus thought St. Croix looked like a lush garden when he first saw it. Today, the island is a combination of graceful Danish architecture, modern development and natural beauty. There are two main towns, Christiansted on the northeast coast and Frederiksted on the west. Christiansted, designed by the Dutch West Indies Company as a planned community, shows its Dutch influence plainly, but it is more than just historic buildings. There is modern shopping, excellent dining, wonderful little bars and numerous outstanding resort hotels. Guarded by Fort Frederik, Frederiksted is a very quiet community on the west seashore, differing substantially from Christiansted because many of the original buildings were destroyed by a hurricane and high waves in 1867 and the fire of 1878. The real pleasure in Frederiksted is its bustling, colorful port, attracting freighters, cruiseships and navy vessels, vying for sleeping quarters in the well-kept harbor. For years, divers and macrophotography buffs around the world have known the famous **Frederiksted Pier** as one of the Caribbean's premier dives for all kinds of marine life. The port of Frederiksted has endured a major expansion, with vendor kiosks in Victorian gingerbread style lining the waterfront and two shaded bus stops installed in General Buddhoe Park. The old pump station has been converted into a hospitality lounge for tourists, a police substation, and a VITRAN bus token station. The best place to watch the glorious sunsets of St. Croix is now an old clock tower adjacent to the park that has been renovated to include a second-story observatory.

Bird's Eye View

Lying 75 miles east of Puerto Rico and 40 miles south of St. Thomas, St. Croix (rhymes with "boy"), is the largest of the U.S. Virgin Islands (which also include St. John and St. Thomas)—in fact more than two times larger than St. Thomas, but only 50,000 people live there. With a land mass 29 miles long by seven miles (82.2 square miles), St. Croix is separated from St. Thomas and St. John by 32 miles and a 12,000-foot oceanic trench. Rocky terrain fills the eastern sector, while the west end has higher elevation and more forests. Salt River on the north coast has now been approved as a National Park, including not only the sight where Columbus first landed, but also the underwater Salt River drop-off and canyon. Among the many natural attractions are wildlife refuges for birds and leatherback turtles, rain forest, botanic gardens, three nature preserves and three parks—one under the sea.

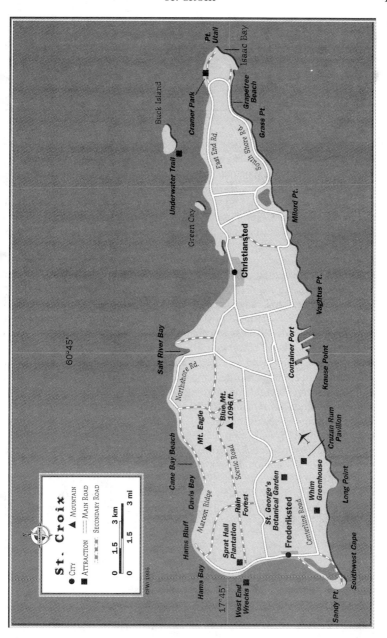

History

Columbus and his crew first came ashore at St. Croix's Salt River in 1493, but native Caribs did their best to fight them off. In haste he named the island Santa Cruz (Holy Cross) and sailed on to lay claim to St. John and St. Thomas. Eventually he renamed the entire group—including the British Virgin Islands at the time—for the legendary 11,000 virgin followers of St. Ursula. Today, we know that he wildly exaggerated the number of islands in the area. Soon after Columbus' departure, British, Dutch and French colonists began to establish farms on St. Croix, and in 1653, the island was awarded the crusaders' Order of St. John, better known as the Knights of Malta. France took control a few years later, and for the next 50 or so years, possession alternated between the French and the Spanish. As St. John and St. Thomas became acquired by the Danish West India Company and Guinea Company, St. Croix remained in the background. In 1773 the Danes also purchased St. Croix, attracted by its already burgeoning slave population and sugarcane fields. Planters and pirates mingled together during this golden age; some secluded coves are still said to harbor buried treasure. As the sugar beet was introduced to Europe, and the uprisings of slaves threatened the status quo, commercial interest in the island began to flag. Over the past 250 years, seven different conquerors took control of the island, though the Danish influence has remained the most lasting. During World War I, the Danes, sensing the sugarcane industry had all but dissolved, looked for buyers, finding the U.S. which was seeking a Caribbean base from which it could protect the Panama Canal. Eventually a great deal was struck between the two powers—$25 million dollars for three islands. The opening of the Carambola Beach Resort and Golf Club attracted a new wave of visitors to St. Croix starting in 1986. Though St. Croix was hard hit by Hurricane Hugo in 1989, islanders were not daunted and threw themselves body and soul into renovating the tourist facilities.

People

People born on St. Croix are called Crucians. The majority are of African descent, with a cultural mix from many other Caribbean islands. There is even a community of people from the island of Vieques (Puerto Rico). Lots of ex-pats from the U.S. also settle here. As well, there is a smattering of French, Germans and Italians who create their own small enclaves. A few Danes, stemming back to the original owners of the island, can even be found here.

Beaches

Buck Island offers guided tours of underwater snorkeling trails.

All beaches on St. Croix are public and free of charge, but if you go to a beach that is maintained by the resident hotel, you may have to pay a small fee for facilities. Lying 1.5 miles off northeast St. Croix, **Buck Island**, an 850-acre national monument, has some of the best beaches in the St. Croix area, reachable by boat from Christiansted; the six-mile trip takes 45 minutes to an hour. Some concessionaires that offer sail or motorboat tours also include a picnic lunch and an overland hike to the island's 400-foot summit with terrific views. Turtles also lay their eggs there. **Cane Bay** also has a stunning beach on the island's north side. Other fine beaches can be found at **Protestant Cay**, **Davis Bay**, **Cramer Park** on the east shore, and **Fredriksted Beach** to the north of town. The latter two have changing facilities and showers. Surfing is best on the north coast, and you'll find great shells on the northwest coast, from **Northside Beach** to **Ham's Bay**, as well as on **Sprat Hall Beach**.

Underwater

St. Croix offers a splendid, immense wall, a trench that stretches the island's northern coast from Christiansted west past Maroon Ridge and rivals similar attractions off Cozumel and the Caymans. The wall alone makes St. Croix the best dive destination in the U.S. Virgins. In particular, two areas along the northern coast, **Cane Bay** and **Salt River Canyon**, are among the best locations in the Eastern Caribbean; the first is a prime access to the sheer wall (and accessible from shore), the latter is an unusual formation in a sprawling undersea valley. The original **Fredriksted Pier**, famed for its profusion of sea horses and other macro life, is no more. In a controversial decision, it was torn down and replaced by another facility which is better able to accommodate shipping needs. Fortunately, sea life, including the delightful horses, is slowly regenerating on the new pilings and in a few years it may almost mirror the old site. Although a decent site showcasing four wrecks has been created off Butler Bay, if you're a sunken ship devotee, you'll want to head for St. Thomas or the British Virgins. St. Croix's visibility averages 75 feet year-round but can approach 100 feet in the summer. First-time snorkelers have been delighted for years by the underwater trail at **Buck Island**, just north of St. Croix's eastern tip, but the never-ending crowds can be a bit overwhelming. Additionally, Buck Island's conditions vary, causing jaded snorkelers to shrug off the site if visibility is poor or if fish are percolating elsewhere. Other good snorkeling sites are **Cane Bay**, **Green Cay** (a short swim off Chenay Bay), and Grapetree Beach (on the south coast near eastern tip).

Cane Bay Drop-Off

Possibly the best sites on St. Croix's wall are located around Cane Bay, highlighting an incredible diversity of sponge life: blood-red fire sponges, yellow tube sponges, red rope sponges, and many more, along with rare deep water coral life. Not much in the way of big fish (they run scared), but plenty of reef fish. An intermediate site with over a dozen possible profiles.

Jimmy's Surprise

The big fish hang out at Jimmy's, a seamount (60–95 feet) located east of Cane Bay. The west side of the pinnacle is sprinkled with sea fans, the east by barrel sponges, while groupers and nurse sharks are sometimes ensconced in a plunging crevice; gray angelfish trail divers eagerly. Currents, which can be a problem, make this strictly an advanced dive.

Northstar (a k a Twin Anchors)

A coral lip at 35 feet drops steeply to mushrooms of brain coral amid a dense staghorn forest. Beautifully encrusted old Dutch anchors are found, along with green morays and stingrays and, at 130 feet, a ledge that steps off into the abyss. An advanced shore dive from Davis Bay or intermediate from a boat.

Salt River Canyon

It's not a river but an underwater gorge carved into the Salt River Bay. Its west wall is probably the most popular boat dive on the island (25–130 feet), viable for both beginners and advanced. When the waters are clear, "it's like looking across the Grand Canyon," said one happy diver reminded of the pinnacles and valleys of the American southwest. The geography allows for plenty of swim-throughs amid green morays and barracudas, while lion's paw sea cucumbers loll about. A great night dive when basket stars, octopus and other nocturnal critters dance through the plankton-rich, bioluminescent waters.

The West End Wrecks

Four wrecks litter this floor off Butler Bay on the west coast. The best is a 177-foot steel-hulled freighter sunk in 1986, the Rosaomaira, which sits upright on a floor 110 feet down, encrusted and delicately spiced with red and pink sponges. Minimal penetration is available at any of the sites, but a well-oriented diver can see all four hulks in one dive. Novices should start with the North Wind, a 75-foot tug about 45 feet under and work their way deeper to the other sites (if abilities warrant). Also possible as a shore dive.

Dive Shops

Anchor Dive Center

Salt River Bay; ☎ *(800) 532-3483 or (809) 778-1522.*
Centrally located within ten minutes of all wall sites; two-tank dive $65. Nightly excursions to Salt River Canyon for superb nocturnal dives, $55. Limits boats to six divers. PADI Five Star dive center with courses from beginner to instructor.

Cane Bay Dive Shop

Cane Bay; ☎ *(809) 773-9913.*
Shore dives available in front of the shop to St. Croix's wall (two dives, $52.50 including all equipment). Regular two-tank dive from Zodiacs, $70. PADI affiliated.

Dive Experience PADI

Christiansted; ☎ *(800) 235-9047 or (809) 773-3307.*

A PADI Five Star facility and Instructor Development Center. Fish-feeding dives to Chez Barge, which features sociable morays and barracudas. Two-tank dive $70 including all equipment. Custom videos of your dive, $75, or you may rent video equipment.

V.I. Divers

Christiansted; ☎ *(800) 544-5911 or (809) 773-6045.*

PADI five-star facility (handles NAUI referrals) and the first shop on St. Croix (25 years old), Maximum group size, 12. Two-tank dive, $70. Resort course, $85. Snorkel trips to Green Cay, $35.

On Foot

It doesn't have St. Thomas' cosmopolitan infrastructure nor St. John' well-established National Park system. Neither fish nor fowl, St. Croix appears to be pondering a more environmentally conscious use of its interior. But its recently anointed **Salt River Bay National Park** lacks the funds to develop a trail system, and there is, so far, little organization of the paths and dirt roads which lead through the rainforest and hills surrounding **Blue Mountain** (the island's highest, 1096 feet). Interestingly, from afar, the island's fledgling environmental movement seems to be an outgrowth of community concerns, particularly the island's beautification program (originating from Hurricane Hugo) and a new recycling program (due to a landfill approaching capacity). It would appear that the island will soon be diversifying its forest management to include eco-tourism.

East End Beaches

Follow the East End Road to Cramer Park Beach. Begin your hike on the dirt road which continues east, passing "pocket" beaches on the way to Point Udall, the easternmost point of the United States (named for former Secretary of the Interior, Mo Udall). The dry point features bird watching and a variety of cactus and succulents. A vague trail can be located that leads around the tip to the southern coast and a secluded nude beach, Isaac Bay. From here, continuing west will bring you to Jack Bay, and another path that winds north back over the Goat Hills to Cramer Park. Allow two hours for the round-trip to Point Udall or three hours for the entire loop.

The Rain Forest

If you follow Route 63 four miles north of Frederiksted, you'll arrive at Hams Road, where a rough, sparsely-traveled four-wheel-drive track climbs Caledonia Valley. The hike begins here and ascends via the road through increasingly dense forest, passing a sugar mill and leading to the main ridge of St. Croix's north-coast spine. You'll soon encounter a junction; turn right, and take another right at an intersection soon thereafter. You are now on Creque Dam Road, in the heart of the island's rainforest (technically, a "subtropical moist forest") dominated by kapok trees, royal palms and hanging vines. The descent along Creque brings you back to Route 63, about two miles south of where you began. Although the entire trail is on a road open to vehicles, traffic is sparse, and this represents the best access into St. Croix's most untouched forests. Allow three to four hours.

Trekking Tours

St. Croix Environmental Association

Christiansted; ☎ *(809) 773-1989.*
Recently organized nonprofit provides guided nature hikes to East End Beaches, Salt River Bay and the rainforest. Tours average three hours and leave every morning; $20.

By Pedal

Easily the best cycling destination in the Virgins, St. Croix is less hilly and more spread out than its neighbors and features at least two inviting possibilities that visit the island's most scenic areas. The first starts one-and-a-half miles north of Frederiksted and uses Creque Dam Road—the easiest climb into St. Croix's rainforest—to access the main ridge (average elevation 700 feet), which snakes toward Salt River Bay. The other route is about 25 miles and takes in the rolling hills east of Christiansted: follow the East End Road along the north coast out to **Point Udall**, returning via the South Shore Road; the **Seven Hills** rising between these two roads offer excellent off-road and single-track potential and are frequented by the island's local riders. Those wanting easier pastures should stick to the area between Christiansted and Salt River Bay or to the fields along the southern coast (west of the airport), although both areas are subject to heavy vehicular traffic.

Bike Rental Shops

St. Croix Bike and Tour

Cotton Valley; ☎ *(809) 773-5004.*

Five-hour, 14-mile tours from Frederiksted through the rainforest, $45, including lunch and complementary water bottle. KHS 21-speed bike rentals, $25 day ($1 for half-day) including drop-off at hotel.

What Else to See

There are two major towns to see in St. Croix, the largest which is **Christiansted**, and the place most ships dock, **Frederiksted**. Christiansted is homey and culturally stimulating urban center, full of attractive 18th century buildings, many considered U.S. national historic sites. Covered walkways, mortar arches and colonnades lend an 18th century tropical ambiance. Take a look at the 17th-century French fortress, **Fort Chritiansvaern**, full of dungeons and cannons, from which there are excellent views of the harbor. A block away is the **Steeple Building**, today a historical museum with a small collection of Carib and Arawak relics and photos of the city from the 1800. Also historically intriguing is the old **Scalehouse**, built in 1856 to house the huge scale used to weigh merchandise being shipped abroad, and the **Government House**, now home to the U.S. District Court, but still one of the most beautiful Danish colonial buildings in the islands. Saturday morning is the best time to visit the outdoor markets at **"Shan" Hendricks Square**, chock full of tropical fruits and vegetables for sale, including the island's favorite–green genips. The harbor itself is a joy to contemplate; nearby, on the waterfront and **Company Street**, you'll find lots of stores.

On the western end of the island is Frederiksted, usually asleep until a cruise liner docks at port. In contrast to the colonial Danish style of Christiansted, Frederiksted is more Victorian gingerbread. Pick up a free walking tour guide from the visitor's bureau at the end of the pier. **Fort Frederiks**, on the far side of Lagoon Street, was the site of the 1848 proclamation freeing the slaves. **The Market Place** is two blocks south and one block east of the fort. Feel free to browse up and down streets and alleys here—the best way to glimpse the stunning architecture. One especially pretty building on Strand Street (along the waterfront) is the **Old Customs House** from the 18th century, now the headquarters of the Energy Commission, and the gingerbread-trimmed **Victorian House**. Not far from Christiansted is the **Cruzan Rum Factory**, which offers guided tour and drink samples.

North of Frederiksted, the shore road north will take you past **Sprat Hall**, an old plantation home turned guesthouse, all the way to the rain forest, and

he **Scenic Drive**. Heading down Centerline Road you'll arrive at the fully re-
tored **Estate Whim Plantation Museum**, dating back to the 17th century, and
ncluding a main house, and a half-dozen other structures including a wind-
nill and cook house. Other places outside the urban areas include the rain
orest at **St. Croix Leap**, where you will find a talented group of woodcarvers
vho create pieces carved in native mahogany. They practice a form of forest
nanagement, using wood from trees culled for specific purposes only. This is
lovely place to stroll and inspect the remains of a great house and a spec-
acular historical garden hosting some of the original crops of the native In-
ian tribes. Also worth a visit is the **St. Croix Aquarium**, notable for its
cological approach for staffing its tanks and fresh-food-feeding its "staff"
laily, by recycling marine life after they have "performed" for a time in the
quariums. The aquarium houses about 40 species of marine animals and
nore than 100 species of invertebrates.

City Celebrations

rucian Christmas Fiesta ★★★★

Various locations, Frederiksted.

This annual two-week festival celebrates the Christmas season with arts and crafts
exhibits, food fairs, parades (one for children, the other for adults), the selection of
Miss St. Croix, and the coronation of the festival's Prince and Princess. Most events
take place in Christiansted and Frederiksted. Each town has a Festival Village complete with amusement rides and nightly entertainment.

Historical Sites

ort Christiansvaern ★★★★

Downtown, Christiansted, ☎ *(809) 773-1460.*

Hours open: 8 a.m.–5 p.m.

This fort was built by the Danes in 1738 and rebuilt after hurricane damage in
1772. Its five rooms are decorated as they were in the 1840s. The admission charge
(free for those under 16) includes entry to the Steeple Building. The fort's newest
attraction is the St. Croix Police Museum, just opened in 1994. Created by Lt.
Elton Lewis a 20-year veteran of the St. Croix Police Department, the idea behind
the museum is to "promote high morale" and esprit de corps among police officers.
Exhibits include weapons, photos, artifacts and an old police motorcycle from St.
Croix's past.

ort Frederik ★★★

Emancipation Park, Frederiksted, ☎ *(809) 772-2021.*

Hours open: 8:30 a.m.–4:30 p.m.

This fort dates back to 1760, and is now an art gallery and museum. It is best known
as the site where on July 3, 1848, Governor General Peter Von Scholten freed the
Danish West Indies slaves.

teeple Building ★★★★

Downtown, Christiansted, ☎ *(809) 773-1460.*

Built by the Danish in 1754, this was their first Lutheran church, called the Churc of Lord God of Sabaoth. Deconsecrated in 1831, it served as everything from a bak ery to a school, and is now under the auspices of the U.S. National Park Servic Interesting exhibits tell the island's history, with emphasis on Native Americans an African Americans. The entry fee includes admission to Fort Christiansvaern.

Museums and Exhibits

Aquarium ★★▸

On the waterfront, Frederiksted, ☎ *(809) 772-1345.*
Hours open: 11 a.m.–4 p.m.

Opened in 1990 by marine biologist Lonnie Kaczmarsky, this aquarium display some 40 species of marine animals and more than 100 species of invertebrates. Wha makes it really unique is its "recycling" of sea life—after doing a stint in the tank creatures are released back to the open seas. Kaczmarsky is passionate on preservin the ocean environment; this is a good place to pick up hints before diving and snor keling on how to minimize your impact.

Parks and Gardens

St. George Village Botanical Gardens ★★★★▸

St. George Estate, Kingshill, ☎ *(809) 772-3874.*
Hours open: 9 a.m.–5 p.m.

Built among the ruins of a 19th-century sugarcane plantation workers' village, th little slice of paradise is not to be missed. The 17 acres were the site of an Arawa settlement dating to A.D. 100. Stop by the Great Hall to pick up a brochure for self-guided walking tour, then feast your senses on the lovely gardens, whic include 850 species of trees and plants. Each ecosystem of St. Croix is representec from rainforest to desert. The grounds also include restored buildings from th plantation era, including workers' cottages, storehouses and a blacksmith shop Warning: Don't buy the Aqua Venus bottled water in the giftshop. It's literall impossible to open! $1.00 for kids.

Tours

Buck Island Reef National Monument

Buck Island.

No trip to St. Croix is complete without a trip to this national monument islanc located three miles northeast of the mainland. It's a volcanic rock comprising som 300 acres with hiking trails, an observation tower, picnic tables and lovely beache The real attraction, however, is its surrounding 550 acres of underwater coral gar dens, home to more than 250 species of fish. This is a true snorkeler's paradise, wit an underwater trail and visibility of more than 100 feet. Several operators will tak you there and set you up with snorkel equipment: **Big Beard's Adventure Tour** (☎ *773-4482*), **Diva** (☎ *778-3161*), **Llewellyn's Charter** (☎ *773-9027*), **Teroro** (☎ *773-3161*), and **Mile Mark Water Sports** (☎ *773-2628*). Not to be missed!

Cruzan Rum Factory

West Airport Road, Frederiksted, ☎ *(809) 772- 799.*

Tours of the rum distillery and bottling plant are offered Monday-Friday from 9:00 11:30 a.m. and 1:00–4:15 p.m. Check out the colorful mural in the tasting room which depicts an old sugar plantation of the 1840s. You get to sample the product at the conclusion, but unless you're really interested and have never seen a rum factory before, skip this brief and relatively expensive tour (most such factories let you tour for free). One amusing sight: the mango tree, where workers write their names on the ripening fruit to keep the tourists from picking it.

state Mount Washington Planta ★★★

West coast, Frederiksted, ☎ *(809) 772-1026.*
Take a self-guided walking tour through the excavated ruins of a sugar plantation.

state Whim Plantation Museum ★★★★

Centerline Road, Frederiksted, ☎ *(809) 772-0598.*
Hours Open: 10 a.m.–4 p.m.
This partially restored sugar plantation gives a good look at what life was like in St. Croix in the 1800s. The handsome great house, built of lime, stone and coral and boasting walls three feet thick, is beautifully restored and filled with antiques. The grounds also include the cookhouse where you can feast on Johnny cakes ($1 each and well worth it, but the old woman who cooks them is a real crab and forbids pictures, and charges another dollar for the recipe), a woodworking shop, a windmill, and an apothecary. The giftshop is excellent; even if you're not interested in seeing the plantation, it's worth a trip just to peruse the interesting wares for sale. $1 for children.

uided Tours ★★★

Various locations, Frederiksted.
If you choose to leave the driving to someone else, these companies are happy to oblige with guided tours of St. Croix's highlights. Be sure to check in advance if admission charges to attractions are included in the rates. **Eagle Tours** *(☎ 778-3313)*, **St. Croix Safari Tours** *(☎ 773-6700)*, and **Travellers Tours** *(☎ 778-1636)*. **Take-a-Hike** offers walking tours and hikes; call ☎ 778-6997. For a birds-eye view of the island, call **St. Croix Aviation** *(☎ 778-0090)*, which offers sightseeing flights.

alt River Bay National Historical Park ★★★★

Route 80 near Route 75, Frederiksted.
These 912 tropical acres were added to the national park system under the Bush Administration. The park remains in a pristine condition and is home to many threatened and endangered plant and animal species. It is the largest remaining mangrove forest in the Virgin Islands and a great spot for birdwatching. The site includes an old earthen fort, an Indian ceremonial ball court, and burial grounds. This is also the only documented site on U.S. soil on which Christopher Columbus landed. His ill-fated "discovery" in 1493 led to a skirmish with Carib Indians, with fatalities on both sides.

Sports

Sports on St. Croix run the tropical gamut of water games to golf, horse back riding, sailing and sportsfishing. (For diving information, see "Div Sites" above.) Many visitors charter a sailboat to Buck Island or to othe neighboring islands. Prices on charters and boats-for-hire are controlled b the National Parks Service, but they may change, so do your best to negot ate. Scuba packages, which include hotel, often can save you loads of dollar

Golf

Various locations, Christiansted.

Duffers have three choices on St. Croix. **Carambol Golf Club** (☎ *778-5638)* is gorgeous, par-72 course designed by Robert Trent Jones. Located in St. Croix' northwest part, golfing on scenic 18 holes costs $50 per person per day (you can go around as many as you want), plus $18 mandatory cart rental for 18 holes. Nea Christiansted, the Buccaneer course is a challenging 18 holes. Greens fees are abou $25. Call ☎ *773-2100.* **The Reef Club** at Tegue Bay (☎ *773-8844)* is a nine-hol course. Greens fees are $8 for nine holes, $12 for 18.

Paul and Jill's Equestrian Sta

Sprat Hall, near Frederiksted, ☎ *(809) 772-2880.*

Well-regarded for their high-quality horses, this stable takes folks out for two-hou trail rides through the rainforest and past Danish ruins. Jill's family has lived on St Croix for some 200 years. Two-hour rides are about $50, and reservations are essential. Closed Sundays.

Watersports

Various locations, Frederiksted.

For scuba diving, try: **Dive Experience** (☎ *773-3307)*, **Virgin Island Diver** (☎ *773-6045)*, **Anchor Dive Center** (☎ *778-1522)*, **Blue Dolphin Divers** (☎ *773 8634)*, **Cruzan Divers** (☎ *772-3701)*, **Cane Bay Dive Shop** (☎ *773-9913)*, an **Dive St. Croix** (☎ *773-3434)*. For deep-sea fishing: **St. Croix Marin** (☎ *773 7165)*, **Captain Pete's Sportfishing** (☎ *773-1123)*, and **Cruzan Divers** (☎ *772 3701)*. For cruises and boating, try **Mile Mark Chaters** (☎ *773-2628)*, **Sundanc** (☎ *778-9650)*, **Llwewellyn's Charter** (☎ *773-9027)*, **Bilinda Charters** (☎ *773 1641)*, and **Junie Bomba's** (☎ *772-2482)*. For windsurfing: **Lisa Neuburger Wind surfing Center** (☎ *778-8312)* and **Minstral School** (☎ *773-4810)*.

Where to Stay

✪	**Fielding's Highest Rated Hotels in St. Croix**	
★★★★★	**Buccaneer Hotel**	$165–$390
★★★★★	**Westin Carambola Beach Resort**	$165–$330
★★★★	**Villa Madeleine**	$300–$425
★★★	**Cane Bay Reef Club**	$85–$165
★★★	**Club St. Croix**	$120–$194
★★★	**Cormorant Beach Club**	$110–$265
★★★	**Hibiscus Beach Hotel**	$95–$190
★★★	**Hilty House Inn**	$65–$130

♡	**Fielding's Most Romantic Hotels in St. Croix**	
★★★★★	**Buccaneer Hotel**	$165–$390
★★★★	**Villa Madeleine**	$300–$42
★★★★★	**Westin Carambola Beach Resort**	$165–$330

	Fielding's Budget Hotels in St. Croix	
★	**Cactus Inn**	$39–$45
★	**Danish Manor Hotel**	$49–$95
★	**Club Comanche**	$35–$126
★★	**On the Beach Resort**	$55–$110
★	**Cottages by the Sea**	$70–$110

St. Croix's roster of accommodations are varied. Some are intimate properties downtown while others are sprawling complexes including beaches and golf courses. While the accommodations on this island shy away from the cookie-cutter familiarity of typical chain motels, there is no shortage of amenities. The best will have air conditioning, direct-dial telephones, cable color television, and likely will have their own in-house dive service or a clos working relationship with a shop to facilitate their diving clients' conve nience. If you want to be near the beach, don't stay in Christiansted, wher none of the hotels has beachfront property. (The exception is Hotel on th Cay, with its postage-stamp strand.) Restoration since Hurricane Hugo find most properties in shipshape form. Most of the restaurants are in Christian sted, so you will probably need a car to dine out if you are staying along th coast.

Hotels and Resorts

The premier property on most anybody's list (not to mention the most expensive) is the **Buccaneer**, which sprawls down a hillside. It simply boasts the best facilities on the island—with three beaches, 18-hole golf course, jogging trail, spa, shops and a full water sports program. In any property on the beach, ask for rooms above the first floor, so you will feel safe leaving the window open to the breeze at night.

Christiansted

Anchor Inn   **$80–$145**   ★ ★

58-A King Street, ☎ *(800) 524-2030, (809) 773-4000, FAX (809) 773-4408.*
Single: $80–$125. Double: $90–$145.

This small hotel is set on the waterfront in the heart of Christiansted's National Historic District. Rooms have cable TV, refrigerators, air conditioning and telephones. some have porches as well. The on-site restaurant features American and West Indian fare. Other facilities include a lounge and pool. There's lots to see and do within walking distance.

Buccaneer Hotel   **$165–$390**   ★ ★ ★ ★ ★

Gallows Bay, ☎ *(800) 223-1108, (809) 773-2100.*
Double: $165–$390.

Set on a landscaped peninsula and encompassing 240 acres with three beaches, this deluxe property is located two miles east of Christiansted. A former sugar plantation has been transformed into a well-polished resort that the same family has run since its inception in 1946. Accommodations vary widely, through all are comfortable and include refrigerators and patios or balconies. The best rooms are right on the beach, and there are also beautifully decorated suites, rooms atop the hillside, and one-bedroom, two-bath cottages, also on the hill. Guests are kept busy with lots of recreational facilities, including an 18-hole championship golf course, eight tennis courts, two pools, a health club with sauna, and a shopping arcade. There are lots of organized activities and watersports. Four restaurants, four bars and nightly entertainment round out the action. Resort lovers are kept happy.

Club Comanche   **$35–$126**   ★

1 Strand Street, ☎ *(800) 524-2066, (809) 773-0210, FAX (809) 773-0210.*
Single: $35–$126. Double: $45–$126.

This hotel dates back to 1948 and it shows—not necessarily because of historical charm, but because it would really benefit from an overhaul. Guest rooms are small and simple; most have TV sets. The premises include two good restaurants and a pool. There's nothing special about this budget choice except the fine food, but the rates are quite reasonable.

Cormorant Beach Club	$110–$265	★ ★ ★

4126 La Grande Princesse, ☎ *(800) 548-4460, (809) 778-8920, FAX (809) 778-9218. Single: $110–$265. Double: $125–$265.*

Located three miles west of Christiansted on the north shore, this intimate resort makes for a great getaway. Guest rooms are in three-story beachfront villas, tastefully decorated with rattan furniture, bright fabrics, island artwork, and luxurious touches like bathrobes and fresh flowers. The grounds include a large free-form pool, two tennis courts, croquet, and a library. Guests can choose from several plans that include meals and drinks. The beach is excellent, and this spot gets high marks for service. No kids under five during the winter.

Hibiscus Beach Hotel	$95–$190	★ ★ ★

4131 La Grande Princesse, ☎ *(800) 442-0121, (809) 773-4042, FAX (809) 773-7668. Single: $95–$170. Double: $105–$190.*

Located three miles outside of Christiansted, this fine hotel just opened in 1992. Accommodations are in two-story buildings that line the palm-studded beach. All have ocean views off the balcony or patio, and are nicely done, though the baths are on the small side. There's a pretty pool on-site, as well as a beachfront restaurant and lounge. Snorkel equipment is included in the rates, and other watersports (which cost extra) are found nearby. Nice and small, with the feel of a resort but not the cost of one. Inquire about special golf, dive and all-inclusive packages.

Hotel Caravelle	$79–$255	★ ★

44A Queen Cross Street, ☎ *(800) 524-0410, (809) 773-0687, FAX (809) 778-7004. Single: $79–$255. Double: $89–$255.*

This waterfront hotel is in Christiansted's downtown historic district, overlooking the bay. Guestrooms are comfortable and pleasant, with modern furnishings and colorful fabrics. There's a pool on-site and watersports nearby. The waterfront restaurant and bar are lively and popular with boaters. A good in-town choice, and the rates are reasonable.

Hotel on the Cay	$95–$198	★ ★ ★

Protestant Cay, ☎ *(800) 524-2035, (809) 773-2035, FAX (809) 773-7046. Single: $95–$188. Double: $95–$198.*

Located on a small cay in Christiansted Harbor, a two-minute ferry ride from the mainland, this imaginatively landscaped hotel offers great seclusion, though boat service to Christiansted is frequent. Guest rooms are comfortable and pleasing, with extras like coffeemakers, VCRs, and private terraces with water views. The grounds are dotted with waterfalls, canals and bridges, lending a welcome tropical feel. Recreational options include a pool, tennis court and watersports on the small beach. Nice, if you don't mind the isolated location.

King Christian Hotel	$80–$135	★ ★ ★

59 King's Wharf, ☎ *(800) 524-2012, (809) 773-2285, FAX (809) 773-9411. Single: $80–$125. Double: $100–$135.*

Located in the heart of town overlooking Christiansted Harbor, this hotel opene
in 1940, though the building it is housed in is some 200 years old. Guest rooms ar
spacious and air-conditioned; the best ones have large furnished balconies with har
bor views. Those counting every penny can stay in one of the 15 budget room
which have no views but are clean and comfortable. There's a restaurant and coffee
shop on the premises, as well as a pool and dive center. Boats to Buck Island leave
right from their dock. A great in-town choice.

St. Croix by the Sea   **$90–$145**   ★★★
St. John's Estate, ☎ *(800) 524-5006, (809) 778-8600.*
Single: $90–$145. Double: $90–$145.
This family-run resort is located three miles west of Christiansted. Guestrooms ar
contemporary and comfortable enough, but not particularly special. The ground
include a large saltwater pool, (the site of scuba lessons), four tennis courts, two res
taurants and a bar. A European plan is available for an extra $10 per person per day.

Westin Carambola Beach Resort   **$165–$330**   ★★★★★
Kings Hill, ☎ *(800) 228-3000, (809) 778-3800, FAX (809) 778-1682.*
Double: $165–$330.
Situated on 26 acres on the north shore of Davis Bay, this property reopened in th
summer of 1993 after renovations and joining the Westin hotel family. Guestroom
(which any other property would rightfully call suites) are found in villa-style, red
roofed buildings surrounded by lush landscaping. All are quite extraordinary, with
sitting areas, coffeemakers, minibars, enormous bathrooms and lovely English
country furnishings. Best of all are the large screened porches—the perfect spot to
while away the hours far from mosquitoes' harm. The only drawback is that many
rooms are not right on the beach, though it's only a quick stroll to the sand
Request a second-floor unit, which offers better views, higher ceilings and more pri
vacy. Facilities include 18 holes of golf, a pool, four tennis courts, three restaurants
two bars and watersports, including a dive shop. Very fine, and the beach is divine.

Frederiksted

Sprat Hall Plantation   **$95–$220**   ★★
Route 63N, ☎ *(809) 772-0305.*
Single: $95–$215. Double: $110–$220.
This family-run hotel is structured around the island's oldest great house, which
dates back to 1670. Located just north of Frederiksted, accommodations range
from nonsmoking, antique-filled rooms in the great house to air-conditioned con
temporary seaview units, some with TV. There are also several one-bedroom cot
tages with kitchenettes for rent. The grounds are lush and inviting, and dinner is a
somewhat formal affair. No kids under 16 in the great house rooms. You'll be need
ing a car.

Apartments and Condominiums

Self-catering is easy, and most properties—from private homes to condos—are avail
able with maid service. Supermarkets are modern and well-stocked, and fresh local fruits
and vegetables can be bought at market. You will probably need to count the cost of a car
rental into most choices.

Christiansted

| Cane Bay Reef Club | $85–$165 | ★★★ |

1407 Kingshill Street, Kingshill, ☎ (800) 253-8534, (809) 778-2966, FAX (809) 778-2966.
Single: $85–$165. Double: $85–$165.
Located about 20 minutes from both Christiansted and Frederiksted, this property was rebuilt after Hurricane Hugo's extensive damage. All units are one-bedroom apartments with modern kitchens, tiled balconies and ceiling fans. The best choices are the two condominium units—the only ones that are air-conditioned—which are much more nicely furnished. There's a restaurant, bar, and saltwater pool on-site; the beach is a three-minute walk. You'll definitely want a rental car, as this place is fairly remote.

| Caribbean View All-Suites | $80–$120 | ★ |

66 La Grande Princesse, ☎ (809) 773-3335, FAX (809) 773-1596.
Single: $80–$120. Double: $80–$120.
Located a half-mile from the sea and 10 minutes from downtown Christiansted, this complex consists of two-story apartment buildings. Each has four one-bedroom units with VCRs, kitchens, terraces and maid service. Facilities are limited to a pool and shuffleboard court; you'll need a car to get around. Decent for the rates.

| Club St. Croix | $120–$194 | ★★★ |

3280 Golden Rock, ☎ (800) 635-1533, (809) 773-4800, FAX (809) 778-4009.
Single: $120–$194. Double: $120–$194.
This friendly beachfront condominium resort is one mile out of Christiansted. Accommodations include well-furnished studios, a penthouse, and one- and two-bedroom apartments, all with full kitchens, cable TV, private balconies, ceiling fans and air conditioning. A nearby oil refinery sometimes taints the air if the wind comes from the east. Recreational choices are good for a condo operation, with three tennis courts, a large pool, Jacuzzi, limited watersports, a catamaran for cruising the high seas and a bar and restaurant. Inquire about special packages.

| Colony Cove | $130–$290 | ★★ |

3221A Golden Rock, ☎ (800) 524-2025, (809) 773-1965, FAX (809) 778-4009.
Single: $130–$290. Double: $130–$290.
Set on the beach two miles from Christiansted, this condominium complex offers two-bedroom, two-bath units with full kitchens, laundry facilities, private balconies and ocean views. Each is individually owned and decorated, but all can be counted on for clean, comfortable living. The premises includes a restaurant, two tennis courts, a business center and a pool. Watersports await on the wide beach.

| Cormorant Cove | $105–$230 | ★★★ |

4126 La Grande Princesse, ☎ (800) 548-4460, (809) 778-8920, FAX (809) 778-9218.
Single: $105–$230. Double: $105–$230.
Set right on the beach near its sister property, the Cormorant Beach Club, this condo complex has 16 units of one to three bedrooms. All are luxuriously furnished, air-conditioned, and have fully equipped kitchens, private terraces, maid service, washers and dryers and Jacuzzis. The grounds include a large pool and two

tennis courts. Guests can use all the facilities at the Cormorant Beach Club, so it works out as the best of both: apartment living and hotel amenities.

Gentle Winds Resort $230–$305 ★★

9003 Gentle Winds, ☎ (809) 773-3400, FAX (809) 778-3400.
Single: $230–$305. Double: $230–$305.

Set on the beach some eight miles northwest of Christiansted, this contemporary condo complex offers two- and three-bedroom units. All are air-conditioned, have two or three baths, full kitchens, VCRs, telephones, and nice sea views. There's a pool, two tennis courts, games room, and a beach bar, but you're on your own for meals. Guests can get reduced rates at the Carambola Beach Golf Course, eight miles away. Ideal for families.

Horizons $1400–$5000 ★★★

Kings Hill, ☎ (609) 751-2413, FAX (609) 751-2414.
Double: $1400–$5000.

Horizons combines the privacy and luxury of a private villa along with full resort amenities. Located on the grounds of the Carambola Beach Hotel, the house has four master bedrooms each with its own bath and air conditioner, a gourmet kitchen, a 40-foot great room with stereo, cable TV, VCR and a video library, a full-sized pool, expansive sundecks and a whirlpool bath. The fee, which is for seven nights, includes maid service and transfers to and from the airport. Guests can use the services at Carambola and get discounted greens fees at its golf course.

Schooner Bay Resort $145–$295 ★★

5002 Gallows Bay, ☎ (800) 524-2025, (809) 773-9150, FAX (809) 778-4009.
Single: $145–$295. Double: $145–$295.

You can walk to downtown Christiansted from this three-story condominium resort, which overlooks the harbor. Two- and three-bedroom units are plush, with full kitchens, nice decor, living and dining areas, VCRs, radios, telephones, washer/dryers, and private balconies. The three-bedroom condos have an upstairs and downstairs. There's a pool, Jacuzzi, and tennis court on-site, but you'll have to look elsewhere for meals.

Sugar Beach Condominiums $110–$250 ★★

3245 Estate Golden Riock, ☎ (800) 524-2049, (809) 773-5345, FAX (809) 773-1359.
Single: $110–$250. Double: $110–$250.

Situated on a reef-protected beach beside a historic sugar mill in a residential neighborhood two miles out of Christiansted, this condo complex has studios and apartments with one to three bedrooms. All have full kitchens, seaview balconies, and modern, comfortable appointments. You'll pay extra for maid service. There are two tennis courts, a pool, and the private beach, but no restaurant.

Villa Madeleine $300–$425 ★★★★

19A Teague Bay, ☎ (800) 548-4461, (809) 778-7377, FAX (809) 773-7518.
Single: $300–$425. Double: $300–$425.

This deluxe operation is set on a hill between two beaches, some 15 minutes from Christiansted, with sweeping views of Buck Island and Duggins Reef. Accommodations are in one- and two-bedroom villas beautifully done and including sitting rooms, modern, full modern kitchens, four-poster beds and chaise lounges in the bedrooms, two full baths, and—best of all—decent-sized private pools. Really luxurious! The on-site restaurant draws raves for its gorgeous decor and smashing food, and there's also a bar, billiards room and tennis court. This is one of St. Croix's best properties, and all is quite sophisticated and elegant. The only drawback is the distance to the beach—you'll have to drive.

Waves at Cane Bay $85–$195 ★★

Kingshill, Kingshill, ☎ (800) 545-0603, (809) 778-1805, FAX (809) 778-4945.
Single: $85–$195. Double: $85–$195.

Located on the north shore a short walk from Cane Bay Beach, this operation offers large studios with kitchens, screened porches, ceiling fans and TVs. Only some are air-conditioned, but all are quite comfortable. Maids tidy up six days a week. The pool is a natural sea-fed grotto and the snorkeling is great off the small beach. There's a bar but no restaurant, and you'll definitely need a car, as this spot is somewhat remote.

Frederiksted

Chenay Bay Beach Resort $125–$210 ★★

Estate Green Cay, ☎ (800) 548-4457, (809) 773-2918, FAX (809) 773-2918.
Single: $125–$180. Double: $125–$210.

This cottage colony is located on 30 acres three miles from Christiansted. The West Indian-style cottages are scattered about well-landscaped grounds; all have kitchenettes and patios, and most are air-conditioned. The grounds, surrounded by a 14-acre wildlife preserve, include a pool, two tennis courts, watersports (snorkeling and kayaking are free), the beach, and a casual restaurant and bar. Nice and relaxing, but you'll want a car to get around.

Cottages by the Sea $70–$110 ★

127A Smithfield, ☎ (800) 323-7252, (809) 772-0495, FAX (809) 772-0495.
Single: $70–$110. Double: $70–$110.

Located on the western end of the island just outside of Frederiksted, this basic complex is right on the beach. The 20 wood and fieldstone cottages are simply furnished and have kitchenettes, patios, and air conditioning. Maids tidy things up daily. Three large patios are situated on the beach for sunning and barbecueing. No children under eight at this agreeable spot.

On the Beach Resort $55–$110 ★★

☎ (800) 524-2018, (809) 772-1205, FAX (809) 772-1757.
Single: $55–$90. Double: $65–$110.

No kids under 14 at this small hotel, which draws a largely gay clientele. Accommodations are spacious and tropically furnished; most have kitchens but only some have balconies. The premises includes a good beach for snorkeling, a pool, a bar and a bistro open for breakfast and lunch. You'll want a car to get around, though downtown Frederiksted can be walked to in about 10 minutes.

Inns

Most of the inns on St.Croix are located in historic buildings in Christiansted, rife with Danish colonial architecture. A few are situated on the shores. All exude the personality of the owners, who tend to be extremely personable.

Christiansted

Anchor Inn of St. Croix   **$80–$150**   ★★

58 King Street, ☎ *(800) 524-2030, (809) 773-4000, FAX (809) 773-4408.*
Single: $80–$130. Double: $95–$150.

This friendly little spot is located in downtown Christiansted in a courtyard at the harbor's edge. Due to motel-like furnishings and tinted windows that keep the sun out, rooms are on the drab side. There's a pool, restaurant, coffeeshop, and bar on-site, as well as extensive watersports—everything from scuba to deep-sea fishing. Popular despite its uninspired accommodations.

Hilty House Inn   **$65–$130**   ★★★

2 Hermon Hill, ☎ *(800) 524-2026, (809) 773-2594, FAX (809) 773-2594.*
Single: $65–$160. Double: $85–$130.

This bed and breakfast was built on the ruins of an 18th-century rum distillery, 1.5 miles from the beach. Guest rooms are individually decorated and have private baths, but no air conditioning. There's also two one-bedroom cottages with kitchenettes. TV can be watched in the library, and there's a large pool on-site. Most rooms at this pleasant spot are under $100.

Pink Fancy Hotel   **$70–$120**   ★★

27 Prince Street, ☎ *(800) 524-2045, (809) 773-8460, FAX (809) 773-6448.*
Single: $70–$120. Double: $80–$120.

It is indeed pink (the shutters, anyway) and it is indeed somewhat fancy at this popular inn, which comprises four buildings, the oldest dating to 1780. Located downtown within walking distance of shops and restaurants, this intimate inn is loaded with charm. Guest rooms are immaculate, and each boasts West Indian decor, air conditioning, and a kitchenette. The grounds are lush with lots of plants, and include a nice pool and hammocks for lazy afternoons. The rates include continental breakfast and free drinks.

Low Cost Lodging

Since lodging is based on the scale of the American dollar, not much is to be found in the category of cheap, unless you can bear very small rooms and basic furnishings. Make sure the property is close enough to a beach or stores/restaurants if you can't afford to rent a car. **Danish Manor** takes advantage of its location in the center of Christiansted, although you'll need to take a bus to the beach.

Christiansted

Cactus Inn   **$39–$45**   ★

48 King Street, ☎ *(809) 692-9331.*
Single: $39. Double: $45.

As the rates suggest, you won't find much in the way of amenities here. But if you're seeking a decent, no-frills room with air conditioning, cable TV, and private bath, they'll do right by you.

Danish Manor Hotel   **$49–$95**   ★

2 Company Street, ☎ *(800) 524-2069, (809) 773-1377, FAX (809) 773-1913.*
Single: $49–$85. Double: $59–$95.

This downtown inn consists of an old West Indian-style manor house and a newer
addition. The motel-style guestrooms are small and simply furnished, but do have
private baths, air conditioners, refrigerators and cable television. There's a pool,
Italian restaurant, and bar on the premises. Good value for the rates, and lots
(including the beach) within walking distance.

Frederiksted

Frederiksted Hotel   **$80–$110**

20 Strand Street, ☎ *(800) 524-2025, (809) 772-0500, FAX (809) 772-0500.*
Single: $80–$100. Double: $90–$110.

This small hotel overlooks the harbor at the edge of town. The air-conditioned
guest rooms are comfortable enough, but lack phones and are somewhat dark. Ask
for a seaview room, by far the best accommodations. There's a pool and pool bar,
the site of entertainment on the weekends. The restaurant serves breakfast only. A
free shuttle transports guests to the beach and nearby tennis courts.

Where to Eat

Fielding's Highest Rated Restaurants in St. Croix

★★★★★	Cafe Madeleine	$18–$26
★★★★	Kendrick's	$14–$26
★★★	Blue Moon	$10–$20
★★★	Harvey's	$8–$20
★★★	Le St. Tropez	$10–$25
★★★	Mahogany	$26–$36
★★★	Top Hat	$14–$28

Fielding's Special Restaurants in St. Croix

★★★★★	Cafe Madeleine	$18–$26
★★★	Blue Moon	$10–$20
★★★	Harvey's	$8–$20
★★	Comanche	$9–$21
★★	Picnic in Paradise	$10–$20

Fielding's Budget Restaurants in St. Croix

★	Mango Grove	$5–$8
★★	Tivoli Gardens	$6–$20
★★★	Harvey's	$8–$20
★★★	Blue Moon	$10–$20
★★	Comanche	$9–$21

The best restaurants are in Christiansted, though you can find a handful of good ones in Frederiksted. New ones sprout up all the time; it's best to ask your hotel to recommend the latest trend-setters. Prices are not cheap and could run you up to $100 for two (without wine) for the top-class options

's always safer to make a reservation than not to; on the weekends it's es-
:ntial, particularly if you are headed for a show afterwards. Grilled fish are
ιe specialty of the island, particularly **Comanche Restaurant**, which adds ex-
:emely exotic sauces. **Chart House** has a terrific view of the boat-filled harbor.

Christiansted

ntoine's   **$$$**   ★ ★

58A King Street, ☎ *(809) 773-0263.*
International cuisine. Specialties: Omelets, goulash, wienerschnitzel, lobster.
Lunch: 11 a.m.–2:30 p.m., entrees $14–$32.
Dinner: 6:30–9:30 p.m., entrees $14–$32.
Many visitors get their wakeup javas at this second-floor charmer in the Anchor Inn.
The breakfast menu boasts at least a dozen omelets loaded with interesting combi-
nations. But that's not all that's here—bartenders proffer tropical concoctions and
a huge selection of beer to a lively crowd. At dinner, hearty and tasty German and
Middle-European food appears on the generous plates—despite the restaurant's
French name. From the terrace, there's a great view of seagoing vessels on the wharf
below.

anana Bay Club   **$$$**   ★ ★

44A Queen Cross St., ☎ *(809) 778-9110.*
Seafood cuisine.
Lunch: 7 a.m.–4 p.m., entrees $15–$25.
Dinner: 4–11 p.m., entrees $15–$25.
Sit surrounded by 18th-century buildings and 20th-century businessfolk who
gather for gossip and low-key deal-making in this open-air eatery known for fresh
seafood, burgers and steaks. The Banana Bay Club is located in the Caravelle Hotel,
one of downtown's lodging bargains. You don't have to pay high prices for unsur-
prising, well-prepared food and a great view of the Christiansted harbor.

afe Madeleine   **$$$**   ★ ★ ★ ★ ★

Estate Teague Bay, Teague Bay, ☎ *(809) 773-8141.*
Italian cuisine.
Dinner: 6–10 p.m., entrees $18–$26.
The crowning glory of the Villa Madeleine, the romantic haven on the east coast of
the island, this restaurant recalls a posh plantation house of bygone days. It's all
dolled up in butter-yellow paint, and the patio bursts with bright blooms. The pri-
marily Italian-continental cuisine is some of the finest on the island, with specialties
like lamb served with rosemary and garlic in a Barolo wine glaze and open ravioli
with fresh lobster in a sauterne sauce. On Sundays, brunch is served from 11:00
a.m.-2:00 p.m. for $16.

hart House   **$$$**   ★ ★

59 King's Wharf, ☎ *(809) 773-7718.*
American cuisine. Specialties: Prime rib, mud pie.
Dinner: 6–10 p.m., entrees $14–$26.
Most stateside visitors are familiar with this chain restaurant based in California.
Christiansted's version does not disappoint—the waitstaff is perky, the prime rib is
cut the way you like it, the copious salad bar is one of the best on the island, and it's

constantly mobbed. There's no outdoor dining, but the decor is nautical and it's s
close to the water that it really doesn't matter, especially when you're lucky to get
seat with a harbor view.

Comanche $$ ★ ★

1 Strand Street, ☎ *(809) 773-2665.*
International cuisine.
Lunch: 11:30 a.m.–2:30 p.m., entrees $9–$21.
Dinner: 6–9 p.m., entrees $9–$21.

A pianist tickles the ivories nightly at this intimate and consistently reliable terrac
restaurant in the Comanche Inn. Decor is south-seas style, with wicker chairs an
fans, and the cuisine runs the gamut from Chinese specialties to conch chowde
Serving three meals a day, the Comanche is also known for a filling West India
lunch.

Dino's $$$ ★ ★

4-C Hospital Street, ☎ *(809) 778-8005.*
Mediterranean cuisine. Specialties: Fresh pasta.
Dinner: entrees $14–$20.

After a tour of the nearby 17th-century Fort Christiansvaern, repair to this historica
house serving thoroughly modern Italian fare. Chef Dwight deLude makes his past
fresh every day, and he likes to experiment; sometimes there's ravioli made wit
sweet potatoes or other interesting vegetables. Sauces are always intensely flavore
and made with fresh garden herbs.

Harvey's $$ ★ ★ ★

11 Company Street, ☎ *(809) 773-3433.*
Latin American cuisine.
Lunch: entrees $8–$20.
Dinner: entrees $8–$20.

Motherly Sarah Harvey is the chef-owner of this small West Indian dinner hous
and local hangout. Timid diners won't remain so for long, because Harvey likes t
visit at every table, and since there's no real menu, she'll discuss what's cookin' fo
the evening. Sometimes there's goat water or local seafood in butter sauce, and
mountain of island-grown veggies and starches. The decor could be described bes
as thrift-shop modern: plastic tableware and folding chairs.

Kendrick's $$$ ★ ★ ★ ★

52 King Street, ☎ *(809) 773-9199.*
International cuisine.
Dinner: 6–10 p.m., entrees $14–$26.

Dine among the antiques in yet another restored old Danish home that's one of the
island's toniest (and priciest) eating establishments. The nattily attired and well
trained wait staff keeps wineglasses full and dishes cleared deftly between courses
Chef David prepares island-inspired French cuisine and his specialties often include
a luscious pork loin with a roasted pecan crust or rack of lamb marinated with
crushed herbs and served with roasted garlic and thyme sauce. There are three din
ing rooms, and you'll be equally well-treated no matter which one you end up in.

Mahogany $$$ ★★★

Kings Hill, ☎ (809) 778-3800.
Seafood cuisine.
Dinner: 6–10 p.m., entrees $26–$36.
This gourmet outlet at the Westin Carombola is open only on Tuesday, Thursday and Saturday. The formal dining room has a high, high beamed ceiling and pretty furniture for a gracious atmosphere. The menu features such delicacies as French snails sauteed in garlic, shallots and pernod and wrapped in chicken tenderloins; pan-seared mahi mahi encrusted with hazelnuts; and West Indian shrimp filled with backfin lump crabmeat and fine herbs. There are also beef and lamb dishes for carnivores. Men are requested to don collared shirts and slacks.

Mango Grove $ ★

King and Queen Cross streets, ☎ (809) 773-0200.
American cuisine.
Lunch: from 11 a.m., entrees $5–$8.
Dinner: to late, entrees $5–$8.
I couldn't resist checking this place out after spotting their sign out front: "Hostess is getting a pedicure. Please seat yourself." That about sums up the casual atmosphere at this cool little spot in a nicely shaded courtyard. Munch on typical salads, burgers or sandwiches and quaff a cool beer at this friendly spot—and be sure to compliment the hostess on her perfect feet.

Picnic in Paradise $$ ★★

Cane Bay, ☎ (809) 778-1212.
Italian cuisine.
Dinner: entrees $10–$20.
It's worth a drive up the north coast to dine at this lovely indoor-outdoor restaurant in a protected coral cove near Cane Bay. Whether on the deck or in a breeze-filled dining room, meals are generally well-prepared and often include conch fritters, filet mignon and other West Indian-Continental specialties. If not quite paradise, it comes pretty close, if only for an hour.

Saman $$$ ★

Kings Hill, ☎ (809) 778-3800.
American cuisine.
Dinner: 6–10 p.m., entrees $15–$20.
The best reason to come to this restaurant at the Westin Carombola is to sit outside, enjoy the sea breeze, and groove to the excellent live jazz every Tuesday evening (other nights see steel, calypso and island bands). The menu offers up seafood, steaks, chicken and pasta dishes; the caesar salad with char-grilled shrimp, salmon or chicken is especially good. Wednesday nights are given over to a seafood buffet ($29), while Friday is a pirate theme night with limbo dancers and other entertainment (also $29).

Tivoli Gardens $$$ ★★

39 Strand, ☎ (809) 773-6782.
International cuisine.
Lunch: 11:15 a.m.–2:30 p.m., entrees $6–$15.

Dinner: 6–9:30 p.m., entrees $11–$20.

There's a fairyland of lights and greenery on the spacious porch of this popula saloon facing Christiansted harbor. A surprising carnival of eclectic treats are pre pared with aplomb—witness Hungarian goulash and a Thai curry on the sam menu. The frequently served chocolate velvet cake is wicked on the waistline an heaven on the tastebuds.

Top Hat   **$$$**   ★★

52 Company Street, ☎ (809) 773-2346.
Seafood cuisine. Specialties: Herring appetizers, frikadeller with red cabbage, gravlax.
Dinner: 6–10 p.m., entrees $14–$28.

Probably the only Danish restaurant on the island, Top Hat has consistently please visitors and residents for 20 years. The Danish owners—chef Bent Rasmussen an his wife Hanne—run a spic-and-span operation on the top floor of a charming gir gerbread trimmed-house. Located above a shopping center, it's painted in mute tasteful tones.

Frederiksted

Blue Moon   **$$**   ★★

17 Strand St., ☎ (809) 772-2222.
International cuisine.
Dinner: entrees $10–$20.

Hot jazz and hot food draw folks to this restaurant and club in a quaint Victoria building in the heart of funky, laid-back Frederiksted. The place bustles Frida night for live jazz concerts and at Sunday brunch, and this bistro's creative chefs ar always experimenting with different cooking styles. Some nights, specials could b Cajun, or at other times French-influenced Asian temptations. Usually there are on or more chocolate delights on the dessert menu. Closed July-September.

Le St. Tropez   **$$$**   ★★

67 King Street, ☎ (809) 772-3000.
French cuisine.
Lunch: entrees $10–$25.
Dinner: entrees $10–$25.

This amiable bistro is a corner of Gallic charm in the center of the West Indian tow of Frederiksted. Familiar favorites like quiche, roast duck and frog legs are serve on a terrace or in a romantic dining room. The woodsy bar is a little dark, but that how many people like it.

Where to Shop

Shopping only seems to get better on this island, though the brick or stone sidewalks and some hefty flights up may make it difficult for those with knee problems or the elderly. If you're healthy and able, pray that your ship docks in Christiansted's **Gallows Bay** (where there are more stores than at Frederiksted). Some new complexes near the water (**Pan Am Pavilion** and **Caravelle Arcade**) are more walker-friendly. If you are turned on by low prices, look for substantial savings on fine china and crystal (30–50 percent), perfume, liquor (60 percent cheaper), cigarettes (40 percent cheaper), watches, gold jewelry and imported cosmetics. If you're in need of resort wear and Indonesian style sarongs, head for **Java Wraps** in the Pan Am Pavilion. **Wayne James Boutique**, a famous native designer, offers excellent ladies' fashions. Also recommended are the gift shop at Estate Whim Plantation and the 1870 Town House Shoppes in Christiansted. U.S. citizens are allowed to bring home $1200 worth of goods tax-free and five-fifths of liquor (six, if one is locally produced, plus up to $100 in gifts.

St. Croix Directory

ARRIVAL

American Airlines offers nonstop service to St. Croix from Miami, with connecting service from NYC, Newark and Raleigh/Durham via Miami on San Juan. (Flights into San Juan connect into St. Croix on convenient commuter airlines.) **Carnival Airlines** flies nonstop from Miami, NYC, Orlando and Newark to San Juan with connecting flights on commuters. **Continental** flies direct from Newark to St. Croix, with connecting service from Boston, Chicago, Detroit and Philadelphia via Newark. **Delta** flies direct from Atlanta to St. Croix, nonstop from Atlanta to San Juan. **Trans World Airways** flies nonstop from NYC, St. Louis and Miami to San Juan. **United Airlines** flies nonstop from Dulles International (Washington, D.C.) to San Juan. **USAir** flies nonstop from Baltimore, Charlotte and Philadelphia to San Juan. Once you're in the Caribbean you might consider **Air Anguilla**, which flies direct from Anguilla to St. Croix, and returns via St. Thomas. **American Eagle** flies daily from San Juan to St. Croix and back. **LIAT** flies from St. Croix to other Caribbean islands to the south and return. **Sunaire Express** offers frequent jet-prop and daily service between St. Croix and St. Tho mas, and San Juan to St. Thomas and St. Croix and return. **Virgin A** makes passenger/freight service between San Juan and St. Croix and i lands to the south. It also has a charter ambulance.

One of the joys of the USVI is the ability to island hop. Inexpensiv transportation via ferry is available among the **USVI** and the **BVI** as we opening up other possibilities for day trips. Year-round Caribbea cruises from San Juan, Miami and other stateside ports go to St. Croi and return.

BUSINESS HOURS

Stores open weekdays 9 a.m.–5 p.m., some later in Christiansted. Bank generally open Monday–Thursday 9 a.m.–2:30 p.m. and Friday 9 a.m. 2 p.m. and 3:30–5 p.m.

CLIMATE

Temperatures during the summer, cooled by eastern trade winds, kee the temperature around 82 degrees F. Brief showers also keep thing cool. Winter temperatures rise to 77 degrees F. Rainiest months ar September–January, and about 40 inches of rain fall per year. A ligh sweater is needed in winter.

DOCUMENTS

U.S. citizens need not carry a passport, although some proof of identit will be required upon leaving the islands. A passport is a good idea sinc the nearby British Virgin Islands are so accessible from St. John and St Thomas. If you wish to dive the Rhone or snorkel amid the fantasti granite boulders at the baths on Virgin Gorda, you'll need to first clea BVI Customs with a passport and an $8 entry fee.

ELECTRICITY

Current runs at 110 volts at 60 cycles.

GETTING AROUND

Transportation on the islands is handled either by taxi or rental car Remember, that driving is on the left side of the road. Many renta companies in Cuz Bay offer competitive rates. Expect to pay rough $60 per day, plus gas and insurance for a Suzuki Sidekick (with fou wheel drive to accommodate the blind switchbacks and extreme moun tain inclines).

LANGUAGE

The official language is English, but the special lilt to the accent is calle cruzan. Some locals speak a musical patois called English Creole— blend of English, African and Spanish. Many people also speak goo Spanish.

MEDICAL EMERGENCIES

St. Croix has a 250-bed **hospital** ☎ *(809) 778-6311*, with 24-hour emergency service. Ask your hotel about doctors on call when you check-in.

MONEY

The official currency is the U.S. dollar.

TELEPHONE

The area code is *809*. Since USVI is an incorporated territory, toll-free numbers that operate in the U.S. work here. You can also dial direct to the mainland. Normal postage rates apply.

TIME

Atlantic Standard Time, one hour later than New York City; during Daylight Saving Time, it is the same as New York.

TIPPING AND TAXES

Some hotels include a 10–15 percent service charge; this should include all tips for both restaurant and room service, unless the attention was extraordinary. If no service is added, leave a 15 percent tip for the waitress, $1–2 a day to the maid; bartenders and wine stewards should be tipped always. Tip the bellboy and porter at least 50 cents a bag. Taxi drivers should receive a 15 percent tip if you are satisfied with the service.

TOURIST INFORMATION

The **St. Croix Tourist Office** ☎ *(809) 773-0495* is located at the Christiansted Wharf. It is open daily.

WHEN TO GO

The Fiesta Food Fair is held on Jan. 5 at the Agriculture Fair Grounds in Estate Lower Love, featuring native cooks and their cuisine, arts and crafts, and steel and quelbe bands. Organic Act Day is June 21. Oct. is one of the busiest months. The Champagne Mumm's Cup Regatta sets sail on Oct. 8–10. Columbus Day/Puerto Rican Friendship Day is celebrated on Oct. 6–10, a week-long celebration featuring parade, horse racing and native foods and music. The St. Croix Jazz & Caribbean Music & Arts Festival takes place in mid-October. The Golden Hook Challenge is slated for Oct. 21–23, a sportsfishing contest. Veterans Day is celebrated on Nov. 11,with island-style parades of steel bands, calypso and partying. The Crucian Christmas Fiesta, the traditional two-week event that features parades, pageants, food and music starts Dec. 11–Jan. 7. The Crucian Christmas Festival Food Fairs in Christiansted and Frederiksted is held in the third week of Dec. The Festival Village in Christiansted takes place on Dec. 29. Frederiksted's Village opens on Dec. 30, with nightly reggae, calypso and Latin music. A Carnival-like Christmas celebration takes place from several days before Christmas to about a week after New Year's.

ST. CROIX HOTELS	RMS	RATES	PHONE	CR. CARDS
Christiansted				
★★★★★ Buccaneer Hotel	149	$155–$340	(800) 223-1108	A, CB, D, MC, V
★★★★★ Westin Carambola Beach Resort	151	$160–$330	(800) 228-3000	A, D, MC, V
★★★★ Villa Madeleine	20	$305–$425	(800) 548-4461	A, MC
★★★ Cane Bay Reef Club	9	$85–$165	(800) 253-8534	A, MC
★★★ Club St. Croix	54	$120–$194	(800) 635-1533	A, CB, D, MC, V
★★★ Cormorant Beach Club	38	$110–$265	(800) 548-4460	A, MC, V
★★★ Cormorant Cove	38	$105–$230	(800) 548-4460	A, MC, V
★★★ Hibiscus Beach Hotel	38	$95–$190	(800) 442-0121	A, D, MC, V
★★★ Hilty House Inn	6	$65–$130	(800) 524-2026	None
★★★ Horizons			(609) 751-2413	
★★★ Hotel on the Cay	55	$95–$198	(800) 524-2035	A, MC, V
★★★ King Christian Hotel	39	$80–$135	(800) 524-2012	A, CB, D, MC, V
★★★ St. Croix by the Sea	65	$90–$145	(800) 524-5006	A, MC, V
★★ Anchor Inn of St. Croix	31	$80–$150	(800) 524-2030	A, CB, D, MC, V
★★ Colony Cove	60	$130–$290	(800) 524-2025	A, D, MC
★★ Gentle Winds Resort	66	$230–$305	(809) 773-3400	None
★★ Hotel Caravelle	43	$79–$255	(800) 524-0410	A, CB, D, MC, V
★★ Pink Fancy Hotel	13	$70–$120	(800) 524-2045	A, MC
★★ Schooner Bay Resort	62	$145–$295	(800) 524-2025	A, D, MC
★★ Sugar Beach Condominiums	46	$110–$250	(800) 524-2049	A, MC, V
★★ Waves at Cane Bay	12	$85–$195	(800) 545-0603	A, D, MC
★ Cactus		$39–$45	(809) 692-9331	
★ Caribbean View All-Suites	18	$80–$120	(809) 773-3335	A, CB, D, MC, V
★ Club Comanche	42	$35–$126	(800) 524-2066	A, MC
★ Danish Manor Hotel	35	$54–$99	(800) 524-2069	A, MC, V
Frederiksted				
★★ Chenay Bay Beach Resort	50	$125–$210	(800) 548-4457	A, MC
★★ Frederiksted Hotel	40	$80–$110	(800) 524-2025	A, MC, V
★★ On the Beach Resort	13	$55–$110	(800) 524-2018	A, CB, D, MC, V

ST. CROIX HOTELS	RMS	RATES	PHONE	CR. CARDS
★★ Sprat Hall Plantation	16	$95–$220	(809) 772-0305	
★ Cottages by the Sea	20	$70–$110	(800) 323-7252	A, D, MC

ST. CROIX RESTAURANTS	PHONE	ENTREE	CR. CARDS

Christiansted

American			
★★ Chart House	(809) 773-7718	$14–$26••	A, DC, MC, V
International			
★★★★ Kendrick's	(809) 773-9199	$14–$26••	A, MC, V
★★ Antoine's	(809) 773-0263	$14–$32	A, MC, V
★★ Comanche	(809) 773-2665	$9–$21	A, MC, V
★★ Tivoli Gardens	(809) 773-6782	$6–$20	A, MC, V
Italian			
★★★★★ Cafe Madeleine	(809) 773-8141	$18–$26	A, DC, MC, V
★★ Picnic in Paradise	(809) 778-1212	$10–$20••	A, MC, V
Latin American			
★★★ Harvey's	(809) 773-3433	$8–$20	None
Mediterranean			
★★ Dino's	(809) 778-8005	$14–$20••	None
Seafood			
★★★ Top Hat	(809) 773-2346	$14–$28••	A, MC, V
★★ Banana Bay Club	(809) 778-9110	$15–$25	A, MC, V

Frederiksted

French			
★★★ Le St. Tropez	(809) 772-3000	$10–$25	A, MC, V
International			
★★★ Blue Moon	(809) 772-2222	$10–$20••	A

Note: • Lunch Only

•• Dinner Only

SINT EUSTATIUS

Over half of the 17,000 visitors to Sint Eustatius each year are cruise ship passengers.

Sint Eustatius is the least touristic of the Leewards Islands with mediocre beaches, an oil refinery and an unprepossessing landscape. What is marvelous about Sint Eustatius is that it is relatively cheap—the same salad that goes for $25 on St. Barts is a mere $6 here. And it's a must for history buffs. Forever hymned in the United States as the first place to salute the rebel stars and stripes in 1776, the free port of Oranjestad was a constant thorn in the side of the British until Admiral George Brydges Rodney was sent to raze it, making his base in what is now the excellent museum in the beautiful old Gin House Hotel on the water's edge. Often called Statia, the island today is also a paradise for hikers, even if there are no parks, picnic tables or water fountains. Instead you can find at least 17 different kinds of orchids, iguanas, huge land crabs and pristine coral reefs teeming with fish. Self-reliant and rugged adventurers will also find the trails underwater exciting—and gloriously deserted. Simply, Statia is a place where you make your own schedule and nobody cares whether you follow it or not. Best of all, packing for Statia is a cinch since there is absolutely no reason to dress up for any occasion anywhere on the island.

Bird's Eye View

Sint Eustatius lies 35 miles south of St. Martin and 17 miles southeast of Saba. The island is eight square miles with a population of 1800. The highest point of the island, at its southern end, is the 2000-foot high **Quill**, a geologically young volcano that is extinct. The classic volcanic cone harbors a beautiful crater filled with dense tropical rain forest (where towering kapok trees grow and at least 15 types of wild orchids). Statians once cultivated cocoa, cinnamon and coffee here in the crater's fertile soil; today bananas are the solitary crop. At night locals hunt for land crabs inside the crater. Contorted cloud forests carpet the summit of **Mazinga Peak**, where on a clear day, you can see St. Kitts, Nevis and Anguilla. The **Panorama track** rewards with glorious views of Sint Eustatius, Saba, St. Martin and St. Barts. There are five wildly diverse trail options for climbing to the rim, around it and into the bowl-shaped crater.

History

Columbus discovered Sint Eustatius on his second voyage, but a Spanish settlement never followed. The Dutch founded the first settlement in 1636, building Fort Orange but the Dutch claim it was never finalized until 1816, after the island changed hands 22 times. During the 18th century, the island became extraordinarily prosperous, as more than 8000 swarmed to the island, half of whom were slaves. Trade became the most profitable way to make a living, and the island gained the nickname "The Golden Rock."

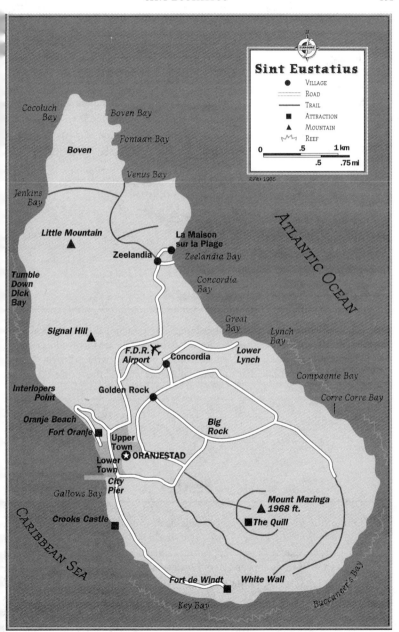

Sint Eustatius

- ● VILLAGE
- ROAD
- TRAIL
- ■ ATTRACTION
- ▲ MOUNTAIN
- 〰 REEF

0 .5 1 km
.5 .75 mi

ATLANTIC OCEAN

Cocoluch Bay
Boven Bay
Fontaan Bay
Boven
Venus Bay
Jenkins Bay
Little Mountain ▲
Zeelandia ● La Maison sur la Plage ●
Zeelandia Bay
Concordia Bay
Tumble Down Dick Bay
Great Bay
Lynch Bay
Signal Hill ▲
F.D.R. Airport ✈ **Concordia** ● **Lower Lynch**
Compagnie Bay
Golden Rock ● *Corre Corre Bay*
Interlopers Point
Oranje Beach
Fort Oranje ■ **Big Rock**
Upper Town
✪ **ORANJESTAD**
Lower Town
City Pier
Gallows Bay
▲ **Mount Mazinga 1968 ft.**
Crooks Castle ■
■ **The Quill**
CARIBBEAN SEA
Fort de Windt ■ **White Wall**
Key Bay
Buccaneer's Bay

Statia has a long and unique relationship with the United States. At th
time of the War for Independence, Statia was a major port from which arm
were shipped to General Washington's troops via Boston, New York an
Charleston. On Nov. 16, 1776, the island unknowingly fired the first initia
salute to the just-declared nation, but the British retaliated, the port bein
taken in 1781 by Admiral George Brydges Rodney, who captured 150 mer
chant ships and 5 million pounds before the French expelled him the nex
year.

After that, the economy began to decline as control of the island change
power numerous times, and merchants were banished by changing rules
The Emancipation Act of 1863 significantly squashed any hope for a planta
tion industry. Most natives were reduced to sustenance farming and receiv
ing monetary assistance from relatives abroad.

People

There are numerous nationalities represented on Sint Eustatius because th
island has changed hands several times. Most people are involved in farming
fishing, trading and a small oil industry. Locals are extraordinarily friendl
and there is great hope that tourism will be the wave of the future. At presen
there is no crime.

Beaches

One of the loveliest beaches is **Oranje Baai**, stretching for a mile along th
coast away from the Lower Town. The strand is perfectly safe for swimming
with a large expanse of sand appearing January-July. Other times the beac
narrows and even disappears. Avoid **Zeelandia** for swimming, but you can se
interesting geological formations in the cliff and even nesting sea birds. (A
dangerous undertow here can be deadly and there is no lifeguard to sav
you.) After a rain, you can find lots of shells and driftwood on the beach—
hikers love it. The beach itself, however, is especially lovely and two mile

ong. **Lynch Beach**, also on the Windward side, is a bit safer for swimming if you do not venture far out into the surf.

Underwater

int Eustatius is a diver's dream with coral reefs, marine life and many hipwrecks to explore.

Still emerging from the shadow cast by her better-known little sister Saba, int Eustatius is possibly the best-kept dive secret in the Eastern Caribbean, nd it's easy to understand why. If you're looking for an island with beaches, ightlife and resorts to complement a vivid underwater scene, you are kindly equested to skip Statia. This is a minimally developed destination visited by nly a few hundred divers each year. But do head for Statia if you desire an ff-the-wall vacation to an island your friends have never heard of (and all our dive buddies know of Saba by now). The payoff, for those willing to rough it" without a disco, is pristine diving through deep volcanic canyons nd fissures, over shallow reefs and plunging walls, and around a bevy of qui-tly disintegrating 17th- and 18th-century trading ships. And those are just 1e documented sites; there are a number of unexplored areas offering true irgin dive possibilities.

Statia's wrecks provided a delightful bounty to early diver visitors. So much o that, although their wooden hulls were long gone, the government even-1ally ruled that nonresidents may dive only when accompanied by a local ive operator; today, the occasional bottle or pewter utensil unearthed will be donated to the Oranjestad museum. Fortunately, there are still plenty o antiquities to see, but the reefs are the real star of Statia's underwater show and you won't have to elbow your way in to do it. The spectacular and rar flying gurnard is regularly spotted on Statia, and larger pelagics frequent number of the sites. Humpback whales cruise the area December throug February. Perhaps the best snorkeling site is found 70 feet from shore at **City Wall** (in front of Dive Statia's shop), a barricade that once represented th old sea wall for Lower Town and is now inhabited by reef fish and inverte brate life; watch for sea urchins. A steep trail leads to calm **Jenkins Bay** in th northwest or to **Corre Corre Bay**, off the eastern side of the island (see "O Foot"), both providing excellent snorkeling. There's one professional div operator on Statia at present, but rumors are swirling about competitio coming to town.

Barracuda Reef

The island classic, centered on a 700-foot-long mini-wall (depth to 70 feet), the ree lives up to its name with schools of barracuda touring the colorful wall that is plas tered with soft corals and sea fans. Many smaller creatures lurking in the nooks and crannies, plus a resident porcupine fish that circles the site. French angels, spotted morays, lobsters and sporadic nurse sharks also share the area with the namesak predators. Best visited in the morning, when the sunlight streams in from the eas and lights up the reef's kaleidoscope of colors.

The Cliffs

A spectacular wall off the southern coast of the island, the Cliffs begins in a cora garden at 70 feet, which leads to the lip of the drop-off which descends 250 feet Friendly groupers call the wall home, while brightly colored hard and soft corals accent the area for photographers.

Double Wrecks

The premiere "archeological dive" on the island is... you guessed it, two wrecks, one on top of the other! Suitable for all levels of divers, the two 250-year-old caravels lie at 60 feet, strewn with delicate anemones, red vase sponges and shards of pottery Thousands of fish swarm the site, while a variety of conch, including the rare rooste conch, sprawl in the grassy sands that surround the wrecks.

The Five Fingers (a k a, Caroline's Reef)

A series of coral-encrusted lava flows and sponge-covered ledges create the main topography of this dynamic dive. The coral creates spokes (or fingers) which con verge at a hub where a tiny hole serves as a passage between reefs for the smaller fish Lobsters, sea turtles and nurse sharks also call the site home.

Grand Canyon

A local favorite, Grand Canyon is comprised of a series of volcanic fissures pouring a never-ending stream of sand into the depths. The wall at this location tops out at 70-to-80 feet, and is suitable for beginners, while more experienced divers will want to swim over the brink to the more dramatic vistas which descend to 450 feet.

Dive Shops

Dive Statia

Oranjestad; ☎ *(599) 38-2435.*

The island's oldest shop is a small, low-key operation, with all sites within 15 minutes of the dock. Two-tank dive, $72, including equipment. Resort course $80; night dives and underwater photography courses available. PADI instructors provided on all dives. Two mountain bikes are also available for rent at $10 per day.

On Foot

Good things come in small packages and, for hikers, Statia is a small treasure. With only 12 square miles to cover, the island realistically can be seen entirely on foot, albeit by dedicated walkers. But more sedate visitors will still want to climb **The Quill**, the classically shaped volcanic cone that dominates the island from every vantage point (although the best view is actually obtained from nearby St. Kitts). It represents one of the Caribbean's easier "high points" and rewards its guests with a lush crater rainforest (the only one on an otherwise arid island), where islanders hunt land crabs after dark. A three-hour guided tour of **Oranjestad** is easily arranged with local historians through the island museum or tourist office; they will also provide a walking map featuring a few trails and donkey tracks not listed below.

Corre Corre Bay

Take the road east out of Oranjestad (referred to as Behind the Mountain Road) toward Round Hill, which continues right around the Quill to a large rock painted with an exclamation point. The trail begins opposite the rock and crosses private land (the owners permit hikers), passing the ruins of an old plantation that once oversaw fields of sugarcane and cotton. Once you arrive at isolated Corre Corre Bay, you'll find good snorkeling on the outer reef.

The Quill

Not yet classified as extinct (it's been a few thousand years since the last activity), the 1968-foot Quill represents the northernmost point of the active volcanic range that stretches through the Eastern Caribbean from Grenada north to Statia. At least four possible routes—detailed in the hiking brochure provided by the tourist office—lie on the Quill's slopes, but the following represents the main route. A sign on a telephone pole at the south end of Oranjestad denotes Quill Track 1. The path ascends the western slope through shrub and woodlands to Sign No. 5, which marks a fork; either track leads to the crater rim, but the left-hand side is steeper and difficult after wet weather. Once at the top, trails lead around the rim and to the actual summit, called Mazinga Peak (great views), and into the densely vegetated crater itself (check locally to see if a guide is advised). The verdant interior has been cultivated over the years with bananas, coffee, cinnamon and cacao, but now is primarily a home to huge kapok trees.

By Pedal

Judging from the fact that only Dive Statia (see "Under Water") can provide visitors with bike rentals—and only two at that!—Statia can be considered virgin mountain biking territory. The island is small, but the main road will reward cyclists with relaxed touring. The trail to the Quill is said to be unrideable, but perhaps it's just waiting for the right pair of muscles? One caution: off-roading appears inviting, but invites stickers and thorns; carry a patch kit.

What Else to See

Upper Town the main urban center, can be seen in an eyeblink. There is **Fort Oranje**, the government center and where you go to hear the latest gossip. (On an island as small as this, gossip ranks high on the list of entertainment options.) The island museum is the **Doncker-De Graf House**, where you can see relics from Statia's history. Archeological digs are often underway so check with the tourist board about possible sites. One site recently discovered was a synagogue built in 1738. For trekking expeditions, see above under "Treks."

Historical Sites

Fort Oranje ★★★

Upper Town, Oranjestad.

This fort dates back to 1636. It was restored in honor of the U.S. Bicentennial in 1976. St. Eustatius was the first foreign entity to support the United States in the Revolutionary War, and a plaque here, presented by Franklin D. Roosevelt, gives thanks. The British retaliated by sacking the then-rich town and its harbor, and much of the rebuilding was done with U.S. funds. The tourist office out front is a good place to pick up brochures and maps and hire a guide.

Museums and Exhibits

t. Eustatius Historical Museum   ★ ★ ★

Wilhelmina Way, Oranjestad.
Hours Open: 9 a.m.–5 p.m.

This museum is housed in a beautifully restored 18th-century building once lived in by British Admiral Rodney during the American Revolution. (Not a popular man, as he's the one who ordered the town destroyed after it acknowledged the fledgling United States as an independent country.) The museum's eclectic exhibits focus on sugar production, slave trading, 18th-century antiques, and pre-Columbian artifacts.

Tours

he Quill   ★ ★ ★ ★

Southern portion, Oranjestad.

The island's highest point at 1968 feet, the Quill is an extinct volcano with a lush rainforest in its crater. Twelve marked trails offer all level of hikes, from simple treks to strenuous trips to the summit. Pick up a brochure at the tourist office, or hire a guide to take you for about $20. Excellent birdwatching. Locals come at night to catch the large crabs that live in the crater. You can accompany them and get your hotel to cook your quarry. Inquire at the tourist office for details.

Sports

Sports on the island are limited to hiking, climbing, diving and swimming. Softball, basketball and volleyball can be played at the Community Centre on Rosemary Lane.

ennis

Rosemary Lane, Oranjestad.

St. Eustatius is not the place to come to play tennis—there's one lone court on the entire island. The concrete court at the Community Center is open every day and lit for night play, but you'll have to bring your own racquet and balls, though they do have changing rooms. The fee is about $5.

Watersports

Lower Toen, Oranjestad.

Dive Statia is the island's most complete (and virtually only) watersports center. They offer deep-sea fishing trips, snorkeling equipment, and scuba instruction and excursions. St. Eustatius is a diver's paradise, with all sorts of interesting undersea items to explore, including myriad sunken ships and their booty. Snorkelers can see a lot too, as the depths are often only about 10 feet.

Where to Stay

Fielding's Highest Rated Hotel in Sint Eustatius

★★★	Old Gin House	$125–$225

Fielding's Most Romantic Hotel in Sint Eustatius

★★	La Maison sur la Plage	$60–$95
★★★	Old Gin House	$125–$225

Fielding's Budget Hotel in Sint Eustatius

★★	Airport View Apartments	$60–$75
★★	Talk of the Town	$54–$81
★★	La Maison sur la Plage	$60–$95
★★	Golden Era	$75–$93
★★★	Old Gin House	$125–$225

Forget about big fancy resorts on Sint Eustatius. It's just not that kind of island. There are four small hotels and a number of apartments and rooms to rent. Little is to be expected in regards of style. Basic comfort is the most prevailing feature. The French-inspired **Maison Sur La Plage** is located on a lovely beach but the **Old Gin House** ranks as the most stylish, erected amid the ruins of an old cotton gin.

Hotels and Resorts

Golden Era   **$75–$93**   ★★

> *Lower Town,* ☎ *(599) 3-82445, FAX (599) 3-82445.*
> *Single: $75. Double: $93.*
> This small hotel sits right at the water's edge, but you'll have to travel a half-mile for the beach, as the shoreline here is rocky. Guest rooms are quite basic, but comfortable with air conditioning, phones and tiny private balconies. The restaurant serves decent Caribbean cuisine. The saltwater pool is the only other facility. Acceptable for the rates, but nothing too exciting.

a Maison sur la Plage $60–$95   ★★

Zeelandia, ☎ (599) 3-82256, FAX (599) 3-82831.
Single: $60–$80. Double: $60–$95.

Located on the northeastern coast, this small property took a real pummeling during Hurricane Hugo, and has yet to return to its predestruction days. That's not to say that all is in ruins, but some repairs have a slapdash quality. Accommodations are in cottages with basic furnishings, private terraces and bright artwork. Facilities include a gourmet French restaurant, a bar, a TV lounge (you won't find one in your room), a small library and a pool. The beach stretches for two miles, but the sea is too rough for most swimmers.

Talk of the Town $54–$81   ★★

Oranjestad, ☎ (599) 3-82236, FAX (599) 3-82640.
Single: $54–$65. Double: $68–$81.

This small hotel is set off the beach, but does have a pool. Rooms are quite basic but nice, with air conditioning, locally made furnishings, telephones, and cable TV. The downstairs restaurant is fine. Though frills are few, this is still one of the better choices on this tiny island.

Apartments and Condominiums

Ask the tourist board for help in finding just the right house or apartment for your needs. Bring your own staples from home.

Airport View Apartments $60–$75   ★★

Golden Rock, ☎ (599) 3-82474.
Single: $60. Double: $75.

Like the name implies, these units are indeed near the airport. Each unit is a studio with just the basics—refrigerator, coffeemaker, cable TV—but not complete kitchens, though there is a barbecue area where you can grill meals. There's also a bar and restaurant on the premises, but not much else, not even a pool.

Inns

Old Gin House $125–$225   ★★★

Lower Town, ☎ (599) 3-82319, FAX (599) 3-82555.
Single: $125–$150. Double: $175–$225.

This elegant inn is by far the nicest place to stay on St. Eustatius, and also by far the most expensive. Housed in a restored 18th-century cotton gin factory, rooms are spacious and individually decorated with good artwork, antique furnishings and ceiling fans (no air conditioning). Request one of the rooms in the original inn as they have the most character, though the ones in the newer building across the street are also quite pleasant. There's a restaurant, small pool and library on the premises, and the beach is steps away. No children under 10 permitted.

Low Cost Lodging

There are a few guest houses in Oranjestad in which you can rent rooms. Rather than reserve from afar, it's best to see in person the situation before you part with your money. The tourist office, which you should contact upon arrival, will also help you find a suitable room.

Where to Eat

★★★	**Fielding's Highest Rated Restaurants in Sint Eustatius**	
★★★	La Maison Sur La Plage	$15–$25
★★★	Old Gin House	$10–$22
★★★	Talk of the Town	$5–$20

	Fielding's Special Restaurants in Sint Eustatius	
★★★	La Maison Sur La Plage	$15–$25
★★	L'Etoile	$7–$20
★★	Stone Oven	$10–$15

	Fielding's Budget Restaurants in Sint Eustatius	
★★	Kim Cheng's Chinese	$5–$10
★★	Cool Corner	$8–$10
★★	Stone Oven	$10–$15
★★★	Talk of the Town	$5–$20
★★	L'Etoile	$7–$20

Don't expect to eat cordon bleu here. No one's heard of it. Even credit cards are looked at with quizzical looks; do everybody a favor and pay in cash. The best restaurants are the **Old Gin House** (for atmosphere and cuisine) **Maison Sur La Plage** (for the windswept view of the beach), **Talk of the Town** (for sandwiches Dutch style); **Kim Cheng's Chinese Restaurant** (for the expected fare), and **L'Etoile** (for home-cooked meals).

Cool Corner   **$**   ★★

> *Fort Oranjestraat,* ☎ *(599) 38-2523.*
> *International cuisine.*
> *Lunch: 10 a.m.–4 p.m., entrees $8–$10.*
> *Dinner: 4 p.m.–midnight, entrees $8–$10.*

This hot spot (for Statia) beckons with a prime location near the local tourist office. A good place to meet the friendly townspeople, Cool Corner stays open late to serve the needs of the few night owls who may be prowling. Fare is Caribbean-Chinese, with curry plates and Cantonese specialties available.

m Cheng's Chinese $ ★ ★

Prinsesweg, Upper Town, ☎ (599) 30-2389.
Chinese cuisine.
Lunch: entrees $5–$10.
Dinner: entrees $5–$10.

Sometimes called The Chinese Restaurant this tiny eatery manages to produce plates heaped with hearty food in rather cramped surroundings. The fare is actually a potpourri of dishes encompassing West Indian, creole and Chinese.

toile $$ ★ ★

6 Van Rheeweg, ☎ (599) 38-2299.
Latin American cuisine.
Lunch: Noon–4 p.m., entrees $7–$20.
Dinner: 4–10 p.m., entrees $7–$20.

What appears to be a roadhouse is really a warm, welcoming room proffering tasty island specialties prepared by the amiable Caren Henriquez. Its location on a hillside is a little out of the way for the average tourist, so it's mainly frequented by a crowd of regulars. Along with hamburgers, tasty spareribs and hotdogs, Henriquez prepares goat stew or stuffed crab.

Maison Sur La Plage $$$ ★ ★ ★

Zeelandia Beach, Zeelandia, ☎ (599) 38-2256.
French cuisine.
Lunch: entrees $15–$25.
Dinner: entrees $15–$25.

In what's considered to be an out-of-the-way location for Statia, La Maison sur Plage is the only fine French restaurant on Zeelandia beach, which is only a few miles from Oranjestad. Meals are served on a breezy, trellised terrace overlooking windswept sands and the Quill. Expect traditional Gallic specialties like duck breast or beef fillets with green peppercorn sauce, and crepes for dessert.

d Gin House $$$ ★ ★ ★

Lower Town, ☎ (599) 38-2319.
American cuisine.
Lunch: Noon–2 p.m., entrees $10–$22.
Dinner: 6:30–8 p.m., prix fixe $10–$22.

Dinner at the Mooshay Bay Dining Room of this venerable hotel is one of the best deals in town. A delicious four-course meal that often includes chateaubriand or lobster and two kinds of wine is available for $22 per person. The 18th-century tavern room is spiffily decorated with burnished pewter and gleaming crystal, and it faces the pool. Across the street, the Terrace Restaurant, which has an ocean view, is a nice place for burgers or steak and chicken plates.

one Oven $$ ★ ★

16A Feaschweg, Upper Town, ☎ (599) 38-2247.

Latin American cuisine.
Lunch: entrees $10–$15.
Dinner: entrees $10–$15.

This cozy, coconut-palm fringed bar and danceteria serves as a West Indian eater depending on who's available to cook. When the burners are going, it's a good spot for goat water or conch. Check out the wild party animals swinging on Friday night when it stays open until the last guest moseys on home.

Talk of the Town   **$$**   ★ ★ ★

L.E. Saddlerweg, Upper Town, ☎ (599) 38-2236.
International cuisine.
Lunch: 11:30 a.m.–2 p.m., entrees $5–$20.
Dinner: 7–10 p.m., entrees $5–$20.

A Dutch family owns and operates this plant-filled, indoor-outdoor restaurant near the airport. It has a reputation for the best creole meals in town, but the cuisine jumps often from one exotic clime to the next. Specialties include lobster stew which can be ordered in advance. Good deals include the Dutch-style breakfast buffet with some American standards thrown in—all for under $10.

Where to Shop

Statia is no St. Thomas. You'll find a few items imported from Holland, including cosmetics, perfumes, liquors, cigarettes and jewelry at the **Mazinga Gift Shop** in Upper Town (Fort Oranjestraat). One good native buy is **Masinga Mist** (schnapps made from soursop) which you can pick up at **Dive Statia boutique** near the Old Gin House. The museum at Fort Oranje has a small selection of books and postcards.

Sint Eustatius Directory

ARRIVAL AND DEPARTURE

You can reach Sint Eustatius several times a day on 20-minute flights from St. Maarten on **WINAIR**. WINAIR also flies to the island from St. Kitts, which takes only 10 minutes. WINAIR also offers flights from Sint Eustatius to Saba. All flights are in small planes, but be sure you look out the window when you land and take off to get a great view of The Quill, the island's volcano. There is a departure tax of $3 if you are going to the U.S., $3 if you are going on to any other Caribbean island.

BUSINESS HOURS

Shops generally open weekdays 8 a.m.–noon and 1–4 p.m. Bank (there's only one) open Monday–Thursday 8:30 a.m.–1 p.m. and Friday 8:30 a.m.–1 p.m. and 4–5 p.m.

CLIMATE

Daytime temperatures hover in the mid-80s during the day and drop to the 70s during the evening, year-round. Only 45 inches of rain fall a year.

DOCUMENTS

U.S. and Canadian citizens need to show only proof of citizenship (current passport or one that expired less than five years ago, or voter's registration card or birth certificate with raised seal and a photo ID), plus an ongoing or return ticket.

ELECTRICITY

Current runs 110 volts, 60 cycles, same as in the U.S. No converter or transformer necessary.

GETTING AROUND

Most destinations are within walking distance, but several taxi drivers make excellent guides. A tour around the island runs about $35. Cars can be hired at the airport, but you must show your own driver's license or an international driver's license. Driving is on the right, but the cows, sheep and goats who casually graze over the roadways don't seem to know. You should drive slowly to avoid hitting them.

LANGUAGE

The official language is Dutch (most of the signs are written so), but everyone speaks English. If you meet someone on the street, use the national greeting; "Awright, ok-a-a-y."

MEDICAL EMERGENCIES

Most emergencies are immediately flown to Sint Maarten (though you may want to charter a flight to San Juan, Puerto Rico), but there is a small hospital on the outskirts of Oranjestad.

MONEY

The official currency is the Netherlands Antilles florin (abbreviated NAf), also called the guilder. American dollars are generally accepted everywhere, but Canadians should change their money into florins (Barclays Bank in Wilhelminaweg) or in St. Maarten before coming. Only hotels and a few restaurants will accept credit cards. Imagine you are out in the middle of nowhere.

TELEPHONE

The country code is *599*. To call from the States, dial *011* (international access code), plus *599* (country code) plus *38* (city code) plus 4-digit local number. You may need to use a different code when calling from another Caribbean island.

TIME

Atlantic Standard Time, one hour ahead of New York, except during Daylight Saving Time, when it is the same.

TIPPING AND TAXES

Restaurants, hotels and bars all add a 15 percent service charge. You don't need to tip anyone on top of this. Taxi drivers should get $1–2. No porters to worry about, so be prepared to carry our own luggage.

TOURIST INFORMATION

There are three tourist offices on the island: at the airport, in Lower Town opposite Roro Pier, operated by the Sint Eustatius Historical Society, and in the village center. For more information, call ☎ (599) 82433. In the U.S. ☎ (800) 344-4606.

WHEN TO GO

The Queen's Coronation Day on April 30 is a big island bash with fireworks, music, dancing and sports events. Carnival is celebrated in July. Statia-America Day is commemorated on Nov. 16, honoring the first salute to the American flag by a foreign government. Boxing Day is celebrated the day after Christmas on Dec. 26.

SINT EUSTATIUS HOTELS		RMS	RATES	PHONE	CR. CARDS
Oranjestad					
★★★	**Old Gin House**	20	$125–$225	(599) 38-2319	A, CB, MC, V
★★	**Airport View Apartments**	9	$60–$75	(599) 38-2474	A, MC
★★	**Golden Era**	20	$75–$93	(599) 38-2445	A, D, MC
★★	**La Maison sur la Plage**	10	$60–$95	(599) 38-2256	A, MC
★★	**Talk of the Town**	18	$54–$81	(599) 38-2236	A, MC

SINT EUSTATIUS RESTAURANTS		PHONE	ENTREE	CR. CARDS
Oranjestad				
	American			
★★★	**Old Gin House**	(599) 38-2319	$10–$22	A, DC, MC, V
	Chinese			
★★	**Kim Cheng's Chinese**	(599) 30-2389	$5–$10	None
	French			
★★★	**La Maison Sur La Plage**	(599) 38-2256	$15–$25	MC, V

SINT EUSTATIUS RESTAURANTS	PHONE	ENTREE	CR. CARDS
International			
★★★ Talk of the Town	(599) 38-2236	$5–$20	A, MC, V
★★ Cool Corner	(599) 38-2523	$8–$10	None
Latin American			
★★ L'Etoile	(599) 38-2299	$7–$20	None
★★ Stone Oven	(599) 38-2247	$10–$15	None

Note: • Lunch Only

•• Dinner Only

ST. JOHN

Constant trade winds off St. John thrill windsurfers.

For many die-hard ecotourists, St. John is one of the greatest natural wonders of the three U.S. Virgin Islands. In fact, the two major diversions here are climbing and "limin" (that is, "laying back," Caribbean style)—the latter preferably done before *and* after the former. Unlike so many other flat, arid Caribbean isles, the U.S. Virgin Islands (which also include St. Croix and St. Thomas), are beautifully sculpted and vividly green, and St. John has more than its fair share of emerald green bays, snow-white beaches, and lushly carpeted mountain peaks; in fact, almost two-thirds of the island's land area, plus another 5600 acres underwater, compose the U.S. Virgin Islands National Park, donated to the United States by Laurence Rockefeller. As such, there are terrific adventures both above and under water, so untrod that many visitors come for weeks and never get beyond the gorgeous **Trunk Bay Beach**. All it takes is a good pair of boots and a little guidance to mash one's way through densely packed rain forest or hike over well-marked nature trails that lead past 200-year-old plantation houses. Underwater the views are just as spectacular, with rock formations, grottoes and wrecks that rate as some of the best in the Caribbean. The absence of sales tax here has been known to drive some visitors to frenzy, but once the shopper's dust settles, they find that the most pleasant thing to do on St. John is just to lay back, drink in hand, shades in place, and soak up the rays.

Bird's Eye View

The U.S. Virgin Islands lie 1500 miles southeast of New York and about 1000 miles south of Miami. A mere 18 degrees above the equator, they are bounded to the north by the Atlantic Ocean and the south by the Caribbean Sea, except for St. Croix, which is surrounded by the Caribbean. St. John is two miles east of St. Thomas, and a mere 20-minute ferry ride away. A three mile expanse called Pillsbury Sound separates St. John from St. Thomas, and between the two islands lie a few, smaller, mostly uninhabited ones, or so Christopher Columbus fantasized when he named the group St. Ursula and her 11,000 virgins. The highest peak is **Bordeaux Mountain** at 1277 feet. Most of St. John's 2500 residents live in the area surrounding **Cruz Bay**, a tiny ramshackle town, where ferries and cruise-ship tenders dock, tourists shop and islanders go about their very laid-back business. Scenic overlooks provide a glimpse of broad expanses of white sand lapped by a turquoise sea. Closer inspection reveals a sugary white sand and interesting snorkeling off shore. When the ferry landing was built in Cruz Bay, opening a gateway to St. Thomas and her airport, the closest to St. John, Coral Bay sank slowly into seclusion. It's a pass-through for those on their way to Salt Pond Beach or Don Carlos Mexican Seafood Cantina. The new eateries like Skinny Legs and Shipwreck Landing are beginning to lure crowds to Coral Bay.

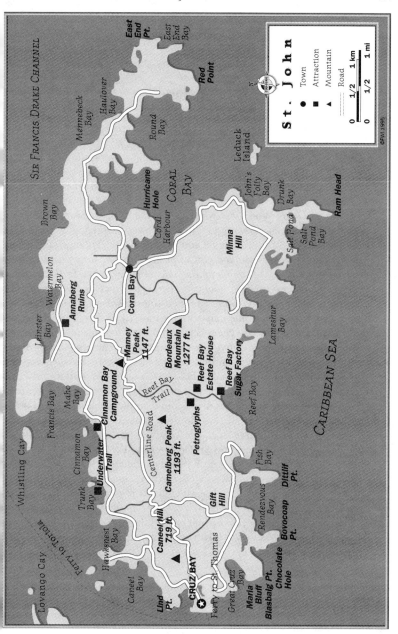

St. John

Town ●
Attraction ■
Mountain ▲
Road ------

0 — 1/2 — 1 km
0 — 1/2 — 1 mi

©FM 1995

SIR FRANCIS DRAKE CHANNEL

East End Pt.
East End Bay
Red Point
Haulover Bay
Memebeck Bay
Round Bay
Leduck Island
CORAL BAY
Brown Bay
Watermelon Bay
Hurricane Hole
Coral Harbour
John's Folly Bay
Drunk Bay
Ram Head
Salt Pond Bay
Salt Pond Bay
Leinster Bay
Annaberg Ruins ■
Coral Bay ●
Mamey Peak 1147 ft. ▲
Minna Hill
Francis Bay
Maho Bay
Cinnamon Bay
Cinnamon Bay Campground ▲
Bordeaux Mountain 1277 ft. ▲
Reef Bay Estate House ■
Reef Bay Sugar Factory ■
Lameshur Bay
Whistling Cay
Trunk Bay
Underwater Trail ■
Reef Bay Trail
Centerline Road
Petroglyphs ■
Camelberg Peak 1193 ft. ▲
Reef Bay
Fish Bay
CARIBBEAN SEA
Hawksnest Bay
Caneel Bay
Caneel Hill 719 ft. ▲
Gift Hill
Rendezvous Bay
Dittlif Pt.
Bovocoap Pt.
Ferry to Tortola
Lovango Cay
Lind Pt.
CRUZ BAY ✪
Ferry to St. Thomas
Great Cruz Bay
Chocolate Hole
Maria Bluff
Blasbalg Pt.

History

Archaeologists have yet to decide whether the Arawaks or Caribs (the island's first pre-Columbian inhabitants), African slaves or a combination thereof were responsible for the primitive etchings along the Reef Bay trail. In 1493, Columbus discovered the islands of St. Croix, St. John and St. Thomas, and then shoved off to Puerto Rico. A hundred years later saw the arrival in St. John of Sir Francis Drake as he prepared to confront the Spanish troops in San Juan. While St. Croix changed hands between the French and Spanish, St. John (along with St. Thomas) was appropriated by the Danish West India Company, becoming a hub of business (St. Thomas), and a magnet for sugarcane, tobacco and cotton plantations (St. John). In 1717, the Danes established St. John's Coral Bay as a permanent port. In 1733, a great slave rebellion devastated the country, when a large mass of slaves, ostensibly carrying bundles of wood, were admitted to Fort Berg in Coral Bay. Once inside, they brandished cane knives and massacred hundreds of settlers and the entire Danish garrison. The rebels held the fort for nine months until the Danes, with the support of two French warships and an army from Martinique, recaptured the island and rebuilt the factories. In 1848, slavery was abolished, though planters tried to hold onto their crops until the advent of the European sugar-beet soured their profits. When the planters eventually left the island, the former slaves divided up their properties and relied on the land and the sea to provide their sustenance. In 1917, with a view to protect its interest in the Panama Canal, the U.S. bought the Virgin Islands package—St. John, St. Thomas and St. Croix—from the Danes for a mere $25 million. Starting in the 50s, tourism began to strategically raise the standard of living. In 1956, Laurence Rockefeller took a shine to the island and erected his Caneel Bay resort, which gave visitors full opportunity to enjoy the pleasures of the park. With the advent of the Maho Bay resort in 1976, more ecologically oriented travelers arrived on St. John's shores, ready to scale and sail the challenging resources. Luxury entered with the opening of the Virgin Grand, now the Hyatt Regency, with a slew of high-class condos following in its wake.

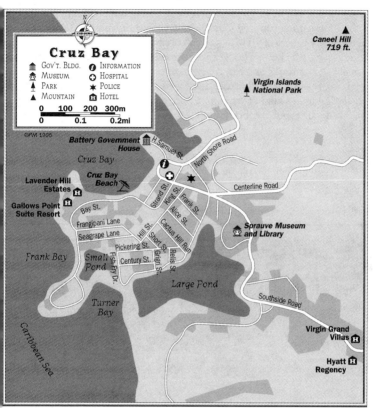

People

There are only about 3500 people who live on St. John, many of them not quite sure they want their small island overrun with tourists. That may be the reason why visitors are sometimes treated with a measure of distance. Locals take time to warm to conversation, and while they stop traffic talking among themselves, few may laugh with you. (To be fair, just one look at how American cruise passengers sometimes treat islanders—with an air of patronization left over from the master-slave dynamic—should fully explain their cool-

ness.) Reggae is a major passion, as is the Rastafarianism influence, and belie
in the supernatural runs high: natives still believe the jumbies (spirits) cause
the closing of the Reef Bay Sugar Factory in 1916. You'll find a number o
American ex-pats here, who, keen to the laid-back lifestyle, spend their day
casually selling wares in Cruz Bay. If you can leave your cellular phone and
datebook at home, it will take only a few days to understand the Virgin vibe
called "limin"—a kind of wrinkle in time phenomenon that makes it impos
sible to do anything else but lounge, sip cool drinks and daydream.

Beaches

Hawk's Nest Bay on St. John has two good reefs offshore with elkhorn coral.

The island's best beach, **Trunk Bay**, is the most photographed spot in the
Caribbean, but underwater it's beginning to show wear and tear. Non-divers
can use a unique snorkeling scuba system (SNUBA) that involves an air-sup
port raft attached to a 20-foot line allowing the snorkeler the thrill of diving
There are also snorkel rentals and lockers for hire, as well as snack bars. The
beach, however, should be well avoided on days when cruise ships pull into
port. **Hawks Nest Bay Beach**, a rollercoaster ride from Caneel, is a favorite
beach. It's a 15-minute walk from the reception area of the **Caneel Bay** resort,
and is usually very deserted. **Cinnamon Bay** is long and powdery, and the na-

onal park maintains a little historical museum. Difficult to reach over a tor-
uous road, **Maho Bay** is beautiful and calm, full of turtles, and well worth
the effort. Coves unreachable by car are **Solomon** and **Honeymoon** behind the
Cruz Bay Center. The short hike will fill a morning (nudists prefer it, even if
here is an official law against taking it all off). Palm trees fringe both coves
and a rocky outcropping separates them, providing excellent snorkeling. **Reef
Bay**, in the south, is reached by a 2.5-mile trail descending through a shady
moist rain forest, after which comes a dry scrub forest. **Salt Pond** is also especially good for snorkeling and features a hearty climb to **Ram's Head**.

Underwater

Although there's plenty of beautiful underwater life to mirror the island's
lush above-ground geography, diving on St. John tends to be shallow and
mild, which makes it a great place to learn, or to visit if you've just been certified. There are relatively few surface conditions to complicate matters, although the northern coast is subject to swells in the winter (which usually
renders these sites inaccessible). Several operators visit the wreck of the
Rhone off the BVIs (you'll need a passport or birth certificate), and dives off
eastern St. Thomas are easily accessible from Cruz and Cinnamon bays.
Trunk Bay has a 225-yard self-guiding underwater trail that will thrill first-
time snorkelers, but the best snorkeling lies off **Cinnamon Bay**, **Hawksnest
Beach** or in **Leinster Bay** (at nearby Watermelon Cay).

Carvel Rock

An exciting, intermediate dive (20-80 feet) with a good current you can ride, Carvel
lies just off Cinnamon Bay. You'll cut through a narrow passage (gloves recommended), to the reef area, revealing schools of tiny silversides so thick you can't see
through the swarm, which are usually followed by a couple dozen hungry tarpon
eager for lunch, darting and snapping. Lavender gorgonians shelter basket stars
along the floor, while manta rays sometimes cruise the sands.

Grass Cay

A lovely fringe reef (20–50 feet) features enormous coral heads, gorgonians, star
corals and rope sponges. Plenty of tropicals, including trumpetfish and Spanish hog-
fish. Terrific for beginners, and an east-to-west current can be located to create a
pleasing drift dive.

The Leaf

Ideal for intermediates, the Leaf is a large reef (40–60 feet) just west of Ram's Head,
featuring rock shelves, six-foot-high fingers of coral extending from the reef and

Caribbean spiny lobsters housed in the numerous crevices. Wrasse, schools of angel
and pelagics also frequent the site.

Wreck of the *Major General Rogers*

A 120-foot Coast Guard cutter that was sunk as an artificial reef in the'70s, the *General Rogers* sits upright in the channel between St. John and St. Thomas. Considerable barnacle growth and sponge life decorate the hull, with parrotfish, grouper
and hungry yellowtail nearby. At just 60 feet to the deck, this is a relatively easy
wreck dive, although a slack tide is necessary to avoid strong tidal currents.

Dive Shops

Coral Divers

Coral Bay; ☎ *(809) 776-6850.*
Situated on the quieter east end of St. John's, Coral Divers is a four-year-old NAUI
training facility. Offers two-tank and night dives for $65. Resort course, $65.

Cruz Bay Watersports

Cruz Bay; ☎ *(800) 835-7730 or (809) 776-6234.* The biggest operator on the
island. Two-tank dive $78, or book it through St. John Watersports ☎ *(809-776-6256)* for $73. Snorkel trips, $25.

Low Key Watersports

Cruz Bay; ☎ *(800) 835-7718.*
PADI five-star and I.D.C. facility with classrooms. Offers three-day "Executive"
course with videos and manuals shipped to home address ($350); open water certification after dives on the island. Three vessels, group size under 12; weekly trips to
the Rhone on Fridays ($130 with lunch, customs fees and all equipment). Two-tank
dive $75, including equipment.

Paradise Watersports

Caneel Bay; ☎ *(809) 776-6111 or 693-8690.*
Smaller PADI and NAUI operation limits groups to eight with sites chosen by consensus. Resort courses and pool sessions; close to many of the eastern St. Thomas
sites and occasional trips to the Rhone. Two-tank dive, $75.

On Foot

If you've been looking for something to thank the Rockefellers for, look no
further than St. John. After falling in love with its pristine, untouched beauty, in 1954 Lawrence Rockefeller bought and donated 5000 acres of prime
St. John real estate to the U.S. government, which turned around and created the unique **Virgin Islands National Park**, eventually comprising about two-
thirds of the island's above-water territory (and a decent chunk of its under

ater coral reefs and offshore islands). As such, there is virtually no compar-
son between St. John and the other U.S. Virgins when it comes to hiking;
's where the Virgins, well... practically live up to their name. With the pos-
ible exception of Martinique and Guadeloupe, St. John has the best-devel-
ped trail system in the Caribbean, offering a variety of short jaunts.
lthough the two longest trails come in under two-and-a-half miles, it's pos-
ible to make a few itinerary adjustments to create memorable all-day excur-
ions, particularly in the vicinity of **Lameshur**. The shorter trails under a mile
re not listed here, but many are worth a look. Pick up a copy of the free trail
uide available at the visitor's center, which outlines 22 hiking possibilities;
etter yet, purchase a waterproof *Trails Unlimited* topo map (available
hroughout Cruz Bay) for a more detailed look at the island's geography. If
ou're visiting from St. Thomas for the day, two trails leave from the vicinity
f Cruz Bay leading to **Caneel Hill** and **Lind Point**, and can be combined (us-
ng the Caneel Hill Spur trail) for a shorter hike. Another enticing offering is
he Park Service's guided outing which buses guests to the start of the **Reef**
ay Trail, near the top of Mamey Peak, for a mostly downhill and casual stroll
ast petroglyphs and sugar factory ruins to **Reef Bay**. Here hikers can swim
nd snorkel before being ferried back to Cruz Bay late in the afternoon.
ther guided hikes are available and will provide an informative glimpse into
he Caribbean ecosystem and the history of the Virgin Islands.

ordeaux Mountain Trail

A dirt road leads south from Centerline Road near Mamey Peak. Shortly after passing Bordeaux Mountain on this road, a precipitate trail leads off to the right and
drops 1000 feet in just over a mile through wildflowers and kapok trees to Lameshur Bay. You may return using either the same route, or via a considerably longer
loop using the Lameshur Bay trail, Reef Bay trail and the Bordeaux Mountain Road
(nearly five miles back to the starting point).

aneel Hill Trail

For day-trippers docking at Cruz Bay, the surest introduction to St. John's wild terrain is the steep ascent of Caneel Hill, the mountain overlooking the ferry landing.
Caneel's 719-foot elevation is attained in three-quarters of a mile, and leads to
another climb to 848-foot Margaret Hill. The 2.4-mile trail then descends through
the forest down to the North Shore Road, at the turnoff for Caneel Bay. An easier
variation is to turn around at Caneel's summit, descend, and rather than heading
back into Cruz Bay, take the Caneel Hill Spur midway down toward the Visitor
Center. By crossing the North Shore Road, you also may access the Lind Point
Trail.

hnny Horn Trail

Begin this less-used trail at the Emmaus Moravian Church in Coral Bay. The hike
climbs and descends briskly through upland dry forest and scrub. About a mile into
the hike, the Brown Bay Trail heads off to the right (east), while Johnny Horn con-

tinues down to Watermelon Bay (good snorkeling) and Leinster Bay Road. If you've arranged for a pickup, it's 1.8 miles and under two hours to this point. Or you may create a semi-loop by returning to the Brown Bay trailhead, which ventures over unmaintained tracks to a ridge overlooking Hurricane Hole; this hike ends at the shoreline below, 1.2 road miles east of the church where you began (allow four hours).

The Ram Head Trail

This isolated trail begins from a parking area 3.9 miles south of Coral Bay. Highlighting St. John's driest vegetation, the rollercoaster path to Ram Head first traipses past Salt Pond, then over a hill to a unique, blue cobble beach. Continue over exposed coastal cliffs (watch your footing) to the cactus-peppered Ram Head, which rewards with views of the British Virgins and, on occasion, St. Croix to the south. A short spur trail to Drunk Bay (near the start of the Ram Head hike) also is worth exploring; allow two hours to see the whole area.

The Reef Bay Trail

This excellent hike starts from Centerline Road, 4.9 miles east of Cruz Bay, and descends steadily from the ridge through tropical forest. Identifying markers are provided for much of the vegetation, as well as for the historical sights (the trail passes the ruins of four sugar estates and a petroglyph site). A spur trail to Lameshur Bay takes off from behind the ruins of the Reef Bay Great House. As you continue down and your elevation decreases, the plant life along the path evolves into drier scrub and cactus. After 2.2 miles, the trail ends at the isolated beach fronting Reef Bay, where picnic tables are available. You may return via the same trail or, if you've arranged a ride, take the one-and-a-half mile Lameshur Bay trail.

By Pedal

Other islands are bigger or taller, but few concentrate as many steep grades into a compact area as St. John. While some residents view cycling here as a form of masochism, those who delight in long hills will be delighted and challenged. Buck up, my well-toned friends, and head up to **Centerline Road**, which traces the island's main east-west ridge; once you've climbed the initial hill on either side, it rolls more gently through gorgeous forests. Somewhere near the navel of the island, the dirt Bordeaux Mountain Road follows another ridge southeast to **Bordeaux Mountain**. Just east of this mountain is a steep, four-wheel-drive road which drops down to Coral Harbor; if you're at all unsure about descending extreme grades, walk it. The North Coast Road west of Cinnamon Bay passes one beautiful beach after another; however, this also is the most trafficked stretch on the island. Instead, head east out of Cinnamon Bay to the **Annaberg Ruins** where quieter roads visit more beaches; riding as far as Watermelon Bay and over to Francis Bay will create a relative easy half-day trip of about eight or nine miles. The best moderate ride on the island leaves from Coral Bay and follows the Salt Pond Road south and over to **Lameshur Bay**. This is about eight mile round-tip ride and, although it ascends several hills in each direction, none exceed a few hundred feet above sea level. The East End Road is all but impossible for cyclists: don't say we didn't warn you. Throughout St. John, watch out for the slick concrete you'll find spanning ravine crossings (it's usually covered in algae). One final note: Although you may use the numerous marked dirt roads, bikes are strictly forbidden on all walking trails.

Bike Rental Shops

Coral Bay Watersports
Cinnamon Bay; ☎ *(809) 776-6330.*
A small selection of bikes available, with no charge for a drop-off. $10 per hour, $20 for a half day, $25 for a full day; multi-day discounts available when renting more than one bike.

By Paddle

Sea kayaking is quickly finding a niche in the U.S. and Virgin Islands. The classic tour leaves from Virgin Gorda or Peter Island in the BVIs and heads toward St. John, the wind on your back for most of the way. En route on this idyllic trip, stops at **Beef**, **Cooper**, and **Jost Van Dyke** islands reward with hidden beaches and pristine snorkeling. You can stay at hotels and guest houses in a real bed nightly—which minimizes your load factor to a change of clothes, fresh water, swimsuit, a towel, mask and snorkel, sunscreen (essential) and hat—or, play "no-see-um" on beaches by pulling onto shore late, camping and leaving early before anyone catches you. If planning such a trip, you can take a kayak on the ferry to the British Virgins, but don't forget to bring your passport. Keep in mind summer sun can be intense, best combated with water, sunscreen and a fashionable, wide-brimmed hat. Although the trip can be done in a few days, allow a week for maximum enjoyment. Sea conditions in the Virgins are usually calm, however, an overnight trip is not suitable as a beginner's excursion; make sure you have adequate training and experience before undertaking such an adventure. In addition to the rental and tour options below, it's now possible to purchase collapsible kayaks for relatively easy air transport.

Paddle Tours & Rentals

Arawak Expeditions
Cruz Bay; ☎ *(800) 238-8687 or (809) 693-8312.*

Offers fully supported camping trips starting at Peter Island and winding their way back to St. John, $850 for the five day trip, $1095 for seven days (slightly less during summer months). Half/full-day guided tours, $30-55. Arawak uses fiberglass kayaks and all trips are suitable for beginners.

Coral Bay Watersports

Cinnamon Bay; ☎ *(809) 776-6330.*

Avails off-premise kayak rentals and will help coordinate overnight trips. Half/full day guided tours, $40–60. Single-seat kayak weekly rentals, $120 off-season, $140 in high; double-seat kayaks, $160–$200. Day rates for single-seat kayaks: $10 per hour or $35 for 24 hours; double-seat kayaks, $17 per hour or $60 for 24 hours. $10 per kayak drop-off/pickup charge. High season in effect mid-December to mid-April.

FIELDING'S CHOICE:

Sign up for the National Parks Service tour, whose guided adventure hikes acquaint you with native wildlife, including rippled tail man lizards, black spiny sea urchins, and peely barked "tourist trees."

What Else to See

Most of your time on St. John will want to be spent hiking, climbing and limin', but a few historical sites are worth the effort (some are even located on trails). Among the most interesting is the **Annaberg Sugar Mill Ruins**, operated by the National Parks Service, which gives living history demonstrations of how islanders managed to survive in the post-slavery years. The **Elaine Ione Spauve Library** and the **Museum of Cultural Arts** in Cruz Bay occupy an 18th-century plantation house that contains photos and artifacts illustrating the survival of island arts. A trip to **Caneel Bay**, the resort launched by Laurence Rockefeller, is worth a visit, even if you aren't staying there, to enjoy the dazzling view of the bay from the North Shore road. **Catherineberg Plantation** down Centerline Road, approachable from a rocky road, also has stupendous views, as well as a now crumbling windmill, full of stupendous views.

Museums and Exhibits

Elaine Ione Sprauve Museum ★ ★ ★

Cruz Bay, ☎ *(809) 776-6359.*

Hours Open: 9 a.m.–5 p.m.

This small museum has exhibits on St. John's Danish West Indian history, as well as displays of locally created artwork.

Parks and Gardens

Virgin Islands National Park ★★★★★

Cruz Bay, ☎ *(809) 776-6201.*

No visit to St. John—or any of the U.S. Virgins—would be complete without at least a day spent at the breathtaking national park. It encompasses 12,624 acres and has 20 miles of trails to explore. Stop by the Visitors Center (open daily from 8:00 a.m.to 4:30 p.m.) to peruse the exhibits, pick up a map, and get details of special ranger-led events. Highlights on the park include the Annaberg Ruins, a sugar plantation and mill from the 1780s; the Reef Bay Trail, which passes plantation ruins and petroglyphs); and Trunk Bay, a picture-postcard beach and the start of a marked underwater trail well-loved by snorkelers.

Tours

Guided Tours

Cruz Bay.

The St. John Taxi Association will show you around the island for about $30 for one or two people, $13 per person for three or more. The **St. John Island Tour** *(*☎ *774-4550)* lasts two hours and costs $12 per person. Ranger-led tours are popular at **Virgin Islands National Park**; call ☎ *776-6201* for details. Finally, local personality **Miss Lucy** *(*☎ *776-6804)* tailors private tours to individual interests, while **John Abraham** *(*☎ *776-6177)* offers a friendly, insider's look at his island.

BEST VIEW:

Le Chateau de Bordeaux clings to the edge of a mountain top along Centerline Road, which gives spectacular views of Bordeaux Mountain, St. John's highest peak, and the serpentine Sir Francis Drake Channel, with the British Virgin Islands scattered below. And the cuisine is superb.

Sports

Watersports are an integral part of the St. John lifestyle. At Trunk Bay, a new sport called SNUBA has become very popular—a combination of snorkeling and scuba diving that doesn't require lengthy certification courses. Both campgrounds offer extensive sports packages, including scuba and trekking. The Virgin Islands are famous for spectacular deep-sea fishing for blue marlin, with many world records to prove it. Anglers from all over the world head here for the **Blue Marlin Fishing Tournament** in August. No deep-sea fishing is allowed in the National Park, but you can rod-and-reel fish from the beaches in St. John. Excellent sea conditions with balmy weather and numerous covers and sheltered anchors create unparalleled conditions for sailing. Every type of vessel, from sailfish to oceangoing yachts, can be hired. Boats may be chartered with a full crew or bareback, but know what you are doing if you choose to leave the crew behind. There are many half-day and full-day boat excursions; check first with your hotel, which probably has a full list and can recommend what will best suit your needs. Operators in St. John are based in Cruz Bay and Coral Bay. Because of the constant trade winds, windsurfing also finds a large group of fans. The winds, whipping down the **Sir Francis Drake Channel** north of St. John, are funneled by two hills through the Narrows to the Windward Passage. About five miles north of Trunk Bay, on the north side of **Johnson's Reef**, the conditions are simply perfect. Windsurfers can also sail cross **Pillsbury Sound** to St. Thomas. (See trails for hiking under "On Foot" above. For more information on diving, see "Underwater" above.)

Watersports

Various locations, Cruz Bay.

St. John's two lavish resorts, the Hyatt Regency and Caneel Bay, have their own watersports facilities. Otherwise you're probably on your own. For general equipment rentals, try: **Coral Bay Watersports** (☎ 776-6850), **Paradise Watersports** (☎ 693-8690), **Low Key Watersports** (☎ 693-8999), **Cinnam Bay Watersports Center** (☎ 776-6330), and **Cruz Bay Watersports** (☎ 776-6234). The latter four also offer diving instruction and excursions. For deep-sea fishing, try **Gone Ketchin** (☎ 693-8657), **World Class Anglers** (☎ 779-4281), and **Low Key Watersports** (☎ 693-8999). For kayaking and windsurfing, in addition to other rentals, call **Paradise Aqua Tour** (☎ 776-6226).

FIELDING'S CHOICE:

No other sport will bring you closer to the spirit of the original Arawaks and Caribs than sea kayaking, and the best Caribbean waters for it are found among the sheltered cays and coves of the British and the U.S. Virgin Islands. Arawak Expeditions offers a challenging trip of 3 hours paddling a day, 5–6 miles a day, 5 days in a row. The tour begins in St. John, where you're briefed and supplied with rows, sleeping bag, tents and sleeping pad. Then you and your two-person 20-foot-long kayak are taken by launch to Virgin Gorda, so you'll be paddling downwind back to St. John. Itineraries vary, depending on weather and tides, but can include stops at Ginger, Peter, Norman and Jost Van Dyke islands.

FIELDING'S CHOICE:

To avoid the afternoon breezes and blustery seas, you do most of the traveling before lunch, then pitch camp on a deserted beach. You don't even have to know which way to point the kayaks. The company gives you full instructions how to slip in, button up, manage the paddles, and get back in when you flip. First-timers from 14–73 have returned. Arawak Expeditions, P.O. Box 853, Cruz Bay, St. John, USVI 00831, ☎ (800) 238-8687. Five-night cruises cost $750 per person, seven days $925 year-round, including kayaks, camping equipment, meals and drinks, minimum four guests per tour.

Insider Tip:

Wednesday is cruise day, so hunker down and stay clear away from Cruz Bay.

Where to Stay

![Fielding logo]	**Fielding's Highest Rated Hotels in St. John**	
★★★★★	Caneel Bay Resort	$225–$695
★★★★★	Hyatt Regency St. John	$195–$515
★★★★	Estate Concordia	$95–$190
★★★★	Harmony	$95–$180
★★★	Gallows Point Suites	$140–$360
★★★	Maho Bay Camp Resort	$60–$95

![Heart logo]	**Fielding's Most Romantic Hotels in St. John**	
★★★★★	Caneel Bay Resort	$225–$695
★★★★★	Hyatt Regency St. John	$195–$515

![Budget logo]	**Fielding's Budget Hotels in St. John**	
★★★	Cinnamon Bay Campground	$15–$98
★	Cruz Inn	$55–$90
★★	Inn at Tamarind Court	$40–$110
★★★	Maho Bay Camp Resort	$60–$95
★★	Raintree Inn	$60–$115

On St. John, you can choose from the super-luxurious, the ecologically sound or the charmingly simple. Demand in some cases is excessive, so expect unreasonably high prices. Many people choose to camp because it's cheaper, and because they've come to brave the great outdoors anyway. The camping properties at Cinnamon Bay and Maho Bay are more than agreeable for those used to roughing it. Make reservations far in advance.

Hotels and Resorts

You have two resorts to choose from. **Caneel Bay**, the heart child of Laurence Rockefeller and the premier property on St. John, has been spruced up for the '90s but still reains an ideal serenity at the same time providing the services of an all-inclusive: seven beaches, seven tennis courts, and it's actually in the park. (The most published line about Caneel Bay is "for the newly wed and the nearly dead.") The **Hyatt Regency** is modern, luxurious, with a huge pool, but only six courts!

Caneel Bay Resort · · · · · · · · · · · · · · · $225–$695 · · · · · · · · · · · · ★★★★★

Caneel Bay, ☎ *(800) 928-8889, (809) 776-6111, FAX (809) 693-8280.*
Single: $225–$695. Double: $225–$695.
Set on a 170-acre estate, this distinguished resort continues to do much right, as it has since Laurence Rockefeller bought it in 1956, when it was already in operation for 20 years. Accommodations are scattered about in recently renovated, spacious cottages. All are quite gorgeous and include patios, minibars and coffeemakers (you'll have to pay to brew a cup of Joe), but lack air conditioning, TV and tele- phones, and the bathrooms are rather small. Though they say they don't need air conditioning because ceiling fans and constant breezes do the job, they're wrong— and at these rates, it's nice to have the option of cooled air, especially at night. The rooms overlooking the tennis courts and garden areas offer the most serenity (and are cheaper), while those on the beach are understandably more popular. The extensive grounds offer up 11 tennis courts (play is free), three restaurants, a lounge with nightly entertainment, a small pool, and a new air-cooled exercise room. There are seven lovely beaches from which to choose, with all the watersports one could want. The grounds, which abut Virgin Islands National Park, are kept in gorgeous condition year-round. This is one of the Caribbean's finest resorts, but it's not for everyone. You're required to dress for dinner, there's very little nightlife, and the rates keep out most young folks. No children under five are allowed. If you're going to be out past midnight, you must let them know in advance or you'll be literally locked out of the main gate. In fact, everything is a long walk at this sprawling resort, and while shuttle buses ply the grounds frequently, the impatient may feel, well, impatient with this arrangement. Note: Be sure to go over your bill meticu- lously when you check out. Many guests have complained of being grossly over- charged. And be sure to look into special packages that can save you bucks at this very expensive spot. One final note: Meal plans run from $65 to $85 daily, and as St. John has a variety of gourmet restaurants, you're probably better off dining a la carte.

Hyatt Regency St. John · · · · · · · · · · · · · $195–$515 · · · · · · · · · · · · ★★★★★

Great Cruz Bay, ☎ *(800) 233-1234, (809) 693-8000, FAX (809) 693-8888.*
Single: $195–$360. Double: $240–$515.
This glamorous resort attracts a younger set than at the Caneel Bay, but it too is quite expensive. Set on 34 landscaped acres opening onto a lovely beach, the Hyatt puts guests up in plush guestrooms near the beach and pool. All have modern com- forts, but only some have balconies. There are also seven one-bedroom suites and 14 two-bedroom townhouses. Dining options range from Chinese to Italian to West Indian specialties. Recreational facilities include six tennis courts, a large pool, gym, watersports (there's a charge for scuba, sailing and fishing), and organized activities for the kids at "Camp Hyatt." Very very fun and very very nice, but this is

the kind of crowded, busy resort that turns some people off. If you're looking for true island flavor, stay elsewhere, but if you're a luxurious resort lover, look no further.

Apartments and Condominiums

Rental properties have become extremely popular here for their affordable prices. First-class private homes and villas and plush condos outnumber traditional vacation accommodations on the island. Most villas or beachfront homes offer fully equipped kitchens, plus VCRs, stereos, patio grills and beach toys. Maid and chef service are often available. Choices range from massive, multi-room resort homes that hug the hillside overlooking Cruz Bay to simply decorated one-bedroom condos with a bay view. Villa rentals year-round average $1200–$2000 per week. Condos run $105–$360 per night per unit. For more information contact your nearest USVI tourist board. Check with several rental agencies before you settle on something. Prices vary greatly, and you can choose between simple one-room apartments or more elaborate private homes. Food in supermarkets runs high in St. John; better to stock up in St. Thomas or bring staples from home.

Estate Concordia   **$95–$190**   ★★★★

Maho Bay, ☎ (800) 392-9004, (212) 472-9543, FAX (212) 861-6210.
Double: $95–$190.

Owned by the same folks who developed Maho Bay Campground and Harmony, this property offers deluxe accommodations in an off-the-beaten-track setting on St. John's southeastern coast. The 51-acre estate looks out on Salt Pond Bay with lovely views of the beach below, which is best reached by car. The nicest unit is the loft duplex, which has 20-foot cathedral ceilings, a wraparound deck, two bathrooms, a full kitchen, two twin beds, ceiling fans, and a queen-size sofabed. There's also a vaulted studio with a full kitchen and efficiency suites with kitchenettes. The grounds include a 20- by 40-foot swimming pool, laundry room, and store. As with Harmony, the property was built to be sensitive to the surrounding ecosystem.

Gallows Point Suites   **$140–$360**   ★★★

Cruz Bay, ☎ (800) 323-7229, (809) 776-6434, FAX (809) 776-6520.
Single: $140–$325. Double: $170–$360.

All accommodations at this oceanfront resort are suites. Garden units have sunken living rooms, while the larger upper suites have loft bedrooms and two baths. All are spacious, with quality furnishings, fully equipped kitchens, living and dining rooms, and ceiling fans (no air conditioning, but breezes generally do the job.) There's a restaurant and two bars on the premises, and they'll shuttle you into town (a five-minute walk) for free. The beach is quite small, but the free-form pool is large and inviting. Very nice. No kids under five.

Harmony   **$95–$180**   ★★★★

Maho Bay, ☎ (800) 392-9004, (212) 472-9453, FAX (212) 861-6210.
Double: $95–$180.

As the name implies, these cottages were built as much in harmony with nature as possible. Set high on a hill over the Maho Bay Campground (and owned by the same folks), each unit is powered by the sun and wind and was built using recycled materials—even the nails came from recycled steel. Guests can keep track of their energy use on computers installed in each unit. The spacious, one-room cottages are quite nicely done, with tile floors, wicker furniture, kitchenettes, living and dining areas, interesting artwork, ceiling fans, high wood-beamed ceilings, and nice decks. The shower-only baths are small but functional. There are no phones or TV, and for some reason, all the beds are twins (easily pushed together). It's a five- to seven-minute walk to the beach down a steep road—you're better off driving.

Lavender Hill Estates $135–$265   ★★

Cruz Bay, ☎ *(800) 562-1901, (809) 776-6969, FAX (809) 776-6969.*
Single: $135–$210. Double: $160–$265.
Set on a hillside within walking distance of Cruz Bay shops and restaurants, this complex offers condominium living. Each of the 12 units has full kitchens, nice views off the balconies, spacious living rooms, and one or two bedrooms. All are quite nice and have TVs and phones, but rely on ceiling fans instead of air conditioners. There's a large pool on the premises.

Serendip Condominiums $90–$145   ★

Cruz Bay, .
Single: $90–$145. Double: $90–$145.
This secluded mountainside resort consists of eight one-bedroom units and two studios, each with kitchens, limited maid service, and dining areas. Furnishings are simple but adequate. There are no facilities on-site, but beaches and watersports can be found nearby at the national park.

Inns

Three inns are available on the island; for a tad more sophistication (some private bathrooms), try the Inn at Tamarind Court, which comes with a complimentary breakfast.

Cruz Inn $55–$90   ★

Cruz Bay, ☎ *(800) 666-7688, (809) 776-7688.*
Single: $55–$90. Double: $55–$90.
Accommodations at this basic guesthouse range from simple guest rooms with shared baths to efficiencies with private baths and kitchen facilities. You'll pay extra for air conditioning. Continental breakfast is served daily, and there is entertainment three times a week in the busy bar. Okay for the rates.

Inn at Tamarind Court $40–$110   ★★

Cruz Bay, ☎ *(809) 776-6378.*
Single: $40–$110. Double: $70–$110.
Most rooms for two at this simple spot are around $75, making it one of St. John's least-expensive properties. Most share baths and seem to be decorated with garage sale specials. There are also a few suites and a one-bedroom apartment. Despite its somewhat rundown accommodations, the Tamarind Court does a brisk business with penny-watching young people, and the atmosphere is friendly and fun. A bar and restaurant are on the premises.

Raintree Inn $60–$115   ★★

Cruz Bay, ☎ *(800) 666-7449, (809) 693-8590, FAX (809) 693-8590.*
Single: $60–$100. Double: $70–$115.

The rooms here are as simple as the rates suggest, but very comfortable and with private baths. No air conditioning, but each room has a ceiling fan. There are also loft bedrooms and kitchens in three of the units. Smoking is forbidden. The restaurant serves dinner only. Not bad for the price.

Low Cost Lodging

Camping is a popular alternative on St. John, since the park is so conducive to nights under (or at least near) the stars. Both Cinnamon Bay and Maho Bay campgrounds feature tent-type dwellings (Cinnamon Bay has a few cottages), cafeteria, communal bathrooms and sports activities. Maho Bay even hosts marriages and offers massage facilities and a great view. Reserve both far in advance (in some cases, a year). If you're torn between the two keep in mind that Cinnamon Bay has the prettier site, while Maho Bay has much nicer accommodations.

Cinnamon Bay Campground   **$15–$98**   ★★★

Cinnamon Beach, ☎ *(809) 776-6330, FAX (809) 776-6458.*
Single: $15–$95. Double: $30–$98.

Set in the woods in beautiful Virgin Islands National Park, this park-run campground offers everything from bare sites on which to pitch a tent to rather ugly cottages with electricity, simple cooking facilities, and two trundle beds. There are also small tents with wooden floors that lack electricity but do have gas lanterns and stoves. Four bath houses provide toilets and showers. Meals can be had in the cafeteria. There's no pool, but the nearby beach is grand, and many watersports are complimentary. This spot is prettier than the campground at Maho Bay, but its accommodations are much more rustic. Two-week maximum stay.

Campgrounds

Maho Bay Camp Resort   **$60–$95**   ★★★

Maho Bay, ☎ *(800) 392-9004, (809) 776-6226, (212) 472-9453, FAX (212) 861-6210.*
Single: $60–$95. Double: $60–$95.

Set on 14 forested acres in the Virgin Islands National Park, this gorgeous spot is for nature lovers who like to camp without sacrificing too many creature comforts. Accommodations are in three-room tent-style cottages, with kitchenettes, a screened dining area, sofabeds, twin beds, living areas, private decks and electricity. Five communal bath houses have toilets and showers. The grounds include a sandy beach, simple restaurant and watersports. Each site is limited to two adults and two kids. Quite comfortable and nice, and very popular. The only drawback is that it's a steep walk to the beach.

Where to Eat

Fielding's Highest Rated Restaurants in St. John

★★★★★	Equator	$27–$32
★★★★	Asolare	$18–$24
★★★★	Le Chateau de Bordeaux	$20–$30
★★★★	Paradiso	$17–$25
★★★	Chow Mein	$11–$24
★★★	Don Carlos	$9–$17
★★★	Ellington's	$17–$25
★★★	Mongoose	$6–$50
★★★	Morgan's Mango	$7–$22
★★★	Pussers	$6–$25

Fielding's Special Restaurants in St. John

★★★★★	Equator	$27–$32
★★★★	Asolare	$18–$24
★★★★	Le Chateau de Bordeaux	$20–$30
★★★	Morgan's Mango	$7–$22
★★★	Vie's Snack Shack	$2–$6

Fielding's Budget Restaurants in St. John

★★★	Vie's Snack Shack	$2–$6
★★	The Lime Inn	$3–$20
★★★	Don Carlos	$9–$17
★★	Cafe Roma	$11–$16
★★★	Morgan's Mango	$7–$22

Restaurants in St. John favor American, British, West Indian and Italian cuisines. Atmosphere can range from an outdoor patio with neighborhood strays, a West Indian gingerbread house, the peak of a mountain, or the ruins of a sugar mill—almost all are open to the wind. The best selection is in Cruz Bay, where you can also find elegant dining. Outside Cruz Bay is **Le Chateau de Bordeaux**, the island's most ambitious restaurant, a comfortable low-ceiling room set atop the 1277-foot **Bordeaux Mountain**, St. John's highest point. The menu ranges from scrumptious pumpkin soup to West Indian curry to Peking duck. **Asolare** offers up spicy Asian-influenced fare in a lovely setting. **Etta**, at the Inn at Tamarind Court, is perfect for callaloo soup—a delicious thick seafood porridge with okra and spinach—and other West Indian delights. Remember **Morgan's Mango** for creative neo-Caribbean cuisine in a gingerbread setting. One of the most romantic settings on the island is Caneel Bay's **Equator**, a pretty stone building open to the fresh air. Their pan-fried flying fish makes a memory. For a quick, agreeable pub lunch in Cruz Bay, try **Pusser's** waterfront balcony.

Asolare $$$ ★★★★

Route 20, ☎ *(809) 779-4747.*

Asian cuisine.

Dinner: 5:30–8:45 p.m., entrees $18–$24.

When the owners of five-star Chateau de Bordeaux decided to open a second restaurant, they searched high and far for a name until stumbling upon the Greek work *asolare*, which means "the purposeless, agreeable and leisurely passing of time." Except for the purposeless part, the moniker perfectly sums up this new restaurant, just opened in November 1994. Dine on a large deck overlooking Cruz Bay and the twinkling lights of St. Thomas, or in a charming stone-walled room dominated by a rock fireplace. The eclectic menu has a decidedly Asian bent, with local fish seasoned with the herbs and spices of India, Thailand, Vietnam and China. Try five-spice barbecued tuna with chilled Szechwan noodles, dry-fried long beans and red onion crisps; glass noodle prawns with wok-crisp Chinese greens and a roasted tomato, garlic, red chili and cilantro sauce; or roasted swordfish with scallion vermicalli cake, braised greens and a black bean-clam sauce. The combinations may sound odd, but the results are spectacular. Afterwards, slip off to the nearby Bad Art Bar (Route 10, Cruz Bay, 693-8666), a lively joint that lives up to its name with the tackiest decor imaginable, including, of course, a velvet Elvis.

Cafe Roma $$ ★★

Cruz Bay, ☎ *(809) 776-6524.*

Italian cuisine. Specialties: Pizza, shrimp with garlic sauce.

Dinner: 5–10 p.m., entrees $11–$16.

A touch of Italy in the tropics, this pretty trattoria overlooks the sights and sounds of Cruz Bay from a second-floor perch. No slouch on gustatory or olfactory senses either, the place is noted for dynamite pizza—there's a choice of a white or traditional tomato sauce as a base for several tasty toppings. Seafood is also a standout,

especially shrimp with garlic sauce. An excellent choice for a varied selection of tropical drinks.

Chow Mein $$$ ★ ★ ★

Great Cruz Bay, ☎ (809) 693-8000.
International cuisine.
Dinner: 6–9:30 p.m., entrees $11–$24.
This restaurant's name has changed a few times since its inception (it used to be
called Ciao Mein), but the cuisine atop the sprawling, atrium-style Hyatt Regency
St. John has remained a successful melange of Asian and Italian culinary concoc-
tions. Guests can watch the lobby action below while dining on wok-stirred sea-
food, pot stickers, or pasta with vegetables.

Don Carlos $$ ★ ★ ★

10-19 Estate Carolina, ☎ (809) 776-6866.
Mexican cuisine.
Lunch: 11 a.m.–4 p.m., entrees $9–$17.
Dinner: 4–9 p.m., entrees $9–$17.
This upscale cantina buzzes with zingy waiters delivering foaming margaritas and
zippy fajitas (this stateside chain is famous for them) to happy customers. Don Carlos also features lots of lively entertainment three nights a week. You might see
island favorites like conch fritters slipped in here and there on the menu along with
south of the border staples.

Ellington's $$$ ★ ★ ★

Gallows' Point, ☎ (809) 693-8490.
International cuisine.
Dinner: 6–10 p.m., entrees $17–$25.
Some of the best seafood on the island is prepared here at this view spot positioned
near the ferry dock. On a clear day, you can see St. Thomas from a front-row seat
on the terrace. After a tasty drink, dine on hearty seafood chowder followed by the
daily special, which could be blackened something, or shrimp in an exotic fruit
sauce. A light breakfast is also served from 8 to 10 a.m.

Equator $$$ ★ ★ ★ ★ ★

Caneel Bay, ☎ (809) 776-6111.
International cuisine.
Dinner: 6:30–9 p.m., entrees $27–$32.
Dine in a restored horse-powered sugar mill located on the lovely Caneel Bay
Resort grounds. It's a cavernous round room, formerly called the Sugar Mill, with
a large terrace where many patrons begin their meals with a luscious peach daiquiri.
The new menu features favorite foods and spices from countries close to the equator—specialties from such diverse locales as Morocco, Bombay, Indonesia and Brazil are among the eclectic choices. Especially appealing is the red chili-glazed
calamari served on a curry noodle pancake and the red lentil-crusted snapper. Afterwards, take a stroll along one of the resort's seven spectacular beaches.

Le Chateau de Bordeaux $$$ ★ ★ ★ ★

Junction 10, Centerline Road, Bordeaux Mountain, ☎ (809) 776-6611.
French cuisine. Specialties: Saffron pasta.

Dinner: 5:30–9.00 p.m., entrees $20–$30.

This petite dazzler clings to the cliffs of Bordeaux Mountain in the center of the island, and its terrace commands an unparalleled view of the setting sun and rising moon. (If you're on St. John during a full moon, dinner here is a must!) Despite its unprepossessing exterior, within is a cozy room with hand-crocheted tablecloths flickering oil lanterns and eclectic chandeliers. It's no surprise many honeymooners end up here, as this place just oozes romance. The cuisine is as good as the atmosphere—don't miss the saffron pasta (shaped to resemble an angle fish) stuffed with smoked salmon and sauteed in a sauce of capers, leeks, tomatoes and white wine Other choices include pan-seared Norwegian salmon in light fennel bouillabaisse with cultured mussels over bow-tie pasta, roasted rack of lamb, and grilled pork loin. This is one of the Caribbean's few nonsmoking restaurants, though there's a deck where smokers can slip off to get their fix.

Mongoose $$$ ★★★

Mongoose Junction, Mongoose Junction, ☎ *(809) 693-8677.*
International cuisine.
Lunch: 11:30 a.m.–5 p.m., entrees $6–$10.
Dinner: 5–10 p.m., entrees $10–$50.

A pleasant refueling spot for tired shoppers souvenir hunting at the Tony Mongoose Junction arcade, this eatery and bar offers a bevy of cooling fruity alcoholic drinks and plates of fresh seafood. Patrons poise themselves on a tree-shaded wooden deck or at the bar, which serves light meals until midnight.

Morgan's Mango $$ ★★★

Cruz Bay, ☎ *(809) 693-8141.*
Latin American cuisine.
Dinner: 6–10 p.m., entrees $7–$22.

There's often a crowd at this very popular dining spot in a gingerbread trimmed-house painted in pastels. One reason is an excellent bar and unusual Argentinian specialties interspersed with local seafood and chicken. Another is the woodsy patio where guests sit surrounded by trees and greenery. A plate-crowding hunk of prime beef comes accompanied by the piquant Pampas-style chimmichurri sauce—a spicy melding of oregano, peppers, lots of garlic and olive oil.

Paradiso $$$ ★★★★

Mongoose Junction, Mongoose Junction, ☎ *(809) 693-8899.*
Italian cuisine. Specialties: Lobster fra diavolo.
Dinner: 6–10 p.m., entrees $17–$25.

The words "suave" and "chic" appropriately describe this Italian restaurant all dolled up in burnished woods and marble. Dine in air-conditioned comfort on lobster or a daily seafood special prepared with their signature fra diavolo sauce. Paradiso also has an impressive wine list and well-mixed drinks.

Pussers $$$ ★★★

Wharfside Village, ☎ *(809) 693-9080.*
International cuisine. Specialties: Mud pie.
Lunch: 11 a.m.–6 p.m., entrees $6–$10.
Dinner: 6–10 p.m., entrees $15–$25.

The purveyors of the British Royal Navy's favorite rum have been successful in expanding their small chain of souvenir shops/pub establishments into U.S. Virgin territory with this open-air crowd pleaser. Offering special meal deals that should satisfy all but the very fussy, there are all-you-can-eat Alaskan king crab nights on Friday and Caribbean specials on Thursdays. Sandwiches, seafood plates, and gooey desserts are also available, including the famous mud pie. Don't miss the "Pusser Painkiller" drinks—good for whatever ails you.

The Lime Inn   **$$**   ★★
Cruz Bay, ☎ *(809) 776-6425.*
International cuisine. Specialties: All-you-can-eat shrimp.
Lunch: 11:30 a.m.–3 p.m., entrees $3–$10.
Dinner: 5:30–10 p.m., entrees $3–$20.
The local practice of limin' is strictly adhered to here (it means "hanging out") and the congenial group of limers include veteran travelers" as well as residents. Settle for a terrace seat to while away the hours with a bowl of goat water, seafood, or a sandwich. Hungry bargain hunters crowd the place Wednesday nights for the well-regarded, all-you-can-eat shrimp extravaganza, but no reservations are taken, so line up early.

Vie's Snack Shack   **$**   ★★★
East End, ☎ *(809) 693-5033.*
Latin American cuisine.
Lunch: 10 a.m.–5 p.m., entrees $2–$6.
This is probably the best local cooking in town—but it's only open four days a week, and only for lunch. But if you're in town when Vie's at the stove, don't miss it for fritters both sweet and savory, homemade fruit drinks and spicy chicken.

Where to Shop

Duty-free shopping is the major incentive to pull out your wallet here, and aside from attractive pricing on watches, china, gems, electronics and jewelry, there is no sales tax and a $1200 per person exemption from duty when returning to the U.S. Liquor is also a bargain and anyone over 21 years of age can return to the States with five bottles duty-free (or six, if one is produced in the USVI). Island clothing and T-shirts are also good buys. Stop by Bamboula in Mongoose Junction for ethnic folk art and artifacts.

St. John Directory

ARRIVAL

For North America, the major carriers are **American, Continental, Delta** and **U.S. Air,** with **Tower Air** scheduled several times each week out of New York's JFK Airport, and **TWA** connecting via Puerto Rico. Some arrivals will first stop at St. Thomas and some will stop first on St. Croix, but with only 32 miles separating the two islands, both are included on most itineraries. Virtually any North American gateway provides easy access to the USVI. In addition to these air arrivals, about one-half of the 1.8 million visitors to these islands arrive via cruise ships, most of which dock in St. Thomas Harbor at Charlotte Amalie.

For interisland air transport, both **Sunaire** and **American Eagle** fly between St. Croix and St. Thomas, offering hourly departures all day long. There is no airstrip on St. John, but ferryboat rides from downtown and Red Hook on St. Thomas operate on an hourly basis until 11 p.m. Schedules are subject to change and not every carrier operates every day, so for more complete and current information, on USVI travel connection, call ☎ *(800) USVI-INFO.*

BUSINESS HOURS

Shops generally open weekdays 9 a.m.–5 p.m. Banks generally open Monday–Thursday 9 a.m.–2:30 p.m. and Friday 9 a.m.–2 p.m. and 3:30–5 p.m.

CLIMATE

Temperatures during the summer, cooled by eastern trade winds, keep the temperature around 82 degrees F. Brief showers also keep things cool. Winter temperatures rise to 77 degrees F. Rainiest months are September-January, and about 40 inches of rain fall per year. April-August are the calmest sea conditions with the best visibility, although days of stunning clarity in excess of 100 feet are not unusual in winter.

DOCUMENTS

U.S. citizens need not carry a passport, although some proof of identity will be required upon leaving the islands. A passport is a good idea since the nearby British Virgin Islands are so accessible from St. John and St. Thomas. If you wish to dive the Rhone or snorkel amid the fantastic granite boulders at the baths on Virgin Gorda, you'll need to first clear BVI Customs with a passport and an $8 entry fee.

ELECTRICITY

Current runs at 110 volts at 60 cycles.

GETTING AROUND

Many rental companies in Cruz Bay offer competitive rates. Expect to pay roughly $60 per day, plus gas and insurance, for a Suzuki Sidekick (with four-wheel drive to accommodate blind switchbacks and extreme mountain inclines). And be prepared to drive on the left.

LANGUAGE

The official language is English. Some locals speak a musical patois called English Creole—a blend of English, African and Spanish. Many people also speak good Spanish.

MEDICAL EMERGENCIES

Police ext. *915*, fire ext. *921*, ambulance ext. *922*.

MONEY

The official currency is the U.S. dollar.

TELEPHONE

The area code is 809. Since USVI is an incorporated territory, toll-free numbers that operate in the U.S. work here, normal postage rates apply. You can also direct dial to the mainland.

TIME

Atlantic Standard Time, one hour later than New York City; during Daylight Saving Time, it is the same as New York.

TIPPING AND TAXES

Some hotels include a 10–15 percent service charge; this should include all tips for both restaurant and room service, unless the attention was extraordinary. If no service is added, leave a 15 percent tip for the waitress, $1–2 a day to the maid; bartenders and wine stewards should be tipped always. Tip the bellboy and porter at least 50 cents a bag. Taxi drivers should receive a 15 percent tip if you are satisfied with the service.

TOURIST INFORMATION

The **St. John Tourist Office** ☎ *(809) 776-6450* is located around the corner from the Cruz Bay ferry dock by the post office. It is open daily. In the U.S. call ☎ *(212) 332-2222*.

WHEN TO GO

St. John's Carnival events take place from June 18-July 4, including a food fair, boat races and the recreation of a carnival village. The St. John Carnival Parade takes place on July 4.

The area code is *809*. Since USVI is an unincorporated territory, toll-free numbers that operate in the U.S. work here, normal U.S. postage rates apply. You can also direct dial to the mainland.

ST. JOHN HOTELS	RMS	RATES	PHONE	CR. CARDS
Coral Bay				
★★★★★ **Caneel Bay Resort**	171	$225–$695	(800) 928-8889	A, DC, MC, V
★★★★★ **Hyatt Regency St. John**	285	$195–$515	(800) 233-1234	A, CB, D, MC, V
★★★★ **Estate Concordia**	10	$95–$190	(800) 392-9004	

ST. JOHN HOTELS		RMS	RATES	PHONE	CR. CARDS
★★★★	Harmony	8	$95–$180	(800) 392-9004	
★★★	Cinnamon Bay Campground	113	$15–$95	(809) 776-6330	A, MC
★★★	Gallows Point Suites	60	$140–$360	(800) 323-7229	A, DC, MC, V
★★★	Maho Bay Camp Resort	113	$60–$90	(800) 392-9004	None
★★	Inn at Tamarind Court	20	$40–$110	(809) 776-6378	A, MC
★★	Lavender Hill Estates		$135–$265	(800) 562-1901	A, D, MC, V
★★	Raintree Inn	11	$60–$115	(800) 666-7449	A, CB, D, MC, V
★	Cruz Inn	14	$55–$90	(800) 666-7688	A, MC
★	Serendip Condominiums	10	$90–$145	(809) 773-5762	A, MC

ST. JOHN RESTAURANTS		PHONE	ENTREE	CR. CARDS
Coral Bay				
Asian				
★★★★★	Asolare	(809) 779-4747	$10–$24••	DC, MC, V
French				
★★★★	Le Chateau de Bordeaux	(809) 779-4078	$6–$28	DC, MC, V
International				
★★★	Chow Mein	(809) 693-8000	$11–$24••	A, DC, MC, V
★★★★★	Equator	(809) 776-6111	$27–$32••	A, DC, MC, V
★★★	Ellington's	(809) 693-8490	$17–$25••	A, MC, V
★★★	Mongoose	(809) 693-8677	$6–$50	A, DC, MC, V
★★★	Pussers	(809) 693-9080	$6–$25	A, MC, V
★★	The Lime Inn	(809) 776-6425	$3–$20	A, MC, V
Italian				
★★★★	Paradiso	(809) 693-8899	$17–$25••	A, MC, V
★★	Cafe Roma	(809) 776-6524	$11–$16••	MC, V
Latin American				
★★★	Morgan's Mango	(809) 693-8141	$7–$22••	A, MC, V
★★★	Vie's Snack Shack	(809) 693-5033	•$2–$6	None
Mexican				
★★★	Don Carlos	(809) 776-6866	$9–$17	A, MC, V

ST. JOHN RESTAURANTS   **PHONE**   **ENTREE**   **CR. CARDS**

Note: • Lunch Only

       •• Dinner Only

Hurricane Update

Some hotels and restaurants on St. John suffered damage from Hurricane Marilyn but most expected major repairs to be completed by the start of 1996.

ST. KITTS

Local and international regattas are held at St. Kitts.

Imagine empty beaches, the lushest of flora, dark, humid rain forests, spectacular dive sites, and even fat black ladies sashaying down country roads with pumpkin-sized washing atop their proud heads—St. Kitts has a little something for everybody. With its sister island Nevis, St. Kitts forms a Caribbean nation that just declared its first decade of independence, but the pace of life hasn't changed here in centuries. The epitome of the "limin' life," Kittian culture is still propelled by that "stop for a beer anytime" attitude—an almost ecological spirit, since, despite a lot of dream schemes, the coastline hasn't yet been marred by too much construction. Simply, unhampered tranquility reigns in St. Kitts, and the noisiest thing you'll ever hear will be the gentle skittering of the surf across the black and blonde sands. At one time, St. Kitts was distinguished only by its array of small inns fashioned from old plantations. Today, after the once-pristine Frigate Bay has been developed into an enclave of condos and package-tour hotels, Kittians are understandably nervous about change, even as the island struggles to recover from losses incurred from the demise of Pan Am and 1989's Hurricane Hugo, which did serious damage. Nevertheless, there's an unmistakable stir in the breezy Kitts air, and new luxury hotels are not the only signs of resurgence. A waterfront warehouse has been restyled into a lively duty-free mall and concerned citizens are busily recycling fine old buildings in the capital city into boutiques, restaurants and offices. With just a few more trendy stores and cafes added to its vast array of water activities, St. Kitts could easily become the next Caribbean nexus.

Bird's Eye View

Untrammeled by tourism, St. Kitts is a stunning combination of volcanic mountains, rain forest and golden beaches.

Part of the northern chain of the Leeward Islands in the Eastern Caribbean, St. Kitts covers an area of 68 square miles, divided by three volcanic mountains split by deep ravines and a low-lying peninsula in the southeast. From the air, both St. Kitts and Nevis look like two green blips floating

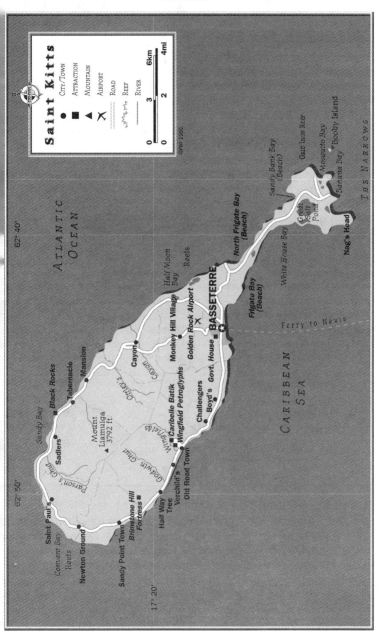

between St. Martin and Montserrat. St.Kitts' curious layout—three island in one—recalls the shape over an oversized tennis racket. The "head" to th northwest is dominated by the 3793-foot **Mount Liamuiga** and a rain fores ringed by sugarcane plantations and a rugged shoreline; the neck is a low lying isthmus known as **Frigate Bay;** and the "grip" is the hilly southwest pen insula, until 1992 reachable only by boat or four-wheel-drive buggy. Fc many years the Southeast Peninsula was considered the "Caribbean Shangri La," blessed with palm-fringed coves that resemble lagoons, rugged, lush to pography and a large salt pond. Today the peninsula is also a reserve fo many of the green vervet monkeys and white-tailed deer that roam about.

The "last frontier of the Caribbean" was considered to be the beach of Si Timothy Thornhill, once approachable only by a rugged stony trail that lec to the southernmost tip of St. Kitts. The massive natural barrier, coverec with steep slopes, thorn bushes and spiky acacia trees, daunted many a bathe in search of the 23 beautiful peninsula beaches that had nearly become leg end. Today the seven-mile Dr. Kennedy Simmonds Highway allows motor ists to traverse the hill in minutes. To preserve the pristine beaches, only few select hotels have been allowed to build on the site.

St.Kitts' capital of **Basseterre** (pop. 20,000) seems to boom with an irre pressible West Indian vigor. The traffic police are crisply dressed, and regga blasts from music stores and cafes. Already being built is a $16.23 millior deep-water cruiseship facility, which will include an expanded shopping are and sailing; the position allows debarking passengers to step off their ship and find themselves less than a block away from the Berkeley Memoria Clock.

History

Columbus first sighted the island of St. Kitts, dubbing it —with a touch o self-aggrandizement—St. Christopher. (The title was later shortened to St Kitts by British tobacco planters, who ignored Spanish claims and moved ir with their African slaves.) For years the island remained lost in obscurity, in habited by cohiba-smoking Carib Indians who found nourishment from the island in the form of turtles, iguanas and mawby liquor. In 1623, a daring group of settlers led by Sir Thomas Warner plopped themselves on the is land, soon having to share the beach uneasily with some French colonists On June 20, 1690, during a French occupation, the Englishman Sir Timo thy Thornhill led a party of soldiers in the dead of night through Friars Bay and over a rocky hill full of thorn bushes and spiky acacia trees to catch the French sentries off guard, who thought the British could only attack from the sea. After taking Basseterre, the island's main city, the English troops spiked the fortress cannons so that other English troops could land in safety. The hill was later named Sir Timothy in honor of Thornhill, but remains a daunting natural barrier, stretching from steep cliffs on the Atlantic to even steeper cliffs on the Caribbean. (The 1783 Treaty of Versailles finally awarded sovereignty to the Brits.) Independent from Britain since 1983, St. Kitts is dealing peacefully with the challenges of economy, but still maintains affectionate ties with the mother country. In fact, Queen Elizabeth II visited St. Kitts in 1985 and her portrait continues to grace island bank notes.

Jewish communities on both islands can be traced back to the 17th century. The earliest date on the nineteen tombstones in the Jewish cemetery on Nevis goes back to the 1680s, and records in England suggest that the Nevis synagogue is older than the 1732 synagogue in Curaçao. Recently, a "mikvah," or ritual bath, was discovered by an island historian. When large populations of Jews fled to the islands to escape the Spanish Inquisition, the majority of those who came to Nevis were from Brazil.

People

Friendly and cricket-loving, Kittians are still living the remains of British gentility at the same time catering to the Caribbean rhythm of life. A little fishing, a little gardening, long pauses to chat—that's the pattern of a day's dally. Kittians were delighted with Queen Elizabeth's comments about the unspoiled beauty, an opinion shared by Christopher Columbus. The beauty, however, seems to have dazzled residents into a slumber that doesn't inspire too much art. A few are notable, such as the sculptor Valentine Brown, who lives in Dieppe Bay and is known for his finely crafted sculptures of faces and figures out of cedar. Style in St. Kitts is casual, but tourists are advised not to wear short shorts, bikinis or bare chests in public places. Today, the British are still aground, running many of the inns and hotels on the island.

Beaches

Most of the Kittian beaches are a dramatic black, born from rich volcanic sand, although the beaches at Frigate Bay and Salt Pond, on the southern peninsula, are brilliantly white. The best beaches are generally located in the south—**Major's Bay**, **Banana Bay**, **Cockleshell Bay** and **Mosquito Bay**—connected today by a new road that makes them fully accessible. Talcum white beaches can also be found in the southeast peninsula. Most of the water sports activities are centered around Frigate Bay, and swimming is especially good, as is snorkeling. Banana Bay and Cockleshell Bay are twin beaches where conditions are also excellent for swimming, and there are cottage beach resorts with watersports facilities operated by Ocean Terrace Inn in Basseterre. **Conaree Beach**, two miles from Basseterre, and **Friar's Bay**, a peninsula where you can see the Atlantic and the Caribbean meet, are also considered user-friendly. Although all beaches are public, you may have to pay a small fee to use the facilities of a hotel located on the beach you choose. (For beaches in Nevis, see the chapter on Nevis.)

The southern beaches of St. Kitts, Frigate Bay and Salt Pond have long been considered the "Caribbean Shangri-La."

Underwater

Hundreds of wrecks are thought to rest off the sloping reefs of St. Kitts. Few of them have been discovered, and most are presumed to be long disintegrated, yet the island inspires the dedicated sunken ship fan. For the rest of us, the west coast offers inviting reefs, particularly at distant **Sandy Point** near the island's northern end, and in the channel between St. Kitts and Nevis, **the Narrows**. Probably the best overall area is named **Grid Iron**, a six-mile undersea shelf rising to within 15 feet of the surface, located on a map by drawing a line between the coastline east of the St. Kitts airport, and the coast just off the Nevis airport (tiny Booby Island lies almost in its path). Although there are a number of dives on this formation, the star is **Monkey Shoals** (see "Nevis"). Just a few dozen divers a week visit St. Kitts, and three shops, one of them recently opened, compete for their favor.

Brimstone Shallows

Multilevel wall diving a mile out of the Basseterre harbor. Lovely soft corals and little current, but a more advanced location owing to the 100-foot depth. Hefty barrel sponges sit amid a collection of anchors left behind by the British fleet stationed at Brimstone Hill Fort.

Nags Head

Unpredictable currents off the southern tip of St. Kitts sometimes make this a more advanced dive (15–80 feet), but one that rewards with plentiful large pelagic activity and even occasional whales. Sand chutes at 60 feet provide pleasant viewing areas for eagle and southern stingrays while, beyond the car-sized boulders, blacktip reef sharks lurk faintly in the distance.

Sandy Point

St. Kitts' most photogenic reef is an intermediate dive (50–90 feet), generously laden with coral-encrusted anchors. Big barrel sponges adorn the wall, which drops to 200 feet, seducing groupers, snapper and 300-pound jewfish into the neighborhood. The site lies 15 miles northwest of Basseterre and dive operators typically require a group to justify the long haul up the coast, usually bussing divers to a rendezvous point at Sandy Point Town.

Wreck of the *River Taw*

Resort courses frequent this 144-foot freighter, which settled on sand 50 feet down following Hurricane David in 1985. Although not one of the region's best wrecks, it makes a good night dive, visited by barracuda, turtles, angelfish and lobster. A good beginner's site.

Wreck of the *M.V. Talata*

St. Kitts' best known carcass, a 120-foot regional freighter that sunk mysteriously one night in 1985, the *Talata's* hull sits on a reef (65 feet) drawing many smaller tropicals including pufferfish, surgeonfish, angelfish and occasional turtles. A more intermediate dive, the *Talata* is surrounded by old cars which were deposited to create an artificial reef. Beware of murky conditions after storms.

Dive Shops

Kenneth's Dive Centre

Basseterre; ☎ *(809) 465-2670.*

Four decades of operation makes Kenneth, an ex-fisherman who used to free-dive for lobster 120 feet down, one of the standard-setters in the region. PADI affiliated with training through Instructor. Two-tank dive, $60, including all gear.

Pro Divers

Turtle Beach; ☎ *(809) 465-3223.*

Nicely located at the southern tip of St. Kitts with easy access to Nevis sites. A PADI outfit with training through Assistant Instructor. Shore dives available. Two-tank dive $60, including all gear ($50 if you bring your own).

St. Kitts Scuba Ltd.

Basseterre; ☎ *(809) 465-8914.*

A PADI and NAUI certified outfit based at Bird Rock Hotel, St. Kitts Scuba began operation in 1995. Two tank dive $60, including equipment.

On Foot

Defined trails to notable sights on St. Kitts are difficult to locate, a situation the government seems in no hurry to change (perhaps, refreshingly, eco tourism has not been identified as a potential money-churner?). St. Kitts' big volcano hike is easier than those on some islands, but is sufficiently spectacular to amply reward intrepid vacationers. One attractive trek not listed below, the Mansion Source Trail, ascends **Verchild's Mountain**, a 3100-foot summit one mile southeast of Mount Liamuiga that features a pond surrounded by dense tropical vegetation. A variation, sometimes referred to as a **Nine Turn Ghaut**, also ascends the area below Verchild's, but continues through a valley to Molineux on the other side of the island; trail conditions vary and may require a guide. Another spot worth exploring is **Black Rocks**.

n the northern shoreline beneath the Belle View Estate, which represent he pyroclastic remains of Liamuiga's last activity. Topographic maps are available but most of the island's trails are not detailed as the government has not yet assembled hiking information or identified and maintained major trails.

Northern St. Kitts is dominated by Mount Liamuiga and a rugged shoreline.

Mount Liamuiga

A two-mile dirt road from Belmont Estate leads straight up the northern slopes of Liamuiga—once nicknamed Mount Misery—to about 1200 feet above sea level. Where the road ends, park and continue on foot along a ridge and then ascend the main ghaut (ravine) through lush virgin forests. Toward the top of this gully, you'll enter a cloud forest brimming with moss, orchids and other epiphytes, and soon reach the rim (2700 feet), which overlooks the imposing, dramatically sculpted crater. The actual summit, rising to 3792 feet, lies on the opposite side of the crater, but the steep, awkward rim is difficult to climb and should be endeavored only with a guide. Although it was once possible to descend the 400 feet to the floor of the crater via roots and vines, the passage was destroyed by Hurricane Hugo and has not been reestablished (check locally for the latest information). The round-trip to the lower rim takes four to five hours; if you can find a guide to take you to the actual summit or to the crater floor, allow an additional two to three hours. The summit area is usually brimming with moisture and can be windy or rainy: bring proper clothing.

The Southeastern Peninsula

A dry, narrow finger of land rises south of Basseterre, pointing directly toward Nevis. Although a paved road now slices through these once untrammeled lands, it still makes for a pleasurable walk at dusk when the sun has lost some of its ferocity.

The peninsula's knolls rise as high as 1047 feet and wrap around several comel beaches and ponds that offer excellent birding. The walk from Frigate Bay to Grea Salt Pond is five miles (bring water, there is little shade) and passes Sand Bank Bay a large cove just northeast of the pond, that is one of St. Kitts' most beautif beaches.

Trekking Tours

Greg's Tours

Basseterre; ☎ *(809) 465-4121.*

Explore the interior of the island with a naturalist bent. The all-day hike up Mt. Lia muiga is $50 per person (minimum group of four), the shorter trip through th rainforest is $35 each (minimum of three).

By Pedal

Bicycling has yet to be discovered on St. Kitts. Although a few locals ex plore the island's sugarcaned slopes on mountain bikes, no dedicated rent. outfits exist at this writing. For those importing their own wheels, an ide ride follows the road from Frigate Bay down the southern peninsula to **Mos quito Bay**; two modest hills are encountered on the 14-mile round-trip. Th main highway circling St. Kitts is a pleasant journey of about 31 miles wit numerous "r and r" possibilities en route. Alternatively, one can construct more demanding circuit off-road by using the maze of dirt tracks whic more-or-less parallel the main highway, transecting the sugarcane fields, par ticularly along the Atlantic coast. These roads connect the plantations an are still used for cane harvesting, but are relatively free from thorns and stick ers. It's possible to avoid the main highway on all but a few miles of this ci cumnavigation. Finally, **Nevis** is but a 45-minute ferry ride away and, if yo smile nicely, you may not be charged for bringing the bike. **Jack Tar Villag** has a small supply of mountain bikes for its customers; if you really want t ride and aren't staying at the resort, you can purchase a day pass for $5 which will avail their bikes, and all other facilities (check on the quality of th bikes provided before signing up).

What Else to See

St.Kitts' capital of Basseterre (pop. 20,00) is in the midst of a booming revival. Decimated by fire in 1867 and rebuilt in the Franco-British colonial style, Basseterre today boasts such delightful Caribbean nuances as high-pitched, no-awning roofs (to lessen their vulnerability in storms); shutters to reduce sun glare but retain the essential movement of air through the hot interior spaces); and occasional outbursts of carpenter Gothic trim. Many of the renovations are due to the efforts of the "Basseterre Beautiful" organization, which is working hard to restore sections of the old town, opening up new stores and courtyard cafes, and keeping the frilly, high-roofed architecture. A bit of the old St. Kitts can be seen in **St. George's Anglican Church**; its wood pews and dusty gravestones in the unruly cemetery point to another era. History buffs interested in the archaeological dig undertaken on the supposed site of a 17th century synagogue in Nevis should contact the historian **Dr. Vincent K. Hubbard in St. Kitts** ☎ *(809) 469-1817*, FAX *(809) 469-1794.*

Brimstone Hill Fortress, the most photographed tourist attraction on St. Kitts, is considered one of the most magnificent fortresses in the West Indies—the second largest of its kind in the hemisphere. Set on a mountainous ridge of volcanic origin, the fortress was adapted to the existing geological conditions of the hill, giving it a maximum potential for defense. Walking around the ruins, only partially restored and deep in weeds, you can easily imagine the violent struggles waged here between the British and the French, the latter who thought they captured the "Gilbraltar of the West Indies" in 1782, only to be ejected for the final time a year later. If you climb the hefty staircase, you'll discover a small museum that gives an overview of the island, and you'll be able to inspect the cannon; if you're lucky, you might even be visited by a local vervet monkey. The view from here gives a marvelous panorama of the ocean and the two cone-shaped islands of Saba and St. Eustatius.

Old Carib rock drawings can be found in **Old Road Town Village** and the ravine at **Bloody Point**, where more than 2000 Indians died in a massacre in 1626.

Twenty minutes north of Basseterre, along the west coast, stands the **Romney Manor**, home of **Caribelle Batik**, where island craftswomen use Indonesian techniques to create a dazzling array of fabrics and clothes unique to the

Caribbean. Also, make a tour of the sugar refinery and taste the pride and jo of Baron Edmund de Rothschild, who distills his own subtle brand of CSI (Cane Spirits Rothschild).

For trekking possibilities, see the section under "On Foot" above.

Historical Sites

Brimstone   ★★★★★

> *Main Street, Basseterre.*
> *Hours open: 9:30 a.m.–5 p.m.*
> This national park houses one of the Caribbean's largest and best-preserved fortresses, called the "Gibraltar of the West Indies" due to its sheer size. It dates back to 1690, covers 38 acres, and saw several skirmishes between the French and the British, who alternated in their control of the fort. Today it is quite nicely restored and you can see the officer's quarters, barracks, hospital and kitchen. A museum is devoted to military history. The park also includes numerous nature trails through its dense vegetation and stunning views of neighboring islands.

Romney Manor   ★★★★

> *Old Road, Basseterre,* ☎ *(809) 465-6253.*
> *Hours open: 8:30 a.m.–4 p.m.*
> Romney Manor is a beautifully restored 17th-century plantation great house, and is home to Caribelle Batik. You can watch local artists produce batik clothing and wall hangings in the same way it's been done for more than 2000 years. Prepare to drop a bundle in the duty-free shop. One of the best reasons to come is to stroll the ground's five acres of colorful gardens. The highlight is a saman tree said to be 350 years old.

Sports

Watersports activities on St. Kitts are focused on Frigate Bay, where you find options from sailing to scuba to windsurfing. Facilities for nearly any sport can be found at the **Jack Tar Village**; the 18-hole Robert Trent Jones designed golf course is particularly popular. The best locations for windsurfing are **Banana Bay** and **Frigate Bay**, and equipment may be rented from watersports operators at hotels and resorts. The coast from **Cades Bay** and **Oualie Beach** to **Newcastle** is also excellent for windsurfing due to strong winds. Tennis courts can also be found there, as well as a few other resorts. Chartering a one-day cruise on a sailboat (picnic included) to Nevis is a wonderful way to spend the day. Horseback riding on St. Kitts can take the form of half-day outings available in Conaree from **The Stable at Trinity Inn**. Inquire whether the sport has been taken up again in the southeastern peninsula, temporarily stopped due to construction in the area.

Horseback Riding

Various locations, Basseterre.

Several outfits offer trail rides along the beach or through the rainforest: **Royal Stables** (☎ *465-2222*) and **Trinity Stable** (☎ *465-3226*).

Royal St. Kitts Golf Club

Adjacent to Jack Tar Village, Frigate Bay, ☎ *(809) 465-8339.*

Hours open: 7 a.m.–6 p.m.

St. Kitts' lone golf outlet is an 18-hole championship course designed by Robert Trent Jones. Greens fee are about $30.

Watersports

Various locations, Basseterre.

General watersports equipment and instruction can be found at **R.G. Watersports** (☎ *465-8050*) and **Pro-Divers** (☎ *465-3223*). **Tropical Tours** (☎ *465-4167*) and **Pelican Cove Marina** (☎ *465-2754*) offer deep-sea fishing excursions. For scuba diving, try **Kenneth's Dive Center** (☎ *465-7043*) and **Pro-Divers** (☎ *465-3223*). For boating and cruising, call **Kantours** (☎ *465-2098*), **Leeward Island Charters** (☎ *465-7474*), and **Tropical Tours** (☎ *465-4039*).

Where to Stay

Fielding's Highest Rated Hotels in St. Kitts

★★★★	Golden Lemon Inn & Villas	$175–$950
★★★★	Ottley's Plantation Inn	$155–$460
★★★★	Rawlins Plantation	$175–$380
★★★	Frigate Bay Beach Hotel	$75–$200
★★★	Jack Tar Village	$110–$340
★★★	Ocean Terrace Inn	$76–$350
★★★	St. Christopher Club	$100–$235
★★★	White House	$270–$375

Fielding's Most Romantic Hotels in St. Kitts

★★★★	Golden Lemon Inn & Villas	$175–$950
★★★★	Ottley's Plantation Inn	$155–$460
★★★★	Rawlins Plantation	$175–$380
★★★	White House	$270–$375

Fielding's Budget Hotels in St. Kitts

★★	Fort Thomas Hotel	$75–$115
★★	Fairview Inn	$75–$145
★★★	Frigate Bay Beach Hotel	$75–$200
★★	Leeward Cove Condominiums	$50–$275
★★★	St. Christopher Club	$100–$235

While the inns of St. Kitts offer unique and intimate vacation experiences, diversified accommodations are increasing, from the familiar hotels of Basseterre (**The Ocean Terrace Inn** and **Fort Thomas Hotel**) to the burgeoning condo resorts along the vast beach of Frigate Bay (where the **Jack Tar Village Beach**

Resort and Casino typifies the luxury of the Carib's all-inclusives) to the major complexes such as **Hyatt Regency** and the couples-only **FDR Resort** in the Southwest Peninsula, recently linked to the rest of the island by an ambitiously engineered, but scenic, "highway of progress." In general, standards of rooms and cuisine are generally high, although air conditioning is not always available, particularly in the old plantation inns. A few of the 35 sugar mill ruins have been converted to guest accommodations, such as the honeymoon suites of **Olden Rock Estate** on Nevis and **Rawlins Plantation** on St. Kitts. In Nevis, **Pinney's Beach Hotel** and the **Four Seasons Resort** are the only two properties located on the coconut palm-lined Pinney's Beach overlooking the narrow of St. Kitts.

Hotels and Resorts

The **Jack Tar Village at Frigate Bay** is the island's premier all-inclusive, about 20 minutes from the airport. Because of the private country club atmosphere, most clients stay a week, or even longer. Nearby, the Colony's **Timothy** beach resort, on one of the finest beaches on St. Kitts, is also near the golf course. **Ocean Terrace Inn** has a marvelous honeymoon package that includes seven nights with an ocean view, a romantic Saturday evening gourmet dinner, a bottle of wine, welcoming cocktail, champagne served in the Jacuzzi, local fruit basket, a rain forest tour and airport transfers. You can also receive a $375 "Get Married on St. Kitts" supplement that includes legal documents, a minister, bouquet and boutonniere.

Bird Rock Beach Hotel   **$75–$310**   ★ ★

Basseterre, ☎ (809) 465-8914, FAX (809) 465-1675.
Single: $75–$180. Double: $85–$310.
This small hotel is located on a bluff overlooking its own 200-foot crescent-shaped beach, one mile from town. Accommodations are in one- or two-room units with air conditioning, balconies and cable TV; some have kitchens. Two restaurants serve continental and local cuisine, and there are also two bars a pool and a tennis court on the premises. The beach is especially good for snorkeling, and a new on-site dive shop supplies watersports equipment.

Casablanca Resort   **$240–$355**   ★ ★

Cockleshell Bay, ☎ (800) 231-1945, (809) 497-6999, FAX (809) 497-6899.
Single: $240–$355. Double: $240–$355.
This new resort is on the island's southeast peninsula, facing a white sand beach. Accommodations are in air-conditioned suites or villas, all with living rooms, minibars, VCRs, refrigerators and balconies. On-site facilities include three restaurants, two bars, a stylish lobby, pool, fitness center, and six tennis courts.

Fort Thomas Hotel   **$75–$115**   ★ ★

Basseterre, ☎ (800) 851-7818, (809) 465-2695, FAX (809) 465-7518.
Single: $75–$90. Double: $90–$115.
Built on the site of an old fort, this hotel reopened in 1993 after extensive renovations. It caters mainly to business travelers who don't mind the fact that the beach is four miles away (they'll shuttle you over for free). Guest rooms are spacious but

nothing special, though you can count on modern amenities and good housekeeping. The dining room serves West Indian and international dishes. There are a few bars and a pool.

Jack Tar Village $110–$340   ★★★

Frigate Bay, ☎ *(800) 999-9182, (809) 465-8651, FAX (809) 465-1031.*
Single: $110–$185. Double: $100–$340.

Set on 20 acres overlooking Lake Zuliani on the isthmus between the Caribbean and Atlantic, this is a popular all-inclusive resort. Guest rooms and suites are scattered about the grounds in two-story buildings. Rooms are simple but comfortable and have modern conveniences; the more expensive suites provide a higher level of pampering. Just about everything is included in the rates, from scuba lessons to tennis on four courts to nightly entertainment. Even the greens fees at a nearby golf course are covered—but you'll need your own cash in the casino. Children under six stay and eat free at the resort, and tykes from 3 to 12 are kept happy in supervised programs, available from 9:00 a.m. to 4:30 p.m. most days.

St. Christopher Club $100–$235   ★★★

Frigate Bay, ☎ *(809) 465-4854, FAX (809) 465-6466.*
Single: $100–$175. Double: $135–$235.

This oceanfront hotel is located just outside of town. Accommodations range from traditional guest rooms to spacious studios to one- and two-bedroom suites with kitchenettes. All are pleasant and comfortable and have air conditioners, phones and TV. There's a restaurant, bar and pool on the premises.

Timothy Beach Resort $105–$380   ★★

Frigate Beach, ☎ *(800) 777-1700, (809) 465-8597, FAX (809) 465-7723.*
Single: $105–$190. Double: $105–$380.

This basic condominium complex is just off the beach. Accommodations range from standard guest rooms to one- and two-bedroom suites, some with full kitchens. All have air conditioning, phones, private balconies, and coffeemakers. There's a cafe and bar on-site, as well as an inviting pool and tennis court. Watersports await at the beach. Good value for the rates.

Apartments and Condominiums

The recent trend in St. Kitts is to set up housekeeping along **Frigate Bay**, a fantastic beach area, in one of the many newly built apartment complexes. Some clusters have their own grocery, but food is never cheap on these islands, so bring your own necessities from home. Among the most elegantly furnished are the **Golden Lemon Villas**, created by the famous New York interior designer Arthur Leaman. Both the **Sun 'n Sand Beach** and **St. Christopher Beach Hotel** can take advantage of being near the facilities of the Jack Tar resort.

Frigate Bay Beach Hotel $75–$200   ★★★

Frigate Bay, ☎ *(809) 465-8935, FAX (809) 465-7050.*
Single: $75–$150. Double: $100–$200.

Set right on the beach as the name implies, the condominium hotel consists of four three-story buildings that face either the pool or the hills. Accommodations are air conditioned and nicely done; many, but not all, have kitchens. There's a swim-up bar in the Olympic-size pool and a bar and restaurant on the premises. Watersports and an 18-hole golf course are within an easy walk.

Island Paradise Village $98–$285 ★★

Frigate Bay, ☎ (809) 465-8035, FAX (809) 465-8236.
Single: $98–$170. Double: $155–$285.

This condominium complex on the beach consists of one- to three-bedroom units, all with fully equipped kitchens, living/dining areas, and balconies or patios. Some have TV and air conditioning, but not all, so be sure to make your reservations accordingly. There's a pool and Italian restaurant on the premises, while golf, tennis and a casino are within walking distance.

Leeward Cove Condominiums $50–$275 ★★

Frigate Bay, ☎ (809) 465-8030, FAX (809) 465-3476.
Single: $50–$80. Double: $60–$275.

This condominium complex occupies five acres in the Frigate Bay area. All units are air-conditioned and have one or two bedrooms, full kitchens, living and dining areas, and patios or balconies. Some also have TVs and phones. Standard guest rooms are also available, for about $80 to $110 per couple. Guests who stay a week get a free rented car—not a bad deal. All can golf for free at the municipal course. There are no facilities on the premises, but many within an easy walk.

Sun 'n Sand Beach Resort $120–$250 ★★

Frigate Bay, ☎ (809) 465-8037, FAX (809) 465-6745.
Single: $120–$150. Double: $120–$250.

Adjacent to Jack Tar Village, this complex consists of air-conditioned cottages that house studios or two-bedroom, two-bath units. All have phones, cable TV, kitchens and patios. There are two pools on-site (one for kids), two tennis courts, and a beach bar and restaurant. The golf course is just across the street, and restaurants and shops are within walking distance. A nice combination of self-catering and resort amenities.

Inns

A true "backwards in time" experience can be had in a number of great plantation houses now beautifully restored and converted into inns. American designer Arthur Leaman has worked his magic into the antique restoration at **Golden Lemon Inn**, though it remains an adults-only complex. A true West Indian feeling, congenial and without attitude, prevails at the **Rawlins Plantation**, also known for its excellent authentic cuisine. Only twelve rooms are available at **The White House**, giving an extra-intimate ambiance.

Fairview Inn $75–$145 ★★

Base of Ottley's Mountain, ☎ (080) 223-9815, (809) 465-2472, FAX (809) 465-1056.
Single: $75–$145. Double: $75–$145.

Located some ten minutes from Basseterre, this complex consists of cottages set around an 18th-century great house. Guest rooms, housed in the cottages, are quite small and motel-like, but decent enough. Only some are air-conditioned, and not all have ceiling fans, so be sure to make your requests accordingly. The site includes a pool, West Indian restaurant and a bar. You'll need a car to get around.

Golden Lemon Inn & Villas $175–$950   ★★★★

Dieppe Bay, ☎ (800) 633-7411, (809) 465-7260, FAX (809) 465-4019.
Single: $175–$435. Double: $175–$950.

One of the best inns in all the Caribbean, the Golden Lemon is located on a black-sand beach at St. Kitts' northwestern tip. Each of the 24 guest rooms are located in the 18th-century great house, beautifully restored with lots of fine antiques. Each room is individually furnished, all with smashing results, sporting antiques, Oriental rugs, West Indian art, raised four-poster beds, ceiling fans (no air), and verandas. The site also includes 14 villas, each with a private pool. Complementary afternoon tea is a refined treat. Creole, American, and continental fare. There's also a pool and tennis court. No kids under 18 allowed at this very tony operation. Those who enjoy life's finer things will not be disappointed.

Ocean Terrace Inn $76–$350   ★★★

Basseterre, ☎ (800) 524-0512, (809) 465-2754, FAX (809) 465-1057.
Single: $76–$175. Double: $100–$350.

This informal inn, set on lushly landscaped hilltop grounds, overlooks the bay. Great sea views from all the air-conditioned rooms, which are modern and tasteful. There are also several one- and two-bedroom apartments and six suites. Two restaurants and three bars keep guests sated. Facilities include two pools, a business center and free transportation to the nearby beach at Turtle Bay, a 20-minute ride. Popular especially with business travelers.

Ottley's Plantation Inn $155–$460   ★★★★

Basseterre, ☎ (800) 772-3039, (809) 465-7234, FAX (809) 465-4760.
Single: $155–$360. Double: $190–$460.

This charming inn sits on a 35-acre estate at the foot of Mt. Liamuiga. Accommodations are in the 1832 great house or in cottages, all air-conditioned and sporting antique and wicker furniture, ceiling fans, phones, combination baths and verandas. The large pool is spring-fed and built into the ruins of a sugar mill, and there are nature trails for exploring the adjacent rainforest. They'll shuttle you to the beach, but it's so nice here you'll hate to leave. The restaurant is wonderful—as is everything here.

Rawlins Plantation $175–$380   ★★★★

Mount Pleasant, ☎ (809) 465-6221, FAX (809) 465-4954.
Single: $175–$250. Double: $255–$380.

Located on 12 acres at the base of Mt. Misery, wonderful views abound everywhere at this charming inn. It was built around the ruins of a 17th-century sugar mill on well-landscaped grounds. Guest rooms are in cottages decorated with good local artwork, nice fabrics, four-poster beds, and antiques. No air conditioning, but breezes generally do the job. Guests can relax at the small spring-fed pool, play tennis on a grass court, enjoy croquet, or take advantage of the free transportation to the beach. Afternoon tea, included in the rates, is a nice touch. The food in the West Indian restaurant is really great. You'll want a rental car to get around, though it's so peaceful and relaxing here you'll have to really get motivated to move on.

White House   **$270–$375**   ★ ★ ★

St. Peters, ☎ (800) 223-1108, (809) 465-8162, FAX (809) 465-8275.
Single: $270–$275. Double: $275–$375.

Located in the foothills above Basseterre, this inn centers around a gorgeous plantation great house that dates to 1738. Accommodations are in a converted stable, coach house and cottage. All are nicely done with four-poster beds, antiques, fine linens, ceiling fans (no air) and private baths. The dining room serves up island cuisine in high style. They'll take you to the beach for free, or you can enjoy the pool, grass tennis court and croquet lawn on the premises. The rates include afternoon tea and laundry service.

Low Cost Lodging

Cheap rooms on St. Kitts offer the most basic of furnishings and facilities. **Conaree Beach Cottages** makes up for any lack of luxury by being right on the beach. Lots of back-to-basics Europeans tend to cram into the cottages at **Trade Winds**, also on Conaree Beach. You can ask around for rooms in private homes, but you should do so in person.

Where to Eat

Fielding's Highest Rated Restaurants in St. Kitts

★★★★★	The Royal Palm	$8–$45
★★★★	Golden Lemon	$7–$50
★★★★	Rawlins Plantation	$23–$35
★★★	Ballahoo	$5–$55
★★★	Chef's Place	$5–$20
★★★	Fisherman's Wharf	$8–$22
★★★	PJ's Pizza	$5–$20
★★★	The Georgian House	$14–$21
★★★	The Patio	$26–$30
★★★	Turtle Beach Bar & Grill	$16–$24

Fielding's Special Restaurants in St. Kitts

★★★★★	The Royal Palm	$8–$45
★★★	Fisherman's Wharf	$8–$22
★★★	The Georgian House	$14–$21
★★★	The Patio	$26–$30

Fielding's Budget Restaurants in St. Kitts

★★★	Chef's Place	$5–$20
★★★	PJ's Pizza	$5–$20
★★★	Fisherman's Wharf	$8–$22
★★★	The Georgian House	$14–$21
★★★	Turtle Beach Bar & Grill	$16–$24

For such a small island, St. Kitts has a wide spectrum of dining experiences, from gourmet delights in historical settings to the homey kitchens of casual local hangouts. All four plantation inns have delightful outdoor patios for candlelit dinners. In Basseterre, dinner at the 400-year-old **Georgian House** is a leisurely elegant evening in a high-ceilinged salon, with aperitifs enjoyed in the walled garden beneath the big mango tree. At the **Ocean Terrace Inn**, the award-winning chef James Vanterpool makes a stunning Two-Flavor Soup (pumpkin and broccoli) and a carrot cake with local sugarcane sauce. Good West Indian food can be found at **The Ballahoo**, overlooking the town center. Some typical delicacies of the island include goat dishes, fried plaintains, creole bean soup, boiled saltfish, goat water (actually, a rich lamb stew), conch chowder, and poached parrotfish with grilled yams. Don't miss an opportunity to try a swig of the island brew called **Royal Estra Stout**, or a glass of mauby, made from tree bark.

| Ballahoo | $$$ | ★★★ |

Fort Street, at the Circus, ☎ *(809) 465-4197.*
Latin American cuisine.
Lunch: 8 a.m.–6 p.m., entrees $5–$55.
Dinner: 6:30–10 p.m., entrees $25–$55.

This upper-level eatery overlooks the bustling downtown district that is Basseterre's version of Piccadilly Circus. The restaurant's customer base is a hodgepodge of cruise ship passengers, businesspeople and shoppers who are apt to find a wide variety of items to munch on, including fresh parrotfish fillets, rotis, burgers and yummy desserts. The place prides itself in presenting reasonably priced French wines. It's also a great location for West Indian or American-style breakfasts—be adventurous and have saltfish with your eggs instead of bacon.

| Chef's Place | $$ | ★★★ |

Church Street, ☎ *(809) 465-6176.*
Latin American cuisine. Specialties: Souse, lamb stew.
Lunch: 8 a.m.–6 p.m., entrees $5–$10.
Dinner: 6–11 p.m., entrees $5–$20.

Get friendly owner Oliver Peetes to describe the West Indian specialties on the daily blackboard—he'll probably oblige. Then settle down around picnic tables outdoors with a streetside view and await generous helpings of souse (pigs feet stew with a special sauce) or lamb stew. Main dishes will be rounded out with rice, a tasty salad and island vegetables. Beverages are also homemade and may include *mauby*, a bittersweet and spicy brew made from tree bark, or fresh ginger beer for the less adventurous.

| Coconut Cafe | $$$ | ★★ |

Frigate Bay Beach, Frigate Bay, ☎ *(809) 465-3020.*
American cuisine.
Lunch: 7:30 a.m.–4 p.m., entrees $6–$45.
Dinner: 4–11 p.m., entrees $25–$53.

Open to the sea breezes and steps away from the sand on the island's most popular swimming beach, this cafe dispenses three meals a day, but it's most popular for sunset cocktails and fresh seafood suppers to follow. There's steel band entertainment on Saturday evenings, and the bar stays open 'till the wee hours.

Fisherman's Wharf $$ ★★★

Fortlands, ☎ *(809) 465-2754.*
Seafood cuisine.
Dinner: 7–12 p.m., entrees $8–$22.
Eating here is like a beach cookout, with diners choosing meat, fish, or chicken to be grilled to order, and serving themselves from a salad and condiments buffet. Orders are taken to long wooden tables facing the oceanfront. Everything is reliably good, but the fresh lobster and shrimp are standouts. A steel band entertains on Friday.

Golden Lemon $$$ ★★★★

Dieppe Bay Town, Dieppe Bay, ☎ *(809) 465-7260.*
International cuisine.
Lunch: 11:30 a.m.–3 p.m., entrees $7–$12.
Dinner: 7–10 p.m., entrees $35–$50.

Some returning visitors would never dream of leaving the island without at least one visit to this exquisite boutique inn's fine restaurant. The three-course, prix-fixe dinners are rotated frequently; owner Arthur Leaman creates the internationally themed menus himself. Gleaming antiques and crystal chandeliers accentuate the dining room and a breezy patio is a gathering spot for Sunday brunch and cocktails. While touring by car, stop by for lunch, which features more informal offerings, including sandwiches, salads and fish dishes.

PJ's Pizza $$ ★★★

North Frigate Bay, Frigate Bay, ☎ *(809) 465-8373.*
Italian cuisine. Specialties: Pizza, subs.
Lunch: 10 a.m.–6 p.m., entrees $5–$20.
Dinner: 6–10:30 p.m., entrees $10–$20.
A reputation for some of the most creative pizza toppings in the Caribbean chain is putting this small place on the culinary map. Refried beans embellish the Mexican pizza and a Rastafarian Ital pie is capped with island veggies in the Rasta colors of gold, red and green. The rest of the offerings are basically Italian, with hero sandwiches made on homebaked bread. Dinner plates usually include lasagne and chili.

Rawlins Plantation $$$ ★★★★

Mt. Pleasant, Mt. Pleasant, ☎ *(809) 465-6221.*
International cuisine.
Lunch: 12:30–2 p.m., prix fixe $23.
Dinner: 8 p.m. Seating, prix fixe $35.
Cap off a tour of the island with lunch or dinner at this splendidly restored estate on the northwest coast. A varied buffet of creole specialties is served to diners on the terrace of the estate's great house, and offerings often include curries, fritters, salads, vegetables and several international specialties. Call before noon to make a reservation for a fixed-price dinner of four courses with soup, salad, entree and a tantalizing

dessert—possibly chocolate terrine with passion fruit sauce. Closed mid-August-mid October.

he Georgian House $$$ ★★★

Independence Square, ☎ (809) 465-4049.
International cuisine.
Dinner: 6–10 p.m., entrees $14–$21.
This beautifully restored home, decorated with Georgian-era reproductions, is a showcase for owner-chef Roger Doche, who prepares a continental menu of seafood, chicken, and steaks, prepared with West Indian flourishes. Peas and rice accompany some of the main courses. Dinner is served nightly on a patio behind the house.

he Patio $$$ ★★★

Frigate Bay Beach, Frigate Bay, ☎ (809) 465-8666.
Latin American cuisine.
Dinner: 7–11 p.m., entrees $26–$30.
The father-daughter cooking team of Peter and Helen Mallalieu prepare island-inspired continental suppers served with a flourish on the patio of their Frigate Bay Beach home. Diners face one of the prettiest private gardens on the island while feasting on specialties like pepper pot stew, broiled fresh seafood, and tropical desserts. Wines and liqueurs are included with dinner.

he Royal Palm $$$ ★★★★★

Ottley's Estate, ☎ (809) 465-7234.
International cuisine.
Lunch: Noon–3 p.m., entrees $8–$18.
Dinner: 8 p.m. Seating, prix fixe $45.
Possibly the most creative food on the island is served at this restaurant located in Ottley's Plantation Inn. Chef Pam Yahn's new "island cuisine" has been glossied on the pages of national magazines, including *Food and Wine*. Her ever-changing menu has included delights like lobster quesadillas and sweet treats like mango mousse with raspberry sauce. Lunches, dinners and Sunday brunch with champagne are served in a location that couldn't be lovelier—the dining room skirts a nearby rainforest. Fixed-price brunch is $20, and served from 12 to 2 p.m.

urtle Beach Bar & Grill $$$ ★★★

S.E. Peninsula Road, Turtle Beach, ☎ (809) 469-9086.
American cuisine.
Lunch: 8 a.m.–6 p.m., entrees $16–$24.
Combine an afternoon of snorkeling (the preferred activity), scuba diving, or just plain loafing on the beach with a notable barbecue of chicken, fish, meat, or lobster prepared at this solar-powered eatery on the southeast coast. Operated by the Ocean Terrace Inn in Fortlands, the Grill is also a cool place Sundays for a well-regarded West Indian buffet replete with live entertainment. Dinner is served only on Saturdays, from 7:30-10 p.m. Equipment for watersports can be rented here as well.

Where to Shop

Shopping is mostly concentrated at several shops and boutiques in and around the traffic circus less than a block from the waterfront. There are at least 57 stores on the island, including the famous **Caribelle Batik**, the island's world-famous designs manufactured at Romney Manor. Also good buys can be found at **Pelican Mall**, a 26-shop arena that features traditional Kittian architecture and pastel colors that resemble a Caribbean market. Duty-free items are available at **A Slice of the Lemon Duty-Free Gift Shop**, on Fort Street, where you can browse through pottery, teas, spices and condiments lower that those in St. Maarten or the USVI. **Splash** at the TDC Mall carries very attractive resort wear and colorful fabrics. Any groom in need of a tux can find one at **Valentino's Men's Wear** on Fort Street. **Windjammer & Caribbean Scents**, in the Pelican Mall, sells outstanding Caribbean resort wear and a fine selection of Caribbean perfumes, as well as **Jamaica's Blue Mountain coffee**. One gallery that shouldn't be missed is the **Plantation Picture House**, featuring the work of Kate Spencer, known for her portraits, landscapes and still lifes. Her designs are available on stone-washed silk and may be worn as scarves.

St. Kitts Directory

ARRIVAL AND DEPARTURE

American Eagle offers daily connections to St. Kitts from American's hub in San Juan. **LIAT** and **WInair** serve St. Kitts from either San Juan, Antigua, or St. Maarten.

Apple Vacation operates a series of 28 Saturday charter departures from Chicago's O'Hare International Airport to St. Kitts and Nevis, available only through retail travel agents. It is the only direct link between the Chicago area and the two-island nation. For information call ☎ *(800) 365-2775.*

Modestly priced taxi fares are available for all island destinations and three-hour, round-island tours can be arranged for about U.S. $40. Fares are usually quoted in EC dollars.

Rental car rates start around $3 per day. Be sure to obtain a $12 island driving license at the police station on Canyon Street in Basseterre—drive on the left side.

A U.S. $10 departure tax is charged all tourists leaving the Golden Rock International Airport and for non-St. Kitts flights departing from Newcastle Airport on Nevis.

BUSINESS HOURS

Shops open Monday–Saturday 8 a.m.–noon and 1–4 p.m. Most close earlier on Thursday. Banks open Monday–Thursday 8 a.m.–3 p.m. and Friday 8 a.m.–5 p.m.

CLIMATE

The climate is pleasant and moderate, with an average temperature of 79 degrees Fahrenheit. Humidity is low and constant northeast trade winds keep the islands cool. Although there is no rainy season, annual rainfall averages 55 inches.

DOCUMENTS

U.S. citizens must present proof of citizenship (passport, voter's registration, or birth certificate), along with return or ongoing tickets. There is a departure tax of $8.

ELECTRICITY

The current runs 230 volts, 60 cycles AC. While the electricity supply at some hotels is 110 volts, AC transformers and adapters are generally needed.

GETTING AROUND

Local transportation is available via minibuses and taxis. Automobiles may be rented from a variety of agencies; ask your hotel. A visitor's driver's license is required and can be obtained from the Police Traffic Department for a fee. Driving is on the left side of the street.

Among the agencies: **Avis**, located at South Independence Square ☎ *(809) 465-6507*, **Choice Car Rental** on Cayon Street in Basseterre ☎ *(809) 465-4422*.

The passenger ferry, *The Caribe Queen*, operates on a regular schedule between the two islands. The crossing takes about 45 minutes and costs $8 round trip.

LANGUAGE

The official language of both St. Kits and Nevis is English.

MEDICAL EMERGENCIES

There is a 24-hour emergency room at **Joseph N. France General Hospital** in Buckley ☎ *(809) 465-2551*. Also ask your hotel about physicians on call.

MONEY

The official currency is the Eastern Caribbean dollar. Make sure you understand which dollar is quoted on bills.

TELEPHONE

Area code is *809*. International calls, telexes and telegrams can be made from **Skantel**, *Cayon Street, Basseterre* ☎ *(809) 465-2219*, Monday-

Friday from 8 a.m.–6 p.m., on Saturday 8 a.m.–2 p.m., and on Sundays and holidays from 6–8 p.m.

TIME

Atlantic Standard Time. That is to say, it's one hour ahead of New York time, except during Daylight Saving Time, when it is the same.

TIPPING

Expect a 10 percent service charge added to most hotel and restaurant bills. If it isn't, be prepared to tip 10–15 percent.

TOURIST INFORMATION

Good brochures and information can be found at the **St. Kitts Tourist Board**, *Pelican Mall, P.O Box 132, Basseterre;* ☎ *(809) 465-2620/ 4040,* FAX *(809) 465-8794.* In the U.S. ☎ *(212) 535-1234.*

WHEN TO GO

Carnival Celebrations take place in a week-long spectacle the last week of December, featuring calypso competitions, queen shows, street dancing and festivals. Tourism Week in Nevis is an annual fair in February. Museum Day is May 18, usually an open house at various museums. Culturama 20, in Nevis the last week of July, is a 20-year-old festival of native arts, crafts and music. Every other month the St. Kitts-Nevis Boating Club provides races and relays for residents and tourists alike. On the last Sunday of every month the Golden Rock Golf Club presents a day of fun golf played on a nine-hole fun course. The Nevis Jockey Club has scheduled nine race days throughout the year to coincide with national holidays.

ST. KITTS HOTELS		RMS	RATES	PHONE	CR. CARDS
Basseterre					
★★★★	Golden Lemon Inn & Villas	32	$175–$950	(800) 633-7411	A, MC, V
★★★★	Ottley's Plantation Inn	15	$155–$460	(800) 772-3039	A, MC, V
★★★★	Rawlins Plantation	9	$175–$380	(809) 465-6221	A, MC, V
★★★	Frigate Bay Beach Hotel	64	$75–$200	(809) 465-8935	A, MC, V
★★★	Jack Tar Village	244	$110–$340	(800) 999-9182	A, MC, V
★★★	Ocean Terrace Inn	53	$76–$350	(800) 524-0512	A, DC, MC, V
★★★	St. Christopher Club	32	$100–$235	(809) 465-4854	MC, V
★★★	White House	8	$270–$375	(800) 223-1108	A, MC, V
★★	Bird Rock Beach Hotel	38	$75–$310	(809) 465-8914	A, D, MC, V
★★	Casablanca Resort	66	$240–$355	(800) 231-1945	A, MC
★★	Fairview Inn	27	$75–$145	(800) 223-9815	A, D, MC, V
★★	Fort Thomas Hotel	64	$75–$115	(800) 851-7818	A, MC, V

ST. KITTS HOTELS	RMS	RATES	PHONE	CR. CARDS
★★ **Island Paradise Village**	62	$98–$285	(809) 465-8035	None
★★ **Leeward Cove Condominiums**	10	$50–$275	(809) 465-8030	A, MC, V
★★ **Sun 'n Sand Beach Resort**	68	$120–$250	(809) 465-8037	A, D, DC, MC, V
★★ **Timothy Beach Resort**	36	$105–$380	(800) 777-1700	A, MC, V

ST. KITTS RESTAURANTS	PHONE	ENTREE	CR. CARDS
Basseterre			
American			
★★★ **Turtle Beach Bar & Grill**	(809) 469-9086	$16–$24•	A, V
★★ **Coconut Cafe**	(809) 465-3020	$6–$53	A, DC, MC, V
International			
★★★★★ **The Royal Palm**	(809) 465-7234	$8–$45	A, MC, V
★★★★ **Golden Lemon**	(809) 465-7260	$7–$50	A, DC, MC, V
★★★★ **Rawlins Plantation**	(809) 465-6221	$23–$35	A, MC, V
★★★ **The Georgian House**	(809) 465-4049	$14–$21••	A, MC, V
Italian			
★★★ **PJ's Pizza**	(809) 465-8373	$5–$20	A, MC, V
Latin American			
★★★ **Ballahoo**	(809) 465-4197	$5–$55	A, MC, V
★★★ **Chef's Place**	(809) 465-6176	$5–$20	None
★★★ **The Patio**	(809) 465-8666	$26–$30••	MC, V
Seafood			
★★★ **Fisherman's Wharf**	(809) 465-2754	$8–$22••	A, MC, V

Note: • Lunch Only

•• Dinner Only

ST. LUCIA

Waterskiing and parasailing are popular activities around St. Lucia.

Watching a local cook an egg in steamy sulphur pools might be cliché now in lovely St. Lucia, but the rest of the island's attractions are far from worn out. Bit by bit St. Lucians are getting the ecotourism bug, finally figuring out that this Caribbean island's biggest draw is its lush natural resources—from exclusive beaches fringed with forests to waterfalls that change color from yellow to purple. In fact, it should be made mandatory for every visitor to drive the steep roads that wind the emerald hills at the island's southern end, where jungle flowers scent the air and giggling children soap themselves under roadside water faucets. To get the full Lucian experience, however, you must get out and trod toe to heel over the dramatic countryside, breathe in the rain forest, and even bathe in the volcano's hot mineral baths. But the spirit of St. Lucia lies not only in the land but in the people as well—friendly musical and forever ready to party. Festivals carve the rhythm of life here and ones such as the two flower festivals, La Rose and Marguerite, and Carnival—a calypso explosion two days before Ash Wednesday—shouldn't b missed.

Bird's Eye View

The second largest of the former West Indies Associated States, the avocado-shaped St. Lucia lies between Martinique and St. Vincent in the Windward Islands chain of the eastern Caribbean. It sprawls over a total area c 238 square miles, a majority of which is covered with dense tropical flora such as hibiscus, frangipani, orchids, jasmine and poinciana. By contrast, the northern end of the island seems positively cosmopolitan. Castries, the capital, is still in need of beautification, but marinas and resorts are filling in the coastline. (The proliferation of all-inclusive resorts is starting to rankle local businesspeople—especially struggling restaurateurs.) Though tourism ha been growing rapidly, the principal sector is agriculture (especially banana and coconut) along with manufacturing, with more than 40 relatively diver sified enterprises.

History

The first inhabitants of St. Lucia were surely Arawak Indians, and later Car ibs, who did not appreciate the British invasion of their island in the early 17th century; for some time they managed to successfully fend off colonization. In 1650, the French overcame the resistance and settled a colony, completing a treaty with the Caribs in 1660. Over the next 164 years, the island exchanged hands 14 times between the French and British in an almost comical seesaw play of power. It was not until the issue of the 1814 Treaty o Paris that the British finally secured all rights. During this time, the Carib Indians were played as a pawn between the two powers until the British finally—and unceremoniously—exiled them to a still-existing reservation or

Saint Lucia

- ✪ CAPITAL
- ● CITY/TOWN
- ✕ AIRPORT
- PRIMARY ROAD
- SECONDARY ROAD
- ▲ MOUNTAIN
- RIVER

| 0 | 3 | 6km |
| 0 | 2 | 4mi |

©BW 1995

SAINT LUCIA CHANNEL

Pigeon Island
61°

Gros Islet

Gros Islet

Monchy

Bon Air

Vigie Airport

CASTRIES

Babonneau

14°

Ciceron

Forestière

La Croix Maingot

*Piton Flore
1871 ft.*

**Dernière
Rivière**

CARIBBEAN
SEA

Anse la Raye

Grand Riviere

Millet

Canaries

Dennery

*Mt. Gimie
3118 ft.*

*Mt. Tabac
2224 ft.*

Praslin

Mon Repos

Soufrière

*Mt. Grand
Magazin
2022 ft.*

*Petit Piton
2461 ft.*

Fond St. Jacques

*Gros Piton
2619 ft.*

Micoud

Desruisseaux

Choiseul

Laborie

Hewanorra Airport ✕

ATLANTIC
OCEAN

Vieux Fort

SAINT VINCENT PASSAGE

Dominica. Although the island gained control of its own government o
Feb. 22, 1979, its official head of state still remains the British throne, rep
resented by a Governor General, who appoints the eleven members of S
Lucia's Senate. The House of Assembly is elected by popular vote.

People

As in neighboring states, about 75 percent of the inhabitants of St. Luci
are descendants of African slaves who were imported as plantation laborers i
the 17th and 18th centuries. (Two percent are descended from indenture
servants brought from India and another two percent are of European ori
gin.) The rich mixture has produced a highly musical local patois, a combi
nation of French, English and Spanish words utilizing a French and Africa
grammatical structure. Although tourism is conducted in English, most pri
vate conversations, jokes, street jibe and some court cases are conducted i
patois. Friendly and helpful, St. Lucians have retained a love of African an
Caribbean rhythms; in fact, they so love to party that dancing has practicall
become a national sport. Every small town and village holds dances regular
ly, propelled by a little beer, rum, smoking weed, and ear-splitting speakers
Friday block parties in the village of **Gros Islet** are especially welcoming to
tourists; other neighborhoods are more closed. Despite all the spontaneou
partying, about 80 percent of the population still remains self-acclaimed
Roman Catholics. Most of the older island women continue to wear the Ma
dras head-tie and a modern version of the panniered skirt. A blend of Frenc
and British cultures, islanders share a passion for both savory French-Creol
cooking and their beloved sport of cricket. St. Lucia has also given birth to
two Nobel Laureates: Sir W. Arthur Lewis won the Nobel Prize in econom
ics in 1979 and the poet Derek Walcott won the 1992 Nobel Prize in litera
ture.

Beaches

St. Lucia's prime goal is to keep beaches open to the public but as pristine as possible; therefore, you'll only find a few with restrooms, changing facilities and snack bars. The best way to find *your* beach is to hire a sailboat and scope around the dozens of nearly deserted possibilities. Because shade is not always available, make sure you always travel to the beach with hat or umbrella, towel and liquid refreshment. Among the best beaches is **Anse Chastanet**, just north of Soufriere, which some claim offers the Windward Islands' only "perfect beach dive," with its steep dropoff, colorful fish, and variety of sponges (parts of *Superman II* were shot here). Anse Couchon beaches feature black, volcanic sand, calm waters for swimming, and a tropical, romantic setting accessible only by boat. Lying at the foot of the Pitons, the crescent-shaped bay of Anse des Piton rates as one of St. Lucia's most dramatic beaches. Facilities are few at Anse LaRaye, a small village beach just beyond Marigot Bay, but there are plenty of shady palm trees. **Cas en Bas**, just opposite Gros Islet on the island's north end, is a windsurfer's dream, comparable to the excellent conditions of Silver Sands on Barbados. Some of the island's major hotels are located on the nearly perfect **Reduit Beach**, chock full of shady palms, white sand and a full range of watersports facilities. Swimmers should avoid the strong currents at **La Toc Bay**, south of Castries Harbor, where the majestic **Cunard La Toc Hotel** lies, though the view is lovely for lunch and sunbathing. One of the most popularly frequented beaches is **Choc Bay**, a long, sweeping stretch of sand and coconut palms, not far from Castries and the major hotels along the northeastern coast. At the southernmost tip of the island you'll find **Vieux Fort**, where the beach makes up for the lack of facilities with gloriously white sand and miles of shady coconut palms.

Underwater

Over the past several years, St. Lucia has emerged as one of the premier dive destinations in the Eastern Caribbean. The island has stunning, pristine reefs and vertigo-inducing walls, the latter best exemplified by a quick glance at St. Lucia's shoreside signature peaks, **the Pitons**, which plunge precipitously into the sea below. The resulting publicity in the dive community has created a popular product, similar to St. Lucia's neighboring attractions. Dominica and St. Vincent. Fortunately, diving was commercialized relatively recently on the island and the government has maintained a firm hand on the number of dive businesses it will license (and, therefore, the number of dive visitors). The area surrounding the Pitons boasts many of the best dive sites and is where the marine park is centered. A faint current runs along the coast, sometimes providing drift opportunities off **Soufriere Bay**, and visibility generally exceeds 75 feet. The coral is unusually clean on St. Lucia, with currents washing over shallower sites to give them an added sheen. Shore diving, among the best in the Eastern Caribbean, is available at **Anse Chastanet Reef**, immediately below the similarly-named hotel. It's a great place for experienced divers to start their St. Lucia adventure. A surprisingly diverse collection of unusual marine life can be found here: frogfish, sea horses, octopus, electric rays and much more (it's also an excellent night dive). Sea conditions allowing, most of the sites below are accessible to beginners.

Anse La Raye

Two excellent sites are found off the beach at the village of Anse La Raye: the first is a shallow, boulder-strewn slope featuring vivid fire corals, purple vase sponges, barrel sponges and soft corals. A sheer mini-wall tucked against a seaside cliff provides the second dive; the wall slips to 80 feet, and is visited by jacks, Bermuda chub, spotted drums and schools of creole wrasse. These sites are close to the wreck of the *Lesleen M.*

Fairy Land

The point off Anse Chastanet marks the island's prettiest dive location, a headland washed by strong currents producing excellent visibility and coral so clean it sparkles. A plateau provides the entrance, sloping gently to 60 feet, while the extraordinarily diverse coral and sponge selection will remind some visitors of a Disneyland, hence the name.

Keyhole Pinnacles

A real favorite, these four striking seamounts reach to within a few feet of the surface just north of Petit Piton, ten minutes from the docks at Soufriere. Colorful vase and large barrel sponges are the backdrop for a multitude of macro life: sea horses, arrow crabs, octopus and squid cavort amid substantial fish activity. Depths to 100 feet.

Superman's Flight

Named after the brief shot that appeared in *Superman II* (of Christopher Reeve flying down the cliff), this popular site lies at the base of the sheer Petit Piton wall, and usually allows divers to "fly" (via currents) over colorful soft corals, sponges, sea whips, gorgonians and large featherduster worms. Several dynamite dives lie along this wall, which drops a thousand feet or more, all just a few minutes from the docks at Soufriere.

Wreck of the *Lesleen M*

An artificial reef was created in 1986 when this 165-foot freighter was sunk just southwest of Anse La Raye, creating an intermediate dive site. The top of the *Lesleen* rises to within 35 feet of the surface, and the pilothouse, engine room and passageways, strewn with deepwater gorgonians, can be explored by careful divers. The hull, sitting upright, 65 feet down, is embraced by an increasing number of soft corals and hydroids.

Dive Shops

Scuba St. Lucia

Soufriere; ☎ *(809) 459-7000.*
The region's only SSI facility (an instructor-trainer facility for Divers Alert Network); also a PADI Five Star facility. Ideally located at Anse Chastanet beach, this is St. Lucia's biggest and oldest operation, with a staff of 22. Two-tank dive, $66. Also features a two-day, four dive introductory course for those wanting more than a resort course, but less than certification (starts at $200).

Dolphin Divers

Marigot Bay; ☎ *(809) 451-4974.*
A PADI Five Star facility and an Instructor Development Center with courses through Assistant Instructor. Opened in 1992 and works with smaller groups off a 32-foot catamaran dive boat. Two tank dive, $70, including equipment ($60 if you bring your own).

On Foot

St. Lucia is one of the largest of the islands dotting the Eastern Caribbean. It is also one of the most heavily populated, yet still contains extensive and marginally explored rainforest within the range of mountains which form a spine leading down the western side of the island. **Mount Gimie** (3118 ft.) is St. Lucia's highest peak, but no marked trails lead to its summit, leading peak-baggers to two other points: **Gros Piton**, the larger of the spectacular spires rising above the town of Soufriere, and **Piton Flore**, a peak within easy reach of the north coast resorts. The excellent *Ordnance Survey* topographical map of St. Lucia can be located at a few bookstores in Castries. Be forewarned, however, that the considerable network of enticing tracks displayed on the map frequently are found to be overgrown and/or impossible to follow. Paths are often muddy, particularly following rain, of which the island's

interior receives an ample share. A guide is advised for the difficult ascent o
Gros Piton and any other extensive explorations; the helpful staff of the **For
est and Lands Department** can provide trail and guide information (☎ *(809,
450-2231 or (809) 450-2078)*. Also, beware of the rare fer de lance, the poi
sonous snake which lurks in St. Lucia's backyard; bites are infrequent, bu
can be deadly (see "On Foot" introductory chapter). Finally, for those seek
ing a gentler stroll, the **Union Nature Trail**, offers a 45-minute gravel-pavec
loop through dry woodland forest; it is located in the hills beneath the com
munity of **Babonneau**, east of Castries.

The road to St. Lucia's volcanic spikes, The Pitons, is surrounded by forest.

Piton Flore

Not to be confused with *the* Pitons, this 1871-foot peak four miles southeast of Castries, is the location of the last known sighting of the Semper's warbler, an endemic bird now presumed to be extinct (it has not been spotted since 1970). Drive through the village of Forestiere to the end of the road; the start of the hike is behind the Forestry Department office on the left. The trail ascends through forestry plantations into the thick of the rainforest. The path divides at a concrete blockhouse; take the sparse, right-hand track and proceed up the steep route to the top, where generous views of the entire northern part of the island, including Castries, are offered. Allow about two hours round-trip.

Hikers on St. Lucia have a choice of several beautiful panoramic views.

Gros Piton

No landmark in the Caribbean is as striking and identifiable as the twin Pitons of St. Lucia. They are the towering remnants of an immense volcanic crater (possibly long-cooled "plugs" of lava), and stir the imagination of all visitors, hikers or not. The larger and taller of the two, Gros Piton (2619 feet), is the easier ascent, although the trail is every bit as steep and difficult as it looks. After climbing through montane forest, the angle increases to approximate real climbing, although ropes and equipment are not necessary on the main trail. Near the top, a particularly intrepid section ascends a narrow chimney, which leads to the exhilarating, if picayune summit. The view encompasses the western coast of St. Lucia, St. Vincent to the south and, on very clear days, Martinique to the north. A guide is strongly advised, but hire one recommended by the Forestry Department. **NOTE:** Slender Petit Piton has been the sight of several climbing accidents in recent years and is now officially "off limits." Guides still make themselves available in Soufriere, but readers are cautioned to contact the Forestry Department and obtain trail conditions before hiring anyone for the ascent.

The Rainforest Walk

A tropical storm devastated the original rainforest trail from Fond St. Jacques in 1994, but a new trail system opened in mid-1995 that takes visitors deep into St Lucia's rainforest environment. The two new trails, **Barre de Lisle** and **Des Catiers** are five and seven miles in length, respectively, and hike into the forest reserves east of Soufriere Bay. This area is home to a variety of birdlife, including the Jacquot parrot, a rare endemic species numbering only 300 in the wild (compared to a million at the time of Columbus' arrival). Until these trails are better established, it's probably wise to consult with the Forestry Department for additional details.

By Pedal

St. Lucia offers extensive and challenging options for hard-core cyclists The only problem is that the island's road network is a maze of switchback and indirect paths, with few obvious loop trips available. An even bigge issue is hectic road traffic; the island's fledgling cycling organization nearly folded after a series of fatal biking accidents (the organization is now rebuild ing and hopes to host a four-day "Tour de St. Lucie" in August, 1996). A such, a bike rental firm has not established a footing on the island at thi writing. By the time you read this, however, things may have changed.

The popular road from **Castries south to Soufriere** is the most appealing des tination, but riders should be aware this is a serious all-day package involving major ascents along the winding coastal road; it's further than it looks and climbs to 1000 feet before reaching sea level **Canaries**, then to over 1600 fee near **Mount Tabac**. An easier outing visits the gentler area **north of Castries** skirting resorts, golf-courses and tony residential areas. One itinerary cover ing this region would head inland from Castries to **Babonneau**, then north to **Monchy** and **Gros Islet**, and return to Castries via the busy coastal route. This ride involves one moderate climb to about 1200 feet. But perhaps St. Lucia' nicest, most relaxed riding lies on the quieter **eastern coast** (which also is the area furthest removed from the tourism infrastructure). The ride from **Dennery** south to **Vieux Fort** stays below 400-foot elevation and visits less-traf ficked areas, with numerous asphalt fingers climbing from the coast into the rainforest for impromptu exploration possibilities; the road from Castries to Vieux Fort (via Dennery) is about 38 miles.

What Else to See

t. Lucia's dramatic countryside includes emerald hills, waterfalls, rain forest, olcanic mineral baths and pristine beaches.

The best time to experience the hustle and bustle of West Indian port life Castries, the island's capital, is on Saturday at the morning market, when mall farmers and artisans lay out their tropical wares for serious barter. Not uch else is of interest in the city, which has been rebuilt and decimated by re several times over, except perhaps for **Columbus Square**, where a 400-car-old samaan tree shades the Cathedral of the Immaculate Conception uilt in 1897. Afternoons are the best time to visit the tiny fishing villages of **nse-la-Raye** and **Canaries**, where you can watch the boats arrive with their aily catch. North of Castries, the **Pigeon Island National Park** offers the op-ortunity to relive the days when France and England waged over St. Lucia. George Rodney, the British admiral who defeated the French in the Do-iinica Passage, raised pigeons as a hobby—hence the name.) Friday nights, he fishing town of **Gros Islet** is a wild "jump-up" scene, noisy with soca and eggae, traditional beats of the Caribbean. The new marketplace at Soufriere the south is also exceptional, decorated with colorful murals and ginger-read trim; the shabby town itself still retains a Third World aura. The dor-

mant "Drive-in Volcano" of nearby **Mt. Soufriere** presents a face akin to a B
horror movie, complete with open pits of boiling sulfur. (You'll need
guide, available at the entrance of the park.) If you want to linger under cas
cading waterfalls and bathe in natural and more aromatic springs, go to th
nearby **Diamond Falls**, where the Diamond Mineral Baths are located on th
Soufriere Estate. Legend has it that King Louis XVI himself partook of th
healing waters here during a French occupation.

Pigeon Island is a 40-acre islet connected by causeway to St. Lucia's wes
coast near the Rodney Bay resort area. The site of St. Lucia's annual jazz fes
tival, the area also boasts two beaches, a restaurant and the remnants of th
18th-century British naval garrison. The new **Pigeon Island Museum and Inter
pretive Centre** is housed in the elegant former British officers' mess buildin;
and provides a hands-on display of the island's natural and political history.

BEST VIEW:

*A startling panoramic view can be glimpsed from the Fort Charlotte fortress
at the top of Morne Fortune, the same sight used by French and British
troops alternately to defend the island. To the north is Pigeon Island, to the
south the Pitons, and the entire scope of the capital's harbor and the Virgie
Peninsula. While you're at the fort, notice the difference between the French
architecture and the walls built by the British at different stages.*

Historical Sites

Fort Charlotte ★★★

Morne Fortune, ☎ *(809) 456-1165.*
Set atop a hill 853 feet above sea level, this fortress was started by the French in
1764 and finished 20 years later by the British. Today it holds government and education offices, but it's worth a trip for the great views if nothing else. The grounds
include a military cemetery that dates back to 1782 where French and British soldiers are buried as well as six former governors of the island.

Parks and Gardens

Maria Islands Nature Reserve ★★★

Half a mile offshore, ☎ *(809) 454-5014.*
Hours Open: 9:30 a.m.–5 p.m.
This reserve consists of two small islands in the Atlantic—one 25 acres, the other
just four. It is home to a thriving population of birds and rare snakes and lizards.
Great snorkeling off the larger island, Maria Major.

Pigeon Island National Park ★★★★

Pigeon Point, ☎ *(809) 452-5005.*
Hours Open: 9 a.m.–4 p.m.
This 40-acre island is connected to the mainland by a causeway. It has a long history
and was used for all sorts of things before becoming a national park—pirates hid out
here in the 1600s, the French and British militaries used it as a fort, and long before
any of them, the Arawak Indians lived here. Ruins from some of these days still exist

on the island, but this is primarily a place to picnic and hang out on its picturesque beaches.

Tours

iamond Falls and Mineral Bath ★★★★

Soufriere Estate, Soufriere.
Hours open: 10 a.m.–5 p.m.
The water in these sulfuric mineral baths averages a toasty 106 degrees Fahrenheit. Louis XVI ordered them built in 1784 so French stationed in the area could soak in the supposedly curative waters. Bring your suit so you, too, can "take the waters."

a Soufriere ★★★

Soufriere.
Hours open: 9 a.m.–5 p.m.
Called the world's only drive-in volcano, this spot encompasses a seven-acre crater complete with pools of boiling mud and sulfurous waters.

he Pitons ★★★★

Soufriere.
These dramatic twin cones are St. Lucia's most identifying landmark. Formed by a prehistoric volcano eruption, Petit Piton rises to 2619 ft., Gros Piton (the fatter of the two) to 2461 ft. Most folks just admire them from the land or sea, but the truly hardy can climb through their lush foliage to the top. You'll need a permit from the **Forestry Division** *(☎ 452-3231)*, and it's best to hire a guide for the very strenuous hike.

Sports

Most hotels boast tennis courts and watersports facilities, including windsurfing, water skiing, and small sailboats. Windsurfers all head for Anse de ables, the bay on the southeastern tip of the island between Moule-a-Chique and the Maria Islands. Actually, conditions for windsurfing are ideal ll along the entire south coast, on both the Atlantic and the Caribbean des. Beginners normally like the calmer waters of the Caribbean while the hore daring windsurfers take advantage of the rougher, choppy waters on he Atlantic coast. Golfers can enjoy two challenging golf courses. Half-day nd full-day fishing charters are available and can be arranged through hotels nd resorts, or at the marinas at Rodney Bay and Castries. The two main shing seasons run between January to June (for tuna, kingfish and dolphin) nd July to December (where the catch is closer to shore). As St. Lucians de-end on fishing for their livelihood, the ways and means are many—you can join fishermen using lines and pots to catch snapper, lobsters and reef fish. Yachtsmen and day-trippers from Castries tend to congregate at Soufrier Bay. One of the region's major charters is **The Moorings**, which offers cruise for 4–6 passengers with lunch and drinks—bareboat or with crew. Other similar cruises can be found at Rodney Bay; **Stevens Yachts** is one of the foremost names in the region. Horseback riding through the forest is also available.

Golf

Two locations.

The choices for duffers are limited to two courses, both nine holes but set up so you can go around twice. **Cap Estate Golf Club** *(452-8523)* is open to the public while the course at **Sandals St. Lucia** *(452-3081)* is only available when not fully booked by guests at the island's two Sandals resorts.

Horseback Riding

Various locations.

Three stables await the horseman (and woman): **North Point** *(450-8853)*, **Trim** *(452-8273)*, and **Jalousie Plantation** *(459-7666)*.

Watersports

Various locations.

If your hotel doesn't offer the watersports you're seeking try one of these. Deep-sea fishing: **Mako Watersports** *(452-0412)* and **Captain Mike's** *(452-7044)*. Scuba diving: **Dive Jalousie** *(459-7666)*, **Moorings Scuba** *(451-4357)*, **Scuba St. Lucia** *(459-7355)*, **Buddies Scuba** *(452-5288)*, and **Windjammer Diving** *(452-0913)*. **Mistral Windsurfing** *(452-8351)* specializes in board rentals and instruction. For cruises and snorkel expeditions, call **Captain Mike's** *(452-0216)*, **Surf Queen** *(452-8351)*, **Brig Unicorn** *(452-6811)*, and **Cat Inc.** *(450-8651)*. Finally, **St. Lucia Watersports** *(452-8351)* offers waterskiing and parasailing in addition to general equipment rentals.

Where to Stay

Fielding's Highest Rated Hotels in St. Lucia

★★★★★	Le Sport	$245–$905
★★★★	Anse Chastanet Hotel	$95–$505
★★★★	Jalousie Plantation	$345–$655
★★★★	Sandals St. Lucia	$396–$664
★★★★	Windjammer Landing	$185–$355
★★★	Club St. Lucia	$175–$445
★★★	Ladera Resort	$180–$655
★★★	Marigot Bay Resort	$90–$220
★★★	Royal St. Lucian Hotel	$215–$385
★★★	Wyndham Morgan Bay Resort	$250–$580

Fielding's Most Romantic Hotels in St. Lucia

★★★★	Anse Chastanet Hotel	$95–$505
★★★★	Jalousie Plantation	$345–$655
★★★	Ladera Resort	$180–$655
★★★★★	Le Sport	$245–$905

Fielding's Budget Hotels in St. Lucia

★	Caribbees Hotel	$50–$75
★★	Tapion Reef Hotel	$50–$80
★★★	Doolittle's Resort	$65–$95
★★	Candyo Inn	$75–$90
★	Green Parrot Inn	$65–$115

St. Lucia offers a full-range of lodging, from the very expensive all-inclusiv resorts (some of the best in the Caribbean) and luxurious five-star hotels t intimate inns surrounded by lush greenery and talcum-soft beaches; ther are also numerous self-catering options in villas and apartments. Throughou the entire island, there are 29 hotels, 23 guest houses, and 10 villas an apartment complexes. Many properties offer the optional Modified Amer can Plan (MAP), which includes breakfast and dinner. You can get up to 5 percent discounts during the summer season. In most circumstances you wi receive a 10 percent service charge on the hotel bill, plus an eight percer government tax. Families tend to do best at all-inclusive resorts since yo don't have to run around trying to find an activity to please everybody (ev erything you need is right outside your doorstep). Properties not located o the south side (where the airport is located) will incur an extra fee for trans fer.

Hotels and Resorts

Sandals, the St. Lucia version of the famous all-inclusive Caribbean resort, has winte rates starting at $1575, going up to $3000 (per week), the highest on the island. A sec ond Sandals resort, **Sandals Halcyon**, opened in 1994 on the site of the former Halcyo Beach Club at Choc Bay, offering breathtaking seaviews from its restaurant, **The Pie House**, which extends over a 150-foot pier. Guests can use all the super sports facilities a the mother resort. It's been said that if you begin your stay at Ladera, you won't want t go anywhere else, so fabulous is the setting. Special spa facilities characterize **Le Spor** where the beach, tennis courts, golf course and apartments are only steps from each oth er. The all-inclusive **Rendezvous** bans kids (couples only), and there are some package that include airfare.

Anse Chastanet Hotel	**$95–$505**	★★★★

Anse Chastanet Beach, ☎ *(800) 223-1108, (809) 459-7000, FAX (809) 459-7700.*
Single: $95–$355. Double: $135–$505.

Situated on a 500-acre hillside beachfront plantation, this unique resort is locate on the southwest coast, north of Soufriere. The grounds are wonderfully lush an steeply lead down to a black-sand beach. Accommodations are found on the hillsid or on the beach. Each is large, individually decorated, and quite posh. The ground include an excellent dive center (lots of scuba enthusiasts stay here), two good res taurants, two bars, and a tennis court. No pool or air conditioning, but no one' complaining. Best suited to the fit, as there are steep stairs everywhere.

Candyo Inn	**$75–$90**	★★

Rodney Bay, ☎ *(809) 452-0712.*
Single: $75–$90. Double: $75–$90.

You can walk to the beach in five minutes from this small hotel. The four gues rooms are standard and well-kept, with modern amenities like phones, TV, an clock radios. The eight apartments have kitchens and more room to spread out; al accommodations are air-conditioned. Facilities are limited to a snack bar, mini-mar ket and pool. There are many restaurants within walking distance, and this small operation is a good deal.

Club Med St. Lucia $800–$1300 per wk. ★★★

Vieux Fort, ☎ *(800) 258-2633, (809) 454-6546, FAX (809) 454-6017.*

This Club Med is set on 95 acres at Savannes Bay, on the southeast coast—a fairly remote region, so you'll have to depend on organized tours (or rent a car) to see the island. Many of the guests here are families with children; this is not a swinging singles Club Med. Accommodations are small, with air conditioning, twin beds and balconies. As with all Club Meds, there's always tons going on, and lots of activities for the youngsters, including an intensive English riding program for kids eight and above (which, like scuba and island tours, costs extra). Among the recreational options are tennis on eight courts, circus workshops, all watersports, a fitness center, exercise classes, archery, rollerblading, and on and on and on. Great for families; singles may want to look elsewhere. Rates are $800 to $1300 per week per adult, and $520 to $845 per week per children 2–11. They occasionally take small children (ages 2–5) free; ask for details. It also costs $30 for a one-time initiation fee (per family) and $50 per person annual dues.

Club St. Lucia $175–$445 ★★★

Cap Estate, ☎ *(809) 450-0551.*
Single: $175–$445. Double: $235–$445.

This all-inclusive resort appeals to romantics—they even have two wedding chapels for those who get so carried away they decide to tie the knot. Guest rooms and suites are large and nicely done; most, but not all, are air-conditioned (those without rely on ceiling fans). There are two pools, nine tennis courts, a health club, a disco, nightly entertainment, and supervised children's programs year-round. Watersports await on two beaches. The rates include all activities (including golf nearby), meals and drinks. A good deal for the price.

Doolittle's Resort $65–$95 ★★★

Marigot Bay, ☎ *(800) 322-3577, (809) 451-4974, FAX (809) 452-0802.*
Single: $65–$80. Double: $80–$95.

This new hotel is perched on a verdant hillside above Marigot Bay and accessible only by a short ride on a gingerbread-trimmed ferry. Accommodations are found in pleasant inn-like rooms with cathedral ceilings, ceiling fans, small kitchenettes and large, screened porches. Further up the hill are 10 one- and two-bedroom villas with screened, open-air living areas and kitchens; these require a three-night minimum stay. The constant trade winds ensure you won't mind the lack of air conditioners. The hotel caters mainly to divers, with an on-site PADI shop as well as a variety of complimentary watersports, boutiques, a pool and a good bar and restaurant. Diving packages cost $975 per person per week and include accommodations, breakfast and dinner, transfers and unlimited boat dives.

East Winds Inn $225–$465 ★★

La Brelotte Bay, ☎ *(809) 452-8212.*
Single: $225–$345. Double: $345–$465.

This small all-inclusive resort accommodates guests in duplex cottages right on the beach. Each unit has a living area and kitchenette, and relies on ceiling fans to keep things cool. The beach bar and dining room are in a thatched hut, and there's also a library and pool on the premises.

Hummingbird Beach Resort　　　　**$80–$165**　　　　　　　★★

Soufriere, ☎ (809) 459-7232, FAX (809) 459-7033.
Single: $80–$125. Double: $105–$165.

This small resort is private and secluded. Guest rooms have ceiling fans (no air), mosquito netting over the beds, and balconies. The grounds are very nicely landscaped and open onto a public black-sand beach. Facilities are limited to a fine restaurant and a pool. Decent for the rates, and don't miss the giftshop, which has a lovely array of batik articles created by the owner.

Islander Hotel/Apartments　　　　**$80–$135**　　　　　　　★★

Rodney Bay, ☎ (809) 452-8757, FAX (809) 452-0958.
Single: $80–$125. Double: $85–$135.

Guests at this resort can choose from standard rooms (nicely done and very comfortable) and one-bedroom apartments with fully equipped kitchens. All are air-conditioned and benefit from maid service. The grounds include a restaurant, terrace bar and pool. The beach is nearby, and there are lots of eateries within walking distance. Quite a bargain.

Jalousie Plantation　　　　　　　**$345–$655**　　　　★★★★

Soufriere, ☎ (800) 392-2007, (809) 459-7666, FAX (809) 459-7667.
Single: $345–$655. Double: $485–$655.

Environmentalists with a conscience probably wouldn't consider staying at this all-inclusive resort, as it was developed in a pristine area that many believe should have been left alone. The setting is gorgeous, perched on a hillside between the Pitons on beautifully landscaped grounds. Most accommodations are in one- and two-bedroom cottages with air conditioning, refrigerators, cable TV, verandas and plunge pools. Twelve suites are housed in a former sugar mill. The extensive grounds include many dining options, four tennis courts, a spa, and private beach.

Ladera Resort　　　　　　　　　**$180–$655**　　　　　★★★

Soufriere, ☎ (800) 841-4145, (809) 459-7323, FAX (809) 273-5302.
Single: $180–$655. Double: $180–$655.

Set on a lush hillside 1000 feet above sea level, this resort offers great views of the Pitons and beyond. Accommodations are in nine villas and nine suites, all quite luxurious with four-poster beds and antiques. The best feature in each is the completely open wall that affords breathtaking views. Some units also have private plunge pools or Jacuzzis. The food in the restaurant is as fine as the views; a bar and communal pool round out the facilities. This unique spot is really special and very popular with those who like luxury combined with peace and privacy.

Le Sport　　　　　　　　　　　**$245–$905**　　　　★★★★★

Cap Estate, ☎ (800) 544-2883, (809) 450-8551, FAX (809) 450-0368.
Single: $245–$305. Double: $405–$905.

Prepare to be pampered, spoiled and primped at this all-inclusive resort situated at the island's northwestern tip and encompassing some 1500 acres. The health spa, called the Oasis, is a sterling facility with exercise classes, yoga programs, and wonderful treatments like massages, facials and body wraps. Guest rooms are as plush as everything else. Meals are wonderfully prepared, with lots of delicious dishes that are also low on calories and—could it be true?—good for you. There's also tennis, watersports, nightly entertainment and bicycles. Indulge!

Rendezvous $2470–$3420 per wk.   ★★★
Malabar Beach, ☎ (800) 544-2883, (809) 452-4211, FAX (809) 452-7419.
This all-inclusive resort used to be a Couples, but is now independent (though still open only to twosomes). Encompassing seven acres with two miles of beachfront, it houses guests in garden or oceanfront rooms, all with air conditioning, modern amenities, and balconies or patios. The rates include all meals, drinks, and activities, and there's plenty to do: two pools, two tennis courts, all watersports, and exercise classes in the gym. There's daily entertainment in the Terrace Bar, and night owls appreciate the Piano Bar, which stays open until the last guest leaves. Rates range from $2470 to $3420 per couple per week. Tipping is not allowed.

Royal St. Lucian Hotel $215–$385   ★★★
Reduit Beach, ☎ (800) 255-5859, (809) 452-9999, FAX (809) 452-9639.
Single: $215–$385. Double: $215–$385.
Located north of Castries on the beach, all accommodations at this hotel are suites with all modern conveniences. The hotel's centerpiece is the large pool, a series of interconnected waterholes complete with falls and a swim-up bar. Great food in the two restaurants, and guests can spend hours whiling away the time in the gorgeous marbled atrium lobby. Tennis and watersports await at the adjacent St. Lucian, the hotel's sister property. Very elegant.

Sandals Halcyon $810–$1020 (3 days)   ★★★
Choc Beach, ☎ (800) 726-3257, (809) 452-5331, FAX (809) 452-5434.
This all-inclusive resort just joined the Sandals family in 1984 after a previous incarnation as the Halcyon Beach Club Hotel. Open only to opposite-sex couples, the resort is set on a nice beach four miles outside of Castries. The rates cover everything from soup to nuts, with three restaurants and seven bars from which to choose. Recreational facilities include two tennis courts, two pools, watersports, plenty of organized tours and activities, and nine holes of golf at Sandals St. Lucia. Rates are $810 to $1020 per person per three days, the minimum stay.

Sandals St. Lucia $2775–$4650 per wk.   ★★★★
La Toc, ☎ (800) 726-3257, (809) 452-3081, FAX (809) 452-1012.
This 155-acre resort is set in a valley 10 minutes outside of Castries. Open only to heterosexual couples, it follows the all-inclusive plan that has made its resorts so popular in Jamaica. Guests are housed in standard rooms very nicely done with four-poster beds and modern amenities; there are also 54 suites with living rooms, VCRs, refrigerators, and terraces. Some even have private plunge pools. The rates ($2775–$4650 per couple weekly) include virtually everything, including tennis on five courts, nine holes of golf, watersports, fitness classes, and lots of activities. Fun.

St. Lucian Hotel $59–$165 ★★★

Reduit Beach, ☎ *(800) 255-5859, (809) 452-8351, FAX (809) 452-8331.*
Single: $59–$165. Double: $59–$165.

Set on one of the island's best beaches, this sprawling Rex resort houses guests in typical rooms that are air-conditioned and comfortable enough, but a bit on the worn side. The grounds include two restaurants, three bars, a very happening disco, a pool, two tennis courts, and all watersports, including a certified windsurfing school. Not the most luxurious resort on St. Lucia by any means, but the rates are quite reasonable, and the active set is kept happy.

Wyndham Morgan Bay Resort $250–$580 ★★★

Gros Islet, ☎ *(800) 822-4200, (809) 450-2511, FAX (809) 450-1050.*
Single: $250–$415. Double: $355–$580.

This all-inclusive resort is located a mile from Castries on a small beach. Guest rooms and suites are modern and attractive, with all the creature comforts associated with Wyndham. The rates include all meals, drinks and activities, and there's plenty to keep guests busy: four tennis courts, fitness center, watersports (scuba, snorkeling, and fishing costs extra), and nightly entertainment. Children are kept occupied in organized programs.

Apartments and Condominiums

You can rent either luxurious villas or more basic digs that come with kitchenettes. Decide whether you want to be closer to the tourist hub or away from it all; apartments in Soufriere and Gros Islet will seem more secluded. Fruits and vegetables can be picked up at the local market, and fish can be bought right off the boats.

Harmony Marina Suites $123–$291 ★★

Rodney Bay, ☎ *(809) 452-0336, FAX (809) 452-8677.*
Single: $123–$205. Double: $193–$291.

This all-suite hotel is set on Rodney Bay Lagoon, some 200 yards from the beach. Standard suites are air-conditioned and include coffeemakers and minibars; some also have kitchens. Deluxe units have four-poster beds and Jacuzzis. All are serviced by maids. The grounds include a pool, mini-market, and restaurant. Popular with families.

Marigot Bay Resort $90–$220 ★★★

Marigot Bay, ☎ *(800) 334-2435, (809) 451-4357, FAX (809) 451-4353.*
Single: $90–$160. Double: $90–$220.

Located seven miles from Castries, this resort encompasses several buildings that offer everything from studios to two-bedroom cottages. Its marina attracts the yachting set, and the property is split in two by the lovely bay; water taxis provide transportation back and forth. Guests are put up in an inn, villas, and pretty cottages, all with nice decor and full kitchens. The grounds include two restaurants, two bars, a pool, and extensive watersports—this place is home to both a windsurfing school and a dive shop. You'll need a car to get around, as it's pretty isolated here.

Tapion Reef Hotel $50–$80 ★★

Tapion Bay, ☎ *(809) 452-7471, FAX (809) 452-7552.*

Single: $50–$60. Double: $60–$80.

This cliffside hotel attracts those carefully watching their budget and business travelers. Guestrooms have twin beds, small baths, air conditioning, and kitchenettes. Facilities are limited to a restaurant, bar, pool, and TV room. (You can also get TV in your room for an extra $5 per night.) The beach is within walking distance. Not bad for the rates.

Windjammer Landing	**$185–$355**	★ ★ ★ ★

Labrelotte Bay, ☎ *(800) 743-9609, (809) 452-0913, FAX (809) 452-9454.*
Single: $185–$275. Double: $185–$355.

Set on 55 landscaped acres on a hillside overlooking a white sand beach, this luxurious enclave consists of Spanish-style villas with one to four bedrooms. All are spacious and beautifully done, with living and dining rooms, kitchenettes, air conditioners in the bedrooms, and all the modern conveniences. Two- to four-bedroom villas each have a private plunge pool. This resort combines the best of self-sufficient housing with all the pampering of a resort, with maid service, nightly turndown, four bars and restaurants, four swimming pools, two tennis courts, a fitness center, and watersports. Parents can stash their kids in the daily supervised programs, available year-round. A wonderful spot, and, while not cheap, gives great value for the money.

Inns

Green Parrot Inn	**$65–$115**	★

Morne Fortune, ☎ *(809) 452-3399, FAX (809) 453-2272.*
Single: $65–$95. Double: $80–$115.

Located on a mountainside with nice views of Castries and the sea, this inn houses one of St. Lucia's best gourmet restaurants. Guest rooms are air-conditioned and have balconies, but won't win any prizes for decor or ambience. There's a large pool on the premises but no other facilities. You'll want a car to get around. Okay for the rates, but you're probably better off just eating here (that's a delight) than staying overnight.

Low Cost Lodging

Depending how many people you can stuff into an apartment will determine how much you pay per person. Ask the Tourist Board for other cheap rooms for rent, but don't always trust a description sight unseen. Don't expect much decor or air conditioning in inexpensive guesthouses.

Caribbees Hotel	**$50–$75**	★

La Pansee, ☎ *(809) 452-4767.*
Single: $50–$60. Double: $65–$75.

This small hotel offers low-cost rates for those who don't mind sacrificing a beach location. Guest rooms are air-conditioned and simple, with phones, TVs, and patios or balconies. There's a bar, restaurant and pool on the premises, but not much else. You'll want a car for mobility.

Where to Eat

Fielding's Highest Rated Restaurants in St. Lucia

★★★★	Dasheene Restaurant	$35–$45
★★★★	Jimmies	$14–$28
★★★	Bistro	$14–$24
★★★	Capones	$11–$24
★★★	Chart House	$11–$30
★★★	Chez Paul	$20–$35
★★★	Green Parrot	$33–$40
★★★	Hummingbird	$9–$26
★★★	Marina Steak House	$13–$19
★★★	San Antoine	$15–$32

Fielding's Special Restaurants in St. Lucia

★★★	Capones	$11–$24
★★	Eagle's Inn	$8–$10
★★	Kimlan's	$3–$5
★★	Naked Virgin	$15–$25

Fielding's Budget Restaurants in St. Lucia

★★	Kimlan's	$3–$5
★★	Eagle's Inn	$8–$10
★★	Ginger Lily	$7–$11
★★★	Paul's Place	$7–$10
★★★	Key Largo	$6–$17

Excellent international cuisine can be found on St. Lucia. The fertile volcanic soil supports a cornucopia of exotic fruits and vegetables; the six types of bananas are particularly delicious. Island chefs make inventive use of papayas, soursops, mangos, passionfruit and coconuts. Most restaurants try to take advantage of the unparalleled natural beauty, so beautiful views have become almost commonplace. One of the most atmospheric eateries is **San Antoine**, perched in the hills overlooking Castries, which incorporates the walls of a 19th-century greathouse, with antique tableware to match. Try the delicious swordfish at **Jammer's** at Windjammer Landing, a villa complex, with pole beams, table linens and bridal-white cane furniture. **Naked Virgin** in Castries is a good bet for traditional West Indian and creole specialties such as callaloo, curries and pepperpot stew. Excellent jerk chicken, a Jamaican specialty, can be had at **Jimmie's**.

A-Pub	**$$$**	★★

The Waterfront, Rodney Bay, ☎ *(809) 452-8725.*
International cuisine.
Lunch: entrees $15–$30.
Dinner: entrees $15–$30.
A convivial yachtie hangout and local watering hole fronting Rodney Bay, the A-Pub serves up terrific steaks, fish and chips, West Indian specialties, and a few international dishes. Join the crowd for a friendly happy hour each evening.

Bistro	**$$$**	★★★

Waterfront, Rodney Bay, ☎ *(809) 452-9494.*
Seafood cuisine.
Dinner: 5–10:30 p.m., entrees $14–$24.
The British owners provide pub offerings like steak and kidney and shepherd's pie along with a varied, extensive seafood menu. Dining is on a wide elevated deck perched on the waterfront. Nautical types and others like the 20 percent discount on food items before 6:30 p.m., sort of a Caribbean early bird special.

Capones	**$$$**	★★★

Reduit Beach, Rodney Bay, ☎ *(809) 452-0284.*
Italian cuisine.
Lunch: 11:30 a.m.–4:30 p.m., entrees $11–$24.
Dinner: 4:30–10:30 p.m., entrees $11–$24.
Patrons are served by waitpersons dressed like 1930s mobsters who present the dinner check in a violin case. But it's all a lot of fun, and the Italian food is skillfully prepared. Dishes include fresh pasta, osso bucco, and juicy steaks. If the atmosphere is too heavy in the main dining room, there's a pizza parlor adjacent serving decent pies, burgers and sandwiches.

Chart House	**$$$**	★★★

Reduit Beach, Rodney Bay, ☎ *(809) 452-8115.*
American cuisine.
Dinner: 6–10:30 p.m., entrees $11–$30.

The most popular dining room on the island could be this all-American chain steakhouse overlooking the yacht harbor. Guests like the attentive service by a loyal staff (very little turnover here) and the food, which is steak, lobster (in season), tangy baby back ribs, and some Caribbean specialties, all familiar and well-prepared. The restaurant is a fern-filled wood-frame house that exudes warmth.

Chez Paul $$$ ★★★

Derek Walcott Square, Rodney Bay, ☎ *(809) 452-3022.*
International cuisine.
Lunch: 9 a.m.–4 p.m., entrees $20–$35.
Dinner: 4–11 p.m., entrees $20–$35.

Chez Paul is a more streamlined version of Rain, the South Pacific-themed restaurant that has held court on this spot since 1885. The drinks are still heady and rum-based, but the food, which was never the real attraction, is now a more sophisticated melding of European, Asian and Caribbean influences. It's open for sandwiches and lighter meals all day long. The tin-roofed house overlooks Derek Walcott Square, which is named after St. Lucia's distinguished Nobel Prize winner.

Dasheene Restaurant $$$ ★★★★

Ladera Resort, Soufriere, ☎ *(809) 459-7850.*
International cuisine.
Lunch: entrees $35–$45.
Dinner: entrees $35–$45.

The view from this hilltop aerie is unbeatable, nestled between the Pitons in Soufriere, an old French fishing community known for its sulphur springs. Located in a rustically chic villa resort, Dasheene is named after an exotic leaf used in cooking, and the menu, which changes often, incorporates locally grown produce, prime meats and seafood. The Austrian chef favors kingfish, which he likes to smoke and serve with mango or avocado and coconut sauces. Fish and shellfish are delivered to the restaurant daily.

Eagle's Inn $ ★★

Reduit Beach Road, Rodney Bay, ☎ *(809) 452-0650.*
Latin American cuisine.
Lunch: entrees $8–$10.
Dinner: entrees $8–$10.

This small funky spot, which is one of a friendly string of similar joints in Reduit Beach, serves French-inspired West Indian food. The atmosphere is very low-key and romantic, with an eagle-eye view of Gros Ilet in the distance. A good place for curry and fish dishes.

Ginger Lily $ ★★

Reduit Beach, Rodney Bay, ☎ *(809) 452-8303.*
Chinese cuisine.
Lunch: 11:30 a.m.–2:30 p.m., entrees $7–$11.
Dinner: 6–11 p.m., entrees $7–$11.

Cantonese specialties are on hand at this popular restaurant near the tourist hotels in Reduit Beach. There's always a long list of familiar favorites, which pleases residents who flock here often when the urge hits. Lunch specials are available, with several courses for under $8.

Green Parrot   **$$$**   ★ ★ ★

Red Tape Lane, Morne Fortune, ☎ *(809) 452-3399.*
International cuisine.
Lunch: Noon–3 p.m., entrees $33–$40.
Dinner: 7 p.m.–midnight, prix fixe $33–$40.

Chef Harry brought his years of culinary expertise learned at Claridge's in London home to St. Lucia, and now cooks and entertains nightly at this lively spot on a hilltop in Morne Fortune, overlooking Castries. His spiced pumpkin creation, "soup oh la la" will make you say just that when you taste it. Known for a scrumptious lunch buffet where you can heap your plate with West Indian goodies for under $8, Green Parrot is also a wild scene several nights a week when belly or limbo dancers (including Harry) reign. There's a well-chosen wine list.

Hummingbird   **$$$**   ★ ★ ★

Anse Chastenet Road, Soufriere, ☎ *(809) 459-7232.*
French cuisine.
Lunch: entrees $9–$26.
Dinner: entrees $9–$26.

Combine lunch with a plunge in the pool at this restaurant located in a rustic resort on the Soufriere waterfront. Visitors flock here when the house specialty, freshwater mountain crayfish, is in season. At other times, enjoy other seafood dishes, steaks, sandwiches and rich desserts.

Jimmies   **$$$**   ★ ★ ★ ★

Vigie Cove Marina, Rodney Bay, ☎ *(809) 452-5142.*
Latin American cuisine.
Lunch: 11 a.m.–4 p.m., entrees $14–$28.
Dinner: 4–11 p.m., entrees $14–$28.

Jimmies' bar has long been known as the place to meet and greet, but the cuisine, authentic West Indian specialties prepared by a local chef who trained in fine restaurants in England, is also worth noting. Jimmie cooks with a light touch, and his pancakes and crepes stuffed with vegetables and seafood are sublime.

Key Largo   **$$**   ★ ★ ★

The Marina, Rodney Bay, ☎ *(809) 452-0282.*
Italian cuisine.
Lunch: 11:30 a.m.–4 p.m., entrees $6–$17.
Dinner: 4–10 p.m., entrees $6–$17.

Sophisticated pizzas on a patio are served at this small restaurant with its own outdoor brick oven. All manner of Italian coffee drinks are dispensed here as well. Try the house specialty, a pizza made with artichokes and shrimp.

Kimlan's   **$**   ★ ★

Micoud Street, Rodney Bay, ☎ *(809) 452-1136.*
Latin American cuisine.
Lunch: 7 a.m.–4 p.m., entrees $3–$5.
Dinner: 4–11 p.m., entrees $3–$5.

A local family runs this upper-level West Indian restaurant with a terrace positioned
directly across from Columbus Square. Steaming bowls of curry or fish stews are
served with rice and salad. A good spot for people watching, and for lighter snacks
and ice cream.

Marina Steak House $$$ ★★★

The Marina, Rodney Bay, ☎ (809) 452-9800.
Seafood cuisine.
Dinner: 5 p.m.–midnight, entrees $13–$19.
You'll find steak and seafood in a series of dim rooms with a bar where jazz piano
can be heard playing on Friday nights. The restaurant, a converted private home in
Rodney Bay Marina, is a reliable spot for American-style meals with vegetables and
a baked potato served alongside.

Naked Virgin $$$ ★★

Marchand Road, Marchand, ☎ (809) 452-5594.
Latin American cuisine. Specialties: Flying fish.
Lunch: entrees $15–$25.
Dinner: entrees $15–$25.
This graceful West Indian building in the suburb of Marchand is the home of an
excellent punch that gives the restaurant its provocative name. The brew is so
potent, it might encourage you to take your clothes off. Be that as it may, the Virgin
also has a loyal following of regulars who admire chef/owner John Paul's traditional
creole cooking.

Paul's Place $ ★★★

Bridge St., Rodney Bay, ☎ (809) 452-3398.
International cuisine.
Lunch: 9 a.m.–4 p.m., entrees $7–$10.
Dinner: 4–10 p.m., entrees $7–$10.
Paul's provides a tasty lunch buffet to office workers who crowd the place at noon.
Those who don't want to brave the line can choose from a menu of rotis, sand-
wiches, and plate meals. Dinner is more subdued, with innovatively prepared fish,
chicken and steak dishes. It's not always up to par, but when it is, it shines brightly.

San Antoine $$$ ★★★

Old Morne Rd., Morne Fortune, ☎ (809) 452-4660.
International cuisine.
Lunch: 11:45 a.m.–2:15 p.m., entrees $15–$32.
Dinner: 6:15–9:30 p.m., entrees $15–$32.
The surroundings are old fashioned and gracious, with meals served in the main
house of the old San Antoine Hotel. The dining room, lit by candles at night, is run
by an English couple who keep things purring along smoothly. Those looking for a
special night out often choose this salon, which overlooks the twinkling lights of the
harbor. The menu includes French and continental specialties, including seafood in
parchment, pepper steak, or filet mignon with crayfish stuffing.

Where to Shop

St. Lucia's shopping won't disappoint. A new harborfront shopping complex called **Pointe Seraphine** features a large variety of duty-free imports such as designer perfumes, crystal and china. You'll also find native crafts and resort wear there, but try to avoid the complex when a cruise ship has docked. Market day (Saturday) at the Castries' 100-year-old market will give you a chance to kibitz with farmer's wives displaying luscious tropical fruits and vegetables, spices and local crafts; don't be shy about asking to sample a bite of tamarind, but keep a watch on your handbag and wallet. Good buys are woven fruit baskets for the kitchen back home; a good place to shop is the **government handicraft store** at the waterfront. A number of shops also sell locally made baskets, wood carvings and pottery. Hand-screened clothing and colorful batik apparel are featured buys, especially at the famous **Caribelle Batik** store. St. Lucia's artists tend to specialize in designs and portraits of the island's flora and fauna. If you want to see craftspeople working in their studios, stop by the **Arts & Crafts Development Centre**, near Choiseul, on the southwest coast; baskets, dishes, tapestries and woodcarvings are good buys. Some shops are being developed on the west coast, south of Castries. In general, prices at hotel and resort boutiques run much higher than elsewhere.

St. Lucia Directory

ARRIVAL AND DEPARTURE

American Airlines serves St. Lucia nonstop from New York/JFK every Sunday and daily from its San Juan, Puerto Rico hub, with connecting service to major U.S. cities. **BWIA** flies nonstop to the island twice a week from New York/JFK through Sept. 14, and three times a week from Miami. St. Lucia is now directly accessible to six U.S markets, with charter programs beginning out of Boston (GWV), Chicago (Club Med) and Detroit (Keytours), in addition to those already available from Atlanta, Cincinnati and St.Louis.

The airport departure tax is U.S. $11.

BUSINESS HOURS

Shops open weekdays 8 a.m.–12:30 p.m. and 1:30–4 p.m. and Saturdays 8 a.m.–noon. Banks open Monday–Thursday 8 a.m.–3 p.m., Fri-

day 8 a.m.–5 p.m. Some in Rodney Bay also open Saturday from
a.m.–noon.

CLIMATE

Temperatures year-round average between 70 and 90 degrees F. Constant trade winds keep the air cool and the humidity from becoming
oppressive.

DOCUMENTS

U.S. and Canadian citizens need to show a full and valid passport. British citizens need no passport if their stay does not exceed six months.
French citizens must show an ID card. An ongoing or return ticket
must also be shown.

ELECTRICITY

Current runs 220 volts, 50 cycles, with a square three-pin plug. A few
hotels use 110 volts, 50 cycles. Bring an adapter and converter plug.

GETTING AROUND

Travel between Castries and other towns including Soufriere and Vieux
Fort can be done in minibuses, usually overcrowded and stocked with
local produce; you may have to share your seat with a carton of tomatoes. Buses leaving for Soufriere and Vieux Fort can be picked up in
front of the department store on Bridge Street. To get to Cap Estate
take the bus near the market on Jeremy Street in Castries.

Taxis are all over the island. They have excellent experience with the
small, winding roads outside the capital. Many taxi drivers are guides
and have been trained in showing tourists around the city and island.
Cars are unmetered, but official rates have been set by the government.
Before setting off for a destination, verify the price in advance, and in
what currency. When someone says dollar, you must specify whether it
is the American dollar or the Eastern Caribbean dollar that is being
talked about.

Rental cars are available in St. Lucia, but roads are difficult in the countryside and driving is on the left—always a bit hazardous for drivers
used to the right side of the road. A driver's license is required and may
be obtained from the Immigration Office upon arrival. It remains valid
for three months. Stick with the top American names in agencies. You
have assurance that you can use your credit card, arrangements can be
easily made in advance before you leave, and if anything goes wrong,
you can easily contact the head office back home. **Budget** ☎ *(809)
452-8021*; **Avis** ☎ *(809) 353-2046*; and **Hertz** ☎ *(809) 452-0679*. Of
the three Hertz is the most expensive. It's best to get collision insurance; membership in auto clubs may lower the price in certain circumstances. Budget is the least expensive, about $300 per week for its least
expensive car. All agencies can have cars waiting at the airport, or you
can contact their office at the airport when you arrive. If it is the first
time you are driving on the left-hand side of the road, it's a good idea

to be traveling with a companion and allow him or her to spot the road for you. In foreign situations or one in which there are many distractions, or late at night, it is very easy to become forgetful and cross to the wrong side of the road, especially when you are turning or looking for directions.

LANGUAGE

The official language is English, though a local patois is spoken.

MEDICAL EMERGENCIES

A 24-hour emergency room is available at St. Jude's Hospital, Vieux Fort ☎ *(809) 454-6041* and Victoria Hospital, Hospital Road, Castries ☎ *(809) 452-2421.*

MONEY

The currency is the Eastern Caribbean dollar.

TELEPHONE

The area code is *809.* Local numbers have seven digits, all of which should be dialed. International phone calls, as well as cables, can be made at the offices of the **Cable & Wireless** in the George Gordon Building on Bridge Street in Castries ☎ *(809) 452-3301.* Placing calls through your hotel or from your hotel room usually results in an enormous surcharge that is best avoided; some tourists have just been paralyzed by seeing the final bill tallying all their carefully monitored calls home.

TIME

Atlantic Standard Time, all year round, one hour earlier than New York time. During Daylight Saving Time, however, it is the same hour.

TIPPING AND TAXES

The government imposes an 8 percent occupancy tax on hotel room rentals. Sometimes hotels and restaurants add a 15 percent service charge, but check your bill carefully. In restaurants it is customary to tip waiters or waitresses 10–15 percent if it has not already been added to the bill. Airport porters usually receive about 75 cents a bag.

TOURIST INFORMATION

The **St. Lucia Tourist Board** is located at Point Seraphine in Castries ☎ *(809) 452-5968.* It's always worth stopping by to see if they have any brochures or suggestions for hikes, excursions, etc. It is also a source to find out what is happening in the community. In the U.S. call ☎ *(800) 456-3984.*

WHEN TO GO

January 1 and 2, which is the New Year's celebration, culminates in a two-day street fair offering local foods, island music, and dancing and games for children. Carnival is celebrated February 14 and 15 with elaborate costumes, dancing before dawn and national calypso contests. The annual St. Lucia Jazz Festival usually takes place in the middle of

May. June 29 is the feast of St. Peter, a Fisherman's Day, where pries
bless the fishermen's brightly decorated boats. August 30 is the Feast
St. Rose of Lima, a spectacular flower festival dating back to the 18
century where members of the La Rose Flower Society sing and dan
in the streets in costumes. September hosts an annual island-wide cul
nary competition. September 30–August 4 is an annual Internation
Billfish tournament, with anglers from the region and North Ameri
participating. November 22 is St. Cecilia's Day, celebrated by musician
serenading the streets of Castries. Early December hosts the Atlant
Rally for Cruisers with the world's largest annual transocean yacht rac
Christmas, on December 25, is usually celebrated by early morning se
enaders visiting homes and sampling holiday gourmet fare.

ST. LUCIA HOTELS	RMS	RATES	PHONE	CR. CARD
Castries				
★★★★★ Le Sport	102	$245–$905	(800) 544-2883	A, MC
★★★★ Anse Chastanet Hotel	48	$95–$505	(800) 223-1108	A, D, MC, V
★★★★ Jalousie Plantation	115	$345–$655	(800) 392-2007	A, MC
★★★★ Sandals St. Lucia	209	$2775–$4650	(800) 726-3257	A, MC, V
★★★★ Windjammer Landing	114	$185–$355	(800) 743-9609	A, MC
★★★ Club Med St. Lucia	265	$800–$1300	(800) 258-2633	A, MC
★★★ Club St. Lucia	312	$175–$445	(809) 450-0551	A, CB, D, MC, V
★★★ Doolittle's Resort	22	$65–$95	(800) 322-3577	A, MC, V
★★★ Ladera Resort	16	$180–$655	(800) 841-4145	A, D, MC
★★★ Marigot Bay Resort	40	$90–$220	(800) 334-2435	A, MC
★★★ Rendezvous	100	$2470–$3420	(800) 544-2883	A, MC
★★★ Royal St. Lucian Hotel	98	$215–$385	(800) 255-5859	A, CB, MC, V
★★★ Sandals Halcyon	180	$810–$1020	(800) 726-3257	A, MC
★★★ St. Lucian Hotel	260	$59–$165	(800) 255-5859	A, MC, V
★★★ Wyndham Morgan Bay Resort	238	$250–$580	(800) 822-4200	A, CB, D, MC, V
★★ Candyo Inn	12	$75–$90	(809) 452-0712	A, MC
★★ East Winds Inn	10	$225–$465	(809) 452-8212	A, MC, V
★★ Harmony Marina Suites	30	$123–$291	(809) 452-0336	A, D, MC
★★ Hummingbird Beach Resort	10	$80–$165	(809) 459-7232	A, D, MC
★★ Islander Hotel/ Apartments	63	$80–$135	(809) 452-8757	A, D, MC, V

ST. LUCIA HOTELS	RMS	RATES	PHONE	CR. CARDS
★★ Tapion Reef Hotel	30	$50–$80	(809) 452-7471	A, MC
★ Caribbees Hotel	18	$50–$75	(809) 452-4767	A
★ Green Parrot Inn	60	$65–$115	(809) 452-3399	A, MC

ST. LUCIA RESTAURANTS	PHONE	ENTREE	CR. CARDS

astries

American			
★★★ Chart House	(809) 452-8115	$11–$30••	A, DC, MC, V
Chinese			
★★ Ginger Lily	(809) 452-8303	$7–$11	A, MC, V
International			
★★★ Chez Paul	(809) 452-3022	$20–$35	A, DC, MC, V
★★★ Green Parrot	(809) 452-3399	$33–$40	A, MC, V
★★★ Paul's Place	(809) 452-3398	$7–$10	A, MC, V
★★★ San Antoine	(809) 452-4660	$15–$32	A, MC, V
★★ A-Pub	(809) 452-8725	$15–$30	A, V
Italian			
★★★ Capones	(809) 452-0284	$11–$24	A, MC, V
★★★ Key Largo	(809) 452-0282	$6–$17	MC, V
Latin American			
★★★★ Jimmies	(809) 452-5142	$14–$28	A, MC, V
★★ Eagle's Inn	(809) 452-0650	$8–$10	A, MC, V
★★ Kimlan's	(809) 452-1136	$3–$5	None
★★ Naked Virgin	(809) 452-5594	$15–$25	A, MC, V
Seafood			
★★★ Bistro	(809) 452-9494	$14–$24••	A, MC, V
★★★ Marina Steak House	(809) 452-9800	$13–$19••	A, MC, V

oufriere

French			
★★★ Hummingbird	(809) 459-7232	$9–$26	MC, V
International			
★★★★ Dasheene Restaurant	(809) 459-7850	$35–$45	A, MC, V

ST. LUCIA RESTAURANTS	PHONE	ENTREE	CR. CARD

Note: • Lunch Only

•• Dinner Only

SINT MAARTEN/ ST. MARTIN

Sailing excursions from St. Martin to other islands are easily arranged.

Half-Dutch, half-French, the island of Sint Maarten/St. Martin gives a bi-polar vacation for the price of one. Sint Maarten, the Dutch side, is part of the trio of islands that make up the Dutch Windwards (including Sint Eusta-ius and Saba), while only a few steps away, St. Martin belongs to the French West Indies. A mere welcoming sign acts as the only border between the two sides—nary a customs officer in sight—but the contrasts are startling, if quite tantalizing. Not only are the native languages different (though most people speak English as a common dominator), the ambience of each sovereign state nation bears its own unique personality. Quiet and more refined, St.

Martin's capital of Marigot is the place to go if you're looking for goo (duty-free) shopping, fine Creole cooking, and French haute cuisine; you're looking to sail, frenzied Philipsburg, Sint Maarten's capital, has th best port. The Dutch side also boasts a dozen casinos; the one at **Port de Plai sance** is the nicest. Beaches are good all around the island, and scuba dive and snorkelers will find very exciting conditions. Some of the Caribbean' most luxurious (and most expensive resorts) are situated on the island, bu most tourists let themselves be lured to the sea at least for one day (if not week) to sail to some of the other glorious islands nearby.

Bird's Eye View

Simpson's Bay lagoon is spectacular at sunset.

St. Martin/Sint Maarten lies at the top of the Guadeloupe archipelago 144 miles east of Puerto Rico. The total land mass is 37 square miles. The main airport and seaport are located on the Dutch side, which occupies the southern part of the barely triangular island. The western coast is low-lying and mostly comprised of **Simpson Bay Lagoon**, where small craft find a safe harbor. The rest of the Dutch side is very hilly, almost conical scrubland though a good strong rain can turn it into a lush garden. Two ranges cros the island, in-between lies **Great Bay** and its **Salt Pond**, the valley of **Belle**

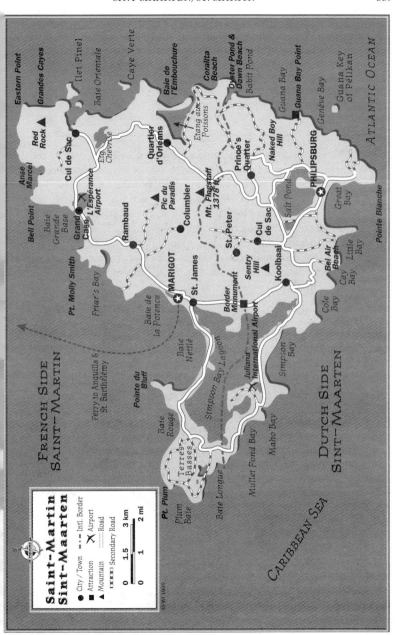

Saint-Martin
Sint-Maarten

- City / Town
- Attraction
- Mountain
- Intl. Border
- Airport
- Road
- Secondary Road

0   1.5   3 km
0   1   2 mi

FRENCH SIDE
SAINT-MARTIN

DUTCH SIDE
SINT-MAARTEN

ATLANTIC OCEAN

CARIBBEAN SEA

Eastern Point
Grandes Cayes
Îlet Pinel
Caye Verte
Baie Orientale
Baie de l'Embouchure
Coralita Beach
Oyster Pond & Dawn Beach
Babit Pond
Guana Bay
Guana Bay Point
Guana Key of Pélikan
Genève Bay

Red Rock ▲
Cul de Sac
Anse Marcel
Quartier d'Orleans
Etang aux Poissons
Etg. Chevrise
Prince's Quarter
Naked Boy Hill
PHILIPSBURG
Salt Pond
Great Bay
Pointe Blanche

Bell Point
Pt. Molly Smith
Baie Grande Base
Grand Case
L'Espérance Airport
Rambaud
Plc du Paradis ▲
Columbier
Mt. Flagstaff 1378 ▲
St. Peter
Cul de Sac
Bel Air Beach
Little Bay
Cay Bay

Friar's Bay
MARIGOT
St. James
Sentry Hill ▲
Border Monument ■
Koolbaai
Cole Bay

Baie de la Potence
Pointe du Bluff
Baie Nettlé
Baie Rouge
Pt. Plum
Plum Baie
Baie Longue

Ferry to Anguilla & St. Barthélémy

Juliana International Airport
Simpson Bay Lagoon
Simpson Bay
Maho Bay
Mullet Pond Bay
Terres Basses

©WI 1996

Plaine, and the smaller salt ponds at **Le Galion**. Dotting the coastline are numerous bays that make for excellent beaches.

History

Columbus discovered and named St. Martin in 1493, and by the 1630 both the Dutch and French had settled on the island. Pirates combed th craggy shores and secret coves of the island, burying treasure and booty the had won at sea. It was in St. Martin that Peter Stuyvesant (the last Dutc governor of New York) lost his leg in a struggle with the Spanish in 1640 According to legend, the binational division of St. Martin was determine when a Dutchman and a Frenchman stood back to back, then circled the i land until they encountered each other again, face to face. (Since the Frenc side is somewhat bigger than the Dutch, leading devotees of this legend lik to believe that the Dutchman was fatter and slower.) More legitimate histo rians tend to suppose that a small group of French and Dutch prisoners es caped their Spanish captors and drew up an agreement to divide the islan between them. In 1946, Guadeloupe, of which St. Martin is a dependency became an Overseas Department of France and in 1974, an Overseas Regio of France.

A cannon on St. Maarten is a reminder of days when pirates roamed the shores

People

As of 1994, there were about 28,000 residents on the French side and 32,000 on the Dutch side, but ask residents what they want to be called and nobody knows. The confusion lies in the multilinguistical nature that divides the island as well as the genuine amiability that unites it. On the Dutch side, children in primary school study in English, while students on the French side don't learn English until secondary school. Still, there's no real overt competition, and the signs separating the Dutch from the French side are truly ones of welcome, rather than declarations of partisanship. To make matters even more confusing, there are many different accents among English speakers (one distinctly Jamaican) and even a lively street dialect called *papiamento*, a hefty Caribbean mix of English, Spanish, Portuguese, Dutch and African languages. There's enough interest in Papiamento to warrant its own newspaper.

With all the French sophistication and the Dutch gentility, superstition and backwoods lore are still strong and thriving in St. Martin, including the belief in *jumbies* (evil spirits) and *soucouyants*, a kind of vampire woman. The fetish for calypso is also pure Caribbean, though the lyrics lack the political bite known on more dissident islands, and contests and parties are held regularly throughout the year. Lasana Sekou singularly upholds the literary tradition as the island's only published poet, rich in the local dialects and slang.

Beaches

St. Martin has 37 white sand beaches in excellent condition; many still wait to be discovered. Colors are dazzling, from deep blue to turquoise to emerald green. Take your pick from coastal crescent-shaped stretches noted for their seclusion to broad swatches of pristine virgin sand. Access to public beaches is easy, usually through little roads off the highway and even in high season, you won't find them uncomfortably crowded. In addition to the mile-long beach at **Great Bay** in Philipsburg, there is **Little Bay**, within a walk-

ing distance from town, with excellent watersports activities. At the west end
of **Cupecoy**, you can bathe au naturel, but there are no facilities. Reachable
more easily by boat are the more secluded beaches of **Plum Bay** and **Rouge
Beach** (no facilities). You'll find a nudist beach (and clothes-optional hotel)
at one end of **Orient Bay**. No roads go directly to the beach; rather, one must
park on tracks off the main road at the north or south end of the beach and
walk a few hundred feet to the water. Orient Bay also has lots of shops, restaurants and watersports facilities.

Underwater

Diving on St. Martin is buried within the shadows of the island's glittering
nightlife and rippling canvas sails. The sport seems virtually an afterthought
on St. Martin, most obviously displayed by the fact that day trips to Saba, St.
Barthélémy and Anguilla are promoted eagerly through local dive shops.
Sites close to shore have been overfished and the coral degraded, and wind
frequently whip up the seas, making access a bit rocky. As locals will quietly
explain, St. Martin simply is not a major dive destination. And yet, there are
at least two good wrecks—one ancient, the other very new—and the shallow
reef structure is extensive, stretching for more than two miles off St. Martin's
coast. An excellent site, **One Step Beyond**, is not listed below; rough waters
rarely make the location (seven miles southeast of Philipsburg) available to
divers, but it yields large pelagics, coral arches and tunnels. The best of the
rest are concentrated on the south coast around Philipsburg and visibility averages 60 to 80 feet (better in winter). Dive prices are a little steeper than in
most parts of the Eastern Caribbean. There are a few small operators on the
French side, but using them requires familiarity with the French system of
diving. In sum, most anyone serious about exploring the depths will visit a
couple St. Martin sites then beeline to nearby Saba, where the real excitement lies, but beginners and less of worldly divers will be kept sufficiently
happy on St. Martin. Snorkelers will find the island's coves and inlets ideal
settings; try Mullet Bay or the waters off Green Cay, Tintamarre or Ilet
Pinel.

Hen and Chicks

As close to a wall dive as you'll find on St. Martin, this pleasant site drops down
gracefully (25–60 feet) past elkhorn and staghorn coral forests, then down a 45-
degree incline through plate and brain coral. Dolphins sometimes visit this part of
the reef, while big eels and solid fish life lurk lower down.

Pelican Rock

A series of small rock outcroppings off the southeastern shore starts at sea level, like stepping stones out to 50 feet; many sponges, sea fans and whips, soft corals, grassy sand area with rays (50 feet).

Wreck of the *Proselyte*

Built in 1770, the Danish war frigate *Proselyte* crashed against St. Martin's reefs in 1801, providing one of the region's oldest identifiable wreck sites. The wooden hull is long gone, but 26 cannons have been located, along with three large anchors, brass barrel hoops (from water and powder kegs), brass monkeys and ballast bars. The wreckage starts at 15 feet and descends to 50 feet.

Wreck of *Teigland*

The island's most recent sinking is a 135-foot island freighter, sunk deliberately in 1993. The ship landed upright on Cable Reef in 70 feet of water and is already drawing fish activity. Although intact, the *Teigland* can be penetrated.

Dive Shops

Ocean Explorers Dive Center

Simpson Bay; ☎ *(599) 545-252.*
A smaller, independent operation, the oldest on the island (35 years); PADI and NAUI affiliation, with courses to Assistant Instructor. Two-tank dive, $80 including equipment; maximum group size, 10 divers.

Trade Winds Dive Center

Philipsburg; ☎ *(599) 575-176.*
Conveniently located five minutes from major dive sites. Twelve-year-old operation; PADI and SSI-affiliated, with courses to Assistant Instructor. Two-tank dive, $85 including equipment ($5 per dive discount if you bring your own gear).

On Foot

One of the better local legends has it that St. Martin's national boundaries were determined by having two statesmen, one French, one Dutch, walk the island's perimeter to establish an equal territorial claim for each nation. Whether the Frenchman was a faster walker or, as some suggest, the Dutchman was slowed by inebriation, the French wound up with the larger chunk of land. Since this point several hundred years ago, hiking has faded into the background, while shimmering beaches have become firmly established as St. Martin's principle outdoor attraction. It doesn't help matters that this densely populated island has little room left for explorations on foot. But

there are unexpected options, which will quietly appear on backcountr
roads, particularly on the less densely populated French side and on Terre
Basses, the peninsula west of Simpson Bay. Keep your mind open to these
sporadic strolls and you will be rewarded.

Horses can be rented on St. Maarten/St. Martin for excursions over the hills o
Anse Marcel to the beaches of Petite Cay or Cole Bay.

Cole Bay To Cay Bay

Just west of Philipsburg lies a series of hills that shelter three quiet coves. This trail
follows an equestrian trail beginning at the Crazy Acres Riding Center, climbing
out of Cole Bay to a hillside viewpoint that takes in St. Barthélémy, St. Kitts, Saba
and St. Eustatius. The trail continues, meandering down into secluded Cay Bay,
where swimming is peaceful. Allow two hours round-trip.

Paradise Peak

A worn road leads to the top of St. Martin's highest point, but there's no reason you
can't walk it. The summit road starts a quarter-mile east of the turnoff for Colom-

bier. Where the road splits, bear to the left, drive as far as the last house and park for the hiking portion of the trip. The path ascends through St. Martin's lushest forests for three-quarters of a mile to the airy 1378-foot summit. Note the signs that lead to the best of several viewpoints. From the communication tower, it's possible to work back down using a series of paths on the south and east sides that eventually lead to Orient Bay and Orleans.

By Pedal

Over the past three years, St. Martin residents have fervently embraced bicycles, creating the latest fitness craze to strike this affluent island. On Sundays, it's not uncommon to see a hundred or more cyclists tooling around **Simpson Bay Lagoon**, and although primary arteries are fast-paced, there are usually viable alternatives. The main road circling St. Martin rolls past most of the island's best scenery, as well as topping nine good-sized hills; several routing possibilities are available, but figure about 35 miles (including the loop around Simpson) for the whole circuit. A shorter, relatively flat option is the 13-mile ride around Simpson Bay, while quieter dirt roads west of the lagoon lead to **Terres-Basses**, a peninsula sprinkled with lovely beaches and posh residences. Off-roaders will find lovely riding along the coast immediately north of Marigot, and on the hillsides leading to **Paradise Peak**. In general, the best mountain biking lies on the less-crowded French side, though Cay Bay (near the GEB water plant) is an idyllic area. The island offers little respite from heat other than bars and restaurants, so riders are well-advised to carry plenty of water for any extensive undertakings.

Frog's Legs

Marigot; ☎ *(590) 87-05-11.*

Rents Specialized mountain bikes for about $15 per day, with two-hour tours starting at $35.

Tri-Sport

Simpson Bay; ☎ *(599) 554-384.*

A bicycle/triathlon shop with an adjacent health food restaurant, The Carrot. The growing inventory of Trek Mountain Bikes rent for $15 per day (or 24 hours), with discounts for week-long rentals.

What Else to See

St. Maarten's shops at Simpson's Bay offer French fashions, batiks from St Barts, jewelry, perfumes and quality gift items.

Unless you have a fort fetish, there's not much to see in St. Martin; bette stay on the beach, cruise to a neighboring island, or go shopping in **Marigot** a kind of St. Tropez of the Caribbean that sports its own jet-set scene, nud beach, sidewalk cafes and fishing boats. The **Port La Royale Marina** makes ar interesting pitstop (you may be there anyway, chartering a schooner), anc the museum Saint-Martin **On the Trail of the Arawaks** can be worth the trou ble if you have any interest in Native American history. A good view of th French capital can be seen from the top of **Fort St. Louis** but be prepared fo a hefty climb. To take your choice among the island's top restaurants, heac for **Grand Case**, whose "Restaurant Row" has earned this tiny beachfron town the title "Gastronomic Center of St. Martin."

Don't miss the pastoral hamlet of **Orléans** (also known as the French Quar ter), the oldest French settlement on the island. Here you'll find handsome small homes set among gardens alive with such tropical blossoms as bouga invillea, wisteria, flamboyant and hibiscus. **Roland Richardson**, a neighbor-

ood artist, conservationist and historian, welcomes visitors to his studio on
hursdays.

Philipsburg, the capital of the Dutch side, boasts **Great Beach Bay**, perhaps
ne of the cleanest city beaches in the world. You can find more about the
story of the city at the **Museum Arcade** on *111 Front Street*. Fauna and flora
om the island can be glimpsed at the zoo, at **Madam Estate**, close to the
few Amsterdam Shopping Center.

Historical Sites

rt St. Louis   ★★★
Just off Rue de la Republique, Marigot.
This old fort, dating back to 1786, is well preserved with some original cannons still
intact. It's worth the very steep climb (bring water) for the splendid views of Marigot alone.

Museums and Exhibits

ourthouse of St. Maarten   ★★★
Front Street, Philipsburg, Dutch Side.
Located north of the town square on bustling Front Street, this 1793 building was
recently restored with glorious results. The second floor still functions as a court-
house, while the first floor is a post office. You'll definitely want to snap a picture of
this colorful edifice.

aint-Martin museum, On the Trail of the Arawaks   ★★★★
Sandy Ground Road, Marigot.
This new museum is located next to the Royal Marina on the lagoon side. Exhibits
focus on pre-Columbian artifacts, including remains of indigenous inhabitants dating back to 1800 B.C. and ceramics from 550 B.C. There's also a reproduction of
a 1500-year-old Indian burial site (just discovered in 1994), early 20th-century
photographs of the island, and displays on the plantation and slavery periods. Open
Monday-Saturday from 9 a.m.–1 p.m. and from 3–7 p.m.

imartn Museum   ★★★
111 Front Street, Philipsburg, Dutch Side.
Hours open: 10 a.m.–6 p.m.
This small museum is housed in one of the few remaining 19th-century West
Indian-style cottages on the island. Exhibits are on a changing basis, most focusing
on the island's history and culture. There are some upscale specialty boutiques on
the premises. Not worth a special trip, but a nice way to kill an hour or two if you're
in the neighborhood.

Parks and Gardens

utterfly Farm   ★★★★★
Le Galion Beach Road, Orient Bay.
Hours Open: 9 a.m.–5 p.m.
If you're never given butterflies a second thought (or look) before, you certainly
will after visiting this tranquil spot near Orient Bay. Hundreds of rare and exotic
butterflies fly free in a large screened-in garden replete with fish ponds, fountains

and tropical foliage. Interesting exhibits showcase their egg laying, caterpillar an
pupa stages, and you'll get to see butterflies emerge from their cocoons and fly o
into the great beyond (or at least around their 900-square-meter home). It's tru
fascinating, and a tour, offered at no additional charge, is a must to really appreciat
the exhibits. Butterflies are free...but this tour costs $10 for one or two people, $2
for three and $7.50 each for a group of four.

Tours

Pinel Island   ★ ★ ★ ★

Cul de Sac Bay.

Just five bucks will get you a roundtrip boat ride to this tiny island off the coast o
French St. Martin. There you can snorkel (they rent equipment), sunbathe or din
in the casual restaurant.

St. Maarten Zoo   ★ ★ ★

Madame Estate, Philipsburg, Dutch Side.
Hours open: 9 a.m.–5 p.m.

This small zoo is especially suited to children (who get in for $2), with its play
ground and petting zoo. The grounds include botanical gardens, two walk-throug
aviaries, and caged animals from the Caribbean and South America.

Seaworld Explorer   ★ ★ ★ ★

Grande Case Pier, Grande Case.

This semi-submarine has an open-air deck and underwater observatory hull that let
you view sealife in air-conditioned comfort—and without getting your hair wet
Trips depart from Grande Case Pier and explore the waters surrounding Creol
Rock. A diver feeds the fishies to make sure tourists have lots to see. Tours cost $3(
for adults, $20 for kids 2-12. Add $10 each ($7 for kids) for roundtrip transporta
tion from your hotel.

BEST VIEW:

*At 1278-feet, Paradise Peak, called Pic du Paradis, offers a breathtaking view
of both the French and Dutch capitals.*

Sports

Almost every beachfront hotel has facilities for windsurfing and sunfish sail
ing; windsurfing lessons average about $20. Waterskiing and parasailing are
offered by a few hotels.

Sailing is one spectacular sport in St. Martin. From bases in Marigot, as well as Anse Marcel and Oyster Pond near the French/Dutch border, you can find any number of yacht charters. Recommended moorings on the French side of St. Martin include: **Bai Rouge** (good anchorage), **Nettlé Bay** near Marigot, **Marigot Bay** (for shopping), **Friar's Bay** (calm), **Happy Bay** (beach-grazing) and **Grand Case Bay**, a charming fishing village with a dock grocery, pharmacy and excellent restaurants. A top-class marina can be found at **Port Louvilliers** at Anse Marcel, with docking space for 60 boats (29–73 feet) and boutiques, grocery, cafe and **La Capitanerie**, a ship chandlery. At **Oyster Pond** you'll also find a large marina and **Captain Oliver's**, a popular restaurant and hotel, plus a small grocery and a ship chandlery. Sailing excursions from St. Martin to other islands (Anguilla is a favorite, but boats also go to St. Barts, Saba, St. Kitts, Nevis and St. Eustatius) can be arranged by most hotels. Rates for a day trip with snorkeling, open bar and picnics run between $65–$70 per person.

Caid & Isa, a horseback riding facility located at Meridien L'Habitation at Anse Marcel, is operated by longtime pro Brigitte Sacaze. Paso Finas can be hired for 2.5-hour excursions over the hills of Anse Marcel to the private beach of **Petite Cayes**. Other facilities include the **OK Corral** at the Coralita beach (including one pony for children) and **Crazy Acres** at Cole Bay (on the Dutch side).

Sport-fishing finds big fans on St. Martin. Half-and full-day charters with tackle, bait and snacks are readily available at **Bobby's Marina**, **Great Bay**, **Simpson Bay** and **Port La Royale Marina**. December to April is the season for kingfish, dolphin and barracuda; tuna is available year-round.

Boating is available on two types of vessels: large catamarans holding 25 or more passengers that sail to St. Barts for the day, or small sailboats that hold six to ten passengers for excursions to secluded beaches. Boats depart from **Bobby's Marina** and **Great Bay Marina** in Philipsburg, **Simpson Bay Lagoon**, and **Port La Royale Marina** at Marigot Bay. A new marina is located at **Port Lonvilliers** at the north end of the French section.

There are numerous tennis courts on the island. **Le Privilege**, overlooking Meridien L'Habitation, has six lighted courses and **La Belle Créole** has four lighted Omni courts. **Laguna Beach** has three lighted hard-surface courts. Other hotels include **Nettlé Bay Beach Club**, **Mont Vernon**, **Simson Beach**, **Oyster Bay**, **Grand Case Beach Club**, **Coralita**, **Esmeralda Resort** and **Green Cay Village**.

Golf

Mullet Bay Resort, Philipsburg, Dutch Side.
The island's only links are an 18-hole course designed by Joseph Lee. It is quite scenic and very challenging, but often open only to guests at the Mullet Bay Resort—if your heart is really set on golfing, play it safe and stay at this well-run resort.

Greens fee for nonguests (when they are allowed) are about $100, and considerab
less for guests—another reason to stay here.

Horseback Riding

Various locations, Philipsburg, Dutch Side.

On the Dutch Side, horses can be rented at **Crazy Acres** (☎ *5-42793*). On t
French Side, try **Caid and Isa** (☎ *87-32-92*) and the **O.K. Corral** (☎ *87-40-7.*
The going rate is about $40 for a two-hour trail ride.

Watersports

Various locations, Philipsburg, Dutch Side.

If your hotel doesn't offer the watersports you're seeking, a slew of companies a
happy to help. Dutch Side: for boating and cruises, try **White Octopus** (☎
23170), **Caribbean Watersports** (☎ *5-42801*), **Bobby's Marina** (☎ *5-22366*), a
Bluebeard (☎ *5-52898*). For deep-sea fishing, try **Wampum** (☎ *5-22366*), **S
Brat** (☎ *5-24096*), and **Bobby's Marina** (☎ *5-22366*). Scuba divers can call **Le
ward Island Divers** (☎ *5-242268*), **Tradewinds** (☎ *5-54387*), **St. Maarten Dive
(☎ *5-22446*), and **Ocean Explorers** (☎ *5-45252*), which also runs a unique unde
water walk on which non-swimmers can stroll with the help of special helmets th
supply oxygen.

Where to Stay

Fielding's Highest Rated Hotels in Sint Maarten/St. Martin

★★★★★	La Belle Creole	$205–$455
★★★★★	La Samanna Hotel	$28–$995
★★★★	Dawn Beach Hotel	$105–$290
★★★★	Green Cay Village	$257–$557
★★★★	Le Meridien l'Habitation	$175–$655
★★★★	Oyster Pond Hotel	$120–$310
★★★★	Point Pirouette Villas	$161–$845
★★★★	Port de Plaisance	$220–$600
★★★★	Privilege Resort & Spa	$196–$580
★★★	Divi Little Bay Resort	$110–$350

Fielding's Most Romantic Hotels in Sint Maarten/St. Martin

★★★	Hevea	$75–$125
★★★	Horny Toad Guesthouse	$103–$185
★★★	L'Esplanade Caraibes Hotel	$100–$290
★★★★★	La Samanna Hotel	$28–$995
★★★★	Oyster Pond Hotel	$120–$310

Fielding's Budget Hotels in Sint Maarten/St. Martin

★	Beach House	$53–$100
★★	La Residence	$75–$98
★★	Royale Louisiana	$49–$129
★★	Hotel le Belvedere	$85–$120
★★	Summit Resort Hotel	$55–$150

Dream about it and you've got it in St. Martin, provided you can pay for
Lodging runs from the fabulously chic resort to intimate inns tucked in
beachside coves around the island. There are small, family-run establish
ments where you can make friends with the mom-and-pop owners, or tim
share condos where you will never meet the owner. Even if you aren't in t
Prince Charles tax bracket, you can still find digs worthy of your wallet.
1995, the number of hotels totaled 50, with more than 3500 rooms. The
are also apartment-hotels with cooking facilities, as well as privately staff
villas and homes for rent by the week or month. You could save money bu
ing package deals. Inquire when you are making your reservation wheth
you can pay by credit card.

Hotels and Resorts

Some fabulous resorts have been built during the boom that hit the French St. Mart
in the past decade. **Le Meridien L'Habitation** is now integrated with **Le Domaine**, sportin
a French attitude in service, but fortunately also in quality. **La Samanna** is nearly an in
mate resort inn out of the Riviera; if you don't want twin beds, make sure you specify. I
Belle Creole resembles a Mediterranean fishing village; the most special rooms are th
three-story villas. Mont Vernon, built in 1990, boasts its own duty-free shopping mal
large swimming pool and full sports facilities.

Sint Maarten

Dawn Beach Hotel   **$105–$290**   ★★★ ★

Oyster Pond, ☎ (800) 351-5656, (599) 5-22929, FAX (599) 5-24421.
Single: $105–$290. Double: $105–$290.

This resort is located three miles from Philipsburg in a relatively remote area. Gues
are accommodated in recently renovated cottages (set too close together) on th
hillside or beach, each holding studios with rattan furnishings, living and dinin
areas, full kitchenettes, and private balconies or patios. The pretty pool is accente
by a waterfall. There are also two tennis courts, a restaurant and watersports on th
very nice beach. You'll need a car to get around.

Divi Little Bay Resort   **$110–$350**   ★★ ★

Philipsburg, ☎ (800) 801-5550, (599) 5-22333, FAX (599) 5-23911.
Single: $110–$350. Double: $110–$350.

Located a mile out of Philipsburg and set on a wide, sandy beach, this resort date
back to 1955, making it one of the island's oldest. Accommodations run the gam
from standard guestrooms to casitas to suites with one to three bedrooms. All ar
quite comfortable, air-conditioned, and feature refrigerators and balconies or patio
with nice ocean views. Guests can choose from two restaurants and two bars; othe
facilities include a pool on three levels, three tennis courts, shops and watersports o
the pretty, quiet beach. The adjacent casino is small and friendly. It's abut a 20
minute walk into town. Decent for the price.

Great Bay Beach Hotel   **$164–$285**   ★★ ★

Philipsburg Bay, ☎ (800) 223-0757, (599) 5-22446, FAX (599) 5 23859.
Single: $164–$245. Double: $125–$285.

The Great Bay is one of the island's few all-inclusive resorts. Guest rooms are adequate, but nothing to write home about. The 10 junior suites have very large bathrooms with whirlpool tubs, but are not necessarily worth the bump in price. There are two restaurants and three bars, one with entertainment and shows nightly. The grounds also include two pools, a casino, a tennis court, gym, and all the usual watersports at the pleasant beach.

Holland House Beach Hotel $69–$195 ★★

Philipsburg, FAX (599) 5 22572.
Single: $69–$180. Double: $84–$195.

This hotel is right in the center of Philipsburg on a small palm-dotted beach. Air-conditioned guest rooms have sitting areas, twin beds, TVs, and private balconies, though not all have views. The larger junior suites also have small kitchenettes. Be sure to book a room on the beach side, or you'll suffer from the din of the noisy street. There's a beachfront restaurant and bar, but no other facilities—much within walking distance, however. As many rooms can be had for just under $100 a night, this is a good in-town bet.

Maho Beach Hotel & Casino $140–$460 ★★★

Maho Bay, ☎ (800) 223-0757, (599) 5-52115, FAX (212) 969-9227.
Single: $140–$315. Double: $155–$460.

Set on a rocky bluff above the beach, this bustling resort (the island's largest) is near the airport and can suffer from the roar of jets. Accommodations are quite nice and feature private balconies and large baths, all with bidets and some with whirlpool tubs. There are also 57 efficiency units with small kitchenettes. Facilities include nine restaurants, two cafes, a nightclub and several bars, a large casino, two pools, four tennis courts, a full-service health club, and all the usual watersports. This spot appeals to conventioneers and those who like busy resorts with all the accompanying activity.

Mullet Bay Resort $270–$765 ★★★

Mullet Bay, ☎ (800) 468-5538, (599) 5-52801, FAX (599) 5-54281.
Single: $270–$515. Double: $270–$765.

Located seven miles from Philipsburg on 172 beachfront acres, this mega-resort is situated around the island's only 18-hole golf course. Accommodations include 300 guest rooms and 300 suites with kitchens. All are spacious and comfortable with refrigerators, modern conveniences, and views of the ocean, lake, or golf course. Guests can choose from six restaurants, eight bars, a casino, and a host of recreational options: 14 tennis courts, two pools, aerobics classes in the fitness center, all watersports, and lots of organized programs. There's also an arcade with more than a dozen tony boutiques, so bring lots of cash. The grounds are nicely landscaped and include a boardwalk and nature path for scenic strolls. Very nice for resort lovers, but lots of conventioneers can make things crowded. Those who like large and thriving resorts will not be disappointed.

Oyster Pond Hotel $120–$310 ★★★★

Oyster Pond, ☎ (599) 5-22206, FAX (599) 5-25695.
Single: $120–$310. Double: $120–$310.

This intimate hideaway is located in a secluded cove and surrounded on three sides by water. Accommodations are beautifully done in white wicker and pastel fabrics; each room is individually decorated and has ceiling fans, air conditioners, and sea-view patios. The 20 suites are especially luxurious. The French restaurant is romantic and highly regarded, and there's also a comfortable lounge for quiet respites. The mile-long beach is quite lovely but not the greatest for swimming; most guests prefer the saltwater pool. All is quite chic at this fine resort.

Point at Burgeaux Bay $70–$395   ★★

Philipsburg, ☎ *(599) 5-54335, FAX (516) 466-2359.*
Single: $70–$395. Double: $70–$395.

This three-story hotel is located in a residential area, 15 minutes from downtown Philipsburg. It fronts the ocean, but the beach is a bit of a walk. Accommodations range from standard rooms to one- and two-bedroom suites with kitchens and terraces. Maids tidy up daily. Facilities are limited to a swimming pool and Jacuzzi.

Port de Plaisance $220–$600   ★★★★

Simpson Bay, ☎ *(800) 732-9480, (599) 5-45222, FAX (599) 5-42315.*
Single: $220–$455. Double: $220–$600.

Set just to the Dutch side of the border, this hotel has a great location for those who want to experience both the French and Dutch sides of the island. The sprawling complex has junior suites and one- and two-bedroom suites with all modern amenities, plus fully equipped kitchens and large terraces with garden or marina views. The grounds include five restaurants (including a spa bar for the health-conscious), a shopping arcade, a spa and tennis center and a picturesque marina. It also boasts the nicest casino on the island, a truly elegant room with a gorgeous painted ceiling, upscale chandeliers and a very professional staff.

Summit Resort Hotel $55–$150   ★★

Simpson Bay Lagoon, ☎ *(599) 5-52150, FAX (599) 5 52150.*
Single: $55–$135. Double: $65–$150.

Perched on a bluff and overlooking the lagoon, this complex consists of gingerbread-trimmed cottages clustered very closely (too closely) together. Accommodations are either studios or duplexes, all air-conditioned and boasting sitting areas and verandas. Some also have kitchens. There's a restaurant and bar on the premises, and the large saltwater pool is very nice. They'll shuttle you to the beach and Philipsburg, but you'll probably want a car so you can travel on your own schedule.

St. Martin

Coralita Beach Hotel $115–$140   ★★

Marigot, ☎ *(590) 87-31-81.*
Single: $115. Double: $140.

This small hotel is family run. As the name implies, it's located right on the beach, about four miles from the center of town. Rooms are pleasant and air-conditioned, but could use a little work; some boast kitchenettes. Facilities include a bar, restaurant, pool and a tennis court. They'll arrange horseback riding, watersports and even yoga classes.

Esmeralda Resort **$180–$300**

Baie Orientale, ☎ (800) 622-7836, (590) 87-36-36, FAX (590) 8-73518.
Single: $180–$300. Double: $180–$300.
Situated on secluded grounds overlooking the bay, this property consists of 15 villas that can be rented in their entirety or partially as standard guest rooms. All are nicely decorated and have all the modern conveniences; some units have kitchenettes as well. Each villa has its own pool, but you may be sharing it, depending on how much of the villa you rent. There are two restaurants, a bar, a large communal pool and three tennis courts. Watersports await on the mile-long beach, one of the island's best.

Golden Tulip St., Martin **$95–$140**

Cul de Sac Bay, ☎ (800) 344-1212, (590) 87-49-19, FAX (590) 8-74923.
Single: $95–$140. Double: $95–$140.
The on-site beach is not the greatest, but guests can easily make their way to the better sands at Orient Beach. The luxurious Golden Tulip has spacious villa-style guestrooms with all the modern amenities and nice ocean views off the terrace. Facilities include five pools, a bar and restaurant, daily shopping trips to Marigot and Philipsburg and watersports. Nice digs for the price.

Hotel Anse Margot **$138–$261**

Baie Nettle, ☎ (800) 742-4276, (590) 87-92-01, FAX (590) 8-79213.
Single: $138–$247. Double: $169–$261.
Located a mile out of Marigot and fronting the lagoon, this hotel is a popular spot. Nine three-story buildings with pretty gingerbread trim house the guestrooms and suites, all quite pleasant with air conditioners, refrigerators, and private balconies. The restaurant is a beautiful spot for a romantic meal, and there's also a bar, two pools, and watersports on the beach. The clientele is predominantly European.

Hotel Mont Vernon **$105–$160**

Baie Orientale, ☎ (800) 223-0888, (590) 87-62-00, FAX (590) 8-73727.
Single: $105–$125. Double: $135–$160.
Situated on a mile-long beach, all accommodations here are in suites, all rather large, comfortable and pleasant. The free-form pool is the island's largest, and there are also two tennis courts and a fitness room for energetic types. The beach has all watersports and many topless bathers. Supervised programs keep little tykes busy during holidays and high season, and a free shuttle makes getting into Marigot and Philipsburg easy. Lots of conventioneers at this bustling resort.

L'Esplanade Caraibes Hotel **$100–$290**

☎ (590) 87-06-5, FAX (590) 8-72915.
Single: $100–$250. Double: $130–$290.
This new hotel is set high on a hill overlooking Grande Case and the sea; both are an easy, five-minute walk. Accommodations are in suites with fully equipped kitchens, color TV, direct-dial phones, central air conditioning and ceiling fans, and furnished balconies. One-bedroom and loft suites have a king bed and a sleeper sofa in the living room; lofts have an additional half-bathroom downstairs. The rooms are pleasant, but don't quite live up to the splendor of the hotel's pretty facade. Facili-

ties are limited to a small pool and a bar that's open only in the high season. It offers sandwiches at lunch, but that's it in terms of food service, so you'll definitely want to stock the kitchen (breakfast is a 15-minute walk.) Friendly service and a sophisticated French ambience make this property a winner—but they really could use a restaurant.

La Belle Creole $205–$455   ★★★★★

Marigot, ☎ (590) 87-66-00, FAX (590) 8-75666.
Single: $205–$455. Double: $205–$455.

Designed to resemble a Mediterranean village, this resort encompasses 25 acres and has two beaches. Guest rooms are found in villas linked by picturesque pathways. All are very spacious and luxuriously appointed. The 18 suites, which run from $900 to $1320 per night, are as posh as can be (at that rate, they'd better be!). The grounds include a lovely plaza, four tennis courts, a croquet lawn, pool, complete watersports including a dive center, and exercise classes in the fitness center. Dining choices range from casual to elegant and there's frequent entertainment in one of the three bars. The beaches are not the greatest, but no one seems to mind at this lovely enclave.

La Residence $75–$98   ★★

Marigot, ☎ (800) 365-8484, (590) 87-70-37, FAX (590) 8-79044.
Single: $75–$80. Double: $92–$98.

This small hotel is in the heart of Marigot, one mile from the beach. Rooms are air-conditioned, modern and comfortable, and a few accommodations offer kitchens. The French restaurant is quite good, and there's also a bar for unwinding. Popular with business travelers, as there is much within an easy walk.

La Samanna Hotel $28–$995   ★★★★★

Baie Longue, ☎ (590) 87-64-00, FAX (590) 8-78786.
Single: $28–$825. Double: $280–$995.

This tony spot is set on 55 beachfront acres and is designed to resemble a Moorish Mediterranean village. Accommodations are in the main building and in villas scattered about the beach. All are on the small side but very elegant and spotless. Large patios, minibars, refrigerators, and air conditioning are standard throughout; massive renovations a few years ago did the job splendidly. The resort's well-heeled guests can play tennis on three courts, partake in all watersports, and splash about in the nice pool. The food is grand, and la Samanna gets high marks for seclusion and sophistication. Attentive service and extra touches like daily fresh flowers make this one of the Caribbean's finest resorts—and one blessedly free of pretension.

Laguna Beach Hotel $70–$185   ★★★

Baie Nettle, ☎ (800) 333-1970, (590) 87-91-75, FAX (590) 8-78165.
Single: $70–$180. Double: $80–$185.

This Victorian-style hotel overlooks the lagoon and its beach. Guests are housed in standard rooms to studios with two baths and kitchenettes. All are air-conditioned and have modern comforts like cable TV and hair dryers. The grounds include a large pool, restaurant and bar, and three tennis courts. Watersports can be rented on the public beach. Decent for the rates.

Le Flamboyant **$115–$364**

Baie Nettle, ☎ *(800) 221-5333, (590) 87-60-00, FAX (590) 8-79957.*
Single: $115–$364. Double: $115–$364.

This large beach hotel houses guests in tropically decorated standard rooms; the more expensive one- and two-bedroom suites have kitchenettes. Many resort amenities at this busy spot, including two pools, a tennis court, and watersports. Many on the beach go topless. Two restaurants offer a choice of elegant or casual dining.

Le Meridien l'Habitation **$175–$655**

l'Anse Macel, ☎ *(800) 543-4300, (590) 87-33-33, FAX (590) 8-73038.*
Single: $175–$655. Double: $175–$655.

Situated on 170 acres, this sprawling resort consists of the 251-room l'Habitation and the 145-room Le Domaine. All the guest rooms are nicely decorated and comfortable, though those in Le Domaine are larger, have oversized tubs, and are the better choice. Many rooms have kitchenettes; be sure to ask if this is important to you. The extensive grounds cater to resort lovers, with four restaurants, three bars, two lovely pools, six tennis courts, racquetball and squash courts, a marina and full watersports at the gorgeous beach. Most activities are included in the rates. Guests can also use the adjacent Le Privilege Fitness Center and Spa, a luxurious spot to work up a sweat or get a massage. Nice, but a bit isolated.

Privilege Resort & Spa **$196–$580**

Anse Marcel, ☎ *(800) 874-8541, (590) 87-38-38, FAX (590) 8-74412.*
Single: $196–$580. Double: $196–$580.

Located on St. Martin's northern shore, this deluxe choice has Creole architecture outside and luxurious rooms and suites within, with central air, minibars, TVs and VCRs and quality tropical furnishings. The spiffy spa offers hydrotherapy baths and every possible pampering service. Other facilities include six tennis courts, four squash courts, two racquetball courts, aerobics classes, a high-tech exercise room, two restaurants, two bars and a disco. There's also a marina and heliport that offer excursions to neighboring islands. Nice.

Royale Louisiana **$49–$129** ★★

Marigot, ☎ *(590) 87-86-51, FAX (590) 8-74412.*
Single: $49–$129. Double: $67–$129.

Located in downtown Marigot above several shops, this hotel is a great bargain—if you don't mind the fact that a decent beach is a good 20-minute walk away. (There's a small one closer, but it's nothing to brag about.) Air-conditioned guest rooms are simple but comfortable, with telephones and VCRs. Facilities are limited to a restaurant and bar, but there's much within walking distance. Since the beach is not terribly convenient, it's unfortunate that this hotel does not have a pool.

St. Tropez **$120–$215**

Orient Bay Beach, ☎ *(800) 622-7838, FAX (203) 849-1892.*
Single: $120–$215. Double: $120–$215.

This new hotel offers accommodations in modern junior suites, all with air conditioning, king-size beds, sitting areas, terraces, TV, phone and refrigerator. Facilities include a pool ad watersports.

Apartments and Condominiums

You can actually spend as much money on a fabulous villa as you would at a chic resort. Or you can find more modest digs and cook your own meals in a fully equipped kitchenette. The self-catering options in St. Martin are that vast. If you don't have a car, it will be important to be near the beach so you don't have to hire a taxi; the best on the shore are Dawn Beach Hotel, Belair Beach Hotel, Laguna Beach Hotel and the Pavilion Beach Hotel. Contact villa rental companies such as **Carimo** ☎ *(590) 87-57-58*, **Immobilier St. Martin Caraibes** ☎ *(590) 87-55-21*, and **West Indies Immobilier** ☎ *(590) 87-56-48*.

Sint Marteen

Beach House   **$53–$100**   ★

Philipsburg, ☎ *(590) 87-57-58.*
Single: $53–$90. Double: $63–$100, FAX (599) 5-30308.

Located on Great Bay, a 10-minute walk from downtown Philipsburg, this guesthouse provides air-conditioned efficiencies with maid service. All have terraces and simple furnishings, as the rates suggest. You can cook in or saunter over to one of the many restaurants in the area.

Beachside Villas   **$160–$405**   ★★★

Simpson Bay, ☎ *(590) 87-55-21.*
Single: $160–$405. Double: $160–$405.

These Mediterranean-style villas are set on the beach and are quite elegant. All are individually owned but identically decorated, with two bedrooms, fully equipped kitchens, combination baths, living and dining areas, VCRs, and decks. Maids tidy up daily. Facilities are limited to a small pool, but there are many restaurants and shops in the area. The only downside is the proximity to the airport, which means loud roars when jets take off and land.

Belair Beach Hotel   **$165–$375**   ★★★

Little Bay Beach, ☎ *(800) 933-3264, (599) 5-23362, FAX (599) 5-25295.*
Single: $165–$300. Double: $190–$375.

This all-suite hotel is situated on the beach, next to the Divi Little Bay. The condos at this Mediterranean-style hotel are individually owned and rented out when the owners are elsewhere. Each unit has two bedrooms, two baths, full but small kitchens, living and dining rooms, VCRs, and private patios or balconies, and can sleep up to six. Facilities include a bar and restaurant and a tennis court—no pool, but the beach is right there, where watersports equipment can be rented. Request a unit on an upper floor for more privacy. Good for families.

Captain Oliver's Hotel   **$100–$200**   ★★★

Oyster Pond, ☎ *(590) 87-40-26.*
Single: $100–$165. Double: $110–$200.

Located on the French/Dutch border and fronting the lagoon, this charming complex gets high marks for its peaceful grounds and reasonable rates. Guests are housed in attached pink bungalows that hold junior suites with kitchenettes, rattan furnishings, air conditioners, and private balconies. The well-landscaped grounds feature two restaurants, a bar, a 100-slip marina, a dive center, and a pool. Watersports can be found at Dawn Beach, reached via water taxi.

upecoy Beach Club $100–$650 ★★★

Cupecoy Lowlands, ☎ (215) 885-9008, FAX (215) 572-7731.
Single: $100–$225. Double: $105–$650.
Situated on white sandstone cliffs that overlook Cupecoy Beach (whose size varies, depending on the tides), this Mediterranean-style complex offers suites with one to three bedrooms. All have full kitchens, nice decor and spacious terraces. There's a pool and bar on the premises, and they'll help arrange other activities and watersports. A restaurant and casino await across the street. They have no local phone; the number shown is in Pennsylvania.

lorizon View Beach Hotel $90–$300 ★★

Frontstreet, ☎ (599) 5-32120, FAX (599) 5-32123.
Single: $90–$300. Double: $90–$300.
If you want to be in the heart of Philipsburg—not, incidentally, one of the island's most desirable locations—this hotel will fit your needs. Each unit is air conditioned and offers cable TV, direct-dial phones and fully equipped kitchenettes. Only half have oceanfront balconies, however. Accommodations range from studios to one- and two-bedroom suites. There's a restaurant on site, and much shopping and nightlife right out the front door. The beach is small and not especially picturesque.

lorny Toad Guesthouse $103–$185 ★★★

Simpson Bay, ☎ (599) 5-53316, FAX (599) 5-53316.
Single: $103–$185. Double: $103–$185.
This former governor's residence combines guesthouse ambience with apartment living. It is located on a lovely beach that sometimes suffers from jet noise at the nearby airport. Each one-bedroom apartment is individually decorated and quite charming, with fully equipped kitchens, fresh flowers and maid service. The friendly owners, Earle and Betty Vaughn, treat renters like personal guests, providing a gracious touch lacking in the fancier resorts. There are no facilities on-site, but there's plenty to do within walking distance. No kids under seven.

Pelican Resort & Casino $125–$585 ★★★

Simson Bay, ☎ (800) 626-9637, (599) 5-42503, FAX (599) 5-42133.
Single: $125–$345. Double: $125–$585.
This full-service resort combines the best of both worlds: condo living with full resort amenities. The air-conditioned accommodations range from studios to three-bedroom suites, all colorfully done in tropical decor and with fully equipped kitchens with dishwashers and microwaves. Facilities include three restaurants, a large casino, a full-service health spa, six pools—two with swim-up bars—six tennis courts, and a marina. Extensive watersports include cruises aboard the property's catamaran. There's even a doctor's office! With all that going on, this resort isn't for everyone—it's not exactly an idyllic escape, more like a teeming mini-city, and to get to the beach you'll have to brave steep hillsides. Especially suited to families with its two kiddie pools, playground and poolside barbecue areas.

Point Pirouette Villas $161–$845 ★★★★

Simpson Bay Lagoon, ☎ (599) 5-44207, FAX (599) 5-42338.
Single: $161–$700. Double: $161–$845.

This villa complex is situated on a private peninsula in the lowlands area. The Med*
iterranean-style villas have one or two bedrooms. All are air conditioned and hav*
living and dining rooms, VCRs, stereos, full kitchens, and small private pools, an*
all are quite posh. Facilities include a tennis court and gym; restaurants, shops, an*
casinos are within walking distance.

Royal Islander Club   **$180–$320**   ★★★ ★
Philipsburg, ☎ (599) 5-52388, FAX (599) 5-52585.
Single: $180–$250. Double: $180–$320.
This time-share property shares the beach and facilities with its sister property, th*
Maho Beach Hotel & Casino. Guests, therefore, have the convenience of condo liv*
ing combined with the bells and whistles of a full resort. Accommodations rang*
from studios to one- and two-bedroom suites, all very tastefully done with kitchen*
and all the modern comforts. There's an Olympic-size pool on the grounds, an*
guests can take advantage of the restaurants, bars, tennis courts and other extensiv*
facilities next door. Nice.

Town House Villas   **$130–$305**   ★★
Philipsburg, ☎ (599) 5-22898, FAX (599) 5-22418.
Single: $130–$305. Double: $130–$305.
Located on the outskirts of Philipsburg and right on the beach, this complex con-
sists of 11 duplex villas. Each has two bedrooms, 1.5 baths, living and dining rooms
and full kitchens. Patios are set along a nice courtyard. Maids keep things tidy. N*
facilities on the premises, but lots of shops and restaurants are a short stroll away*
Reasonable rates make this a popular choice.

Tradewinds Beach Inn   **$61–$155**   ★
Simpson Bay, ☎ (599) 5-54206.
Single: $61–$115. Double: $61–$155.
This small inn is located on the beach at Simpson Bay. Guests can choose from stu-
dios and one- and two-bedroom apartments, all air-conditioned and with kitchen-
ettes and maid service. Facilities are limited to a pool.

St. Martin

Club Orient Resort   **$120–$320**   ★★
Baie Orientale, ☎ (800) 828-9356, (590) 87-33-85.
Single: $120–$275. Double: $140–$320.
This resort has a "clothes-optional" policy which means that most (if not all) guests*
are nudists. Located on a peninsula on the Atlantic side of the island, guests are*
housed in rustic wooden chalets that have living rooms, full kitchens and large*
porches. No air conditioners, but ceiling fans generally do the job. Facilities include
a casual beachside restaurant, a bar and two tennis courts. No pool, but you're right
on the beach. You'll need a car for mobility.

Grand Case Beach Club   **$95–$425**   ★★★
Grand Case, ☎ (800) 447-7462, (590) 87-51-87, FAX (590) 8-75993.
Single: $95–$260. Double: $95–$425.
Located on a crescent beach, this apartment complex consists of six white stucco
buildings that offer nice ocean views. Accommodations include studios and one-

and two-bedroom suites, all air conditioned and with rattan furnishings, fully equipped kitchens, satellite TV, wet bars and nice balconies. Facilities include a restaurant, bar, tennis court and complete watersports. No pool, but the beach is fine for swimming. This quiet spot is a great value and very popular, so book early.

Green Cay Village   **$1800–$3900**   ★★★★

Orient Bay Beach, ☎ (590) 87-38-63, FAX (590) 8-73927.
Double: $1800–$3900.
Perched atop Orient Bay, each villa at this Creole-inspired complex has its own small swimming pool. The villas are quite spacious and include a large living room with an entertainment center (VCR, cable TV, CD player), a full and modern kitchen, two dining areas, food for your first evening and a barbecue grill. Facilities include concierge services and a tennis court. Prices quoted are for a one-bedroom villa for seven nights; two- and three-bedroom villas run from $2300 to $3900 per week. Rates include airport transfers and daily maid service.

Hotel le Belvedere   **$85–$120**   ★★

Cul de Sac, ☎ (800) 221-5333, (590) 87-37-89, FAX (590) 8-73052.
Single: $85–$120. Double: $85–$120.
Located on the northeast coast, all accommodations at this property are suites that are on the small side but offer kitchenettes and all the creature comforts. There's a large free-form pool and a bar and restaurant on the premises, and guests are transported free of charge to Pinel island where watersports await. You'll want a car, as this place is fairly remote, but the rates are very reasonable for what you get.

Le Pirate Beach Hotel   **$110–$180**   ★★

Marigot Bay, ☎ (800) 666-5756, (590) 87-78-37, FAX (590) 8-79567.
Single: $110–$180. Double: $110–$180.
Set on the beach just outside of Marigot, this condominium hotel houses guests in air-conditioned studios with kitchenettes and terraces; each can sleep up to four. There's a bar and restaurant on the premises, as well as watersports and an activities desk for booking sightseeing excursions. Several restaurants are within walking distance, so renting a car is not as important as at some of the more remote resorts.

Marine Hotel Simpson Beach   **$101–$230**   ★★

Baie Nettle, ☎ (800) 221-4542, (590) 87-68-68, FAX (590) 8-72151.
Single: $101–$230. Double: $111–$230.
This property combines self-catering units with resort amenities. Accommodations are found in five-story Creole-style buildings, each decorated with rattan furniture and sporting kitchenettes on the balcony. There are also 45 duplex units with two bedrooms and two baths. The premises include a restaurant, bar, pool, tennis court and watersports. Not bad for the rates.

Nettle Bay Beach Club   **$100–$450**   ★★★

Baie Nettle, ☎ (800) 999-3543, (590) 87-95-24, FAX (590) 8-72151.
Single: $100–$450. Double: $140–$450.
Accommodations here range from villas to garden suites, all with full kitchens. Villas are large and bright though rather sparsely furnished, and come in one- and two-bedroom configurations. The garden suites are one-bedroom units with smaller

kitchen areas. All are air-conditioned and have private terraces or patios. The grounds include three tennis courts, five pools and a restaurant.

Pavillion Beach Hotel   **$95–$255**   ★★★

Marigot, ☎ *(590) 87-96-46, FAX (590) 8-77104.*
Single: $95–$255. Double: $125–$255.

This small hotel is set right on the beach, with a sea view from each of its 16 rooms. Accommodations are either studios or suites, all large and inviting and boasting kitchenettes. Request an upper floor for more privacy. There are no on-site facilities, but the central location puts much within walking distance.

Inns

Inns range in quality and cost. The smallest have now merged into a group called **Inns of Sint Maarten/St. Martin**; ask the Tourist office for more information. At Horny Toad, you may have to wave off landing planes at the nearby airstrip, but the beach is lovely and the management is family-friendly.

Sint Maarten

Mary's Boon   **$80–$155**   ★★★

Juliana Beach, ☎ *(599) 5-54235, FAX (599) 5-53403.*
Single: $80–$155. Double: $80–$155.

Located next to the airport, 15 minutes from Philipsburg, this is an authentic West Indian inn—not someone's idea of one. The beach is quite nice, but can disappear during high tide. Accommodations are in large studios with kitchenettes, patios, and ceiling fans in lieu of air conditioners. Public spaces are nicely accented with island art, tropical prints, and antiques. There's a restaurant and bar, but no other facilities. As with all the properties in this area, occasional airport noise is intrusive.

Pasanggrahan Royal   **$73–$153**   ★★

Great Bay, ☎ *(599) 5-23588, FAX (599) 5 22855.*
Single: $73–$153. Double: $73–$153.

This inn, housed in a 19th-century governor's house and the former residence of Queen Wilhelmina, sits on a small strand of Great Bay Beach. The smallish Guest rooms are decorated in wicker and have balconies or patios; not all are air-conditioned and some are fairly run down. The studios are a better bet with their superior furnishings and kitchenettes. Guests forego modern amenities like phones and TV but are rewarded with a good dose of historical charm, especially noteworthy on this modern and developed island. The bar and restaurant are popular with locals, and afternoon tea is a treat. Lots within walking distance.

St. Martin

Hevea   **$75–$125**   ★★★

163, Boulevard Grande Case, ☎ *(590) 87-56-85, FAX (590) 8-78388.*

Located just across the street from the beach, this inn is housed in a restored Creole mansion. It has two guestrooms, three studios and three suites. Five units are air conditioned; the other three make do with ceiling fans. All are quite pleasant, and the French restaurant of the same name is highly regarded.

Low Cost Lodging

The way to save money in St. Martin is to stuff as many people as you can in an apartment or villa, go in off season, or cook your own food. Even small hotels can have big rates, so don't be misled by the size of the building. Cheap rooms usually mean noise, few furnishings and no tub. If you're savvy, you might be able to bargain down some prices.

Where to Eat

Fielding's Highest Rated Restaurants in Sint Maarten/St. Martin

★★★★	Bye Bar Brazil	$8–$19
★★★★	L'Auberge Gourmande	$15–$31
★★★★	Le Perroquet	$18–$26
★★★★	Saratoga	$16–$26
★★★	Antoine's	$15–$36
★★★	Captain Oliver Restaurant	$16–$24
★★★	Hevea	$22–$38
★★★	Hevea	$30–$50
★★★	La Nadaillac	$16–$32
★★★	Le Bec Fin	$16–$31

Fielding's Special Restaurants in Sint Maarten/St. Martin

★★★★	Bye Bar Brazil	$8–$19
★★★★	Le Perroquet	$18–$26
★★★	Antoine's	$15–$36
★★★	La Nadaillac	$16–$32
★★★	The Wajang Doll	$21–$30

Fielding's Budget Restaurants in Sint Maarten/St. Martin

★★★	Mark's Place	$3–$13
★★★	The Grill & Ribs Co.	$5–$11
★★★	Drew's Deli	$3–$15
★★★	Cheri's Cafe	$6–$17
★★★	David's	$6–$17

With its strong French influence, St. Martin almost has a legal obligation to
serve world-class cuisine, and it doesn't disappoint. Out of 50 restaurants in
Marigot, and another 20 in Grand Case and two dozen scattered throughout the island, many have top gourmet French kitchens; there are also fine
Italian, Swiss, Vietnamese and Chinese eateries. Don't miss the **lolos**, family-
run food stalls along Boulevard Grande Case. American junk food is always
within reach. Seafood is omnipresent, and French wines are in abundance.
At some restaurants, you can dine to the tune of jazz, reggae and pop, and
bars stay busy until midnight. In Philipsburg, the best French restaurant is
surely **Le Bec Fin**, where the Dutch royal family dines. In Philipsburg, good
burgers and conch chowder for prices that won't break can be found at **The
Greenhouse**, and cheap Chinese restaurants can be found on Back Street. Reserve for most elegant dining, especially during high season. Prices for a
three-course meal for two, without wine, can run from $60–$120 and up-
wards. Service charges are often added inconspicuously in the wrong place
on credit card charges, so always peruse your slip carefully before signing or
adding more tip. The legal age for drinking and gambling is 18.

Sint Maarten

Antoine's   **$$$**   ★★★

55 Front Street, Philipsburg, ☎ (599)5-22964.
French cuisine. Specialties: Fresh local crayfish.
Dinner: 4-10 p.m., entrees $15–$36.
A gorgeous setting on a breezy patio above Great Bay makes this restaurant a
romantic choice for a celebration dinner. Cuisine is classic French with Italian
touches. Some specialties offered bring back memories of an uncomplicated past; to
wit, duck with cherries, lobster thermidor and chocolate mousse. When in season,
fresh local crayfish makes a welcome appearance.

Cheri's Cafe   **$$**   ★★★

Cinnamon Grove Center, Maho Beach, ☎ (599) 55-3361.
American cuisine. Specialties: Steaks, seafood.
Lunch: 11 a.m.-4:30 p.m., entrees $6–$12.
Dinner: 4:30-1:30 p.m., entrees $12–$17.
Cheri Batson, owner of the legendary cafe and bar that bears her name, must share
the honors for the success of her hugely popular eating establishment with her steak
purveyor—customers are always raving about the quality and quantity of the grilled
beef. A huge sirloin steak fills out a plate for a modest $10.95. A lot of customers
think the place is just plain fun—nobody sits down for long when the house band,
Ramon, starts to play. Great burgers are also on the menu, along with the inevitable
grilled seafood.

Chesterfield's   **$$**   ★★★

Great Bay Marina, Pointe Blanche, ☎ (559) 5-23484.
American cuisine.
Lunch: 11:30 a.m.-2:30 p.m., entrees $7–$12.
Dinner: 5:30-10 p.m., entrees $7–$20.

Rub epaulets with the boating crowd at this pierside restaurant with a casual, congenial ambience. The food is well-prepared, with a host of seafood, duckling and beef dishes served with flair at lunch and dinner. A companionable group often gathers for happy hour on a daily basis.

Greenhouse   **$$$**   ★ ★

Bobby's Marina, Philipsburg, ☎ (599) 5-22941.
American cuisine.
Lunch: 11 a.m.-5 p.m., entrees $6–$10.
Dinner: 5-10 p.m., entrees $11–$25.

An all-purpose eatery that serves American favorites and exotic Indonesian specialties, the Greenhouse has a harbor location and a dining room lush with plant life. Guests can play pool, throw darts and dance as well as dine. It jumps daily at happy hour, which actually lasts a little longer; good for twofers and gratis hors d'oeuvres.

L'Escargot   **$$$**   ★ ★ ★

76 Front Street, Philipsburg, ☎ (599) 5-22483.
French cuisine.
Lunch: 11 a.m.-3 p.m., entrees $8–$23.
Dinner: 6:30-11 p.m., entrees $18–$29.

Snail fanciers will enjoy a meal at this venerable grande dame of a restaurant, which has been in the same spot for over 20 years. The delectable delicacy is a specialty and it shows up stuffed in mushrooms and in various other ways. The rest of the menu is largely French, encompassing duck, seafood and meat dishes.

Le Bec Fin   **$$$**   ★ ★ ★

119 Front Street, Philipsburg, ☎ (599) 5-22976.
French cuisine.
Dinner: 6-10 p.m., entrees $16–$31.

Ascend a flight of stairs to this second-floor dining salon in the courtyard of the St. Maarten Museum. At night, the ambience is candlelit and intimate, during the day try to snag a table overlooking the sea; there are only a few of them available. The kitchen really shines with its seafood preparations, especially lobster, served grilled or flamed in brandy.

Le Perroquet   **$$$**   ★ ★ ★ ★

72 Airport Road, Simpson Bay, ☎ (599) 5-41339.
French cuisine.
Dinner: 6-10 p.m., entrees $18–$26.

This restaurant, situated in a typical West Indian house near the airport, serves very atypical meals. Once seated, servers wheel a cart to your table with a choice of nightly specials—which often include filets of ostrich or boar steaks. Surprisingly, ostrich tastes more like beef, rather than the expected chicken. For less adventurous palates, fresh red snapper or beef dishes are usually available. Simpson Bay Lagoon can be viewed from the plant-filled porch.

Saratoga   **$$$**   ★ ★ ★ ★

Simpson Bay Yacht Club, Simpson Bay, ☎ (599) 5-42421.
Seafood cuisine.
Dinner: 6:30-10 p.m., entrees $16–$26.

A perennial favorite, this yacht club restaurant in a mahogany-panelled dining room features a changing menu of very fresh seafood offerings. Although pricey, its faithful following returns for specialties like scallops seviche or salmon in puff pastry with spinach and mushrooms. Leafy salads feature at least two kinds of greens, served with two homemade dressings. Steaks and beef dishes are also available.

he Grill & Ribs Co. $ ★★★

Old Street Shopping Cntr., Philipsburg,
American cuisine.
Lunch: 11 a.m.-4 p.m., entrees $5–$11.
Dinner: 4-10 p.m., entrees $5–$11.

This informal place is the island's best-known and best-loved ribarama. For a reasonable price of $12.95, diners can chow down on an unlimited amount of pork or beef ribs. The Grill & Ribs Co. has two locations to choose from: a second story alfresco terrace eatery at the Old St. Shopping Center, or the rib place behind Pizza Hut on Simpson Bay Beach. Other offerings include chicken fajitas, burgers, chicken and sandwiches heaped with a side of fries.

he Seafood Galley $$ ★★★

Bobby's Marina, Philipsburg,
Seafood cuisine.
Lunch: 11 a.m.-3 p.m., entrees $7–$18.
Dinner: 6-10 p.m., entrees $7–$18.

Although this pier-side establishment has a clubby restaurant offering hot plates of fresh fish and seafood, some people bypass it and head straight for the adjoining raw bar. There they can graze all night from a generous menu of oyster shooters, clams on the half shell, or crab claws. Lunchtime is popular for the view and the hearty sandwiches and egg dishes.

he Wajang Doll $$$ ★★★

134 Front Street, Philipsburg,
Asian cuisine. Specialties: Rijstaffel.
Dinner: 6:45-10 p.m., entrees $21–$30.

It helps to come here with a big group and a healthy appetite for this restaurant's 20-item Javanese feasts. This cuisine, known as *rijstaffel* (rice table), originated in the former Dutch colony of Indonesia. Seemingly endless plates of savory and spicy seafood, meats and chicken are devoured over a mountain of fragrant rice. They can be embellished with "try them if you dare" hot pepper sambals. Couples and singles won't feel left out, as smaller and cheaper versions are available as well as a la carte dishes.

St. Martin

3ye Bar Brazil $$ ★★★★

47 Boulevard Grande Case, Grand Case, ☎ *(590) 87-76-49.*
Latin American cuisine.
Dinner: 7–3 a.m., entrees $8–$19.

Locals love to hang out here and talk literature and politics with Michel, the opinionated (but gracious) owner of this laid-back spot in the heart of Grande Case. Michel is famous for his *caipirinha*—a wonderful concoction of rum, sugar and lime—as well as his selection of 38 whiskeys, including 16 single malts from Scotland. You can try three shots for $10. The Brazilian and French food is great, too, and the entire wine list is available by the bottle and by the glass, something we'd like to see more restaurants offer. Save room for the *manjar*, a coconut dessert, then try the *batita de coco*, a drink of coconut milk and rum that's an excellent digestive. This place is not to be missed!

Captain Oliver Restaurant $$$ ★★★

Oyster Pond, Marigot, ☎ *(590) 87-30-00.*
Seafood cuisine.
Lunch: Noon–3 p.m., entrees $16–$24.
Dinner: 7–11 p.m., entrees $16–$24.

A popular outdoor restaurant/snackbar/store on a pier facing the sea, Captain Oliver's sits across from its namesake resort. A thoroughly democratic place, the good Captain has provided a choice of eateries to fit every budget. There's a snack shack dispensing le chili dog and other light meals, with a grocery store attached. The centerpiece, though, is the oceanfront restaurant, where creative international cuisine, with an emphasis on seafood, is served for lunch and dinner. Soups are delicious and different, and the fresh tuna, when available, is stellar.

Cha Cha Cha's $$$ ★★★

Boulevard de Grand Case, Grand Case, ☎ *(590) 87-53-63.*
Latin American cuisine.
Dinner: 6–11 p.m., entrees $11–$20.

This colorful cafe draws the au courant set who like to behave a little outre. The menu is a melting pot of piquant Latin and Gallic specialties that usually taste as good as they read. Skillfully grilled or steamed fresh seafood is served with tropical salsas. Some people never make it to the dining room, preferring to graze on a daring tapas menu while sipping a blender drink in a whimsical garden. Come before 7 p.m. to save a little money on a generous prix-fixe, three-course supper for under $20.

Coco Beach Bar $$$ ★★★

Orient Beach, Marigot,
International cuisine.
Lunch: entrees $15–$30.
Dinner: entrees $15–$30.

By day Coco Beach bar is just one of five plain open-air eateries competing for the tourist dollar on clothing-optional Orient Beach. But at night, it becomes a quaint little candlelit restaurant, with tastefully set tables and a diverse menu, which includes caesar salad, filet mignon, and lobster with pasta. Softly lapping ocean waves provide atmospheric background music. Despite an often-full house, service is among the best on the island.

David's $$ ★★★

Rue de la Liberte, Marigot, ☎ *(590) 87-51-58.*
English cuisine.
Lunch: 11:30 a.m.–2:30 p.m., entrees $6–$17.
Dinner: 6–10 p.m., entrees $6–$17.

When it's crowded, David's can be a convivial place, with word games or darts providing the entertainment while waiting for light pub fare or full dinners. An interesting menu of hearty soups, meat and pasta dishes are all reasonably priced, and freshly caught seafood is a standout. The bar stays open until the witching hour and the scene can be boisterous or dull, depending upon who shows up.

ew's Deli $ ★★★
French Cul-de-Sac, Marigot,
American cuisine. Specialties: Cheeseburgers, cheesecake.
Lunch: 11 a.m.–3 p.m., entrees $3–$15.
Dinner: 7–9:30 p.m., entrees $3–$15.
North of Orient Bay lies the little community of French-Cul-de-Sac, where Drew from Wisconsin, a wonderful host, grills up some of the best bacon cheeseburgers around. Cole slaw and New York-style cheesecake with the burger provides a well-balanced vacation diet. The place is a little cramped, but the friendly reception might urge you to sit a spell. Full meals are also offered.

vea $$$ ★★★
163 Boulevard de Grand Case, Grand Case, ☎ (590) 87-56-85.
French cuisine.
Dinner: 6:30–10 p.m., entrees $22–$38.
Set in a restored Creole mansion that is also an intimate inn, this 10-table French eatery is charming and romantic. The size of the dining room ensures the consistently fine quality of the French cuisine served here. The proprietors, who hail from Nice, use only the finest ingredients and believe that simplicity is key. Sauces made with fresh herbs, wine, or wild mushrooms are often used to subtly accentuate, never overpower, lamb, duck breast, or a signature red snapper en papillote. Closed Mondays from April 15-December 14.

Auberge Gourmande $$$ ★★★★
89 Boulevard Grand Case, Grand Case, ☎ (590) 87-73-37.
French cuisine.
Dinner: 6:30–10 p.m., entrees $15–$31.
The setting is a quaint, converted residence sporting jalousied windows. Guests dine by candlelight in a comfortable room, although increased noise on the streets of Grand Case may affect a romantic tete-a-tete. Soups are a specialty and are interestingly prepared, including a brew of mussels with orange. Grilled fish is reliable, although the roast pork and roast lamb were only average on one occasion and the once-impeccable service has slipped of late.

le Flottante $ ★★
Boulevard Grande Case, Grand Case, ☎ (590) 87-89-46.
French cuisine.
This open-air French bakery is just about the only place to get breakfast in Grande Case. They offer up wonderful pastries and delicious cafe au lait, but don't expect service with a smile—unless you're a local. Open daily from 6:00-10:00 a.m.

Maison sur Le Port $$$ ★★★
rue de Republique, Marigot, ☎ (590) 87-56-38.
French cuisine.

Lunch: Noon–2:30 p.m., entrees $11–$14.
Dinner: 6–10 p.m., entrees $17–$34.

Chef Christian Verdeau presents impeccably prepared but rather small portions ᴏ
duck, lobster and other prime meats and seafood on an outdoor patio with a harbᴇ
view. Prices remain stable, though, for the excellent quality of the ingredients, an
a warm welcome is reserved for all comers.

La Nadaillac $$$ ★★

Rue de la Liberte, Marigot, ☎ (590) 87-53-77.
French cuisine.
Lunch: Noon–2:30 p.m., entrees $16–$32.
Dinner: 6:30–9:30 p.m., entrees $16–$32.

This intimate gem, albeit a very dear one (as in prices), is the province of Fernan
Mallard, from the Perigord. Appropriately enough, most specialties involve proc
ucts from that region of France, including preserved goose. The restaurant is on a
attractive patio facing the harbor, nestled among the chic clothing stores in th
Galerie Perigourdine.

Lolos $

Boulevard Grande Case, Grand Case,
Seafood cuisine.

The food stalls that line a section of Grande Case Boulevard are known as *lolᴄ
These mom-and-pop operations offer the freshest seafood and local treats each dᴀ
for amazingly low prices. Most open from noon on, but it's a catch-as-catch-cᴀ
type of business. Well worth checking out.

Mark's Place $ ★★★

French-Cul-de-Sac, Marigot, ☎ (590) 87-34-50.
Latin American cuisine.
Lunch: 12:30–2:30 p.m., entrees $3–$13.
Dinner: 6:30–9:30 p.m., entrees $3–$13.

The West Indian food served here is hearty, plentiful and varied—on a given nigʜ
you could have lobster bisque with a curry of conch or goat, or a crab back appetizᴇ
and swordfish, but sometimes the quality is unexceptional. It's hard to quibble wiʈ
the reasonable prices, but you get what you pay for. And the crowds keep coming–
Mark's Place is usually jammed.

Mini-Club $$$ ★

Rue de la Liberte, Marigot, ☎ (509) 87-50-69.
French cuisine.
Lunch: Noon–3 p.m., prix fixe $32.
Dinner: 7–10:30 p.m., entrees $18–$35.

Locals who like to stuff themselves silly with food as good as mother makes aʀ
grateful for the continuing success of the gargantuan French-creole buffet servᴇ
here on Wednesdays and Saturday nights. The setting is lots of fun too: a junglʏ
tropical terrace suspended over the water. The feast includes all the wine you cᴀ
drink, so bring a friend who can help you down the stairs. On other days sample aʀ
unparalleled lobster souffle and other French specialties. The buffet is $40 per peʀ
son.

rf Club South $ ★★

Boulevard Grande Case, Grand Case,

American cuisine.

New Jersey natives will do a double take as they come upon the Garden State Parkway, Turnpike and other highway signs prominently displayed on Boulevard Grande Case. Jersey expatriots run this funky spot, which boasts of a "New Jersey menu" (lots of burgers and cheese steaks). It's a happening spot, especially on Sunday, when they give out free drinks from 10 a.m.–2 p.m. and live music kicks in at 6 p.m. All the locals come and party, then head over to Jimbo's when the Surf Club closes at 10 p.m.

FIELDING'S CHOICE:

Little known to the outside world is the special purple and bittersweet guavaberry liqueur produced on the island ever since Dutch colonists settled in the 18th century. During the Christmas holidays, it's customary to go from home to home serenading for samples. Every family makes a different brew, which is usually fully consumed by the end of the Christmas season. The Sint Maarten Guavaberry Company now makes the liqueur locally, and offers shade, seating and a few samples at its midtown production area at the Guavaberry Shop on 10 Front St. Try a guavaberry colada (blended with cream of coconut and pineapple juice), or a guavaberry screwdriver (mixed with orange juice). A bottle of guavaberry sells for less than $15 and is considered duty-free because it is an island craft.

Where to Shop

St. Martin's duty-free port carries all the typical products one would expect find at 25–50 percent discounts: china, jewelry, crystal, perfumes and shions. Usually prices are quoted in American dollars and sales clerks speak nglish. Local art shown in galleries and artist's studios make great buys; besdes **Roland Richardson** in Orleans, seek out the work of **Genevieve Curt** ☎ *(590) 87-88-52*, at the **Tropical Gallery**. Other fine names are the painter lexandre Minguet and the Lynn family (husband, wife and two sons). Both ne Dutch and French side have some of the most sophisticated fashion ops in the Caribbean, but be prepared to pay in francs on the French side if ou want a good exchange. (Hours on the French side are iffy, but usually

run Monday-Saturday 9 a.m.–12:30 p.m. and 3–7 p.m.) Some stores adju
their schedules to accommodate cruise ships on Sunday and holidays.

Philipsburg, capital of Dutch St. Maarten, is full of shops and markets.

Philipsburg may seem more crowded and junk-oriented than Marigot, b
you can find highly memorable leather (**Domina**), clothes (**Maurella Senes**
and jewelry (**Caribbean Gems**). Shopping on Grand Case is limited to narro
main street. Best shops in Marigot are at the **Marina Royale**. Don't miss th
lively **early morning market in Marigot** where locals sell their spices, handicraf
and tropical fruits and vegetables. **Port La Royale** is a beehive of activity aft
dawn; hang out here if you want to meet yachties and even local schoon
captains cruising in from other islands with new goods. High-fashion d
signs can be found in the **Galerie Périgourdine** shopping complex, across fron
the post office.

Sint Maarten/St. Martin Directory

ARRIVAL AND DEPARTURE

American Airlines offers flights from New York, Miami, Dallas, R
leigh/Durham and San Juan, Puerto Rico. **Continental** flies out
Newark. **BWIA** flies from Miami. **Air St. Barthélémy** flies daily to an
from St. Barts, as does **WINAIR** (Windward Islands Airways). Inte
island service is provided by **ALM, Air Martinique, LIAT** and **WINAIR**. A
flights arrive at Juliana Airport on the Dutch side of the island as do
Air Guadeloupe, which offers daily flights to and from Guadeloupe
There is a $10 departure tax from Juliana Airport on the Dutch side.

For its daily 10-minute flights to St. Barts, **Air Guadeloupe** and **Air St. Barthélémy** also use Espérance Airport, a small domestic terminal near Grand Case on the French side. There is a 15 French franc (about $3) departure tax from Espérance Airport on the French side. The latter is already calculated into tickets written and sold on St. Martin. If it is not shown on the ticket, then you will be expected to pay in cash at the departure gate—have the francs ready.

BUSINESS HOURS

On the Dutch side, shops open Monday–Saturday 8 a.m.–noon and 2–6 p.m. Banks open Monday–Thursday 8 a.m.–1 and Friday from 8:30 a.m.–1 p.m. and 4–5 p.m. On the French side, shops open Monday–Saturday 9 a.m.–12:30 p.m. and 3–7 p.m. Some shops take a longer or shorter siesta, so call ahead. Banks open weekdays 8:30 a.m.–1:30 p.m.

CLIMATE

Sunshine prevails on the island and it is warm year-round. Temperatures during the winter average 80 degrees F, in the summer, it gets a little warmer. Constant trade winds keep the climate pleasant.

DOCUMENTS

U.S. citizens entering via the Dutch side (Juliana Airport) for stays of up to three months need a valid passport, or one that has expired no longer than five years prior, or a notarized or original birth certificate with raised seal, or a voter's registration card. Canadian citizens must have a valid passport. U.S. residents and Canadians who are not citizens must have a green card or multiple re-entry stamp. Travelers must also show a return or onward ticket.

U.S. citizens and Canadians traveling as tourists and entering via the French side (Espérance Airport) for stays up to three weeks must have proof of citizenship in the form of a valid passport, a passport that has expired no more than five years prior, or other proof of citizenship, in the form of a birth certificate (original or official copy), or a voter's registration card, plus a government-authorized identification with photo. For stays over three weeks, or for nontourist visits, a valid passport is necessary. Resident aliens of the U.S. and Canada, and visitors from countries other than those of the Common Market (E.E.C.) and Japan, must have a valid passport and visa. A return or onward ticket is also required for all visitors.

ELECTRICITY

Current runs 220 AC, 50 cycles. American and Canadian appliances require French plug converters and transformers.

GETTING AROUND

Taxis from Juliana Airport to Marigot run about $8, double that for Grand Case. Between 10 p.m. and midnight, rates rise 25 percent, after midnight 50 percent. The taxi center in Marigot is near the tourist office ☎ *(590) 87-56-54*; in Grand Case ☎ *(590) 87-75-79*. Car rentals can be made at Juliana Airport or delivered free to hotels. Most hav automatic transmission, many are air-conditioned. All foreign driver' licenses are honored. Major credit cards are accepted, and a tank of ga should last a week. Cars cost about $25–$55 per day, depending o make and unlimited mileage is offered. One rental company to try i **Sunset** ☎ *(590) 87-32-93;* book your car well in advance, especially i winter.

Scooters rent for about $18–$23 per day from **Rent 2 Wheels** in Bai Nettlé ☎ *(590) 87-20-59,* or **Moto Caraibes** ☎ *(590) 87-25-9* Given the hilly terrain of St. Martin, mopeds, scooters and motorbike should only be rented by experienced riders.

Buses run from 6 a.m.–midnight, leaving from Grand Case, and can b flagged down anywhere. Buses run to Marigot, Cole Bay, Simson Bay Mullet Bay, etc., as well as Marigot/Philipsburg and French Quarter, Philipsburg. The fare is $1 within the French side and $1.50 if you cros to the Dutch side.

LANGUAGE

French is the official language of St. Martin and Dutch is the officia language of Sint Maarten, but English is spoken everywhere.

MEDICAL EMERGENCIES

There is a hospital in Marigot ☎ *(590) 87-50-07* and another in Phi ipsburg ☎ *31111.* Hotels can contact English-speaking physicians fo you. There are about 18 doctors practicing general medicine, six den tists, and specialists in many varied fields. In addition, French St. Martin has several pharmacies.

MONEY

The official currency on the French side is the French franc and th guilder on the Dutch side, but U.S. dollars are accepted everywhere Prices are often quoted in U.S. dollars. The rate of exchange is subjec to change due to currency fluctuation.

TELEPHONE

The international country code for St. Martin is *590.* To call the Dutc side, dial the code *599-5.* French side numbers have 6 digits, the Dutc side 5. The cheapest way to make calls is with a telephone card on pub lic phones (8 on the square in Marigot and 2 in Grand Case in front o the pier). It's a toll call when phoning from one side of the island to th other.

TIME

St. Martin is one hour ahead of East Standard Time in New York French St. Martin uses the 24-hour system of telling time; hence, 1 p.m. in the afternoon is 13 hours.

PPING AND TAXES

Most hotels include tax and service quoted in room rates, which together add 10–15 percent to the bill. If no service charge is added, feel free to leave 10–15 percent on restaurant bills.

URIST INFORMATION

The St. Martin Tourist Office is located at the Waterfront in Marigot ☎ *(590) 87-57-21*, FAX *(590) 87-56-43*. A good source for history, architecture and art on the island can be found in the beautiful four-color magazines called *Discover St. Martin*, available free at hotels and tourist sites. A slew of other free publications are available, including *What to Do*, *St. Maarten Nights*, *St. Martin's Week* and *Focus*, among others. Some of the larger hotels distribute to guests free of charge a daily *Times* FAX in conjunction with the *New York Times*. In the U.S. ☎ *(212) 989-0000*.

HEN TO GO

Mardi Gras is held on February 28, a frenzied carnival with dancing filling the streets of Marigot and Grand Case. Another carnival, with calypso, "jump ups," floats, steel bands and bright costumes takes place the last two weeks in April and early May, mostly on the Dutch side, but with some French participation. The Marlin Open de St. Martin on May 29–June 3 is an invitational organized by the Sailfish Caraibes Club. June 6 is the African Festival with arts, crafts, music and dance lectures. Bastille Day on July 14 is celebrated with fireworks, parades and sports contests. Schoelcher Day, on July 21, in honor of the French parliamentarian who led the campaign against slavery, is celebrated with boat and bike races. Halloween is a wild affair in Grande Case, when locals go crazy with exotic costumes. Concordia Day, on November 11, starts the season off with parades and ceremonies. New Year's Eve, called Réveillon de la Saint Sylvestre, is celebrated noisily with balloons, late-night dancing and dining at hotels and restaurants.

SINT MAARTEN/ ST. MARTIN HOTELS		RMS	RATES	PHONE	CR. CARDS
Marigot					
★★★★	La Belle Creole	160	$205–$455	(590) 87-66-00	A, CB, MC, V
★★★★	La Samanna Hotel	80	$28–$995	(590) 87-64-00	A, MC, V
★★★★	Green Cay Village	16	$257–$557	(590) 87-38-63	A, MC, V
★★★★	Le Meridien l'Habitation	396	$175–$655	(800) 543-4300	A, CB, MC, V
★★★★	Privilege Resort & Spa	20	$196–$580	(800) 874-8541	
★★★	Esmeralda Resort	54	$180–$300	(800) 622-7836	A, D, MC, V
★★★	Golden Tulip St. Martin	94	$95–$140	(800) 344-1212	A, D, MC, V

SINT MAARTEN/ ST. MARTIN HOTELS	RMS	RATES	PHONE	CR. CARD
★★★ Grand Case Beach Club	71	$95–$425	(800) 447-7462	A, DC, MC, V
★★★ Hevea	8	$75–$125	(590) 87-56-85	
★★★ Hotel Anse Margot	96	$138–$261	(800) 742-4276	A, D, MC, V
★★★ Hotel Mont Vernon	394	$105–$160	(800) 223-0888	A, MC, V
★★★ L'Esplanade Caraibes Hotel	24	$100–$290	(590) 87-06-5	D, MC, V
★★★ Laguna Beach Hotel	62	$70–$185	(800) 333-1970	A, MC, V
★★★ Le Flamboyant	271	$115–$364	(800) 221-5333	A, CB, DC, MC,
★★★ Nettle Bay Beach Club	230	$100–$450	(800) 999-3543	A, MC
★★★ Pavillion Beach Hotel	16	$95–$255	(590) 87-96-46	A, D, MC
★★★ St. Tropez	84	$90–$300	(800) 622-7838	
★★ Club Orient Resort	83	$120–$320	(800) 828-9356	A, CB, D, MC, V
★★ Coralita Beach Hotel	24	$115–$140	(590) 87-31-81	A, CB, MC, V
★★ Hotel le Belvedere	130	$85–$120	(800) 221-5333	A, MC, V
★★ La Residence	21	$75–$98	(800) 365-8484	A, D, MC, V
★★ Le Pirate Beach Hotel	60	$110–$180	(800) 666-5756	A, MC, V
★★ Marine Hotel Simpson Beach	165	$101–$230	(800) 221-4542	A, CB, MC, V
★★ Royale Louisiana	75	$49–$129	(590) 87-86-51	MC, V

Philipsburg

	RMS	RATES	PHONE	CR. CARD
★★★★ Dawn Beach Hotel	155	$105–$290	(800) 351-5656	A, MC, V
★★★★ Oyster Pond Hotel	40	$120–$310	(599) 5-22206	A, CB, DC, MC,
★★★★ Point Pirouette Villas	85	$161–$845	(599) 5-44207	A, MC
★★★★ Sheraton Port Plaisance	88	$225–$600	(800) 732-9480	A, DC, MC, V
★★★ Beachside Villas	14	$160–$405	(590) 87-55-21	A, MC
★★★ Belair Beach Hotel	72	$165–$375	(800) 933-3264	A, MC, V
★★★ Captain Oliver's Hotel	50	$100–$200	(590) 87-40-26	A, MC
★★★ Cupecoy Beach Club	126	$100–$650	(215) 885-9008	None
★★★ Divi Little Bay Resort	147	$110–$350	(800) 801-5550	A, DC, MC, V
★★★ Great Bay Beach Hotel	285	$164–$285	(800) 223-0757	A, MC, V
★★★ Horny Toad Guesthouse	8	$103–$185	(599) 5-53316	None
★★★ Maho Beach Hotel & Casino	600	$140–$460	(800) 223-0757	A, D, MC, V

SINT MAARTEN/ ST. MARTIN HOTELS		RMS	RATES	PHONE	CR. CARDS
★★★	Mary's Boon	12	$80–$155	(599) 5-54235	None
★★★	Mullet Bay Resort	570	$270–$765	(800) 468-5538	A, DC, MC, V
★★★	Pelican Resort & Casino	655	$125–$585	(800) 626-9637	A, CB, MC, V
★★★	Royal Islander Club	135	$180–$320	(599) 5-52388	A, D, DC, MC, V
★★	Holland House Beach Hotel	54	$69–$195	(599) 5-22572	A, D, MC, V
★★	Horizon View Beach Hotel	30	$90–$300	(599) 5-32120	
★★	Pasanggrahan Royal	30	$73–$153	(599) 5-23588	A, MC
★★	Point at Burgeaux Bay	14	$70–$395	(599) 5-54335	None
★★	Summit Resort Hotel	50	$55–$150	(599) 5-52150	A, MC, V
★★	Town House Villas	12	$130–$305	(599) 5-22898	A, MC, V
★	Beach House	10	$53–$100	(590) 87-57-58	A, MC
★	Tradewinds Beach Inn	10	$61–$155	(599) 5-54206	

SINT MAARTEN/ST. MARTIN RESTAURANTS		PHONE	ENTREE	CR. CARDS
Marigot				
American				
★★★	Drew's Deli		$3–$15	A, MC, V
English				
★★★	David's	(590) 87-51-58	$6–$17	
French				
★★★★	L'Auberge Gourmande	(590) 87-73-37	$15–$31••	
★★★	Hevea	(590) 87-56-85	$22–$38••	A, MC, V
★★★	La Maison sur Le Port	(590) 87-56-38	$11–$34	MC, V
★★★	La Nadaillac	(590) 87-53-77	$16–$32	None
★★	Mini-Club	(590) 87-50-69	$32–$35	A, MC, V
International				
★★★	Coco Beach Bar		$15–$30	A, MC, V
Latin American				
★★★	Cha Cha Cha's	(590) 87-53-63	$11–$20••	MC, V
★★★	Mark's Place	(590) 87-34-50	$3–$13	A, MC, V

SINT MAARTEN/ST. MARTIN RESTAURANTS	PHONE	ENTREE	CR. CARDS
Seafood			
★★★ Captain Oliver Restaurant	(590) 87-30-00	$16–$24	A, MC, V

Philipsburg

	PHONE	ENTREE	CR. CARDS
American			
★★★ Cheri's Cafe	(599) 5-53361	$6–$17	None
★★★ Chesterfield's	(599) 5-23484	$7–$20	None
★★★ The Grill & Ribs Co.		$5–$11	None
★★ Greenhouse	(599) 5-22941	$6–$25	A, MC, V
Asian			
★★★ The Wajang Doll		$21–$30••	A, MC, V
French			
★★★★ Le Perroquet	(599) 5-41339	$18–$26••	A, MC, V
★★★ Antoine	(599)5-22964	$16–$32	A, MC, V
★★★ L'Escargot	(599) 5-22483	$8–$29	A, MC, V
★★★ Le Bec Fin	(599) 5-22976	$16–$31••	A, MC, V
Seafood			
★★★★ Saratoga	(599) 5-42421	$16–$26••	A, MC, V
★★★ The Seafood Galley		$7–$18	A, MC, V

Note: • Lunch Only

        •• Dinner Only

Hurricane Update

The pictures glimpsed by CNN fanatics of the awesome destruction on
Sint Maarten/St. Martin were enough to make anyone reconsider a late
summer Caribbean getaway. Hurricane Luis tossed boats onto the island's
shore, sinking many others into the depths of Simpson Bay, while 40-foot
waves rolled violently into coastal resorts, reaching as high as the third-floor
restaurant of the Great Bay Beach Hotel, where 200 guests were sitting out
the storm. Dutch tourism officials, who initially tried to prevent news cam-
eras from recording the horrible scenes of destruction in the days following
the hurricane, were quickly chastised by the media as placing too high a priority on spin control—censoring the images of disaster to preserve what they
could of the island's once-prosperous tourism infrastructure.

The island's principle attraction, its famed beaches all evolved during the hurricane; Cupecoy and Maho beaches suffered erosion at the hands of wind and water while, at the end of the day, Dawn and Philipsburg beaches were enlarged. Damage to the island's scrubby interior was extensive, and will take many months to recover.

Except as noted, all of the hotels listed in the book were open at press time following the hurricane, or received minimal damage and expect to re-open by the end of 1995. La Belle Creole, Club Orient, Dawn Beach Hotel, Divi Little Bay and Great Bay Beach Hotel all suffered major structural damage and will be closed until well into 1996.

Club Orient

"Wiped Out"

Dawn Beach Hotel

Sustained serious damage; could re-open by Summer, 1996.

Divi Little Bay

Structural damage; closed until further notice.

Great Bay Beach Hotel and Casino

Major structural damage; hopes to reopen within one year.

La Belle Creole

Badly damaged; closed until further notice.

ST. THOMAS

t. Thomas has 34 dive sites and offers excellent snorkeling.

St. Thomas is the most cosmopolitan of the U.S. Virgin Islands, if not the most unabashedly commercial. Lots of Caribbean islands boast white sands, aquamarine seas and lush mountains, but few display luxury goods in such abundance. A commercial hub long before Blackbeard who prowled its waters, St. Thomas is now a prime destination for cruise ships, whose passengers rush ashore—not unlike the 19th-century buccaneers—in hot pursuit of duty-free booty.

Others still come to get away from it all, even if the wave of development that followed Hurricane Hugo in 1989 gave a jolt to urban American reality. Along with new resorts and fast-food restaurants there is now a K-mart and a Hard Rock Cafe, and luxurious homes have blossomed like frangipani on the

northern and eastern hillsides. Gridlock in paradise today aptly describes th
sidewalks and narrow alleyways of downtown Charlotte Amalie (pronounce
ah-MAHL-ya), the territorial capital and St. Thomas's only real town. B
beyond the city bustle, there lies another St. Thomas, with more than 4
beaches, rides aboard an Atlantic submarine, golf, tennis, parasailing, boar
sailing, big game fishing—the activities of an endless summer. Simply, S
Thomas is an ideal destination for the couple in which one shops and th
other grumbles. Just one word of warning: whatever you do, avoid the cit
scape when cruise ships dock in port (and if you're on a cruise ship yourse
duck!).

Bird's Eye View

The tram to Paradise Point gives a bird's eye view of the St. Thomas harbor.

St. Thomas lies about 40 miles north of St. Croix and 75 miles east o
Puerto Rico. Only 14 miles by three miles long, it is literally built on
mountain—the reason it's called "Rock City"—with its one main town
Charlotte Amalie, situated on the central south shore. At its highest peal
Crown Mountain, it measures 1550 feet high. A scenic road around the island
Skyline Drive (Route 40), allows a simultaneous view of both sides of the is
land. Beach resorts dot most of the coastline; private homes with bright rec

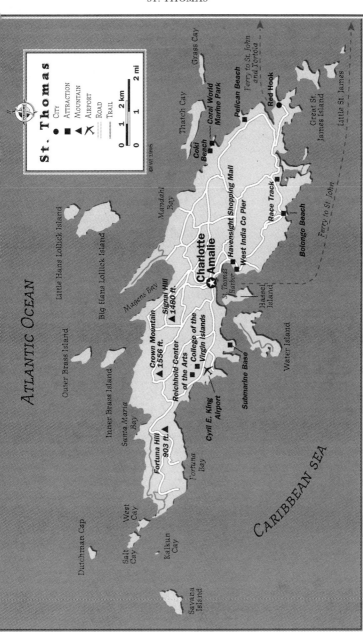

roofs of corrugated iron nestle into the hillside in the wooded interior. The island is easy to navigate by automobile, but there are the inevitable daily traffic jams that clog downtown Charlotte Amalie at rush hour. An excellent view of grassy hills, talcum-white beaches and blue waters can be glimpsed from the Crown Mountain Road, west off Harwood Highway. On the outskirts of town (follow Veterans Drive along the waterfront and turn left at the Villa Olga sign) you'll discover Frenchtown, a community of Swedish descendants from the time Sweden invaded St. Bart in the late 18th century. (Locals still speak a Norman French dialect.)

History

As with St. Croix and St. John, Columbus discovered these islands on his third voyage in 1493. A plan for colonizing St. Thomas was signed by Frederick III of Denmark, but the first settlement failed. Charlotte Amalie, St. Thomas's first permanent European settlement, dates back to 1671. Set on a grand circular harbor, the town was laid out by planners in Denmark who had never seen the mountainous 32-square mile island. Danish control of the Virgin Islands ended when the U.S. bought St. Croix, St. Thomas and St. John for $25 million in order to protect its interests in the Panama Canal. Today, the self-governing unincorporated territory has a nonvoting delegate to the U.S. House of Representatives.

Beaches

Though St. Thomas endures a lot of visitors, beaches have remained appealing, with fine white sand sloping into beautiful bays. The heart-shaped **Magen's Bay**, the largest bay along St. Thomas' rugged northeast coast, is often considered one of the prettiest beaches in the world. It's also the only beach with an admission charge (50 cents, 25 cents for children under 12 and under, $1 for parking), but it also has all the conveniences of civilization, including parking, lifeguards, equipment rental, changing rooms, restaurants and bars. The calm waters are good for swimming, first-time sailors

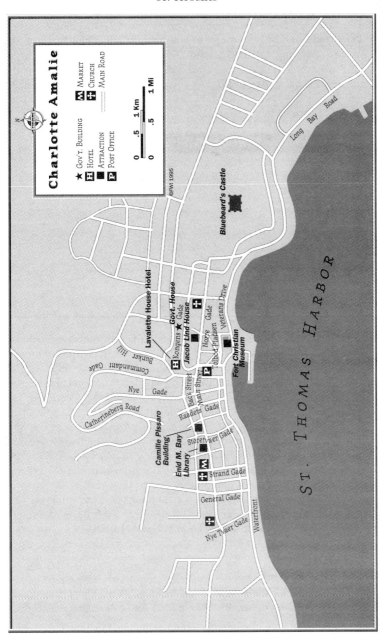

Charlotte Amalie

★ Gov't. Building
H Hotel
■ Attraction
P Post Office

M Market
✝ Church
— Main Road

N

0   .5   1 Km
0   .5   1 Mi

©PM 1995

Bluebeard's Castle

Lavalette House Hotel

Govt. House

Kongens Gade
Jacob Lind House
Commandant Gade
Bunker Hill

Norre Gade
Olbod Madsen
Veterans Drive

Fort Christian Museum

Nye Gade

Catherineberg Road

Back Street
Raadets Gade
Main Street

Camille Pissaro Building
Enid M. Bay Library

Storefrraer Gade
Strand Gade

General Gade

Waterfront

Nye Tvaer Gade

ST. THOMAS HARBOR

Long Bay Road

and a small craft can be rented on the beach (for about $20 hourly). On the northeast shores, **Coki Point** is sterling (stop by the 80,000-gallon aquarium at **Coral World** and the underwater observatory), as is **Sapphire Beach** on the east coast, pointing toward St. John and the **British Virgin Islands**. In the south, two excellent beaches are **Lindbergh Bay**, in front of a hotel near the airport, and **Morning Star**, in front of a resort just east of Charlotte Amalie. There are few deserted beaches here, which is just as well, because isolated areas tend to attract more crime.

FIELDING'S CHOICE:

From January to April, pilot whales frequent the breeding grounds off the north end of the island. Inquire at your sports activity center about whale-watch tours.

Underwater

St. Thomas probably does more dive business than any other destination in the Eastern Caribbean, generating a profusion of operators. Most of the diving is easily accessible and not difficult, and certification and resort courses are very popular. Make sure the dive shop you select is not one of the cattle-drive operators geared toward massive groups of cruise-ship passengers. Locals will reluctantly point out that St. Thomas (like St. John) doesn't offer a lot of big fish and no walls, but decent reef dives are available off the cays, which cluster around the island, particularly on its eastern half (see "St. John" for some of the shared destinations in the Pillsbury Sound). Shore diving is nice from **Coki Bay**. Several good wrecks ornament the St. Thomas depths, and local dive shops offer weekly trips to the wreck of the *Rhone* in the British Virgins; prices vary, but be sure to bring your passport if you want to make the trip. Visibility averages 80 to 100 feet normally. A recompression chamber is available at the St. Thomas Naval Hospital.

Cow and Calf Rocks

Located just south of the island's eastern tip in a newly created marine sanctuary, this is probably St. Thomas' most popular reef site: two rocks that just break the surface. There are swim-throughs, caves and overhangs, abundant tropicals and horse-eye jacks navigating the stands of elkhorn coral. The occasional surge makes this a more intermediate site.

French Cap

A prominent rock formation several miles south of Bolongo Bay, French Cap is a pyramid-shaped seamount which is usually dived to a depth of 80 feet. The structure is home to a rainbow variety of colored and barrel sponges, elkhorn coral, reef fish and sporadic visits by rays. An intermediate or advanced dive with excellent visibility.

Tunnels and Arches at Thatch Cay

Eight swim-through arches, plus two long tunnels are a dramatic feature of this intermediate and very colorful dive. Glassy sweepers brush over the forests of brain, mushroom and whip coral that decorate the area's dynamic rock formations (to 30 feet). Claustrophobics be warned!

Wreck of the *West Indies Trader* (a k a W.I.T. Shoal).

The U.S. Virgins' premiere wreck dive is an awe-inspiring 385-foot freighter that sits upright, soaring 70 feet toward the surface, eerily surrounded by nothing but sand (110 feet). Complete penetration, down stairwells and into the wheelhouse (just 40 feet below the surface) is available, and the spectacularly encrusted freight-loading crane with its 100-foot boom is a special highlight. The *West Indies Trader* is located five miles from shore (southwest of the airport) in strong currents; some hairy near-accidents certify this a very advanced wreck dive.

Dive Shops

Admiralty Dive Center, Inc.

Charlotte Amalie; ☎ *(809) 777-9802.*

Smaller boutique operation visiting outlying sites; maximum group size, six divers. PADI and NAUI affiliated, training to Divemaster. Two-tank dive $70, including equipment. Snorkel/hiking trips to St. John, $60.

Chris Sawyer Dive

Redhook; ☎ *(800) 882-2965 or (809) 775-7320.*

NAUI and PADI affiliated (a Five Star facility), with four separate shops spread around the island. Groups limited to six divers, perfect safety record over 14-year operation. Two-tank dive, $70. Handicapped instruction.

Coki Beach Dive Club

Coki Beach; ☎ *(800) 474-2654 or (809) 775-4220.*

Resort courses and easy access to shore dives off Coki (two-tanks, $40). PADI and SSI affiliated with courses through Divemaster. Two-tank boat dive, $65.

St. Thomas Diving Club

Bolongo Bay; ☎ *(800) 538-7348 or (809) 776-2381.*

A PADI five-star facility with training through Instructor. Popular with locals, offers private charters. Two-tank dive, $80.

On Foot

Bustling St. Thomas is undeniably beautiful, but it's also one of the most heavily developed and densely populated islands in the Eastern Caribbean. Its relatively compact size, 32 square miles, coupled with a population exceeding 50,000, means that truly virgin territory is long gone. Paved roads lead to the island's highest point, **Crown Mountain** (1556 feet), and snake to the crests of other scenic vistas. So, where does a walker go? In addition to the paths listed below, your best opportunities for escape lie on the two islands just south of Charlotte Amalie. **Hassel Island** (recently adopted as part of the National Park) features nice beaches and a long-abandoned ruin, Fort Cowell, but is currently reachable only by private boat. Nearby **Water Island**, the fourth largest of the U.S. Virgins, was an Army base during WWII and later, its (now-closed) hotel served as inspiration for Herman Wouk's *Don't Stop the Carnival*. The island has a small population and a manufactured, quarter-mile strip of sand; impromptu ferry service is provided to Water Island by its residents. A St. Thomas walking itinerary also should include a tour of charming **Charlotte Amalie**, which buzzes with activity when cruise ships are docked (as many as five a day), and even when they aren't. For ample appreciation of the capitol's history, pick up a *Historic District Guide* from the tourist office.

Bordeaux Beach and Stumpy Bay Beach

Drive west on Route 30, passing the airport, and ascend the hills on the west end of the island. Near the top of the ridge, on the right, a four-wheel drive road leads down to the northern coastline and is suitable for hiking. At the first intersection, head right for about a mile down to Stumpy Beach, an isolated, little-visited cove that offers swimming and snorkeling (beware of sea urchins). Returning to the intersection, head right one-and-a-half miles down to cliffs and a picnic area that overlooks Bordeaux Bay. Allow three hours to visit both beaches, a little more to include sunning.

Sandy Bay and Botony Bay

The island's most deserted lands lie on the western tip, which can be reached by driving west on Route 30 to its end near Bordeaux Hill. Follow the dirt road west, descending into Sandy Bay, with Botony Bay a short distance northeast. There is a parcel of private land surrounding Botony Bay and some controversy about allowing visitors onto it, but U.S. law specifies that all beaches are public. Another trail begins at the same road-end: head south down to **David Point** for views of **Fortuna Bay** and the airport. Allow about an hour round-trip for either hike.

By Pedal

Bicycling on St. Thomas is not to be taken lightly. The island's heavily traveled roads are complicated by steep grades and switchbacks, making cycling a brain-rattling experience, not for the timid. No bike rental outfits exist at present and are unlikely to appear anytime soon.

What Else to See

Sailboats leave Charlotte Amalie for excursions to St. John and the British Virgin Islands.

A look around Charlotte Amalie can be done in less than a morning; choose a rainy day if you can find one. The Government House is a bit of a bore, as is the Virgin Islands Museum, though Fort Christian itself might harbor a few detectable ghosts since it was the center of social and political activity for the island over several hundred years. Somewhat captivating is the **Estate St. Peter Greathouse Botanical Gardens**, sprawling over 11 lush acres high atop the volcanic peaks of the north side of the island. Opened in 1992 after a renovation that was completely destroyed by Hurricane Hugo (and then renovated again by a hearty New England couple), the meticulously landscaped gardens offer self-guided nature trails through such exotic flora as the umbrella plant from Madagascar, the cane orchid from China and the bird of paradise from South Africa. You can also spend time here visiting an **orchid jungle**, **rain forest**, **waterfalls** and **monkey habitat**. Superb views from the outdoor observation deck renders 20 other Virgin Islands. Some visitors plant themselves on the deck's benches and sit for hours. Open 9 a.m.–5 p.m., admission is a rather steep $8 ($4 kids under 12).

The second-oldest synagogue in the U.S. and its territories is located at St. Thomas in Charlotte Amalie, picturesquely situated on a narrow street high above the harbor. It was built in 1833 and is worth visiting for its architecture and its fittings. Its sand floor is said to commemorate the Exodus. Tourists are welcome not only during the religious services but also during the week. An international Bicentennial celebration slated for 1995–96 is commemorating 200 years of Jewish life in St. Thomas. Visitors of all faiths will travel to St. Thomas in honor of the St. Thomas Synagogues' proud history. For more information contact the St. Thomas Tourist Board.

Coral World has an underwater observatory ☎ *(809) 775-1555* that provides a 360-degree look at coral life. At 2 p.m. divers hand-feed sharks in the Predator Tank. Admission is $16, $10 for children 3 and over. Open daily from 9 a.m.–6 p.m.

Reinhold Center for the Arts at the University of the Virgin Islands, located on a hillside overlooking Brewers Bay, holds many cultural events. Don't miss folk dances performed by the **Caribbean Dance Company**. Call ☎ *(809) 774-8475*.

Tillett Gardens in the Tutu area, the site of funky and fascinating arts and crafts studios, often hosts classical concerts ☎ *(809) 775-1929*. It's well worth a trip anytime for great shopping. Closed Sunday.

Carnival follows Easter in the Virgin Islands. The Carnival Food Fair offers a chance to sample dishes such as **kallaloo** (a stew of meat, seafood and greens) and drinks prepared with sea moss and soursop, a local fruit. A pre-dawn dance through the streets, called the J'Ouvert Morning Tramp, is followed by the Children's Parade that day. On April 30, the Adults' Parade is led by Mocko Jumbies, stilt dancers in extravagant, brightly covered costumes.

Most tourists make at least one excursion to **St. John**, two-thirds of which is the Virgin Islands National Park, where each uncrowded beach seems to surpass the one before ($3 one way for a 20-minute ferry that leaves every hour from Red Hook on the East End, $7 for the 45-minute ride from Charlotte Amalie.)

BEST VIEW:

From atop the 1500-foot Mountain Top, on St. Peter's Mountain, you can see a panoramic view of both sides of the island as well as a multitude of islands stretching east to Virgin Gorda.

FIELDING'S CHOICE:

To experience the scuba thrill without getting wet, take a ride on the Atlantis Submarine, a 46-passenger underwater craft that takes passengers for an hour's ride at depths of 50-90 feet. The sub's large windows give good views of corals reefs and a multitude of marine life. Hours are generally 10 a.m.-2 p.m., but call first for reservations. The boat ride leaves from the West Indies dock at Havensight Mall on the outskirts of Charlotte Amalie. For more information ☎ (809) 775-1555.

Historical Sites

Fort Christian ★★★

At the harbor, ☎ *(809) 776-4566.*
Hours open: 8:30 a.m.–4:30 p.m.
This brick fortress is the oldest building in the Virgin Islands and a U.S. national landmark, dating back to 1672. It has housed everything from the entire St. Thomas colony to a jail to a church over the years, and is now home to an art gallery, police station, book store, and, in the former dungeons, the Virgin Islands Museum, which traces the island's history. It's currently under renovation, so access may be limited.

Historic Churches ★★★★

Various locations.
Charming Charlotte Amalie is home to several historic churches well worth a look. The Frederick Lutheran Church (Norre Gade) is the Western Hemisphere's second-oldest Lutheran church. All Saints Anglican Church on Garden Street was built in 1848 to celebrate the end of slavery. The Dutch Reformed Church on Nye Gade was built in 1844, but actually dates back to 1744 (the original was destroyed by a fire in 1804). Finally, the Cathedral of St. Peter and St. Paul in Kronprindsens Alley was built in 1848 and is enhanced by murals done in 1899 by Belgian artists.

St. Thomas Synagogue ★★★★

Synagogue Hill, ☎ *(809) 774-4312.*
Hours open: 9 a.m.–4 p.m.

This is the oldest synagogue in continuous use under the American flag, and th
second-oldest in the Western Hemisphere. The floor is sand, symbolic of the dese
through which Moses and the Israelis wandered for 40 years. A bicentennial cele
bration, commemorating 200 years of Jewish life on St. Thomas, takes place i
1995-96, with art shows, celebrity guests, special events and Jewish cultural produc
tions. Call for a schedule once on the island.

Museums and Exhibits

Seven Arches Museum ★★★

Government Hill, ☎ *(809) 774-9259.*
Hours open: 9 a.m.–3 p.m.

This Danish house was built in 1800 and is now a private home, but they'll let yo
in to see its historic furnishings and antiques. The grounds include a separat
kitchen and a walled garden, the perfect spot to quaff the drink included in th
admission fee.

Parks and Gardens

Estate St. Peter Greathouse Gardens ★★★★

Route 40 and Barrett Hill Road, Above Hull Bay, ☎ *(809) 774-4999.*
Hours open: 9 a.m.–5 p.m.

As you stroll the grounds of these new gardens, it's hard to believe this verdant spo
was completely leveled by Hurricane Hugo in 1989. Owners Sylvie and Howar
DeWolfe did an amazing job restoring everything to its former glory. These gar
dens, reopened in late 1992, are perched 1000 feet above Hull Bay and Magens Ba
Beach on the island's north side. Self-guided trails lead through more than 200 vari
eties of Caribbean plants and trees, as well as imported treasures like the tropical da
lily from Asia and South African bird of paradise. There are also ponds, waterfall
and a rainforest—not to mention sweeping views from the large deck, where yo
can spot more than 20 other Virgin Islands. The recreated great house is filled wit
contemporary Caribbean furnishings and locally done artwork. A treat!

Tours

Coral World ★★★★

Coki Point, ☎ *(809) 775-1555.*
Hours Open: 9 a.m.–6 p.m.

Nonswimmers can see what all the fuss is about at this five-acre marine park, hom
to 21 aquariums, a touch tank, an 80,000-gallon tank showcasing the world's larg
est living man-made reef, an exotic bird habitat, and semi-submarine rides. The
highlight is the underwater observatory, an air-conditioned room 20 feet below se
level through which you can observe all sorts of sea life, an especially exciting sigh
at feeding time. The grounds also include duty-free shops, a bar and restaurant, and
a pretty beach where they rent snorkel and scuba equipment (showers and changing
rooms are available). Kids get in for $10.

Guided Tours

Various locations.

St. Thomas is easily explored on your own, but if you'd like to spare the expense o
renting a car, take a guided tour. **Destination Virgin Islands** *(☎ 776-2424)* offer

walking tours, beach and shopping trips, and excursions to St. John and St. Croix. Prices vary. The **St. Thomas Islands Tour** (☎ *774-7668*) explores the island in two hours for $14 per person; another excursion takes in the many splendid views and costs $20. **Tropic Tours** (☎ *774-1855*) offers various shopping and scenic tours; call for prices. Also try **Smitty Island Tour** (☎ *775-2787*), which goes to Coral World, Drakes Seat, Mountain Top and Magen's Bay ($35); and **Timmy Island Tour** (☎ *775-9529*), whose 2.5-hour tour includes Red Hook, Sapphire Beach overlook, Coral World, Magen's Bay, Mountain Top, and Charlotte Amalie ($25).

Paradise Point Tramcom, Inc. ★★★

Havensight Area, ☎ *(809) 774-9809.*
Hours open: 8:30 a.m.–6:30 p.m.
When this $2.8-million tramway opened in August 1994, it brought back a popular attraction that ceased to exist in the 1970s. The 3.5-minute ride—not recommended for those afraid of heights—gives a bird's eye view of the harbor and stops at 697-foot-high Paradise Point, where you can wander among the shops, have a quiet drink or just soak up the scenery. When going up, try to snag the last car; when coming down, hop in the first car for the best unobstructed views. $5 for kids under 13; kids under six are free.

Robinson Crusoe Excursion ★★★★

☎ *(809) 776-7880.*
It's not cheap ($325 per couple), but if you're in love and solvent, here's a great day trip you'll always remember. A private helicopter takes you on a scenic ride to an uninhabited island, where you're left to your own devices for several hours. They'll give you a cooler of ice, but you'll have to pack your own lunch, drinks and towels. The four-hour trips leave at 9:30 a.m. 1:30 p.m.

Seaplane Adventure ★★★★★

Charlotte Amalie Harbor, Charlotte Amalie, ☎ *(809) 777-4491.*
Amazing views abound on this 45-minute flight aboard the twin-engine seaplane Vistaliner. Bring lots of film, because you'll be snapping away like mad as you fly over some 100 islands of the U.S. and British Virgin Islands. The entire tour takes 1.5 hours (it's exciting to take off and land from the ocean) and is greatly enhanced by extra-large windows, lively narration via headphones (which can also be plugged right into your video camera) and an interesting booklet that gives details on the islands spotted. Great fun!

Sports

All watersports activities are enjoyed on St. Thomas. Sportfishing on S
Thomas is devoted primarily to the blue marlin. In March, April, May an
June they can be found in the south in the Caribbean, north in the Atlant
in July-September. On the Atlantic side of the Virgins is the **100-fathom drop
off**, bordering on the Puerto Rico Trench, the deepest hole in the Atlanti
Ocean. Because the Virgin Islands lie in the Trade Winds Belt, fishing can a
ways be done on the leeward side. **Redbook**, at the main center of St. Tho
mas, is the main center for boat operators. Many operators offer half- an
full-day boat excursions on any number and variety of craft; full-day fishin
expeditions can come with equipment, picnic, ice and beer. The water
northeast of St. Thomas are prime fishing grounds, helping the Virgin Is
lands live up to their reputation as a superb site to catch blue marlin. Surfin
attracts lots of fans during the winter since the sea huskily rolls in with a blas
at Hull Bay on the north coast of St.Thomas. Windsurfing here is best at th
eastern end where winds peak during noontime; the roughest conditions ar
at Hull Bay, the gentlest at Morningstar in the south. Even novices are invit
ed for a two-hour lesson of windsurfing at the Windsurfing St. Thomas,
School of Boardsailing at St. Pleasant. Kayaking is popular, as is sportfishing
Horse racing is a party event on St. Thomas, involving thoroughbred horses
panmutuel, and daily double betting. Events are approximately monthly
usually on a local holiday or Sunday. English-style riding lessons are availabl
at **Rosenthal Riding Ring**, which also offers trial rides. St. Thomas has a spec
tacular 18-hole championship course, designed by George and Tom Fazio
at **Mahogany Run**. There are six public tennis courts on St. Thomas, as well a
private ones at many hotels. Play in the early morning or late afternoon unti
you get used to the weather.

Mahogany Run Golf Course

Mahogany Run Road, North Shore, ☎ *(809) 775-5000.*
Hours open: 7 a.m.–4:50 p.m.

St. Thomas' only golf course is an especially scenic and challenging one, a par-70
known for its dramatic 13th and 14th holes, which hug cliffs overlooking the Atlantic Ocean. If you play holes 13, 14 and 15 (the "Devil's Triangle") without a pen-
alty shot your first time on the course, they'll give you a prize. A new 270,000-
gallon desalination plant keeps everything lush and green (in the past, the course
was in a constant battle with Mother Nature). Designed by George and Tom Fazio,

greens fees vary depending on the time of year, and range from a high of $70 for 18 holes to a low of $50. Nine holes can be played before 8 a.m. and after 3 p.m.; discount twilight rates kick in after 2 p.m. Tee times are taken 48 hours in advance and run daily from 7 a.m.–4:50 p.m. Several resorts, including Grand Palazzo, Renaissance Grand and Secret Harbour offer golf packages.

atersports

Various locations.

If your hotel doesn't offer the equipment you need, these companies are happy to help out. For boating, try: **Island Yachts** *(☎ 775-6666 or (800) 524-2019)*, **Avery's Marine** *(☎ 776-0113)*, **Coconut Charters** *(☎ 775-5959)*, **Nightwind** *(☎ 775-4110)*, and **New Horizons** *(☎ 775-1171)*. For scuba and snorkel instruction and excursions, try: **Seahorse Dive** *(☎ 774-2001)*, **Adventure Center** *(☎ 774-2990)*, **Dean Johnston's Diving** *(☎ 775-7610)*, **Hi-Tec Water Sports** *(☎ 774-5650)*, **Aqua Action** *(☎ 775-6285)*, **Underwater Safaris** *(☎ 774-1350 or (800) 524-2090)*, and **Dive In** *(☎ 775-6100)*. Deep-sea fishers can call **Fish Hawk** *(☎ 775-9058)* and **St. Thomas Sportfishing Center** *(☎ 775-7990)*.

Where to Stay

Fielding's Highest Rated Hotels in St. Thomas

★★★★★	**Grand Palazzo**	$250–$1325
★★★★★	**Marriott Frenchman's Reef & Morning Star**	$160–$395
★★★★	**Anchorage Beach Villas**	$195–$235
★★★★	**Bolongo Bay Beach & Tennis Club**	$195–$235
★★★★	**Elysian Resort**	$200–$630
★★★★	**Island Beachcomber**	$95–$150
★★★★	**Renaissance Grand Beach**	$215–$895
★★★★	**Sugar Bay Plantation**	$180–$370
★★★	**Sapphire Beach Resort**	$190–$395
★★★	**Secret Harbour Resort**	$179–$480

Fielding's Most Romantic Hotels in St. Thomas

★★★★★	**Grand Palazzo**	$250–$1325
★★★	**Hotel 1829**	$60–$290

Fielding's Budget Hotels in St. Thomas

★	**Island View Guest House**	$60–$100
★★	**Mafolie Hotel**	$65–$97
★★	**Heritage Manor**	$45–$135
★★★	**Blackbeard's Castle**	$75–$140
★★★	**Carib Beach Hotel**	$79–$145

Bluebeard's Castle gets high marks for retaining historic touches while providing modern amenities to hotel guests/visitors.

Accommodations can run wild in St. Thomas—from a posh resort that features live alligators in the moat to historical inns reputed to be haunted. In between are congenial inns, high-rise hotels and faux Italiante villas. Many big resorts offer the use of tennis courts, fitness centers and nonmotorized watersports equipment at no extra charge to guests. Not all lodgings are in the best of shape; ironically, some of the best ones today suffered the worst damage during Hurricane Hugo and now sport new faces and interiors. Most people head for the large congregations of lodgings on the south coast, near Charlotte Amalie. Other good locations include the Pineapple Beach curve of Water Bay, where the Renaissance Grand Beach Hotel is located, and near Red Hook on the east coast.

Hotels and Resorts

With more than 14 resorts to choose from, you need to first set down your priorities. Do you want to be near shopping or near private coves? Do you want an all-inclusive, such as the Bolongo Limetree, where you pay one price for everything, or would you rather take advantage of a special "Land and Sea" package that would get you close to the British Virgin islands (Windward Passage Hotel)?

Not all hotels have air conditioning, not a necessity if you are on the windward side of the island, important if you need a refuge from the hot sun. If your hotel is on the beach, you can save considerable money by not taking a sea view, but if you stay in your room a lot, the lack of fresh breeze and view may not be worth it.

Blackbeard's Castle   **$75–$140**   ★ ★ ★

Waterfront Veterens Drive, ☎ (800) 344-5771, (809) 776-1234, FAX (809) 776-4321.

Single: $75–$110. Double: $95–$140.

This inn, a national historic landmark, is built around a stone tower once reportedly used by pirates. Guestrooms are quite small but charming enough with simple furnishings, air conditioners, and tiny balconies. There are also several one-bedroom suites with more amenities. The grounds include a large pool, a highly regarded restaurant, and a bar with nightly jazz bands. Wonderful views abound everywhere. The beach and downtown Charlotte Amalie are within walking distance.

Bluebeard's Castle Hotel $140–$235 ★★★

P.O. Box 7480, Bluebeard's Hill, 801, ☎ (800) 524-6599, (809) 774-1600, FAX (809) 774-5134.
Single: $140–$235. Double: $140–$235.

Set high up on a hill with splendid views of the harbor and beyond, this venerable hotel is built around a 17th-century tower. Lodgings are found in villas and range from studios to one-bedroom suites, all air-conditioned, nicely decorated, and boasting balconies or terraces. There's nightly entertainment in the lounge, two well-regarded restaurants, a large pool, two tennis courts, and a fitness center. They'll shuttle you over to the beach for free. Nice, but group business dominates here, so individual travelers can feel lost in the shuffle.

Bolongo Bay Beach & Tennis Club $195–$235 ★★★★

Cowpet Bay, 802, ☎ (800) 524-4746, (809) 775-1800, FAX (809) 779-2400.
Single: $195. Double: $235.

This busy property, also known as Club Everything, offers full resort amenities and a lovely palm-studded beach. Guestrooms have two entrances, white tile floors, two double or king beds, shower-only baths and a small refrigerator and stove top. The west wing is quietest, while those in the center have the nicest views, but all are quite close to the beach. Definitely request a second-floor unit for more privacy. The grounds include four lit tennis courts, a pretty pool complete with swim-up bar, several restaurants, a barbecue area and all the watersports one could want, including daily boat trips and a dive shop. Complimentary supervised programs for children are offered daily except Sunday. Excellent for families.

Bolongo Limetree $1250–$2918 per wk. ★★★

☎ (800) 524-4746, (809) 776-4770, FAX (809) 779-2400.

St. Thomas' only all-inclusive resort draws mainly a younger crowd. Besides meals and drinks, the rates include three trips on a 100-foot catamaran (all-day sail, a half-day snorkel trip and a cocktail cruise). Guestrooms are quite small but ingeniously built on two levels, giving a feeling of space. Each has pretty rattan furnishings, white tile floors, and small shower-only baths. The junior loft suites, with a king bed upstairs and a sofa bed below, are quite nice. Unfortunately, all rooms lack a terrace or balcony. On the plus side, each is quite close to the beach. Facilities include two lit tennis courts, several restaurants, a pretty wedding gazebo (they do some 300 weddings each year), a fitness center and a disco. Three theme nights each week get guests mingling. Guests can also take the free shuttle to use the facilities at sister property Bolongo Bay Beach & Tennis Club. Double-occupancy rates are $1250 for four days/three nights (the minimum stay) and $2918 for eight days/seven nights.

Elysian Resort $200–$630 ★★★★

6800 Estate Nazareth, Cowpet Bay, 802, ☎ (800) 524-4746, (809) 775-1000, FAX (809) 779-2400.
Single: $200–$350. Double: $225–$630.
This resort, set on a hill above a peaceful cove, houses guests in nicely done guestrooms or loft units with full kitchens and one to three bedrooms. Sporting facilities include a large and elaborate pool, a tennis court, an excellent and well-equipped health club and complimentary watersports. Dining choices range from the elegant Palm Court to the casual Oasis outdoor grill. This property is more luxurious than its Bolongo siblings, but there's also less going on—a plus or minus, depending upon your preference. If you're looking for action, you can always hop the free shuttle that takes you to the Bay Beach Club or Limetree.

Emerald Beach Resort $139–$239 ★★★

8070 Lindbergh Bay Beach, Lindbergh Beach, 802, ☎ (800) 233-4936, (809) 777-8800, FAX (809) 776-3426.
Single: $139–$200. Double: $149–$239.
Located just a mile from the airport, this smaller hotel has decent guestrooms that won't win any prizes for originality, but are quite modern and comfortable nonetheless. Facilities include a bar and restaurant, pool and tennis court. There's watersports for hire at the very nice public beach, just steps away.

Grand Palazzo $250–$1325 ★★★★★

Great Bay, ☎ (800) 545-0509, (809) 775-3333, FAX (809) 775-5635.
Single: $250–$865. Double: $250–$1325.

The rates are high, but those who can afford it will be happily impressed with this deluxe Italian renaissance-style resort. Accommodations are in plush junior suites with expensive and luxurious furnishings and wonderful views of St. John and the British Virgin Islands off the terrace. There's also a handful of one- and two-bedroom suites. Facilities include a large free-form pool, four tennis courts, a full health club with modern exercise equipment and pampering services, a 56-foot catamaran for ocean cruises, two elegant restaurants, several bars, and watersports, including a dive shop. The rates include such niceties as afternoon tea, ice delivered to your room twice daily and a weekly cocktail party. The grounds are simply gorgeous and the beach is fine. They don't come much better!

Island Beachcomber $95–$150 ★★★★

P.O. Box 302579, Lindbergh Beach, 803, ☎ (800) 982-9898, (809) 774-5250, FAX (809) 774-5615.
Single: $95–$145. Double: $100–$150.
Set right on a fine beach, this hotel took a licking in Hurricane Hugo, but has been rebuilt to the joy of its faithful clientele—some 80 percent of the guests are repeat visitors. This casual spot houses guests in comfortable, air-conditioned rooms facing the lush garden or beach; all have cable TV, phones, refrigerators, and patios or porches. The restaurant is open-air and reasonably priced, and there's also a beach bar. No pool, but the sea is calm and good for swimming. Snorkeling equipment

and water rafts are complimentary (other watersports cost extra), and they'll shuttle you into town for free. A pleasantly informal spot with the kind of friendly staff we'd like to see at all Caribbean resorts.

Mafolie Hotel $65–$97   ★★

P.O. Box 1506, Mafolie Hill, 804, ☎ *(800) 225-7035, (809) 774-2790, FAX (809) 774-4091.*

Single: $65–$87. Double: $80–$97.

Set high on a hill overlooking Charlotte Amalie, this Mediterranean-style villa hotel is only for those who can handle steep climbs. Guestrooms are simple and basic; only some have air conditioners and none sport TVs or phones. There's a pool and two restaurants on the grounds, and the views are stunning. They feed you breakfast for free, and the shuttle to Magen's Bay Beach is also gratis. The reasonable rates (most rooms are under $100) make Mafolie worth considering.

Magens Point Hotel $105–$305   ★★

Magens Bay, ☎ *(800) 524-2031, (809) 775-5500, FAX (809)776-5524.*
Single: $105–$255. Double: $118–$305.

Set on a hillside next to the Mahogany Run Golf Course and overlooking the beach, this informal operation consists of motel-style guestrooms and 22 studio and one- and two-bedroom suites with cooking facilities. There's a restaurant, bar, pool, and two tennis courts on-site, and they'll shuttle you to the beach (about a half mile away) at no charge. All here is quite casual, including, sometimes, the maintenance, but it's pleasant enough and the rates are relatively reasonable.

Marriott Frenchman's Reef & Morning Star $160–$395   ★★★★★

#5 Estate Bakkaroe, ☎ *(800) 524-2000, (809) 776-8500, FAX (809) 776-3054.*
Single: $160–$395. Double: $160–$395.

This full-service resort complex, which incorporates both Frenchman's Reef and Morning Star, has so much going on at all hours that you'll never have to venture outside its boundaries. Guests are housed in accommodations right on the beach (Morning Star) or on a rocky promontory surrounded by water on three sides (Frenchman's Reef). Whichever you choose, you can count on modern and comfortable living, though the rooms on Morning Star are more luxurious (and expensive). Facilities include a huge pool, four tennis courts, watersports on the fine beach, a dinner theater, and six restaurants, several bars, and a disco. Live entertainment is frequently scheduled, as are all sorts of activities. A water taxi will whisk you into town if you can tear yourself away from the happenings here. On the downside, the property hosts a lot of conventions, so you'll be sharing the facilities with name tag-wearing business folk. This is a grand spot for those who covet full resorts, but if you're looking for a laid-back tropical escape, look elsewhere. Ditto if you hate long walks.

Point Pleasant Resort $200–$380   ★★★

Estate Smith Bay, ☎ *(800) 524-2300, (809) 775-7200, FAX (809) 776 5694.*
Single: $200–$275. Double: $260–$380.

This property takes up 15 acres on a lush hillside overlooking Smith Bay. Guests are put up in large standard rooms or spacious suites with full kitchens and living and dining areas. If you choose not to do your own cooking, two restaurants will do the job. Facilities include a small beach, tennis, three pools, and complimentary watersports. Guests also get free use of a car for four hours each day; a welcome idea we'd like to see more resorts follow. A better beach is found next door at the Stouffer Grand, which guests are welcome to use. Very nice.

mada Yacht Haven Hotel $90–$225   ★★★

5400 Long Bay, 802, *(800) 228-9898, (809) 774-9700, FAX (809) 776-3410.*
Single: $90–$200. Double: $90–$225.

Guests sacrifice a beach for the relatively reasonable rates at this so-so hotel. Located on a large marina from which you can watch the cruise ships come in, accommodations are found in six low-rise buildings. Rooms have modern amenities like VCRs but are a bit run down. The grounds include two pools (one with a swim-up bar) and two restaurants and bars. They'll shuttle you over to the beach at the Marriott for free.

naissance Grand Beach $215–$895   ★★★★

P.O. Box 8267, Water Bay, 801, *(800) 468-3571, (809) 775-1510, FAX (809) 775-2185.*
Single: $215–$895. Double: $215–$895.

Set on a lush hillside sloping to a small beach, this former Stouffer is another full-service resort that keeps guests pleasantly occupied. As with other large resorts, there's not a lot of true island flavor here, but no one seems to mind (or even notice). Guestrooms, just redone in 1995, are quite plush; a few hundred dollars more buys a two-story townhouse suite or a one-bedroom unit with an indoor whirlpool. Recreational options include six tennis courts, two pools, an excellent health club, and lots of watersports. There's also a sprinkling of restaurants and bars, and organized programs for the kids. Like most of St. Thomas' beaches, the one here is quite narrow and not as pretty as at some competing properties. The grounds are quite lush, though—in fact, the resort is a certified botanical garden with some 500 species of plants. You'll find all you want at this large spot, but be warned the clientele is dominated by conventioneers.

ugar Bay Plantation $180–$370   ★★★★

Estate Smith Bay, *(800) 927-7100, (809) 777-7100, FAX (809) 777-7200.*
Single: $180–$370. Double: $180–$370.

Located on the island's east end, this resort just opened in 1992. A large complex of nine buildings, it has all the usual resort diversions and very pleasant guestrooms and suites, all with coffeemakers, refrigerators, and nice views off the balcony. The grounds include three interconnected pools complete with bar and waterfalls, seven tennis courts, a fitness room, two restaurants, four bars, and watersports at the small beach. Kids are kept busy (and parents relaxed) with supervised programs year-round. A good, all-around resort.

indward Passage $125–$235   ★★

P.O. Box 640, 804, ☎ *(800) 524-7389, (809) 774-5200, FAX (809) 774-1231.*
Single: $125–$230. Double: $135–$235.

The rates are fairly reasonable at this busy commercial hotel, located downtown an overlooking the harbor. Guestrooms are basic but fine, and the 11 more expensi suites offer sitting areas, hair dryers and refrigerators. There are a few restauran and bars and a pool, but no other facilities. Most of the guests are business travele as the beach is beyond walking distance.

Apartments and Condominiums

Apartments and villas are numerous in St. Thomas, and the common language and t familiar U.S-style supermarkets make self-catering a breeze. The one shock will be ho high the prices for food are. You can always bring staples from home, soft packages soup, etc., that can fit easily into the corners of a suitcase.

Anchorage Beach Villas   **$195–$235**   ★★★

Cowpet Bay Point, Bluebeard Hill, ☎ *(800) 524-6599, (809) 774-1600, FAX (80 774-5134.*
Single: $195–$235. Double: $195–$235.

Located on the beach near the island's eastern tip, this complex consists of 30 villa that are large and modern. Each has two bedrooms, two baths, full kitchens, sky lights, large decks, and washer/dryers. Most sleep up to four, while the loft uni can accommodate six. Maids tidy up daily. Facilities include a pool, two tenn courts, and a fitness center. There's a restaurant for those who don't feel up cooking in. The weekly manager's cocktail party is a nice opportunity to meet you fellow guests. The beach is small but decent, and they'll shuttle you about for a fee

Bolongo Bay Beach Villas   **$235–$475**   ★★

☎ *(800) 524-4746, (809) 775-1800, FAX (809) 779-2400.*
Double: $235–$475.

Located on the grounds of Bolongo Bay Beach & Tennis Club, this villa comple offers the best of the self-catering and resort worlds. Villas are individually deco rated and include full kitchens, one or two bedrooms and very large balconies. Vill guests have their own pool, and can also use all the facilities at Bolongo Bay, whic include four lit tennis courts, watersports, a sprinkling of bars and restaurants an free programs for the kids.

Cowpet Bay Village   **$247–$420**   ★★★

6222 Estate Nazareth, Cowpet Bay, ☎ *(800) 524-2038, (809) 775-6220, FAX (80 775-4202.*
Single: $247–$300. Double: $247–$420.

This complex, located on the beach at Cowpet Bay, consists of 30 two- and three bedroom villas. All are spacious and airy, with fully equipped kitchens, living/dinin areas, balconies, washer/dryers, and maid service. There's a restaurant on site, an guests can borrow snorkeling equipment for free. There's no pool, but the beach i right at hand. You'll need a car for mobility.

Crystal Cove   **$126–$273**   ★★

Route 6, Sapphire Bay, 802, ☎ *(809) 775-6220, FAX (809) 775-4202.*
Single: $126–$205. Double: $131–$273.

This 25-year-old complex shows its age, but the rates are reasonable for self-suffi cient types who want kitchen facilities. Accommodations are in condominiums tha range in size from studios to one- and two-bedroom units, all with complete kitchens, balconies, and basic furnishings. Maid service is available every day but Sunday. Facilities include a saltwater pool and two tennis courts. There's no restaurant on site, so you'll want a car.

avilions & Pools	**$180–$260**	★ ★ ★

Estate Smith Bay, ☎ *(800) 524-2001, (809) 775-6110, FAX (809) 775-6110.*
Single: $180–$260. Double: $180–$260.

This villa resort is located seven miles from Charlotte Amalie, near Sapphire Beach. Each of the 25 air-conditioned villas has one bedroom, living/dining areas, complete kitchens, VCRs, and private, decent-sized pools. Maids tidy up daily, and the rates are quite reasonable for self-sufficient types. There's a restaurant and open-air bar that occasionally hosts live entertainment. Guests can play tennis on the courts at the nearby Sapphire Bay Beach Resort for free; watersports equipment can be rented there as well.

apphire Beach Resort	**$190–$395**	★ ★ ★

P.O. Box 8088, Sapphire Bay, 801, ☎ *(800) 524-2090, (809) 775-6100, FAX (809) 775-4024.*
Single: $190–$395. Double: $190–$395.

Located on one of St. Thomas' best beaches, this villa resort encompasses 35 picturesque acres. It's a bit out of the way, so you'll want to rent a car to get around. The accommodations are quite posh with large balconies, fresh flowers, and fully equipped kitchens; most are right on the beach. The largest units have two baths, two balconies, and two queen-size sofa beds in addition to the bedroom, so can sleep six. Maids tidy up daily, and room service is available. Watersports and supervised children's programs are free. There's also a restaurant, pool with nice views of neighboring islands, two bars, and a 67-slip marina. Kids under 12 stay and eat for free.

ecret Harbour Resort	**$179–$480**	★ ★ ★

6280 Estate Nazareth, 801, ☎ *(800) 524-2250, (809) 775-6550, FAX (809) 775-1501.*
Single: $179–$310. Double: $179–$480.

All accommodations are in suites at this secluded resort set on a private beach. Lodging is in spacious studios and one- and two-bedroom condos with full kitchens, quality tropical furnishings, air conditioning and ceiling fans, and enormous balconies. Facilities include an extensive watersports center, a pool, full-service health club and two tennis courts. Two restaurants and a few bars complete the scene. The narrow, coconut tree-dotted beach is lovely, and the sea here is so calm it sports one of the island's few swim floats. This operation combines the best of self-sufficient and resort living.

ecret Harbourview Villas	**$140–$360**	★ ★ ★

P.O. Box 8529, Nazareth Beach, 801, ☎ *(800) 874-7897, (809) 775-2600, FAX (809) 775-5901.*
Single: $140–$281. Double: $140–$360.

Set on a cliff above the beach, this condominium resort offers studios and one- and two-bedroom units, all with complete kitchens, balconies, and maid service. Facili-

ties include a restaurant, pool, and three tennis courts. Guests can use the beach a
facilities at the nearby Secret Harbour Beach Resort. While they offer shuttle servi
into town (for a fee), you'll probably want to rent a car for independence.

Watergate Villas $73–$375   ★★★

Route 7, Estate Bolongo Bay, 803, ☎ *(800) 524-2038, (809) 775-6220, FAX (8(
775-2298.*

Single: $73–$247. Double: $142–$375.

Set on a hill on the south coast 15 minutes out of Charlotte Amalie, this compl
offers individually decorated villas that are rented out in their owners' absenc
Configurations range from studios to one-, two-, and three-bedroom units, all wi
complete kitchens, living/dining areas, maid service, balconies, and contempora
furnishings. There are three pools, two tennis courts, and a restaurant on the pr
mises. Good for self-sufficient types, but you'll want to rent a car to get around.

Inns

Inns in St. Thomas are especially homey, and reminiscent of the days when a wea
traveler could find sustenance and a room along the wayfaring highway. A number of c
lonial houses have been restored by owners who use the main area as a restaurant and re
out a few rooms in the back. (Imagine the wonderful cooking smells you can enjoy a
day!) Some are located on hillsides; others are situated on some of the best beach
around.

Admiral's Inn $79–$149   ★

Villa Olga, 802, ☎ *(800) 544-0493, (809) 774-1376, FAX (809) 774-8010.*

Single: $79–$149. Double: $79–$149.

This inn is not in one of St. Thomas' better neighborhoods, but on the other han
the area is home to many fine restaurants. Guestrooms, located on the hillside, a
air-conditioned and have private baths and cable TV, but the furnishings have see
better days. The inn's four acres include two restaurants, a pool, and a small mar
made beach good for snorkeling. Continental breakfast is included in the rates.

Heritage Manor $45–$135   ★

P.O. Box 90, 1A Snegle Gada, 804, ☎ *(800) 828-0757, (809) 774-3003, FAX (80
776-9585.*

Single: $45–$130. Double: $55–$135.

Located in the historical district, this small inn dates back to the early 1800s and w
originally the home of a Danish merchant. All rooms are air-conditioned an
include such niceties as ceiling fans, refrigerators and brass beds, but only the tw
apartments, which boast kitchens, have private baths. There's a tiny pool on sit
(built in an old Danish oven!) and an honor bar, but little else, though you can wal
(in daylight) to shops and restaurants. The neighborhood is a bit iffy, so spring fo
a cab at night. Most rooms are under $75, making this one of St. Thomas' rare bud
get choices.

Hotel 1829 $60–$290   ★★

Government Hill, 804, ☎ *(800) 524-2002, (809) 776-1829, FAX (809) 776-4313.*

Single: $60–$280. Double: $70–$290.

This atmospheric inn was built in (you guessed it) 1829 by a French sea captain for his bride. It's located right in the heart of the city, so you'll have to drive or take a taxi to the beach (beautiful Magen's Bay is 15 minutes away). Now a national historic site, the hotel accommodates guests in charming rooms enhanced with antiques, air conditioners, minibars and VCRs. The price you pay depends on the size of your room, which varies widely—definitely request one in the original building (the rest were added in the late 1920s and are not as nice). The continental restaurant is well-regarded, and there's also a wonderful bar and a tiny pool. Not especially suited to small children or the physically challenged, as there are many steep stairs to negotiate and no elevator to help things along.

Low Cost Lodging

A budget consciousness does exist in St. Thomas, and there are several options under $50 per double in small, unassuming hotels. Camping is becoming ever more popular on the island. Checking out your room ahead of time is essential; insist on seeing the room you will be renting since the conditions could vary from apartment to apartment. The Tourist Office in Charlotte Amalie could also help you find arrangements; also peruse the Virgin Island daily newspapers under the classified section.

Carib Beach Hotel   **$79–$145**   ★ ★ ★

70-C Lindberg Bay, Lindbergh Beach, 802, ☎ (800) 792-2742, (809) 774-2525, FAX (809) 777-4131.
Single: $79–$145. Double: $79–$145.

This Best Western hotel just reopened in 1994 after damage from Hurricane Hugo forced it to close in 1989. Located on a very small, man-made beach (you can tan but there's no ocean access, so calling this place a "beach hotel" is really stretching it), each basic room is air-conditioned and has a private balcony, cable TV and telephones. Facilities include a pleasant restaurant and a small pool. Located just a stone's throw from the airport, so expect some noise from jets. Though this place is rather bare-bones compared to St. Thomas' many glittering resorts, there's something quite agreeable about it.

Island View Guest House   **$60–$100**   ★

P.O. Box 1903, Constant Hill, ☎ (800) 524-2023, (809) 774-4270, FAX (809) 774-6167.
Single: $60–$94. Double: $65–$100.

This informal guest house is five minutes out of Charlotte Amalie and perched high on a hill with great harbor views. Guestrooms are quite simple, as suggested by the rates (most are under $100), but comfortable enough. Most, but not all, have private baths, and those who want air conditioners will pay an extra fee. The high-priced units have kitchenettes. There's a restaurant, honor bar and small pool on the premises, and continental breakfast is complimentary. Ask about special packages.

Where to Eat

Fielding's Highest Rated Restaurants in St. Thomas

★★★★	Cafe Normandie	$25–$39
★★★★	Craig and Sally's	$11–$26
★★★★	Cuzzin's	$10–$20
★★★★	Old Stone Farmhouse	$23–$29
★★★★	Palm Terrace	$22–$32
★★★★	Virgilio's	$13–$39
★★★	Hotel 1829	$20–$32
★★★	Palm Court	$14–$32
★★★	Raffles	$15–$29
★★★	The Frigate	$15–$30

Fielding's Special Restaurants in St. Thomas

★★★★	Cafe Normandie	$25–$39
★★★★	Cuzzin's	$10–$20
★★★★	Old Stone Farmhouse	$23–$29
★★★★	Virgilio's	$13–$39
★★★	Victor's New Hide Out	$9–$20

Fielding's Budget Restaurants in St. Thomas

★★★	Epernay Champagne Bar	$6–$10
★	Palm Passage	$6–$12
★	Glady's Cafe	$6–$13
★	Art Geckos	$5–$16
★★★	Cafe Sito	$4–$19

Locals dine out as frequently as visitors on St. Thomas, which accounts for the extraordinary range of dining options, with cuisines hailing from nearly every corner of the world. Splurging on Sunday brunch is a national pastime. Restaurants are generally informal and open-air, but prices can rival those of Manhattan's most elegant dining rooms. Casual dress, even shorts, generally pass muster, but reservations are advisable. Each of the big hotels has several restaurants and a few have gained renown. One of the newest, most elegant spots is the **Grand Palazzo Hotel's Palm Terrace**, where excellent spa-style "light" cuisine dubbed "Floribbean" (Florida meets Caribbean) is serenaded by a pianist in a white diner jacket. A taste of France can be found at **Provence**, in funky Frenchtown, where you can sample such delights as hearty soups, casseroles and a fine antipasto bar. One delicacy not to pass up are the liqueur-flavored milkshakes such as the one with Jamoco-chocolate ice cream, coconut ice cream and Kahlua that you can find at **Udder Delite Dairy Bar** near Magens Bay. ☎ (809) 775-2501. Sorry to say, but St. Thomas is one of only two Caribbean islands with a **Hard Rock Cafe**. Go only if you feel homesick.

Agave Terrace $$$ ★★★

6400 Estate Smith Bay, Water Bay, ☎ *(809) 775-4142.*
Seafood cuisine.
Lunch: 10 a.m.–6:30 p.m., entrees $18–$24.
Dinner: 6:30–10 p.m., entrees $18–$24.
It may be a little hard to find, with a resort-hotel location on the northeastern end of the island. But even nonguests should try to make it here for a leisurely breakfast or dinner on the patio while the light is still good for an unparalleled view of the Caribbean sea in the distance. The cuisine is mostly Mediterranean style seafood, and the chef is delighted to create any dish (within reason) that a customer requests.

Art Geckos $$ ★

Tillet Gardens, Smith Bay Road, ☎ *(809) 775-4550.*
American cuisine.
Lunch: 11 a.m.–4:30 p.m., entrees $5–$8.
Dinner: 6–11:30 p.m., entrees $6–$16.
Enjoy burgers, sandwiches and salads at lunch, plus fresh seafood and grilled Jamaican jerk chicken at dinner at this casual open-air cafe in Tillett Gardens. If you're lucky, you'll get to watch the daily iguana feedings. The restaurant is a true oasis in a peaceful garden setting, though the real reason to come here is to check out the fascinating artisans' shops that surround it. Besides the famed maps and underwater seascapes by Jim Tillett, you'll find a goldsmith shop, African mahogany carvings, a tea shop and beautiful hand-painted gifts. A must!

Blackbeard's Castle $$$ ★★★

P.O. Box 6041, Blackbeard Hill, ☎ *(809) 776-1234.*
American cuisine.
Lunch: 11:30 a.m.–2:30 p.m., entrees $8–$13.
Dinner: 6:30–9:30 p.m., entrees $18–$29.

Feel like Blackbeard the pirate surveying his domain from this stunning aerie wit an eagle eye view of the harbor and the city. The international cuisine has won man awards from local publications several years in a row. It's hard to have a meal her without sampling from a varied array of homemade soups, salads or creative appe tizers. Entrees include a choice of veal, excellent seafood, beef filets or a devilish rich pasta. Lighter meals can be had in the lounge or by the pool, where non-gues can swim. There's a bountiful buffet Sundays from 11:00 to 3:00 pm.

Cafe Normandie   **$$$**   ★★★★
rue de St. Barthélémy, Frenchtown, ☎ *(809) 774-1622.*
French cuisine.
Dinner: 6–10 p.m., entrees $25–$39.

In an informal survey, island residents anointed this cozy, elegant French restauran with a bright yellow painted exterior as their favorite overall dining out spot a fev years ago. Food, service and location are all exceptional, but I suspect people retur again and again for the sinful chocolate fudge pie. There's a well regarded five course, prix-fixe supper available nightly that includes a palate-cleansing sorbe Make sure to reserve in season, as it is small and popular. Closed Mondays in sum mer.

Cafe Sito   **$$**   ★★★
21 Queens Quarter, ☎ *(809) 774-9574.*
Mediterranean cuisine.
Lunch: entrees $4–$19.
Dinner: to 11 p.m., entrees $4–$19.

This new spot, just opened in 1995, is a real winner. The long dining room ha wood-beamed ceilings, white-washed walls and pretty wooden cases displaying a good wine selection (featuring a $120 bottle of Dom Perignon). The cuisine i tapas, with such delicacies as sizzling shrimp in virgin olive oil with saffron and gar lic, paellas, fish and chicken, and the most wonderful salad of vine-ripe tomatoes hearts of palm and gorgonzola cheese. Highly recommended!

Chart House   **$$$**   ★★★
P.O. Box 3156, Villa Olga, ☎ *(809) 774-4262.*
American cuisine.
Dinner: 5–10 p.m., entrees $13–$37.

Salad bar lovers flock here for a huge spread of many items, including passable cav iar. Dinner specialties include sizzling steaks, juicy prime rib, chicken and lobster the salad bar is included. All this bounty is consumed on a terrace overlooking the sea, situated in a 19th century building which was once home to Russian diplomats Don't overlook the famous "mud pie" if you still have room.

Craig and Sally's   **$$$**   ★★★★
22 Estate Honduras, Frenchtown, ☎ *(809) 777-9949.*
International cuisine.
Dinner: 6–10:30 p.m., entrees $11–$26.

A talented husband and wife team combine his knowledge of fine wines and her culinary expertise in the operation of this muraled restaurant in Frenchtown. Although there are several dining areas, it's often crowded; the word is out on the creative Mediterranean and Asian specialties prepared here. Sun-kissed tomatoes, broiled peppers or salsas made with market picked fruits are used liberally on plump scallops, chicken or swordfish. Sally's desserts recall a childhood learning to bake at mother's elbow; there's key lime pie and killer chocolate cakes.

Cuzzin's $$ ★★★★

Back Street, Charlotte Amalie, ☎ *(809) 777-4711.*
cuisine.
Lunch: entrees $10–$20.
Dinner: 5–9:30 p.m., entrees $10–$20.
Authentic island cuisine awaits in this local's hangout, a cute yellow brick building with wooden shutters. Specialties include stewed conch, curried chicken and other local dishes and drinks like sea moss (milk, sugar, seaweed and nutmeg). Each entree comes with a choice of three side dishes such as potato stuffing, rice and beans, yams and macaroni and cheese. The daring will like the homemade hot sauce that accompanies some meals. Closed for dinner on Mondays.

Epernay Champagne Bar $ ★★★

24 B Honduras Street, Frenchtown, ☎ *(809) 774-5343.*
International cuisine.
Dinner: 4:30 p.m.–1 a.m., entrees $6–$10.
Before or after a night on the prowl, nestle here for champagne by the glass; sample up to six different varieties. A grazing menu of sophisticated snacks covers the globe; there's sushi, caviar and goat cheese. Food is served from 5 p.m. to 12 a.m.; it's open later on weekends. Wine and desserts are also available.

Eunice's Terrace $$$ ★★

66-67 Smith Bay, Route 38, Smith Bay, ☎ *(809) 775-3975.*
cuisine.
Lunch: 11 a.m.–4 p.m., entrees $6–$11.
Dinner: 6–10 p.m., entrees $10–$28.
Don't let the junk yard out back put you off. An island success story, Eunice's establishment grew like topsy from a simple food stand to a two-story building with a popular bar in Smith Bay. The West Indian cuisine that built her reputation is possibly the best on the island. There's a daily menu, but conch fritters and an incomparable tropical rum cake are usually available.

Glady's Cafe $$ ★

17 Main Street, ☎ *(809) 774-6604.*
cuisine.
Lunch: entrees $6–$13.
This spot, set in an alleyway in Charlotte Amalie, is where locals congregate for breakfast (served from 6:30 a.m.) and Caribbean-style lunches. Besides the standard burgers and sandwiches, the menu offers up conch in lemon butter sauce and sauteed shrimp. The brick walls, covered in murals, feature pigs flying; check out the blackboard for Glady's thought of the day, such as the recent "The effect of hope is astounding."

Hard Rock Cafe $$ ★★★

International Plaza, Charlotte Amalie,

American cuisine.
Lunch: 11 a.m.–4 p.m., entrees $7–$16.
Dinner: 4 p.m.–midnight, entrees $7–$16.

This memorabilia-laden retro-rock burger palace draws a more subdued crowd tha those in mainland cities, but there's the requisite antique auto suspended over th entrance. Bob Marley mementoes are also included with the gold Beatle record behind glass frames. Among the wall exhibits is a red and gold neon sign proclaim ing "No drugs or nuclear weapons allowed" inside. Good burgers barbecue rib nachos and fajitas are served.

Hook, Line and Sinker $$ ★★★

#2 The Waterfront, Frenchtown, ☎ (809) 776-9708.
International cuisine.
Lunch: entrees $5–$10.
Dinner: entrees $6–$20.

Yachties tie up to this seaside eatery that's nothing special, but it's a good meet an greet place. There's a nice outdoor deck, and offerings are reasonably priced. It's convenient stop if you're in the area, especially for a burger or steak lunch.

Hotel 1829 $$$ ★★★

30 Kongens Gade, Charlotte Amalie, ☎ (809) 776-1829, (800) 524-2002.
American cuisine.
Dinner: 5:30–10 p.m., entrees $20–$32.

Streamlined service and stellar food are served in a restored Government Hill hotel Tables on the terrace are well-sought after for the terrific views, but wherever yo sit, the cuisine is pleasing. Specialties include a wilted spinach salad and dessert souf fles; and the raspberry chocolate is especially toothsome.

Il Cardinale $$ ★★

Back Street, ☎ (809) 775-1090.
Italian cuisine.
Lunch: until 4 p.m., entrees $11–$19.
Dinner: 5:30–11 p.m., entrees $11–$19.

This air-conditioned spot offers a quiet and dignified respite from the teeming streets of Charlotte Amalie. Located upstairs in the Taste of Italy shopping mall, the decor is subdued, with large oil paintings dominating the walls and tables clothed in white linen. Among the choices are homemade crepes, salmon in champagne sauce, a highly regarded chicken salad and *pasta e fagiolo* soup. Nice. After your meal stroll the adjacent gallery that spotlights local artwork.

L'Escargot $$$ ★★★

#12 Submarine Base, Charlotte Amalie, ☎ (809) 774-6565.
Seafood cuisine.
Lunch: 11:45 a.m.–2:30 p.m., entrees $7–$15.
Dinner: 6–10 p.m., entrees $15–$27.

A long-established dining room, this classic French restaurant is one of a few eater ies located at a submarine base west of Charlotte Amalie, near the airport. Meals are taken in a patio overlooking the ocean. Specialties are old favorites like rack of lamb or lobster thermidor; all simply and impeccably prepared.

mon Grass Cafe $$$ ★★

Bakery Square, Back Street, ☎ *(809) 777-1877.*
cuisine.
Lunch: 11 a.m.-3:30 p.m., entrees $7–$16.
Dinner: 6–10 p.m., entrees $16–$20.

The menu changes often at this pretty spot located in a scenic courtyard. Dine outdoors next to the lily pond, or inside, where gleaming woods, stone walls and ceiling fans create a lovely atmosphere. Entrees range from salads and burgers to roast salmon, grilled swordfish and pork and lamb dishes. Sunday brunch (10:30 a.m.–2:30 p.m.) is followed by a "tea dance" with a mini menu from 5–9 p.m.

d Stone Farmhouse $$$ ★★★★

Mahogany Run, ☎ *(809) 775-1377.*
cuisine.
Dinner: 6:30–10 p.m., entrees $23–$29.

Considered one of St. Thomas' fining dining outlets, the Old Stone is built in the ruins of a 200-year-old dairy farm near Mahogany Run Golf Course (on the north side, 20 minutes from Charlotte Amalie). A pianist lends just the right amount of ambience to this lovely room of thick stone walls and varied antiques. Entrees include such imaginative offers as filet mignon with cheese and a red onion marmalade and snapper in a potato crust. Whatever you choose, you'll be well pleased.

alm Court $$$ ★★★

Red Hook, ☎ *(809) 775-1000.*
cuisine.
Dinner: 6:30–10 p.m., entrees $14–$32.

Located steps from the beach at the Elysian Resort, this fine dining spot offers tables inside or, better yet, out under the stars. Entrees run the gamut from fresh seafood to beef, lamb, poultry and pasta dishes. Such specialties as a grilled portabella mushroom served with carmelized onions and port wine sauce and swordfish in ginger lime butter with poached peaches in dark Cruzan rum keep patrons happy. Heavenly!

alm Passage $ ★

Off of Main Street, ☎ *(809) 779-2708.*
Italian cuisine.
Lunch: 11 a.m.–3:30 p.m., entrees $6–$12.

Located in a scenic courtyard and surrounded by art galleries, Palm Passage is a nice place for a tasty lunch of risotto, roasted garlic, pizza or grilled eggplant salad. The menu also features burgers and sandwiches.

alm Terrace $$$ ★★★★

Great Bay, ☎ *(809) 775-3333, (800) 545-0509.*
International cuisine.
Dinner: 6:30–10 p.m., entrees $22–$32.

A chef with a background in cooking for luxury health spas in California and Florida holds court at this, the Grand Palazzo resort's crown jewel. Weight watchers can delight in the fact that many of the delectable meals are prepared in natural juices and infusions, instead of heavy cream sauces. Alas, the calories await in the desserts, one of which is caramel ice cream encased in chocolate. Apparently, this ensures a return to the fat farm. The surroundings here are some of the most luxurious on the island; everything exudes a rosy glow and all is pretty in pink. A pianist helps further the romantic mood. Divine!

Piccola Marina Cafe $$$ ★★★

6300 Smith Bay, Red Hook, ☎ *(809) 775-6350.*
American cuisine.
Lunch: 11 a.m.–5:30 p.m., entrees $5–$14.
Dinner: 5:30–10:30 p.m., entrees $13–$24.

This alfresco restaurant on a Red Hook Marina dock is a fun place, with a selection of pastas for your dining pleasure. Sauces range from tomato marinara to a creamy alfredo. Others can order sandwiches, chicken, fresh seafood or quaff a brew or two. Sunday brunch is served in the winter from 10 a.m. to 3 p.m.

Provence $$$ ★★★

Honduras Street, Frenchtown, ☎ *(809) 777-5600.*
French cuisine. Specialties: Antipasto Table.
Dinner: 6–10:30 p.m., entrees $15–$19.

Chef and restaurateur Patricia La Corte, who created the well-regarded Fiddle Leaf on Government Hill is now roosting at this country-French bistro on the second floor of a wooden building in funky Frenchtown. The warmly-decorated room, with arched doorways and potted palms, offers a wharf-side view. Specialties include lamb shank with hearty chakerny and rosemary sauce on a bed of mashed potatoes and oven roasted garlic chicken. Nibblers go into grazing heaven with La Corte's reasonably priced antipasto table, served daily until 11:00 p.m.

Raffles $$$ ★★★

The Marina, Compass Point, ☎ *(809) 775-6004.*
Seafood cuisine.
Dinner: 6:30–10:30 p.m., entrees $15–$29.

This south-seas themed restaurant is a favorite with residents, who enjoy the steak flambeed at tableside. Ladies especially like the high-backed peacock chairs in the salon cooled by ceiling fans and ocean breezes. Other specialties include fresh fish and stuffed leg of lamb.

Rain Forest Cafe $ ★

Mountain Top Shopping Mall, Mountain Top, ☎ *(809) 774-2400.*
American cuisine.

The best reason to come to this new cafe is to check out its amazing views—probably the best on an island that abounds with sweeping vistas. The offerings are simple—deli sandwiches, salads, pastries—the better to leave room for at least one banana daiquiri. The frothy drink was reportedly invented here in 1949 by British restaurateur Conrad Graves. Cheers!

Terrace Restaurant $$ ★

Next to the airport at the Carib Beach Resort, Lindbergh Bay, ☎ *(809) 774-2525.*
American cuisine.
Lunch: 11:30 a.m.–2:30 p.m., entrees $5–$7.
Dinner: 6–9:30 p.m., entrees $7–$19.

No need to make a special trip here (the food's merely adequate), but if you have a long wait at the airport, stroll on over to this pleasantly informal outdoor spot at the Carib Beach Resort. The menu features typical salads, burgers, steak, chicken and the catch of the day. On Friday nights from 6:00-9:45, a steel band helps liven things up. A great place to catch the moon rise, and it sure beats sitting in the airport. Also open for breakfast from 7:00-10:30 a.m.

he Frigate   **$$$**   ★ ★ ★

P.O. Box 1506, Mafolie Hill, ☎ (809) 774-2790, (800) 225-7035.
Seafood cuisine.
Dinner: entrees $15–$30.

An awe-inspiring ocean view and tender steaks hot off the charcoal broiler continue to please the regulars that ascend to this small, charming hotel dining room on Mafolie Hill. Non-red meat eaters will be pleased with fresh seafood, chicken and a salad bar. There's a smaller branch in Red Hook (No 18-8) near the Marina, 775-1829.

ictor's New Hide Out   **$$$**   ★ ★ ★

103 Submarine Base, Charlotte Amalie, ☎ (809) 776-9379.
International cuisine.
Lunch: 11:30 a.m.–3:30 p.m., entrees $9–$11.
Dinner: 5:30–10 p.m., entrees $11–$20.

Chef Victor left quiet Montserrat for more action, and he cooks his West Indian specialties for an appreciative crowd of locals, tourists, and the occasional celebrity. The ubiquitous conch and curried chicken dishes are available, as well as his signature dish, Lobster Montserrat, cooked with fruit and cream sauce. Newcomers should probably arrive by taxi, as the hilltop hideaway is a little hard to find.

irgilio's   **$$$**   ★ ★ ★ ★

18 Dronningens Gade, ☎ (809) 776-4920.
Italian cuisine.
Lunch: until 4 p.m., entrees $13–$22.
Dinner: 4–10:30, entrees $16–$39.

It looks like a dump from the outside, but a true haven awaits inside this wonderful restaurant. The walls are covered with eclectic artwork, the ceilings twinkle with tiny lights and display cases proudly spotlight the Caribbean's largest wine collection— 400 bottles, plus an extensive collection of cordials. The food is as good as the atmosphere. The huge menu offers up 40 kinds of homemade pastas, fish, chicken and vegetarian specialties. Save room for a luscious dessert such as bananas foster or crepes suzette prepared tableside. You'll find few tourists among the upscale locals who dine here regularly.

Where to Shop

Since Charlotte Amalie was declared a free port in 1755, opening it fo
trade with the European powers and growing American colonies, the island
have moved to a mercantile beat. Jewelry, liquor and electronics stores, in
terspersed with shops offering china, linens and perfume crowd Main Stree
Jitneys take cruise ship passengers downtown; most stores also have outle
at the Havensight Mall near the dock.

U.S. residents may bring home $1200 in goods free of duty, with the ne:
$1000 each subject to 5 percent duty. Members of a household may make
joint declaration, entitling a family of four to a $4800 duty-free allowanc
There is no sales or luxury tax. Best buys include unmounted gems (duty
free for Americans, no matter the price), gold jewelry and watches. Befor
stepping into a store, know what you are looking for and what the price
back home. Finesse in bargaining goes a long way.

Reputable establishments offer dealer warranties and certificates of auther
ticity and generally avoid the sidewalk barker come-ons that grow more shri
as one moves west on Main Street. Most visitors leave toting at least one bot
tle of rum. Local brands such as Cruzan cost less that $3 a fifth, and if yo
buy any spirits produced in the territory, you are allowed to take six bottle
rather than the normal five bottles back to the States duty-free.

Must-see for shoppers are several specialty stores that showcase the impres
sive work of artisans from Jamaica, Haiti, Dominican Republic, Martiniqu
and others. Start with **Down Island Traders** next to Post Office Alley on th
Waterfront, where you can choose everything from edible delicacies such a
marmalades and jellies to sweet Caribbean rum balls, fiery mustards, tast
fruit chutneys and exotic spices, as well as extensive Haitian and Jamaica
wall hangings, handmade cloth and wooden dolls, including the legendar
Caribbean worry doll. (According to an ancient island tale, these precious
looking figures will take away your troubles if you hand them over. The big
ger the worry, the bigger the doll—one worry per doll.) Upstairs is **The Gal
lery**, a two-room studio featuring fine Caribbean folk art, including wor
from some of the island's top primitivists. The **Caribbean Marketplace** in Ha
vensight Mall specializes in exotic condiments as well as "Sunsations," a nev
line of flower, fruit and herbal extracts for bath gels, body splashes and skii
oils. Handmade steel-pan drums can also be found here. At **Mango Tango** ir

ie Al Cohen Building (across the street from Havensight), you can stock up
n wooden masks from Jamaica, wooden earrings from Trinidad and origi-
al and print work from the Virgin Islands. **Tillet Gardens Craft Complex**, lo-
ated in Tutu across from Four Winds Plaza, features the work of Jim
illett's screen-painted maps of the Caribbean, cruising maps of the Virgin
slands and abstract paintings by himself and other local artists. Also in the
ime complex is **Okidanokh**, where goldsmith Abel Fabri's original jewelry in-
ludes such precious stones as tourmaline, sapphire, topaz and agate. The
olor of Joy is a boutique that features watercolors and prints by St. Thomas
ainter Corinne Van Rensselaer, as well as varied gifts from the islands; the
aribbean Enamel Guild—a small annex—features hand-painted jewelry,
oxes and various accessories. The best time to visit Tillett Gardens is during
ie popular Arts Alive arts and crafts fairs, held on-site three times a year. For
iore information call ☎ *(809) 775-1929* about the next festival.

St. Thomas Directory

RRIVAL

American Airlines offers nonstop service from Miami, NYC and Ra-
leigh-Durham to St. Thomas, connecting from all parts of the world via
NYC. **Carnival Airlines** flies nonstop from Miami to San Juan, with
connections on convenient carriers. **Continental Airlines** flies nonstop
from Newark to St. Thomas, connecting from Boston, Chicago, Detroit and Philadelphia via Newark. **Delta Airlines** flies nonstop from Atlanta to St. Thomas, continuing to St. Croix. **Trans World Airways** flies
nonstop from NYC, St. Louis and Miami to San Juan, with connections
to St. Thomas in convenient carriers. **Virgin Island Paradise Airways**
flies direct from Newark to St. Thomas via St. Croix, connecting from
Chicago, Dallas, Houston and Philadelphia.

Inter-island flights include daily service from St. Croix, St. Kitts-Nevis
and Anguilla to St. Thomas on **Air Anguilla**. **Air Calypso** offers daily service between St. Croix, St. Thomas and San Juan. **American Eagle** offers daily service from San Juan to St. Thomas/St. Croix, and between
St. Croix and St. Thomas. Also check service on **Sunaire Express**,
Windward Island Airways and **Leeward Island Air Transport** (LIAT).

USINESS HOURS

Shops generally open weekdays 9 a.m.–5 p.m. Banks generally open
Monday–Thursday 9 a.m.–2:30 p.m. and Friday 9 a.m.–2 and 3:30–
5 p.m.

LIMATE

Summer temperatures, cooled by eastern trade winds, hover around 82
degrees Fahrenheit. Winter temperatures range from 77 degrees, dip-
ping to 69 degrees at night and rising as high as 84 degrees. The rainy

season runs September-January, though the sun shines nearly every day. The average rainfall is about 40 inches per year, and showers are usually brief.

DOCUMENTS

U.S. citizens need no passport. But if you plan to visit the British Virgin Islands, you must show proof of citizenship (passport, or birth certificate with photo ID). Canadians must have a valid passport.

ELECTRICITY

Current runs at 110 volts, 60 cycles.

GETTING AROUND

Taxis at the airport usually stand at the far left end of the new terminal, not at all close to where inter-island flights land. Cabs are not metered, but each driver must carry the most up-to-date list of fares. Rates quoted are for one passenger, extra passengers are charged more. If you decide to go to a destination not on the official list of rates, negotiate firmly ahead of time. And be warned they like to pile lots of people in the cabs, regardless of where they're going. You'll need to be patient!

There are public buses every 20 minutes from the terminal to the town (about $1).

Rental cars are widely available, including the large name agencies in the U.S. Rates are about $35 a day.

Ferry boats are an easy way to get around the islands. You can catch one from Red Hook to St. John (every hour from 8 a.m.- midnight); it takes 20 minutes one way, about $3. There's also a ferry at Charlotte Amalie to St. John (45 minutes, about $7), as well as one from downtown to Frenchman's Reef Hotel and Morningstar Beach ($3)—it's a cool way to get to the beach and only 15 minutes long.

Seaboard Seaplane (☎ *(809) 774-4491*) offers daily service to and from St. Croix for about $100 round-trip.

LANGUAGE

English is the official language. Locals also speak a native patois, a mixture of English, African and Spanish. Many people are bilingual in Spanish.

MEDICAL EMERGENCIES

Police ext. *915*, fire ext. *921*, ambulance ext. *922*.

MONEY

The official currency is the American dollar. There is no sales tax.

TELEPHONE

The area code is *809*. Since USVI is an unincorporated territory, toll-free numbers that operate in the U.S. work here, normal postage rates apply. You can also direct dial to the mainland.

TIME

Atlantic Standard Time, which means an hour later than New York City, except during Daylight Saving Time, when it is the same.

TIPPING AND TAXES

Some hotels include a 10–15 percent service charge; this should include all tips for both restaurant and room service, unless the attention was extraordinary. If no service is added, leave a 15 percent tip for the waitress, $1–$2 a day to the maid; bartenders and wine stewards should be tipped always. Tip the bellboy and porter at least 50 cents a bag. Taxi drivers should receive a 15 percent tip if you are satisfied with the service.

TOURIST INFORMATION

The **St. Thomas Dept. of Tourism** has information booths at the airport ☎ *(809) 774-8784*, at Emancipation Garden at Charlotte Amalie ☎ *(809) 774-8784*, ext. *147*; and in Havensight Mall near the cruise ship dock ☎ *(809) 774-8784*. You can also pick up brochures, rest your feet, and even check shopping bags at an island-sponsored hospitality lounge in the Old Customs House next to Little Switzerland.

WATER

There is ample water for showers and bathing, but you are asked to conserve water whenever possible. It's safe to drink.

WHEN TO GO

The Calypso Competition is held at the University of the Virgin Islands cafeteria on March 4. Arts Alive & Crafts Festival, where Caribbean vendors sell handmade crafts and arts, is held on March 17–19. The Caribbean Chorale, one of the most popular groups in the USVI, performs a blend of classical, West Indian and native compositions on April 2. The 10th annual Easter Bonnet Contest takes place on April 17. The Virgin Islands Carnival Events, with nightly competitions in music and costumes, takes place on April 18–22. The 22nd Annual International Rolex Cup Regatta is April 21–23 (tentative). Virgin Islands Carnival Village features local foods, drink, and rides on April 24–29. STARfest 1995, a star-studded tribute to Caribbean talent, is May 13. The 8th Annual American Yacht Harbor Billfish tournament is July 13-18. Arts Alive Arts & Crafts Festival is August 11–13. The Hebrew Congregation of St. Thomas Bicentennial Celebration Gala Opening Weekend, featuring a celebration of Jewish History, is September 15-17. Hebrew Congregation of St. Thomas Bicentennial Celebration Interfaith Succot Service is October 6–8. The Hebrew Congregation of St. Thomas Bicentennial Celebration Jewish Musical Performance starts October 24 for four weeks. St. Thomas/St. John Agriculture Food Fair is November 18–19. Arts Alive Arts & Crafts Festival is November 24–26. The Hebrew Congregations of St. Thomas Bicentennial Celebration, featuring an authentic Sephardic Service and Chanukah Celebration is December 22.

ST. THOMAS HOTELS		RMS	RATES	PHONE	CR. CARDS
Bolongo Bay					
★★★	Bolongo Bay Beach Villas	39	$235–$475	(800) 524-4746	A, DC, MC, V
★★★	Bolongo Limetree	84	$178–$416	(800) 524-4746	A, DC, MC, V
Charlotte Amalie					
★★★★★	Grand Palazzo	150	$250–$865	(800) 545-0509	A, D, DC, MC, V
★★★★★	Marriott Frenchman's Reef & Morning Star	520	$160–$395	(800) 524-2000	A, CB, D, DC, MC, V
★★★★	Anchorage Beach Villas	30	$195–$235	(800) 524-6599	A, D, DC, MC, V
★★★★	Island Beachcomber	48	$95–$150	(800) 982-9898	A, CB, D, DC, MC, V
★★★★	Renaissance Grand Beach	297	$220–$560	(800) 468-3571	A, D, DC, MC, V
★★★★	Sugar Bay Plantation	300	$180–$370	(800) 927-7100	A, D, DC, MC, V
★★★★	Watergate Villas	100	$73–$375	(800) 524-2038	A, D, DC, MC, V
★★★	Blackbeard's Castle	25	$75–$140	(800) 344-5771	A, D, MC, V
★★★	Bluebeard's Castle Hotel	170	$140–$235	(800) 524-6599	A, CB, D, DC, MC, V
★★★	Carib Beach Hotel	69	$79–$139	(800) 792-2742	A, MC, V
★★★	Emerald Beach Resort	90	$139–$239	(800) 233-4936	A, CB, D, DC, MC, V
★★★	Hotel 1829	15	$55–$285	(800) 524-2002	A, D, MC, V
★★★	Pavilions & Pools	25	$180–$260	(800) 524-2001	A, D, MC, V
★★★	Point Pleasant Resort	134	$200–$380	(800) 524-2300	A, D, MC, V
★★★	Ramada Yacht Haven Hotel	151	$90–$225	(800) 228-9898	A, CB, D, DC, MC, V
★★★	Sapphire Beach Resort	171	$190–$395	(800) 524-2090	A, MC, V
★★★	Secret Harbour Resort	60	$179–$310	(800) 524-2250	A, MC, V
★★★	Secret Harbourview Villas	30	$140–$360	(800) 874-7897	D, DC, MC, V
★★	Admiral's Inn	16	$79–$149	(800) 544-0493	A, D, MC, V
★★	Crystal Cove	50	$126–$273	(800) 524-2038	A, DC, MC, V
★★	Heritage Manor	8	$50–$135	(800) 828-0757	A, MC, V
★★	Mafolie Hotel	23	$65–$97	(800) 225-7035	A, MC, V
★★	Magens Point Hotel	54	$105–$305	(800) 524-2031	A, CB, DC, MC, V

ST. THOMAS HOTELS	RMS	RATES	PHONE	CR. CARDS
★★ Windward Passage	151	$125–$235	(800) 524-7389	A, CB, DC, MC, V
★ Island View Guest House	15	$60–$100	(800) 524-2023	A, MC, V

Red Hook

	RMS	RATES	PHONE	CR. CARDS
★★★★ Bolongo Club Beach Resort	200	$195–$235	(800) 524-4746	
★★★★ Elysian Resort	118	$210–$690	(800) 524-4746	A, D, DC, MC, V
★★★ Cowpet Bay Village	30	$247–$420	(800) 524-2038	A, D, DC, MC, V

ST. THOMAS RESTAURANTS	PHONE	ENTREE	CR. CARDS

Charlotte Amalie

American			
★★★ Blackbeard's Castle	(809) 776-1234	$8–$29	A, MC, V
★★★ Chart House	(809) 774-4262	$13–$37••	A, DC, MC, V
★★★ Hard Rock Cafe		$7–$16	A, MC, V
★★★ Hotel 1829	(809) 776-1829	$20–$32••	A, MC, V
Caribbean			
★★★★ Cuzzin's	(809) 777-4711	$10–$20	A, MC, V
French			
★★★★ Cafe Normandie	(809) 774-1622	$25–$39••	A, MC, V
★★★ Provence	(809) 777-5600	$15–$19••	A, MC, V
International			
★★★★ Craig and Sally's	(809) 777-9949	$11–$26••	A, MC, V
★★★ Epernay Champagne Bar	(809) 774-5343	$6–$10••	A, MC, V
★★★ Hook, Line and Sinker	(809) 776-9708	$5–$20	A, MC, V
★★★ Victor's New Hide Out	(809) 776-9379	$9–$20	A, MC, V
Seafood			
★★★ L'Escargot	(809) 774-6565	$7–$27	A, MC, V
★★★ The Frigate	(809) 774-2790	$15–$30••	A, MC, V

Red Hook

American			
★★★ Piccola Marina Cafe	(809) 775-6350	$5–$24	A, MC, V

ST. THOMAS RESTAURANTS	PHONE	ENTREE	CR. CARDS
International			
★★★★ Palm Terrace	(809) 775-3333	$22–$32••	A, MC, V
Latin American			
★★ Eunice's Terrace	(809) 775-3975	$6–$28	A, MC, V
Seafood			
★★★ Agave Terrace	(809) 775-4142	$18–$24	A, MC, V
★★★ Raffles	(809) 775-6004	$15–$29••	A, MC, V
Note: • Lunch Only			
•• Dinner Only			

Hurricane Update

After suffering serious destruction from Hurricane Marilyn, government officials said St. Thomas hoped to have 60 percent of the islands hotel rooms back in operation by the end of 1995. Many shops and restaurants sustained major damage but will be working hard to be back in business as soon as possible.

ST. VINCENT AND
THE GRENADINES

Picturesque St. Vincent's terrain ranges from rugged cliffs to lush valleys and beaches with golden and black sand.

The Grenadines is a small archipelago, a short boat hop south of St. Vincent that offers some of the best cruising possibilities in the Caribbean. Only a few of the islands have any touristic infrastructure, though many of them are so primitive and paradisiacal that most visitors arrive at least for the day to snorkel, trek and sunbathe in complete privacy. Collectively the islands total about 30 square miles of land mass, and while some are uninhabited, those that have residents are mostly populated by descendants of African slaves. The chain perhaps acquired its name from the French word for passionfruit, *grenadine*, of which there are many on the islands. Other historians believe that the chain was discovered at the same time Grenada was, hence "little grenada" or grenadine. The lifestyle in general is extremely laid-back and simple. Islands such as Mustique, Pal Island, Petit St. Vincent and Young are privately owned, and have the most luxurious resorts. Others such as Union, Bequia and St. Vincent are definitely for the vagabond on a budget.

St. Vincent

Boat excursions and hiking trails lead to cascading waterfalls and mineral springs on St. Vincent.

Green and volcanic, St. Vincent is the main island of the Grenadines, more rugged than Grenada and offering a vast array of nature-oriented activities. From Bequia, motor vessels make the nine-mile run to St. Vincent (locally called the mainland here). Although the area is just now awakening to tourism, yachtsmen and sailors have long used the island as a jumping port for fabulous cruises through the surrounding islets; recently many visitors are staying on the island to experience the superb nature trails, stunning waterfalls and the demanding hike to the crater of La Soufriere that last erupted in 1979. The western and eastern side of the island are wonderful areas to explore by bus; along the west, the coastline descends to beaches so golden they seem to glitter in the sun. At other times, the beaches turn coal black. In between are incredibly verdant landscapes flourishing with coconut, breadfruit, bananas, sweet potatoes and cocoa. Wild scenic excursions can be found along the rocky, rugged Atlantic coast, where, the farther you go, the more primitive the houses become. This is an island where you can see residents carrying their own water and pulling up arrowroot, a kind of skinny white radish which has become the island's major export (used for dressing wounds). The capital of Kingstown can claim the oldest botanical garden in the Western hemisphere, begun in 1765. Among its exotic specimens on the beautifully kept grounds is a breadfruit tree brought to the island in 1793 by

Captain Bligh of the Bounty. Endangered St. Vincent parrots can also b found here.

Bird's Eye View

Roughly 18 miles long by 11 miles wide, St. Vincent sprawls over 13 square miles while the Grenadines make a total of 17 more square miles. Th highest peak on the island is **La Soufriere** on the leeward and windwar coasts, an active volcano in the north rising to 4000 feet. It last erupted i 1979, when glowing avalanches rushed down the mountain and the se boiled off the north coast, but careful monitoring succeeded in evacuatin everybody before it blew. Today there is a dome of lava that extruded durin this eruption and during an earlier disturbance in 1973. The steep mountai range of **Morne Garu** rises to 3500 feet and runs southward with spurs to th east and west coasts and the steep hills are forested. Most of the centr mountain range and the steep hills are forested. Dominating the island ar beaches of both golden and volcanic black with lush valleys and rugged cliffs

The capital, **Kingstown**, is located on a sheltered bay, in the southern coas of the island.

History

Columbus marked the presence of St. Vincent on his third voyage in 1498 but luckily didn't go ashore since the resident Carib Indians might have can nibalized him. The native tribes here were more tenacious than other islands keeping the European conquistadors at bay longer than any other island. In 1763 a treaty allowed the British to take control of the island. Sixteen year later, they found themselves battling the French, but the Treaty of Versailles in 1783 gave the power back to England.

Some years later, Captain Bligh took off for Tahiti from England with his crew of the *Bounty*, only to be mutinied by them and pushed out to sea. In 1793 he finally reached St. Vincent on his own, equipped with a canoeful o

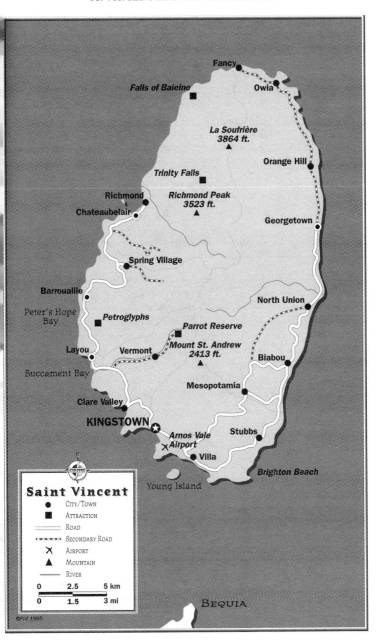

Fancy

Owia

Falls of Baleine

La Soufrière
3864 ft. ▲

Orange Hill

Trinity Falls

Richmond

Richmond Peak
3523 ft. ▲

Chateaubelair

Georgetown

Spring Village

Barrouallie

North Union

Peter's Hope
Bay

Petroglyphs

Parrot Reserve

Layou

Vermont

Mount St. Andrew
2413 ft. ▲

Biabou

Buccament Bay

Mesopotamia

Clare Valley

KINGSTOWN ✪

Arnos Vale
✕ Airport

Stubbs

Villa

Brighton Beach

Young Island

Saint Vincent

● City/Town
■ Attraction
— Road
▪▪▪ Secondary Road
✕ Airport
▲ Mountain
— River

0   2.5   5 km
0   1.5   3 mi

©FWI 1995

BEQUIA

breadfruit seedlings, which became the progenitors of a crop that woul eventually make the island famous. In 1795, the native population side with the French and burned down British plantations during a ferocious bat tle; a year later the Brits triumphantly quelled the rebellion. At that time, th Brits decided to deport the rest of the native Indians to British Hondura (now known as Belize), where their ancestors live today. Until 1979 the is land was under British rule, at which time it received independent statehood along with the other Grenadines, within the Commonwealth. It is governe by a governor-general appointed by the Crown on the advice of the prim minister. The Parliament's House of Assembly is elected every five years.

People

Locals of St. Vincent and the Grenadines are unusually generous and cour teous people, who have a gift for making others feel at home. A British for mality, however, still runs through their behavior, a type of gentility that i also expected of visitors. Any trace of Gallic influence is tempered by a Wes Indies flavor, which is heard in the lilt of the language as well as the spices in the food. Service at most hotels, which are generally small, is characterized by enormous personal attention and care. Little serious crime ever happens on the islands, though valuables should never be left unguarded or ostenta tiously displayed. The farther you travel into the interior, the more primitive the lifestyle.

Beaches

If you're looking for white-sand beaches, stay around Kingstown; the black ones are located around the rest of the island. Beautiful white sands can be found at **Villa Beach**, on the calm western coast. Also fine for swimming is the black **Questelle's Bay** and the black **Buccament Bay**. Dive shops are located at Villa beach and the CSY Yacht Club. The exposed Atlantic Coast is consid ered too rough for swimming, but the view of the crashing waves can be very exciting. None of the beaches here sport lifeguards, so take precautions; even

xperienced swimmers should have someone spotting them, particularly
vhen the water is rough. No beach or changing facilities are located on the
vindward side.

Underwater

For now, diving in St. Vincent and the Grenadines still appeals to the ad-
enturous spirit. The reefs remain pristine and new sites continue to be dis-
overed. As on Dominica and St. Lucia, visibility is usually excellent despite
ignificant rain runoff, because the main island's soil is mostly volcanic (and
leavier), allowing it to sink quickly to the depths rather than mucking up the
vaters. However, unlike the aforementioned destinations, St. Vincent is not
:nown for its walls. This is a place for reefs, which flourish on the tongues of
ıncient lava flows snaking into the sea, and for its extensive fish activity.
There is an abundance of smaller life, including the unusual and rare frog
ish, and frequent sightings of seahorses. Additionally, black coral, which
ısually grows deeper than recreational diving allows, is found much nearer
ea level here, in some spots as close as 27 feet below the surface. Somehow,
:hese beautiful underwater forests, whose branches come in six different colors, have not been leveled. Diving on St. Vincent is concentrated on the
iouthwestern coast, generally close to the two main operators on the island;
:he Grenadines have several dive shops, described under their respective sec-
:ions. With the notable exception of **St. Vincent Dive Experience**, diving does
10t come cheaply in this country. Four affiliated dive shops (**Dive St. Vincent**,
Dive Bequia, **Dive Canouan** and **Grenadine Dive** on Union Island) have worked
out a mix-and-match package which will appeal to island-hoppers: 10 dives
spread among the four shops for $400, including all equipment. Other pack-
ages (which lock you into one location) are also available. Snorkelers comfortable in water depths of 25 feet or more can explore each of the following
three prime locations.

The Gardens

The Gardens slope gently from 25 feet down through pillar coral and an astounding
array of reef fish. The rare and stunning cherubfish (the world's smallest angel), is
usually spotted, along with huge king crabs, gray snapper, creole wrasse and soldierfish among the diverse selection of regulars. Perfect for beginners.

New Guinea Reef

The local favorite, New Guinea begins at 25 feet and drops, sometimes steeply through vivid gorgonians, sponges, and huge sea fans up to eight feet across. A cave 80 feet down showcases all three species of black coral in a panoply of colors accented by a swarming crowd of reef fish. An overhang is home to morays, while the sandy bottom, 100 feet down, is inhabited by burrowing garden eels. An outstanding dive.

The Wrecks

In 1984, two freighters collided with each other in Kingstown's Harbor and capsized, creating an artificial reef. The Nomad's top deck rises to within 15 feet of the surface, while the 120-foot Seimstrand sits on a floor which slopes to 80 feet. The decks have begun to nurture a forest of black coral, and groupers, angels and eels now call the ships home. The two ships can easily be seen on one dive, along with an important new find: the remains of a 19th-century slave ship stirred up by Hurricane Hugo (only the second known wreck of its kind to be discovered).

Dive Shops

Dive St. Vincent

Young Island Dock; ☎ *(809) 457-4928.*
Oldest operator on the island (since 1977), featuring resort courses and entry level certifications, and handling referrals. PADI and NAUI affiliated. Two tank dive $90, including equipment. Owner Bill Tewes made it onto the local .45-cent postcard stamp.

St. Vincent Dive Experience

Villa; ☎ *(809) 457-5130.*
The island's other shop, open since 1992. Two tank dive $70, including all equipment. Groups limited to 10, with three scheduled dives daily. NAUI affiliated, with some PADI instructors, courses to Divemaster.

On Foot

Somehow, St. Vincent feels like a forgotten outpost in the Eastern Caribbean. Many tourists use the island simply as a jumping-off point for the exclusive resorts of the Grenadines, while briefly-glimpsed bare-boat charterers make up another transient portion of the tourism infrastructure. For an island of over 100,000 residents, surprisingly, St. Vincent still has the magical milieu of a backwater place, waiting to be discovered. There is a smoldering volcano, **La Soufriere** (up until recently the most actively-monitored in the Caribbean), treks into rain forests which are home to the few remaining St

'incent parrots, and several splendid waterfalls worth visiting. The Forestry
)epartment has guides to some of the island's trails, and the 1:50,000 *Ord-*
·ance Survey map is helpful for exploration. Hikers should carry insect repel-
:nt (mosquitoes are prevalent), and be prepared for rainy weather and
nuddy trails.

Mount St. Andrew

The obvious summit rising north of Kingstown, this trail follows the Mt. St.
Andrew road, which you'll locate off the main artery heading north out of Kingston
The hike begins in the tiny suburb of Lowmans and ascends the rutted track
through vegetable gardens and fields of bananas before entering the rain forest. The
trail climbs for about two-and-a-half miles to the 2413-foot summit, which provides
eye-filling views of Kingstown, the Mesopotamia Valley and the Grenadines to the
south. Bird-watching is excellent along this accessible trail; allow three hours.

La Soufriere

St. Vincent's spectacular volcanic crater, La Soufriere, was the location of a violent
1902 eruption which caused over 2000 deaths. Activity in April, 1979 deposited a
blanket of ash over the island, destroying many crops, and forced vulcanologists to
take the mountain more seriously (20,000 residents around the volcano were
quickly evacuated). Today, La Soufriere is quiet for the moment and supports two
very separate trails leading to its gaping crater. The traditional route ascends the
eastern slope: drive to Georgetown and, a few hundred feet after crossing the
Rabacca Dry River, follow the road left and up through banana and coconut plantations to the trailhead. Beginning at an elevation of about 1200 feet, it is a three-
hour, three-mile climb along an obvious path through tropical rain forest brimming
with bromeliads and tree ferns. The track eventually arrives at the lip of the crater,
3000 feet above sea level; the actual summit on the opposite side of the cone rises
to 3864 feet. If the mountain isn't enveloped in clouds, the view into the magnificent crater and around the island is breathtaking. The secondary route starts from
just north of Richmond on the western coast: the trail begins near sea level and is
longer and less-defined, ascending a muddy ravine to the rim; because it is frequently overgrown, a guide is a good idea. Ideally, hikers could ascend the less
arduous eastern slope and descend the leeward side, but this requires transportation
coordination and, again, probably the services of a guide. Allow five-to-six hours for
the actual hike, plus transportation time to the trailhead (an hour each way from
Kingstown).

Trinity Falls

Perhaps the prettiest of St. Vincent's waterfalls, Trinity is set deep in a lush canyon
below La Soufriere's western flank. The trailhead is found by driving the leeward
coast road through Chateaubelair to the Richmond Vale Academy, where a side
road leads about a mile further, eventually to become a four-wheel drive track. Follow this path into the deep valley to the falls, about a 45-minute hike. A hot spring,
which emerged after the 1979 eruption, is a recent addition to the remote canyon.

Vermont Forest Nature Trail

Your best chance to see the endangered and beautiful St. Vincent parrot lies in th
Buccament Valley above the village of Vermont, about three miles north of King
stown. The spot is so accessible, you can reach it via local bus out of Kingstown. *
well-marked trailhead leads to the one-and-a-half mile loop, which traverse
through a serene tropical rain forest on the slopes of 3000-foot Grand Bonhomme
Midway, a viewing area sometimes rewards with a glimpse of the parrot in flight; the
bird has a white head and golden brown body, with a rainbow-hued tail. The bes
time to see the parrot, numbering only about 500 in the wild, is at dawn, or late in
the afternoon.

By Pedal

Although St. Vincent's road network is hardly extensive, there are pictur
esque villages and coconut plantations lining the island's coasts which mak
for very pleasant two-wheeled excursions. A complete circuit of the island, a
is possible on most other Caribbean islands, is not feasible by road (th
maintained roads form the shape of a "U" on a map). However, the rugge
trails to La Soufriere (see On Foot) can be ridden in parts, and complete
with the bikes hoisted over your shoulders. This is a true he-man adventure
not to be taken lightly; if you originate in Kingstown, ride up one side of L
Soufriere and down the other, you are undertaking a walloping loop c
about 65 miles (including several on foot). Regardless of your ability—an
you'll need to be in terrific shape—do not attempt this trip by yourself; a
injury in the mountains would be a serious problem. A rough road travel
north from Georgetown along the windward coast to the poor and isolate
villages of Sandy Bay and Fancy. The coastline here is pummeled splendidl
by the Atlantic and relatively few tourists visit the area. In general, if yo
stick to the road closest to the shoreline, the east coast offers easier riding
than the leeward side. A splendid half-day loop trip would follow the eas
coast as far as North Union, then head inland along the Union River and
into fertile Mesopotamia Valley. From here, the road climbs steadily ove
rolling hills toward Eyry Hill (1050 feet) before descending steeply into
Kingstown. Off-roading is better on the west coast, particularly around
Palmyra, in the hills above Chateaubelair.

Bike Rental Shops

Sailor's Cycle Center

Kingstown; ☎ *(809) 457-1712.*

Rents a variety of both mountain and road bikes for $10 per day. Owner Trevor Bailey is the head of the local cycling association and leads impromptu treks into the rain forest.

What Else to See in Kingstown

As St. Vincent's capital and commercial hub, Kingstown bristles with the excitement of a busy port. A trip down to the waterfront is mandatory, to peruse all the island schooners and fishing boats delivering and exchanging goods with their colorful sails flapping in the wind. Take a pilgrimage to the 19th-century **St. Mary's Catholic Church**, which presides in the center of town, a strange concoction of architectural styles designed by a rather eccentric Flemish monk, who loved to pit Romanesque against Baroque, Gothic and Moorish styles. On the north side of town stands the remains of **Fort Charlotte** (all cabs end up there, as does every cruise passenger, it seems). The winding road there passes through lush landscape, the view from the top, at 636 feet, is superb. "Charlotte" was the wife of King George III, whose countrymen built the fortress to defend themselves against French invaders. Driving east of the fort you'll discover one of the most placid places on the island—the **Botanical Gardens**, founded in 1765, and considered the oldest in the Western hemisphere. On the grounds is a breadfruit tree grown from the seedling originally brought to the island by Captain Bligh. Here you'll also find the **National Museum**, which contains ancient Indian artifacts.

Saturday mornings, take yourself down to the southern corner of town for the weekly market that draws farmers, vendors and fishermen from all over the island to sell their exotic-looking fruits, fresh fish and interesting crafts. If you are involved in self-catering accommodations, it's a good place to pick up your weekly rations.

Historical Sites

Fort Charlotte ★ ★ ★

Kingston, ☎ *(809) 456-1830.*

Hours open: 6 a.m.–6 p.m.

Construction on this fort was started around 1791, and it was completed in 1812. It's mostly in ruins today, but well worth a visit for the stunning views from its perch some 650 feet above sea level of Kingston and the Grenadines. Check out the murals that tell the history of black Caribbeans.

Parks and Gardens

Botanical Gardens   ★★★★

> *Kingston,* ☎ *(809) 457-1003.*
>
> *Hours open: 7 a.m.–4 p.m.*
>
> Located on a hillside north of town, this 20-acre garden is the oldest in the Western Hemisphere, dating back to 1765. Among the teak, mahogany and cannonball trees and exotic plants and flowers are breadfruit trees descended from seedlings brought over by Captain Bligh in 1793. The lush grounds also include a pagoda, lily pond and the Archeological Museum, located in a West Indian house and displaying artifacts from pre-Columbian days. Admission to the gardens is free, but once there, it's well worth a couple of dollars to hire a guide for an hour-long tour. Garden lovers should also checkout **Kingston's Montreal Gardens** *(458-5452)*, which are not as well-tended.

Tours

Soufriere Volcano   ★★★★★

> *The north side.*
>
> St. Vincent's dominant feature is the Soufriere Mountains, home to a volcano that has been active for centuries. The most devastating eruption occurred in 1812 and claimed some 2000 lives. Another in 1902 created the mile-wide crater; in 1972 still another eruption created the lava rock island in the crater lake. The latest eruption, in 1979, caused thousands to evacuate but happily took no lives. Two trails climb through rainforest to the crater rim; the easiest (that's a relative term) starts 26 miles out at Kingston at Rabacca. It takes at least three hours to get to the top, though it's only a three-mile trek. Hiring a local guide is strongly advised.

Sports

Sport fishing is only in its early stages of development in these parts, though there are abundant marine life, both in the waters around St. Vincent and in the Grenadines. Deep-sea fishing, however, can be arranged through watersports operators. Better yet, talk to a local fisherman and convince him to let you go along for the day's ride. As for sailing, the Grenadines hold a world reputation for some of the best conditions in the Caribbean. Yachts can be easily chartered, holding up to 10 people. The **St. Vincent Tourist Board** has extensive information on how and from whom to charter. Most yachts come with food, drink and full facilities. If you don't know much about sailing, your best bet is to hire a yacht with crew; it's also easier and less troublesome and you can spend the time relaxing. Passengers are rou-

nely briefed before leaving the harbor and you should be prepared to ask
ny questions you need to. A full week can be spent touring the islands, with
he skipper doubling as chef and chambermaid. There is a windsurfing
hool on St. Vincent on the southern coast, and all islands in the Grena-
nes with resorts have windsurfing equipment. Horseback riding is available
nly in Mustique, at the Carlton House Hotel.

Watersports of all kinds can be arranged through hotels. Scuba certification
available on St. Bequia and St. Vincent, utilizing the terrific marine sources
the region. (For more information, see under "Dive Sites" above.) Sport
shing is not yet formally organized, but dive shops can arrange a fishing
oat; you should bring your own gear. (Spearfishing is not allowed here ex-
ept by special permission). Tennis is available on several courts on St. Vin-
ent (Prospect Racket Club, Emerald Valley Hotel and Grand View Beach
Hotel, among others. The Cotton House on Mustique also has one.) Wind-
urfing lessons are offered at the Young Island resort, as well as the Cotton
House on Mustique. There is a squash court in Kingstown at the Cyril Cyrus
quash Complex on St. James Place.

The region was made for sailing, and every effort should be made to take at
east a one-day cruise. Crafts from Sunfish to Sailfish are available for hire;
nany hotels have their own fleet. Young Island, Palm Island and Petit St.
Vincent regularly offer day sails. Bareboat and skippered yachts can be char-
ered as well on St. Vincent. An exciting sojourn would be a speedboat trip
long the western coast to the **Falls of Baleine**, a 60-foot waterfall. You can
lso sail on a 36-foot sloop, moving in slow motion, to the Falls of Baleine.

For trekking, see under "On Foot" above.

Watersports

Various locations.

Most watersports can be found at your hotel, and those staying on the Grenadines
should be amply outfitted at the exclusive resorts. Otherwise, try one of these. For
boating and cruising, call **Barefoot Yacht Charters** (☎ *456-9526)* or **Lagoon
Marina** (☎ *458-4308)*, both on St. Vincent. On Bequia, call **Frangipani Yacht Services** (☎ *458-3255)*. For scuba, call **Dive St. Vincent** (☎ *457-4714)* and **St. Vincent Dive Experience** (☎ *456-9714)*, both on St. Vincent. On Bequia, call **Dive
Bequia** (☎ *458-3504)* or **Sunsports** (☎ *458-3577)*. **Grenadines Dive** (☎ *458-
8138)* handles diving on Union Island, while **Dive Mustique** (☎ *456-3486)* takes
care of that island's needs.

Where to Stay

Fielding's Highest Rated Hotels in St. Vincent and The Grenadines

★★★★★	Young Island Resort	$160–$555
★★★★	Canouan Beach Hotel	$108–$316
★★★★	Cotton House	$225–$730
★★★★	Petit Byahut	$125–$145
★★★★	Petit St. Vinvent Resort	$210–$685
★★★★	Plantation House	$140–$330
★★★	Friendship Bay Hotel	$115–$200
★★★	Grand View Beach Hotel	$100–$335
★★★	Palm Island Beach Club	$140–$325
★★★	Saltwhistle Bay Club	$200–$340

Fielding's Most Romantic Hotels in St. Vincent and The Grenadines

★★★★	Cotton House	$225–$730
★★★	Palm Island Beach Club	$140–$325
★★★★	Petit Byahut	$125–$145
★★★★	Petit St. Vinvent Resort	$210–$685
★★★★★	Young Island Resort	$160–$555

Fielding's Budget Hotels in St. Vincent and The Grenadines

★	Kingston Park Guest House	$25–$28
★	Umbrella Beach Hotel	$38–$53
★	Julie & Isola Guesthouse	$36–$59
★	Heron Hotel	$49–$65
★	Beachcombers Hotel	$50–$75

Accommodations on St. Vincent can range anywhere from the most enchanting resorts on earth to the bare-bones primitive. You can shell out over $600 for top-class luxury, a moderate $125–$150 for two during winter (some with two meals), or a mere $450 for a bed, nightstand and place to hang the clothes. A great bargain is the 30 percent discount you can usually wrangle during the summer season. Most of the lodgings lie along the lovely south coast, a few minutes from the center of downtown Kingstown. Most do not have air conditioning and rely on the trade winds and a ceiling fan to cool the heat, quite adequately, though mosquito screens are de rigeur.

Hotels and Resorts

St. Vincent simply hasn't gone the way of the high-rise resort. The closest is the property at Young Island, which covers the entire islet, but Sunset Shores gives off the ambience of a enclosed conclave, fortunately air-conditioned, with a family ambience running through the management.

Beachcombers Hotel $50–$75 ★

P.O. Box 126, Villa Beach, ☎ (809) 458-4283, FAX (809) 458-4385.
Single: $50–$55. Double: $75.
This basic property accommodates guests in five different buildings, with all rooms air-conditioned and sporting TVs and private patios. Facilities are limited to a bar and restaurant, with watersports available on the beach.

Grand View Beach Hotel $100–$335 ★★★

P.O. Box 173, Villa Point, ☎ (809) 458-4811, FAX (809) 457-4174.
Single: $100–$215. Double: $125–$335.
A former plantation house is the focal point of this quiet property, located on a promontory overlooking a small private beach. And, as the name suggests, the views here are indeed grand. Lodgings are simple yet comfortable, and while all share the splendid views, not all have air conditioners. The hotel's eight acres include tennis and squash courts, a small pool, a health club, a reading room, and a restaurant serving West Indian fare. Don't come looking for nightlife, but do come for tranquil surroundings and friendly, family-run service.

Lagoon Marina & Hotel $80–$105 ★

P.O. Box 133, Blue Lagoon, ☎ (809) 458-4308, FAX (809) 457-4716.
Single: $80–$105. Double: $85–$105.
This simple hotel overlooks Blue Lagoon and its marina, and is often filled with sea folk. Rooms are basic and you'll pay a bit extra for air conditioning, but all have large patios nice to while away the hours on. The bar and restaurant do a brisk business with marina customers, and there's also a pool and watersports center on the black-sand beach.

Sunset Shores Beach Hotel $115–$210 ★★

849 Villa Street, Villa Beach, ☎ (809) 458-4411, FAX (809) 457-4800.
Single: $115. Double: $115–$210.
The name makes it sound something like a retirement community, but in fact this motel-like property is one of St. Vincent's few commercial hotels. Guestrooms are air-conditioned and comfortable enough; they form a horseshoe around an attrac-

tive courtyard. Facilities include a small pool, a bar and restaurant favored by locals
and nearby watersports on the beach. Kingston is some 10 minutes away.

Villa Lodge Hotel $105–$185   ★ ★

P.O. Box 1191, Indian Bay, ☎ (809) 458-4641, FAX (809) 457-4468.
Single: $105–$140. Double: $115–$185.
Set on a hillside and overlooking the sea, this converted home is popular, friendly
and family run. Guestrooms are air-conditioned and simply furnished; most have
balconies or patios. The restaurant serves West Indian fare, and the large pool is a
nice alternative to the small beach, which is easily within walking distance. The
occasional poolside barbecues attract a lot of locals and are great fun, especially
when steel bands liven things up.

Young Island Resort $160–$555   ★ ★ ★ ★ ★

Young Island, ☎ (809) 458-4826, FAX (809) 457-4567.
Single: $160–$555. Double: $250–$555.
Set on its own private island 200 yards offshore St. Vincent, this resort offers the
kind of tropical pleasures most folks have in mind when they dream of a Caribbean
vacation. In this case, the dream is restricted to those who can afford the high rates
and honeymooners blowing the bank. Accommodations are scattered along a hill
side or set on the beach, and while the pricing determines what you get, all are spa
cious, cooled by ceiling fans, tropically decorated, and have private patios. Most also
have unique rock showers that are open-air but very private. There are no phones or
TVs, the better to appreciate nature by. Facilities include a lagoon-style pool, a ten
nis court, two yachts that whisk guests over the Grenadines, a tiny, picturesque
beach, a bar and restaurant, and most watersports. The lushly landscaped 25 acres
include cages of exotic birds, a floating bar off the beach, and charming stone walk
ways and steps. Despite the high rates, the atmosphere is casual and informal; this is
not so much luxurious as it is the ultimate escape. Everyone seems to be in love, so
singles beware.

Apartments and Condominiums

Options are easy to find, since self-catering has long been a tradition on the island.
Food is readily available in the market at Kingstown, as is fresh fish. Everyone seems to
know someone who has a fishing boat—they might still be squiggling. Staples that are
strictly American-made should be brought from home, as are any special delicacies you
can't leave without.

Indian Bay Beach Hotel $55–$85   ★

Indian Bay, ☎ (809) 458-4001, FAX (809) 457-4777.
Single: $55–$60. Double: $70–$85.
This small apartment hotel offers one- and two-bedroom units with kitchens,
patios, telephones, and living and dining areas. Furnishings are simple but adequate.
Indian Bay's beach is small and rocky, but the snorkeling just off the coast is good.
There's a restaurant and bar on the premises, and the rates are certainly reasonable.

Umbrella Beach Hotel $38–$53   ★

Villa Beach, ☎ (809) 458-4651, FAX (809) 457-4930.
Single: $38–$43. Double: $48–$53.

The rates are incredibly low, and the lodgings prove that you get what you pay for, but if you're on a tight budget and want the convenience (and economy) of having a kitchenette, this may be just the spot. As noted, the rooms are very basic and rely on ceiling fans for sleeping comfort, but they are clean and the location is handy, right near the beach and several restaurants.

Inns

Most accommodations in St. Vincent come with an "inn" feeling about them. That's the nature of the St. Vincent life. Some can be found in Kingstown, others in the highlands away from the hustle of city life.

| obblestone Inn | $60–$75 | ★★ |

P.O. Box 867, ☎ *(809) 456-1937, FAX (809) 456-1938.*
Single: $60. Double: $75.
This harborside inn dates back to 1814 and was originally intended as a sugar warehouse. Guestrooms are cozy (read small) but comfortable and air-conditioned, and all have private combination baths. Request one in the back to avoid street noise, but be warned that all are rather dark. The bar and restaurant are popular with locals, and the in-town location attracts mostly business travelers. There's no pool, which is unfortunate since the beach is a 10-minute drive away.

| Kingston Park Guest House | $25–$28 | ★ |

☎ *(809) 456-1532.*
Single: $25. Double: $28.
This 18th-century plantation house, a private home, is set in a garden overlooking the town and, further out, the Grenadines. As can be expected by the rates (among the island's cheapest), the rooms are nothing too exciting, and many share baths. You'll need a car, which may offset the savings on your accommodations.

Low Cost Lodging

It is possible to find cheap lodgings in simple hotels in the Kingstown area. The style is usually West Indian, with very basic furnishings. Cleanliness is usually not a problem.

| leron Hotel | $49–$65 | ★ |

☎ *(809) 457-1631, FAX (809) 457-1189.*
Single: $49–$51. Double: $55–$65.
Located on the waterfront within walking distance of the town center, this is another of St. Vincent's economical and simple guesthouses. The rooms are very basic and quite old-fashioned, and lack modern amenities like TV but at least have air conditioners and private baths. The restaurant is similarly no-frills, but the reasonably priced meals are tasty enough.

Campgrounds

| Petit Byahut | $125–$145 | ★★★★ |

Petit Byahuat Bay, ☎ *(809) 457-7008, FAX (809) 457-7008.*
Single: $125–$140. Double: $130–$145.
The rates are high for camping, but guests are pampered at this remote spot a bit more than at your typical tent site. Set in a 50-acre valley that's reached only by boat from Kingston (included in the rates), this isolated spot accepts only 14 people at a time, and kids are not allowed. Accommodations are in large tents with wooden

floors, queen-size beds, decks, and sun-warmed showers. The rates include all meal and watersports off the black-sand beach. Dinner is served by candlelight overlook ing the bay. Inquire about weekly and scuba packages. Not for everyone, but well loved by those seeking an offbeat alternative, and the surrounding rainforest is jus gorgeous.

Where to Eat

★★★★★	Fielding's Highest Rated Restaurants in St. Vincent and The Grenadines	
★★★★★	Mac's Pizzeria	$7–$30
★★★★★	The French Restaurant	$6–$16
★★★★	Basil's Bar & Raft	$4–$28
★★★	Basil's Bar & Restaurant	$11–$15
★★★	Cobblestone Roof Top	$5–$6
★★★	Gingerbread Cafe	$4–$18
★★★	Heron Restaurant	$5–$10

	Fielding's Special Restaurants in St. Vincent and The Grenadines	
★★★★★	The French Restaurant	$6–$16
★★★★	Basil's Bar & Raft	$4–$28
★★★	Cobblestone Roof Top	$5–$6

	Fielding's Budget Restaurants in St. Vincent and The Grenadines	
★★★	Cobblestone Roof Top	$5–$6
★★★	Heron Restaurant	$5–$10
★★★	Gingerbread Cafe	$4–$18
★★★★★	The French Restaurant	$6–$16
★★★	Basil's Bar & Restaurant	$11–$15

No one visits these islands in search of the last great chef; he's not hiding out here. There is almost a unilateral menu for the island's casual cafés: a handful of West Indian dishes (callaloo soup, local fish or lobster prepared creole style), fried chicken baskets with french fries and hamburgers—what locals believe that tourists like. The most sophisticated food is found at the hotel restaurants. One island diversion is to visit as many bars as you can and make a serious study of the varieties of rum punch—each bartender take great pride in his or her own unique recipe.

Basil's Bar & Restaurant $ ★★★

Bay Street, Kingston, ☎ *(809) 457-2713.*
International cuisine.
Lunch: 10 a.m.–4 p.m., prix fixe $11.
Dinner: 4 p.m.–midnight, entrees $3–$15.

Those who can't get to Basil Charles' Fantasy Island overwater bar in Mustique make the scene at his second namesake hangout with food on the ground floor o the Cobblestone Inn. Lunchtime buzzes with hungry diners going back and forth from a tasty all-you-can-eat buffet. The spread includes salads and desserts, and a la carte burgers, sandwiches, egg dishes, and seafood are also available. Nighttime i more romantic, with candlelit tables and simple grills on the menu, plus French wines at decent prices. There's a Chinese buffet on Friday evenings.

Cobblestone Roof Top $ ★★★

Bay Street, Kingston, ☎ *(809) 456-1937.*
Latin American cuisine.
Lunch: 7:30 a.m.–3 p.m., entrees $5–$6.

Whatever business is conducted on this leisurely island is usually done at breakfas or lunchtime from this eatery atop the Cobblestone Inn. Housed in a quaint restored early 1800s-era warehouse, the restaurant serves substantial West Indian lunches along with good burgers and fish and chips.

Heron Restaurant $ ★★★

Upper Bay Street, Kingston, ☎ *(809) 457-1631.*
International cuisine.
Lunch: Noon–1:30 p.m., entrees $5–$10.
Dinner: 7–10 p.m., prix fixe $5–$10.

A friendly local couple run this budget hotel and restaurant that's popular with residents for American bacon and eggs breakfasts. Lunch features soups, salads, and sandwiches, and a soup-to-nuts supper is served daily for a set price. Market fresh vegetables are a standout. There's always a lot of action here, and reservations are required for dinner.

The French Restaurant $$ ★★★★★

Villa Beach, Villa Beach, ☎ *(809) 458-4972.*
French cuisine. Specialties: Lobster.
Lunch: 7 a.m.–9 p.m., entrees $6–$14.
Dinner: 7–9:30 p.m., entrees $8–$16.

Behind a homey white picket fence lies an excellent restaurant that dazzles with its simplicity. Guests sit on plain folding chairs, feet planted on rough wooden floors in a windowless structure open to salty breezes. Succulent lobster couldn't get much fresher, retrieved as they are live from an on-site pool. The Parisian chef serves the juicy crustaceans flambeed in brandy, sliced in crepes, or broiled. All dishes are prepared with island-grown herbs and spices. The dining room overlooks Villa Beach and Young Island.

Where to Shop

St. Vincent and the Grenadines is simply not a paradise for shoppers—there is no duty-free sport— but there are some interesting handicrafts to be discovered. Batiks and tie-died fabrics are the province of **Batik Caribe**, a famous name in the Caribbean. The **St. Vincent Craftsman** is a cooperative featuring the work of local artisans; the quality rates among the best crafts in the Caribbean. Many of the crafts represented here are a revival of very ancient techniques, rejuvenated through an unusual program sponsored by the United Nations. If you're headed down the road leading from the banana-boat docks, stop at the shop on the **Old Cotton Ginnery**; while you're there, ask about how you can visit some of the artists in their own homes in the countryside. Other crafts can be found at **Noah's Arkade**, next to the Batik Caribe, where you can also pick up history books about the West Indies. Drop by the local markets to pick up a few bottles of sun-dried peanuts (great for the beach) and local spices. West Indian hot sauce is infamous for making eyes run. Philatelists will adore picking up a bunch of colorful stamps of the islands, available at the post office.

The Grenadines
Bequia

Bequia (BECK-we), a three-hour schooner-run from Union, is a chain of islets between St. Vincent and Grenada attracting escapists of all kinds– from advertising execs who live in homes carved from caves to writers and painters in search of a last-ditch inspiration. It has a great natural beauty, warm, small world flavor, and an endearing innocence; everyone here seems to have a cousin who works on a ship or tanker. (Every time a Bequia grandmother has to visit her offspring on the mainland of St. Vincent, she has to brave the choppy seas on the two islands.) Port Elizabeth's main street bordering Admiralty Bay is but a a few blocks of pavement, then turns into footpath weaving past shops and small hotels and restaurants under the canopy of trees at the water's edge. Long a favorite of Caribbean insiders and yachties, the island was accessible only by boat until mid-1992 when an airport accommodating small planes was built. Some visitors, especially Americans, return to Bequia yearly. Local buses will get you around— actually, just pickup trucks with benches built into the truck bed with a canvas roof. On small islands, your hotel will probably give you a lift. Main beaches are **Friendship Bay**, **Lower Bay** and **Spring Bay**, the latter graced by restless coconut palms. Each has a restaurant or snack bar and sometimes even beach chairs.

In general, Bequia is a place for shuffling between beach and bed, pool to beach, from bar to bar to dinner. The best way to sightsee is to stroll around with your intuitive antennae out for a good round of spontaneous adventure. No major fortresses or historical plantations, but there are some interesting shops including the **Crab Hole Island** (artifacts), **Melinda's** (original handprints), **Maurice's Model Boat Shop** (model boat making is a renowned Bequia craft), the **Bequia Sailing Club** (distinctive T-shirts), the **Wearable Art Shop** and the **Bequia Bookstore**.

To get to Bequia, you can either arrive by small plane via LIAT, or by boat from Kingstown, St. Vincent. The mail boat is an option as is any one of a number of motor launches or chartered yachts.

Bequia Underwater

With its western coast part of a marine park, Bequia features several excellent dive locations, all within a few minutes of the main boat dock. **Devil's Table** is a flat reef sitting in Bequia's harbor, with channels of sand amid the coral structure; terrific detail, including occasional frog fish and sea horses. **The Wall** is a sheer, dramatic plunge from a ledge at 30 feet to a sandy floor 120 feet down, while **The Boulders** is a delightful drift dive among coral encrusted monoliths.

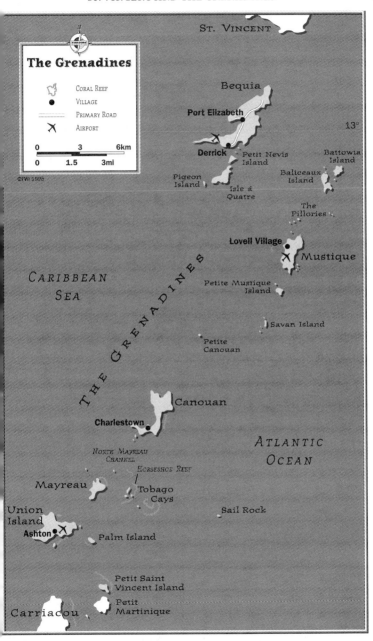

The Grenadines

CORAL REEF
VILLAGE
PRIMARY ROAD
AIRPORT

0   3   6km
0   1.5   3mi

©FWI 1998

ST. VINCENT

Bequia

Port Elizabeth

13°

Derrick   Petit Nevis   Battowia
                Island   Island

Pigeon   Baliceaux
Island   Island

        Isle à
        Quatre

                The
                Pillories

Lovell Village

                    Mustique
CARIBBEAN
        Petite Mustique
SEA   Island

                    Savan Island

THE GRENADINES

        Petite
        Canouan

                Canouan

Charlestown

ATLANTIC
NORTH MAYREAU
CHARLES
                OCEAN
        HORSESHOE REEF

Mayreau   Tobago
                Cays

Union   Sail Rock
Island
Ashton   Palm Island

        Petit Saint
        Vincent Island

        Petit
Carriacou   Martinique

Dive Bequia

Port Elizabeth; ☎ *(809) 458-3504.*

Bob Sachs conducted much of the original dive exploration in and around Bequia opening his shop in 1983. PADI and NAUI affiliated, with courses to Divemaster Two tank dive, $75 with your own equipment (or $85 without).

On Foot in Bequia

In Bequia, hikes from Admiralty Bay lead over unpaved roads and foot paths, but are relatively easy, and arrive at such places as **Mt. Pleasant**, where there is a spectacular view of Bequia. A favored destination also is Hope Bay where the waves are good for body surfing. The northern part of the island covered with gentle hills good for hiking; in the central and southern sections, more mountainous areas give hikers a chance to view incredible vistas There are no roads or cars on Mayreau, but from the bay you can take a track to the tiny hilltop village in the center of the island; here you can see a great view of **Tobago Cays**. Tobago Cays is considered one of the most serene paradises in the Caribbean—four uninhabited islets ringed by pure white beaches and clear blue waters. From a beach anywhere here, you can walk/paddle to see clusters of tropical fish swimming through the coral gardens. **Petit Rameau**, the northernmost cay, has a short trail through heavy mangrove along a sandy beach.

Sports in Bequia

The **Frangipani** and **Plantation House** hotels have fully equipped dive facilities. You can also find windsurfing and sunfish sailing in **Admiralty Bay** and snorkeling around **Spring** and **Friendship Bays**. To find a new beach, hop on water taxi to **Lower Bay**. Or rent a bicycle at the **Almond Tree** boutique and toot over to Spring or Friendship Bay. Evening entertainment revolve around whichever hotel is sponsoring a jump-up, a beach barbecue with bamboo bands and vigorous, sexy dancing.

Where to Stay

Lodging in Bequia is geared for total relaxation. Nearly each property is unique and exudes a certain personal ambiance. Prices for rooms are not exorbitant and many are within a reasonable range.

Hotels and Resorts

Accommodations range from the very expensive Plantation House, a series of 1, 2, and 3 bedroom cottages, to the still expensive Spring on Bequia, a 200-year-old working plantation house to relatively inexpensive **Blue Tropic Apartments** ☎ *(809) 458-3573* with kitchens and balconies overlooking Friendship Bay.

Friendship Bay Hotel   **$115–$200**   ★★★

Friendship Bay, ☎ *(809) 458-3222, FAX (809) 458-3840.*
Single: $115–$130. Double: $130–$200.

Set on a palm-studded cove and a sandy beach, this casual complex provides motel-like lodging in stone buildings scattered around picturesque grounds. The rooms are basic but comfortable enough, with ceiling fans, private baths and verandas. Facilities include a bar and restaurant popular with locals, a watersports center (some rentals are complimentary), and a tennis court. The weekly barbecues and jump-ups are not to be missed, and the beach is quite fine.

antation House $140–$330   ★★★★

P.O. Box 16, Belmont Backway, Admiralty Bay, ☎ *(809) 458-3425, FAX (809) 458-3612.*
Single: $140–$245. Double: $185–$330.

Located on 10 handsome acres, this property's focal point is the pretty colonial-style main house with a wide veranda on three sides, a great place for people watching and gazing at the harbor. Accommodations are in the main house, cottages, and (relatively) deluxe cabanas. Those in the main house are air-conditioned, while the rest rely on ceiling fans and sea breezes. All are nicely done and quite comfortable. There's a pool, tennis court, health club, restaurant and beach bar on the premises, and a dive shop and watersports center on the beach. Inquire about dive and sailing packages.

ring on Bequia $75–$195   ★★★

Spring Bay, ☎ *(809) 458-3414, FAX (809) 457-3305.*
Single: $75–$180. Double: $95–$195.

Set on a hillside on the grounds of a 200-year-old working plantation, this rather isolated spot practically oozes tranquillity. Don't come here for the beach life, the nearest one is 10 minutes away and nothing great, but do come if you're looking for a true escape in pastoral surroundings. Lodging is found in three stone and shingle buildings; all rooms are clean and comfortable, and kept cool by constant breezes. There's a tennis court and pool on-site, and the Sunday curry buffet is a popular hit.

Apartments and Condominiums

It's always a good idea to fully check out a property before committing yourself to it. s such, it's best to save the self-catering option until your second visit to Bequia, or at ast station yourself at a hotel and investigate the possibilities. There are numerous pri-te homes that are rented in the owner's absence; some are quite luxurious; others sim-er with adequate kitchen facilities.

Inns

rangipani Hotel $30–$130   ★★

Frangipani Beckway, Admiralty Bay, ☎ *(809) 458-3255, FAX (805) 458-3824.*
Single: $30–$130. Double: $80–$130.

This small inn dates back to 1920 and was once the childhood home of the island's current prime minister. Guestrooms are found in the main building, a New England-style house, or in superior garden units in the rear. All are simply furnished and rely on fans to keep things cool and mosquito netting over the beds to keep the pests at bay. Not all have a private bath. The beach is a 10-minute walk and there's no pool, but you can swim in the harbor. Facilities are limited to a restaurant, bar, tennis court and watersports center. Nice for casual types.

Low Cost Lodging

The cheapest lodging is found in simple guesthouses. Ask the tourist board for assistance.

Julie & Isola Guesthouse   **$36–$59**

P.O. Box 12, Port Elizabeth, ☎ (809) 458-3304, FAX (809) 458-3812.
Single: $36. Double: $59.

It's as basic as basic can be, which explains the rates, but the rooms, located in two buildings, are clean, though they can be uncomfortably hot. Not all have private baths, and showers are not always hot. Facilities are limited to a bar and small restaurant serving up good West Indian fare.

Where to Eat

No great claims to chefdom here, but do get ready for home-style island cooking with lots of fresh seafood. Most of the eating places are along the waterfront within walking distance of each other.

Gingerbread Cafe   **$$**   ★★

P.O. Box 1, Gingerbread Complex, Admiralty Bay, ☎ (809) 458-3800.
International cuisine.
Lunch: entrees $4–$10.
Dinner: 7:30-6:30 p.m., entrees $4–$18.

This cute Hansel and Gretelish stone cottage is the place to go for Italian coffee, puckery-fresh limeade and fruit juices, and the appropriate cakes and breads to go with them. Sit here at leisure all day at an outdoor table with a book and gaze out at the activity in the harbor. Next door, the Gingerbread Restaurant serves full meals and sandwiches, and is a nice spot for happy hour rum drinks and music.

Mac's Pizzeria   **$$$**   ★★★★

Box 23, Belmont Beach, Port Elizabeth, ☎ (809) 458-3474.
International cuisine. Specialties: Lobster Pizza.
Lunch: 11 a.m.-4 p.m., entrees $7–$30.
Dinner: 4-10 p.m., entrees $7–$30.

Bequia veterans daydream about the 15-inch lobster pizzas that this terraced restaurant is famous for. Besides the dream pies, Mac's homebakes all its scrumptious breads and bakery goods, and the banana bread, plump with raisins and flavored with rum, is especially toothsome. The menu also features East Indian samosas (fried pastries stuffed with curried vegetables or meats), crunchy conch nuggets, and chunky pita bread sandwiches. This place is a winner.

Where to Shop

Bequia isn't a shopper's fantasy, but you can discover a number of stores featuring various handicrafts and unusual clothing. Visit **Crab Hole**, next to the Plantation House, to watch cotton fabrics being silk-screened. **Garden Boutique** in Port Elizabeth features stunning batik dresses and hand-dyed blouses. Local artwork can be found at **Made in the Shade** in Port Elizabeth. At **Mauvin's Model Boat Shop** you can order a model made of your yacht.

Canouan

Where to Stay

Hotels and Resorts

nouan Beach Hotel   **$108–$316**   ★★★★

Canouan Beach, ☎ *(809) 458-8888, FAX (809) 458-8875.*
Single: $108–$316. Double: $249–$316.

This all-inclusive resort is located on a peninsula on the island's west side. Accommodations are in nicely furnished bungalows that have air conditioners and patios. Facilities include a very good restaurant, large bar, tennis court and watersports. The beach is really pretty and a catamaran takes guests to neighboring islands at no extra charge. The rates include all meals, drinks and activities, but those not speaking French may feel left out. Though it has only 43 rooms, this is St. Vincent's largest and most modern resort.

Mayreau

Where to Stay

Hotels and Resorts

ltwhistle Bay Club   **$200–$340**   ★★★

Mayreau, ☎ *(809) 493-9609.*
Single: $200–$300. Double: $300–$340.

This casual hideaway is the island's only lodging choice. Guests are housed in spacious, one-bedroom stone bungalows that rely on ceiling fans to keep things cool. The setting is idyllic—lovely tropical grounds, fine sandy beaches, and a crystal-clear that well-appreciated by divers. Facilities include a bar, restaurant and most watersports free of charge, though you'll pay extra for scuba and catamaran excursions to neighboring islands. There's virtually nothing in the way of nightlife; this spot has an early-to-bed, early-to-rise charm.

Mustique

Where to Stay

Hotels and Resorts

otton House   **$225–$730**   ★★★★

☎ *(809) 456-4777, FAX (809) 456-5887.*
Single: $225–$730. Double: $225–$730.

Built on the remains of an old sugar plantation, this deluxe operation is Mustique's only hotel, and it's quite lovely (and pricey). Guests are accommodated in elegant cottages that house standard guestrooms, junior suites, or full suites, all nicely decorated and sporting balconies or patios. The grounds include a highly regarded restaurant, bar, two beaches and most watersports at no extra charge. Horseback

riding can be arranged, and there's also a pool, two tennis courts, and occasion
live bands. This exclusive spot pampers guests and attracts the well-heeled set.

Apartments and Condominiums

Mustique Villas $2500–$15,000 per wk. ★★

☎ (800) 225-4255, (809) 458-4621, FAX (809) 456-4565.

These 38 privately owned villas are located on Mustique's northern end. Sever
were designed by Oliver Messel, the late architect and stage designer. Each is ind
vidually decorated and has from one to six bedrooms and full kitchens. Each
staffed with a maid, cook and gardener, and the rates include free use of a Lan
Rover. Rates are on a weekly basis and range from a low of $2500 to a high «
$15,000 for the five- and six-bedroom mansions. One of the pools belongs to Pri
cess Margaret!

Where to Eat

Basil's Bar & Raft $$$ ★★★

Britannia Bay, Mustique, ☎ (809) 458-4621.
International cuisine.
Lunch: entrees $4–$26.
Dinner: entrees $4–$28.

Basil's is not just a bar, it's a way of life. Possibly the most beautiful watering ho
in the world, this unique establishment is a thatch-roofed structure built over th
turquoise waters of Britannia Bay in Mustique. Owner Basil Charles has a grea
thing going; this is the only nightlife spot on the island. Everyone ends up her
sooner or later, including titled lords and ladies and *People* magazine cover girls an
boys. There's good seafood served daily and a $28 barbecue on Wednesday night
It's open from 10:00 am until the last guest goes home.

Palm Island

Where to Stay

Hotels and Resorts

Palm Island Beach Club $140–$325 ★★

Palm Island, ☎ (809) 458-8824, FAX (809) 458-8804.
Single: $140–$205. Double: $215–$325.

Located on its own private 130-acre island, this is another of the Grenadines' para
dise-on-Earth choices. It's not cheap, but the rates are much more affordable tha
some of the nation's other tropical resorts, and this spot remains popular for it
lovely grounds and fine hospitality. Accommodations are in 12 duplex cottages an
eight villas, all very comfortable and cooled by ceiling fans. The resort boasts fiv
lovely beaches, where watersports await (most cost extra). There's also a good res
taurant, bar, and tennis court, and supervised activities for kids.

Petit St. Vincent

Where to Stay

Hotels and Resorts

Petit St. Vincent Resort $210–$685   ★ ★ ★ ★

Petit St. Vincent, ☎ (809) 458-8801.
Single: $210–$530. Double: $435–$685.
Another of the Grenadines' private islands-turned-resorts, this deluxe property is surrounded by white, sandy beaches and an impossibly clear sea. Accommodations are in large one-bedroom wood and stone cottages with large and luxurious baths. If you want room service, hoist a yellow flag; if you prefer privacy, raise the red one. The rates include most watersports, and there's also a tennis court, fitness trail and weekly entertainment. The emphasis here is on privacy, and those who can afford it return again and again.

Union Island

Union Island is 3520 acres in size and attracts many American and Europeans, especially French, who are ready to fish, dive, beachcomb and sail. Many land at the airstrip and walk to the adjacent dock of the posh Anchorage Yacht Club, where they board their charter or private boats. Not much happens in tiny Clifton, so head outside town to deserted **Big Sand Beach** and to the crest of **Fort Hill** with its magnificent view. Trekkers are attracted to the jagged, slab-faced mountainous slopes, especially the 999-foot-high **Mt. Tabor**, the Grenadines' highest peak. A foot trail leading inland from Ashton around Rock Fall ends up in Chatham Bay.

Union Island Underwater

Although Union Island offers good snorkeling and decent diving, the best sites are just a couple miles away, off **Tobago Cays** and **Mayreau Island**. One area, named **Mayreau Gardens**, allows three different drift dives of intermediate difficulty; the strong current discourages fishermen from visiting the reef. There is an excellent wreck, the *HMS Purina*, a 140-foot English gunship which went down in 1918 just off Mayreau. Much of its superstructure is still intact, and with a maximum depth of just 40 feet, the site is terrific for beginners. For experienced divers, ten miles east of Union Island is **Sail Rock**, a dynamic and isolated location which requires very calm seas to visit; the rock outcrop draws barracudas by the dozens and a plethora of nurse sharks. **Horseshoe Reef**, which wraps around the Tobago Cays, offers superb snorkeling.

Grenadines Dive
Clifton; ☎ (809) 458-8138.

Owner Glenroy Adams, a NAUI instructor, has been on Union Island since 1988. His staff is all PADI, with courses to Divemaster. Two-tank dive, $90, including equipment. Dives Mayreau Island and Tobago Cays.

Where to Stay

Anchorage Yacht Club $95–$165 ★★

Union Island, ☎ (809) 458-8221, FAX (809) 458-8365.
Single: $95–$165. Double: $95–$165.

Most who come to this motel-like property are en route to the Grenadines, though this is a decent-enough spot to while away your entire vacation. Guestrooms are spacious and air conditioned and have nice harbor views off the balconies. The twice-weekly jump-ups are well attended; the fine restaurant and bar keep guests occupied the rest of the time. The hotel sits right on a nice beach, where a dive shop handles watersports rentals. There's also a shark pool on the premises, as well as a busy marina.

St. Vincent Directory

ARRIVAL AND DEPARTURE

The departure tax from St. Vincent and the Grenadines is U.S. $6 (E.C. $15). A 5 percent government tax is added to all hotel and restaurant bills. Hotels regularly add a 10 percent service charge. If a 10 percent service charge is not added to your restaurant check, it would be very acceptable (and expected) for you to do so.

BUSINESS HOURS

Most shops open weekdays 8 a.m.–noon and 1–4 p.m., Saturday 8 a.m.–noon. Banks open Monday–Thursday 8 a.m.–1 or 3 p.m. and Friday 8 a.m.–5 p.m. Some banks take a two-hour break from 1–3 p.m. on Friday.

CLIMATE

Temperatures all year round are around 78–80 degrees F, cooled by gentle northeast trade window. Rain is heavier in the mountains of St. Vincent than in the Grenadines, which are generally flatter. Hurricanes can ravish the islands in the fall, while summers attract high humidity. Mosquito repellent is a must between July to November.

DOCUMENTS

U.S. and Canadian citizens must have a passport; all visitors must hold return or ongoing tickets. Visas are not required.

ELECTRICITY

Current runs 220/40 v. 50 cycles.

GETTING AROUND

Island roads are like roller coasters, so if you're not used to such challenging driving, you're probably better off hiring a taxi to get around.

Potholes are everywhere and increase the possibility of accidents and car damage.

Taxis fares run about $3–$4 around Kingstown, $8 from Kingstown to Villa Beach. A good way to see the island is to hire a taxi by the hour (about $15). Rates are fixed by the government, but most drivers try to get twice as much.

Public buses in the form of minivans are the cheapest way to get around; they tend to be boisterous, noisy and crowded, and full of local color. All you need to do is wave at the driver and he will stop for you. The terminal is at Market Square in Kingstown.

Rental cars run about $45–$50 a day. Driving is on the left. Since roads are not well maintained, do get as many directions as possible before you get behind the wheel. You might even take a minibus tour of the island first to get acquainted with the potholes. To rent a car, you will need a Vincentian license, unless you already have an international license.

LANGUAGE

English is spoken everywhere, often with a Vincentian patois or dialect.

MEDICAL EMERGENCIES

The government hospital, called **General Hospital** ☎ *(809) 61185*, is located at the west end of Kingstown. There is also **Bequia Casualty Hospital** at Port Elizabeth ☎ *(809) 83294*.

MONEY

The official currency is the Eastern Caribbean dollar, although U.S. and Canadian dollars are accepted at all but the smallest shops. Most establishments would prefer to take the Eastern Caribbean dollar. When quoted a price, make sure you know what dollar is being referred to. You can get a slightly higher exchange rate at banks; hotels are notoriously low and sometimes charge a fee.

TELEPHONE

The area code for St. Vincent and the Grenadines is *809*. At press time, only AT&T offered direct dial to the area, but check with the Sprint and the MCI offices in your area to verify the latest service. Before dialing other countries from St. Vincent, ask the operator; sometimes there are special codes. Also verify in advance the probable cost, surcharge and government tax; your hotel will probably also add another fee, which can send the bill sky-high. When dialing a local number from your hotel, you can drop the 45-prefix. Few hotels have phones in the rooms.

TIME

Atlantic Standard Time, one hour ahead of New York time, except during Daylight Saving Time, when it is the same.

TIPPING AND TAXES

Hotels tend to add 10–15 percent service charge. If so, you won't be expected to tip chambermaids as well, but the gesture is always appreciated. Restaurants usually charge 10 percent for service. Tip taxi drivers 10 percent of the fare.

TOURIST INFORMATION

The **St. Vincent Department of Tourism** is located at Administrative Centre, Bay St., Kingstown, ☎ *(809) 457-1502*. Stop by and pick up brochures on lodging and sightseeing options. The St. Vincent and the Grenadines tourist guide called *Escape* contains useful tips and suggestions for excursions. The office is only open Monday–Friday.

Bequia has its own office on the waterfront in Port Elizabeth, ☎ *(809) 458-3286*, closed on Saturday afternoons. In the U.S. call ☎ *(212) 687-4981*.

WHEN TO GO

Carnival is a huge week-long celebration in early July, one of the most fantastic parties in the entire eastern Caribbean. Here you'll be able to witness and participate in calypso and steel-band competitions. Do be around when the queen and king of Carnival are crowned, a spectacular event.

ST. VINCENT AND THE GRENADINES HOTELS	RMS	RATES	PHONE	CR. CARDS
Bequia				
★★★★ Plantation House	25	$140–$330	(809) 458-3425	A, D, MC, V
★★★ Friendship Bay Hotel	27	$115–$200	(809) 458-3222	A, D, MC, V
★★★ Spring on Bequia	10	$75–$195	(809) 458-3414	A, MC, V
★★ Frangipani Hotel	15	$30–$130	(809) 458-3255	A, D, MC, V
★ Julie & Isola Guesthouse	20	$36–$59	(809) 458-3304	None
Canouan				
★★★★ Canouan Beach Hotel	43	$108–$316	(809) 458-8888	A, CB, DC, MC, V
Mustique				
★★★★ Cotton House	20	$225–$730	(809) 456-4777	A, DC, MC, V
★★★ Mustique Villas			(800) 225-4255	A, DC, MC, V
St. Vincent				
Kingstown				
★★★★★ Young Island Resort	29	$160–$555	(809) 458-4826	A, D, MC, V
★★★★ Petit Byahut		$125–$145	(809) 457-7008	None

ST. VINCENT AND THE GRENADINES HOTELS	RMS	RATES	PHONE	CR. CARDS
★★★ Grand View Beach Hotel	19	$100–$335	(809) 458-4811	A, MC, V
★★ Cobblestone Inn	19	$60–$75	(809) 456-1937	A, MC, V
★★ Sunset Shores Beach Hotel	32	$115–$210	(809) 458-4411	A, D, MC, V
★★ Villa Lodge Hotel	10	$105–$185	(809) 458-4641	A, D, MC, V
★ Beachcombers Hotel	12	$50–$75	(809) 458-4283	A, MC, V
★ Heron Hotel	15	$49–$65	(809) 457-1631	D, MC, V
★ Indian Bay Beach Hotel	14	$55–$85	(809) 458-4001	A, D, MC, V
★ Kingstown Park Guest House	20	$25–$28	(809) 456-1532	None
★ Lagoon Marina & Hotel	19	$80–$105	(809) 458-4308	A, MC, V
★ Umbrella Beach Hotel	9	$38–$53	(809) 458-4651	A, DC, MC, V
The Grenadines				
★★★★ Petit St. Vincent Resort	22	$210–$685	(809) 458-8801	None
★★★ Palm Island Beach Club	24	$140–$325	(809) 458-8824	A, D, MC, V
★★★ Saltwhistle Bay Club	10	$200–$340	(809) 493-9609	None
★★ Anchorage Yacht Club	10	$95–$165	(809) 458-8221	D, MC, V

ST. VINCENT AND THE GRENADINES RESTAURANTS	PHONE	ENTREE $	CR. CARDS
Bequia			
International			
★★★★★ Mac's Pizzeria	(809) 458-3474	$7–$30	MC, V
★★★ Gingerbread Cafe	(809) 458-3800	$4–$18	A, MC, V
St. Vincent			
Kingstown			
French			
★★★★★ The French Restaurant	(809) 458-4972	$6–$16	A, MC, V
International			
★★★ Basil's Bar & Restaurant	(809) 457-2713	$11–$15	A, MC, V
★★★ Heron Restaurant	(809) 457-1631	$5–$10	None

ST. VINCENT AND THE GRENADINES RESTAURANTS	PHONE	ENTREE $	CR. CARDS
Latin American			
★★★ **Cobblestone Roof Top**	(809) 456-1937	$5–$6•	A, MC, V
Mustique			
International			
★★★★ **Basil's Bar & Raft**	(809) 458-4621	$4–$28	A, MC, V

Note: • Lunch Only

       •• Dinner Only

TOBAGO

The quiet turquoise waters of Tobago are great for snorkeling.

The sister island of nearby Trinidad, Tobago remains largely unknown, though its assets, cultural to ecological, are more than fantastic. Whereas Trinidad is emboldened by the rhythms and harmonies of steel pan bands, Tobago runs to the more subtle natural sounds of the jungle and countryside. The proximity to South America has given Tobago its Latin-based heritage that, combined with African, East Indian, Chinese and European influences, have created a rich cultural stew. And it's a heritage evident in every aspect of life, from the look of the people to the musical cadences of the language to the spicy flavors of the cuisine. A favored destination for South Americans and Europeans as well as Trinidadians, Tobago has remained somewhat a secret to North Americans, though that is beginning to

change. What has saved Tobago from overdevelopment is 24,700 acres o
rain forest set aside in 1765 by British growers, who intuitively realized mor
than 200 years ago that there was a connection between the amount of avail
able water for crops and the number of standing trees. As such, the natura
resources of Tobago have been ably preserved, today embodying a kind o
frozen Fujichrome beauty—from rolling fields of tall, stately coconut palm
swaying in the wind to steep, thickly overgrown, emerald-green hills, to th
bright hues of fishing boats anchored on beaches that range in color fron
pale vanilla to rich butterscotch. If you stay in Trinidad, don't hesitate t
take the ferry to Tobago, which, incidentally, has the best beaches in the re
gion. The proliferations of plant, animal and reptile life residing within th
island's several nature reserves make marvelous opportunities for ornitholo
gists and biologists who can indulge in miles and miles of trekking. Diver
should not miss the stupendous experience of swimming with Atlanti
manta rays, usually dangerous marine creatures that have been subtly traine
by locals to carry humans on their backs.

Bird's Eye View

Tobago, 27 miles by seven miles wide, lies in the extreme southeastern cor
ner of the Caribbean, just 70 miles from Venezuela, on the northeasterr
shoulder of South America. It is separated from Trinidad by a narrow chan
nel less than 20 miles wide; by plane the trip takes a mere 12 minutes. From
the lowlands of the southwest end (home to Scarborough, Tobago's capita
and center of population) the island slowly climbs in elevation until it reach
es the northeast end. Here, the hills form steep, thickly jungled slopes pop
ulated by a wide variety of parrots and other birds. The end of this island is a
popular with bird-watchers as it is with divers. Divers will be happy to know
that the island is surrounded by fringing and patch reefs that take a broad va
riety of forms, including rolling fields of coral, sloping coral walls, huge
blocks of invertebrate, and sponge-encrusted stone with offshore rock struc
tures and pinnacles.

The island's development is concentrated in the southwestern corner,
where visitors will find long, palm-lined stretches of beaches and a sea made
for scuba, diving, waterskiing, wind surfing and snorkeling, especially at the
spectacular **Buccoo Reef**, a shallow-water spot about a half-mile offshore. But
the remaining two-thirds of the island is relatively untouched. Mountains

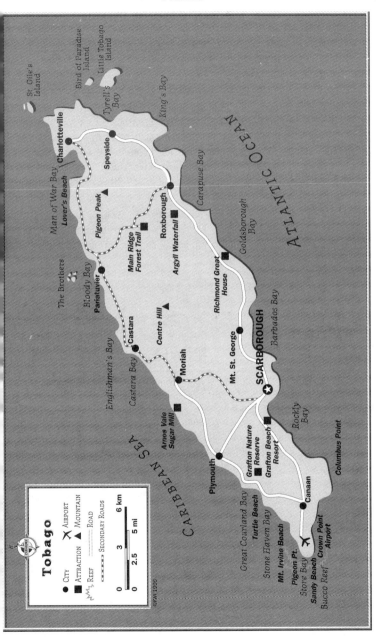

Tobago

- City
- Attraction
- Airport
- Mountain
- Reef
- Road
- Secondary Roads

| 0 | 3 | 6 km |
| 0 | 2.5 | 5 mi |

St. Giles's Island

Bird of Paradise Island

Little Tobago Island

Man of War Bay

Lover's Beach

Charlotteville

Tyrrel's Bay

King's Bay

Speyside

The Brothers

Bloody Bay

Parlatuvier

Pigeon Peak

Main Ridge Forest Trail

Roxborough

Argyll Waterfall

Carapuse Bay

ATLANTIC OCEAN

Englishman's Bay

Castara

Centre Hill

Richmond Great House

Goldsborough Bay

Castara Bay

Moriah

Mt. St. George

SCARBOROUGH

Barbados Bay

CARIBBEAN SEA

Arnos Vale Sugar Mill

Rockly Bay

Columbus Point

Grafton Nature Reserve

Plymouth

Grafton Beach Resort

Great Courland Bay

Turtle Beach

Canaan

Stone Haven Bay

Mt. Irvine Beach

Pigeon Pt.

Store Bay

Sandy Beach

Crown Point Airport

Bucco Reef

rise to 1900 feet; hiking trails weave through stands of giant ferns, bamboo and calabash and saman trees. Farms and plantations of brilliant green do the deeply indented coastlines. Fishing villages drowse in the sun, their brightly painted pirogues hauled up on beaches beneath coconut palms and sea grapes.

Several areas in Tobago have been designated as protected reserves or sanctuaries. The rain forest of the **Main Ridge** is the oldest forest reserve in the western hemisphere, dating back to 1764. Another important sanctuary is **Little Tobago Island**, which lies just offshore from the fishing village of Speyside. Here can be found important nesting grounds for an enormous number of species, including Audubon's shearwater, the red-footed booby, the sooty fern, the red-billed tropic-bird and at least 600 species of butterflies—a lepidopterists's dream.

Renovations and new constructions in recent years have spruced up Tobago's tourist facilities. A monster runway now makes it simple for visitors to arrive from Trinidad. In July 1992, a $20 million terminal for cruise ships was inaugurated in Scarborough.

History

Most historians believe Tobago was discovered by Columbus in 1498, who supposedly dubbed it "Bella Forma" (beautiful form). Its present name was derived from the word tobacco, which the native Caribs cultivated. In 1642 a Baltic duke received permission to settle a number of Courlanders on the north side of the island, but the Dutch took over in 1658, remaining in control until 1662. For the next few centuries the island changed hands at least a dozen times among world powers who considered the island a treasure worth fighting for. Not only the Dutch, but the French and English fought each other for control, not to mention pirate invasions and settlers from Latvia. Some of the conflicts had the stuff of legend about them. Bloody Bay, on the island's west coast, earned its name after a 17th-century clash between combined French and Dutch forces against a British fleet (the latter was the victor). History records that the battle was so "sanguinary" that the water became red with blood. In another ferocious struggle, more than 1700 lives were lost in the battle of Roodklyn Bay, fought between the Dutch and the French. Eventually Tobago was declared neutral territory and promptly became a haven for pirates and treasure hunters. (In fact, rumors of easure still buried on Pirate's Bay abound today.) During the early 19th century, Tobago was a leading contender in the British and French sugar-cane industry, producing more sugar per square acre than any other island. When the sugar industry went bust, Tobago also went bankrupt, and in 1888 the island was tacked to nearby Trinidad by a British colonial government that didn't know what to do with it. In 1962, both islands gained independence from Britain and became a republic within the Commonwealth in 1976. Today Tobago has its own 12-seat House of Assembly, which runs many local services. (For more information, also read the history section in the Trinidad chapter.)

People

Tobago's population numbers about 51,000; about 90 percent of Tobagonians are of African descent, and their food, folklore, music and religion are all African-based. Although the official language on both islands is English, Tobagonians speak with a more lilting, softer accent than Trinidadians. In general, locals on Tobago are extremely friendly and helpful, and perhaps because the island's economy depends on tourism, visitors seem to receive special attention. There is also much less crime on Tobago than on Trinidad. Linguistically original, Tobagonians have invented their own rich local idioms, among them: *beat pan* (play the steel pan); *free up* (relax); *dougla* (a person of mixed Indian and African parentage); *maco* (a person who minds other people's businesses); and *lime* (spend time talking, laughing and watching the girls or boys go by).

About two-fifths of Trinidad and Tobago's people are descended from India, and major Hindu and Muslim festivals are recognized as public holidays. "Eid mubarak!" is the official greeting for Eidul-Fitr on March 14, marking the end of the Ramadan during which Muslims observe a daytime fast. Muslims celebrate this day by fasting and going to the mosque to say prayers, as well as giving alms to the poor. During this time, there is much hospitality extended, even to foreigners, homes are cleaned and decorated, and lavish meals mark the end of the abstinence. In November thousands of tiny deyas (clay pots with oil-fueled wicks) appear in parks and sidewalks to mark the Hindu Festival of Divali, in honor of Lakshmi, the goddess of light and beauty. If you drive through the towns and villages at sunset, you will find them transformed into a gentle wonderland. One of the most beautiful festivals to witness takes place on March 27, marking the Hindu New Year in India and the arrival of spring. Singing groups gather in villages and temples to perform the festive choral songs, and bonfires are lit to mark the triumph of light over darkness. Festivities the following day feature Phagwah bands, tassa drumming and singing, and colored water is sprinkled over everyone in sight. Hardly traditional, Easter is an enormously festive occasion, celebrated with goat and crab races.

To really tap into the traditions of Tobago, try to attend the Tobago Heritage Festival in July, when you can witness old-time weddings, hear traditional local music played with fiddles and tambourines, and hear about the complex courting rituals and codes and dances of days gone by. Each village presents one aspect of the island's heritage, showing off its own versatility in music, dance, drama, cooking and costuming.

Beaches

By all accounts, the best beach on the island is **Pigeon Point**, called by some the "archetype of paradise." Its quiet turquoise waters are good for swimming and the sunsets along the coast are fantastic. The land, however, is privately owned, and a small fee is charged for use, but you'll find seaside bars, boutiques, boats for hire and most watersports. Near the airport, **Store Bay** is Tobago's most happening beach, where young rastas sell locals arts and crafts; expect the vibe to be lively, if not noisy. The land, however, is privately owned, and a small fee is charged for use. Turtle Bay is also a well-kept beach. **Buccoo Reef** is excellent for snorkeling. **Salybia Bay** is delightfully secluded and good for swimming. Leatherback turtles can be seen nesting at certain times of the year on Matura Beach (see below). Surfers should head to **Mt. Irvine Bay**, home of the famous "Irvine wave"; the occasional whale has been sighted in this area.

For those who like clambering over slippery rocks, head for the so-called **Crusoe's Cave**, on the lowlands coast behind Crown Point Airport. The cave, which is gouged on to the coral, was originally the mouth of the tunnel that was thought to have twisted inland for miles. Today fallen rocks have blocked any explorations further than a few feet into the cave. Access to the cave is through private property. Expect to pay a small fee.

FIELDING'S CHOICE:

Leatherback Turtles, by the hundreds, come out of the water to nest during the months of March-June. This is one of the few places in the Caribbean where this occurs. Organized turtle watches allow visitors to witness the awesome spectacle while also protecting the nesting sites. Watchers help their guide measure each turtle and gather relevant statistics, which are sent to the U.S. turtle research stations. The primary location is along the southwestern shore from Great Courland Bay to Turtle Beach. On one June night last year, 80 giant leatherbacks as much as six feet long came up on Grand Riviere beach, while tiny hatchlings, emerging from eggs laid in the sand, were making their way to the sea. For more information, contact Thalia Moolochan of the Grande Riviere Environmental Trust ☎ (809) 670-8458, who is in charge of the program. Trinidad and Tobago Sightseeing Tours ☎ (809) 628-1051, FAX (809) 627-0856, has turtle-watching trips for $50, Caroni Swamp tours for $34, Buccoo Reef tours for $20, including hotel transport.

Underwater

Unlike the murky reefs of its poor sibling to the south, Tobago is an excellent dive location which is only on the cusp of being discovered by Americans. Big pelagics are frequently spotted here, closer to the surface than in most of the Eastern Caribbean, including manta rays, dolphins, and even the occasional hammerhead or droll whale shark. As on Trinidad, Venezuela's Orinoco River filters freshwater nutrients onto Tobago's reefs, courtesy of the Guyana Current, but usually without the heavy dose of silt found off the larger island. The Orinoco can still limit visibility in the "bad water" rainy season (July through November), but the good news is that the multitude of currents which swirl around Tobago make drift diving a dependable specialty. On the Atlantic side, currents of up to three knots are a regular occurrence, although the patterns and directions shift constantly, requiring the insight of a local dive operator. The island's best diving is sprinkled around **Little Tobago Island** (two miles off Speyside), although an area referred to as **The Shallows**, in the channel between Trinidad and Tobago, features several excellent advanced dives. **Kelliston Deep** is famous as the location for the world's biggest known brain coral, some 16 feet high. Year-round visibility at Little Tobago averages 80 to 100 feet; on the southern half of the island expect 50 to 60 feet in the dry season, and 40 or 50 during the rainy season Sections of famed **Buccoo Reef** have been overused and abused for years, in part by glass-bottom boat operators which encourage visitors to walk on the reef. The result: much of Buccoo is now a heap of dead coral attracting few fish. If you take a snorkel trip to Buccoo, make sure you're visiting its living sections or, better, head for some of the other bays which curl along the island's Caribbean coast and usually feature good snorkeling. **Pirate Bay**, just north of Man of War Bay, is a particularly idyllic setting, and **Tyrrel's Bay** (of Speyside) also features spots accessible from the shore.

Diver's Dream

An advanced site surrounding a submarine plateau at The Shallows, this dive offers a good chance of bumping into almost anything: hammerheads, black tips, eagle rays, large turtles and barracudas. The terrain is visually striking, creating a raw foreboding theatre of cracks, crevices and caves; well-suited for divers weary of colorful detail and hungry for rugged drama.

Japanese Gardens

A series of scenic gardens nurture fluttering damselfish, angels and parrotfish amid a wide-ranging palette of tube sponges and, further down, black coral. Then, you'll ride a current which sweeps you along the side of Goat Island, turning right to cut through a canal between two large rocks, and then whooshes you into quieter waters. Here, the reef and sand floor sparkle in the sun and mantas are sometimes seen. Suitable for all levels.

Manta City

Tobago's most famous dive location draws the magnificent titular characters almost year-round (though fewer sightings occur during the summer). The dive starts over a reef, winding up over a more barren landscape of boulders and brain corals (depth to 50 feet). But the mantas are the stars, hovering along the edge of a vast drop-off and have gradually grown accustomed to human contact, usually altering their flight patterns to circle and peruse divers.

Mount Irvine Wall

A shallow wall off Mt. Irvine Bay drops to 50 feet and reveals a series of swim-through caves and tunnels. The area attracts many of the more unusual critters including seahorses, short-nosed batfish, spiny lobsters and eels, along with an assortment of reef fish and occasional eagle rays. Night dives reveal octopus, morays and orange ball anemones.

Dive Shops

Aqua Marine Dive Ltd.

Scarborough; ☎ *(809) 660-4341.*

PADI International Resort and training facility, based at Blue Waters; expects to be Five Star facility Fall 1995. Courses available to instructor level. Two-tank dive, $70. Two scheduled dives daily; groups limited to 15.

ive Tobago, Ltd.

Pigeon Point; ☎ *(809) 639-0202.*
Oldest shop on Tobago (since 1977), catering primarily to Europeans. Three dives daily in small groups of 6 to 8. Two-tank dive $80 with equipment, or $70 if you bring your own. PADI and NAUI-affiliated, with certification to Divemaster.

lan Friday Diving

Charlotteville; ☎ *(809) 660-4676.*
Five-year-old, PADI-affiliated shop with courses to Divemaster. Groups limited to 6, prefers to work with experienced divers. Two-tank dive, $70.

bago Dive Experience

Black Rock and Speyside; ☎ *(809) 639-0191.*
Two-tank dive, $70. PADI and NAUI affiliated, with courses to Divemaster. Two locations; the Speyside shop is part of Manta Lodge, a new diver's hotel.

On Foot

Relaxed and unspoiled, Tobago has plenty of exploration possibilities, but ew identified trails at this writing from which to springboard into the wilderness. Coupled with Trinidad, the island is riding the eco-tourism boom nd more trails are in the works. **Centre Hill** is Tobago's high point, 1900 eet, around which the island's forest reserve spreads. The **Argyll Waterfall**, ust west of Roxborough, is well worth the 10-minute walk/wade off the main road (guides will make themselves obvious, but are not necessary). There is a book of trails available locally, and the helpful topographical map of Tobago is dependably obtained at the Land and Survey Department in Port of Spain, Trinidad. The **Trinidad and Tobago Field Naturalists' Club** ☎ *(809) 624-3321)* has frequent field trips and welcomes outsiders. The island's complex interior, filled with diverse animal and bird life, invites exploration in the company of a naturalist, who can add greatly to your experience.

ittle Tobago Island

A bird sanctuary, located less than two miles off the bay at Speyside, Little Tobago is typically visited with a local guide, easily arranged through your hotel or by the tourist office (although there are usually short boats on the beach available for transit). Once on the island, there are obvious short trails which lead up the main hill, providing ample opportunity to spot the variety of birds which inhabit Little Tobago. Most notably, look for red-billed tropicbirds (nesting along the eastern cliffs in winter and spring), sooty terns (along the shore in spring and summer), laughing gulls (above Alexander Bay in the summer) and the magnificent frigatebird (which actually nests on nearby St. Giles Islands).

Main Ridge Forest Trail

The island's best-maintained hike, also known as Gilpin's Trace, is an ideal introduction to Tobago's rain forest and wildlife. The loop trail begins at one of two points along the Parlatuvier Road: from the posted trailhead at mile marker 1.25, follow the path through fern forests and past ant and termite hills for about a mile to a small waterfall along the Gold-Silver River. Continue along the trail, passing two more waterfalls, and then climb a steep grade which leads back to the main road. The complete route is about two-and-a-half miles; allow two to three hours for the complete circuit.

Trekking Tours

Pioneer Journeys

☎ *(809) 660-4327 or 660-5175.*

Renson Jack, a local forest ranger, and Pat Turpin organize acclaimed all-day naturalist expeditions into Tobago's wilderness. Groups are limited to 12 people, and rates are $42-55, depending on hike selected.

By Pedal

Lots of winding, hilly roads greet riders, but Tobago is an excellent island to explore by bicycle. The only level area is around the airport, with the island becoming progressively more mountainous as you travel north, even along the coastline. A wonderful, quiet area for mountain biking is the dirt track between **Bloody Bay** and **Man O War Bay**, with another nice ride cutting through the gentle mountains via **Parlatuvier Road**. The roller-coaster road between **Roxborough** and **Charlotteville** is challenging. Trail riding can be sought in the hills above the **Hillsborough Dam**; a rough road wanders through lush rain forest to **Castara** or **Mason Hall** (good birdwatching, too).

Bike Rental Shops

Glorious Ride Bike Rental

Scarborough; ☎ *(809) 639-7652.*

Rents Taiwanese ten-speed mountain bikes; $7 per day.

Bairds Rental

Crown Point Airport; ☎ *(809) 639-2528 or 639-7054.*

12-speed mountain bikes, $8 per day.

What Else to See

The star attractions on Tobago are mostly natural, but one of the main focuses of any excursion should be the delightful, though eccentric, little town
of **Scarborough**, Tobago's capital. Market days on Friday and Saturday are an
explosion of sights, sounds and aromas as the turbaned vendors lay out their
enormous piles of fresh vegetables and fruits. Bargaining is the joy of the
day; but don't try so hard to get a good deal that you miss biting down on a
delicious papaya or a ripe golden tomato. From here, you can start the trek
up to **Fort King George**, the city's most significant historical monument. Built
in the 1770s, it stands a towering 450 feet above the town; today it houses a
small but fascinating museum collection of colonial and Indian artifacts. Just
below is the **Centre of Fine Art**, where you can peruse the products of local talent.

Even if you don't hike, take time to wander the island. Worthwhile is simply the joy of driving from Scarborough in the lowland to the fishing villages
of **Charlotteville** and **Speyside** on the far side of the island. (While in Speyside,
a visit to **Little Tobago**, the bird reserve, is highly recommended; see above.)
As the road leaves the capital and enters the hills, it gradually narrows and
becomes more and more convoluted until it becomes little more than a narrow, barely two-lane road, teetering along the edges of the seaside cliffs and
plunging into palm-filled valleys, only to climb back again. The journey to
the far side goes further back in time the farther you go. The town soon
takes on that true Caribbean look of small fishing villages, covered with zinc
roofs and animals wandering onto the road. Most watersports, golf, fine eat-
ries and nightlife are all found in the southern region. If you want to stay in
nature, stick to the "far side" of Tobago.

Not to be missed is **Charlotteville**, a picturesque fishing village embraced by
high hills. Here, the bay is deep and sheltered; many head for a lively cove
called **Pirate's Bay**, a 20-minute hike through the national forest. Legend has
it that pirate treasure is buried here, but not a single piece of gold has ever
turned up.

If you have time, the drive on the **Northside Road** will show you an uncommonly rugged but beautiful glimpse into rural Tobago. The starting point,
where the ruins of the 17th-century **Fort James** are located, offers a wide-an-
gle, windswept view of the west coast. This is the site of one of Tobago's ear-

liest communities, settled by the Dutch in 1633. A requisite stop is th **Mystery Tombstone**, whose 18th-century epitaph for young Betty Stiven is ; chilling as it is poetic: "A Mother without knowing it and a Wife without le ting her husband know it except by her kind indulgence to him." Drivin north from Plymouth, an excellent place to stop for a spot of tea is th charming **Arnos Vale Hotel**, an old estate house set in a beautifully lush trop cal garden. A nature reserve is nearby (see above under "Treks."). As yo continue north, you enter the heart of rural Tobago; the tiny mountain vi lages come alive with the rhythms of life. In **Golden Lane**, seek out the grav of Gang Gang Sara, an African woman rumored to be a witch who in olde days was said to have flown to Tobago, where she took up residence. Whe she tried to leave, it was said, she lost her power to fly because she had eate salt while on the island.

BEST VIEW:

The view from the top of Fort King George is a panoramic sweep of the surrounding coastline, but for sunsets head for Flagstaff Hill on the island's northernmost tip, to watch the last golden rays penetrate the deep indigo sea. Deep-sea fishing is also available, as is horseback riding, with equipment provided by the Palm Tree Village Beach Resort. The leading beachfront hotels have their own watersports facilities.

Historical Sites

Fort King George   ★★★

Scarborough.

Tobago's best-preserved historical building is this fort perched on a hill above Scarborough. English troops built it in 1779 and over the years it traded hands severa times between the English and French. You can inspect its ruins and cannons, anc on a clear day you can see forever, or at least to Trinidad. The Barrack Guard House is the site of the **Tobago Museum** (☎ *639-3970*), whose exhibits center on Amer indian pottery and relics, military artifacts, and documents from the slave era. It's open weekdays from 9:00 a.m. to 4:30 p.m.

Tours

Adventure Farm and Nature Rese   ★★★

Anros Vale Road, Plymouth.

This 12-acre plantation grows mangoes, citrus, bananas and papaya, and rears sheep and goats in its pasture. You can come and pick your own fruit (they charge market prices) and for birdwatching. Open to the public every day but Saturday from 7:00 a.m.–9:00 a.m. and 5:00–6:00 p.m., when a caretaker acts as guide for an extra $1.

Sports

The leading beachfront hotels boast their own watersports activities program. Deep-sea fishing is also available through the local **Gerard "Frothy" de Silva** ☎ *(809) 639-7108.* Other tour operators can be found in the vicinity of Pigeon Point/Crown Point; in the rural areas, arrangements can be made with local fishermen. The **Palm Tree Village Beach** resort also offers horseback riding (equipment provided) ☎ *(809) 639-4347;* it maintains its own stables. There are several professional sports associations, where like-minded athletes can find each other, such as the **Surfing Association** ☎ *(809) 637-4533;* **Windsurfing Association** ☎ *(809) 659-2457.* Anyone interested in yachting should contact the **Viking Dive and Sail/Yacht Chartering Limited**, inside Pigeon Point Resort at Crown Point; ☎ *(809) 639-9209,* FAX *(809) 639-0414.*

Mount Irvine Golf Course

Mount Irvine Hotel, Scarborough, ☎ *(809) 639-8871.*
Hours Open: 6:30 a.m.–3 p.m.
This 18-hole, par-72 course is among the Caribbean's most scenic, covering 125 acres of rolling hills and overlooking the sea. Great views from the clubhouse, too. Greens fees are about $46.

Watersports

Various locations.
If your hotel can't supply the necessary aqua activity, try one of these. Scuba diving: **Tobago Marine Sports** *(☎ 639-0291),* **Dive Tobago** *(☎ 639-0202),* Man Friday Diving *(☎ 660-4676),* and **Viking Dive** *(☎ 639-9209).* Boating: **Viking Sail/Yacht Chartering Limited** *(☎ 639-9209).* Deep-sea fishing: **Gerald deSilva** *(☎ 639-7108).* Windsurfing: **Windsurfing Association of Trinidad and Tobago** *(☎ 659-2457).* General watersports: **Blue Waters Inn** *(☎ 660-4341),* and **Mt. Irvine Watersports** *(☎ 639-9379).*

Where to Stay

Fielding's Highest Rated Hotels in Tobago

★★★★	Grafton Beach Resort	$160–$245
★★★★	Richmond Great House	$85–$125
★★★	Arnos Vale Hotel	$110–$240
★★★	Kariwak Village Hotel	$65–$95
★★★	Mount Irvine Bay Hotel	$125–$365
★★★	Palm Tree Village	$80–$455
★★★	Turtle Beach Hotel	$110–$200

Fielding's Most Romantic Hotels in Tobago

★★★	Arnos Vale Hotel	$110–$240
★★★★	Richmond Great House	$85–$125

Fielding's Budget Hotels in Tobago

★	Golden Thistle Hotel	$40–$60
★	Coral Reef Guest House	$40–$70
★	Arthur's-on-Sea	$40–$75
★★	Sandy Point Beach Club	$40–$75
★★	Man-O-War Bay Cottages	$55–$70

Accommodations run the gamut from the comfortable family feeling of small, inexpensive bed and breakfast guest homes to the luxury of opulent four-star hotels. Several hotels on the southwest/tourist end of the island are within walking distance of the airport. Most of the favorite vacation hang-outs are near a long, palm-covered sandspit called Pigeon Point and adjacent to the snorkeling at Buccoo Reef. Five miles up the island's Caribbean side there are a few more hotels of ascending levels of luxury, found on a succession of bays along the scalloped coastline. Above the little hamlet of Spey ide, the only bona-fide hotel on this side of the island is the **Blue Waters Inn**, a walk away from **Jemma's** restaurant suspended mysteriously over the branches of an immense almond tree.

Hotels and Resorts

Renovations are on the upswing in Tobago. The **Grafton Grand**, an 88-room hotel, was completed in December 1994. This property is independent of the **Grafton Beach Resort**, but the two properties are connected by way of a bridge and the guests from either property have access to the other's facilities. The former **Crown Reef Hotel** has been given a $23 million facelift. If you want to be close to nesting turtles (in season), stay at the **Turtle Beach Hotel**. They won't be in your room, but the nearby beach will be close enough.

Arnos Vale Hotel $110–$240   ★★★

Arnos Vale Road, ☎ (809) 639-2881, FAX (809) 639-4629.
Single: $110–$160. Double: $160–$240.
This self-contained resort, located 20 minutes from Scarborough, attracts a mostly Italian clientele. The sloping grounds are nicely landscaped and include acres of fruit orchards, the bounty of which often enhance the creole, Italian and international meals. Accommodations are located on the hillside and near the beach; all are air-conditioned and decorated with wood and wicker furniture, and most have private balconies. Facilities include three bars, a disco, pool and watersports.

Grafton Beach Resort $160–$245   ★★★★

Black Rock, ☎ (809) 639-0030.
Single: $160–$245. Double: $160–$245.
This upscale resort, 15 minutes out of Scarborough, attracts a mostly European clientele. Guestrooms are very nicely appointed with teak furnishings, minibars, marble baths and all the modern comforts. The two suites, which go for $555–$600 per night, also have Jacuzzis. There's lots to do: a large pool, shuffleboard, two air-conditioned squash courts, a well-equipped gym, and two restaurants and three bars. A dive shop takes care of sporting needs on the nice beach, and there is frequent evening entertainment. One of Tobago's better choices.

Kariwak Village Hotel $65–$95   ★★★

Crown Point, ☎ (809) 639-8545, FAX (809) 639-8441.
Single: $65–$95. Double: $65–$95.
This authentic island getaway is nicely designed and quite popular with both tourists and locals. Accommodations are in 10 octagonal stucco cottages arranged around a swimming pool. Rooms are simple but comfortable. Couch potatoes can camp out in the TV lounge to get their fix. You can walk to the beach in five minutes or take the free shuttle. The restaurant is a local favorite, and on the weekends, this place is a popular spot to hear live music. They'll help arrange tours and watersports.

Mount Irvine Bay Hotel $125–$365   ★★★

Mount Irvine Bay, ☎ (809) 639-8871, FAX (809) 639-8800.
Single: $125–$365. Double: $145–$365.

This sprawling north shore resort is highlighted by its 18-hole golf course, the best on the island. There's plenty to keep travelers occupied off the greens, too, with two tennis courts, Tobago's largest pool, a health spa, and watersports on the private beach. There's also two restaurants and two bars, with frequent entertainment once the sun goes down. Lodging is in modern and well-appointed guestrooms and in 46 fairly plush cottages that fetch $330 to $432 per night. One restaurant, found in an 18th-century sugar mill, is especially atmospheric.

Pelican Beach Hotel $95–$230   ★★

Whitby, ☎ *(809) 946-7112, FAX (809) 946-7139.*
Single: $95–$130. Double: $130–$230.

This small hotel is situated on six miles of beach. The oceanview guestrooms have ceiling fans and balconies. The premises include a restaurant and bar, with watersports nearby.

Turtle Beach Hotel $110–$200   ★★★

Plymouth Local Road, Great Courland Bay, ☎ *(809) 639-2851, FAX (809) 639-1495.*
Single: $110–$200. Double: $110–$200.

If you're visiting this hotel between May and October, you'll get the chance to see leatherback turtles laying their eggs on the beach, hence the name. It's decent any time of the year here, though, with a lovely beach, full dive shop, two tennis courts, and pool to keep guests happy. Accommodations are comfortable, though central air would be a great improvement over the individual units. Additional facilities include two restaurants and two bars at this well-run spot.

Apartments and Condominiums

Enormous variety exists in the self-catering department; you can splurge on luxury homes and apartments (with a live-in chef and maid) or you can hole up in a cottage and do your own cooking. Several attractive villas are available for rent on the **Mount Irvine Beach Bay Estate**, some right next to the beach, others along the fairways. Opportunities also exist in extremely isolated coves, though you will surely need to rent a car. Most of your supplies will need to be met by the Friday and Saturday fruit and vegetable markets in Scarborough. Bring what staples you will need because you will be hard put to find a supermarket that is sufficient. For more information and rates, contact the **Tobago Villas Agency**, *Box 301, Scarborough;* ☎ *(809) 639-8737, FAX (809) 639-8800.*

Crown Point Beach Hotel $55–$105   ★

Store Bay Beach, Crown Point, ☎ *(809) 639-8781, FAX (809) 639-8731.*
Single: $55–$105. Double: $55–$105.

Set on seven acres overlooking Store Bay Beach, this condominium resort is eight miles from Scarborough. Accommodations are in studios and one-bedroom units with air conditioning and kitchenettes; maids tidy up daily. There's a restaurant, bar, two tennis courts, and a supermarket on the premises.

Golden Thistle Hotel $40–$60   ★

Store Bay Road, Crown Point, ☎ *(809) 639-8521, FAX (809) 639-8521.*
Single: $40–$45. Double: $60.

This low-frills property is two minutes from the airport and houses guests in air-conditioned studios with kitchenettes, twin beds, and TV sets. The beach is walkable, but there's a pool on-site for those feeling especially lazy. A bar and restaurant complete the limited facilities.

Man-O-War Bay Cottages $55–$70 ★★

Charlotteville Estate, ☎ *(809) 660-4327.*
Single: $55–$70. Double: $60–$70.
Set on a 1000-acre cocoa plantation, these modest cottages are located right on the beach. Configurations vary from one to four bedrooms, all with kitchens, fans and verandas. Maid and cook service is available for an extra charge. This spot is especially popular with birdwatchers and those really looking to get away from it all. You'll want a car for mobility.

Palm Tree Village $80–$455 ★★★

Milford Road, ☎ *(809) 639-4347, FAX (809) 639-4180.*
Single: $80–$455. Double: $80–$455.
This self-styled village is located five minutes from Scarborough and is across the street from a busy public beach. Guests can choose to stay in the hotel with its standard air-conditioned rooms, or in 40 villas with two to four bedrooms, large living areas, kitchens and patios. Maid service is available, as are cooks. Facilities include a restaurant, bar, Jacuzzi, steam room, pool, gym and tennis court.

Sandy Point Beach Club $40–$75 ★★

Sandy Point Village, ☎ *(809) 639-8533, FAX (809) 639-8495.*
Single: $40–$70. Double: $50–$75.
This resort, located near the airport, sometimes suffers from the roar of jets. Accommodations are in studios and one-bedroom suites, all with air conditioners, kitchenettes, and pleasing decor. The beach is pretty but not good for swimming, so guests splash about in one of the two pools or take the free shuttle to the beach at Pigeon Point. The casual beachside restaurant serves varied fare for those not into cooking. This friendly spot is a great bargain.

Inns

The following inns are so-called because of their size, rather than any abiding congeniality. The **Blue Waters Inn** in Speyside may be in danger of losing its unofficial "inn" status since it is presently undergoing a 30-room expansion project.

Blue Waters Inn $60–$115 ★★

Batteaux Bay, Speyside, ☎ *(809) 660-4341, FAX (809) 660-5195.*
Single: $60–$100. Double: $70–$115.
Set in a protected cove along a small beach, this property is found 90 minutes from Scarborough. Guestrooms are basic and rely on sea breezes to keep cool. The surrounding rainforest attracts nature lovers and those who like seclusion; rent a car or you may suffer from too much isolation. There's a tennis court, restaurant, and bar on the grounds, but no pool. Birdwatching excursions are frequently offered, and watersports are nearby.

Coral Reef Guest House $40–$70 ★

P.O. Box 316, Milford Road, Scarborough, ☎ *(809) 639-2536, FAX (809) 639-0770.*
Single: $40–$45. Double: $45–$70.

This basic guesthouse has simple air-conditioned rooms with private baths. Eight apartments have one to three bedrooms and kitchenettes. Facilities are limited to a dining room, bar, pool and games room.

Richmond Great House $85–$125   ★★★★

Belle Garden, ☎ *(809) 660-4467, FAX (809) 660-4467.*
Single: $85–$125. Double: $85–$125.

Located on the southern coast on a remote hillside, this unique spot brims with interesting African art and local antiques. The 200-year-old plantation house offers a handful of nicely decorated and colorful rooms, each individually done. The beach is a 10-minute drive.

Salt Raker Inn $45–$130   ★★

P.O. Box 1, Duke Street, ☎ *(809) 946-2260, FAX (809) 946-2817.*
Single: $45–$125. Double: $70–$130.

This small inn dates back to 1835 and was originally a shipwright's home. Rooms are individually decorated and some have air conditioning; there are also three one-bedroom suites. The beach is across the street. Facilities include a charming eight-stool bar, an open-air restaurant, a dive shop and a library. The occasional live entertainment is appealingly informal.

Low Cost Lodging

Bed and breakfasts are the cheapest way to go on Tobago, and are full of charming possibilities that are infused with the personality of the owner who is often the cook, maid and chief bottle washer.

Pentridge Lodge ☎ *(809) 639-4129* is the island's consummate bed and breakfast, featuring rooms the size of small apartments beneath vaulted ceilings. The home is mansion-like with three wings, and completely private. Bird-watchers will be delighted with the parakeet sightings. The owner is a successful dress designer with champagne sensibilities who loves to entertain. Following a good meal, the beach is a welcome 10-minute walk away.

Hillcrest ☎ *(809) 639-9263.* This is a whole house that sleeps 10, with three bedrooms of two double beds and two twin bedrooms. The living room opens onto a wide porch, though the bedrooms are small. It's very secluded up a dirt road. It's the place to be if you have a big family.

Arthur's-on-Sea $40–$75   ★

Crown Point, ☎ *(800) 742-4276, (809) 639-0196, FAX (809) 639-4122.*
Single: $40–$65. Double: $45–$75.

This small hotel is situated on a busy street a few minutes' walk from Store Bay Beach. The air-conditioned guestrooms are simple and basic, with private patios. TVs are available on request. There's a restaurant, bar and pool on the premises.

Where to Eat

Fielding's Highest Rated Restaurants in Tobago

★★★★★	Blue Crab	$4–$20
★★★★★	La Tartaruga	$9–$24
★★★	Dillon's Seafood	$12–$27
★★★	Jemma's Sea View Kitchen	$10–$27
★★★	Miss Jean's	$4–$6
★★★	Old Donkey Cart House	$3–$25
★★★	Papillon	$15–$25

Fielding's Special Restaurants in Tobago

★★★	Jemma's Sea View Kitchen	$10–$27
★★★	Miss Jean's	$4–$6
★★★	Old Donkey Cart House	$3–$25

Fielding's Budget Restaurants in Tobago

★★★	Miss Jean's	$4–$6
★★★★★	Blue Crab	$4–$20
★★★	Old Donkey Cart House	$3–$25
★★★★★	La Tartaruga	$9–$24
★★★	Jemma's Sea View Kitchen	$10–$27

While most of the big hotels and resorts offer "continental" cuisine—that means food that's recognizable back home—local cuisine is a flavorful combination of Indian curries blended with the more traditional Caribbean fare. Favorites include curried crab and dumplings, served in a curry sauce with hard dumplings (be sure to bring a bib, this is a messy one), and *rotis*, chicken or beef and potatoes in a curry sauce wrapped in a thin, unleavened bread.

In the coastal areas, especially around festival times, indulge in a bit of *pacr*
a shellfish concoction that is reputed to have heady aphrodisiacal powers.

Down the street from the airport there are numerous stands advertising
local food—**Miss Jean**, **Sylvia's**, **Alma's**, **Esme's**—offering some of T&T's mos
authentic cuisine. Here you'll be able to sample conch, crab and kingfis
with roti, an especially Indian flat bread stuffed with ground chickpeas (
ubiquitous fast food in this country). At **Jemma's Seaview Kitchen** in Speysid
try the callaloo—a popular T&T "blue food" made from the leaves of th
dasheen plant; her entrées of shrimp, kingfish, crab and chicken run a rea
sonable $10. Also unforgettable is the flying fish at the **Blue Crab** on Robin
son and Main in the funky town of Scarborough ☎ *(809) 639-2737*, entree
from $10.

Blue Crab $$$ ★★★★★

Robinson Street, Scarborough, ☎ *(809) 639-2737.*
Latin American cuisine.
Lunch: 11 a.m.–3 p.m., entrees $4–$6.
Dinner: 6–10 p.m., entrees $12–$20.
The hardworking family that runs this popular spot whips up tasty meals that com
bine the cuisines of East India, Portugal and Creole. Fresh vegetables and fruit
from their own gardens are used in the preparation of such delights as pumpki
soup and homemade ice cream and fruit wines. Lunches are served on the wide ter
race of the traditional West Indian building. Only fish caught that day is used i
their seafood dishes. Treat an island friend to dinner here, which is available by
advance reservation only from Wednesday through Friday.

Dillon's Seafood $$$ ★★★

Airport Road, Crown Point, ☎ *(809) 639-8765.*
Seafood cuisine.
Dinner: 6–10 p.m., entrees $12–$27.
A charter captain and fisherman runs this modern restaurant cooled by air-condi
tioning, which assures that all fish and seafood are so fresh they snap back at you
There's lobster thermidor, or island kingfish in a tomato sauce, and fish soup. Some
of the food though, could use a braver hand with the salt shaker or the spice rack.

Jemma's Sea View Kitchen $$$ ★★★

Windward Road, Tyrell's Bay, ☎ *(809) 660-4066.*
Latin American cuisine.
Lunch: 9 a.m.–4 p.m., entrees $10–$20.
Dinner: 4.–9 p.m., entrees $10–$27.
The kids, big and small, will enjoy eating in a real treehouse overlooking Tyrell's
Bay. They may have to fight for space though, as there are only 10 tables. The
emphasis is on local dishes, served in generous portions by an amiable staff. Special-
ties include callaloo soup, grilled seafood, and crab and dumplings. It's a great place
to stop on a circle-island tour or a day at the beach. Open Fridays from 8 a.m. to
5 p.m. only.

Tartaruga $$$ ★★★★★

Buccoo Bay Beach, Buccoo Bay, ☎ *(809) 639-0940.*
Italian cuisine.
Dinner: 7–11 p.m., entrees $9–$24.

Fresh is the key word at this intimate, friendly spot. The Italian owner and chef prepares delicious pasta that's homemade daily. Sauces are embellished with garden-grown herbs. Fish is delivered to his door from a reliable source. The service, by a well-trained staff, is as quick as it gets on the island. Recommended dishes include spaghetti with dorado in a sauce of olive oil and pepper, served with tomatoes. Stop by for a drink, an espresso, homemade ice cream or luscious deserts such as ricotta cakes, and amaretto cheesecake.

Miss Jean's $ ★★★

Store Bay Beach, Store Bay, ☎ *(809) 639-0211.*
Latin American cuisine.
Lunch: 9 a.m.–4 p.m., entrees $4–$5.
Dinner: 4–10 p.m., entrees $5–$6.

Miss Jean's motto is if you love good food we love to feed you and she means it. All manner of seafood, soups and stews, including the island favorite, crab and dumplings, emanate miraculously from a small shed on the sand in Store Bay. If you like, sample a few things at Jean's and mosey on to Miss Esmie or Miss Trim's place next door. For a carbo load, try the macaroni pie, which is stewed chicken or beef with macaroni, if it's available.

Old Donkey Cart House $$$ ★★★

Bacolet Street, Scarborough, ☎ *(809) 639-3551.*
International cuisine.
Lunch: 11 a.m.–3 p.m., entrees $3–$10.
Dinner: 6:30 p.m.–midnight, entrees $20–$25.

The Viennese owner of this charming restaurant is the island's only authority on German wines, which are a specialty of the place. These fine vintages accompany well-prepared local fish, steaks and pastas. Start your meal with some excellent cheese. At lunch, sandwiches are served on homebaked bread.

Papillon $$$ ★★★

Buccoo Bay Road, Mt. Irvine, ☎ *(809) 639-0275.*
Seafood cuisine.
Lunch: entrees $15–$25.
Dinner: entrees $15–$25.

Chef Jakob Straessle's cuisine may not be on the cutting edge of chic, but the Swiss restaurateur always delivers reliably tasty old favorites like lobster thermidor, served with a choice of soup, rice and salad. Also featured are conch in season, cooked in coconut milk. Dine in air-conditioned comfort in a rustic, out-of-the-way lodge. Closed for lunch on Sundays.

Where to Shop

Compared to the cascades of goods available in Trinidad, Tobago's sha
represents a mere trickle. Three malls cater to the obvious and uninspirin
Scarborough Mall in the center of town, **IDC Mall** at Sangster Hill, and **Breez
Mall** on Milford Road. (Breeze Hall is perhaps a tad more fashionable
You'll find more original items in the designer boutiques such as **The Cotto
House** on Bacolet Street (with smaller outlets at Sandy Point Hotel and P
geon Point, where you can pick up unusually beautiful batiks and tie-dyes
Tobago's own fashion mavens head for **Nairobi**, above the Starting Gate Pu
off Shirvan Road. As for arts and crafts, you can find some of them at th
malls (Scarborough and IDC), but it's more fun to buy them from vendo
hawking their own wares in the market. Good buys are leather sandal
carved gourds and hand-wrought jewelry. Most hotels have small gift shop
but expect the prices to be exaggerated. A couple of nice craft stores can b
found on the road leading to Pigeon Point, a fine beach. The jewele
Jose Andres is especially revered for his unique jewelry made from indigenou
woods, bone, coral and seedpods. The duty-free allowance covers one qua
of liquor, 200 cigarettes/50 cigars, and gifts up to TT$50.

Tobago Directory

ARRIVAL AND DEPARTURE

Multiple flights daily depart from major North American gateways t
Tobago. **BWIA** (British West Indian Airlines), familiarly known as Be
Wee because of its friendly, comfortable service. BWIA is the officia
airline of Trinidad and Tobago and has been providing dependable ser
vice to the Caribbean for more than 50 years. There are daily flight
from Miami, New York and Toronto. The flight to Tobago from
Miami is about 2.5 hours, with a short stop in Port of Spain, Trinidad
to clear customs.

Several companies rent well-maintained cars for about $50 a day, bu
since driving is on the left and the roads are narrow and hilly, most vis
itors prefer to hire a car and driver (about $60).

There is a departure tax of TT $75 (in local currency only-abou
U.S. $120 is collected at the airport.

BUSINESS HOURS

Shops open Monday–Thursday 8 a.m.–4 p.m., Friday 8 a.m.–6 p.m. and Saturday 8 a.m.–noon. Banks open Monday–Thursday 9 a.m.– 2 p.m. and Friday 9 a.m.–noon and 3–5 p.m.

CLIMATE

Weather conditions are very comfortable, with temperatures averaging 83 degrees F. The wet season runs June to December, with rainfall in mostly short sharp bursts. Tobago is slightly cooler and less humid than Trinidad. A scant 11 degrees above the equator, the climate is decidedly tropical.

DOCUMENTS

A passport is required for entry, as is a return or ongoing ticket. A departure tax of about $12 in U.S. currency is collected at the airport. An international driver's license is required for car rentals.

ELECTRICITY

Current runs either 115 or 220 volts at 60 cycles. While many hotels have 115 volt current, it is advisable to travel with a small transformer just in case. These supplies are readily available at low cost.

GETTING AROUND

Although both Trinidad and Tobago are small, you'll need a car to get around. Get one at the airport, from **Singh's** or **Amar**. And ask for maps. Driving is on the left side of the street. A ferry service links Trinidad and Tobago, about a 2.5 hour journey.

Taxis charge fixed fares to the downtown area and major hotels from the airport. Fares from Crown Point International Airport to Crown Point run about $4, to Pigeon Point about $6 in U.S. currency. Taxis to Speyside run about $32, and Roxborough about $22.

Car rentals are mostly local agencies. Among the best are **Auto Rentals Crown Point Beach hotel** ☎/FAX *(809) 639-0644* and **Singh's Auto Rentals, Grafton Beach Hotel** ☎ *(809) 639-0191*.

Bicycles, scooters and motorcycle rentals are available at **Blossom Enterprises**, *Milford Rd., Canaan*, ☎/FAX *(809) 639-8485*. **Toyota Rent a Car**, *177 Tragarete Rd.*, ☎ *(809) 628-5516*; and **Kalloo's Auto Rental** *32 Ariapita Ave., Woodbrook*, ☎ *(809) 622-9073*.

Among the best tour companies are **Pioneer Journeys**, *Man O'War Bay Cottages, Charlotteville*, ☎ *(809) 660-4327*; and **Bruce Ying Sightseeing Tours Around Trinidad and Tobago**, *Bacolet St., Scarborough*, ☎/ FAX *(809) 639-4402*.

LANGUAGE

English is the official language and is spoken with a rich, melodious accent. The old French-based patois has almost died out; some Hindi is still used among the Indian community.

MEDICAL EMERGENCIES

There are hospitals in Port of Spain, Scarborough, Mount Hope large teaching hospital), and Fernando, and an extensive network health centers and clinics, both public and private; both governme and private doctors practice.

MONEY

The official currency is the Trinidad and Tobago dollar (written TT$ which floats against other currencies. Daily rates are listed in the new papers. Credit cards are widely accepted in tourist areas, and by rent car companies, hotels, restaurants and major shops.

TELEPHONE

The country code is *809*. If dialing direct from the U.S. and Canad and much of the Caribbean, dial the number "1" first; from oth countries, including Haiti, Cuba and the Dutch and French Caribbea dial "01." The phone system is digital, and international direct dialin and other standard services are available throughout the system.

TIME

Atlantic Standard Time, one hour ahead of New York City, except du ing Daylight Saving Time, when it is the same.

TIPPING

Many hotels add a 10–15 percent service charge. If the restaurant b does not add a 10–15 percent service charge, feel free to do so.

TOURIST INFORMATION

Local information offices are at **Piarco Airport** ☎ *(809) 664-519* **Crown Point Airport**; ☎ *(809) 639-0509*; **Tobago: N.I.B. Mall**, Scarbo ough; ☎ *(809) 639-2125/3566*. In the United States call ☎ *(80* *232-0082*.

WATER

Tap water is safe to drink; bottled mineral waters are widely availabl and tasty.

WHEN TO GO

Carnival explodes in February with steel bands, parades and lots of loc foods and drink. Tobago Arts Festival occurs March-April. The Roun the Gulf Sailing Competition takes place in March. Goat and Crab race take place in April. The Indo-Caribbean Festival of Arts takes place i May. The Tobago Heritage Festival is in July. The Steelband Festival in August and October. The Tobago Music Festival takes place in No vember and December. The Tobago Christmas Pageant, with loc music and dance, is in December. For more information, contact th tourist board. Also check out "When To Go" at the end of the Trinida chapter.

TOBAGO HOTELS		**RMS**	**RATES**	**PHONE**	**CR. CARDS**
lymouth					
★★★★	**Grafton Beach Resort**	112	$160–$245	(809) 639-0030	A, DC, MC, V
★★★★	**Richmond Great House**	10	$85–$125	(809) 660-4467	None
★★★	**Arnos Vale Hotel**	30	$110–$240	(809) 639-2881	A, DC, MC, V
★★★	**Kariwak Village Hotel**	18	$65–$95	(809) 639-8545	A, DC, MC, V
★★★	**Mount Irvine Bay Hotel**	105	$125–$365	(809) 639-8871	A, DC, MC, V
★★★	**Palm Tree Village**	60	$80–$455	(809) 639-4347	A, DC, V
★★★	**Turtle Beach Hotel**	125	$110–$200	(809) 639-2851	A, DC, MC, V
★★	**Blue Waters Inn**	28	$60–$115	(809) 660-4341	A, MC, V
★★	**Man-O-War Bay Cottages**	6	$55–$70	(809) 660-4327	None
★★	**Pelican Beach Hotel**	14	$95–$230	(809) 946-7112	A, DC, MC, V
★★	**Salt Raker Inn**	12	$45–$130	(809) 946-2260	A, D, MC, V
★★	**Sandy Point Beach Club**	50	$40–$75	(809) 639-8533	DC, MC, V
★	**Arthur's-on-Sea**	15	$40–$75	(800) 742-4276	A, DC, MC, V
★	**Coral Reef Guest House**	24	$40–$70	(809) 639-2536	A, DC, MC, V
★	**Crown Point Beach Hotel**	100	$55–$105	(809) 639-8781	A, DC, MC, V
★	**Golden Thistle Hotel**	36	$40–$60	(809) 639-8521	A, DC, MC, V

TOBAGO RESTAURANTS		**PHONE**	**ENTREE**	**CR. CARDS**
lymouth				
	International			
★★★	**Old Donkey Cart House**	(809) 639-3551	$3–$25	A, MC, V
	Italian			
★★★★★	**La Tartaruga**	(809) 639-0940	$18–$24●●	A, MC, V
	Latin American			
★★★★★	**Blue Crab**	(809) 639-2737	$4–$20	A, MC, V
★★★	**Jemma's Sea View Kitchen**	(809) 660-4066	$10–$27	None
★★★	**Miss Jean's**	(809) 639-0211	$4–$6	None
	Seafood			
★★★	**Dillon's Seafood**	(809) 639-8765	$12–$27●●	A, MC, V
★★★	**Papillon**	(809) 639-0275	$15–$25	A, DC, MC, V

TOBAGO RESTAURANTS   PHONE   ENTREE CR. CARD

Note: • Lunch Only

•• Dinner Only

TRINIDAD

Trinidad's Carnival is the Caribbean's most celebrated annual spectacle with islanders working all year on floats and costumes.

Trinidad is the largest of the Lesser Antilles Islands, home to calypso, steel pan bands and some of the most spectacular aviary habitats in the Western World. Practically ringed with beaches, the island is a cultural smorgasbord of cuisines, festivals and religious rituals that draws tourists despite the almost studied indifference to their comfort. During the '70s, the two-island nation (which includes its sister island Tobago) became the wealthiest, if not the most cosmopolitan, nation in the Caribbean, allowing it to eschew tourism as an unneeded intrusion. As finances plummet in the early '90s, Trinidad is now courting tourism with an attractive come-on, and a special amiability toward foreigners is being seriously cultivated. Even without such

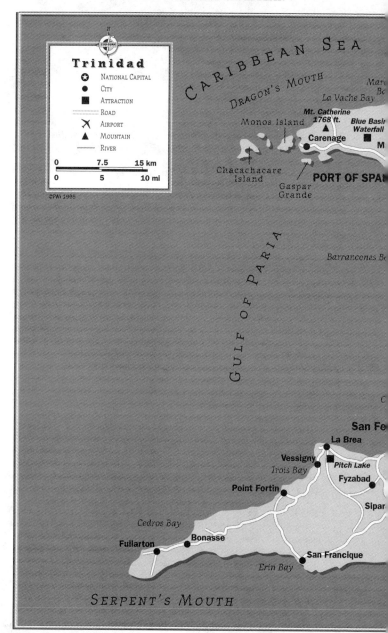

Trinidad

⊗ National Capital
● City
■ Attraction
--- Road
✕ Airport
▲ Mountain
--- River

0   7.5   15 km
0   5   10 mi

CFW 1995

CARIBBEAN SEA

DRAGON'S MOUTH

Mar
Bo
La Vache Bay

Monos Island   Mt. Catherine 1768 ft. ▲   **Blue Basin Waterfall** ■ M
Carenage

Chacachacare Island

Gaspar Grande

PORT OF SPA

GULF OF PARIA

Barrancones B

San Fe
La Brea
Vessigny ■ *Pitch Lake*
Trois Bay   **Fyzabad**
Point Fortin
Sipar

Cedros Bay
Bonasse
Fullarton   **San Francique**
Erin Bay

SERPENT'S MOUTH

Toco Beach

Blanchisseuse Bay

Madamas Bay

Matelot

Toco

rico ay

Blanchisseuse

Asa Wright Nature Centre

Brasso Seco/Paria

Mt. Tucuche ▲ 3072ft.

Aripo Caves

Maracas Waterfall

Mt. Tabor ▲

Mt. Aripo ▲ 3085 ft.

St. Joseph

Arima

Saline Bay

Tunapuna

Arouca

Arena Forest

University of West Indies

Sangre Grande

roni Bird nctuary

Piarco Airport

Matura Bay

Manzanilla Bay

Cunupia

Chaguanas

Mt. Tamana 1009 ft. ▲

Nariva Swamp

ATLANTIC OCEAN

Cocos Bay

Pointe-à-Pierre

Wild Fowl Trust

Rio Claro

Pierreville

Prince's Town

New Grant

Tableland

Mayaro Bay

Devil's Woodyard

Ortoire

Débé

Guayaguayare

Galeota Point

Trinity Hills ▲

Guayaguayare Bay

Moruga

Moruga Beach

81°

10°

natural resources as its fine rain forest, palm-fringed beaches and exotic nature reserves, simple daily life alone in Trinidad makes a fascinating diversion. The island's capital, Port-of-Spain is a vibrant, dizzying waterfront town of colorful gingerbread houses competing with ramshackle stalls and short high-rises as at least seven distinct nationalities stream down the narrow, winding alleyways intent on doing business somewhere between First World and Third. Ecotreks are fabulous on the island, and especially on Tobago, which is a short ferry ride away. Excellent accommodations are available on both islands, but the latest trend is to snuggle up in one of the many bed and breakfast-type inns, where you can forge an intimate relationship with the host, who usually doubles as chef, chambermaid and chauffeur. This is the real way to experience these islands in order to forge memories you can take home and cherish. Of course, Carnival in Trinidad is one of the most spectacular events in the Caribbean, an annual blowout affair whose efforts can be seen year-round in the studious productions of floats, costumes and musical performances.

Bird's Eye View

Trinidad is situated in the Caribbean Sea about 12 kilometers off the northeast coast of Venezuela. Tobago is 30.7 kilometers farther to the northeast. The entire land mass of Trinidad covers 1861 square miles while Tobago has a mere 117 miles. Almost all of Trinidad's hotels and restaurants are confined to the foothills around Port of Spain, the capital city, which has more than 60,000 residents; the entire island has a population of more than 1 million. Below the **Savanah Park**, lined with gingerbread mansions, spreads the city, a jumble of wooden houses and tiny stores whose wares often spill onto the sidewalk.

Just an hour from the city is a primeval rain forest, arrived at by a coiled spring of a road that leads to **Arima Valley**, where wildlife is so profuse that the New York Zoological Society began its first tropical ecology center there in 1949. This was later turned into a neighboring coffee and cocoa estate and a hotel for bird-lovers—the **Asa Wright Nature Centre and Lodge**. The grotto here is the most accessible place in the world to see the rare cave-dwelling oilbird, equipped with batlike sonar.

History

Columbus stumbled upon Trinidad and Tobago in 1498. Since then, the two islands have been a battlefield of contention among the French, Dutch, British and Spanish. Trinidad was long viewed as a source for Amerindian slaves, so the island was fiercely guarded, in contrast to Tobago which was nearly deserted by the Spanish. In 1592, an inland capital was erected at St. Joseph, stimulating interest in the cultivation of tobacco and cocoa. During the middle of the 18th century, plagues swept through the area, decimating the settlement and forcing the Spanish governor to move to a more coastal location, less vulnerable to jungle diseases and Indian raids. Port of Spain took its time to develop, attracting a slow stream of settlers followed by Christian missionaries intent on civilizing the Indians. Both tobacco and cocoa production soon fell into disfavor, the former a victim of competition among the northern islands, the latter a victim of blight. In 1776, the Spanish government offered land grants and tax incentives to Roman Catholic settlers; in response, numerous French planters from French Caribbean countries poured in to establish farms. By the end of the century, prosperous Frenchmen had gained control of the government, spreading the lilt of their patois and their tasty cuisine islandwide. During the Napoleonic Wars in 1797, the British sent a fleet to Trinidad, who swiftly overcame the resident Spaniards who had been too distracted fighting off Indians. In 1815, Tobago itself came under British control and was made a ward of Trinidad in 1897.

In the 1970s, offshore petroleum discoveries propelled Trinidad to the enviable status of the wealthiest nation in the Caribbean. Literacy rose to 90 percent, roads were paved, electricity installed. Signs of abject poverty, common among West Indian nations, nearly disappeared. In 1962, Sr. Eric Williams, the father of Trinidad and Tobago's new independence from British rule, vowed to avoid what he called the mistakes of his Caribbean neighbors, which in his mind, was servile catering to tourists. As such, tourism lay fallow for several decades. However, during the mid-'80s, resources plummeted, and the challenge of the Trinidadian government in this decade will be to re-establish economic stability and ensure conservation of the island's natural resources.

People

Trinidad's population is well over one million people. Their facial features represent a mingling of characteristics from Africa, America, Europe, Asia and the Indian subcontinent. Calypso lyrics hold the soul of the people—often they are editorials that bemoan what the oil bust has done to the country. Yet by all standards, Trinidad and Tobago are prosperous nations; children are kept fed by plentiful fish and fruit, healthy by free medical care, and taught in schools responsible for a literacy rate higher than the United States. Today, the two-island nation is 40 percent black and 40 percent East Indian, plus Chinese, Arab, British and remnant Carib Amerindian stock—only with each passing generation are bloods mixing so much that you can't tell who's who. The cultural jetsam takes its biggest influence from the conquerors who stayed the longest—Spain, France and Holland. Important is the legacy left by the Africans who arrived as slaves, indentured servants from India brought to replace them after abolition, Chinese who proved unfit to harvest sugar but adept at everything else, Syrians bearing textiles, and former British estate owners whose descendants wouldn't leave for anything. Color is less an issue in this country, where intercultural cooperation has received lots of elbow grease. Race relations here are considered a miracle of worked-at harmony.

Music and Carnival are nearly year-round industries. A century ago, the British outlawed African drums in Trinidad, for allegedly inciting passions leading to violence. People switched to beating on bamboo, biscuit tins, hubcaps, and as local petroleum exploitation surged on, musicians used oil drums, which someone noticed tended to change pitch after much pounding, and particularly when dented. Pan music can now be heard everywhere from Sunday mass to jazz ensembles to 120-musician orchestras during Carnival's Panorama. Best of all is the ubiquitous pan yard, especially in the month preceding Carnival, where the neighborhoods gather to hear free rehearsals. Best jam is on Oxford Street. For more information, see the chapter called "Caribbean Culture" in the front of the book.

Beaches

On the subject of beaches, Tobago wins hands down over Trinidad. The latter, however, does have numerous ones—they are simply not as beautiful or as memorable as Tobago's. Most of Trinidad's beaches are on the Caribbean coast from Las Cuevas to Balata Bay, and on offshore islands such as Monos.

One of the most beautiful beaches is **Cyril Bay**, complete with a small waterfall and fantasy sites for picnics. The cove is made of pebbles and sand and can be reached only by foot. Surfers congregate at **Tyrico Bay**, but the beach is small for bathing. Swimmers who are not experienced should avoid the strong undertow. **Maracas Bay** is a favorite among locals who love the long stretch of sand and the ample parking spaces. You can also find food and changing facilities here. Along the north coast you'll find **Las Cuevas Bay**, a very pretty stretch of sand ringed by submerged and partially submerged caves. Some of the best fruit on the islands is sold across the street. Swimmers should avoid the waters because of a fierce current, but the beach is usually serene and uncrowded. **Blanchisseuse Bay** is located about eight miles east, with lovely palm trees for shade and no crowds. Lovers should enjoy the near absolute seclusion.

Northeast beaches take about an hour to reach by car. Bodysurfers particularly like the conditions at **Balandra Bay**. Good swimming can be found in the calm waters of **Salibea Bay**, just past Galera Point. A lovely drive can be had down **Cocal**, the road between Manzanilla Beach and Cocos Bay, lined as it is with towering palm trees who make an arch over the highway. The water at Manzanilla is sometimes polluted by the Atlantic overflow, so avoid swimming if the sea looks muddy.

Underwater

If you ask about diving on Trinidad, you'll be steered straight to Tobago in the blink of an eye. If you pry further, you'll probably be told—in no uncertain terms—"There's no diving on Trinidad." Well, they're right, but only to a degree. Tobago's stunning reefs and giant mantas are stiff competition for any neighboring island, but most particularly for Trinidad, which has a few complicating factors visiting divers need to consider. The first is the Orinoco, Venezuela's massive river, which flows straight to Trinidad. While this has the positive effect of steering rich nutrients into Trinidad's reef system, it also brings silt, making visibility just 20 to 50 feet during the January-through-May dry season, and a ghastly 10 or 20 feet during the June-through-December rainy season. Suffice to say, that "blue water" feeling one attains on most Caribbean islands simply isn't found here. To make matters worse, the Orinoco's colder waters settle into the depths below the surface and create a thermocline, which means that diving down past 35 or 40 feet is like entering a refrigerator, by Caribbean standards, anyway.

Trinidad does have some fair dive sites, mostly concentrated around the tiny islands which lie directly west of Port of Spain: **Monas**, **Heuvos** and **Chacachacare Islands**, all part of the Gulf of Paria. Each of these sites, referred to locally as "down the islands," provide suitable beginner dives. A number of mid-to-late 18th-century wrecks, including three Spanish galleons pepper the vast northern coast. Although nothing is left of their wooden frames, divers can outline the shape of the disintegrated wrecks through cannonballs, ballast, anchors, pottery and bottles strewn around the sites, along with several cannons which are tucked against one shoreline. Shore diving is possible from a number of points along the northern coast, in **Maracas Bay**, and off **Las Cuevas** and **Toco Beaches**; a tender boat is recommended as entry can be rough and buddy separation is not infrequent. Additionally, currents on the north coast are sometimes tricky, making diving here a more advanced pursuit than is found off the Gulf of Paria islands. In sum, Trinidad remains an offbeat dive destination nurtured by locals, and visited by few outsiders, but suitable as a jumping-off point for the more dynamic sites on Tobago. Decent snorkeling is possible at **Toco Beach** (beware again of rough water) or around **St. Peter's Bay**, just west of Port of Spain.

Dive Shops

Ron's Watersports

Port-of-Spain; ☎ *(809) 673-0549.*

PADI certified, with courses through Assistant Instructor. Two tank dive, $60 including equipment. Ron also organizes reasonably-priced day-trips to Tobago.

On Foot

Trinidad is the largest island in the Eastern Caribbean, and not just in geographical terms. The island was once part of the South American continent—some say as recently as 6000 years ago—and, as such, it has more in common with nearby Venezuela than it does with other Caribbean islands. This is most magnificently displayed by the island's diverse wildlife. A few of the four-limbed highlights are the unique golden tree frog, ocelot, armadillo, peccary, porcupine, deer and red howler monkeys. In addition to the almost-extinct bush turkey and the brilliant scarlet ibis, the avian population includes over 400 species of birds, 617 types of butterflies and some 60-odd species of bat. Further, on the ground are 2300 different flowering shrubs and plants, including 700 kinds of orchids and a number of carnivorous species which lurk in swampy areas. To its credit, Trinidad, richly-endowed with oil deposits, began protecting its natural resources well before "ecotourism" became a marketing concept. At this writing, there are 13 official wildlife sanctuaries which shelter much of the island's swamps and mountain forests.

The downside, for adventurous hikers, is that much of the country's wildlife is not easily visited without a guide. There are a growing number of tour operators who are accommodating the growing demand for wilderness exploration. Perhaps the top of the list is occupied by the famous **Asa Wright Nature Center**, a lodge and sanctuary set deep in the rain forest of the Northern Range, at an elevation of about 1200 feet.

Asa Wright Nature Center

A former coffee, citrus and cocoa plantation, Asa Wright (see Where to Stay) has become a world-renowned location for bird-watching, drawing naturalists and biologists to its unique environment. A series of nine hiking trails, up to several miles long, leave from the area around the lodge, but are not generally open to nonresidents. However, the public can tour the grounds as part of the daily one-and-a-half-hour walks (10:30 a.m. and 1:30 p.m.; $6 for nonresidents, reservations recommended).

Maracas Falls

A splendid 300-foot spill, Maracas Falls is situated in the mountains above St Joseph, six miles east of Port of Spain. Take the road leading north out of St. Joseph to an intersection, following the signs a mile further to the waterfall trail. At the trailhead, an easy path (less than a mile) snakes to the base of the falls, where a picnic area is located. A harder trail crosses the river and climbs a narrow track to the lip of the falls; a deep pool upstream offers cool swimming.

Mount Catherine

The arid Chaguaramas Peninsula, a national park, rises west of Port of Spain. A six mile hike to Mt. Catherine (1768 feet) starts in Carenage Bay and ascends through dry scrub woodlands inhabited by the red howler monkey to an airy summit with views down the long Tucker Valley. The length, heat and exposure make this a serious hike; bring sufficient water and allow five-to-six hours round-trip.

Mount Tabor

In the hills north of Tunapuna, the Mt. St. Benedict Monastery marks the start of several trails into the woodlands, a home to numerous winged species, as well as red howler monkeys. The most popular trail—alive with dozens of bird species at daybreak and just before sunset—accesses a fire tower atop Mt. Tabor, with views extending down to the Caroni Plains. Allow one-and-a-half hours round-trip.

What Else to See

Drive Saddle Road north from the Savannah for 30 minutes to beautiful Maracas Bay; continue east to Las Cuevas Bay. In the northeast the nicest beaches are **Ma Tura**, **Salybia**, **Pajes**, **Toco** (take the lighthouse road), **Grande Riviere**, **Shark River** and **Matelot**.

Nariva Swamp, the backdrop to Cocos Bay, is one of the world's great birding regions. **Canoni Swamp**, with its red ibis, four-eyed fish and other wonders, is 20 minutes south of Port of Spain on the Butler Highway toward San Fernando. Call Winston Nanan at **Nanan's Bird Sanctuary Tours** ☎ *(809) 645-1305*.

A stroll in **Queen's Park Savannah** in Port of Spain is obligatory. You'll ramble alongside training thoroughbreds, admire gingerbread mansions, watch sandlot cricket matches and buy fruit, corn or barbecued fish from park vendors, who also sell fresh coconut milk.

City Celebrations

arnival ★★★★★

Port of Spain, ☎ (809) 623-8867.

Trinidad's famous carnival officially lasts just two days, from sunrise on Monday to midnight on Tuesday before Ash Wednesday. However, the unofficial season starts right after Christmas. Started by the French plantocracy 200 years ago, the festival was adopted by the island's blacks as a celebration of the end of slavery. Today, the joyous festival is eagerly anticipated by Trinidadians all year long. Most everyone dons elaborate costumes they've spent months making, then parades through the streets to the beat of steel bands. Tourists are welcome to join a troupe from a few hundred to literally thousands of costumed revelers.

Museums and Exhibits

ational Museum ★★★★

117 Frederick Street, Port of Spain, ☎ (809) 623-5941.
Hours Open: 10 a.m.–6 p.m.

The museum's exhibits center on Trinidad's geography and history through the ages, with artifacts from pre-Columbian times. The highlight is a large art gallery with changing displays and a permanent exhibit on the works of famed 19th-century painter Michel Jean Cazabon.

Parks and Gardens

oyal Botanical Gardens ★★★★★

Queen's Park Savannah, Port of Spain, ☎ (809) 622-3530.
Hours Open: 9:30 a.m.–5:30 p.m.

Located in the two-mile Queen's Park Savannah, these lush gardens cover 70 colorful acres on land that was once a sugar plantation. The grounds include the President's House, an 1875 Victorian mansion home to the president of Trinidad and Tobago, and the **Emperor Valley Zoo** *(☎ 625-2264)*, named after the huge Emperor butterflies common in the area. The gardens, laid out in 1820, showcase specimens from around the world.

Tours

asa Wright Nature Center ★★★★★

Spring Hill Estate, Port of Spain, ☎ (809) 667-4655.
Hours Open: 9 a.m.–5 p.m.

This 191-acre estate turned wildlife sanctuary is a must for bird watchers, with more than 100 species waiting to be glimpsed. The grounds include eight trails, one leading to the world's most accessible colony of nocturnal oilbirds. Guided tours are offered daily at 10:30 a.m. and 1:30 p.m.; reservations are suggested. They also take in guests here; see the entry under lodging for more details.

aroni Bird Sanctuary ★★★★★

Butler Highway, Port of Spain.
Hours Open: 4 p.m.–6:30 p.m.

This sanctuary comprises 40 square miles of mangrove swampland bisected by waterways. Come at sunset to see the national bird, the scarlet ibis, come home to roost, an amazing, colorful sight. Boat tours are conducted by **David Ramsah** (☎ 663-4767) and **Winston Nanon** (☎ 645-1305).

Sports

Deep-sea fishing is available in the cliff-bound **Boca Islands** in the north west where mackerel, kingfish, wahoo, yellowtail tuna, barracuda, red snapper and groupers are in abundance. Your hotel can make all arrangement Much sailing is done on a private basis in Trinidad, though it is in its infan stage commercially. Weekly races are held by the Yachting Association, an you may be able to inquire about renting or hiring boats among the owner There is also a great interest in power-boat racing; the major annual compe tition is the Great Race (90 miles) between Trinidad and Tobago that take place in August. Over the past several years surfing has become a passion o Trinidad. The Surfing Association of Trinidad and Tobago is very warm t visitors and will offer all the assistance it can. There is no particular season fo surfing; conditions are favorable year-round. Four surfing breaks are avai able. The biggest swells happen around **Toco Point**, on the northeast coast o Trinidad. **Chaguaramas Bay** is the prime spot for windsurfing.

Golf

Two locations, Port of Spain.

Trinidad has two courses for duffers. The island's only 18-hole course is at **St Andrew's Golf Club** in Maraval; ☎ 629-2314. The **Chaguaramas Golf Course** ha nine holes; ☎ 634-4349.

Watersports

Various locations, Port of Spain.

A variety of companies are happy to assist with watersports. Deep-sea fishing: **Bay shore Charters** (☎ 637-8711) and **Trinidad and Tobago Game Fishing Associatio** (☎ 624-5304). Boating and sailing: **Island Yacht Charters** (☎ 637-7389). Wind surfing: **Windsurfing Association of Trinidad and Tobago** (☎ 659-2457). Genera watersports equipment and instruction: **Ron's Watersports** (☎ 622-0459) and th **Surfing Association of Trinidad and Tobago** (☎ 637-4355).

Where to Stay

	Fielding's Highest Rated Hotels in Trinidad	
★★★★	Asa Wright Nature Center	$103–$187
★★★★	Trinidad Hilton	$149–$460
★★★	Holiday Inn Trinidad	$100–$300
★★★	Kapok Hotel	$70–$140
★★★	Valley Vue Hotel	$80–$300

	Fielding's Most Romantic Hotels in Trinidad	
★★★★	Asa Wright Nature Center	$103–$187
★★★	Kapok Hotel	$70–$140

	Fielding's Budget Hotels in Trinidad	
★★	Monique's Guest House	$45–$50
★	Bel Air International	$56–$89
★★	Normandie Hotel	$60–$95
★★	Chaconia Inn	$65–$95
★★	Farrell House Hotel	$60–$140

Accommodations in Trinidad run from the traditional high-rise (with U.S. Connections) to the intimate bed and breakfast. Most lodgings are near the Savannah. No hotel in Port of Spain opens onto a beach; to get to the nearest beach you'll have to take a taxi and it's expensive. Anyone with a yen for the wild outdoors will have a memory of a lifetime at the **Asa Wright Nature Reserve**, where you'll feel as if you are sharing the room with the wildlife. During Carnival and culture fests, finding a hotel room on Trinidad can be tricky. On Tobago, it's downright impossible.

Hotels and Resorts

One of the premier hotels, the **Trinidad Hilton**, currently undergoing a multimillion dollar renovation, has unveiled an expanded conference center and refurbished grand ballroom; the second phase of the renovation has encompassed the addition of two new function rooms and executive business center. **The Kapok**, however, is actually more pleasant than the Hilton and less costly. **The Normandie** is a charming work of sculpture in colored concrete, with shops, cafe and an art gallery.

Chaconia Inn $65–$95   ★ ★

106 Saddle Road, Maraval, ☎ (809) 628-8603, FAX (809) 628-3214.
Single: $65–$85. Double: $75–$95.

Located three miles form Port of Spain in a mountain valley, this hotel houses guests in air-conditioned rooms (most with TV). There are also four two-bedroom apartments with kitchenettes for self-catering types. Facilities include two restaurants, a pool and occasional entertainment in the bar. A decent and friendly spot but a bit out of the way.

Farrell House Hotel $60–$140   ★ ★

P.O. Box 4185, Southern Main Road, ☎ (809) 659-2230, FAX (809) 659-2204.
Single: $60–$125. Double: $93–$140.

This government-owned hotel appeals primarily to business travelers. Located on a 15-acre estate in the Point Lisas area, it puts up guests in air-conditioned, motel style rooms, nothing too exciting. Eleven suites have kitchenettes and small living rooms. There's a restaurant and pool, but not much else in the way of extras. Tourists will be happier elsewhere.

Holiday Inn Trinidad $100–$300   ★ ★ ★

Wrightson Road and London Street, ☎ (800) 465-4329, (809) 625-3361, FAX (809) 625-4166.
Single: $100–$300. Double: $110–$300.

This downtown hotel overlooks the harbor and attracts mainly business travelers and conventioneers. Accommodations are standard tried-and-true Holiday Inn modern, air-conditioned, cable TV, and balcony with nice views. Those staying on the executive floor pay extra for upgraded rooms and a private lounge. There's a revolving rooftop restaurant (another HI tradition), dancing in the lounge, a nice pool and a healthclub.

Kapok Hotel $70–$140   ★ ★ ★

16-18 Cotton Street, FAX (809) 622-9677.
Single: $70–$125. Double: $85–$140.

This contemporary hotel is located five minutes from downtown, near Queen's Park Savannah. Guestrooms are spacious and modern, and the six suites have kitchenettes. The two restaurants offer a choice of Caribbean or Chinese/Polynesian fare, and there's also a cocktail lounge and pool. Quite decent for the rates; most rooms are under $85.

Normandie Hotel $60–$95   ★ ★

10 Nook Avenue, ☎ (809) 624-1181, FAX (809) 624-1181.
Single: $60–$85. Double: $70–$95.

This two-story hotel is located in St. Ann's Valley, near the botanical gardens. Taking a cue from the gardens, its own grounds are nicely landscaped and include a restaurant, disco and pool. Guestrooms are air-conditioned and comfortable, but on the dark side. Many of the 12 two-story suites have kitchens and are well worth the bump in price. Right next door is an art gallery and shopping arcade with well-made local wares.

rinidad Hilton   **$149–$460**   ★ ★ ★ ★
Lady Young Road, Belmont Hill, ☎ *(800) 445-8667, (809) 624-3211.*
Single: $149–$460. Double: $161–$460.
This commercial hotel is located a mile from downtown. The air-conditioned guest rooms and suites have all the modern conveniences, and some include fax and computer hookups for business travelers. Facilities include two restaurants, three bars, a pool, and two tennis courts. Guests are mainly American business travelers who appreciate the nice trappings and attentive service.

alley Vue Hotel   **$80–$300**   ★ ★ ★
67 Ariapita Road, P.O. Box 442, ☎ *(809) 624-0940, FAX (809) 627-8046.*
Single: $80–$300. Double: $80–$300.
Located 10 minutes from Port of Spain on a hillside overlooking the city, this modern hotel attracts mostly business travelers. Accommodations are in comfortable air-conditioned rooms; most are under $100. Facilities are plentiful for the number of guestrooms: a restaurant, two bars, disco, business center, a pair of tennis and squash courts, a pool, playground and gym. The Valley Vue also has a small waterpark with three 400-foot waterslides leading to a splash pool.

Inns

Guest houses in Trinidad have a stylish way of approximating inns; the Trinidadian ersonality fills in any gaps with its natural congeniality. There's an elegant casualness to he best inns, where you will feel so at home you may never want to leave. The **Mount St. enedict Guest House** is near-religious in its peaceful ambiance; spiritual seekers can escape to the nearby monastery for a shady refuge, but the views from some of the inn's partments can be objects of profound contemplation.

onique's Guest House   **$45–$50**   ★ ★
114 Saddle Road, ☎ *(809) 628-3334, FAX (809) 622-3232.*
Single: $45. Double: $50.
This friendly guest house is located in the Maravel Valley and surrounded by lush hills. Rooms are nicely furnished, air-conditioned, and spotless. The small restaurant serves bargain fare, and guests can splash about in a nearby pool. One of Trinidad's better guest houses.

Low Cost Lodging

The newest trend on Trinidad and Tobago is bed and breakfasts. There is an association for these kinds of places, but the communication is often informal; if one B&B is illed, the owner will call up her friends for you. Chances are a car will even be sent to pick ou up and hot tea and pastries will be awaiting you on arrival. Best of all, you may find South American family next to your room, or even Finns; the host could be Chinese, frican, Indian or British. To go the B&B route, you need a sense of adventure and a pas-

sion for unexpected experiences. Sometimes you don't get all the privacy you are used t
since B&B's treat you like family—whoever knows where that leads? Because accommo
dations and policies vary widely from home to home, it's best to ask specific question
about what you can expect before you go (i.e., how to get from the airport, childrer
pets, air-conditioning and noise). Some houses are way out of the way, so get specifics.

La Maison Rustique is a B&B with a wonderful tea room and garden. In the Arim
Valley, the Asa Wright Nature Centre and Lodge is a fine accommodation, simple, bu
good local food and unbelievable birding. Meals are included.

Asa Wright Nature Center $103–$187   ★ ★ ★ ★
Spring Hill Estate, ☎ *(809) 667-4655.*
Single: $103–$127. Double: $147–$187.

This special spot is devoted to preserving nature. Located two hours out of Port o
Spain some 1200 feet up, it is a former coffee estate converted into a 191-acre wild
life sanctuary. Two guestrooms are in the main house, which dates to 1908, and ar
quite romantic and furnished with antiques. The rest are located in cottages; all ar
very basic. The lush grounds and neighboring rainforest attract birders from aroun
the world. The rates include afternoon tea and three meals a day, a good thing sinc
this spot is way off on its own. You'll need a car.

Bel Air International $56–$89   ★
Piarco, ☎ *(809) 664-4771, FAX (809) 664-4771.*
Single: $56–$89. Double: $75–$89.
This hotel is found three minutes from the airport, so it attracts mainly travelers i
transit. The air-conditioned guestrooms are rather simple and dated, and could us
soundproofing to buffet airport noise. Facilities are limited to a pool and decent res
taurant. There's no reason to stay here unless you're enroute to someplace else.

Where to Eat

Fielding's Highest Rated Restaurants in Trinidad

★★★★★	Veni Mange	$8–$10
★★★	Breakfast Shed	$5–$7
★★★	Cafe Savannah	$8–$17
★★★	Chaconia Inn	$12–$19
★★★	Hong Kong City	$8–$20
★★★	Michael's	$8–$25
★★★	Philip and Fraser's	$8–$20
★★★	Rafters	$6–$21
★★★	Tiki Village	$6–$13

Fielding's Special Restaurants in Trinidad

★★★	Cafe Savannah	$8–$17
★★★	Monsoon	$5–$5
★★★	Philip and Fraser's	$8–$20

Fielding's Budget Restaurants in Trinidad

★★★	Monsoon	$5–$5
★★★	Breakfast Shed	$5–$7
★★★	Singho	$5–$12
★★★★★	Veni Mange	$8–$10
★★★	Tiki Village	$6–$13

No fewer than seven distinct cultures have influenced the cuisine of Trinidad, from the Spanish settlers who cooked up pastelles to the French who introduced herbs such as broad-leaved thyme and basil. The British brought tamarind from the East Indies for sauces used still today in red snapper. A ten-alarm chile pepper called a *habañero* hails from Mexico. Spicy pastelle are a favorite snack—tamales concocted by placing meats, raisin, capers an fresh herbs atop grated corn or cornmeal and folded in bright green leave instead of the usual corn husks. "Oil-down" is another local specialty, mad from breadfruit, a round starchy yamlike fruit that makes a gooey thick ste when cooked. Before you go, check out the delicacies in *Callaloo, Calypso c Carnival*, a new cookbook from The Crossing Press in Freedom, Californi by Dae De Witt and Mary Jane Wilan. Most nights, calypso or pan music heard at the exceedingly friendly **Mas Camp Pub** *(French St., at Ariapita Ave* ☎ *(809) 623-3745*, $2). There are also frequent concerts at **Spektakula Forum** *(Henry St.,* ☎ *(809) 623-2879*, about $5.)

Breakfast Shed $ ★★★

Waterfront, Wrightson Road, ☎ *(809) 627-2337.*
Latin American cuisine.
Lunch: 5 a.m.–3 p.m., entrees $5–$7.
Break bread with the wharf rats on huge platters of homestyle West Indian food near the cruise ship dock and the Holiday Inn. Fellow diners are working people and early risers who like the fish breakfasts served from 5 a.m. Lunch (the only other meal served) is accompanied by plantains, rice and peas and other plate stretchers. So down home, the hall-like room is called the "Holiday Out" by regulars.

Cafe Savannah $$ ★★★

16-18 Cotton Hill, St. Clair, ☎ *(809) 622-6441.*
Latin American cuisine.
Lunch: 11:45 a.m.–2:15 p.m., entrees $8–$9.
Dinner: 6–10:15 p.m., entrees $8–$17.
Possibly the best callaloo soup on the islands is served at this intimate restaurant on the lower level of the Kapok Hotel. Prepared with a rich stock of *dasheen* (taro leaf) and okra, it's filled with pumpkin, coconut and crabmeat. Other specialties include lobster Soucouyant and pork steak in zippy mustard sauce. There's a prix fixe lunch of several courses, but sandwiches and salads are available.

Chaconia Inn $$$ ★★★

106 Saddle Road, Maraval, ☎ *(809) 628-8603.*
Latin American cuisine.
Lunch: 11 a.m.–2 p.m., entrees $12–$19.
Dinner: 7–11 p.m., entrees $12–$19.
The dining rooms of this motel-like resort in a Port of Spain suburb serve a double purpose: at lunch in the Lounge, business folk gather for a no-frills lunch of fish, pasta, pork and some vegetarian offerings. Sandwiches are tasty and moderately priced. And once a week, a West Indian barbecue is the attraction at the modern, plant-filled alfresco Roof Garden atop the hotel. A bar serves drinks until 2 p.m.

Hong Kong City $$ ★★★

86 Tragarete Road, Newtown, ☎ *(809) 622-3949.*
Chinese cuisine.
Lunch: entrees $8–$20.
Dinner: entrees $8–$20.

Spicy, creative Tri-Chi food is served amidst gaudy red and gold trappings. Bright Oriental lanterns hang from an intricately decorated ceiling. Chinese-food loving Trinidadians favor pepper shrimp, pork with dasheen and other delights. Karaoke nights sometimes, for those who enjoy that sort of thing. For more Chinese food around town, try: **New Shay-Shay Ten**, *81 Cipriani Blvd., 627-8089*, and in San Fernando area **Soong's Great Wall**, *97 Circular Road, 652-2583*.

Michael's   **$$$**   ★ ★ ★

143 Long Circular Road, Maraval, ☎ (809) 628-0445.
International cuisine.
Dinner: 6–10:30 p.m., entrees $8–$25.
Michael's offers toothsome Italian food livened with local produce. His version of proscuitto is served with vividly-flavored fresh papaya instead of the more common melon. Pastas are a standout; they're all homemade. Filet mignon, fish and chicken are also served. Decor is modern, chairs are comfortable and hug the back, floors are polished hardwood. Located in a townhouse in the suburb of Maraval, the service is notably efficient.

Monsoon   **$**   ★ ★ ★

72 Tragarete Road, Port of Spain, ☎ (809) 628-7684.
Indian cuisine.
Lunch: 11 a.m.–4 p.m., entrees $5.
Dinner: 4–10 p.m., entrees $5.
This brisk, but stylish East/West Indian restaurant is probably the most popular in town for curries and the flatbread (*paratha*). Lunch is a fast-paced affair, and very busy; many people take advantage of the take-out service. Complete meals built around shrimp, chicken, and fish include several veggies, lentils and rice. There are great rotis, or dough wrapped around spiced conch or chicken, and fresh squeezed, exotic drinks. The Wednesday night buffets are a good bet for a well-rounded feast in quieter surroundings.

Philip and Fraser's   **$$**   ★ ★ ★

16 Phillips St., Port of Spain, ☎ (809) 623-7632.
International cuisine.
Lunch: 11 a.m.–4 p.m., entrees $8–$12.
Dinner: 4–10 p.m., entrees $8–$20.
All meals are cooked to order at this bastion of new creole cuisine, which translates into smaller, but intensely-flavored dishes. Thankfully, vegetables are very lightly cooked, in the French style, rather than stewed out of all nutrients. Surroundings are tasteful and muted, with plenty of greenery and basketry. There's live jazz on Friday nights. Open Saturdays for dinner only, from 7 to 10 p.m.

Rafters   **$$**   ★ ★ ★

6A Warner Street, Newtown, ☎ (809) 628-9258.
Seafood cuisine.
Lunch: 11:30 a.m.–4 p.m., entrees $6–$21.
Dinner: 4–11 p.m., entrees $6–$21.
Meat and potatoes people and seafood lovers all get their culinary kicks here: On Wednesday, a buffet of fresh local sea creatures is featured, Thursdays, Fridays and

Saturdays chefs carve hunks of roast beef and other meats nonstop until it's all gone
In an adjacent lounge snacks and sandwiches are available for folks with more pru
dent appetites and pocketbooks. The restaurant resides in a lovely old restored dry
goods store.

Singho $$ ★★★

Long Circular Mall, Port of Spain, ☎ *(809) 628-2077.*
Chinese cuisine.
Lunch: 11:30 a.m.–7 p.m., entrees $5–$7.
Dinner: 7:30–11 p.m., entrees $7–$12.

Solidly good Cantonese food is the star at this tony eatery in the gargantuan Long
Circular Mall. Decor features an aquarium, and meals run on the lines of cashew
chicken, spareribs in black bean sauce, and curries. Regulars and tourists like to stop
in Wednesday nights for the Chinese buffet.

Tiki Village $$ ★★★

16-18 Cotton Hill, St. Clair, ☎ *(809) 622-6441.*
Chinese cuisine.
Lunch: 11:30 a.m.–7 p.m., entrees $6–$13.
Dinner: 7:30–9 p.m., entrees $6–$13.

The island's version of Trader Vic's sits atop the plush Kapok Hotel, with a night
vista of the glittering city lights; at lunch, Queens Park Savannah is spread out in all
its glory. Food is good to average, with a dim sum lunch served from 11 a.m. to 3
p.m. on weekends and holidays. Management thoughtfully provides cards for diners
to mark their choices on. The regular menu features Polynesian-style fish, steaks and
chicken.

Veni Mange $ ★★★★★

13 Lucknow Street, St. James, ☎ *(809) 622-7533.*
Latin American cuisine.
Lunch: 11:30 a.m.–2:30 p.m., entrees $8–$10.

Come and eat, say local media star Allyson Hennesey and co-owner and sister Rosemary Hezekiah, in the local lingo. A cross between Julia Child and Oprah Winfrey,
Allyson manages to run the best West Indian lunch spot in town and host her own
TV talk show. Specialties include tasty crab backs, hollowed out crab shells filled
with peppered meat and a spicy mix of peppers and tomatoes. Hearty soups, including pumpkin and callaloo, are also recommended. Open for dinner on Wednesdays
7:30 to 10 p.m., and for drinks on Fridays, from 7 to 10 p.m.

Where to Shop

Fabrics on the island of Trinidad are simply fantastic—a true art in themselves. East Indian silks and cottons come in high-class quality; the best bargains are found in downtown Port-of-Spain on Frederick Street around Independence Square. Even if you don't drink, stock up on local brews such as Angostura Bitters and Old Oak or Vat 19 rum, all which can be bought duty-free and make excellent gifts at Christmas time.

Local artisanry is quite skilled, ranging from fine straw work to cane-inspired creations to miniature steel pans (the large ones, of course are too bulky to ship home, but if you must, shopkeepers will have some interesting suggestions how to lug them home). Island-designed fashions are spectacular at **The Village**, near the Hotel Normandie, and you can find a top-class gallery, **Art Creators**, just around the corner on St. Ann's Road. The latest designs in batik work and island-inspired jewelry can be picked up at **The Cotton House** on Bacolet and Windward Roads. Calypso records are also a favorite buy here. The assistants at **Rhyner's Record Shop** on Prince Street will help you find the latest releases; ask to see some of the old classics. Soca music is also a great buy; many a traveler who just bought albums blindly has come away with great party music, only regretting he hadn't bought more at the time. **Metronome**, in Port-of-Spain, on Western Main Road, is also a good source for music.

Trinidad Directory

ARRIVAL AND DEPARTURE

BWIA offers daily nonstop flights to Piarco Airport, about 30 miles east of Port-of-Spain, from New York and Miami as well as daily direct flights from Toronto. It also offers flights three times a week from London and serves Boston and Baltimore once a week. **American Airlines** and **Air Canada** also have regular nonstop flights. **LIAT** and **BWIA** offer inter-island flights, all landing at Piarco Airport. Most round-trip flights includes airfare to Tobago, so be sure to verify before you pay for the ticket. To fly to Tobago from Trinidad takes about 15 minutes. Departures are available several times a day. LIAT also flies regularly to Trinidad from Barbados.

Taxis are generally plentiful at the airport; a ride to downtown Port-of-Spain runs about $19 in U.S. currency. Buses run on the hour from the airport to the South Quay Bus Terminal, but you will probably need to hire a taxi from there to get to your hotel.

Ferry service is available between Trinidad and Tobago, once a day except Saturdays. The trip takes about six hours. Tickets can be purchased in Port-of-Spain and at Scarborough in Tobago.

The airport departure tax is about U.S. $12.

BUSINESS HOURS

Shops open Monday–Thursday 8 a.m.–4 p.m., Friday 8 a.m.–6 p.m. and Saturday 8 a.m.–noon. Banks open Monday–Thursday 9 a.m.–2 p.m. and Friday 9 a.m.–noon and 3–5 p.m.

CLIMATE

Trinidad has a tropical climate whose dry season runs from January to June, with a wet season the rest of the year. Temperatures are uniformly high year-round. In Port-of-Spain, average temperature in January is 78 degrees F, in July 79 degrees F. Annual rainfall is around 60 inches.

DOCUMENTS

U.S. and Canadian citizens, as well as those of the United Kingdom, may enter the country with a valid passport if they only plan to stay less than two months. An ongoing or return ticket is also required. An immigration card is handed to you upon arrival (or on the plane) which must be filled out and handed in as you depart. Do not lose it. A visa is required for longer stays. Long delays in clearing customs have often been reported. Visitors may bring in 200 cigarettes or 50 cigars, plus one quart of "spirits." To facilitate matters, pack as lightly and unostentatiously as possible.

ELECTRICITY

Current runs 110 or 220 volts, AC 60 cycles. Always inquire of your hotel when you are making reservations what kind of transformer or adapter you will need.

GETTING AROUND

Port-of-Spain is full of crazy drivers who taunt each other into dangerous maneuvers. Do your best to avoid driving yourself around the city, or at least downtown; better conditions are available in the countryside. If you're staying in the suburbs, a car is probably necessary, since you will always be waiting for hired cabs to arrive. You can explore the northern coast by taxi, but a car is more feasible.

Taxis run on fixed rates according to the destination. There is a set route that they follow and will drop off passengers anywhere along that route. There are minibuses as well as regular sedans. Before getting in the car, determine whether you are entering a route taxi or a private one, which will take you anywhere. Even though fares are fixed, drivers are not necessarily honest, and unless you're knowledgeable, expect to be stiffed a few dollars.

Private taxis do not pick up any other passengers and they take you straight to your destination. Take one for longer trips or destinations not on the regular route. Rates are usually not observed during Carnival, when anything goes since the demand is so high. Adjust and go with the flow or you will drive yourself crazy arguing.

Buses are an inexpensive way to get around the island, but they are often too crowded and dilapidated for comfort. Buses depart from the **South Quay Bus Terminal**. Cars can be rented from several agencies including **Auto Rentals** ☎ *(809) 675-2258* and cabs are available from **Bachhus Taxi Service** ☎ *(809) 622-5588*. Roads are fairly well-paved but turn narrow and tortuous in the backcountry. During the rainy season they may be dangerously washed out. Forget driving into downtown Port-of-Spain during rush hour—you'll never get out. Remember that all driving is on the left.

LANGUAGE

The official language is English, spiced with a rich slew of local idioms. There is also some facility in Chinese, Hindi, Spanish and French, due to the large amount of immigrants.

MEDICAL EMERGENCIES

There are several adequate hospitals in Port-of-Spain. Among them are the **Tobago Country Hospital** on Fort Street in Scarborough ☎ *(809) 639-2551;* and **Port-of-Spain General Hospital** on Charlotte Street ☎ *(809) 625-7869*. Ask your hotel to suggest the nearest pharmacy, but bring your own prescription medicine (an extra dose) in case you lose your luggage. Medicine made in the U.S. is far superior to any you could buy in the islands. Severe medical emergencies should be flown to San Juan or back home stateside.

MONEY

The Trinidadian dollar (written as TT$) has been devalued twice in the past few years. You can exchange money in the major hotels in Port-of-Spain, which offer rates comparable to banks. Most shops, hotels and restaurants will accept American dollars if you run short of local money, but they would prefer their own currency.

TELEPHONE

The area code for the two islands is *809*. Telegraphs, telefax, teletype, and telex, can be sent through the textel office at *1 Edward St., Port-of-Spain;* ☎ *(809) 625-4431*. Cables can be sent from the Tourism office and major hotels. To place an intra-island call, dial the local seven-digit number. To reach the U.S., dial 1, the area code, then the local number.

TIME

Atlantic Standard Time.

TIPPING AND TAXES

Restaurants and hotels add a 15 percent Value Added Tax (called VAT). Many hotels and restaurants add an additional 10–15 percent service charge; check your bill carefully. If they don't, do add your own tip, if you find the service satisfactory.

TOURIST INFORMATION

The **Trinidad & Tobago Tourism Development Authority** is located locally at *134-138 Frederick Street, Port-of-Spain;* ☎ *(809) 623-1932.* Stop by for brochures, maps, and advice and assistance in obtaining lodging, especially bed and breakfast situations. In the U.S. call ☎ *(800) 232-0082.*

WHEN TO GO

New Year's Day is January 1. Good Friday and Easter Monday are both holidays. Whit Monday is June 7. Corpus Christi is June 18. Labor Day is June 19. Emancipation Day is August 1. Independence Day is August 31. Republic Day is September 24. Christmas Day is December 25. Boxing Day is December 26.

Fielding's Choice:

Don't miss Divali, the Hindu Festival of Lights, usually celebrated in October. The beauty of pan music is epitomized by the world steel band festivals. The festival, called Pan Is Beautiful, is held in the last week of October. Check with the tourist board for exact dates.

TRINIDAD HOTELS		RMS	RATES	PHONE	CR. CARDS
Port of Spain					
★★★★	Asa Wright Nature Center	20	$103–$187	(809) 667-4655	None
★★★★	Trinidad Hilton	394	$149–$460	(800) 445-8667	A, DC, MC, V
★★★	Holiday Inn Trinidad	235	$100–$300	(800) 465-4329	A, DC, MC, V
★★★	Kapok Hotel	71	$70–$140	(809) 922-6441	A, DC, MC, V
★★★	Valley Vue Hotel	68	$80–$300	(809) 624-0940	A, MC, V
★★	Chaconia Inn	35	$65–$95	(809) 628-8603	A, DC, MC, V
★★	Farrell House Hotel	51	$60–$140	(809) 659-2230	A, MC, V
★★	Monique's Guest House	11	$45–$50	(809) 628-3334	A, MC, V
★★	Normandie Hotel	63	$60–$95	(809) 624-1181	A, CB, DC, MC, V
★	Bel Air International	56	$56–$89	(809) 664-4771	A, DC, MC, V

TRINIDAD RESTAURANTS	PHONE	ENTREE	CR. CARDS
ort of Spain			
Chinese			
★★★ Hong Kong City	(809) 622-3949	$8–$20	A, DC, MC, V
★★★ Singho	(809) 628-2077	$5–$12	A, MC, V
★★★ Tiki Village	(809) 622-6441	$6–$13	A, DC, MC, V
Indian			
★★★ Monsoon	(809) 628-7684	$5–$5	A, DC, MC, V
International			
★★★ Michael's	(809) 628-0445	$8–$25••	A, MC, V
★★★ Philip and Fraser's	(809) 623-7632	$8–$20	A, MC, V
Latin American			
★★★★★ Veni Mange	(809) 622-7533	$8–$10•	None
★★★ Breakfast Shed	(809) 627-2337	$5–$7•	None
★★★ Cafe Savannah	(809) 622-6441	$8–$17	A, DC, MC, V
★★★ Chaconia Inn	(809) 628-8603	$12–$19	A, DC, MC, V
Seafood			
★★★ Rafters	(809) 628-9258	$6–$21	A, DC, MC, V

Note: • Lunch Only

•• Dinner Only

INDEX

Favorite People, Places & Experiences

ADDRESS:	NOTES:

Name

Address

Telephone

Name

Address

Telephone

Name

Address

Telephone

Name

Address

Telephone

Name

Address

Telephone

Name

Address

Telephone

Favorite People, Places & Experiences

ADDRESS:	NOTES:

Name

Address

Telephone

Name

Address

Telephone

Name

Address

Telephone

Name

Address

Telephone

Name

Address

Telephone

Name

Address

Telephone

Favorite People, Places & Experiences

ADDRESS:	NOTES:

Name

Address

Telephone

Name

Address

Telephone

Name

Address

Telephone

Name

Address

Telephone

Name

Address

Telephone

Name

Address

Telephone

Favorite People, Places & Experiences

ADDRESS:	NOTES:

Name

Address

Telephone

Name

Address

Telephone

Name

Address

Telephone

Name

Address

Telephone

Name

Address

Telephone

Name

Address

Telephone

Favorite People, Places & Experiences

ADDRESS:	NOTES:

Name

Address

Telephone

Name

Address

Telephone

Name

Address

Telephone

Name

Address

Telephone

Name

Address

Telephone

Name

Address

Telephone

Favorite People, Places & Experiences

ADDRESS:	NOTES:

Name

Address

Telephone

Name

Address

Telephone

Name

Address

Telephone

Name

Address

Telephone

Name

Address

Telephone

Name

Address

Telephone